DEUTERONOMY

Smyth & Helwys Bible Commentary: Deuteronomy
Publication Staff

President & CEO
Cecil P. Staton

Publisher & Executive Vice President
David Cassady

Vice President, Editorial
Lex Horton

Senior Editor
Mark K. McElroy

Book Editor
P. Keith Gammons

Art Director
Jim Burt

Assistant Editor
Kelley F. Land

Smyth & Helwys Publishing, Inc.
6316 Peake Road
Macon, Georgia 31210-3960
1-800-747-3016
© 2003 by Smyth & Helwys Publishing
All rights reserved.
Printed in the United States of America.

The paper used in this publication meets the minimum
requirements of American National Standard for Information
Sciences—Permanence of Paper for Printed Library Materials.
ANSI Z39.48–1984 (alk. paper)

Library of Congress Cataloging-in-Publication Data

Biddle, Mark E.
Deuteronomy / Mark E. Biddle
p. cm. — (Smyth & Helwys Bible commentary, 4)
Includes bibliographical references and indexes.
ISBN 1-57312-061-8
1. Bible. O.T. Deuteronomy—Commentaries.
I. Title. II. Series.

BS1275.53.B53 2003
227'.1077—dc21

Library of Congress Control Number: 2003001671

SMYTH & HELWYS BIBLE COMMENTARY

DEUTERONOMY

MARK E. BIDDLE

SMYTH&HELWYS
PUBLISHING INCORPORATED · MACON, GEORGIA

ADVANCE PRAISE

This really fine commentary on Deuteronomy combines attention to literary and redactional features of the book with excellent exposition. Mark Biddle's close reading of the text elicits both literary and theological understanding of the text. The reader is aided by the clarity of his writing. Of no small significance are the illustrations and special boxes that offer to the interpreter delightful surprises that would not be expected in the typical commentary.

Patrick D. Miller
Princeton Theological Seminary

Mark Biddle's commentary adds power and luster to the new, rapidly appearing Smyth & Helwys Commentary series. Biddle understands the complexities of the tradition of Deuteronomy and is well versed in critical issues. Beyond that, he makes fine use of the format of the series in order to make pertinent connections to faith issues in the contemporary world. Readers will find this to be an accessible and useful interpretive text.

Walter Brueggemann
Columbia Theological Seminary

TO MY GRANDPARENTS
ARTHUR O. AND EDNA MILLER
IN MEMORIAM

CONTENTS

ABBREVIATIONS USED IN THIS COMMENTARY

Books of the Old Testament, Apocrypha, and New Testament are generally abbreviated in the Sidebars, parenthetical references, and notes according to the following system.

The Old Testament

Genesis	Gen
Exodus	Exod
Leviticus	Lev
Numbers	Num
Deuteronomy	Deut
Joshua	Josh
Judges	Judg
Ruth	Ruth
1–2 Samuel	1–2 Sam
1–2 Kings	1–2 Kgs
1–2 Chronicles	1–2 Chr
Ezra	Ezra
Nehemiah	Neh
Esther	Esth
Job	Job
Psalm (Psalms)	Ps (Pss)
Proverbs	Prov
Ecclesiastes	Eccl
or Qoheleth	Qoh
Song of Solomon	Song
or Song of Songs	Song
or Canticles	Cant
Isaiah	Isa
Jeremiah	Jer
Lamentations	Lam
Ezekiel	Ezek
Daniel	Dan
Hosea	Hos
Joel	Joel
Amos	Amos
Obadiah	Obad
Jonah	Jonah
Micah	Mic

Nahum	Nah
Habakkuk	Hab
Zephaniah	Zeph
Haggai	Hag
Zechariah	Zech
Malachi	Mal

The Apocrypha

1–2 Esdras	1–2 Esdr
Tobit	Tob
Judith	Jdt
Additions to Esther	Add Esth
Wisdom of Solomon	Wis
Ecclesiasticus or the Wisdom of Jesus Son of Sirach	Sir
Baruch	Bar
Epistle (or Letter) of Jeremiah	Ep Jer
Prayer of Azariah and the Song of the Three	Pr Azar
Daniel and Susanna	Sus
Daniel, Bel, and the Dragon	Bel
Prayer of Manasseh	Pr Man
1–4 Maccabees	1–4 Macc

The New Testament

Matthew	Matt
Mark	Mark
Luke	Luke
John	John
Acts	Acts
Romans	Rom
1–2 Corinthians	1–2 Cor
Galatians	Gal
Ephesians	Eph
Philippians	Phil
Colossians	Col
1–2 Thessalonians	1–2 Thess
1–2 Timothy	1–2 Tim
Titus	Titus
Philemon	Phlm
Hebrews	Heb
James	Jas
1–2 Peter	1–2 Pet
1–2–3 John	1–2–3 John
Jude	Jude
Revelation	Rev

Other commonly used abbreviations include:

BC	Before Christ
(also commonly referred to as BCE = Before the Common Era)	
AD	*Anno Domini* ("in the year of the Lord")
(also commonly referred to as CE = the Common Era)	
v.	verse
vv.	verses
C.	century
c.	*circa* (around "that time")
cf.	*confer* (compare)
ch.	chapter
chs.	chapters
d.	died
ed.	edition or edited by or editor
eds.	editors
e.g.	*exempli gratia* (for example)
et al.	*et alii* (and others)
f./ff.	and the following one(s)
gen. ed.	general editor
ibid.	*ibidem* (in the same place)
i.e.	*id est* (that is)
LCL	Loeb Classical Library
lit.	literally
n.d.	no date
rev. and exp. ed.	revised and expanded edition
sg.	singular
trans.	translated by or translator(s)
vol(s).	volume(s)

Selected additional written works cited by abbreviations include:

AB	Anchor Bible
AnBib	Analecta Biblica
ANET	*Ancient Near Eastern Texts Relating to the Old Testament.* J. B. Pritchard, ed. Princeton, 1954.
AnOr	Analecta orientalia
AOAT	Alter Orient und Altes Testament
AThANT	Abhandlungen zur Theologie des Alten und Neuen Testaments
BASOR	*Bulletin of the American Schools of Oriental Research*
BDB	Brown, F., S.R.Driver, and C.A. Briggs, *A Hebrew and English Lexicon of the Old Testament.* Oxford, 1907.
BETL	Bibliotheca Ephemeridum Theologicarum Lovaniensium

Bib	*Biblica*
BiBe	Biblische Beiträge
BibOr	Biblica et orientalia
BibRev	*Biblical Review*
BZAW	Beihefte zur Zeitschrift für die alttestamentliche Wissenschaft
CBQ	*Catholic Biblical Quarterly*
GTA	Göttinger theologischer Arbeiten
HBT	*Horizons in Biblical Theology*
IDB	*The Interpreter's Dictionary of the Bible.* G.A. Buttrick, ed. 4 vols. Nashville: Abingdon, 1962.
Int	*Interpretation*
IOS	*Israel Oriental Society*
ITC	International Theological Commentary
JBL	*Journal of Biblical Literature*
JBR	*Journal of Bible and Religion*
JJS	*Journal of Jewish Studies*
JPS	Jewish Publication Society
JQR	*Jewish Quarterly Review*
JSOTS	Journal for the Study of the Old Testament: Supplement Series
MGWJ	*Monatschrift für Geschichte un Wissenschaft des Judentums*
NAC	New American Commentary
NCBC	New Century Bible Commentary
OBT	Overtures to Biblical Theology
OTL	Old Testament Library
SBLDS	Society of Biblical Literature Dissertation Series
SBLMS	Society of Biblical Literature Monograph Series
SBL.SCSS	Society of Biblical Literature Septuagint and Cognate Studies Series
SBT	Studies in Biblical Theology
SWBAS	Social World of Biblical Antiquity Series
TLOT	*Theological Lexicon of the Old Testament.* E. Jenni, et al, ed. M. Biddle, trans. 3 vols. Peabody, Mass.: Hendrickson, 1997.
TOTC	Tyndale Old Testament Commentaries
TQ	*Theologische Quartalschrift*
VT	*Vetus Testamentum*
VTSup	Supplements to Vetus Testamentum
WMANT	Wissenschaftliche Monographien zum Alten und Neuen Testament
ZAW	*Zeitschrift für alttestamentliche Wissenschaft*

AUTHOR'S PREFACE

I began my academic career in the book of Jeremiah, which requires its students to turn again and again to Deuteronomy, Jeremiah's primary linguistic and theological predecessor. Later studies in Isaiah, Micah — in short, practically everywhere my interests took me — brought me repeatedly to recognize Deuteronomy as perhaps the chief interlocutor among books in the Hebrew canon. Jesus and Paul quote Deuteronomy with regularity. This centrality of Deuteronomy within the canon, alone, renders it worthy of careful, thoughtful study. It is all the more perplexing, therefore, that the church in all its eras has largely disregarded Deuteronomy. I hope in this commentary to open Deuteronomy to new consideration by the church's preachers and teachers so that they may come to see in it something of the significance seen by Jeremiah, Isaiah, Jesus, and Paul.

I am grateful to many people for the parts they played in my life while I undertook this project and before. I dedicate it to the memory of my maternal grandparents, Arthur O. and Edna Miller, whose examples of genuinely pious lives often came to mind as I read Deuteronomy's call to authentic holiness. The collaboration of my editors and friends, Kandy Queen-Sutherland and Samuel Balentine, has been invaluable.

Finally, and especially, of course, I am grateful that my work takes place in the context of life with my wife, Priscilla, and my children, Colin, Alec, Ellen, and Graeme. Deuteronomy's call to faithfully commit the tradition to the next generation sounds poignantly for me.

Mark E. Biddle

SERIES PREFACE

The *Smyth & Helwys Bible Commentary* is a visually stimulating and user-friendly series that is as close to multimedia in print as possible. Written by accomplished scholars with all students of Scripture in mind, the primary goal of the *Smyth & Helwys Bible Commentary* is to make available serious, credible biblical scholarship in an accessible and less intimidating format.

Far too many Bible commentaries fall short of bridging the gap between the insights of biblical scholars and the needs of students of God's written word. In an unprecedented way, the *Smyth & Helwys Bible Commentary* brings insightful commentary to bear on the lives of contemporary Christians. Using a multimedia format, the volumes employ a stunning array of art, photographs, maps, and drawings to illustrate the truths of the Bible for a visual generation of believers.

The *Smyth & Helwys Bible Commentary* is built upon the idea that meaningful Bible study can occur when the insights of contemporary biblical scholars blend with sensitivity to the needs of lifelong students of Scripture. Some persons within local faith communities, however, struggle with potentially informative biblical scholarship for several reasons. Oftentimes, such scholarship is cast in technical language easily grasped by other scholars, but not by the general reader. For example, lengthy, technical discussions on every detail of a particular scriptural text can hinder the quest for a clear grasp of the whole. Also, the format for presenting scholarly insights has often been confusing to the general reader, rendering the work less than helpful. Unfortunately, responses to the hurdles of reading extensive commentaries have led some publishers to produce works for a general readership that merely skim the surface of the rich resources of biblical scholarship. This commentary series incorporates works of fine art in an accurate and scholarly manner, yet the format remains "user-friendly." An important facet is the presentation and explanation of images of art, which interpret the biblical material or illustrate how the biblical material has been understood and interpreted in the past. A visual generation of believers deserves a commentary series that contains not only the all-important textual commentary on Scripture, but images, photographs, maps, works of fine art, and drawings that bring the text to life.

The *Smyth & Helwys Bible Commentary* makes serious, credible biblical scholarship more accessible to a wider audience. Writers and editors alike present information in ways that encourage readers to gain a better understanding of the Bible. The editorial board has worked to develop a format that is useful and usable, informative and pleasing to the eye. Our writers are reputable scholars who participate in the community of faith and sense a calling to communicate the results of their scholarship to their faith community.

The *Smyth & Helwys Bible Commentary* addresses Christians and the larger church. While both respect for and sensitivity to the needs and contributions of other faith communities are reflected in the work of the series authors, the authors speak primarily to Christians. Thus the reader can note a confessional tone throughout the volumes. No particular "confession of faith" guides the authors, and diverse perspectives are observed in the various volumes. Each writer, though, brings to the biblical text the best scholarly tools available and expresses the results of their studies in commentary and visuals that assist readers seeking a word from the Lord for the church.

To accomplish this goal, writers in this series have drawn from numerous streams in the rich tradition of biblical interpretation. The basic focus is the biblical text itself, and considerable attention is given to the wording and structure of texts. Each particular text, however, is also considered in the light of the entire canon of Christian Scriptures. Beyond this, attention is given to the cultural context of the biblical writings. Information from archaeology, ancient history, geography, comparative literature, history of religions, politics, sociology, and even economics is used to illuminate the culture of the people who produced the Bible. In addition, the writers have drawn from the history of interpretation, not only as it is found in traditional commentary on the Bible but also in literature, theater, church history, and the visual arts. Finally, the *Commentary* on Scripture is joined with *Connections* to the world of the contemporary church. Here again, the writers draw on scholarship in many fields as well as relevant issues in the popular culture.

This wealth of information might easily overwhelm a reader if not presented in a "user-friendly" format. Thus the heavier discussions of detail and the treatments of other helpful topics are presented in special-interest boxes, or Sidebars, clearly connected to the passages under discussion so as not to interrupt the flow of the basic interpretation. The result is a commentary on Scripture that focuses on the theological significance of a text while also offering the reader a rich array of additional information related to the text and its interpretation.

An accompanying CD-ROM offers powerful searching and research tools. The commentary text, Sidebars, and visuals are all reproduced on a CD that is fully indexed and searchable. Pairing a text version with a digital resource is a distinctive feature of the *Smyth & Helwys Bible Commentary.*

Combining credible biblical scholarship, user-friendly study features, and sensitivity to the needs of a visually oriented generation of believers creates a unique and unprecedented type of commentary series. With insight from many of today's finest biblical scholars and a stunning visual format, it is our hope that the *Smyth & Helwys Bible Commentary* will be a welcome addition to the personal libraries of all students of Scripture.

The Editors

HOW TO USE
THIS COMMENTARY

The *Smyth & Helwys Bible Commentary* is written by accomplished biblical scholars with a wide array of readers in mind. Whether engaged in the study of Scripture in a church setting or in a college or seminary classroom, all students of the Bible will find a number of useful features throughout the commentary that are helpful for interpreting the Bible.

Basic Design of the Volumes

Each volume features an Introduction to a particular book of the Bible, providing a brief guide to information that is necessary for reading and interpreting the text: the historical setting, literary design, and theological significance. Each Introduction also includes a comprehensive outline of the particular book under study.

Each chapter of the commentary investigates the text according to logical divisions in a particular book of the Bible. Sometimes these divisions follow the traditional chapter segmentation, while at other times the textual units consist of sections of chapters or portions of more than one chapter. The divisions reflect the literary structure of a book and offer a guide for selecting passages that are useful in preaching and teaching.

An accompanying CD-ROM offers powerful searching and research tools. The commentary text, Sidebars, and visuals are all reproduced on a CD that is fully indexed and searchable. Pairing a text version with a digital resource also allows unprecedented flexibility and freedom for the reader. Carry the text version to locations you most enjoy doing research while knowing that the CD offers a portable alternative for travel from the office, church, classroom, and your home.

Commentary and Connections

As each chapter explores a textual unit, the discussion centers around two basic sections: *Commentary* and *Connections*. The analysis of a passage, including the details of its language, the history reflected in the text, and the literary forms found in the text, are the main focus of the *Commentary* section. The primary concern of the *Commentary* section is to explore the theological issues presented by the Scripture passage. *Connections* presents potential applications of the insights provided in the *Commentary* section. The *Connections* portion of each chapter considers what issues are relevant for teaching and suggests useful methods and resources. *Connections* also identifies themes suitable for sermon planning and suggests helpful approaches for preaching on the Scripture text.

Sidebars

The *Smyth & Helwys Bible Commentary* provides a unique hyperlink format that quickly guides the reader to additional insights. Since other more technical or supplementary information is vital for understanding a text and its implications, the volumes feature distinctive Sidebars, or special-interest boxes, that provide a wealth of information on such matters as:

- Historical information (such as chronological charts, lists of kings or rulers, maps, descriptions of monetary systems, descriptions of special groups, descriptions of archaeological sites or geographical settings).

- Graphic outlines of literary structure (including such items as poetry, chiasmus, repetition, epistolary form).

- Definition or brief discussions of technical or theological terms and issues.

- Insightful quotations that are not integrated into the running text but are relevant to the passage under discussion.

- Notes on the history of interpretation (Augustine on the Good Samaritan, Luther on James, Stendahl on Romans, etc.).

- Line drawings, photographs, and other illustrations relevant for understanding the historical context or interpretive significance of the text.

- Presentation and discussion of works of fine art that have interpreted a Scripture passage.

Each Sidebar is printed in color and is referenced at the appropriate place in the *Commentary* or *Connections* section with a color-coded title that directs the reader to the relevant Sidebar. In addition, helpful icons appear in the Sidebars, which provide the reader with visual cues to the type of material that is explained in each Sidebar. Throughout the commentary, these four distinct hyperlinks provide useful links in an easily recognizable design.

AΩ

Alpha & Omega Language

This icon identifies the information as a language-based tool that offers further exploration of the Scripture selection. This could include syntactical information, word studies, popular or additional uses of the word(s) in question, additional contexts in which the term appears, and the history of the term's translation. All non-English terms are transliterated into the appropriate English characters.

Culture/Context

This icon introduces further comment on contextual or cultural details that shed light on the Scripture selection. Describing the place and time to which a Scripture passage refers is often vital to the task of biblical interpretation. Sidebar items introduced with this icon could include geographical, historical, political, social, topographical, or economic information. Here, the reader may find an excerpt of an ancient text or inscription that sheds light on the text. Or one may find a description of some element of ancient religion such as Baalism in Canaan or the Hero cult in the Mystery Religions of the Greco-Roman world.

Interpretation

Sidebars that appear under this icon serve a general interpretive function in terms of both historical and contemporary renderings. Under this heading, the reader might find a selection from classic or contemporary literature that illuminates the Scripture text or a significant quotation from a famous sermon that addresses the passage. Insights are drawn from various sources, including literature, worship, theater, church history, and sociology.

Additional Resources Study

Here, the reader finds a convenient list of useful resources for further investigation of the selected Scripture text, including books, journals, websites, special collections, organizations, and societies. Specialized discussions of works not often associated with biblical studies may also appear here.

Additional Features

Each volume also includes a basic Bibliography on the biblical book under study. Other bibliographies on selected issues are often included that point the reader to other helpful resources.

Notes at the end of each chapter provide full documentation of sources used and contain additional discussions of related matters.

Abbreviations used in each volume are explained in a list of abbreviations found after the Table of Contents.

Readers of the *Smyth & Helwys Bible Commentary* can regularly visit the Internet support site for news, information, updates, and enhancements to the series at <**www.helwys.com/commentary**>.

Several thorough indexes enable the reader to locate information quickly. These indexes include:

- An *Index of Sidebars* groups content from the special-interest boxes by category (maps, fine art, photographs, drawings, etc.).

- An *Index of Scriptures* lists citations to particular biblical texts.

- An *Index of Topics* lists alphabetically the major subjects, names, topics, and locations referenced or discussed in the volume.

- An *Index of Modern Authors* organizes contemporary authors whose works are cited in the volume.

INTRODUCTION

Deuteronomy, the last of the five books of the Torah, as they are called in Hebrew, or of the Pentateuch (from the Latin expression for "five books"), preserves the three addresses Moses delivered to the people of Israel just prior to his death and their entry into the promised land. Its name, which means "second law," derives from the title assigned it in the Septuagint, the ancient Greek translation of the Hebrew Bible. The Greek name, in turn, probably reflects the Greek translator's misunderstanding of the reference in Deuteronomy 17:18 to a "copy" of the Torah to be made for the king's personal use as a reference to a "second law." In a sense, however, the name is still appropriate; the substance of Moses' addresses to the people of Israel is an explication of the one covenant given at Mt. Horeb/Sinai (Deut 1:5). In other words, Deuteronomy does not represent a "second" law in the sense of a different (alternative or additional) covenant. It does, however, represent a *reiteration, explication,* and, to a degree, *expansion*, of the sole covenant between YHWH and Israel. [God's Proper Name]

Deuteronomy within the Canon of the Hebrew Bible

In many ways, Deuteronomy is the lynchpin of the Old Testament canon. Evidence suggests, for example, that the discovery in the Jerusalem temple of a prototype of the current book during the reign of King Josiah may have given impetus to the collection of the canon itself. According to 2 Kings 22–23, King Josiah instituted a series of religious reforms based upon an otherwise unidentified "Torah scroll" discovered in the Jerusalem temple during renovations (c. 623/622 BC). The account of this discovery immediately raises a number of questions. Perhaps the first and foremost has to do with the likely identity of the scroll. Theoretically, the phrase "Torah scroll" could have been a reference, as it usually is today, to the entirety of the Pentateuch, to some portion of it (all or part of one of the five books of Moses that constitute the Torah) or to some other document no longer preserved that could lay claim to Torah status. The fact that Josiah's officials could read aloud the entirety of the scroll in a relatively brief period and that, later, Josiah would have the entire document read aloud to the people gathered in solemn assembly tends against the first option. Similarly, the seriousness with which

God's Proper Name

AΩ The Hebrew Bible employs a variety of divine names and titles for the God of Israel. Except for the Song of Moses (Deut 32), the book of Deuteronomy normally restricts itself to two of the more common designations used in conjunction with one another, YHWH ʾĕlôhîm. This compound phrase consists of God's proper name, YHWH, and the noun meaning "God, god" or "gods," which can also refer to a deity (or deities) other than the God of Israel. Grammatically, ʾĕlôhîm is a plural form of the noun ʾēl, "god" in virtually all the Semitic languages (compare Arabic, ʾallâ). Occasionally, as in Deut 3:24, Deuteronomy employs the additional title ʾădonāy, "my Lord," a form of an honorific title that can also be used in reference to human beings. In modern Hebrew, in fact, ʾadôn can be rendered by the English terms "sir" or "Mr." Jewish scribes distinguished between uses of ʾadôn, "lord," and ʾădonî, "my lord," in reference to human beings, and ʾădonāy, "my Lord," in reference to God, by reserving the (probably artificial) spelling with –āy for the deity.

It is important to remember that, whereas ʾĕlôhîm refers to a deity or deities generically, and ʾadon(î) is a title of respect suitable for beings other than God, YHWH is the proper name of Israel's God. It is a name shrouded in mystery. Neither its origins, its meaning, nor even its pronunciation are certain. Exod 3:14-15 maintains that God revealed this name, presumably for the first time, to Moses at the burning bush. Portions of Genesis, in contrast, place it on the lips of the patriarchs, generations earlier, and even attribute knowledge of the name to the second or third generation of humanity (Gen 4:26). The origins of Israel's worship in the name of YHWH lie in Israel's obscure past. The name may be attested outside Israel in a few unclear instances of Babylonian personal names dating as far back as the third millennium.

The meaning of the name is equally unclear. According to Exod 3:14 ("I am that I am"), it is related to the Semitic verb *hyh/hwh*, "to be" (*y* and *w* are sometimes interchangeable in Semitic languages). Many scholars consider this etymology very probable. In this case, the name would mean "the one who is," "the one who causes to be," "the one who is or will be present [to help]," or the like. Alternative suggestions include the view that the short forms *yāh* and *yāhu* attested in personal names may point to origins as a cultic exclamation, that the name is related to the Arabic root *hwy*, "to be passionate," or to the Ugaritic root *hwy*, "to speak," or that it means "the one who sends down [lightning or rain]." In any case, YHWH does not mean "Lord," as it is conventionally rendered. This convention traces to the Septuagint, and probably reflects the Hellenistic practice of referring to deities as *kurios*, "lord."

Even the proper pronunciation of the name is unknown. Prompted by fear of inadvertently violating the commandment against improper use of the divine name, Jewish practice discourages pronouncing the name at all. Semitic languages, including Hebrew, were originally written without vowels. When scribes copied manuscripts of the Hebrew Bible that incorporated an innovative system of vowel notation, they supplied the divine name with the vowels of the terms ʾĕlôhîm or ʾădonāy—a circumstance that led to the artificial English pronunciation "Yehovah/Jehovah"—to remind readers not mistakenly to pronounce the name, but one of the substitutes.

English translations often follow a convention that permits those who do not know Hebrew to recognize whether the Hebrew Bible employs God's proper name, the common noun, or the honorific title. YHWH is typically translated "Lᴏʀᴅ" or, when it appears in conjunction with ʾădonāy, "Gᴏᴅ" (in either case spelled with small capitals); ʾĕlôhîm is translated "God" or "god/gods" depending on its referent; ʾădonāy is translated "Lord" with only an initial capital.

Since only the four consonants, YHWH, are assured, the name is sometimes called the "Tetragrammaton" (Greek for "four letters"). This commentary will employ "YHWH" in order to refer to the God of Israel by name.

Josiah, his officials, and the people took the document renders it unlikely that, having been found, it would once again be lost to posterity. The likeliest hypothesis argues that the book discovered in the temple should be identified with all or part of one of the five books of the biblical Torah. As it turns out, the language of the account in 2 Kings provides significant clues that link Josiah's scroll with the book of Deuteronomy. Josiah assembled the people to hear the scroll read and to ratify the covenant it described in a fashion reminiscent of Moses' convening of the so-called

Deuteronomy and the Josianic Reform

AΩ The following phrases found in 2 Kings 23 are typically Deuteronomic and point to the close relationship between the two documents:

"to keep his commandments, and his statutes, and his testimonies" (2 Kgs 23:3; Deut 6:17; compare Deut 4:40, 45; 6:2, 20; etc.)

"with all his heart and all his soul (and all his might)" (2 Kgs 23:3, 25; Deut 4:29; 6:5; 10:12; 11:13, 18; 13:4; 26:16; 30:2, 6, 10)

burning the vessels of Asherah (2 Kgs 23:4, 6, 15; Deut 7:5; 12:3)

"the sun, the moon, the stars, and the hosts of heaven" (2 Kgs 23:5; Deut 4:19: 17:3)

"beat it to dust" (2 Kgs 23:6, 15; Deut 9:21)

"male cult prostitutes" (2 Kgs 23:7; Deut 23:18)

"to cause his son or his daughter to pass through the fire" (2 Kgs 23:10; Deut 18:10; compare Deut 12:31)

"broke the masseboth" (2 Kgs 23:164; Deut 12:3; compare 7:5)

"provoke YHWH to anger" (2 Kgs 23:19, 2; Deut 4:25; 9:18; 31:29; 32:16, 21)

"mediums and wizards" (2 Kgs 23:24; Deut 18:11)

"idols (*gillulîm*) and abominations (*šiqqûṣîm*)" (2 Kgs 23:24; Deut 29:16)

"[YHWH's] name there" (2 Kgs 23:27; Deut 12:5, 11, 21; 14:23, 24; 16:2, 6, 11; 26:2)

"Covenant Renewal in Moab" described in Deuteronomy 29:1 [2 Eng]–31:13. For his part, Josiah covenanted to keep the provisions of this covenant "with all his heart and all his soul," just as Deuteronomy exhorts its readers to do in the famous passage known as the "Shema" (especially, Deut 6:5). In an effort to conform Judean religious practices to the provisions of the newly found scroll, Josiah instituted a number of reforms described in 2 Kings 23. Almost without exception, they correspond to provisions outlined in the book of Deuteronomy. [Deuteronomy and the Josianic Reform]

If, as seems likely, Josiah's scroll was some form of Deuteronomy, a second question arises from the account of its discovery. What was the status of the previously unknown law scroll prior to its discovery? This question has the potential to provide significant insight not only into the role of Deuteronomy in seventh-century Judah, but also into the development of the canon of the Hebrew Bible. To rephrase the question as pointedly as possible, one may well ask: How could ancient Israel have misplaced and forgotten a book of the Bible? The answer, of course, is that had Israel, at any moment prior to finding the scroll in the temple, regarded it as Scripture—as a book of the Bible—the scroll would not have suffered such a fate. For one thing, there would have been more than one copy. For another, had Deuteronomy already enjoyed canonical status, it would have commanded appropriate respect. It is inconceivable that a book with scriptural authority would fall into disuse to be forgotten! Apparently, in Josiah's time, the first major section of the Hebrew Bible, the Torah, was either incomplete (missing at least the book found in the temple) or, as seems more likely given the fact that the Pentateuch gives evidence of having reached its final form in the post-exilic period, only in the seminal stages of formation. In fact, since all of the books of the Hebrew Bible outside the Pentateuch date to around the time of Josiah or later, Josiah's mystery Torah scroll is arguably the first biblical book mentioned in the historical sources. How did the book come to be where it was? Although scholars speculate that refugee priests from the conquered northern kingdom may have brought with them a copy of a law scroll in use in the north, the history of the scroll prior to 622/23 is entirely hypothetical, if not downright conjectural. This much is certain: The idea of authoritative "Scripture"

Authorship

Did Moses himself write the book of Deuteronomy? Since the eighteenth century, scholars have focused considerable attention on the authorship of the Pentateuch in general, and the book of Deuteronomy in particular. The classical theory, the so-called "Documentary Hypothesis" or "JEDP Theory" widely accepted in the late nineteenth and early twentieth centuries, holds that the Pentateuch is a composite of four anonymous ancient written sources (J, E, D, and P), identifiable by differences in literary style, varied forms of the divine name, theological perspectives, clues as to dates of composition, etc. At the moment, no consensus opinion as to details prevails among scholars other than the conviction that the Pentateuch is probably a composite.

The question has always been controversial. Conservatives charge those willing even to consider the possibility that Moses may not have written every word in the Pentateuch with irreverence, at best, if not outright heresy. Critical scholars respond that they are simply trying to understand and explain phenomena observable in the Pentateuch, and that the issue is not whether the Pentateuch contains material that traces back to Moses, but whether a single author can have written the Torah. In terms of a tenet of faith, the question involves whether God can inspire anonymous authors.

What evidence can be brought to bear? Both Jewish and Christian traditions have long considered Deuteronomy one of the five "books of Moses." Even the New Testament and Jesus refer to the writings of Moses (see John 1:45; 5:46, for example), although these statements can be interpreted as references to the legal material within the Pentateuch and not to the entirety of all five books. The books of Genesis, Exodus, Leviticus, Numbers, and

Deuteronomy are anonymous; the ancient manuscripts have no title pages or headings. Tradition and the Bible clearly associate these books with Moses as the source of the material, but they make no absolute claim that Moses wrote every word in them.

As for evidence found within the books, one need read no farther than Deut 1:1-5 before encountering specific indications that someone other than Moses was responsible for committing Deuteronomy to writing. Every reference to Moses in this introduction is in the third person. Moses speaks in the first person beginning only in v. 6 in the quotation introduced in v. 5. The introduction refers to the site of Moses' address as "beyond (on the other side of) the Jordan," indicating that the author writes from Palestine, west of the Jordan. Moses never crossed west of the river. Similarly, if one assumes that one (or more) editor(s)/compiler(s) gathered authentic Mosaic traditions, the difficulties associated with place names in Deut 1:1 (see commentary) can also be explained. Later editors may not have been familiar with these ancient place names.

Even the ancient Jewish rabbis recognized that Moses probably did not compose the entirety of the books associated with his name. "Our masters taught: . . . Moses wrote his own book, as well as the oracles of Balaam, and Job. Joshua wrote the book that bears his name and the last eight verses of the Five Books" (*b. B. Bat* 14b-15a). Another rabbinic tradition speculates that Samuel may have also contributed to the Torah.

In other words, whether or not Moses wrote the words of Deuteronomy (and he probably did not), they have scriptural authority because they are faithful to Moses' teaching and because they present an authentic unfolding of it. God can also inspire anonymous authors.

per se was a relatively new phenomenon in Israel. Furthermore, since this "law scroll"—whether Deuteronomy or some other portion of the Torah—would have claimed Mosaic authority, its sudden appearance on the stage as late as the seventh century BC suggests that, for ancient Israel, Mosaic "authority" itself cannot have been simply identified with Mosaic "authorship." While it is already exceedingly difficult to imagine that Israel would have misplaced and forgotten a book considered part of the Bible, it is virtually impossible to imagine that Israel would have neglected a book that had been written by Moses. [Authorship]

Structure and Literary Characteristics

As it turns out, however, when seen in the light of this evidence concerning the sudden and late appearance of some form of the book, several internal features of Deuteronomy take on new significance precisely in relation to this question of "Mosaic authority." For example, the structure of the book of Deuteronomy corresponds in interesting ways to the picture of the composition history of the book suggested by 2 Kings 22 and 23. More importantly, taken together, composition history and literary structure provide significant clues to the purpose and message of the book. Introductory formulae divide the book into three major speeches of unequal length and differing character that Moses is to have delivered, just prior to his death, to the Israelites encamped on the plains of Moab awaiting entry into the promised land. The second and longest of these addresses (5:1–28:68), the core of the book, consists of the so-called "Deuteronomic Code," the detailed explication of the Horeb/Sinai covenant (chs. 12–26) through a series of regulations and case law examples. This "Deuteronomic Code" is prefaced (chs. 5–11) by an exhortation to obey the covenant, which it identifies specifically with the Decalogue as expressed most essentially in the commandment to worship YHWH only. A collection of covenant blessings and curses (27–28) concludes the core address. [Outline]

Several literary features of this core address are noteworthy. First, both the Decalogue (ch. 5) and portions of the Deuteronomic Code have parallels elsewhere in the Pentateuch (the Decalogue also appears in Exod 20; for parallels to the Deuteronomic Code, see commentary on Deut 12 and especially [Parallels Between the Covenant and Deuteronomic Codes] and [Parallels Between the Deuteronomic and Holiness Codes]). Why does the Torah include in Deuteronomy a second version of these laws? Did Moses forget that he had already treated these matters in Exodus, Leviticus, and Numbers? Comparison of the duplicate laws reveals that, in many cases, Deuteronomy's version seems to reflect social, economic, and political circumstances much later than the other version (especially when the parallel is found in the so-called "Covenant Code," Exod 21–23). Is it possible that the Deuteronomic Code represents an independent revision of Israel's predominantly oral case-law tradition undertaken in an effort to update the Mosaic tradition?

Second, it may be significant that the Deuteronomic Code is, for the most part, anonymous (exceptions include 18:15-17). In fact, the Code, and the prefatory exhortation and blessings/curses appendix in particular, participate in a sophisticated tri-level scheme of speakers and addressees that governs the rhetorical strategy of the entire book. Three voices can be heard: God, Moses, and an anonymous narrator who is identical with the author(s)

/editor(s) responsible for putting the book in its final form. In effect, the narrator reports the words of Moses who, in turn, reports the words of God. As with any report, the time lapsed between the events reported and the record may have been of any duration. While Moses' address can be dated with relative certainty, the narrator, theoretically, may have written at any time afterward.

These three voices correspond roughly to the three audiences addressed in the book. On the surface, Moses directs his address to the generation of Israel gathered on the plains of Moab. These Israelites were the children of those who had been present at Mt. Sinai. With the passing of Moses, that earlier generation, with the exceptions of Joshua and Caleb, came to an end. Moses spoke to a generation that had *not* participated in the covenant-making at Sinai/Horeb. They needed to hear the substance of the covenant, to learn how to apply it, and to be encouraged to obedience. Yet, at times, the book obscures the distinction between the Sinai/Horeb generation and the conquest generation, addressing the latter as though it had been present at Sinai/Horeb (see 11:7), collapsing, as it were, these two generations into one Israel. At the same time, however, the narrator knows and the reader should not forget that—whereas YHWH may have spoken directly to the generation assembled at Sinai/Horeb, and Moses to the generation gathered in Moab—the book addresses any generation that reads the book: "*You* were shown so that you would acknowledge that YHWH is God . . . He brought *you* out of Egypt with his own presence, by his great power . . . to bring you in, giving you their land for a possession, *as it is still today*" (4:35-38, my emphasis).

In fact, although Deuteronomy makes no systematic effort to differentiate between them, it seems to be aware of the three layers of its own documentary nature. These three layers correspond roughly to the three speakers and the three audiences. The book refers to the Decalogue document, written by YHWH himself to be delivered originally to the Sinai/Horeb generation and thereafter stored in the Ark of the Covenant (10:1-5). The contents of this Decalogue are reproduced *within* Deuteronomy (ch. 5). In turn, Moses is said to have committed his exposition of the Decalogue (1:5), addressed originally to the Moab generation and roughly equivalent to the Deuteronomic Code plus addenda, to writing in a document to be deposited *beside* the Ark of the Covenant (31:26). Finally, the narrator composed the present book of Deuteronomy, containing the Deuteronomic Code, which in turn contains the Decalogue, for Israelites in any generation.

Although the voice of the narrator(s)/editor(s) can be heard throughout the book, it is concentrated in the speeches that comprise the framework around the Deuteronomic Code. The first and last of these speeches consist primarily of narrative instead of exhortation and explication; in fact, they relate a narrative sequence that breaks off at the end of the first speech to be resumed only later in the final speech. Unlike the Code, which develops an explication of the Decalogue, the narrative framework focuses on the person and ministry of Moses. Furthermore, the final speech almost has the character of addendum; it includes a wide variety of genre and perspectives—poems, songs, and a third-person account of Moses' death. Portions of this narrative framework to the book, like portions of the exhortation and consequence framework to the Deuteronomic Code, seem to reflect a very late era in Israel's history. In fact, circumstances that prevailed in Josiah's day and later seem to be assumed in discussions of Israel's fate at the hands of invading enemy nations, for example. (See commentary on Deut 28.) In short, features evident within the book confirm the complicated history of its composition and transmission suggested by the testimony of the Kings account (2 Kgs 22–23).

Deuteronomy in Context

This narrative framework functions to set the Deuteronomic Code in two key and interrelated contexts: (1) Moses' addresses to Israel on the plains of Moab *and* the documentary record of these addresses complete with narrative framework were motivated by concerns arising from Moses' death and the resultant crisis of transition. On every level of speaker/audience/document, the book of Deuteronomy addresses trans-generational issues. The confusion of audiences seems to be entirely intentional. In the book of Deuteronomy, each and every successive generation of Israel finds itself at Moses' feet hearing Moses' challenge to live out the possibilities inherent in the Sinai/Horeb covenant as explicated by the Deuteronomic Code. (2) In a related manner, the narrative framework relates the history of Israel's wandering and the early stages of conquest (the narrative preamble) as a precedent for YHWH's dealings with Israel as a nation (among other nations). The ending, with its linkage to the treaty blessings and curses and its emphasis on the testimonial character of Moses' parting addresses, functions as a prophetic call to obedience, a glance toward the future. Together, they focus the book on the decision Israel always faces: Choose life!

In fact, the consensus of biblical scholarship is that Deuteronomy serves an even broader contextualizing function. Based on similarities in theme, theology, and language, and on the proximity of the date of the scroll's discovery (likely a form of Deuteronomy) to the date of the composition of Israel's major history, scholars theorize that this proto-Deuteronomy must have inspired the intellects and imaginations of the authors who penned the books of Joshua, Judges, 1 & 2 Samuel, and 1 & 2 Kings.[1] In turn, students of the Torah (Genesis–Deuteronomy) recognize its influence on the other four books of Moses. Similarly, the book of Jeremiah, whose ministry dates to just after the discovery of Deuteronomy, and to a lesser extent other books of the prophets, bear the stamp of Deuteronomic theology and language. It would not be unreasonable to claim that, had proto-Deuteronomy gone undiscovered, approaching half the Old Testament would not have been written, or certainly would have been radically different.

Many scholars regard the position of Deuteronomy at the literary juncture between the Torah and the Former Prophets (as the Deuteronomistic History is known in the Hebrew canon) along with the literary peculiarities of the narrative framework of Deuteronomy as evidence, in fact, that Deuteronomy was edited at some point specifically to become the introduction to the Deuteronomistic History. After the discovery of "proto-Deuteronomy" in the temple, and after the composition of Joshua–2 Kings, an editor would have supplied the narrative account of the transition moment in Israel's history and prefaced the newly edited version of Deuteronomy to the whole. At some point, Deuteronomy would have also been included in the five books of the Pentateuch. The result would have been an eleven-volume "canon" that narrated the story of God's people from the creation of the world to the Exile. This literary placement accentuates Deuteronomy's pivotal role—at the juncture between the wilderness and the promised land.

Deuteronomy in the Context of the Christian Canon

The importance of Deuteronomy is not limited to the first half of the Christian canon. According to the Gospel writers, Jesus quoted Deuteronomy more often than any other biblical book. When asked what is the key to authentic faith, Jesus quoted the "Shema" (Deut 6:4-6; see Matt 22:37; Mark 12:29-30; Luke 10:27). Indeed, it has been suggested that the Gospel of Matthew can be considered a "deuteronomistic" work that takes the theology of

Deuteronomy in the New Testament

According to the Gospel writers, apart from citations of the Decalogue (four times: Mark 7:10 [= Matt 15:4]; Mark 10:19 [= Matt 19:18-19; Luke 18:20]; Matt 5:21, 27), which can be attributed to either Deuteronomy or Exodus, Jesus quoted Deuteronomy more often than any other book in the Hebrew Bible (six times: Deut 6:4-6 [Mark 12:29-30 = Matt 22:37 = Luke 10:27]; Deut 8:3 [Matt 4:4 = Luke 4:4]; Deut 6:16 [Matt 4:7 = Luke 4:12]; Deut 6:13 [Matt 4:10 = Luke 4:8]; Deut 24:1 [Matt 5:31]; Deut 19:15 [Matt 18:16]; the Psalter follows closely with five citations; Exodus, Leviticus, and Isaiah are each cited three times and Hosea twice; Genesis, Jeremiah, Daniel, Zechariah, and Malachi are cited once each). Paul quoted most often from Isaiah (twenty-six times), the Psalter (eighteen times), Genesis (fourteen times), and Deuteronomy (ten times; thirteen times including the three citations of the Decalogue—Rom 7:7 [Exod 20:17 = Deut 5:21]; Rom 10:6-8 [Deut 30:12-14]; Rom 10:19 [Deut 32:21]; Rom 11:8 [Deut 29:4]; Rom 12:19-20 [Deut 32:35];

Rom 13:9 [Exod 20:13-17 = Deut 5:17-21]; Rom 15:10 [Deut 32:43]; 1 Cor 9:9 [Deut 25:4]; 2 Cor 13:1 [Deut 19:15]; Gal 3:10 [Deut 27:26]; Gal 3:13 [Deut 21:23]; Eph 6:2-3 [Exod 20:12 = Deut 5:16]; 1 Tim 5:18 [Deut 25:4]). Paul cites eleven other books five times or fewer: Leviticus, Exodus, Hosea, 2 Kings, Jeremiah, Habakkuk, Numbers, Joel, Malachi, Proverbs, Job (in descending order of frequency). In descending order of frequency, the General Epistles cite the Psalter seventeen times; Deuteronomy, including the Decalogue, eight times (Heb 1:6 [Deut 32:43 LXX]; Heb 10:30a [Deut 32:35]; Heb 10:30b [Deut 32:36]; Heb 12:21 [Deut 9:19]; Heb 13:5 [Deut 31:6,8]; Jas 2:11a [Exod 20:14 = Deut 5:18]; Jas 2:11b [Exod 20:13 = Deut 5:17]; Jas 4:5 [Deut 32:11-12, 16-22]); Genesis, Exodus (including the Decalogue), Isaiah, and Proverbs five times each; Leviticus four times; Jeremiah twice; and 2 Samuel, Habakkuk, and Haggai once each. The importance of Deuteronomy to Jesus and the authors of the New Testament is self-evident.

R. Longenecker, *Biblical Exegesis in the Apostolic Period* (Grand Rapids: Eerdmans, 1975), 57-59, 108-11, 164-66, 196-97.

Deuteronomy as the basis for its argument.[2] Paul, the trained rabbi, appeals to Deuteronomy regularly. [Deuteronomy in the New Testament] Yet, in comparison to its significance among and for the other books that comprise the Christian Bible, Deuteronomy is woefully neglected in the preaching and teaching of the church. Given its stature within the canon, the relative neglect of Deuteronomy among Christians is truly astonishing. What accounts for it?

Law and Grace: A False Dichotomy. At least two closely related misapprehensions seem to motivate Christian disregard for the riches of Deuteronomy. First, for most of Christian history, the church has operated with a disdainful caricature of Old Testament "Law." The Law, it has been maintained, consists of a series of rigid, highly specific rules. They were imposed upon ancient Israel as the standards Israel must meet in order to satisfy God's demands for righteousness. Since, however, human beings ultimately fall short of the standards of absolute righteousness, the Law failed as the means to Israel's justification. Because of this failure of the Law—YHWH's covenant with Israel—Jesus came announcing and enacting God's grace. The failed Law, it has been argued, is therefore no longer binding on Christians; Christians have another, better avenue to relationship with God.

As the commentary that follows will repeatedly assert, however, this understanding of Old Testament "Law" is not a faithful representation of reality, especially not as it pertains to Deuteronomy. To begin with, the Old Testament nowhere maintains that relationship with God can be earned. Instead, the biblical statement concerning the establishment of the relationship between God and Israel can be described best under the theological heading of election. The Old Testament consistently maintains that, in an act of unmerited and inexplicable grace, *God chose and redeemed Israel well before and apart from the giving of the Law.* In fact, the Hebrew word often translated "law" can better be rendered "teaching," "instruction," or even "principles." That is, Old Testament "Law" is not a set of restrictive rules, but the principles or guidance for living life as the people of God. In short, God "saved" Israel by grace, but the life God wishes for God's people has a certain principled character. It manifests identity. Life as God's people is neither anarchic nor formless. As Jesus put it, "By their fruits you shall know them" (Matt 7:20). In effect, the "Law" describes the character of the "fruits of grace."

A Biblical Model for Interpretation. Second, Christians have never developed an adequate approach to interpreting Torah, so they neglect it. One of the most obvious features of the "legal" material in the Old Testament involves its antiquity. Quite often, it deals with matters pertinent to ancient Israel's agrarian, pre-modern, Near Eastern culture that are entirely without parallel in the modern western world. Christians read Deuteronomy's discussion of the manumission of slaves, for example, and quickly realize that (fortunately) circumstances have changed. The rules no longer apply. If read closely, however, Deuteronomy both calls for and models a more engaged, nuanced interpretive approach. Deuteronomy recognizes that specific circumstances change. But the basic principles do not. Commitment to the covenant's call for the people of God to live as the people of God requires an approach to the interpretation of the basic principles that will result in new and faithful responses to new situations. In fact, according to Deuteronomy itself, Moses addressed Israel on the plains of Moab, and eventually the book was written precisely because Israel perpetually faced new situations that called for new applications of the basic principles of the covenant. Deuteronomy, then, models how to approach new circumstances on the basis of the fundamental and abiding principles of God's will revealed in Torah. It establishes an authoritative biblical tradition of interpretation.

If the church is to live its life as God's people, responding to the ethical challenges of modern life, embodying the principles of holiness and godliness, it cannot afford to disregard such a rich resource.

NOTES

[1] Scholars refer to this six-volume work as the "Deuteronomistic History (= DH)." For a detailed exposition of the scholarly arguments for the association of these books with Deuteronomy, see M. Noth, *Überlieferungsgeschichtliche Studien: Die sammelnden und bearbeitenden Geschichtswerke im Alten Testament,* SKG.G 18/2, 3rd ed. (Tübingen: Max Niemeyer, 1967); E. Friedman, *The Exile and Biblical Narrative: The Formation of the Deuteronomistic and Priestly Works,* HSM 22 (Chico CA: Scholars Press, 1981); M. Weinfeld, *Deuteronomy and the Deuteronomic School* (Oxford: Clarendon Press, 1972); etc.

[2] See O. H. Steck, *Israel und das gewaltsame Geschick der Propheten: Untersuchungen zur Überlieferung des deuteronomistischen Geschichtsbildes im Alten Testament, Spätjudentum und Urchristentum* (WMANT 23; Neukirchen: Neukirchener Verlag, 1967).

THE INTRODUCTION TO DEUTERONOMY

1:1-46

COMMENTARY

Introduction, 1:1-5

The introduction to the book of Deuteronomy (1:1-5) presents readers with a bewildering array of difficulties. To begin, the grammar of v. 1 and the place names recorded there [Place Names in Deuteronomy 1:1-5] are susceptible to multiple interpretations. The expression "between Paran, Tophel, Laban, Hazeroth, and Di-zahab" may intend to locate a site somewhere in the center of the area circumscribed by these places. The people would have paused there just prior to Moses' death and the crossing of the Jordan. Alternatively, it could refer to the route Israel took on the final leg of their journey in the wilderness. In the latter case, the introduction indicates that Moses spoke "these words" at stages along the way.

If Deuteronomy 1:1 intends to locate the site of Moses' speech as the last stop before Moses' death, it contradicts the standard claim that Moses and Israel paused east of the Jordan opposite Jericho

---

Place Names in Deuteronomy 1:1-5

AΩ The obscurity of several of the place names in the comment opening Deuteronomy complicates its interpretation significantly. Only Paran and Hazeroth can be identified with certainty. Suph may be an abbreviation for *yam-sûp*, the usual Hebrew designation for the Red Sea, including its extensions, the Gulfs of Suez and Aqabah. The LXX, which translates simply "red" here, understands the name in this way. Or it may be the ancient name for the modern Khirbet Sufe, situated southeast of Medeba in Moab. An Egyptian text dated to the reign of Shoshenq I (10th century BC) and an Assyrian text from the time of Sargon II (8th century BC) mention a Laban near the Brook of Egypt, and the itinerary of Israel's wilderness wandering lists a Libnah somewhere on the route from Hazeroth to Paran (Num 33:20-21). One cannot be sure that either should be equated with the Laban of Deut 1:1. Tophel and Di-zahab are otherwise unknown in either the Bible or other ancient texts. Some have associated them with the modern et-Tafile, 15 miles south-southeast of the Dead Sea, and ed-Dhebe in Moab, respectively.

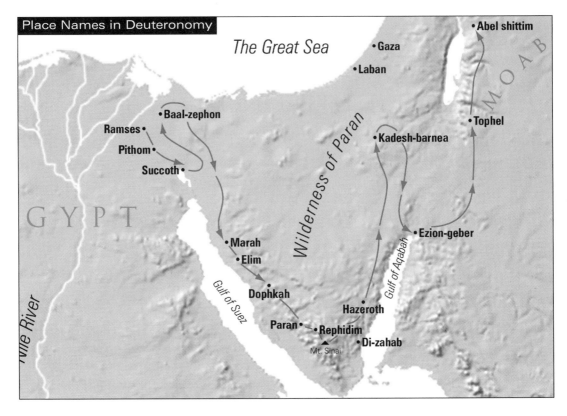

Place Names in Deuteronomy

(Num 22:1; 31:12; 33:50; 35:1), near Shittim (Num 25:1) or in the valley opposite Beth-peor (Deut 3:29)—that is, in Moab just north of the Dead Sea. All the identifiable place names in Deuteronomy 1:1 lie much farther to the south. Should 1:1 mean to suggest that Deuteronomy records a series of Moses' speeches delivered along the journey, as the Targums (ancient Aramaic paraphrases of the Hebrew Bible) seem to have understood, then it contradicts v. 5. Alternatively, it may refer only to the "historical preamble" (1:6–4:40), giving the locations for events summarized as the background for the exposition of the Law that commences in Deuteronomy 5. [Deuteronomy 1:1-5, Introduction to What?] In the end, the precise intention of v. 1 remains obscure.

Despite these difficulties, Deuteronomy 1:1-5 announce several important themes. First, the text places a great deal of emphasis on the unique role of Moses as divine spokesman (vv. 1, 3) and interpreter of the Law (v. 5). N. Lohfink and others[1] have analyzed the literary structure of this passage and found a clearly concentric shape that draws the reader's

Deuteronomy 1:1-5, Introduction to What?

Interpreters debate the significance of the second introduction found in Deut 4:41-44. The discussion of the law announced in Deut 1:5 actually begins only in ch. 5. The obscurity of Deut 1:1, the apparent repetitiveness of introductions (a second introduction is found in 4:41-44), and a series of phenomena noteworthy in Deut 1–4 and 29–34 (the "framework" to the book) have led scholars to consider the current "introduction" to Deuteronomy in relation to the books of Exodus–Numbers, on the one hand, and to the books of Judges–2 Kings, on the other. Do Deut 1:1–4:40 serve as the introduction to the books of Deuteronomy through 2 Kings while Deut 4:41-44 introduce the book of Deuteronomy proper?

attention to the threefold reference to Moses "speaking" (v. 1) "according to all YHWH had commanded him" (v. 3) and "explaining the law" (v. 5):

A. These words
  B. Moses spoke
    C. (place) beyond the Jordan
      D. (time) eleven days journey from Horeb to Kadesh-barnea
        E. Moses spoke as YHWH commanded
      D'. (time) In the 40th year after Horeb
    C'. (place) beyond the Jordan
  B'. Moses explained
A'. this Torah

Second, v. 1 introduces the notion that Moses addresses his words to "all Israel." Deuteronomy repeatedly insists that the covenant with YHWH applies to "all Israel," to every individual Israelite throughout all its generations. Indeed, Moses pauses now, forty years after the giving of the Law at Mt. Horeb, to explain the importance and validity of this covenant to the second generation. They had not freely chosen to enter into covenant relationship with God. Yet, in Deuteronomy Moses insists that, although of those who stood at the foot of the mountain of God, only Joshua and Caleb survive, the relationship with God established in that earlier generation included all subsequent generations. They have the opportunity for and indeed the responsibility of living up to this ancestral identity. They, too, can be "Israel" if they choose as their ancestors did to live in covenant with YHWH.

On the other hand, and thirdly, the introduction subtly reminds readers of the inherent danger that is the flip side of covenant: the danger of rebellion and failure to accept the blessings of covenant. The parenthetical comment that the journey from Mt. Horeb to Kadesh-barnea requires only eleven days juxtaposed with the dating of Moses' speech in the fortieth year after Israel's departure from Horeb calls attention to the senselessness of the forty years in the wilderness. The first generation of Israelites freed from Egyptian slavery could have begun to take possession of the promised land within a matter of weeks after receiving the covenant. Instead, because of their rebellion and unbelief, God sentenced them to forty years of virtual exile in the desert. YHWH offers relationship and blessing to "all Israel," but each generation, indeed every individual, must responsibly accept YHWH's grace.

Finally, v. 5 provides an important clue to the nature and purpose of the book of Deuteronomy: "Moses undertook to *explain* this law." Deuteronomy does not purport to be an additional collection of laws to supplement those given at Horeb. Nor is it merely a restatement, a second edition as it were. Instead, since neither Moses' original audience nor later readers of Deuteronomy were original parties to the covenant, and since Israel was about to encounter a new situation, Moses lays out the purpose, guiding principles, and proper mode of interpretation of the original covenant. In other words, within the Bible itself, Deuteronomy is an exercise in biblical interpretation. As such, it serves as a model for all future generations of God's people.

Moses Appoints Assistants, 1:6-18

Moses' address begins with a historical summary of major events since Israel departed from Mt. Horeb (Sinai). YHWH's instruction to depart incorporates an idealized description of the extent of the territory that was to be Israel (v. 7) and an allusion to the promise God made to the patriarchs (v. 8, see Gen 15:13-16; 26:2-5; 28:13-15) that serve as a link to the account in vv. 9-18. The instruction to leave Horeb and take possession of the vast territory God had promised Israel leads smoothly to the account of measures Moses took in response to the burden of leading a people so numerous (v. 10, also a citation of the patriarchal promise; see Gen 15:5; 26:4) and blessed (v. 11, another allusion, made even more explicit by the phrase, "the God of your ancestors"). [The Promise to the Patriarchs in Deuteronomy] A bracket involving the phrase "at that time (*bāʿēt hahûʾ*, vv. 9, 16, 18)" unifies vv. 9-18.

The Promise to the Patriarchs in Deuteronomy

The reference to God's promise to Abraham, Isaac, and Jacob in Deut 1:8 raises a question of considerable theological and literary significance. Because the book of Deuteronomy consciously hearkens back to earlier generations of Israel as the reference point for its message to the audience of Moses' address (and to the readers of the book), it is important to distinguish between three principal Deuteronomic uses of the phrase "your/our ancestors." Several occurrences of the phrase simply denote ancestors without reference to a particular historical period (for example, 13:6; 28:36, 64; 30:5, 9; 31:16; 32:17). Since the relationship between the generation that entered the land and the generation present at Mt. Sinai constitutes a central theme in Deuteronomy, a second major category of uses of the phrase refers to this Sinai generation. References to this generation of "ancestors" characterize them either as

recipients of the covenant (8:18; 29:25) or as the sinful generation that murmured and rebelled (8:3, 16).

In Deut 1:8 the phrase refers, in a third major usage, to Israel's patriarchs, Abraham, Isaac, and Jacob (see also 6:10; 9:27; 29:13; 30:20; 34:4). In fact, all occurrences of the phrase in this patriarchal meaning refer specifically to certain aspects of the tradition of God's "promises to the patriarchs" in the book of Genesis. Effectively, Deuteronomy ignores the lives of the patriarchs except for God's promise to bless them with a land for the multitudes of their descendants.

Several texts in Deuteronomy mention a covenant with the ancestors (4:31; 5:3; 7:12; 8:18; 29:25). Although a few texts in Genesis describe God's promise to the patriarchs as a covenant (Gen 15:18; 17:2), the contexts of Deut 8:18 (see 8:3, 16) and 29:25 suggest that the references are to the Sinai covenant.

The area described in v. 7 far exceeds the extent of historical Israel, even during the period of David's empire. The "hill country of the Amorites" refers to the central hills of Judah and Ephraim. The Arabah is the depression, actually a continuation of the Jordan rift, extending from the southern tip of the Dead Sea to the northern shore of the Gulf of Aqabah. The Shephelah consists of the hills west of the Judean mountains. The central desert south to the region around Kadesh-barnea is called the Negev. Together with the "coast of the Sea," the broad coastal plain, inhabited in the early Israelite period by the Philistines, this description of the southern boundary of Israel encompasses the southern desert from the Mediterranean to the Gulf of Aqabah. To the north, Phoenicia and Syria mark the other extreme. The "land of the Canaanites" lies between.

The chief critical issue related to this passage involves its similarity to two other passages in the Pentateuch, Exodus 18:13-26 and Numbers 11:10-25. As does Deuteronomy 1:9-18, these passages record Moses' appointment of a group of assistants, administrators, and judges to lighten his burden of leadership. The accounts in Deuteronomy and Exodus bear particularly close resemblance to one another in that both describe the appointment of "commanders of thousands, commanders of hundreds, etc."

Two explanations for the resemblance of these three passages seem possible. First, the Pentateuch may narrate two or three distinct occasions when Moses appointed assistants. But it seems highly improbable that Moses would have established three separate and redundant hierarchies. Second, the three accounts may be different versions of the same story, an interpretation supported to a degree by the fact that Deuteronomy clearly intends to summarize and restate older material. In this case, however, attention shifts from the similarities in the accounts to their differences. In Deuteronomy, Moses decides before leaving Horeb to appoint assistants because Israel has been so richly blessed. The people choose capable men as administrators and judges. Moses details their responsibilities, including the responsibility of bringing the most difficult cases before him for review. In Exodus, Moses' father-in-law, Jethro, suggests, before Israel receives the covenant at Mt. Sinai, that Moses appoint assistants to forestall exhaustion. [The Sequence of Events as Recorded in Exodus] Moses himself chooses administrators and judges to hear minor cases. In Numbers, God ameliorates Moses' frustration at Taberon, on the route from Sinai to Kadesh-barnea, with the suggestion that he gather the elders of

The Sequence of Events as Recorded in Exodus

The order of Exodus 17–19 is somewhat disturbed. According to Exod 17, the people were encamped at Rephidim. Exod 19:2 records their departure from Rephidim and arrival in the wilderness of Sinai. According to Exod 18:5, however, the people were already encamped at the foot of Mt. Sinai when Jethro advised Moses to appoint assistants. Exod 18 also seems to presuppose that the Sinai covenant had already been revealed ("statutes and decisions," vv. 16, 20) and that the "Tent of Meeting" had already been established ("inquire of God," v. 15; cf. Exod 33:7-11). J. Van Seters points out that the departure of Moses' father-in-law recorded in Exod 18:27 is mentioned once again, after the giving of the Law, in Num 10:29-32. Van Seters argues that Exod 18 has been displaced from its earlier location in Num 10.

"Etiology in the Moses Tradition: The Case of Exodus 18," *Hebrew Annual Review* 9 [1985]: 355

Israel to be consecrated as administrative assistants. Their duties are not specified.

Assuming that these are variant accounts of one event rather than separate accounts of three events, scholars offer three major explanations for the variations. Some argue that the author(s)/editor(s) of Deuteronomy fused the older accounts in Exodus and Numbers into the account found in Deuteronomy 1:9-18.[2] Others argue that the accounts in Exodus and Numbers depend literarily on the Deuteronomy account. Deuteronomy 1:9-18 is related, in this view, not to the Exodus and Numbers account, but to the legal material in Deuteronomy 16:18b and 17:8-13, which it foreshadows.[3] These theories of literary dependence fail, however, to account for the rarity of verbal parallels in the three accounts. In other words, while they tell substantially the same story, they do not use the same words to do so—as one would expect if one had served as the model for the others. Consequently, many other scholars argue that the significant differences in the three accounts point to independent narratives based on distinct oral traditions concerning the appointment of assistants.[4]

All three versions start with the recognition that Moses cannot continue to bear the burdens of leadership alone. The Bible consistently portrays its heroes not as wonder-workers with superhuman capabilities, but as normal human beings responding to divine callings. To be sure, they were gifted and talented in their own ways, but they could also succumb to the weaknesses and failings common to humanity. Moses himself resisted God's call (Exod 3–4), grew weary (Exod 17:12), became impatient (Num 11:10-15), and lost his temper (Exod 32:19). YHWH's relationship with Israel, the deliverance from Egyptian bondage, the covenant, and the gift of the land did not depend inextricably on Moses. Joshua would succeed him to lead the people into the promised land.

Moses was an important figure, but not the only one whom God could use. Others had their own parts to play.

In comparison to the Exodus and Numbers versions, the Deuteronomy account manifests a particular interest in the qualifications (v. 13) and responsibilities (vv. 16-17) of these other leaders, especially the judges. Moses directed the Israelites to choose men who were "wise (*ḥăkāmîm*), insightful (*nĕbonîm*), and knowledgeable (*yĕduʿîm*)." These near synonyms emphasize various aspects of the mature discernment required of leaders.

The Hebrew terms for "wise, wisdom," *ḥākām, ḥokmâ*, connote skill and competence, "know-how," sometimes even cunning and craftiness (the meaning implied in Jesus' admonition to be "as wise [sly] as serpents and innocent as doves," Matt 10:16). The craftsmen and artisans who built and furnished the tabernacle and the temple were noted for their "wisdom" (Exod 28:3; 31:6; 35:10; 36:1, 2, 4, 8; 1 Chr 22:15; etc.). Normally, such skill can only be acquired through experience and training (Prov 6:6; 9:9; 13:20; 21:11). Similarly, the wisdom teachers of the books of Proverbs, Job, and Ecclesiastes gained skill in understanding the ways of the world God created (Eccl 8:1, 5, 17; 12:9), including the ways of human kind (Prov 10–24), by learning and careful observation (Prov 1:2-6; 6:6). Because such wisdom required years of study and practice to perfect, the Bible regularly associates wisdom with advanced age.

The basic meaning of the verb *bîn*, here in its plural passive participle form ("those who *bîn*"), is "to perceive" by sight (Prov 7:7), by hearing (Prov 29:19), by touch (Ps 58:10), or by taste (Job 6:30). By extension, it can also mean "to observe carefully" (Prov 23:1) and, thus, "to understand" (Isa 29:16; Prov 1:2, 6; etc.). The connotations and usages of this verb point to the relationship between accurate, careful perception and understanding. In order to understand, one must first listen, observe, consider. Moses asked for inquisitive, perceptive men of keen discernment.

Leaders must also be knowledgeable. The Hebrew verb *yādāʿ*, most often translated "to know," regularly implies an intimate, personal knowledge, as in the Hebrew idiom referring to sexual intercourse ("And Adam knew Eve," Gen 4:1; reflected also in New Testament Greek, "I have never known a man," Luke 1:34). The verb has no object in v. 13: Moses does not indicate what these leaders are to know. Presumably, Moses wanted people with wide, personal knowledge of life and of human nature. [Niebuhr on Realism and Idealism] The translators of the RSV and NRSV correctly sought to convey this connotation by translating "experienced."

Niebuhr on Realism and Idealism

In political and moral theory "realism" denotes the disposition to take all factors in a social and political situation, which offer resistance to established norms, into account, particularly the factors of self-interest and power. In the words of a notorious "realist," Machiavelli, the purpose of the realist is "to follow the truth of the matter rather than the imagination of it; for many have pictures of republics and principalities which have never been seen." This definition of realism implies that idealists are subject to illusions about social realities, which indeed they are.

"Idealism" is, in the esteem of its proponents, characterized by loyalty to moral norms and ideals, rather than to self-interest, whether individual or collective. It is, in the opinion of its critics, characterized by a disposition to ignore or be indifferent to the forces in human life which offer resistance to universally valid ideals and norms. This disposition, to which Machiavelli refers, is general whenever men are inclined to take the moral pretensions of themselves or their fellow men at face value; for the disposition to hide self-interest behind the façade of pretended devotion to values, transcending self-interest, is well-nigh universal. It is, moreover, an interesting human characteristic, proving that the concept of "total depravity," as it is advanced by some Christian realists, is erroneous. Man is a curious creature with so strong a sense of obligation to his fellows that he cannot pursue his own interests without pretending to serve his fellowmen.

Reinhold Niebuhr, "Augustine's Political Realism," in *The Essential Reinhold Niebuhr: Selected Essays and Addresses*, ed. R. M. Brown (New Haven: Yale, 1986), 123.

Moses wanted assistants, then, who were competent, perceptive, and experienced because their judicial responsibilities[5] would require them to "hear" and "judge rightly (*špṭ ṣedeq*)" (v. 16). In order to discern the truth of situations that will come before them and to reach decisions that will restore balance and health to social relationships, they will depend on their powers of observation, their life experience, and their personal competence. [Righteousness and the Righteous]

The text does not assume that the concept of right judgment, of justice, is self-evident. It further defines the duties of these judges in four ways. First, their jurisdiction extends to everyone in Israelite society. Even the "alien (*gēr*)" deserves justice. Second, everyone in Israelite society deserves justice equally. Judges are to be impartial, hearing the cause of the weak and the strong, the poor and the wealthy alike. They are to resist the influence of the powerful. The expression, "do not regard the face of a person," (v. 17; NRSV, "You must not be partial") refers to an individual's reputation and status (compare the Asiatic concept of "saving" or "losing face," or reputation). Third, and most importantly, judges are to remember that their authority and their responsibility derive from God. Justice is God's. In fact, the duty to offer justice to everyone impartially derives from the fact that God, "the Judge of all the earth" (Gen 18:25), shows no favoritism and is unimpressed by status. God wants only justice. Finally, the text calls upon judges to be

Righteousness and the Righteous

AΩ Moses charged the newly appointed judges of Israel to "judge righteously" (Deut 1:16). It is very difficult for modern readers to encounter the term "righteously" or the related terms "righteous" and "righteousness" without thinking primarily, if not exclusively, of a theological or spiritual connotation. The context of Moses' charge to the judges, however, clearly indicates that Moses had in mind legal and social disputes to be adjudicated thoroughly, fairly, and impartially. Apparently, "righteousness," like "beauty" and "goodness," requires further definition. How did the ancient Hebrews understand "righteousness"?

The ancients did not distinguish between the religious and social realms to the extent moderns do. In modern terms, however, the Hebrew concept of "righteousness" is primarily social and relational. The Old Testament employs the family of terms (ṣādaq, ṣedeq, ṣaddîq, ṣĕdāqâ) over 500 times in a wide range of contexts in reference to behavior that promotes harmonious social relationships and contributes to the peace and well-being of involved individuals and groups. Minimally, the righteous are innocent of wrongdoing (Exod 23:6-8; 2 Kgs 10:9). Righteousness is a matter of proper treatment of one's neighbor (1 Kgs 8:31-32), of loyalty and faithfulness to one's family (Gen 38:26), of accurate weights and measures (Lev 19:36; Deut 25:15). The concept implies more than simply avoiding wrongdoing, however. A righteous individual returns a poor man's coat before nightfall although the poor man's debt has not yet been paid (Deut 24:13). In the interests of nurturing and strengthening a relationship, a righteous individual will do more than required (Gen 33:30; 2 Sam 24:18). Later, the good king would be described as one who maintains social harmony (ṣĕdāqâ) and order (2 Sam 8:15; 15:4; 1 Kgs 10:9), especially on behalf of the poor.

Clearly, then, for the ancient Hebrews, "righteousness" was not a private religious matter. In conflicts between members of the same family, social group, or society, the community desired to see harmony and right relationship (ṣĕdāqâ) restored. This desire provides the background for understanding Deut 1:16 and the parallel passages in Deut 16:18 and Lev 19:15. No society that denies this activist justice to the weak by settling for minimal "innocence" can be called "righteous."

humble. Some cases may be beyond their abilities. Rather than arrogantly, and perhaps incorrectly, render decisions of which they are uncertain, judges should refer these difficult cases to a more competent colleague—in this instance Moses.

Israel Declines to Enter the Promised Land, 1:19-46

Deuteronomy 1:19-46 recounts Israel's departure from Mt. Horeb, its arrival at Kadesh-barnea in the southern desert, the reconnaissance mission into Canaan, Israel's refusal to enter the promised land, and YHWH's displeasure. The events narrated in this passage establish the pattern of Israel's rebellion and give the grounds for Israel's period of wandering, for YHWH's prohibition against Moses' entry into the land, and ultimately, for Joshua's career as Moses' successor. The account itself is remarkable for its conciseness and brevity. One might even say for its minimalism.

Once again, certain issues require preliminary attention. The problem of the so-called "number shift" in Deuteronomy and the recurring question of the relationship of Deuteronomy to other Pentateuchal traditions figure prominently in interpreting this passage.

First, Deuteronomy 1:21 and 31 present the initial occurrences of a puzzling phenomenon common in the book of Deuteronomy. Unlike modern English, the Hebrew pronoun system employs distinct singular and plural forms of the second person "you." In keeping with the notion that Moses addressed the assembled people of Israel, plural forms dominate in Deuteronomy. Occasionally, however, singular forms suddenly appear in the midst of plural speech, as in vv. 21 and 31. Scholars struggle to explain the "numbers shift" phenomenon. Do the singular sections represent editorial insertions? Does the alternation play some structural role? Is it a feature of ancient rhetorical style? Or is it simply incidental? To date no explanation offered has gained widespread support in scholarly circles.

Second, as is true for the entire "historical summary" section (Deut 1–3), Deuteronomy 1:19-46 stands in an interesting relationship to parallel traditions elsewhere in the Pentateuch, found in this case in Numbers 13–14. These two accounts of the reconnaissance mission, the people's reaction to it, and God's response clearly refer to the same incident, but they differ in significant details. Once again the question involves whether Deuteronomy depends

---

Amorites

AΩ The first instances of the Akkadian term *Amurru* ("West") seem to be in 3rd millennium BC cuneiform literature where the term refers both to the desert region of Syria to the "west" of Mesopotamia and to the Semites who dwelt there. The name may have originally been a self-designation (the name of a Hanaean clan at Mari) that came secondarily to refer to the region. It is known from mid-2d millennium BC Egyptian, Mesopotamian, and Hittite sources as an administrative district, a kingdom, or a vassal, respectively, located in central Syria with its capital at Mari. The Amorite Hammurapi (c. 1875–1800 BC) conquered Mari, already influential under Zimri-lim, and established the first dynasty of Babylon with control over much of the Euphrates region. Mari itself was destroyed (c. 1595 BC) by the Hittite ruler Mursilis I. Remnants of the once rather powerful political entity, surviving only as a number of independent city-states (Kadesh on the Orontes, for example) succumbed in the 13th century to the conquering Sea Peoples.

The Amorites were an aggressive people. In the late 3rd millennium, they mounted a series of raids into Akkad and Sumer, the two political centers of Mesopotamia at the time, prompting king Shu-Sin of Ur (2037–2029 BC) to build extensive border fortifications. Beginning around 2000 BC, they moved in several phases into Mesopotamia proper to

be assimilated into and, by the 1700s BC, to dominate the Mesopotamian population. Kings in the Babylonian dynasty that included the famed Hammurapi all have Amorite names. Egyptian execration texts (c. 1900 BC) mention rulers to the south of Syria in Palestine and the Transjordan who bear Amorite names. Given the complexity of the archeological picture, uncertainty concerning the defining characteristics of the Amorite dialect, and the volatility of ancient population movements, it is difficult to be more precise about Amorite history and population centers.

The Bible uses the term "Amorite" generally as an ethnic designation for segments of the Semitic population that Israel found inhabiting southern Palestine and the Transjordan (in this sense, the term is nearly synonymous with "Canaanite," Gen 15:16; Exod 3:8; Deut 1:7; Josh 10:5; 24:15; 2 Sam 21:2) and specifically in reference to "the two kings of the Amorites," Sihon, whose kingdom Heshbon was in the southern Transjordan, and Og, king of Bashan (Num 21:13; Deut 3:8; 4:46; Josh 2:10; 9:10; 24:8; Judg 10:8; 11:19-21). Bashan and Heshbon may have been the southernmost examples of the Amorite city-states. As in the Mesopotamian sources, by the time of Israel's arrival in Palestine and certainly thereafter, the term "Amorite" had lost specificity.

literarily on Numbers or vice versa, or whether each represents an independent tradition. As will be demonstrated below, this question is more than an esoteric scholarly concern. A careful comparison of the two versions highlights their specific emphases and nuances.

Deuteronomy 1:19-46 differs from Numbers 13–14 on several points. According to Deuteronomy, the people request the espionage mission; according to Numbers, YHWH suggests it (13:1-2). Numbers describes a much more extensive patrol, reaching as far north as Rehob near Hamat in Syria—the entire length of Palestine (13:21); Deuteronomy mentions only the Valley of Eshcol (1:24). According to Deuteronomy 1:37, YHWH prohibits Moses' entry into the promised land because of the people's unbelief and rebellion; according to Numbers 20:12, YHWH disqualifies Moses when he angrily and disobediently strikes the rock to produce water. Deuteronomy 1:38 anticipates Joshua's commission as Moses' successor (compare Deut 31:7-8, 14-15, 23; Num 27:12-23); Numbers focuses on Caleb's role. Deuteronomy 1:19-46 consistently refers to Israel's enemies as the "Amorites" (vv. 19, 20, 27, 44), [Amorites] while Numbers refers more precisely to the Canaanites and the Amalekites (13:28; 14:25, 43, 45). Similarly, Deuteronomy calls the giants of the land "the sons of the Anakim," understanding the plural term "Anakim" as the name of a people. Numbers, on the other hand, calls them "the sons of Anak," a reflection of the notion that Anak was an individual. [Anakim] Deuteronomy gives the impression that little time elapsed between the spies' return and the people's abortive attempt at conquest; Numbers envisions a period of up to three days (Num 14:1, 40). According to Deuteronomy, YHWH instructed Moses to warn against attempting an invasion (v. 42); in Numbers, Moses issues the warning on his own initiative (14:41-42).

Anakim

AΩ The Anakim are known only from a few references in the Hebrew Bible, almost all of which are associated with the tradition of Calebite possession of Hebron and its environs. The name itself seems to be related to terms that refer to the neck and to jewelry worn around the neck (Deut 15:4; Judg 8:26; Prov 1:9; Ps 73:6; *Cant* 4:9). The Bible employs the term in relation to a people who inhabited southern Palestine prior to the arrival of the Israelites. It occurs in several forms in this usage. One construction, *bĕnê hā'ănāq* (Josh 15:14; Judg 1:20; lit., "sons of the neck," that is, "long-necked men"), and the related *yĕlîdê hā'ănāq* (Num 13:22, 28; Josh 15:14; lit., "children of the neck"), seem to describe the stature of this people. The Bible refers to them more often simply as *'ănāqîm*, "long-necks" (Deut 2:10, 11, 21; Josh 11:21, 22; 14:12, 14; Jer 47:5) or, in a usage that seems to have lost contact with the descriptive origins of the term, as the *bĕnê 'ănāqîm*, "sons of the Anakim" (Deut 1:28; 9:2; lit., "sons of the long-necks"). Even further removed from the original usage, two passages assume that the "sons of Anak" must have descended from an ancestor by that name (Josh 15:13; 21:11).

The Anakim were associated with other obscure, legendary giant races such as the Rephaim (Deut 2:10-11) and the Nephilim (Num 13:33; compare Gen 6:4). They lived in the region surrounding Hebron (Num 13:22, 28; Josh 11:21; 14:12-15; 15:13-14; 21:11-13) and in the area later to become Philistia (Josh 11:21; Jer 47:1-5). In fact, the Bible attributes the earlier name for Hebron, Kiriath-arba, to either the ancestor of Anak (Josh 15:13-14) or a leading member of the group (Josh 14:15). Joshua (Josh 11:21) or Caleb (Josh 14:12-15; 15:13-14) drove the Anakite clans of Ahiman, Sheshai, and Talmai from Hebron (Josh 15:13-14; see also Num 13:22, 28; Judg 1:10, 20). The texts manifest some confusion whether Caleb controlled all of Hebron and its vicinity (Josh 15:13-14) or only the surrounding countryside (Josh 21:11-13).

The Deuteronomy account is also much shorter than that in Numbers 13–14. In fact, Deuteronomy sometimes omits information found in Numbers, necessary for a complete understanding of the sequence of events. For example, Deuteronomy does not list the members of the spying party (see Num 13:4-16). Deuteronomy (v. 25) fails to mention that they found grapes at Eshcol. Numbers focuses on this discovery, calling attention to the fame of the region surrounding Hebron for its grape production (Num 13:24), as part of its explanation of how the tribe of Caleb came into possession of the area. In fact, the name Eshcol means "cluster (of grapes)" and this etiology accounts for the reference. [Etiologies] Deuteronomy does not give the content of the spies' report (compare Num 13:26-29), leaving the people's fearful reaction in Deuteronomy 1:36, 38 without foundation—unless the reader also knows the Numbers account. Deuteronomy is likewise silent concerning Caleb's effort to calm the people (Num 13:30), the people's deliberations concerning the possibility of return to Egypt (14:1-4), their threat to stone Joshua and Caleb (14:6-10), Moses' intercession with YHWH on behalf of the people (14:5-19), the death by plague of the ten spies (14:36-38), and the Ark of the Covenant (14:44). Deuteronomy's final reference to Israel's mourning after its defeat at the hands of the Amorites (1:46) is unparalleled in Numbers.

Since the brevity of the Deuteronomy version results in an incomplete account that presumes information not explicitly stated, most scholars consider it an abbreviation of the Numbers tradition. [Joshua and Caleb] As noted above, the most significant results of this comparison of the two versions, however, is the insight it affords into the purposes of the editor(s) of the book of Deuteronomy. Numbers highlights etiology—explanations of how the Calebites came to possess Hebron and of the forty-year duration of the wilderness wandering—Moses' intercessory role, and YHWH's presence with Israel as symbolized by the *shekinah* glory and the Ark of the Covenant. Deuteronomy, on the other hand, mentions none of these elements and accentuates Israel's astonishing lack of confidence in YHWH's protection, its arrogant

Etiologies

Etiologies explain the origins and backgrounds of names, customs, practices, and other long-standing situations. Folk cultures typically preserve information and pass it across generations in story form. Etiologies answer questions such as "How did X come to have this name?" "Why do we observe this custom?" "Why do we worship at this place? In this way?" "Why do we enjoy such a cordial (or hostile) relationship with our neighbors?" One can easily imagine grandparents or parents telling these stories after dinner to answer children's questions.

Hebrew narrative literature includes many examples of etiology. Why do humans fear snakes? Because of the serpent's temptation of Adam and Eve, human beings and snakes will be perpetual enemies. What do rainbows mean? They signify God's promise to Noah never again to destroy the world by flood. Why do people speak so many different languages? To hinder people from cooperating in follies such as the Tower of Babel, God "confused" the situation by introducing linguistic diversity.

> **Joshua and Caleb**
>
> The problem of the relationship between Num 13–14 and Deut 1:19-46 is complicated somewhat by the fact that the Numbers passage seems to have been edited. The central figure in Numbers is Caleb, the ancestor of the Calebites who gained possession of Hebron because of their ancestor's faithfulness. Several texts mention Caleb as the sole spy in favor of entering the land (13:30) and, thus, the sole member of the exodus generation to be rewarded with the privilege of entry (14:24). Another series of texts refer to Caleb and Joshua (14:6, 30, 38) acting in consort. References to Joshua (14:6) seem to have been added to avoid the impression that Moses' successor was silent on this important occasion. The list of spies that opens the unit mentions "Hoshea the son of Nun" as the spy representing the tribe of Ephraim, further suggesting that, originally, Joshua played no significant role in the account. The editor's comment that Moses called Hoshea "Joshua" (13:16) probably served to facilitate the inclusion of Joshua alongside Caleb. Another instance of editorial expansion can be found in YHWH's double response to Moses' intercessory prayer (14:20-25 // 14:26-30). The first of these responses mentions Caleb only (v. 24) and ends with the command to depart Kadesh-barnea for the wilderness. The second substantially repeats the first, except that Joshua is mentioned alongside Caleb (v. 30), and it refers to the people's fear concerning the fates of their children (v. 31; compare Deut 1:39).
>
> Since Deut 1:19-46 bears closest verbal similarity to the later portions of Num 13–14 (for example 1:39 // 14:31), it is at least possible that Num 13–14 was edited to bring it into closer conformity with Deut 1. In this case, Deut 1:19-46 may have been dependent upon an early form of Num 13–14 that, in turn, was subsequently edited in light of Deut 1:19-46. On the other hand, as discussed in the commentary, these verbal similarities are often unsupported by the text of the LXX, suggesting that late scribes supplemented the text of Deuteronomy on the basis of Numbers in a period well after the Torah had been closed. Obviously, the issue is complicated.

overconfidence in the efficacy of shallow and belated repentance, and the common fate of leader and people.

From Horeb to Kadesh-barnea, 1:19-21

The "travel notice" in v. 19 is the second in a series of such comments in Deuteronomy 1–3 and 31–34 (1:6b, 19; 2:1, 3, 8, 13, 24, 34; 3:1, 4, 29; 31:1; 32:44; 34:1), all in the first person plural, which serve as the narrative skeleton for the so-called "outer framework" of the book. They describe Israel's journey from one point to the next. Then follows the account of an incident and another travel notice. The notice in 1:19 describes Israel's journey from Mt. Horeb toward the "hill country of the Amorites," specifically Kadesh-barnea. This site in the southern desert, probably the modern Tel el-Qudeirat, was located on the King's Highway from Syria to the Arabah, on the threshold of the promised land.

Moses sees no reason for delay. YHWH delivered Israel from Egyptian bondage because of the promise made to the patriarchs, a promise that included the gift of the land of Canaan. Now Israel needs only to "take possession" of the gift (v. 21; the first occurrence of second person singular address). It seems straightforward enough. Moses betrays an awareness, however, that the matter is somewhat more complex than simply receiving: this gift must be taken. Canaan's inhabitants are powerful, well armed, and numerous. At first glance, nomadic Israel appears ill prepared for

Oasis
A view of the Oasis of Barnea with the Tell el Kadesh in Egypt.

the task. Without explicitly stating the reason for his confidence, Moses encourages them not to fear or be discouraged and thereby pinpoints what will become the central issue in the account—Israel's fear.

The Reconnaissance Mission, 1:22-25

The people suggest a commonsense approach to the task ahead (v. 22). None of them have ever been in Canaan. In order better to prepare, they require information. A party should be sent ahead to reconnoiter. What will be the best route? Will they encounter opposition? Where? How strong will it be? Moses sees the wisdom of the idea and chooses a representative from each tribe to undertake the mission. Arriving at the Valley of Eshcol, the spies gather samples of the land's bounty to show their compatriots. They return, then, with both personal testimony[6] and objective evidence of the goodness of the land YHWH has given them.

The People Decline YHWH's Gift, 1:26-28

The people's fearful response to the spies' report is astonishing. One must assume that the report has been abbreviated and that some negative information has been omitted or will be supplied later (see v. 28). Numbers preserves a much fuller version of the report. At any rate, the information given in v. 25 can hardly have occasioned the people's response. The narrator has probably reserved the troubling news to be communicated to the reader in the people's recollection in v. 28 in order to sharpen the dissonance of the people's refusal to take YHWH's gift. Interestingly, presented with an ambivalent report—a bountiful land, but occupied by strong people in fortified cities—the people focus their attention on the negative. How typically human! The reader finds it difficult to resist the suspicion that the suggestion to send spies, which seems a pragmatic measure, may have in fact been motivated by an insidious fear. After all, Moses seems to have sensed the need for encouragement from the outset (v. 21).

Verses 26-28 offer an interesting and insightful example of the relationship between fear and sin. When the people hear that they must actively "take" the land from its current inhabitants, they choose to disobey God, to "rebel against" God's direct command (v. 26). Why would God's people flagrantly disobey a command intended to bring them immediate benefit? Why do people sin? As did Adam and Eve in the Garden (Gen 3:1-13), Israel doubts God's motives. They distrust YHWH. They fear that YHWH, the God of their ancestors, who delivered them from Egyptian slavery, does not truly have their best interests at heart. In the privacy of their tents, they "murmur" that YHWH has brought them to the wilderness there to abandon them. YHWH has acted not out of love, but out of hatred and a desire to see them destroyed (v. 27)! It has all been a trick!

What can be the root of such mistrust? Fear! The spies have told them of great giants and grand fortresses and their "hearts have melted" (v. 28); today one would say that they "lost heart" or that their "knees buckled." Now they can see not God's promise of God's past provision for their need, but only tall men in walled cities!

Moses Encourages Israel to Trust YHWH, 1:29-33

Trust grows out of experience. Moses renews his exhortation that the people need not fear (v. 29). Now, however, he supplements the call to trust YHWH with a recitation of events in Israel's experience of YHWH. Israel can trust YHWH because YHWH has proven trustworthy. Surely the God who defeated the Egyptians on Israel's behalf can help them conquer the inhabitants of Canaan. In fact, Moses says, he "will himself fight for you" (v. 30).

The Masculine Pronoun in Reference to the Deity

AΩ The question of how best to refer to the deity in English is difficult. This commentary seeks to balance the awareness that ancient Israel spoke about and to its God, YHWH, in masculine terms with the awareness that all God-talk is metaphorical and that, since the Bible itself insists that both male and female reflect the image of God, to employ exclusively masculine language in speaking of God is sexist, at best. On the one hand, it would be anachronistic to attribute modern sensibilities to patriarchal Israelite society; on the other hand, it would be improper to fail to acknowledge that the God who created both genders of humankind in God's own image encompasses and transcends masculine and feminine. In the effort to be responsible to both of these concerns, the commentary will employ masculine pronouns when explicating the biblical language, strictly speaking. But when the author of the commentary speaks of God more generally, the author will assiduously avoid sexist references. Admittedly, this approach is a compromise and has deficiencies. It seems, however, the scheme most suited to fidelity to the text of Scripture and the author's understanding of the one God who is both Mother and Father and who transcends all human categories of thought.

[The Masculine Pronoun in Reference to the Deity] Furthermore, Israel has experienced not only the martial God who fights for God's people, but the tender God who cares for them as a father cares for his son (v. 31), and the provident God who leads them to their destination (v. 33). Not only then has God demonstrated the *ability* to deliver Israel, but the *desire* to do so. Israel's best interests motivate God's actions. The deliverance from Egypt constituted only the beginning of a journey to end in Canaan. YHWH did not intend simply to deliver Israel from bondage, but to lead them into bounty and rest. YHWH has promised them the good land because they need it. Nevertheless, Israel cannot bring itself to trust, to believe (v. 32).

YHWH's Reaction, 1:34-40

To this point, only Moses, the spies, and the people have participated in the discussion. Now YHWH himself speaks. The people have disobeyed, they mistrust YHWH, they devalue YHWH's provision for them. Consequently, YHWH is angry (v. 34). [An Angry God]

God's anger at Israel's fear, mistrust, and blatant rebellion move God to impose three sanctions and grant three benefits, in pairs, suited to the people's behavior. First, none of the adults alive at the time (the expression "of this evil generation" in v. 35 is not represented in the LXX; it may be a scribal

---

An Angry God

📖 Many Christians take great pains to downplay biblical texts, especially but not exclusively in the Old Testament, that portray divine emotions. In their view, a perfect deity cannot be subject to change—God cannot change God's mind or God's heart. Many people consider anger, in particular, an ignoble emotion unworthy of God. Typically, interpreters treat texts that speak of God's emotions as vapid metaphors. God does not really regret, change God's mind, or become angry. The texts in question, these interpreters maintain, refer to some indescribable aspect of God's character or they represent accommodations to the constraints of human language. The argument can be made that such interpretations give priority to philosophical assumptions as to the divine nature over the plain sense of the biblical text. If one values the Bible as a primary source for Christian theology—if not *the* primary source—then one must take the biblical witness seriously. Furthermore, if one takes seriously the biblical assertion that the God of Israel is a personal God, then one should be uncomfortable with the abstract, immutable, impersonal deity imagined by the philosophers.

Corporate Responsibility

In contrast to the modern Western emphasis on individualism, ancient Israelite culture embodied a notion of corporate responsibility. Whereas modern society insists that only the individual can be held responsible for wrongdoing, and, conversely, esteemed for accomplishment, the Israelites recognized that individuals represent and reflect their families and communities. As the Rabbis put it, "The talk of the child in the market-place is either that of his father or of his mother" (*bSukkah* 56b). It is possible to draw the distinction too sharply, but it can fairly be said that the ancient understanding seems more down-to-earth, less artificial, than the modern concept. Do abusive parents share some responsibility for the crimes of their delinquent teenagers? Do middle-class stockholders, hungry for dividends and increases in stock values, bear some responsibility for the questionable or even unethical business practices of giant multi-national corporations? Several texts in the Hebrew Bible reflect this concept of collectivism. Modern readers often find them among the more difficult texts in the Bible precisely because of the conflict between the ancient and modern viewpoints. For example, modern readers are often troubled by the apparent injustice manifest in the stoning of Achan and his entire family as punishment for his sin at Jericho (Josh 7). God's refusal to allow Moses to enter the promised land because of Israel's rebellion at Kadesh-barnea (Deut 1:37) offends modern sensibilities in a similar fashion.

Scholars debate the significance of two aspects of this notion of corporate responsibility. First, scholars disagree as to the degree to which ancient Israelites viewed themselves as individuals. In an influential study, the British scholar H. Wheeler Robinson coined the term "corporate identity" to describe this feature of Israelite culture. He argued that, in the earliest periods of Israel's history, individual identities were typically subsumed in the identity of the group—the family, clan, tribe, or nation. Such an analysis would account for the Achan episode, for the biblical practice of regularly identifying individuals as the "son of X, the son of Y, of the clan of Z," (Josh 7:18; 1 Sam 1:1; etc.), and for a number of other phenomena. Since Robinson's article, however, scholars have pointed out that his terminology suggests that Israel had no notion whatsoever of the individual, a suggestion contrary to the evidence (Noah, the individual, was spared judgment; Caleb and Joshua do not suffer the common fate of the rebellious generation).

Second, scholars have come to reject an earlier viewpoint concerning the linear development of Israelite thought from collectivism to individualism, with the turning point usually located in the time of Jeremiah (31:29-30) and Ezekiel (18:2-4). Collectivism and individualism can be found in texts from all periods of Israelite history. Which is it, then? Does the Bible view people as individuals or as members of communities? It may well be that modern interpreters' failure to resolve this tension suggests that the truth is complicated. People are individuals who belong to families and communities.

H. Wheeler Robinson, *Corporate Personality in Ancient Israel* (Facet Books, Biblical Series 11; Philadelphia: Fortress Press, 1964).

insertion, perhaps under the influence of Num 14:35) will be permitted to enter the promised land (v. 35), with the exception of Caleb. As a reader familiar with Numbers 13:30 knows, Caleb had admonished the people to "go up immediately, and take possession of [the land]; for we can well conquer it." Because Caleb "has wholly followed the LORD," God promises that he and his descendants will possess the land Caleb reconnoitered (v. 36).

Second, YHWH prohibits Moses' entry into the land (v. 37) and indicates that Joshua will succeed Moses and lead a future generation into Canaan (v. 38). The text gives no indication of God's reasoning on this point. It seems that God punishes Moses for Israel's rebellion despite the fact that Moses had faithfully executed his role as divine spokesman, encouraging the people to obey God's command and reminding them of God's faithful leadership and providence. Any proposal concerning Moses' implicit guilt or

God's logic will be little more than speculation in light of the text's silence on these issues. It must suffice to call attention to the Hebraic notions of the close identity between leader and people and of "corporate responsibility," the expectation that the fates of individuals and of the groups to which they belong are inextricably linked. The Hebrew recognized that, in a real sense, all members of a community bear responsibility for the actions of other members. [Corporate Responsibility] Although Moses had committed no specific crime on this occasion, he had obviously failed in some way to lead his people into a mature trust in God. Perhaps Moses should not have reinforced the people's timidity by permitting the spy mission. At any rate, as the prophet Hosea (4:9) put it, "like people, like priest." To say more would be indiscreet.

Third, in a reversal of the previous punishment-benefit order, YHWH promises that the minor children, "who this day have no knowledge of good and evil,"[7] will possess the land (v. 39), but their parents will journey in the wilderness until the older generation passes (v. 40). This transference of the promise to the next generation exemplifies a wondrous principle in the book of Deuteronomy: neither is YHWH's relationship with Israel limited to a single generation nor do one generation's failures prevent a later generation from fulfilling the potential of this relationship.

Facile Repentance and Desperate Obedience, 1:41-46

After YHWH pronounces sentence, when it is too late, the people reverse their stance. In the face of God's anger, they quickly—perhaps too quickly and too easily—repent. "We have sinned," they confess (v. 41). Have they truly repented of their mistrust or is their sudden obedience designed to avert punishment? Have they learned to trust God or only to fear God's anger? YHWH wants to give the land to a willing and grateful people, not to coerce obedience. But this people, who have taken God's promise lightly and discounted God's love, now presume upon God's mercy (v. 43).

One can hear echoes of the ancient institution of "holy war" (*ḥerem*) in YHWH's warning that the people will be defeated if they attempt now, too late, to enter the land. According to the "holy war" doctrine, some (not all) of Israel's conflicts were sacred. YHWH declared the war as symbolized by the trumpet blast calling Israel to battle. The army of Israel prepared for battle as if preparing for a religious celebration. The enemies were YHWH's enemies. YHWH led Israel onto the battlefield as symbolized by the presence of the Ark of the Covenant at the head of the column. YHWH fought the battle. Often, Israel was instructed to employ unusual, even foolish techniques (Joshua's army marching around Jericho blowing trumpets, Josh 6:1-21; Gideon's 300 men with trumpets and concealed lamps, Judg 7:16-22) in order to make it clear that YHWH had won the victory, not Israel. Holy War texts frequently mention that YHWH threw the enemy "into confusion," permitting Israel's army to rout them. Territory, living things, and plunder conquered in such a Holy War belong to YHWH, not the people. Israel cannot assume, however, that YHWH endorses all of its military campaigns. YHWH's presence on the battlefield with them is not automatic. In this case, they go into battle falsely confident that, because they have acknowledged their sin, YHWH will accompany them despite his warning to the contrary ("I am not in your midst," v. 42). Ironically, their rebellion yet again (v. 43) demonstrates the insincerity of their earlier repentance. As predicted, the Amorites soundly defeat them, pursuing them "as bees do" (an image associated with warfare in several extra-biblical ancient Near Eastern texts as well). The Amorites pursue Israel all the way to Horman (modern Tel Masos). Afterward, Israel returns to Kadesh to mourn and seek God's forgiveness. Aware of their history of mistrust, unbelief, rebellion, and false repentance, YHWH pays them no mind (v. 45). The unit concludes with a summary notice that Israel spent quite a lengthy period at Kadesh (v. 46).

CONNECTIONS

Interpreting Texts

This question of how properly to interpret authoritative texts and traditions is neither a new problem nor a problem exclusive to biblical interpretation. Since human language is somewhat ambiguous, and since statements of law or principle simply cannot be formulated in such a way as to deal explicitly with every possible future situation, any authoritative document, whether Holy Scripture or the United States Constitution, for example, must be interpreted in order to be applied to new situations. The framers of the Constitution could not have imagined interstate highways, transcontinental telephone systems, radio, TV, or the Internet. Because they knew that new circumstances would arise, however, they chose language that would express basic principles, yet be broad enough to apply to unanticipated new situations ("The

Congress shall have Power . . . To regulate Commerce . . . among the several States . . . ." Art. I, Sect. 8). Because the Constitution is the fundamental, binding, defining document of the Republic, the legislative, executive, and judicial branches seek to apply its basic principles to new situations. In fact, the Supreme Court functions solely to assure that the Constitution is faithfully and reasonably so applied.

In a similar way, the Torah states broad principles, without always defining how to apply these principles in every situation one could conceivably encounter. How does an adult child living in another state "honor" a parent who needs long-term care but who is unwilling to move away from home? In other instances, the Torah states very specific cases that no longer arise. Is there some principle of God's will expressed in the very limited situation involving the ox that gores (Exod 21:28-31)? In either case, as Deuteronomy clearly understands, the Torah, YHWH's revealed will for YHWH's people, must be interpreted and applied or it becomes irrelevant. In fact, Deuteronomy consciously represents the attempt to extrapolate the principles inherent in the covenant established at Mt. Horeb (Sinai) and apply them to the new situation confronting Israel. A generation has passed. A new generation stands poised to enter the promised land. Moses, the only leader and mediator of the covenant Israel has ever known, will not enter the land with his people. At this juncture, Deuteronomy offers a body of authoritative amplifications and clarifications of the basic covenant. It relates to the Decalogue in analogy to the relationship between legislation and the Constitution.

Moments of Transition

Deuteronomy 1:6-18 recounts Moses' initiative at a decisive moment of transition in the life of the nation of Israel—the transition from existence as a band of freed slaves under the leadership of a charismatic and gifted visionary to life as a society requiring organization and governmental structures. All movements, whether revolutionary or religious, idealistic or intellectual, come to such moments of transition. Threatened by its more powerful and politically more stable neighbors, Israel asked Samuel to give it a king (1 Sam 8:5). Centuries later, pressured by growing numbers and thus growing needs, the early church soon chose deacons to minister to its poor widows (Acts 6:1-6). By the end of the New Testament period, the church had also instituted the offices of elder, bishop, deacon, widow, etc. (1 Tim 3; 4:3-22). In modern history, the goal of the American Revolution was not independence from England only, but a new government.

Such moments of transition are both necessary and dangerous. If Israel were to survive as a healthy society, it must be ordered. Inevitably, disputes would arise between individuals and groups. Inevitably, crimes would be committed. Already the people had become so numerous that Moses could not see to all their needs. He found it necessary to establish judicial and governmental institutions or social chaos would ensue. [Realism and Idealism] The challenge lay, however, in establishing institutions that would nurture the genius of the movement instead of feeding on it. Institutions tend toward self-perpetuation, self-service, and self-importance.

Samuel warned Israel that kings become greedy for power and status. Rather than serving, they demand service (1 Sam 8:10-18). True to Samuel's fears, Saul disobeyed God, David took Uriah's wife and then his life, and Solomon lived extravagantly at the expense of his people. By the third century, the leadership of the Christian church had become an institutionalized bureaucracy. The Protestant Reformation, born of a renewed awareness of individual freedom and responsibility before God, soon exchanged the hierarchies of the Roman church for hierarchies of its own. Almost since the ratification of the Constitution, the people of the US have denounced "big government" and "self-perpetuating bureaucracies." Indeed, there is nothing new under the sun.

Moses was aware of the danger. He sought judges with wisdom, sensitivity, and experience. He admonished them to remember that they held their positions not by virtue of their merit, but by divine calling. They were to administer God's justice. This ministry made no room for self-aggrandizement, for partiality, or for arrogance. As Jesus would later say, "The kings of the nations exercise lordship over them; and those in authority benefit from being commissioned. But not so with you; instead, the greater among you shall be as the least, and the leader as the servant" (Luke 22:24-25, author's translation).

Both the need for order and the danger inherent in institutionalized power continue to be felt in modern society and, sadly, in the church. Precisely because they are necessary, the church must always be on guard that its institutions do not become ends in themselves.

The Problem of Trust

The noted psychologist Erik Erikson documented the significant stages in human emotional development. According to his analysis, the infant's first developmental task involves the resolution of the conflict between what he termed "basic trust" versus "basic mistrust." If the infant's caregivers provide consistent, quality care—warmly, lovingly, competently, and regularly meeting the infant's needs for nourishment, affection, and comfort—the infant develops confidence or trust in the benevolence of the world and, reciprocally, a healthy sense of his or her own value. Conversely, inconsistent, capricious care or abuse engenders mistrust (the caregivers are unreliable and therefore the world is impersonal, chaotic, and even malevolent) and a sense of worthlessness (the infant senses that his or her needs are not met because he or she is insignificant).[8]

James Fowler pioneered the study of the development of the human individual's capacity for religious faith.[9] Fowler noted that Erikson's "basic trust" is nearly identical with the basis for religious faith. In more mature forms, of course, religious faith typically involves belief in some deity or divine power, incorporates some system of doctrine and morality, and is manifest in some overtly religious practice. At the foundation of all religious faith, however, lies "undifferentiated faith," the ability and tendency to trust that someone cares and the confidence that this concern makes one worthy. In essence, believers trust that the world is not ultimately random, that it has purpose, and that their lives have value. It is perhaps not too great an oversimplification to say that a core message of the Bible is that God cares about God's creation.

In a modern context, of course, belief in God is most often understood in relation to the question of the *existence* of a deity. Moderns conceive of faith primarily in opposition to atheism or agnosticism. In the context of the insights of Erikson and Fowler, however, one can ask whether granting intellectually the notion that God *exists* is on a par with *trusting* God for care and purpose in life. Erikson commented, for example, on the puzzling inconsistency manifest by "many who profess faith, yet in practice mistrust both life and man [sic]."[10] The Hebrew Bible—the product of an era that knew little of modern scientific skepticism—rarely argues that God exists. It assumes that God created and sustains the world. Instead, faith and faithfulness are, for the Bible, matters of trust and relationship.

The seed of the first sin was neither modern-style doubt nor defiance, but mistrust. The serpent said to Eve, "Did God say, 'Do not eat of any tree of the garden'?" Eve replied, "We may eat the fruit of the trees in the garden, but God said, 'Do not eat the fruit of the tree in the middle of the garden or touch it, lest you die.'" The serpent replied, "You won't die. God knows that when you eat it, your eyes will be opened and you will be like God, knowing good and evil." (Gen 3:1b-5, excerpted)

The serpent insinuated that the God who had created them, who had planted the rich and luxuriant garden to provide for them, who walked with them daily, had intentionally and deceptively withheld from them the best gift of all. Adam and Eve disobeyed God because, in their mistrust, they feared that God might not have provided the best. Thus, they acted on their own initiative and contrary to God's express command.

In the same way, despite everything Israel had seen God do for them in Egypt, at Sinai, and on the journey through the wilderness, at Kadesh-barnea their mistrust and fear gave birth to rebellion and sin. Despite Moses' assurance that God loved them as a parent loves a child, they feared the descendants of giants more than they trusted their Creator.

The problem of trusting God surfaces even when no giant stands in one's path. Everyday concerns can command one's attention and undermine one's confidence in God's provision. Like an infant who has forgotten the comforting sight of mother's face or the soothing sound of father's voice, one can easily come to feel alone, unloved, and unworthy.

Jesus addressed this problem when he said, "Do not be anxious . . . Consider the birds of the air: They do not sow or reap or gather into barns, and yet your heavenly Father feeds them. Are you not more valuable than they? . . . If God clothes the grass of the field, which is alive today and is thrown into the oven tomorrow, is he not more likely to clothe you, O you of little faith? . . . Your heavenly Father knows that you need [food and clothing]!" (Matt 6:25-32, excerpted)

The American poet and philosopher Ralph Waldo Emerson once wrote, "All that I have seen teaches me to trust the Creator for all that I have not seen." Little giants stand in the path ahead. Bills must be paid. Children struggle to adulthood, negotiating obstacles of peer pressure, identity, career, and relationships. Young adults face the uncertainties of a changing economy and shrinking opportunities. Corporations downsize. Careers falter. Aging parents require care. Yet, God created a wondrous world. God gives life and sustains it. Surely God will provide for today and tomorrow.

NOTES

[1] N. Lohfink, "Der Bundesschluss im Lande Moab: Redaktionsgeschichtliches zu Dt 28,69-32,47," *Biblische Zeitschrift* NS 6 (1962): 32 n. 2; J. Lundbom, "The Inclusio and Other Framing Devices in Deuteronomy I–XXVIII," *Vetus Testamentum* 56 (1996): 300-301; D. Christensen, *Deuteronomy 1–11* (WBC 6A; Dallas: Word Books, 1991), 6-7.

[2] See, for example, A. D. H. Mayes, *Deuteronomy* (NCBC; Grand Rapids: Eerdmans, 1979), 118.

[3] See, for example, J. Van Seters, "Etiology in the Moses Tradition: The Case of Exodus 18," *Hebrew Annual Review* 9 (1985): 355-61.

[4] See, for example, G. von Rad, *Deuteronomy: A Commentary* (OTL; Philadelphia: Westminster, 1966), 39-40.

[5] By contrast, Num 11:10-25 omit any reference to judges. See the discussion of the problem of literary dependence above. Although vv. 13 and 15 refer generally to military-administrative officers, the description of duties and responsibilities applies only to judges; in similar fashion, Exod 18:13-26 elaborate the duties of the judge and mention administrative posts only in passing.

[6] The phrase "and brought us word" in v. 25 does not appear in the LXX: a Hebrew copyist may have imported it from the people's proposal for a spy mission in v. 22—"and let them bring us word"—that does appear in the LXX.

[7] Again, the LXX has no equivalent for the phrase "who you said would become a prey." It probably represents a harmonization with Num 14:3, 31.

[8] See, especially, *Childhood and Society* (2d ed.; New York: Norton, 1963), 247-51.

[9] See, especially, *Stages of Faith: The Psychology of Human Development and the Quest for Meaning* (San Francisco: Harper and Row, 1981), 120.

[10] *Childhood and Society*, 248.

PASSAGE THROUGH FRIENDLY AND HOSTILE TERRITORIES

2:1–3:11

Overview of Section, 2:1–3:22

Characteristically, Deuteronomy records none of the details of the long period of Israel's wanderings following the rebellion at Kadesh-barnea. The book summarizes the account of these nearly forty years in the brief statements that Israel "remained at Kadesh many days" (1:46) and that it wandered about in the region of Mount Seir "many days" (2:1). [About Forty Years] Instead, Deuteronomy focuses on events significant for its distinctive theology of history. In particular, it seeks to situate Israel's historical relationship with YHWH in the broader context of YHWH's management of human affairs on a worldwide level. Although God's chosen people, Israel is not immune from YHWH's demands of obedience and justice. Nor is Israel YHWH's sole concern in the world. YHWH provides for other nations as well. Israel's role in human affairs is key, to be sure, but Israel is subject to YHWH's overarching sovereignty. Post-exilic readers of Deuteronomy will have found that the principles that governed Israel's early history in the land continued to operate in their own experience of life among the nations of the world. In this way, Israel's past history serves as a paradigm for all its generations.

About Forty Years

The Pentateuch adheres to a rather well ordered and consistent chronology of the events that transpired on Israel's journey from Egypt to Canaan. The departure from Egypt serves as the reference point for a system of dating that occasionally appears in texts outside the Pentateuch as well (1 Kgs 6:1). The following table details the key elements of the chronology for the period:

Departure from Rameses	15th day, 1st month, 1st year	Num 33:3, 5
Arrival at Sinai	3rd month	Exod 19:1-2
Departure for Kadesh	20th day, 2nd month, 2nd year	Num 10:11
Return to Kadesh	1st month, 40th year	Num 20:1
Arrival at Mt. Hor	1st day, 5th month, 40th year	Num 13:37-38; Deut 2:7; 29:5
Crossing the Zered	38 years after Kadesh rebellion	Deut 2:14
Camped at Beth-peor	before the 11th month, 40th year	Deut 1:3

The Structure of the Passage and Its Relation to Other Traditions

Deuteronomy 2:1–3:22, the account of the final leg of Israel's journey to the promised land, divides into two subsections. Deuteronomy 2:1-23 recounts Israel's passage through the Transjordanian territories belonging to its cousins Edom (vv. 1-8), Moab (vv. 9, 13), and Ammon (vv. 17-19) and incorporates comments concerning the aboriginal inhabitants of these regions (of Moab and Edom, vv. 10-12; of Ammon and Philistia, vv. 20-23) and concerning the passing of the generation of those who rebelled at Kadesh (vv. 14-16). Deuteronomy 2:24–3:22 records Israel's encounters with the enemy kingdoms of Heshbon and Bashan in the upper Transjordan. This second subsection includes reports concerning Moses' division of the upper Transjordan among the tribes of Reuben and Gad and his charge to these tribes that, although they have already received their territory, they must assist the other tribes in conquering Canaan. The demise of the rebellious generation marks the transition from the peaceful encounters in the south to the military conquest of the north. As Israel's abortive attempt to enter Canaan from Kadesh demonstrated, YHWH will not fight on behalf of those who willfully disobey. Passage through Edom, Moab, and Ammon was only possible, therefore, because these nations permitted Israel the privilege of transit. In turn, the conquest of Heshbon and Bashan would have been impossible had not YHWH fought for Israel.

Deuteronomy 2:1-23 exhibits a basic structure governed by the pattern of a divine command to cross friendly territory in peace (2:4-7, 9 and 13a, 18-19) followed by a travel notice recording the passage (2:8, 13b; the notice of the passage through Ammon is missing). While the basic sequence of events recorded here is clear (YHWH commands Israel to pass through Edom, Moab, and Ammon in succession and Israel obeys), the passage presents interpreters with a number of literary, traditional, and geographical puzzles.

First, the familiar interchange of verbs in second person singular (vv. 7, 9ab, 18-19) and plural forms (vv. 3-6, 13) appears in the passage, compounded now by the presence of first person singular (vv. 2, 9aa, 17), first person plural (vv. 1, 8), and third person plural (vv. 10-12, 14-16, 20-23) passages. For the most part, these verb forms reflect the diversity of content in the passage, in itself a puzzle. At certain points, however, the interchange renders it very difficult to determine who speaks to whom (e.g., 2:10-12, 15-16).

The most puzzling aspect of this passage involves its relationship to similar traditions in the book of Numbers. Israel's encounter with Edom (vv. 1-8a, see also v. 29) is also recorded in Numbers 20:14-21; 21:4. Once again, comparison of the two passages reveals several points of contact: both mention the purchase of drinking water (Deut 2:6; Num 20:19); both discuss seeking permission "to pass through" Edomite territory (Deut 2:4; Num 20:17). Yet the differences between the two passages are much more striking and call attention to Deuteronomy's distinctive emphases: Deuteronomy records YHWH's command but mentions no embassy to the king of Edom; Numbers records Moses' embassy to the king of Edom but no divine command. Deuteronomy situates YHWH's command to pass through Edom at the conclusion of Israel's travels around Mount Seir; Numbers places Moses' embassy in the period of Israel's stay at Kadesh. Deuteronomy assumes that Edom will fear Israel's military strength so that YHWH exhorts Moses to reassure Edom of Israel's peaceful intentions; Numbers relates Edom's successful military opposition to Israel's passage. Deuteronomy records only YHWH's instructions concerning the encounter with Edom and assumes that events transpired as planned; Numbers relates a military confrontation in which Israel was rebuffed. Presumably, according to Deuteronomy, Israel transited Edomite territory without incident (see also Deut 2:29); according to Numbers, Israel was forced to detour to the south (Num 21:4 [Textual Problems and Itinerary]) and then to the east of Edom (Num 21:10-12; 33:41-44).

Textual Problems and Itinerary

The reference to the road from Ezion-geber and Elath in Deut 2:8 may be a residue of this tradition preserved in Num 21:4. LXX does not attest to the first two occurrences of the preposition "from (*min*)" in Deut 2:8. Instead, LXX reads "And we approached our brothers the sons of Esau who dwell in Seir by the desert road from Elath and from Ezion-geber . . . ." The textual data supports either of two possible interpretations: (1) LXX preserves the more original meaning and the prepositions have been added to MT in an effort to harmonize it with Num 20:14-21; 21:4. (2) The Hebrew text is the more original, reflecting an earlier stage in the tradition more closely akin to the Numbers tradition. In this case, the LXX translator will have omitted the prepositions to bring v. 8 into closer harmony with Deut 2:1-7, 29.

Again, as with Deut 1:9-18 and 1:19-46, the passage concerning Israel's encounter with Edom raises significant questions regarding the relationship of Deuteronomy to traditions preserved in Exodus and Numbers. Theoretically, several possibilities could account for the unique character of Deuteronomic traditions. Perhaps the simplest explanation would be to argue that Exodus and Numbers record traditions handed down independently of those recorded in Deuteronomy. But this hypothesis, while providing a ready explanation for the peculiarities of the two bodies of tradition, does not easily account for their sometimes verbatim similarities.

Alternatively, one tradition may depend literarily upon the other so that any dissimilarities result from the intentional editorial activity of the compilers of the Torah. Assuming this hypothesis, the next task would be to establish which tradition can claim priority. Several observations suggest the priority of the tradition preserved in Numbers. First, it is more likely that an editor would have chosen to omit any reference to Israel's confrontation with Edom than it is that an editor would have inserted such a reference in a tradition otherwise silent on the issue. Second, the book of Deuteronomy exhibits a pro-Edom tendency (see 23:7), that may have motivated the omission of the account of Edom's refusal to permit Israel passage. Third, if the Hebrew text of Deuteronomy 2:8 is accepted as the more original reading, the Deuteronomy account may, in fact, betray some awareness of the confrontation tradition preserved in Numbers.

The accounts of Israel's encounters with Moab and Ammon, in contrast, are unique to Deuteronomy. Numbers preserves only lists of campsites along Israel's route from Edom to the plains of Moab (Num 21:10-13; 33:41-50). Indeed, Deuteronomy 2 narrates Israel's passage through Moab and Ammon with even greater economy than it does the Edom encounter. In essence, Deuteronomy 2 relates only YHWH's command not to "harass Moab [or Ammon, respectively] or contend with them in battle, for I will not give you any [of their land] as an inheritance because I have given [it] to the sons of Lot for an inheritance" (vv. 9, 19). These commands seem to be modeled after Deuteronomy 2:5. Stylistic variations suggest that a later editor may have supplemented the original Edom account with the Moab and Ammon sections: 2:5 is in the second person plural, 2:9 and 19 are in the second person singular. Verses 9 and 19 add a second prohibition against harassment to the command not to engage in battle shared by all three sections. Verse 9 makes the reference to warfare explicit by the addition of the phrase "in battle (*milḥāmâ*)." (LXX harmonizes the three commands by adding the phrase "in battle [*(eis) polemon*]" to vv. 5 and 19.) Verses 9 and 19 omit the colorful idiomatic expression "not even for the sole of your feet to tread upon" and rearrange the order of the verb ("I gave") and the object ("as a possession") in the final clause. Verse 19 also reorders the sequence of the verb ("I will not give") and the indirect object ("to you") in the middle clause.

Several other observations bolster the impression that the sections dealing with Moab and Ammon may be later expansions of the account. The account in Numbers 21:10-15 seems to suggest, for example, that Israel did not pass through but *around* Moab and Ammon. In fact, several phenomena suggest further that the section dealing with Ammon may be even later than the Moab material. Deuteronomy 2:29 does not mention Ammon in a reference to Israel's passage through the Transjordan. If the passing of the rebellious generation (vv. 14-17) marks a transition from the period in which YHWH was unwilling to fight on Israel's behalf—and thus Israel could only travel unimpeded through uninhabited and friendly regions—to the era of the conquest, vv. 18-23 are misplaced. With the exception of v. 23, comments concerning the displacement of earlier inhabitants of southern Palestine and the Transjordan deal with the settlement of the nations of Edom, Moab, and Ammon in their new territories. The exceptional v. 23 deals with the Caphtorim (= the Philistines?) who displaced the earlier Avvim along the southern seacoast. Not only does it differ from the other such comments in terms of its irrelevance to the region under discussion, but it also departs from the pattern of attributing the dispossession of the early inhabitants to the decision and intervention of YHWH.

All these observations further confirm the perception that the book of Deuteronomy results from a long process of the transmission of oral and documentary traditions and of compiling and editing them into the present form. Hints as to the relatively late date of the author(s) and editor(s) of the final form of the book abound in this passage. Verse 7 assumes that the forty years in the wilderness have already ended (technically it will not end until Moses' death). Verse 12 assumes that Israel has already conquered its inheritance. Verse 23 speaks of the Philistines' arrival in Canaan, which was almost simultaneous with Israel's, as an event in the distant past.

Themes of the Passage

Why have the editors further developed the material in this fashion? Did they capriciously tamper with the older material? In fact, although the passage is quite complicated in terms of the confusion of address forms and the numerous indications of editorial activity, it conveys a clear and consistent matrix of interrelated themes dealing with God's economy of history. First, YHWH does not permit Israel to dispossess, even to harass, Edom, Moab, or Ammon because he has granted these nations possessions in much the same way he has given Canaan to Israel. Here Deuteronomy manifests a sophisticated understanding of the worldwide stage upon which God's plans play out in human history. Because Israel naturally views YHWH's dealings with humankind from the perspective of its own interests and history, the danger of myopic exclusivism always posed a threat. Yes, Israel was the chosen people, promised a land, a heritage, and a central role in human history. But elsewhere in the world, YHWH involved himself in the affairs of other nations, providing for their need and guiding their history as well.

Second, YHWH's favor is discriminate, nuanced. Israel cannot simply assume that because it is the chosen people YHWH will automatically be partisan. Even the chosen can rebel and incur God's anger. Just as God refused to validate Israel's resistance at Kadesh-barnea by intervening on their behalf at Hormah, God does not take the field on their behalf until the rebellious generation has passed away. Election is not a *carte blanche* for irresponsibility.

Finally, as Deuteronomy understands it, YHWH manages the economy of international relations such that election, which clearly benefits one nation, does not unfairly disadvantage another innocent nation. According to Deuteronomy's global concept of history, a concept it shares with other portions of the Hebrew Bible (see especially Gen 15:16), God employs one nation's dispossession of another both as a means to bless the conqueror and to punish the vanquished. Deuteronomy explains that Israel once served as YHWH's instrument of judgment against the Canaanite inhabitants of the promised land. Later, as the first readers of the book knew firsthand, Israel will experience God's sovereignty over the whole world in the form of the Assyrian and Babylonian "conquest" of Israel and Judah. This viewpoint, inherent already in Deuteronomy 2:1-23, becomes especially apparent in the following section, 2:24–3:22.

COMMENTARY

Passage through Friendly Territory, 2:1-23

The Passage through Edom, 2:1-8a

Clearly, the account of the final phase in Israel's journey to the promised land has little interest in narrative detail. It relates only reports of Israel's movement from place to place, divine commands, and ethnographic comments concerning the displacement of aboriginal peoples by new settlers. This disinterest in narrating events points to the passage's chief impetus: reflection on the historical and theological significance of these events.

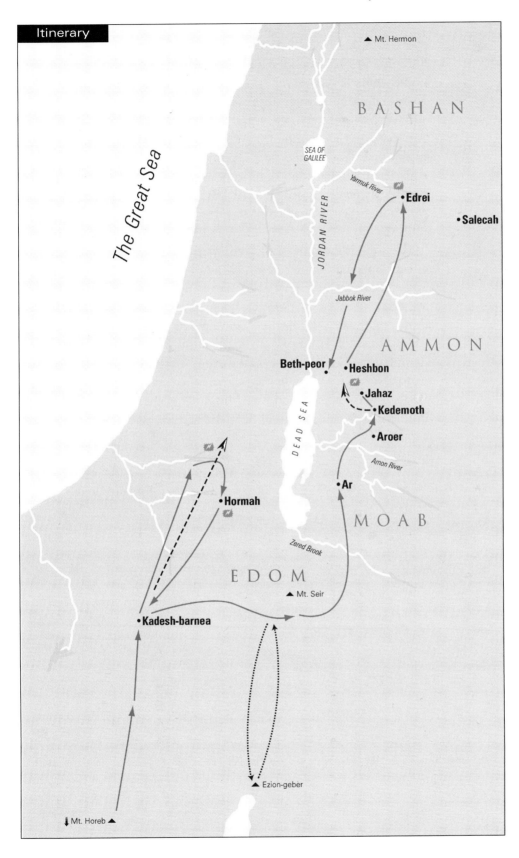

After departing from Kadesh-barnea, Israel spent "many days" in the area around Mt. Seir (2:1). In contrast to rather detailed accounts in Numbers of experiences and encounters at various points along Israel's journey during the interim between the sin at Kadesh and the passing of the sinful generation, Deuteronomy summarizes nearly forty years in this phrase, "many days." Apparently for Deuteronomy, nothing of real significance occurred in this period of waiting for the punishment on the sinners to be completed. Similarly, no significant event signaled the end of the period. After nearly forty years, YHWH simply announced to Moses that the time had come to turn northward, toward Canaan (2:2-3).

The core of the unit (2:4-7) consists of YHWH's instructions concerning the manner in which Israel is to handle its passage across Edomite territory and, especially, the reasons for this approach. First, YHWH stresses Edom's kinship to Israel. YHWH, outlining the next leg in the journey, refers to "your brothers the sons of Esau" (2:4), employing family terms instead of the national designation "Edom" found in the Numbers parallel. These three words (in Hebrew, *ʾăḥêkem bĕnê-ʿēsāw*) efficiently recall the story of Jacob, Israel's ancestor, and Esau, the father of the Edomites—twin brothers, both descendants of Abraham and Isaac. [A History of Fraternal Discord]

A History of Fraternal Discord

Like their eponymous ancestors, the twin brothers Jacob and Esau, the nations of Israel and Edom experienced a long history of always ambivalent and often troubled relations. On the one hand, as evidenced in the respect for Edomite territorial integrity advocated in Deut 2:1-8a, Israel maintained an awareness of its kinship with Edom. One section of the Deuteronomic Code (23:7-8) permits a third generation descendant of an Edomite membership in the congregation of Israel, whereas individuals of Moabite and Ammonite ancestry are permitted this privilege only in the tenth generation (23:3-6).

Despite YHWH's instructions not to infringe on Edomite sovereignty, however, King David (2 Sam 8:13-14; 1 Kgs 11:15-16; 1 Chr 18:13; see Num 24:18) and later King Amaziah of Judah (2 Kgs 14:7; 2 Chr 25:11-12) conquered Edom. Ammon and Moab, too, were subjected to Israelite or Judean domination, despite YHWH's promise of a homeland to the descendants of Esau (Deut 2:5) and Lot (Deut 2:9, 19). In turn, Edom frequently fought against Israel or Judah, often in consort with its cousins Ammon and Moab. Solomon was unable to maintain Israelite control over Edom, for example (1 Kgs 11:14-22). The three Transjordanian nations unsuccessfully invaded Judah during Jehoshaphat's

reign (2 Chr 20). Edom revolted against Judean overlordship once again under Jehoram (2 Kgs 8:20-22; 2 Chr 21:8-10), only to be viciously suppressed by Amaziah (2 Kgs 14:7; 2 Chr 25:11-12).

Tensions between Judah and Edom reached a peak during the Assyrian and Babylonian crises of the 8th and 6th centuries BC, respectively. Edom opportunistically took Judean captives during the Syro-Ephraimitic crisis (734–732 BC; 2 Chr 28:17) and, apparently, again during Judah's troubles with Babylon (587–586 BC; Ps 137:7). Edom's malicious glee over Judah's fate elicited harsh reactions from the prophets (Isa 11:14; 63:1; Jer 49:7-22; Ezek 25:12-14; 35:1–36:7; Obad; see also Lam 4:21-22). In fact, in some passages, Edom becomes an almost apocalyptic symbol of animosity toward Israel—and God (Isa 34).

Edom took possession of portions of southernmost Judah (as far as Hebron and Beersheba) in the exilic and post-exilic periods. Nabateans moved into former Edomite territory. The Hasmonean, John Hyrcanus, forcibly converted the Edomites (Idumeans) to Judaism (Josephus, *Ant.* xii, 9, 1), finally reuniting the descendants of Jacob and Esau as one people (see Amos 9:12; Obad 21). In fact, the Herodian kings were of Idumean descent.

Second, YHWH predicts that the sons of Esau will fear Israel. YHWH gives no reasons for Edom's reaction. Israel's encounter with the Amorites at Hormah, Israel's only previous such contact recorded in Deuteronomy (1:44-45), certainly would not have enhanced its military reputation! Presumably, YHWH has in mind Israel's encounters with the Egyptians (see especially Exod 15:15) and the Amalekites (Exod 17:8-20). This reference to Edom's fear of Israel may offer further confirmation that the authors and editors of the "historical framework" of Deuteronomy were aware of—and assume that their readers also knew—traditions recorded independently in other sections of the Torah. More importantly, it should be noted that, in both the Exodus-Leviticus-Numbers and the Deuteronomy schemas of the period from the exodus to the conquest, the victories over Egypt and Amalek, both of which occurred before Israel reached Sinai and thus before the sins involving the golden calf and the rebellion at Kadesh, were Israel's only successful military encounters until after the passing of the rebellious generation. Edom's fear, then, indicates that a new era will soon begin.

Third, YHWH issues the first of two commands concerning Israel's passage through Edom: Israel is to pass through Edomite territory peacefully. Surely the "sons of Esau," Israel's cousins, deserve familial respect. Although YHWH does not specify the causes for Edom's fear, he explains clearly the reasons Israel must deal tenderly with Esau's sons. Jacob twice defrauded his brother, first of birthright, then of blessing. But Esau, too, descended from Abraham and, as promised, YHWH had provided for all Abraham's descendants, including Esau and his offspring (see Gen 33:1, 4, 9; 36:6-8). The conquest of the land promised Jacob's descendants will begin later. Israel has no claim to Edom's territory. YHWH then issues the second command along with its justification: not only should Israel avoid open conflict with its cousins, but it should not so much as inconvenience them. In a harsh and arid land, food and especially water are precious. Israel is to pay for whatever it consumes. It can afford to do so, for "these forty years YHWH your God has been with you; you have wanted for nothing." The reader thinks almost inevitably of parallels between this command and Jacob's plea that his brother, Esau, accept gifts celebrating their reunion. "I beg you, if I have found favor in your sight, accept my gift from my hand. Truly, to see your face is like seeing the face of God, with such favor have you received me. Please accept the gift I bring you, because God has treated me graciously and because I have enough" (Gen 33:10-11). In keeping

Emim

AΩ The identities and histories of the aboriginal peoples mentioned in 2:10-12, 20-23 have been obscured by the passage of time. For the most part, these nations, by the time of the biblical writers already semi-legendary, are known primarily from a few passing references in the Bible. The Emim appear elsewhere only in Gen 14:5 in a list of nations including the Zuzim (= Zamzummim?) and the Horites. Their name (Hebrew for "terrors") may reflect their reputation as giants, as suggested also by their equation with the Anakim (see [Anakim]) and the Rephaim. The Zamzummim, also identified as a Rephaim group, appear only here and, perhaps, in Gen 14:5. Their name may be etymologically related to the Arabic onomatopoeic noun *zamzamâ*, "smacking," the noise made while eating. Presumably, this designation may correspond roughly to the Greek term *barbaroi*, "barbarians," an onomatopoeic term that refers to the "babbling" of "uncivilized" non-Greek speakers.

Deuteronomy classifies both the "Terrors" and the "Babblers" as Rephaim. Although this term occurs in ancient Near Eastern literature much more frequently, its significance is not fully understood. Etymologically, the noun may be related either to the verb *rp'*, "to heal," or to the verb *rph*, "to sink down, to relax." Furthermore, it seems to appear in two meanings whose relationship to one another remains uncertain. In a series of texts, especially certain cuneiform ritual texts from the ancient city of Ugarit, it clearly refers to the "shades" or ghosts of the dear departed (as those who are capable of healing? or as those who have "sunk down" to the grave?). In another series of texts, including especially biblical references (Gen 14:5; 15:20; Deut 2:11, 20; 3:11, 13; Josh 12:4; 13:12; 15:8; 17:15), it refers to the aboriginal giants of Canaan and the Transjordan. Nothing is known of these giants other than the scanty information given in the Bible.

---

with its lack of interest in incidental details, the text relates in a matter-of-fact manner simply that Israel traversed Edom by way of the Arabah Road that ran from the southern shore of the Dead Sea to the northern tip of the Gulf of Aqabah (2:8a).

The Passage through Moab, 2:8b-13

Again YHWH commands Israel to respect the territorial integrity of a kindred people. This command—which omits reference to any fearful Moabite reaction, to the purchase of food and drink, and to YHWH's provision for Israel—seems to be an abbreviation modeled on 2:5. YHWH has granted Moab, also Israel's cousin (Gen 19:30-38), its homeland as well. In this regard Israel enjoys no advantage.

The parallel structure of the passage suggests that the brief statement in 2:9 implies the provisions and justifications specified in the fuller form in 2:4-7. In order to maintain balance, the writer amplifies the summary with a comment concerning Moab's conquest of its homeland. Similarities between Israel and its cousins extend beyond the fact that YHWH has granted them all a homeland to include the manner in which all came to possess their territories. Moab displaced the aboriginal Emim, an obscure race identified with the equally obscure Anakim and Rephaim. [Emim] As an afterthought (another indication of the editorial nature of this unit?), v. 12 supplies at this point information concerning Edom's displacement of the Horites. [Horites] This supplement, furthermore, describes Edom's conquest of its homeland in terms normally

Horites

AΩ In addition to references to the displacement of the obscure, semi-legendary peoples of the Transjordan, Deut 2:12-23 also mentions three groups of people involved in population shifts in southern Palestine. The identification of the Horites, the Avvim, and the Caphtorim, none of whom are associated with the mysterious Rephaim, is nonetheless difficult owing to the insufficiency or complexity of the evidence.

The Hebrew Bible apparently employs "Horite" (*horî*, plural *horîm*) to refer to two distinct ethnic groups. In one series of texts (Gen 34:2; Josh 9:7), LXX reads "Horites" for the Masoretic Text's "Hivites" (see also Exod 3:28; Isa 17:9). These "Horite-Hivites," inhabitants of central Palestine, may have been related to the Hurrians resident in portions of central Palestine in the ancient period. In this case, the confusion of the names may have resulted from the incidental similarity in the sounds of "Hurrian" (*huru* or *hurw*) and "Horite."

In another group of texts (Gen 14:6; 36:20, 21, 29, 30; Deut 2:12, 22; see also Gen 36:2), "Horite" indicates inhabitants of the southern desert in the vicinity of Mt. Seir. Since there is no evidence of Hurrian occupation of this region, and since the names (Gen 36) of these southern "Horites" are clearly Semitic, not Hurrian, the "Horites" mentioned in Deut 2 and related texts must have been a distinct, otherwise unknown Semitic group.

Similarly, biblical tradition consistently identifies the "Avvim" as the aboriginal Canaanite population in the vicinity of Gaza (Josh 13:3; 2 Kgs 17:31). According to Deut 2:23 they were displaced by the "Caphtorim." Cuneiform literature knows of the *Kaptara*, mentioned in economic texts from Mari and Ugarit. A body of Egyptian texts dating from the period 2200–1200 BC refers to *Keftiu* in contexts suggesting that Crete is in mind. The Bible explicitly equates the Philistines with the Caphtorim in two texts (Jer 47:4; Amos 9:7) and implicitly in Deut 2:23. Evidence suggests that the original home of the Philistines included a wider geographical area than Crete alone. Presumably, by the biblical period, the term Caphtor and Caphtorim had come to indicate broadly the region from which the Philistines came, including but not limited to Crete.

reserved for Israel's conquest of Canaan (esp. Josh 24:8; see also Deut 3:12, 18, 20; etc.; Josh 9:24; 11:14, 20; etc.) and finally draws explicit attention to the parallel (v. 12b). There can be no question that, for Deuteronomy, Israel's awareness of God's activity in its history does not preclude a comprehensive perspective on God's involvement in human affairs.

The "Passage" of the Rebellious Generation, 2:14-16

Thirty-eight years had passed between the rebellion against YHWH's command to enter Canaan at Kadesh-barnea and the entry into Moabite territory. By the end of these nearly forty years, all the "warriors" had died. This reference to warriors may be a satirical allusion to Israel's fear of the Anakim. Even though YHWH was prepared to go before them into battle, these "brave warriors" had cowered. Now, however, with their passing, YHWH's anger with Israel and, thus, the period of YHWH's refusal to fight on their behalf were ended. This section of the account stands out because of the description of YHWH's animosity toward the rebel generation in terms normally reserved for the enemies of YHWH and of Israel (v. 15). These "men of war" had made themselves YHWH's enemies! But now the warfare was ended. Israel had paid for its sins. A later generation of Israel, in all likelihood the generation that furnished the book of Deuteronomy with this historical framework, would have seen the Assyrian and Babylonian crises as another instance in which Israel had become YHWH's enemy through disobedience to the covenant.

The Passage through Ammon, 2:17-23

This unit follows the model established in the section dealing with the passage through Moab. YHWH simply commands Israel not to harass or harm the Ammonites in any way because they, too, are a kindred people and because their homeland is also a divine grant. As in the previous section, comments concerning the former inhabitants of the region balance the brevity of this command. The area that would become Ammon, like the area later known as Moab, had also been previously inhabited by a group of Rephaim, known to the Ammonites as the Zamzummim.

Two new elements appear in this comment. First, the text indicates not only that the Ammonites displaced the Zamzummim, but that "YHWH destroyed them [the Zamzummim] before them [the Ammonites]" (v. 21). Furthermore, as though to supplement the section dealing with the passage through Edom, the text adds for the second time (see v. 12) a comment concerning Edom's displacement of the Horites. Now, however, the text emphasizes that Edom was able to take possession of its inheritance because of YHWH's assistance (v. 22). Following upon the description of the passing of the rebellious generation, these comments make a startling statement about YHWH's activity in human history: YHWH had destroyed the enemies of Ammon and Edom just as he had destroyed an entire generation of Israel! YHWH had fought for non-Israelites and against Israel!

Second, the text adds an extraneous note concerning the Caphtorim's displacement of the Avvim (v. 23). This comment pertains not to a people related to Israel, but to the Philistines, Israel's standing enemy! It refers not to the Transjordan, but to the coastal plain. The text does not explicitly attribute the success of the Caphtorim over the Avvim to the intervention of YHWH nor does it describe the Caphtorim's ownership of the land as a divine grant. The context, however, certainly implies YHWH's interest even in the Philistines!

Passage through Hostile Territory, 2:24–3:11

Unlike Israel's peaceful passage through Edom, Moab, and Ammon, open conflict characterized the final phase of Israel's journey through the Transjordan. Now, after the death of the last of the Kadesh rebels, YHWH was willing once again to intervene on

Israel's behalf. His intervention became necessary because Israel encountered two hostile Amorite kingdoms, Heshbon (2:24-27) and Bashan (3:1-11), ruled by two hostile kings, Sihon and Og. Furthermore, in contrast to Edom, Ammon, and Moab, these nations could claim no divine grant to their territory and no kinship to Israel. In fact, because of their long history of abominable behavior, they were subject to YHWH's judgment through Israelite instrumentality. In a sense, Israel's victories over Sihon and Og exemplify the manner in which YHWH administers justice on the international scale and represent a prelude to the conquest of Canaan.

The passage is literarily and theologically complex. Its overall structure is clearly divided into two major sections corresponding to Israel's conflicts with the two Amorite kingdoms. As in the previous passage concerning Edom, Moab, and Ammon, the first section provides the more complete portrayal while the subsequent section omits details, presumably on the assumption that the reader will supply them on the basis of the fuller account. The pattern of travel report followed by divine instruction, encounter, summary statement of the outcome, and supplemental comment established in the previous passage continues. Of course, the outcome statements now take the form of descriptions of Israel's victory over its enemies and the subsequent occupation of conquered territory.

Once again, however, the interpreter finds the familiar pattern of shifts in person and number. The passage begins (v. 24) with second person plural imperatives and shifts suddenly, within the same verse, to second person singular forms of address. Moses speaks in the first person singular beginning in v. 26 and continuing through v. 29 where the singular gives way to the plural. Plural forms abruptly replace singular midway through v. 30. The extended section reporting Israel's military engagement with Sihon's army and the outcome of this battle, 2:32–3:1, consistently employs first person plural forms. Singular forms return in v. 2 before the passage returns to the plural in vv. 3-8. The final section, vv. 9-11, constitutes a note concerning place names and Og's relationship to the Rephaim in the third person. The problem of the relationship between the material in Deuteronomy and parallel accounts in Numbers (and, for vv. 26-33, in Judges) also resurfaces. The characteristic editorial emphases of the historical preamble to Deuteronomy are evident as well.

From a theological perspective, however, the passage raises two very difficult issues. First, how does one reconcile the fact that God "hardened" Sihon's heart with the larger biblical theme of human free will and responsibility? Second, what place does the harsh, merciless "holy war" theme have in the modern believer's understanding of God? This much is certain, the complexity of these issues demands that the entire passage be considered carefully. It would be perilous to focus on an isolated phrase or concept divorced from the larger context within Deuteronomy, and, indeed, within the Bible as a whole.

The Conquest of Heshbon and Environs, 2:24-37

The source analysis of 2:24-27 provides an important clue to the particular interests of Deuteronomy's version of the encounter with Sihon and the conquest of Heshbon. The Deuteronomic author has apparently supplemented the older tradition with material dealing with the Holy War theme (v. 25, vv. 34-37), with Israel's previous encounter with Edom (vv. 28-29), and with the hardening of Sihon's heart (vv. 30-31). The account moves efficiently from the initial divine instruction to cross the Arnon and confront Sihon (vv. 24-25) to Moses' offer of peace (vv. 26-29), Sihon's negative response (vv. 30-32), and, finally, the report of the outcome of the conflict (vv. 33-37).

The account of Moses' embassy to Sihon and the ensuing military encounter (vv. 26-33) parallels reports in Numbers 21:21-25 and Judges 11:19-26. The three passages substantially agree on the basic course of events, on a number of specific details, and, in the core narrative, even in wording. On the other hand, they differ in equally remarkable ways that raise once more the question of the nature of the literary relationships.

All three passages report that messengers (*malāʾkîm*) were sent (*šlḥ*) to Sihon asking permission for Israel to "pass through" (*ʿbr*) his land (*ʾereṣ*; Num 21:21-22; Deut 2:26-27; Judg 11:19). They agree that Sihon refused the request, choosing instead to attack (Numbers and Judges employ the verb *lḥm*; Deuteronomy has the related noun *milḥāmâ*) Israel at Jahaz with his full army (*kol ʿammô*, literally, "all his people"; Num 21:23; Deut 2:32; Judg 11:21a). All recount that Israel prevailed (literally, Israel "smote [*nkh*]" Sihon; Num 21:24; Deut 2:33; Judg 11:21), ultimately taking possession of Sihon's entire kingdom (Num 21:25; Deut 2:33-36; Judg 11:21b-22).

In addition to these major agreements involving all three passages, two passages concur on several details and phrases. The Numbers passage, especially, bears similarities to the Deuteronomy passages not shared by Judges, on the one hand, and shows similarities to the Judges passages not shared by Deuteronomy, on the

Parallels

Numbers (21:21) and Judges (11:19) have the account in the third person, whereas in Deuteronomy (2:26) Moses reports in the first person. Numbers (21:23) and Judges (11:20) agree that Sihon refused to allow Israel to pass through "his territory" (*ʿābor bigbulô*); Deuteronomy has simply "to pass through" (*haʿābīrēnû bô*, v. 30). Both mention that "Sihon assembled all his people" (Num 21:23; Judg 11:20). Both Numbers (21:24) and Judges (11:22) describe Sihon's conquered territory as extending "from the Arnon to the Jabbok" and as including Heshbon "and her daughters" (Num 21:25; Judg 11:26), an idiom that refers to the cities and villages belonging to the political and economic orbit of a major city, in this case Heshbon, metaphorically envisioned as the "daughters" of the "mother" city (see also Num 32:42; Josh 15:45, 47; 17:11, 16; Judg 1:27, etc.).

Numbers and Deuteronomy both provide details concerning Israel's offer to pass through Sihon's kingdom without inconveniencing the populace, although the exact wording differs (Num 21:22; Deut 2:27-29). Both accounts closely parallel the respective accounts of Israel's encounter with Edom. Num 21:22 virtually duplicates the message sent to the king of Edom (Num 20:17), employing language found only in these two texts. Similarly, Deut 2:27-29 follows the pattern of 2:26. Indeed, it makes explicit reference to the offer made Edom as a precedent. Just as the language of Num 21:22 is peculiar to Numbers, the phrase "turn aside to the right or the left" characterizes Deuteronomy (2:7; 5:32), Deuteronomistic literature (see, for example, Josh 1:7; 23:6; 1 Sam 6:12; 2 Kgs 22:2), and later literature influenced by Deuteronomistic literature (2 Chr 34:2, for example). Both Numbers and Deuteronomy recount that Sihon and his people "came out to meet (*wayyēṣēʾ liqrāʾt*)" Israel at Jahaz (Num 2:23; Deut 2:32). Both refer to Israel's conquest of the many cities associated with Heshbon, Sihon's capital (Num 2:25; Deut 2:34-36).

---

other. [Parallels] Deuteronomy and Judges have only one common feature not found in Numbers, namely the fact that both attribute Israel's victory over Sihon to the fact that "YHWH gave him over" to Israel (Deut 2:33; Judg 11:21).

Assuming, as the high degree of similarity would suggest, that the three passages are somehow related to one another on a literary level, the basis for determining whether one or more of these texts depends on one or more of the other two must be the observation that the simpler Judges account seems to represent an earlier form of the tradition than either of the other two. It straightforwardly recounts the events—without amplification of the message sent to Sihon, for example—in the third person form one would expect of ancient traditions passed on throughout generations of Israel. In this case, the Numbers and Deuteronomy versions would represent expansions of the older tradition in directions characteristic of their current contexts. The first person style of the Deuteronomy account reflects the setting of Deuteronomy as an extended address of Moses, for example, and should not be considered a substantive variant in the tradition. Furthermore, the three sections that are unique to Deuteronomy (vv. 27b-29; 30b-31; 33b-37) represent the theological emphases of the preamble to Deuteronomy instead

Independent Traditions

The question of the relationship between Numbers and Deuteronomy apart from Judges is much more difficult. The consensus scholarly opinion regards the Numbers and Deuteronomy accounts to be independent of one another. In contrast, J. Van Seters sees the elements shared by Numbers and Deuteronomy alone as evidence that the Numbers version was composed utilizing elements of both Judges and Deuteronomy.

J. R. Bartlett responds with the argument that Num 21 is the source for Deut 2 and Judg 11. He correctly observes that Van Seters's arguments do not demonstrate that Numbers depends on Deuteronomy since similarities between the two do not consist primarily of verbal parallels.

On the other hand, Bartlett does not sufficiently address the observation that the simplest of the three accounts, and

therefore the account most suited to have served as the basis for the other two, is the Judges version.

Taking Deuteronomy's first person forms as an editorial revision made to accommodate the account to its context and removing from Numbers and Deuteronomy the material common to all three accounts, the material left in both Numbers and Deuteronomy can be best explained as editorial expansions characteristic of and unique to the authors/editors of the two books. In other words, the simplest solution seems to be to consider the Numbers and Deuteronomy accounts to be independent elaborations of a common tradition derived either from Judg 11 or from an older source accessible to the authors of all three texts.

J. Van Seters, "The Conquest of Sihon's Kingdom: A Literary Examination," JBL 91 (1972): 182-97.

J. R. Bartlett, "The Conquest of Sihon's Kingdom: A Literary Re-Examination," JBL 97 (1978): 347-51.

of integral elements of the ancient tradition. It remains difficult, however, to determine whether Numbers and Deuteronomy relied on Judges for the tradition or knew it independently. [Independent Traditions]

"Cross the Valley of the Arnon," 2:24-25

The brook Arnon flows from the east into the Dead Sea at roughly the midpoint from north to south. It marks the southern boundary of Ammonite territory. Deuteronomy 2:19, 26, 37 do not make it clear whether Deuteronomy envisions Israel actually passing through Ammon or skirting around it to the southwest. At any rate, according to the Bible (Num 21:26; Josh 12:2), the Amorite Sihon had conquered and occupied the western section of Ammon in a campaign celebrated in the song preserved in Numbers 21:27-29 and Jeremiah 48:45-47. Sihon had taken Heshbon, modern Tell Hesban near Amman, as his capital city. From the outset YHWH adopts a decidedly different tone toward Sihon than he had toward the Edomites, Moabites, and Ammonites. Instead of counseling Moses to treat Sihon with respect and care, YHWH announces that Sihon and his kingdom are in Moses' power (the significance of the idiom "in your hand"). In fact, the language of vv. 24-25 derives from the institution of the Holy War (see [Holy War, Just War, and Pacifism]), attested outside Israel throughout the Semitic world (compare the Moabite stone, l. 17[1] and the modern Arab *jihad*). Verse 25 recalls a passage from Moses' song celebrating YHWH's victory over Pharaoh's army as Israel crossed the sea (Exod 15:14,

16). The nations fear Israel not because of its military might, but because YHWH fights for his people (Deut 20:1-4).

"So I sent messengers," 2:26-29

The instructions regulating Holy War in Deuteronomy 20 call upon Israel first to offer surrender terms to enemy cities lying outside Canaan (v. 10). Moses' offer to Sihon surpassed this regulation. After crossing the Arnon to the wilderness region near Kedemoth,[2] Moses sent messengers requesting permission for Israel to pass through Sihon's territory just as it had through Edom and Ammon. Indeed, Moses' message duplicates the offer made to Edom (2:6 = 2:28) and adds the assurances that Moses intends to remain on the road, with no detours through the countryside, and that Israel will be "on foot" (that is, Sihon need not worry about foraging donkeys or camels). Moses presumably referred to the so-called "King's Highway" that runs north-to-south the length of the Transjordan. The Hebrew of Deuteronomy 2:27 is somewhat unusual. Moses promises to pass through *badderek badderek*, literally "on the road, on the road." The duplication of terms may be intended as an intensification of the idea—"We absolutely will not leave the road." Alternatively, some scholars suspect that the text has become corrupt here and suggest emending it to read *běderek hammelek*, "by the King's Highway," as does Numbers 21:22.

In either case, as further evidence of his honorable intentions, Moses cites Israel's peaceful passage through Edom and Moab. As noted, Deuteronomy takes much greater pains than either Numbers or Judges to document the fact that Moses and Israel gave Sihon absolutely no cause for taking offense. They had no interest in Sihon's territory. "The land YHWH [their] God had given [them]" lay "beyond the Jordan" (v. 29). Sihon truly has no cause for concern.

"But Sihon . . . would not let us pass," 2:30-32

For reasons the text does not specify, Sihon responded aggressively to Moses' request. This passage contradicts the depictions of Israel's encounters with Edom and Moab in Deuteronomy 2 and agrees with the accounts in Numbers, namely, that the kings of Edom and Moab refused Israel passage and that, consequently, Israel kept to a wilderness path around their territory. Notably, Judges 11 makes no mention of an embassy to Ammon. Apparently, although Moses and Israel had no designs on Sihon's kingdom, the Amorites' iniquity had ripened. Sihon's sin and YHWH's displeasure converge.

Significantly, the text describes Sihon's reaction in the same terms used to describe Pharaoh's responses to Moses' request that he permit Israel to leave Egypt. The sequence of the elements in this description may be important for understanding the role God played in "hardening" Sihon's attitude. First, Sihon is said to have been "unwilling" (Hebrew *lo' 'ābāh*) to allow Israel to pass through his land. The same verb used earlier of Pharaoh (Exod 10:27) describes the negative reaction of the Moabite king to Moses' request in Judges 11:17, as well as Israel's refusal to heed YHWH's command to take possession of Canaan from Kadesh-barnea, both with no accompanying statement that YHWH hardened the hearts

"And God Hardened His Spirit"

ΑΩ The motif of "hardening" usually occurs in reference to the Pharaoh of the exodus (20x in Exodus and 1 Sam 6:6). The reference to the hardening of Sihon in Deut 2:30 is the only exception. Consequently, the interpretation of Deut 2:30 can be enriched by an examination of the motif in the book of Exodus.

Terminology for the hardening of Pharaoh varies. Verbs employed describe becoming "heavy" (*kābēd*; Exod 8:11, 28; 9:7, 34; 10:1; compare the adjective in Exod 7:14; see also 1 Sam 6:6), "strong" or "firm" (*ḥzq*, 7:13, 22; 8:15; 9:12, 15; 10:20, 27; 11:10; 14:17, of the Egyptians), and "hard" (*qšh*; 7:3; 13:15). Only Deut 2:30 has "spirit" (*rû'aḥ*) as the object of the verb *qšh* and the additional verb *'mṣ*, "to be strong," a circumstance that suggests the secondary character of Deut 2 in relation to the Exodus account. Usages in Exodus fall into two categories with respect to the subject of the verbs. God is the subject in ten instances (4:21; 7:3; 9:12; 10:1, 20, 27; 11:10; 14:4, 8, 17), while Pharaoh is said to harden his own heart in another ten texts (7:13, 14, 22; 8:11, 15, 28; 9:7, 34, 35; 13:15).

Brevard Childs has pointed out that the plague narrative in Exodus seems to have been primarily concerned with the relationship between signs and the recognition that YHWH is God—and not with questions of free will and predestination.

Nevertheless, Deut 2:30 and the "hardening" texts in Exodus have forcefully raised these questions for generations of readers. Fortunately, they also provide the raw materials for at least outlining a biblical response.

First, it is very significant that, in Exodus, God and Pharaoh himself are the subjects of the verbs in equal proportions. In some sense, then, both human and divine agency played roles in determining Pharaoh's response to

Moses. It was Pharaoh's will *and* God's will that Pharaoh resist Moses' request to free Israel.

Second, the moment at which the text states that Pharaoh's heart was hardened, whether by his own choice or God's, may well be significant. Typically, Pharaoh's heart hardens only *after* the plague/sign has been lifted. Thus when the danger has passed, Pharaoh reconsiders whether it will now be necessary to acquiesce to Moses' demands. Perhaps this was the worst plague Moses and his God can inflict; perhaps Egypt can outlast its slaves and their deliverer God.

Third, the sequence of statements concerning Pharaoh's hardening suggests something of the relationship between his will and God's. Surely it is no coincidence that, following the first five signs, Pharaoh is said to harden his own heart. YHWH's hardening activity begins only after the sixth sign, after Pharaoh's willfulness had apparently reached the point of no return.

C. F. Keil and F. Delitzsch describe beautifully the relationship between Pharaoh's free choice and God's will as follows:

> In this twofold manner God produces hardness, not only *permissively* but *effectively*, i.e., not only by giving time and space for the manifestation of human opposition, even to the utmost limits of creaturely freedom, but still more by those continued manifestations of His [sic] will which drive the hard heart to such utter obduracy that it is no longer capable of returning, and so giving over the hardened sinner to the judgment of damnation.

Brevard Childs, *The Book of Exodus: A Critical, Theological Commentary* (OTL; Philadelphia: Westminster, 1974), 174-75.

C. F. Keil and F. Delitzsch, *Commentary on the Old Testament in Ten Volumes; Volume I: The Pentateuch* (Grand Rapids: Eerdmans, 1976), 456.

of the obstinate. In Israel's case, their unwillingness alone was sufficient to bring YHWH's displeasure.

The crucial issue in this passage, however, concerns the phrase "for YHWH hardened his spirit and made his heart obstinate." A more common form of this phrase ("YHWH hardened his heart") appears frequently in the accounts of Moses' dealings with Pharaoh (Exod 7:3; 9:12; 10:1, 20, 27; 11:10; 14:4, 8, 17). Alongside these statements, the story of the Egyptian plagues also frequently attributes Pharaoh's obstinacy to his own act of will (see "Pharaoh hardened his [own] heart" and similar phrases in Exod 8:15, 32; 9:34). [*"And God Hardened His Spirit"*] What is the relationship between human choice (Exod 8:15, etc.) and divine influence (Exod 7:3) implied in these texts?

Unfortunately, the logical force of these statements, including the one made in Deuteronomy 2:30, depends largely on the significance of the sometimes ambiguous Hebrew particle *kî* that regularly introduces clauses concerning divine hardening of a heart. Although translators most often render it "for" here, it can have a number of meanings other than the causal. In addition to the causal use, two others seem plausible here: the temporal meaning, "when," and the consecutive or consequential meaning, "so that, thereupon, therefore." Does Deuteronomy 2:30 mean to indicate that Sihon was unwilling to allow Israel to pass *because* YHWH had so predetermined by "hardening" Sihon's attitude? Or, does it mean to suggest, as J. A. Thompson has commented, "the demands of God, once rejected, became a hardening influence on Sihon's heart . . . ?"[3] Did YHWH effectively abandon Sihon to his own hard-heartedness (see Rom 1:24, 26, 28)? [*Grace and Hardening*]

However one resolves this conundrum, the text considers the moment of Sihon's decision to refuse Israel passage the beginning of his demise (v. 31). Notably, the text devotes much more attention to the process of discussion and decision that culminated in Sihon's actions (vv. 26-31) than to the actions themselves (v. 32). From the perspective of the book of Deuteronomy, Sihon was doomed to defeat well before he took the battlefield. Israel's victory in the battle, fought at or near Jahaz (compare the Moabite Stone, l. 19; it may be either the modern Jalul, Khirbet et-Teim, Umm el-Walid, or, as many scholars prefer, Khirbet Iskander), is a foregone conclusion.

"And YHWH our God gave him over to us," 2:33-37

Deuteronomy demonstrates no interest in the military details of what must have been an extensive campaign. Rather, it focuses on

Grace and Hardening

The crisis moment in the plots of many of the short stories and novels of noted author Flannery O'Connor comes at the point when a major character experiences a "moment of grace," as O'Connor critics term it. These moments of grace mark crossroads in the characters' lives. Some of O'Connor's characters accept the grace offered; others do not. In either case, from this moment, the paths of the characters' lives take decisive turns, for good or ill.

A particularly poignant example of such a moment occurs in O'Connor's masterful short story "A Good Man Is Hard to Find." Bailey, his wife, his mother, and his children, John Wesley and June Starr, are traveling through Georgia on the way to Florida. Driving down a little-used dirt road so the grandmother can show the children a plantation house she remembered from her youth—a side-trip Bailey had not planned—they run off the road, overturning once and disabling the car. Three men in "a big black battered hearse-like automobile" come along. The grandmother recognizes one of them as "The Misfit," an escaped federal convict they had read about in the paper that morning, and unwisely says so.

Throughout the ensuing ordeal, the grandmother repeatedly encourages The Misfit to acknowledge that he is genuinely "a good man at heart," that he "must come from nice people." The Misfit instructs one of the other men to take Bailey and John Wesley further into the woods. The grandmother asks him, "Do you ever pray?" Two shots ring out. "Pray, pray, pray, pray," implores the grandmother. "If you would pray, Jesus would help you." June Starr and her mother join Bailey and John Wesley in the woods. Two more shots. The grandmother pleads, "Jesus, Jesus." The crisis moment for The Misfit comes, now, in the following passage:

> His voice seemed about to crack and the grandmother's head cleared for an instant. She saw the man's face twisted close to her own as if he were going to cry and she murmured, "Why you're one of my babies. You're one of my own children!" She reached out and touched him on the shoulder. The Misfit sprang back as if a snake had bitten him and shot her three times through the chest. Then he put his gun down on the ground and took off his glasses and began to clean them.

Grace calls upon one to choose. Grace can redeem or harden. The effect of grace on an individual's heart often depends on the individual's willingness to accept it. Both Sihon and The Misfit want no part of the offer.

Israel's execution of the requirements of Holy War (vv. 34-35), the precise boundaries of the territory Israel conquered (v. 36), and the care Israel took, as per YHWH's earlier instructions, not to involve the Ammonites in the conflict (v. 37).

English translations usually suggest that the Israelites totally annihilated the populations of Amorite cities in Sihon's territory ("we . . . utterly destroyed every city, men, women, and children; we left none remaining"). According to the regulations governing Holy War, however, Israel was to kill only the adult male population of such cities; women and children were to be taken captive (Deut 20:13-14; see commentary). Comparison of Deuteronomy 2:34-35 and 20:13-14 indicates that the two texts are closely related: 2:34-35, in effect, cites the regulations. [Translation Difficulties and Possibilities]

At Kadesh the spies had discouraged the people with reports that the cities in Canaan were "fortified up to heaven" (Deut 1:28). Now the people boast that, from Aroer (on the north bank of the Arnon; modern `Ara`ir; mentioned on the Moabite Stone, l. 26) to Gilead in the far north, no city was "too high" (that is, "too well fortified") for them. What distinguished Israel's reaction to the

Canaanite fortifications and to Sihon's walled cities? Now, after the death of the rebel generation, "YHWH our God gave all of them into our hands."

The Conquest of Bashan, 3:1-11

The text gives no rationale for Israel's turn northward to Bashan, the region east of the Sea of Galilee noted for its fertile grasslands. They may have feared an exposed flank. At any rate, the account of Israel's conflict with Og, the king of Bashan, is a very abbreviated version of the previous narrative. In contrast to the Sihon account, however, this unit amplifies the description of the extent of the territory taken from Og (vv. 4-8, 10) and includes learned comments concerning the various names for Mt. Herman employed by Israel's neighbors (v. 9) and the fact that Og was of the last of the Rephaim (v. 11).

Instead of the broad claim to have taken "all [Sihon's] cities" (v. 34), the text now boasts that Israel conquered sixty cities (see 1 Kgs 4:13) in Argob, apparently a region within Bashan. Lest the reader underestimate the magnitude of this accomplishment, the text further specifies that these sixty cities were not farm settlements in the countryside, but "fortified cities with high walls, gates, and bars." The number sixty does not include the unfortified villages Israel conquered in the same action. As a result of the campaigns against the two Amorite kings, Israel found itself in control of a significant portion of the Transjordan, from the Arnon in the south all the way to Mt. Herman (v. 8), or all the plains of Moab, Gilead, and Bashan as far north as Salecah (= modern Slkhad) and Edrei (= modern Der`a?).

The core of the account of Israel's encounter with Og, the king of Bashan (Deut 3:1-3), also finds a parallel in the book of Numbers (21:33). Unlike instances of parallels between Deuteronomy and Numbers examined to this point, these two texts are almost identical. There are only three relatively minor variations. First, Deuteronomy opens with first person plural forms ("we turned," etc., v. 1) whereas Numbers has third person plural forms ("they turn," etc., v. 33). Second, as might be expected of Deuteronomy,

Translation Difficulties and Possibilities

AΩ As D. Christensen has pointed out, in Deut 2:34 and again in 3:6, the Masoretic Text of the Hebrew Bible punctuates with a *zaqeph parvum*, roughly the equivalent of a semicolon or period, after *mĕtīm*, "males." Although the Masoretic punctuation was added to the text well into the current era (AD 700–900), and is therefore not considered canonical, it certainly indicates that the Masoretes were aware of the apparent conflict between the regulations and their application in this instance. This punctuation may also point to the possibility of a translation consistent with the Holy War regulations. The phrase 'et-kol-'îr mĕtīm, usually translated "every city, men . . .," may be understood instead to mean "every city of men," or "the male population of every city." Furthermore, the term *śārîd*, normally translated "survivors" or the like, derives from a verb meaning "to escape," and may be understood to refer here to "escapees, fugitives" (*BDB*, s.v. *śārîd*). Verses 34-35 (and 3:6-7), then, may be translated, "we . . . utterly destroyed the male population of every city; we allowed none of the women and children to flee; only the cattle we took as spoil . . .," without doing violence to the Hebrew. This translation conforms entirely to the regulations in Deut 20.

D. Christensen, *Deuteronomy 1–11* (WBC 6A; Dallas: Word, 1991), 55.

Deuteronomistic Influence in Numbers

Assuming that some direct literary dependence accounts for the similarities between the passages, how does one explain this third, more substantive, difference? Does it provide some clue as to the direction of dependence? Three observations suggest, in fact, that the phrase "him, his sons, etc." indicates that Num 21:33-35 depends on Deut 3:1-3. First, the phrase itself occurs only here and in Deut 2:33. Second, it replaces a phrase in Deut 2:3 that an editor may have perceived as redundant ("YHWH gave into our hand," v. 3 // "I will give him into your hand," v. 2). Third, the Numbers version reproduces the first of these recurrent phrases (Deut 3:2 = Num 21:34) in its only occurrence in the book of Numbers. It characterizes Deuteronomy, on the other hand (2:24, 30; 3:2; 7:24; 20:13; 21:10), where it plays a key role in Deuteronomy's theology of the conquest. In sum, then, the language of the passage conforms to the style of Deuteronomy and is foreign to the style of Numbers. The three variants in Num 21:33-35 can be easily explained as revisions intended to facilitate the insertion of the passage into its context in Numbers and to avoid a perceived redundancy.

Moses himself relates YHWH's speech ("And YHWH said to me," v. 2). Numbers has "And YHWH said to Moses" (v. 34). Third, Numbers does not reproduce the statement in Deuteronomy 3:3 concerning YHWH giving Og into Israel's hands, apparently substituting instead the phrase "him, his sons, and all his people" found elsewhere only in Deuteronomy 2:33. [Deuteronomistic Influence in Numbers]

The unit concludes with a curiosity. Og was a giant. Apparently his basalt sarcophagus could still be seen in Rabbath-Ammon in the writer's day. Measuring roughly thirteen and a half by six feet, it must surely have been quite a tourist attraction. This comment is another indication that the book of Deuteronomy took its final form much later than Moses' day.

CONNECTIONS

Election and Egocentrism

What does it mean to be the chosen people? What does the fact that God chooses say about who God is? What does it imply about God's relationship to those who are not chosen? The Bible clearly and repeatedly asserts that God chose Israel (Gen 12:1-3; Exod 19:5-6; Amos 3:1-2; etc.). Theologians refer to this concept as the "doctrine of election" and describe the chosen as "the elect." The biblical idea, as well as its theological formulation, is rich with notions of the unique, special, even personal dimensions of the relationship between God and God's elect. The biblical doctrine emphasizes God's gracious and free choice, God's commitment to the elect, and the blessings that come to the elect, among other aspects of the relationship.

Awareness of one's special status—whether because of God's choice or because of one's race or class, wealth or power, talent or physical appearance—always brings with it the danger of arrogance and egocentrism. Do the elect deserve to be chosen? Does God choose one to the exclusion of others? When God chooses to relate to one individual, family, or nation, does God thereby exclude the possibility of entering into other relationships? Has the elect any right to say, in effect, to all others: "I'm chosen—and you're not"?

History is replete with examples of egocentrism born of a sense of divine chosenness. How many wars have been fought by the motto, "The infidel must die"? The church's claim to be the "new" people of God is deeply entangled in the very roots of the anti-Semitism that fueled the medieval pogroms and the modern Holocaust. Ironically, modern radical Zionism insists that Israel's right to its ancestral land preempts any Palestinian claim to justice. Nationalism and civil religion, in all their forms and incarnations, depend for their energy to some extent on the idea that a given people and culture are special, superior, even divinely ordained. Within Christianity, claims to exclusive status as God's truly chosen have spawned religious wars, persecutions, and inquisitions.

In a theological perversion of this egocentrism of election, one tradition of Christian theology with roots in the thought of Augustine of Hippo and most notably John Calvin extrapolates from the fact that God chooses some the notion that God must also choose to exclude others. Proponents of this doctrine, often known as "double predestination," intend it to honor God's absolute sovereignty. Instead, they risk dishonoring the God whose will is that "none should perish" (2 Pet 3:9). ["Predestination" in the Calvinist Tradition]

To be sure, the biblical story of YHWH's relationship with Israel certainly demonstrates God's tender and intimate concern for God's people. YHWH called Abraham and blessed him. YHWH provided for Jacob and his sons through Joseph. YHWH delivered Israel from Egyptian bondage, defeating Pharaoh's priests, his magicians, and ultimately his armies. But the Bible also makes assertions that challenge any tidy, restricted understanding of election.

YHWH's interest was never focused upon Israel to the exclusion of other peoples. YHWH chose Abraham not to be the exclusive

---

"Predestination" in the Calvinist Tradition

By predestination we mean the eternal decree of God, by which he determined with himself whatever he [sic] wished to happen with regard to every man. All are not created on equal terms, but some are preordained to eternal life, others to eternal damnation; and, accordingly, as each has been created for one or other of these ends, we say that he [sic] has been predestinated to life or to death. (John Calvin, *Institutes of the Christian Religion*, trans. H. Beveridge [London: Bonham Norton, 1959], III:21:v)

In stark contrast to the sophisticated understanding of election displayed in Deut 2, and in the Hebrew Bible as a whole, the theological tradition most often associated with Augustine, bishop of Hippo (AD 354–430), and John Calvin, the great 16th century Swiss Reformer, proposes a concept of election that emphasizes the double effect of God's choice. For this tradition, the notion that God chooses to bless one group of people necessarily implies that God thereby chooses *not* to bless, that is *to condemn* all others. As Calvin put it, incidentally overlooking the fact that God chose Abraham specifically as the means for bringing blessing to "all the families of the earth": "In the person of Abraham, as in a withered stock, one people is specially chosen, while the others are rejected . . . ."

Instead of this harsh dichotomy, the Bible stresses the personal character of God and of God's interactions with human beings. God is able to relate to more than one group. God chose Israel, but not to the exclusion of all others. God also acted benevolently on behalf of Edom, Moab, Ammon, Syria, and Philistia. Election is not exclusion.

Conversely, it is important to remember that God chooses in order to establish relationship, not to grant privilege. The generation sentenced to wander in the wilderness learned that God can turn *against* the elect should they dishonor the relationship through rebellion.

---

recipient of God's grace, but to be the means whereby "all the families of the earth shall be blessed" (Gen 12:3). In perhaps the noblest moment of his life, Abraham pled with God to pardon the innocent righteous, not among the "elect," but among the residents of Sodom and Gomorrah (Gen 18:16-33).

Years later, YHWH called the prophet Jonah to preach a message of repentance in Nineveh, one of the leading cities in Israel's enemy Assyria. Jonah, arguably the prototypical "election elitist," did not welcome God's intention to show mercy to Israel's most feared enemy. He fled rather than serve as an instrument of God's care for the "non-elect" (see esp. Jonah 4:10-11). In a passage reminiscent of Deuteronomy 2, the same prophet, Amos, who emphasized the special character of YHWH's relationship with Israel, scolded Israel for presuming that they alone had benefited from YHWH's attention. YHWH has actively guided and shaped the fortunes of peoples as distinct and distant as the Ethiopians, the Philistines, and the Syrians (Amos 9:7). Indeed, according to Amos, YHWH, whom Abraham called "the Judge of all the earth" (Gen 18:25), expects the same standards of justice from the Philistines, the Phoenicians, the Edomites, and the Israelites (Amos 1–2). YHWH does not hesitate to refer to the Babylonian king, Nebuchadnezzar, as "my servant" (Jer 27:6), nor to the Persian king, Cyrus, as "my

shepherd" (Isa 44:28) and "(my) anointed" (Isa 45:1; Hebrew
mašîaḥ = messiah!).

The centrality of "the sons of Esau" in Deuteronomy 2:1-12 calls
to mind the account of Jacob's deception (Gen 27). When Esau
learned from his father that his twin brother had defrauded him of
his father's blessing, he poignantly expressed the pain of all disfa-
vored siblings. "Have you only one blessing, Father?" he asked
Isaac. Moved by Esau's pain, Isaac was startled from the inertia of
his initial distress finally to bless Esau as well. Surely God, the
creator and judge of all the earth, does not, by choosing to bless,
exhaust the supply of blessings.

Set at the transition between the sinful generation who, although
"elect," had become God's enemies, this reminder that God
has interests beyond Israel must have had sobering effect on exilic
and post-exilic readers. It should have sobering effect on any
generation.

Holy War?

The account of Israel's conquest of the northern Transjordan confronts its modern reader with the fact that the Bible mirrors the
ancient Israelite culture that produced it. In its earliest form,
Israelite religion, like the religions of its neighbors, was nationalistic, particularistic, and sometimes bellicose. Few modern believers
would advocate the idea that the kingdom of God should, or
could, be established by military conquest, and certainly not that
entire populations should be exterminated and enslaved in the
service of the Creator and Redeemer. On the other hand, moderns
should not too hastily dismiss texts such as Deuteronomy 2 on the
grounds that they represent primitive approaches to realities confronted on the international scale. If God is Judge of all the earth
and if God seems intent on employing human agents as instruments of justice, then the question arises as to how God will
respond to the abominations of the Amorites or of the Third Reich
apart from the imprecise, blunt, and violent means of war. [Holy War,
Just War, and Pacifism]

Clearly, texts such as Deuteronomy 2:24–3:11 require a mature
approach to biblical interpretation, beginning with an adequate
appreciation for the human dimensions of the Bible. To be sure,
believers confess the Bible as the authoritative and inspired witness
to God's revelation. Yet, God revealed God's self to a particular
people in a particular historical and cultural context. Ancient Israel
can only have comprehended its experience of God in relation to

Holy War, Just War, and Pacifism

Church historian Roland Bainton outlines the development of Christian attitudes toward war in three stages. At first Christians were consistent pacifists. In the Medieval period, Western Christianity developed a theory of so-called "just war," which the mainline Protestant Reformers later included as doctrine in their creeds, before launching a series of crusades toward the end of the Middle Ages based upon a Christian version of the Holy War. A fourth "realistic" or "national-interest" approach to war was articulated only in the modern, post-Machiavellian period.

The first and last of these approaches to war are the simplest. Pacifism rejects violence, including war, on the principle that killing is immoral. "National-interest" justifies war as an extension of the power of the state beyond its borders and in its own interests. Moral questions need not be considered.

"Just war" and "holy war" theories are more complicated. As outlined by Christian ethicist John Howard Yoder the just war tradition considers war the lesser of two evils in certain circumstances of threat or injustice. Generally, thinkers in this tradition label a war "just" if it meets several specific criteria. Nations are justified in going to war (*jus ad bellum*) if: (1) legitimate authority wages the war (2) for a just cause, (3) motivated, not by hatred or vengefulness, but (4) with peace as the goal, (5) so that war itself will be a means of last resort (6) initiated only if success seems probable. Furthermore, in order to be "just," wars must be conducted according to certain addi-

tional criteria (*jus in bello*); namely, the means must: (7) be necessary to the end, (8) be discriminating in that the force employed not be excessive in magnitude or in terms of those unnecessarily affected (non-combatants, for example), and (9) respect international law.

Yoder outlines the criteria for Holy War (or Crusade in Christian terminology) as follows: (1) A holy war is fought for a holy cause. (2) This cause is made known by divine revelation. (3) As a consequence, the criterion of last resort does not apply. (4) Furthermore, the probability of success need not be weighed. (5) In holy war, the adversary has no rights.

Several ethicists and theologians, including Bainton and Yoder, have pointed out that modern warfare, with its concepts of "total war" and technologies of mass destruction, lacks any foundation in either justice or holiness. Perhaps the ancient Israelite would point out that modern attitudes toward war do not differ so much from those of ancient Israel, after all. Theologically, the problem remains as to how God will influence the course of international affairs in some cases—if God chooses to do so through human agency—without cooperating in human military conflicts. Practically, for believers, the difficulty of distinguishing just causes and just means persists and, indeed, grows in proportion to modern military technology.

Roland Bainton, *Christian Attitudes Toward War and Peace: A Historical Survey and Critical Re-evaluation* (Nashville: Abingdon, 1960), 66.

John Howard Yoder, *When War is Unjust: Being Honest in Just-War Thinking* (Minneapolis: Augsburg, 1984), 17-18, 26-27.

the givens of its culture. But the recognition that the author(s) of Deuteronomy honestly and faithfully recorded God's revelation to Israel as they understood it can easily become an excuse for passing over texts such as Deuteronomy 2, dismissing them as artifacts of an earlier, less sophisticated era. Such an approach is inconsistent, however, with the confession that the Bible, including Deuteronomy 2, is authoritative and inspired Scripture. Responsible interpretation of such difficult texts requires the interpreter to grapple not only with the ancient, human dimensions of the text, but also the timeless, divine message communicated through it.

In contrast to its respect for the national and territorial integrity of Edom, Moab, and Ammon, Israel viciously conquered the kingdoms of Sihon and Og. What accounts for the difference in Israel's attitude? Several significant characteristics distinguished Edom, Moab, and Ammon, on the one hand, from the Amorite kingdoms of Sihon and Og, on the other. First, as the narrative concerning passage through the southern Transjordan makes abundantly clear, Israel recognized the obligations of kinship with its cousin nations. The Amorites were not protected by these ties. Relatedly, and more significantly, Israel's cousins and the Amorites had different roles in YHWH's economy of human history. Because of their relationship to Abraham, YHWH's chosen, the ancestors of Edom, Moab, and Ammon had been promised lands of their own. By specifying that Israel leave them unharmed, YHWH clearly demonstrated that YHWH continued to provide even for the extended family of Abraham. In contrast, because of their long history of abomination, ironically first described also in YHWH's promise to Abraham (Gen 15:13-16, see below), the Amorites stand under YHWH's judgment.

According to Deuteronomy 2, Edom, Moab, and Ammon permitted Israel to pass through, or in Ammon's case pass by, without incident. Sihon and Og, in contrast, aggressively resisted Israel, in effect bringing their fate upon themselves. Significantly, even before Moses contacted Sihon, YHWH announced that YHWH had already given Sihon into Moses' hand (2:24). This announcement of Sihon's opposition before the fact can be explained in part as an example of God's foreknowledge. But God's directive to "begin to take possession, do battle with him" (2:24) seems to express something more than God's ability to foresee Sihon's reaction to Moses' offer of peace. In fact, a number of biblical texts demonstrate that the Amorites, like Edom, Moab, and Ammon, had also found a place in YHWH's economy of human history— although an unfortunate place. According to these texts YHWH viewed the Amorites' idolatry with particular distaste and displeasure. In fact, as canonical tradition interpreted history, YHWH had predicted the encounter between Moses and Sihon as early as the time of Abraham, as recorded in a passage that suggests that in one encounter YHWH planned both to honor his promise of a home for Israel and, at the same time, to bring judgment upon the sinful Amorites.

Then YHWH said to Abraham, "Know for certain that your descendants will sojourn in a land that is not theirs, and will be slaves there, and they will be oppressed for four hundred years; but I will bring judgment on the nation they serve, and afterward they shall come out with great wealth. As for you, you shall go to your fathers in peace; you shall be buried in a good old age. And they shall return here in the fourth generation; for the iniquity of the Amorites is not yet complete." (Gen 15:13-16)

Indeed, the Amorites' reputation for wickedness and idolatry also served as a motivation for Israel's harsh treatment of the conquered Amorite population. The Torah warns that, if the Amorites should be permitted to co-exist with Israel, the dangers of Amorite religious practice influencing Israel would be too great. Israel should make no covenants with the Amorites. Their worship sites must be destroyed. Israelites must not intermarry with them (Exod 23:23; 34:11-16; Deut 7; 20:17; see also Josh 24:15; Judg 3:5-6; 6:10; 1 Kgs 21:26; 2 Kgs 21:11). Idolatry could spread from Amorites to Israel like an infection.

As Deuteronomy understands it, then, Israel's brutal conquest of the kingdoms of Sihon and Og was God's punishment upon a people who had long and well-deserved God's wrath. At the same time, it was a vital prophylactic against the insidious idolatry that would plague Israel for centuries to come and that would eventually result in Israel experiencing a fate not dissimilar to that of the Amorites. In other words, the Amorites did not suffer their fate simply because God preferred Israel (see Deut 7:6-11), but because God had orchestrated history to bring about a moment in which two needs could be met at once: a land for Israel and punishment for the Amorites.

Modern readers of Deuteronomy 2 may still be troubled. War is a very imprecise instrument of justice. Inevitably, as Israel would later learn (see Ps 74; Lam 5), the innocent die alongside the guilty in time of war. Almost inevitably, the party that considers itself the instrument of God's wrath oversteps the bounds of its commission and becomes arrogant (see Jer 49–50). In the modern era especially, with its convoluted international politics and its weapons of mass destruction, it is difficult to imagine that any war can be just. Still, the theological point of the account of God's management of human history, population movements, and military conflicts must not be missed: God uses human instruments, in this case the Israelites, later the Babylonians, to correct the course of human history. What might otherwise be seen merely as geopolitics corresponds in some way with God's system of international justice. Israel ought not to have forgotten this principle demonstrated early in its history, for centuries later it would experience the downside.

NOTES

[1] Also known as the Mesha Stone after King Mesha whose victory over Israelite domination the text celebrates. It dates to the middle to late ninth century BC. A translation of the text of this memorial inscription can be found in *ANET*, 320-321.

[2] Kedemoth, known only from the Bible (Josh 13:18; 21:37; 1 Chr 6:79), is probably to be identified with either modern Kas ez-Za`feran or Khirbet er-Remeil, both near el-Medeiyineh at the far eastern extremity of the modern Wadi Heidan, a northern tributary of the Arnon.

[3] *Deuteronomy* (TOTC; Downers Grove: InterVarsity, 1974), 95.

THE DISTRIBUTION OF ISRAEL'S TRANSJORDANIAN TERRITORY

3:12-22

Deuteronomy 3:12-22 details the arrangements Moses made to apportion the Transjordanian territory Israel had conquered in the campaigns against Sihon and Og. It brings to a conclusion the account of Israel's journey to the border of the promised land (vv. 12-17). Since Moses' career as Israel's military leader is now concluded, he also issues standing orders to the tribes of Reuben and Gad concerning their duty to participate with all Israel in conquering Canaan (vv. 18-20) and to his successor, Joshua, for the conduct of such campaigns (vv. 21-22).

Like the preceding material in this historical summary, the substance of this narrative has a parallel elsewhere in the Torah, in this case a rather lengthy account found in Numbers 32. Once again, comparison of the two accounts illustrates the freedom with which the Deuteronomic author abbreviates and reshapes the tradition to serve other, chiefly theological, purposes. According to the Numbers account, which is much more detailed especially in terms of the dialogue between Moses and the tribes of Reuben and Gad, these tribes suggest to Moses that, since the rich pastureland of Gilead would provide excellent pasturage for their large herds and flocks, they be permitted to stay behind when Israel crosses the Jordan. Irate, Moses likens the action they propose to Israel's refusal at Kadesh-barnea to take Canaan. In response to Moses' anger, Reuben and Gad propose that they be allowed time to build pens for their livestock and cities for their families. Leaving families and belongings behind, they would then be willing to join the rest of Israel in the conquest of Canaan.

In contrast, the Deuteronomy account characteristically accentuates Moses' initiative, totally omitting any reference to interlocutors and stressing the idea that Reuben and Gad took possession of already existing cities assigned them by Moses (i.e., Reuben and Gad did not built cities themselves). The Deuteronomic author may well have been sensitive to the fact that the time between Israel's arrival at

Beth-peor and its entry into Canaan under Joshua's leadership would have been insufficient for Reuben and Gad to build entire cities. According to Numbers 33:38, Israel arrived at Mt. Hor on the way to Edom on the first day of the fifth month of the fortieth year after departing Egypt. They arrived at Beth-peor sometime before the eleventh month of the same year (Deut 1:3).

Moses delivered the addresses that constitute the body of the book of Deuteronomy, commissioned Joshua, and died. Joshua began preparations to cross the Jordan within days of Moses' death (Josh 1:10-11). In the chronology of Deuteronomy, or in the chronology of Numbers, for that matter, there is no time for Reuben and Gad to build cities.

Surprisingly, Deuteronomy draws no parallels between Reuben and Gad and the Kadesh rebels. Given Deuteronomy's interest in establishing Israel's early disobedience as a paradigm—rebellion like that at Kadesh results in YHWH's displeasure, then and now—one would expect attention to be drawn to the reluctance of the Transjordanian tribes. In fact, the book of Joshua disapprovingly relates yet another example of the Transjordanians' tendency toward semi-autonomy and aberrant religious practice (Josh 22:10-34). On this occasion, representatives of the other tribes rebuked Reuben, Gad, and Manasseh for their apparent rebellion likened to the sin at Beth-peor (Josh 22:17; cf. Num 25:3-5) and to Achan's breech of Holy War rules (Josh 22:20; cf. 7:1). "If you rebel against YHWH today, he will be angry with the whole congregation of Israel tomorrow" (Josh 22:18). Deuteronomy's silence at this point is inexplicable.

COMMENTARY

The Apportionment of the Transjordan, 3:12-17

The Numbers account offers a somewhat confusing portrayal of the details of the conquest, apportionment, and settlement of the Transjordan. At first, according to its portrayal, the tribes of Reuben and Gad alone express interest in Jazer and Gilead, territory Israel had already conquered (Num 32:1; see 21:21-35, esp. v. 24). According to variant traditions included in Numbers 32:39-42, however, the Manassite clan Machir alone conquered Gilead (v. 39) or the Manassite clan Jair alone conquered a number of cities in Gilead (v. 40). Yet another isolated tradition reports the independent campaign of a certain Nabah (v. 41). These traditions not only complicate the geographical and chronological picture, but they also seem to stand in tension with Moses' insistence, reported in both Numbers and Deuteronomy, on the need for Israel to act in unison.

Deuteronomy 3:12-17 displays some of the same confusion, although to a lesser degree. From the outset, Deuteronomy 3:12 makes it clear that the tribes of Reuben and Gad received only half of Gilead, while the half-tribe of Manasseh received the other portion along with all of Bashan. This Manassite territory was then further subdivided among the clans of Jair, who received the Argob (= Bashan), and Machir, who occupied the Manassite portion of Gilead.[Manasseh and Machir] Verses 16-17 are redundant in their present position in the final form of the text.

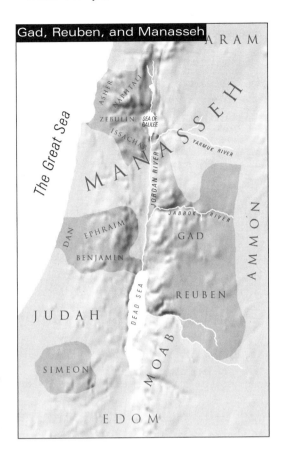

Gad, Reuben, and Manasseh

Standing Order to Reuben and Gad, 3:18-20

As noted above, Moses' instructions to Reuben and Gad reveal none of the tensions that play such a crucial role in the Numbers version of this episode (and in Joshua regarding a later episode). Moses simply and straightforwardly instructs the fighting men (*bĕnê ḥayil*, v. 18) of Reuben and Gad to join their brothers in the conquest of Canaan. The only clear indication that the author of the Deuteronomy account was familiar with the Numbers version or a very similar tradition is Moses' parenthetical remark, "I know you have many cattle" (v. 19). In the Numbers version, concern for the cattle motivates Reuben and Gad to request exemption from crossing the Jordan and excites Moses' displeasure. In Deuteronomy Moses wisely anticipates their concern and peremptorily offers a solution.

Moses' interest, on the other hand, focuses on the duty of Reuben and Gad to join with their brothers—who participated in the defeat of Sihon and Og and thus helped Reuben and Gad to gain their possessions—in the battles to come. This motif is an

Manasseh and Machir

Pre-modern societies often express relationships between national and ethnic groups as kinship ties. As a result, when new population groups arise or disappear, or when existing groups assimilate into a society, it becomes necessary to modify genealogies to account for the new situation. Since the population of ancient Israel was by no means stable and since the Old Testament was produced over many centuries, it is not surprising that the kinship relations described in the various genealogies are often chaotic and sometimes mutually contradictory.

The jagged character of Deut 3:12-17 (and Num 32) reflects this process with regard to the Transjordanian elements of the half-tribe of Manasseh, in particular with regard to the Machirites and the Jairites. Systematic genealogies of the tribe of Manasseh appear in Num 26:29-34 and 1 Chr 7:14-19 (cf. 1 Chr 2:21-24). According to Num 26, Manasseh had one son, Machir, "the father of Gilead." Gilead's six sons were Jezer, Helek, Asriel, Shechem, Shemida, and Hepher. 1 Chr 7:14-19 is very difficult. Virtually all scholars agree that the Hebrew text has become hopelessly corrupt. Among the several difficulties, v. 14 describes Asriel as Manasseh's son (not his great-grandson); it is unclear who "Huppim and Shuppim" are (v. 15, see v. 12); it is unclear whose sister Maacah is (v. 15), especially since she is described as Machir's wife in the next verse; the relationship of Zelophehad (a male) and Hammolecheth (a female) to others in the genealogy is totally obscured; and, finally, a series of names not found in

Num 26 (Peresh, Sheresh, Ulam, etc.) suddenly appears in the Chronicles genealogy.

How does one explain this confusing state of affairs? Notably, several of the names are also place names associated with Transjordanian regions occupied by Machir—Gilead, Jair, and Maacah—and, in fact, according to the Bible, these place names predated the arrival of the Israelite tribes (for Gilead, see Gen 31; for Maacah and Jair, see Deut 3:12-19; Num 32; Josh 13:13; cf. 2 Sam 3:3; 10:8, where Maacah, a Geshurite princess, is Absalom's mother, David's wife). Do the genealogies intend to document the family tree of Manasseh—a state of affairs that cannot change over time (except to grow longer)—or the geographical holdings of the tribe of Manasseh—a circumstance that can vary with time?

Other references to Jair (Deut 3:14) confirm the suspicion that the genealogies reflect geographical control more than family relationships. Jair appears in Deut 3 and Num 26 as a Manassite who conquered the cities referred to as Havvoth-jair. Judg 10:3-4 refers, on the other hand, to a Gileadite judge named Jair who controlled these cities and for whom they were named. Have the circumstances of a later period been transposed into the conquest period? In 1 Chr 2:21-24, Jair is said to be the son of Segub, the son of the Judean Hezron by Ephrathah (another place name), daughter of Machir. According to this genealogy, then, Jair is not properly a Manassite at all, but a Judahite. This seems to represent Judah's efforts to validate its claims beyond its traditional territory in the post-exilic period.

example of Deuteronomy's emphasis on Israel's unity—one God, one covenant, one people. As the Joshua account illustrates, however, the Transjordanians' separatist tendencies not only represent a certain self-centeredness, but also endanger Israel's relationship with YHWH.

Moses' command to Reuben and Gad introduces another significant theme—Israel's rest from its enemies. Although this notion does not surface frequently, and never outside Deuteronomy (12:10; 25:19), the so-called Deuteronomistic history[1] (Josh 1:13, 15; 22:4; 23:1; 2 Sam 7:1, 11 // 1 Chr 22:9, 18; see also 1 Chr 23:25), or very late literature influenced by these earlier instances (2 Chr 14:5-7; 15:15; 20:30; Neh 9:28; Esth 9:16-22; compare Dan 12:13), it represents a theologically rich conception of the meaning of YHWH's gift of the land. In the land God gave, Israel found rest. The concept seems to have been linked particularly closely to the Reuben and Gad tradition. In the earlier literature, only Joshua 23:1 (Joshua's farewell address) and 2 Samuel 7:1, 11 (after subjugating all Israel's neighbors, David and Israel enjoyed rest) employ the term in some other context.

Standing Orders to Joshua, 3:21-22

The logic of Moses' instructions to Joshua is a prototypical example of Deuteronomic thought. Moses argues that: (1) Joshua has been an eyewitness to God's mighty acts on Israel's behalf in the defeat of Sihon and Og (v. 21a); (2) God can be expected to intervene for Israel in the Canaanite campaign (v. 21b); (3) Therefore Joshua[2] need have no fear (v. 22a) because, (4) YHWH fights for Israel (v. 22b). Given Joshua's experience at Kadesh—where Israel's fear led to disobedience—and in the Transjordanian campaign—when Israel defeated a much stronger enemy because it trusted in YHWH's assistance—fear would have been tantamount to unbelief.

Moses' Petitionary Prayer and YHWH's Response, 3:23-29

Having arrived at the border of the land long ago promised the patriarchs, after the struggles with Pharaoh and the harsh journey through the wilderness, Moses now expresses his last remaining desire to the LORD: he wants to see the fruits of his efforts. His prayer, a brief but in many ways model example, elicits YHWH's two-part response. As often in Scripture (compare Elijah's still small voice prayer, 1 Kgs 19:8-18, and Jer 12:1-6), God's response redirects the discussion.

Two verbs, *'br* "to cross (over)" and *rh* "to see," interlace this unit forming its thematic superstructure. Moses asks permission to "cross over" (*'e'bĕrâ,* v. 25) and see the good land "over" (*bĕ'ēber,* v. 25) the Jordan. But YHWH becomes "cross" (*yit'abbēr,* v. 26) with Moses. Moses cannot "cross over" (*ta'ăbōr,* v. 27) to the land. Joshua, his successor, will "cross over" (*ya'bor,* v. 28), leading the people.

Similarly, Moses acknowledges that God has shown (*lĕharôt,* literally, "caused to see," v. 24) him great wonders and asks to be permitted to see (*'er'eh,* v. 25) yet one more. God grants permission to see (*rĕ'ê,* v. 27) the land and refers once again to the land that Moses will have seen (*tir'eh,* v. 28) in the instruction to prepare Joshua. Of course Moses meant to ask permission not just to see the land from afar, but also to enter it. God, however, takes advantage of Moses' choice of words in order to grant Moses' request in part, while denying Moses' actual desires.

Moses Sees the Promised Land from Afar

James Jacques Joseph Tissot. 1836–1902. *Moses Sees the Promised Land from Afar.* The Jewish Museum. New York.

Moses' Prayer, 3:23-25

Moses "entreated" (*ĕthannan*, literally "sought grace for himself," v. 23) the LORD—an expression describing an earnest and formal request. In keeping with the gravity of his petition, Moses begins by addressing God with an honorific title (*ădonāy*, "My LORD") and God's proper name (*YHWH*) in an ascription of praise. In the address, Moses emphasizes YHWH's mighty acts—which he has himself seen—and incomparability. Masterfully, Moses already prepares for his petition in the opening: "You have only begun to show your servant your greatness. . . ." The implication is that YHWH should not prematurely cease to demonstrate his might. Notably, Moses bases his entire prayer not on his own merits or the depth of his desire, but on YHWH's greatness and might. In response to this near-flattery, how can YHWH refuse Moses' modest request that he be allowed to enter the good land YHWH promises?

YHWH's Response, 3:26-28

YHWH answered Moses' prayer, but not as Moses likely expected: "You may certainly see the land—from afar. Prepare your successor to see it firsthand!" Apparently God has grown quite angry with Moses. Why? The narrator supplies only the information that God's anger is "on [Israel's] account." Numbers agrees that YHWH prohibits Moses from crossing the Jordan, but it attributes YHWH's displeasure to a specific situation in which Moses himself sinned (Num 20:10-13; 27:12-23). Deuteronomy's explanation for YHWH's anger is ambiguous.

Commentators have often seen Deuteronomy 3:26 as a prefiguration of the concept of vicarious suffering known from the latter portions of the book of Isaiah (see, especially, Isa 53) and the New Testament. As attractive as this interpretation may be, especially to Christian readers, three observations caution against over-hastily finding the concept—even in an undeveloped form—in Deuteronomy 3. First, the Hebrew term employed (*lēma'an*) means

Legends Concerning Moses' Death

The problem of Moses' death inspired legend and conjecture in the Jewish tradition (see also commentary and sidebars on Deut 34). The medieval *Midrash Petirat Mosheh Rabbenu 'Alav ha-Shalom* contains the following imagined exchange between Moses and YHWH just before Moses' death:

But Moses our Master, peace be with him, said: "It is written, 'Truly God does all these things.' And you deal with your creatures according to your quality of mercy once, twice and thrice, while as to me, You will not pardon my only sin." Said God: "Moses, you have committed six sins, none of which I have reproached you for until now. At the very first, you said to me: 'Send, I pray thee, by the hand of him whom Thou will send' [Ex 4:13]. Secondly, 'For since I came to Pharaoh to speak in Thy name, he has dealt worse with this people' [Ex 5:23]. Thirdly: 'It was not the LORD who has sent me' [Num 16:29]. Fourthly: 'But if the LORD creates a new thing' [Num 16:30]. Fifthly: 'Hear now you rebels' [Num 20:10]. Sixthly: 'And behold you are risen up in the place of your fathers, a brood of sinful men' [Num 32:14]. Were Abraham, Isaac, and Jacob sinful men that you thus addressed their children?"

"Master of the world," said Moses, "I only followed Your example, for You too said: '[remove] the censers of these sinners against their own lives'" [Num 17:3].

But God pointed out to him: "I did not mention their fathers [as sinners]."

"O LORD of the world," pleaded Moses, "how many times has Israel sinned against You and I begged and implored Your mercy toward them and consequently You forgave them. But me You will not forgive!"

"The punishment that is laid upon the community," said God, "is different from the punishment that is laid upon the individual. Furthermore, until today, fate has been in your power."

Cited in R. Kushelevsky, *Moses and the Angel of Death* (Studies on Themes and Motifs in Literature 4; New York: Peter Lang, 1995), 199.

"on account of" or "because of," but does not convey any connotation of "on behalf of" or "for the sake of." Second, Moses' punishment had no redemptive value: no one benefits. Third, and perhaps most significantly, the guilty parties themselves—the Kadesh rebels—had already born the consequences of their own sins. Moses does not suffer banishment from the Holy Land in their place.

Instead, another notion, in some ways equally profound, may resonate here. Deuteronomy seems to suggest that God holds Moses, as Israel's leader, responsible in some sense for his people's failures: like priest like people (Hos 4:9). One could wish that the author had indicated more of his reasoning. [Legends Concerning Moses' Death]

For Deuteronomy, however, the theological significance of Moses' death lies not in the reasons that resulted in YHWH's decision to bar Moses from entering the land, but in the implications of Moses' death for Israel. Moses led the people out of Egypt; he represented YHWH to the people and the people to YHWH at Horeb; he guided the people in the wilderness. In effect, Moses has been the only leader Israel has ever known. Now, at the crucial moment of entry into the promised land, Israel must go on without him. Israel must face the perils awaiting them in Canaan without his wisdom and intimate knowledge of the divine will. Deuteronomy is the response to this crisis of leadership. Although Moses cannot enter the land with Israel, he can leave them with an extensive statement of his insights into the Torah. Deuteronomy converts the crisis of leadership into an opportunity for the establishment of an interpretive tradition.

Final Travel Notice, 3:29

Biblical sources agree that Israel's final station before crossing the Jordan to enter the promised land was in the Moabite plain just north of the Dead Sea and east of the River. The site is variously identified as the Plains of Moab opposite Jericho (Num 21:12; 22:1; 33:50; 35:1), Shittim (Num 25:1), or the valley opposite Beth-peor (Deut 3:29). Moses' summary of Israel's experiences since Mt. Horeb is now complete. The expected continuation of the accounts of the commissioning of Joshua (Deut 3:21) and the death of Moses (3:23-28) appears in the concluding section of the outer narrative framework to the book (31–34).

CONNECTIONS

Rest

From its original usage in Deuteronomy, the significant but infrequent idea of "rest" became a rich source for later biblical writers. The theology of the book of Deuteronomy—adapted by the school responsible for producing the comprehensive historical work Joshua through 2 Kings—emphasizes the paradigmatic character of the generation under Moses' leadership. Just as YHWH withheld protection from those who rebelled at Kadesh, YHWH will "deliver" any future generation of idolaters and rebels "into the hands of their enemies" (Judg 2:11-16). Conversely, YHWH will bring "rest from their enemies" to any generation that repents and turns wholeheartedly to God.

The image of "rest from enemies" comes to describe periods of religious health and national prosperity. The Deuteronomistic History reserves this designation for the period of king David's reign (2 Sam 7:1, 11). The Chronicler, writing some centuries later, reaffirms the Deuteronomistic paradigm (Neh 9:28) and employs the concept of "rest" also to describe the reigns of Asa (2 Chr 14:5-7; 15:15) and Jehoshaphat (2 Chr 20:30). Literature dating from near the close of the production of Hebrew Scripture applies the term to the Jews' victory over Haman and his co-conspirators (Esth 9:16-22) and, in a usage that prefigures inter-testamental, rabbinic, and Christian treatment of the concept, describes the eschaton as a "rest" (Dan 12:13).

Perhaps the most fruitful Old Testament usage of the image can be found in its sole occurrence in the Psalter (Ps 95:11). Here the psalmist recalls Israel's wilderness period and warns against obduracy. They are to respond to YHWH in obedience lest YHWH hinder them too from enjoying the "rest" YHWH offers.

Jewish and Christian literature produced in the Hellenistic period expanded the image of "rest" by employing it in reference to the eschaton (see, for example, Sir 51:27; *Joseph and Asenath* 8:9; 15:7; 22:13; *Sanh.* 99a; 110b; *Gos. Thom.* 50, 51, 60, 90). The author of Hebrews (3:7-4:13) associated the "rest" (Hebrew *nwḥ*, Greek *katapausis*) from enemies with the Sabbath rest (Hebrew and Greek use these same terms for Sabbath rest as well) and utilized Psalm 95 as a point of departure for exhorting his readers to steadfast obedience. Although strictly speaking, the original concept as found in Deuteronomy referred only to historical Israel's security in the land of Canaan, the author of Hebrews appropriately highlighted the open-ended and paradigmatic character of the original concept.

It is important to remember, however, that in Deuteronomy God's gift of "rest" is a gift of security in the land. It is very this-worldly and demonstrates God's concern for the quality of Israel's everyday life. While it is true, as later authors of Scripture emphasize, that God offers rest beyond history, modern readers should not rush too quickly to interpret Deuteronomy in terms of eternity. The paradigmatic character of Deuteronomy calls on its readers to recognize that daily life is lived in relationship to God and under the demands of God's will. Rest and security are conditions of harmony and order with respect to God's will. Chaos and disaster are but expressions of living chaotically and disastrously. The experiences of Israel's wilderness generation warn every subsequent generation of the inherent dangers of being "a people whose hearts go astray and [who] do not regard [God's] ways" (Ps 95:10).

Doing the Will of God

It is difficult not to pity Moses. After his long years of burdensome service, leading a stubborn, childish, grumbling people through the wilderness, justice and equity would seem to require that he be rewarded with more than a distant glimpse of the final goal toward which he has labored. Moses is not alone among biblical heroes. Abraham answered God's call (Gen 12:1-4) only to learn later that

God planned to fulfill the promise by giving the land—not, after all, to Abraham—but to his descendants four hundred years later (Gen 15:15-16)! God called the prophet Isaiah to a ministry of preaching to a people who would not heed his message. He was called to fail! His words were to be committed to writing to serve as a testimony to subsequent generations he would never know (Isa 8:16). Abraham and Isaiah were called upon to trust that, because "the word of YHWH does not return void," some future generation would benefit from their obedience to the call of God.

The questions posed by the experiences of Moses, Abraham, Isaiah, and others, are whether one serves God because God is God or in hopes of some reward (Job 1:9-11) and whether one measures one's life and work according to the standards of immediate and tangible results or to the standards of the kingdom of God and its timetable. If not, has one done the will of God for the sake of righteousness or merely in order to obtain the reward? Does one seek first, foremost, and exclusively the will of God?

In a book-length meditation on the beatitude, "Blessed are the pure in heart, for they shall see God," Søren Kierkegaard remarked that those who do the Good in hopes of reward have "no time to wait, no time, no years, no life to give away—for an eternity."[3]

NOTES

[1] See Introduction, n. 1.

[2] And all Israel—the confusion between second person singular and plural surfaces here. Ostensibly addressed to Joshua, vv. 21-22 function effectively as an address to all Israel; v. 22 is entirely in the plural.

[3] *Purity of Heart Is to Will One Thing: Spiritual Preparation for the Office of Confession*, trans. D. V. Steere (New York: Harper & Row, 1956), 72.

THEOPHANY, COVENANT, IDOLATRY, EXILE, AND MONOTHEISM: PARANESIS AND TRADITION

4:1-40

Deuteronomy 4 consists of three clearly distinct sections of unequal length. The initial section (vv. 1-40) is a lengthy paranesis, or persuasive instruction, concerning various implications of Israel's responsibility to obey the Horeb covenant. The final two sections of the chapter (vv. 41-43 and 44-49) deal with the establishment of the cities of refuge and make the transition from the historical summary in Deuteronomy 1–3 to what follows beginning in Deuteronomy 5. Neither of these concluding units stand in integral relationship to the paranesis in Deuteronomy 4:1-40, nor does 4:1-40 manifest any obvious relationship to the historical survey in chapters 1–3. A. D. H. Mayes observes that the transition from historical summary to paranesis is harshly abrupt, that the summons to hear (v. 1) signals a new beginning, that Deuteronomy 1–3 exhibit no intention to elicit obedience to the Law, and that Deuteronomy 4 does not appeal to the historical events recorded in Deuteronomy 1–3 in support of its argument.[1] The unfulfilled expectation is that accounts of Moses' commissioning of his successor and of his subsequent death will follow 3:23-29, as has already been noted. Observations such as these have led many scholars to conclude that Deuteronomy 4 derives from a late phase in the growth of the book when it was inserted into its current location.

The complicated structure and convoluted logic of the paranesis strengthens the perception that Deuteronomy 4 represents an expansion of the tradition. It repeats itself frequently (compare vv. 1, 6, 14, 23, 40). It resists neat division into sections. Several passages within the paranesis seem at best only very loosely related to their contexts (compare, for example, vv. 21-24). Other passages seem to presuppose knowledge of events dating long after the time of Moses (vv. 25-31). These and other features of the passage have, in fact, occasioned a lively scholarly debate as to whether vv. 1-40 are a homogenous, though loosely structured, unit[2] or the product of a

The Structure of Deuteronomy 4

A sample of scholarly analyses of the structure of Deuteronomy 4 demonstrates the variety of possible solutions. D. Knapp divides the paranesis into the following sections: vv. 1-4 + 9-14 (the oldest portion), 5-8 (an insertion), 15-16a + 19-28, 16b-18 (an insertion), 29-40. A. D. H. Mayes identifies six sections, each save the last beginning with warnings to obey the Law: vv. 1-4, 5-8, 9-14, 15-22, 23-31, 32-40. D. Olson argues that the paranesis is structured concentrically with the introduction (vv. 1-4) paralleling the conclusion (v. 40). An inner framework stresses the "unique greatness of Israel's wisdom and God's nearness" (vv. 5-8 // vv. 32-39). The body of the chapter, vv. 9-31, offers three paradigms for keeping the covenant, namely the "Horeb-Creation-Egypt paradigm from the past" (vv. 9-20), the "Moses-People paradigm of the present" (vv. 21-24), and the "Exile-Return paradigm of the future" (vv. 25-31).

D. Knapp, *Deuteronomium 4: literarische Analyse und theologische Interpretation* (Göttinger theologischer Arbeiten 35; Göttingen: Vandenhoeck & Ruprecht, 1987), 27-42.

A. D. H. Mayes, *Deuteronomy* (NCBC; Grand Rapids: Eerdmans, 1979), 197.

D. Olson, *Deuteronomy and the Death of Moses: A Theological Reading* (OBT; Minneapolis: Fortress, 1994), 31.

long history of redaction and expansion.[3] As a consequence of the loose structure of 4:1-40, the following commentary will deal with units suggested by syntactical features and the sense of the text. Other analyses are possible. [The Structure of Deuteronomy 4]

As will be demonstrated in the commentary below, themes common to several sections of the paranesis receive varied, distinctive, and sometimes nearly contradictory treatments. This observation alone suggests not only that the paranesis developed in stages, but also that it provides a model case of the way in which biblical traditions propagated themselves. Remarkably, this variety, together with the deductive character of the logic of this material and the many apparent allusions to other biblical literature, especially the prophets, lends the paranesis an almost scholastic character. Although it appeals to events at Mt. Horeb/Sinai, it is not concerned with narrating historical tradition. From a rhetorical perspective, it does not seek to encourage or motivate, that is, it is not exhortation. Instead, it represents learned reflection, syllogistic reasoning from the premise of the theophany on the mountain of God. It self-consciously develops theological *assertions* on the basis of historical *experience*. It is probably not incorrect to see it as the record of lengthy discussions among Israel's theologians much like the Talmud will later become the repository for the results of generations of rabbinic debate.

One other phenomenon in Deuteronomy 4, indeed in the entire book, confronts readers in any era quite pointedly with the necessity of a refined sensitivity to the redactional and rhetorical complexity of the book. Deuteronomy 4 employs both the singular and the plural forms of the second personal pronoun with no apparent significance and no apparent pattern—a circumstance already familiar from Deuteronomy 1–3. Furthermore, and much more significantly, the "you" addressed in Deuteronomy 4 clearly represents four distinct audiences treated quite anachronistically as one. Presumably, Moses addressed this speech to those alive at the conclusion of the forty-year wilderness wandering (v. 3). Yet, elsewhere the paranesis presumes this audience to have been present at

Mt. Sinai
Mount Sinai is located in the Old Testament Sinai desert, which is present-day Egypt. The exact location of the mountain is not known, but it is speculated that it is Gebel Musa in the southern Sinai desert. The location, nevertheless, does not carry as much significance as the symbolic nature of the mountain. Mount Sinai represents the place where the Israelites were given the Torah as well as the instructions for the Tent of Meeting.

Horeb and to have witnessed God's great saving acts in the exodus (vv. 9-24, 34-36). Yet again, the text addresses an audience that will experience, or has experienced, the pain of exile (vv. 25-31). As literature, Deuteronomy assumes throughout an audience of readers—a fourth "you." In the end, the relationship between these four audiences proves to be the point of the paranesis. Will readers benefit from the opportunity to identify with and learn from the experience of earlier generations? Can readers place themselves at Mt. Horeb alongside ancient Israel and hear the voice of God, as it were? ["Actualization" and Biblical Interpretation]

COMMENTARY

The Utmost Urgency of Obedience to the Covenant, 4:1-4

The paranesis opens with the abrupt "And now hear, O Israel," which, following 3:23-29, catches the reader totally unprepared. Moses calls Israel to attend "to the statutes and ordinances (*'el-haḥuqqîm wĕ'el hammišpaṭîm*)" that he will "teach" them. This call

"Actualization" and Biblical Interpretation

Theological scholarship on the Old Testament often refers to the process whereby a later generation appropriates earlier traditions as "actualization." Gerhard von Rad popularized the term and concept in his work on Deuteronomy, in particular, which he saw as a prime example of the process (see especially *The Form-Critical Problem of the Hexateuch and Other Essays*, trans. E. Dicken [New York: McGraw Hill, 1966]; *Deuteronomy: A Commentary*, trans. D. Barton, OTL [Philadelphia: Westminster, 1966]; and *Studies in Deuteronomy*, trans. D. Stalker [London: SCM, 1953]). In his wake, many scholars have seen evidence of the "actualization" of traditions in many parts of the Hebrew Bible.

Joseph Groves analyzes varieties of actualization in order to highlight the distinctiveness of actualization as exemplified in Scripture. He terms the first "cultic actualization," characterized as a: (a) regular, (b) dramatic, (c) reality-producing (d) re-enactment of the community's fundamental sacred events which (e) identifies the moment of re-enactment with the moment of the original event. Such cultic actualization envisions time mythically, identifying the present with the mythic past so closely that all distinction is lost.

The second variety, "literary actualization," is the manner in which a new generation handles the traditions of its ancestors. It involves: (a) a recognition of the difference between the two periods, the one that produced the text and the one in which it is read; (b) the awareness of the historically-bound character of the original text; and (c) a primarily hermeneutical perspective, i.e., it is not reality-producing (ibid., 108-12). This type of actualization demarcates the two time periods involved to such an extent that they scarcely have contact with one another.

The third category found in the Hebrew Bible according to this school of scholarship, for which Groves chooses the term "chronological actualization," seeks to resolve the difficulty associated with the problem of relating the two time periods. Through actualization of its tradition, as Brevard Childs has written, Israel was able to experience "an immediate encounter, an actual participation in the great acts of redemption" (see, for example, Exod 13:3-16).

But it was also aware that the tradition is rooted in a unique past. Therefore, it sought to adapt and appropriate the tradition in and for a changed setting. In this regard, the tradition must be validated by later generations in order to have vitality. Until a later generation appropriates and utilizes the tradition, it is sterile, even invalid.

Deut 4 clearly exemplifies this "chronological actualization" in an almost pure form. In this paranesis, generations to come are encouraged and called to keep the tradition alive and to appropriate it ever anew and afresh. Similarities between this process of renewed appropriation of found traditions and the Talmudic concept of the Oral Law are noteworthy.

Joseph Groves, *Actualization and Interpretation in the Old Testament* (SBLDS 86; Atlanta: Scholars Press, 1987), 105-106, 112-16.

Brevard Childs, *Memory and Tradition in Israel* (London: SCM, 1962), 84.

introduces a notion characteristic of Deuteronomy's understanding of its relation to the covenant. Notably, Deuteronomy 4:13 identifies the covenant in a limited sense with the Decalogue, the ten fundamental commandments God gave the people via Moses on Mt. Horeb. Typically, Deuteronomy refers to the fact that YHWH "commanded" (*ṣwh*) Israel to obey the Law, whereas Moses speaks here of "teaching" Israel "statutes and ordinances." Are "statutes and ordinances" synonymous with the basic covenant or do they designate something distinctive?

The etymology and usage of the Hebrew term *mišpāṭ*, "judgments," may provide a clue. This term, a noun formed on the verbal root *špṭ*, "to judge," often refers to decisions or judgments rendered by some judicial authority (Lev 19:15; Num 35:12; 2 Kgs 25:6; Jer 1:16; Ps 105:5; Prov 16:10; 2 Chr 19:6). In this usage, it is analogous not to legislation, but to the modern concept of case law, the body of legal doctrine derived from the actual decisions of the courts. Similarly, *ḥuqqîm* often refers to "boundaries" (Jer 5:22; Mic 7:11; Job 38:10; Prov 8:29) and, by extension, to "principles of order" (Gen 47:26; Judg 11:39; 2 Chr 35:25; Ps 148:6; Job 28:26). "Statutes" and "ordinances," then, seem to refer to specific decisions and regulations that extend, interpret, and apply the fundamental principles of the covenant Decalogue.[4]

As even the most casual reader may observe, while the Decalogue clearly states noble ethical and religious principles, the "boundaries" and "applications" of the principles are often far from clear. What precisely does it mean to honor father and mother in the multitude of circumstances possible in the course of human life? Deuteronomy suggests here that, poised to enter the promised land and begin a settled national existence, Israel needs tools for interpreting and applying the basic requirements of the covenant to specific life situations. It needs the foundations of a tradition of interpretation.

To say that the provisions of the covenant must be interpreted in various life settings is not to say that it is subject to revision, however. The so-called "canonical formula" found in v. 2 is known in covenant texts stemming from throughout the ancient Near East. A scribal convention meant to guard against tampering with legal or treaty documents, it underscores the unalterable validity of a document and its stipulations. [The So-called "Canonical Formula"] While they may require wise interpretation and application, the commandments God gave through Moses are not subject to change in their essence.

The So-Called "Canonical Formula"

AΩ Many Christians familiar with the book of Revelation have understood the concluding statement as a reference to the closing of the canon. Does the phrase "this book" refer to the entire Bible or to the book of Revelation alone?

I warn everyone who hears the words of the prophecy of this book: if anyone adds to them, God will add to him the plagues described in this book, and if anyone takes away from the words of the book of this prophecy, God will take away his share in the tree of life and in the holy city, which are described in this book. (Rev 22:18-19, RSV)

As it turns out, this statement exemplifies a literary device known as the "canonical formula," a formula with a long history reaching back to ancient Mesopotamia. It served the purpose of protecting against tampering with legal texts. It first appeared in Assyrian treaty texts and covenants in forms such as the following formula from a treaty contracted by Esarhaddon.

(You swear that) you will not alter (the covenant text), you will not consign (it) to the fire nor throw (it) into the water, nor [bury (it)] in the earth nor destroy it by any cunning device, nor make [(it) disappear], nor sweep (it) away. (Wiseman)

It also occurs in a number of variations in the Hebrew Bible, first in Deut 4:2 and again in 13:1 (13:2 Eng). Both instances in Deuteronomy function not to close the canon with the book of Deuteronomy, but to highlight the covenantal character of the book and to warn against tampering with the explicit provisions of this covenant. Secondary, i.e., non-covenantal usages in reference to God's majesty and might appear in Eccl 3:14 and in the apocryphal book of Sirach (18:5-6; 42:21; compare Prov 30:6 and Jer 26:2).

D. J. Wiseman, *The Vassal-Treaties of Esarhaddon* (London: British School of Archaeology, 1958), 60, ll. 410-13; see also the epilogue to the Lipit-Ishtar Lawcode (ANET, 161).

The commandments and Moses' instruction by example in their proper interpretation aim to provide Israel the means to life (v. 1). The generation to whom Moses ostensibly addressed the paranesis had "seen with their own eyes" the results of disobedience to the covenant. At Beth-peor some Israelites became involved with Moabite women and, even more detrimentally, in the worship of Moabite deities (compare Num 25:1-15; Hos 9:10; the historical summary in Deut 1–3 betrays no knowledge of this Beth-peor tradition). In wrath, YHWH instructed Moses to have the evildoers executed. On the other hand, all those present at Beth-peor who had maintained fidelity to YHWH were preserved alive.

Notably, given the subsequent development of the theme in Deuteronomy 4, the sin for which YHWH punished Israel at Beth-peor involved violations of the first and second commandments—prohibitions against worshiping gods other than YHWH and against making idols. If the book of Deuteronomy considers the Decalogue to be the core of the covenant, it regards the first two commandments as quintessential.

Israel's Unsurpassed Covenant Relationship, 4:5-8

After the canonical formula (v. 2) and the examples, negative and positive, supporting the claim of the essential importance of obedience to the covenant, the argument resumes. Once again, the text focuses on the nature of Moses' instruction. Moses will "teach" "principles and cases" as YHWH had commanded that he do when the people come to enter the land. This language at least implies that this instruction was foreseen as early as Mt. Horeb and that it can best be understood, not as a supplement to the original covenant—and certainly not as an alternative legal code—but as an explication and application of the principles inherent in the Horeb covenant.

Verse 6 offers a new—indeed virtually unparalleled in Scripture—reason that Israel should adhere to the stipulations of the covenant. Moses prepares to teach "statutes and ordinances" that the nations surrounding Israel will recognize as superior for their wise and insightful conception! Two equally startling rhetorical questions support this claim. Moses first asks whether any other great nation can summon its god in the same way that Israel can summon YHWH (v. 7). Then he asks whether any other nation can boast of laws as "righteous" as those he is about to teach (v. 8). The boastful tone of these questions startles and seems to reflect the concerns and biases of a very late period in Israel's

Buber on Encounters

The You encounters me by grace—it cannot be found by seeking. But that I speak the basic word to it is a deed of my whole being, is my essential deed.

The You encounters me. But I enter into a direct relationship to it. Thus the relationship is election and electing, passive and active at once. An action of the whole being must approach passivity, for it does away with all partial actions and thus with any sense of action, which depends on limited exertions.

The basic word I-You can be spoken only with one's whole being. The concentration and fusion into a whole being can never be accomplished by me, can never be accomplished without me. I require a You to become; becoming I, I say You.

All actual life is encounter.

Martin Buber, *I and Thou* trans. W. Kaufmann (New York: Charles Scribner's Sons, 1970), 62.

history when its encounter with the nations (in exile?) had produced a defensiveness and sensitivity unknown in earlier periods.

Further Elucidation of the Relationship Between the Original Covenant and Moses' Instruction, 4:9-14

The Beth-peor episode served the purposes of the paranesis as an example of the consequences of disobedience. Now the argument turns to Israel's foundational experience. Israel must take care not to forget "the things (*haddĕbārîm*)" they had witnessed. Indeed, memory must be preserved and passed on to subsequent generations (v. 9)—another example of the significance in Deuteronomy of trans-generational relationship to the covenant. What are these "things"? Although portions of Moses' purported audience had only personally witnessed events since Israel's departure from Beersheba during the forty years of wandering, v. 10 speaks of the establishment of the covenant on Mt. Horeb. This fiction boldly embodies the trans-generational emphasis of the book. Although, except for Moses, Joshua, and Caleb, none of those present to hear Moses' speech would have been witness to the Horeb/Sinai event, the book of Deuteronomy has Moses address them as though they had seen for themselves! The God of Israel is known through encounter! [Buber on Encounters] Memory and tradition passed from generation to generation can make later generations witnesses to the events of their ancestors' lives. In a real sense, then, Moses can remind the children and grandchildren of those who had actually been present at Sinai that they, too, had seen YHWH's mighty acts. Israel is never to forget what it saw and heard at Mt. Horeb. [Meditation upon the Law]

The events described briefly in vv. 11-12 receive more complete treatment in Exodus 19:16-25 and 20:18-26. The Exodus and

Meditation upon the Law

R. Chanania ben Teradion said, "If two sit together and interchange no words of the Law, they are a meeting of the scornful, as it is said, *Nor sitteth* [the godly man] *in the seat of the scoffers [Ps 1:1]*; but if two sit together and words of the Law [pass] between them, the Divine Presence abides between them, as it is said, *then they that feared the Eternal spake one with the other; and the Eternal hearkened and heard, and a book of remembrance was written before Him, for them that feared the Eternal, and that thought upon His Name [Mal 3:16]."*
(Abot 3:2)

Deuteronomy accounts agree substantially: While the people gathered together at the foot of the mountain, YHWH appeared to them in a theophany of smoke and fire (Exodus also mentions trumpet blasts and thunder and lightning). The only significant difference between Deuteronomy 4:11-12 (see also Deut 4:33, 36) and Exodus concerns whether Israel heard YHWH's voice intelligibly. Exodus seems to suggest that Israel did not discern YHWH's voice as speech, while Deuteronomy 4:11-12, 33, 36 seem to imply that the whole congregation heard YHWH's voice intelligibly.

At any rate, both passages identify the content of this revelation with the Ten Commandments (see Deut 4:13). In fact, as implied in vv. 1 and 4, v. 14 explicitly distinguishes between the covenant commandments and the "principles and case-law" (see above) that God commissioned Moses to teach Israel later. In other words, the instruction to follow concerning the proper interpretation and application of the Horeb/Sinai covenant was contained implicitly in God's revelation to and through Moses on Mt. Horeb/Sinai.

Another Deduction from the Horeb/Sinai Experience—No Images, 4:15-20

To this point, the paranesis has focused on two themes: (1) the distinction between the covenant, in the strictest sense of the Ten Commandments, and its Mosaic explication; and (2) the importance of the related trans-generational memory. Now, however, it introduces a new theme, deduced as it were from the *nature* of YHWH's epiphany. The logic of this unit is straightforward. First, it calls attention to the fact that Israel saw no discernible form at Mt. Horeb/Sinai (v. 15), highlighting the significance of this observation with a warning to "be very careful (*nišmartem mĕ'od lĕnapšōtêkem*)." YHWH spoke "from the midst of the fire." YHWH did not appear visibly.

The implication drawn from this basic observation is the prohibition against idol worship. Since YHWH appeared in this mysterious fashion, it would be inappropriate, arrogant, and disrespectful to attempt to depict YHWH visually (v. 16). To be sure that the reader understands the radicality of the prohibition, the paranesis goes on to list improper representations of YHWH. YHWH has no gender (v. 16); or, if Genesis 1:18 can be adduced

Sinai Range
Miner Kilbourne Kellogg. 1814–1889. *The Top of Mount Sinai.* c.1844. Oil on canvas. 28.5" x 19.2". Smithsonian American Art Museum, Washington DC.

here, both genders reflect aspects of YHWH's character. To depict YHWH in male or female form would be incomplete, therefore inaccurate, and therefore blasphemous! As the Creator of the universe, YHWH must not, furthermore, be identified with any single created entity. Interestingly, vv. 17-18 list the creations mentioned in Genesis 1, but in reverse order.

Nor should Israel identify YHWH with astral phenomena (v. 19). The phrase "the hosts of heaven (*ṣĕbāʾ haššāmayim*) employed here also frequently occurs in the Hebrew Bible in reference to the angelic hosts (1 Kgs 22:19; Dan 8:10; Neh 9:6; 2 Chr 18:18). Indeed, the Hebrew Bible often refers to God as *YHWH ṣĕbāʾôt* or "YHWH of hosts." This text may reflect, then, the ancient understanding of astral phenomena as manifestations of YHWH's heavenly court. In this sense, the charge that Israel ought not to worship sun, moon, or stars (compare Deut 17:3; 2 Kgs 17:16; 21:3, 5; 23:4, 5; Jer 8:2; 19:13; 33:22, etc.)—unusual in this case because it is based on the assertion that these astral bodies *have been apportioned to the nations*—parallels a remarkably similar statement in Deuteronomy 32:8-9. This passage in the so-called "Song of Moses" claims that the nations have been apportioned in accordance with the numbers of the "sons of God," another expression for the angelic hosts (compare Job 1:6). But, according to Deuteronomy 32, YHWH has reserved Israel for himself! This unit on idols concludes with the reminder that YHWH, not one of the astral hosts, delivered Israel from Egyptian bondage, thereby establishing his claim to them (v. 20).

A Warning by Example: Moses' Death, 4:21-24

The relationship of vv. 21-24 to their context is unclear. This unit departs from the pattern established in previous sections in that the statement concerning the necessity of obedience (v. 23) follows the illustrative case (vv. 21-22). It is also unique in that, in this instance, the event that forms the basis for the argument is not set at Mt. Horeb/Sinai. The unit concludes with a statement of the underlying principle—YHWH's jealousy.

Unlike the tradition found in Numbers (see the discussion above on Deut 3:23-29), Deuteronomy consistently maintains that Moses' punishment came about "because of matters pertaining to" Israel (v. 21). Neither this text nor any other in Deuteronomy clearly states, however, what "things" are in view. Verse 23, with its warning to keep and not forget the commandments, specifically with regard to idol images, suggests that YHWH held Moses responsible for some incident or incidents involving idolatry. The text may refer to the Beth-peor episode cited already in v. 3, although, as attested more fully in Numbers 25, Moses' role in that incident did not contribute to Israel's sin and YHWH expressed no displeasure with him. According to the Numbers tradition, in fact, YHWH prohibited Moses from entering the promised land not because of the people's sin, but because of Moses' own willful arrogance (Num 20:10-13). In its present setting, Moses' punishment can only be loosely related to the idolatry theme.

The concluding statement of principle, on the other hand, masterfully ties together several aspects of the anti-idol polemic developed to this point in the paranesis. The description of YHWH as a "consuming fire" recalls the imagery of the Horeb/Sinai theophany, simultaneously alluding to the fact that YHWH spoke from the fire while also invoking the notion of fiery wrath.

Yet Another Implication Drawn from the Theophany, 4:25-28

The abrupt transition from the formula in v. 24 to the statement concerning the progression of the generations in v. 24 alerts the critical reader to the possibility that the unit so introduced may be a later insertion. The passage of time may result in the diminution of the memory of the exodus and the Horeb/Sinai covenant. Long in the land (*wĕnôšantem*, v. 25; literally, "and you will become inactive, stationary"), the text argues, future generations may "behave corruptly (*wĕhišḥatem*)" and make themselves idols, thereby "provoking (*kʿs*)" YHWH.

This verb represents the second signal that vv. 24-28 may be a very late insertion. It characterizes later Deuteronomistic literature, including the prose portions of the book of Jeremiah (7:18, 19; 8:19; 11:17; 25:6, 7; 32:29, 30, 32; 44:3, 8) and constitutes a major element in the Deuteronomistic theology of history. According to Deuteronomistic thought, the Assyrian conquest of the northern kingdom, and later, the Babylonian conquest of the southern kingdom, were YHWH's acts of punishment in response to a long history of "provocation." The principle established at Kadesh holds true throughout Israel's history. After many generations of rebellion and idolatry, YHWH's patience finally wore thin.

In fact, vv. 24-28 go on to describe events very similar to those of the Babylonian crisis, occasioning suspicions that they represent a *vaticinium ex eventu*, a prediction after the fact. Moses calls "heaven and earth to witness" (Deut 30:19; 31:28; Isa 1:2) that such idolatrous behavior will lead to swift destruction (v. 26). Indeed, YHWH will drive (*hêpîṣ*) idolatrous Israel into exile among the nations (Jer 9:15 [9:16 Eng]; 13:24; 18:17; 30:11; Ezek 11:16; 12:15; 20:23; 22:15; 36:19). Ironically, expelled from the land for idolatry, they will be reduced to worshiping foreign gods of human manufacture, mere wood and stone (Deut 29:16, 36, 64; 2 Kgs 19:18 [= Isa 37:19]; Jer 2:27; Ezek 20:32). [Gods of Wood and Stone] Once again, the language of the anti-idol polemic seems to derive from the rhetoric of a late period in Israel's history and manifests very strong affinities with the prophets, especially Jeremiah.

Repentance and Restoration, 4:29-31

The verb *bqš* in the sense of "to seek YHWH" does not occur elsewhere in Deuteronomy or the Deuteronomistic History, nor does *mṣʾ* in the sense of "to find YHWH." Both occur often in these senses in the prophets. In fact, they occur together in Jeremiah 29:13; Hosea 5:6; and Amos 8:12. Jeremiah 29:13, a passage in Jeremiah's "letter to the Exiles" in which he promises that the Exile will end after a period of seventy years, offers a particularly close parallel (*drš*, "to search for," the third verb in v. 29 also occurs

Gods of Wood and Stone

The book of Deuteronomy concerns itself primarily with encouraging obedience to YHWH, the God of Israel. It does not seem to be interested in establishing the validity of radical monotheism. In fact, the most common assertion in the book of Deuteronomy (and in the "Deuteronomistic History," Joshua through 2 Kings, a body of literature inspired by Deuteronomy) refers to YHWH's incomparability, not to his exclusive status. "O YHWH God, you have only begun to show your servant your greatness and your mighty hand: for what god in heaven or on earth can do such works and mighty acts as yours?" (Deut 3:24; see also 29:25-26; Josh 23:7; Judg 2:12; 1 Sam 12:10; among many other texts). The commentary has already noted the peculiar idea implied in Deut 4:19-20 and its parallel in the Song of Moses that YHWH has assigned the nations of the world to the lesser deities or divine beings while reserving Israel to himself. Abundant evidence in the Hebrew Bible suggests that, both in belief and practice, early Israel accepted the existence of gods other than YHWH.

Alongside these texts that stress YHWH's superiority to other deities, however, one finds a few passages, concentrated in the late Deuteronomistic framework of Deuteronomy and in certain key passages in Joshua through 2 Kings, that emphasize YHWH's exclusive status. YHWH—these texts claim—is not merely superior to other deities: he is the sole God.

The logic of these texts is striking. They argue primarily by means of ridiculing the idea that idols, manufactured things, can be compared to the living God. Deut 4:28 is a parade example of the argument: "And there you will serve gods of wood and stone, the product of human hands, that neither see, nor hear, nor eat, nor smell." Other texts in this family include Deut 4:35, 39; 28:36; 29:16-18; 1 Kgs 8:60; 2 Kgs 17:15; and Jer 2:27.

It should be noted that, unlike the radical monotheism of Isa 40–55—which is based primarily on a sublime meditation on the implications of the doctrine of creation—the idol polemic and monotheistic claims of the Deuteronomic/Deuteronomistic tradition extend the demands of the first two commandments. Gods made with hands cannot be gods at all. The true God of the universe is beyond depiction or location.

---

here). Scholars debate whether Deuteronomy 4:29 depends literarily upon Jeremiah 29:13 or vice versa. The prophetic character of the notions of seeking and finding YHWH suggest Jeremiah 29:13 as the source for Deuteronomy 4:29.

The insertion "predicts" that, in these coming times of distress, all "these words/things will find you," an ambiguous expression referring either to the "words" of the paranesis or the "things" foretold in it. In that time of trouble, Israel will "return" to YHWH and "heed his voice," expressions, once again, reminiscent of the prophets, especially Jeremiah ("return," 3:7; 4:1; 11:10; 18:11; etc.; "heed [YHWH's] voice," 7:23, 28; 9:12; 11:4, 7; 18:10; 22:21, etc.).

The description of YHWH as a merciful God (v. 31) contrasts with the previous portrayal of his consuming jealousy (v. 24). The reference to a "covenant with your fathers"—to which YHWH will demonstrate faithfulness by bringing Israel out of Exile—is ambiguous. Specifically, the question concerns the identity of the "fathers" here. Is this a reference to the exodus generation or to the patriarchs? (See [The Promise to the Patriarchs in Deuteronomy].) A significant strand of tradition in the Hebrew Bible argues that, although YHWH responds in wrath to violations of the covenant, YHWH's covenant with the patriarchs—a covenant based solely upon YHWH's free choice—motivates him again and again to new acts of grace (Isa 63:11; Pss 105:7-9, 42; 106:4, 45; Neh 9:6-7). Notably, these texts stem from the post-exilic period when Israel had confronted its own failures to uphold the covenant. If they had breached covenant fidelity, they must have asked themselves, was God now bound by the covenant? They found it necessary, therefore, to look further back in their history to find a sure basis for relationship with YHWH.[5] In effect, since Israel violated the Sinai covenant, its surest basis for appeal to YHWH was the unconditional covenant with the patriarchs.

YHWH's Exclusive Divinity, 4:32-40

The abrupt return to the earlier motif of God's voice from the midst of the fire further confirms the suspicion that vv. 25-31 have been inserted, either as a unit or in successive operations (vv. 25-28 then 29-31). Whereas prior appearances of the motif emphasized the notion that YHWH did not appear to Israel in any visible form—and, therefore, should not be depicted iconographically—this reprise argues from this motif that YHWH is the sole God. It also differs from v. 12 with respect to details of the means of YHWH's revelation at Mt. Horeb/Sinai (compare v. 36).

The unit opens with a summons to inquire as to whether such a revelation has any precedent or analogy (v. 32). Israel is to investigate the whole of history, all the way back to the beginning of humanity, and to search the whole heavens for any analogy to the Horeb/Sinai experience (v. 32). It is otherwise unheard of that a god should speak to a people in this manner, and even more astonishing that they should survive (v. 33). The fact that God assembled Israel as his people and delivered them in a mighty way from Egyptian bondage is equally unprecedented (v. 34).

The paranesis then draws a somewhat surprising conclusion from the unique nature of these events, namely that these unprecedented experiences imply that YHWH is the *only* god (v. 35). This statement of "radical" monotheism can be seen as another indication of the relatively late date of Deuteronomy 4. There can be little question that for much of Israel's history, its faith can be characterized as having been "monolatrous" or "henotheistic"—as having held

The Development of Monotheistic Faith

Although it might be comfortable to assume that Israel's faith had always been monotheistic, many texts in the Old Testament clearly indicate that the Israelites did not come to a truly monotheistic faith until the exilic or post-exilic period (Gen 14:17-24; 28:20-22; 35:2-4; Josh 24:2; Judg 2:11-15; etc.; 2 Kgs 17:7-18; and many more). Furthermore, archeological evidence of ancient Israelite popular piety supports the conclusion that the worship of deities other than YHWH was widespread. The process by which Israel came to the conviction that their God, YHWH, created all and rules over all, that YHWH must be the sole Lord and God, has been studied in depth by several scholars. The reference list below will provide a useful starting point for those interested in pursuing the question.

Johannes C. De Moor, *The Rise of Yahwism: The Roots of Israelite Monotheism* (BETL 91; Leuven: University Press, 1990).

Diana Vikander Edelman, ed., *The Triumph of Elohim: From Yahwism to Judaism* (Contributions to Biblical Exegesis and Theology 13; Kampen Netherlands: Pharos, 1995); see especially the very helpful bibliography.

M. A. Labuschagne, *The Incomparability of Yahweh in the Old Testament* (Pretoria Oriental Series 4; Leiden: E. J. Brill, 1966).

Bernhard Lang, *Monotheism and the Prophetic Minority: An Essay in Biblical History and Sociology* (SWBAS 1; Sheffield: Almond, 1983).

Martin Rose, *Der Ausschliesslichkeitsanspruch Jahwes: Deuteronomische Schultheologie und die Volksfrömmigkeit in der spaeten Koenigszeit* (BZAW 106; Stuttgart: W. Kohlhammer, 1975).

Morton Smith, *Palestinian Parties and Politics That Shaped the Old Testament* (New York: Columbia University, 1971).

Fritz Stolz, "Monotheismus in Israel," in Monotheismus im alten Israel und seiner Umwelt, BiBe 17, ed. O. Keel (Fribourg: Schweizerisches Katholisches Bibelwerk, 1980), 143-84.

---

that while there may be many gods, only one deserves worship. [The Development of Monotheistic Faith] Surely Israel would not have been so easily and persistently tempted to worship other gods if it had not granted the possibility of their existence! Even the first commandment of the Decalogue seems to acknowledge the existence of other deities when in it YHWH demands that Israel "should have no other gods before [YHWH]." By sometime in the exilic or post-exilic periods, however, as one can see perhaps most clearly in the anti-idol polemic to be found in Isaiah 40–66, at least some segments of Israel had come to the conclusion that the God who created the universe and governs all of human history can have no competitors!

While the logic, for example, of Deutero-Isaiah's monotheistic argument depends upon the idea that creation is one and therefore the Creator must also be one, the logic of the argument here in Deuteronomy 4 is somewhat unique. Strictly speaking, the uniqueness of Israel's experience at Mt. Horeb/Sinai and the fact that YHWH had assembled Israel do not logically require a concept of monotheism. The passage also advances what may be termed a historical argument, however. The fact that YHWH delivered Israel from Egyptian bondage (v. 37) and expelled Israel's enemies from the land he gave it (v. 38) suggests that YHWH is the sole Lord of human history, that "beside him there is no other" (v. 39, *'ên 'ôd*; compare v. 35). YHWH alone presides over the fates of all nations, not just over Israel. YHWH is Lord over the Amorites displaced by Israel because of their sin just as YHWH is Lord over the Babylonians who take Israel captive because of its sin. Israel should, therefore, pause to consider the significance of its experiences of YHWH and acknowledge that YHWH is God both in heaven and over all the earth.

Coupled with this interest in asserting a strict monotheism, this passage (especially v. 36) seems designed to correct any possible misapprehension fostered by v. 12 that YHWH had been "present" in a spatially limited sense in the fire on Mt. Horeb/Sinai. In contrast to the statement that YHWH "spoke from the midst of the fire" (v. 12), v. 36 carefully distinguishes between the fire seen "upon the earth" and the voice of YHWH "from heaven" (its point of origin) heard *through* the fire. There should be no mistake that YHWH's presence was localized. YHWH is, after all, Lord of the universe.

The paranesis concludes with a restatement of its basic theme: obedience to the covenant. The reference to keeping "statutes and commandments (*miṣwôt*)," rather than "statutes and ordinances (*mišpāṭîm*)" is noteworthy, as is the use of the noun *'ădāmâ* "earth" (see also v. 10) instead of *'ereṣ* "land," which is more common in Deuteronomy 4. Seen in the context of the incremental progression of the argument in the paranesis, such minor stylistic variations heighten suspicions that it results from a long process of growth. In essence, if these suspicions are accurate, Deuteronomy can be seen as the record of a lengthy discussion among Israel's theologians concerning the significance of Israel's experiences on Mt. Horeb/Sinai with regard to what might be termed a doctrine of God.

Transition: Establishment of Cities of Refuge and Introduction to the Core of the Book, 4:41-49

Deuteronomy 4:41-49 divides neatly into two, loosely related sections. Verses 41-43 narrate Moses' establishment of three "Cities of Refuge" in the Transjordan. Verses 44-49 offer yet another introduction to the central section of Mosaic teaching concerning the application of the covenant Law. Only an interest in the Transjordan seems to link the two sections. The Cities of Refuge topic receives a much fuller treatment later in the book (Deut 19:1-13) and the introduction contains no information not already disclosed in Deuteronomy 1–3. This passage holds significant information, however, for understanding the literary structure of Deuteronomy and the editorial process that produced it.

Cities of Refuge, 4:41-43

The sudden shift from address to narrative calls attention to the interpolated nature of vv. 41-43. Not since Deuteronomy 1:1-5 has Moses been spoken of in the third person. Verses 41-43 view the Transjordan as lying to the east of the land, a perspective that betrays the post-conquest date of its composition. Finally, the theme of the Cities of Refuge has no connection to the paranesis of vv. 1-40, although the case could be made that it relates the material concerning the conquest of the Transjordan and the settlement of the Transjordanian tribes found in 2:1–3:22. If indeed it does constitute a conclusion to the Transjordan theme, it represents additional confirmation of the late composition of 4:1-40. The insertion of this lengthy paranesis on the significance of God's theophany at Mt. Horeb/Sinai separated vv. 41-43 from their original context immediately after 3:22.

No less than four texts in the Hebrew Bible address the establishment of Cities of Refuge (Num 35:9-15; Deut 4:41-43; 19:1-13; Josh 20:1-9). The literary relationship between these texts is both obvious and difficult to clarify. Numbers 35 records YHWH's instructions to Moses that he commission the people to establish three such cities on either side of the Jordan. Deuteronomy 4 records Moses' sanctification of three cities in the Transjordan. Deuteronomy 19 mentions only the three cities to be established in Canaan, presumably because it is aware that Moses has already established those in the Transjordan, and concentrates primarily on the legal definition of manslaughter and the procedures associated with adjudicating such cases. Joshua 20, however, attributes the founding of all six cities to Joshua (vv. 8-9).

The four texts share certain linguistic similarities in varying degrees. Both Deuteronomy texts refer to "setting apart" (*bdl*) cities, whereas Numbers and Joshua each employ unique verbs. All the texts describe the purpose of these cities as places to which "the manslayer (*rôṣêaḥ*)" may "flee (*sûr*)," although the Deuteronomy texts ("who slays his neighbor without knowing [*bibĕlî-da'at*, that is, without premeditation] and without hating him beforehand [that is, without motive]" define manslaughter, as opposed to murder, more precisely than does the Numbers text ("who smote life unintentionally [*makeh-nepeš bišgagâ*]"). Interestingly, the Joshua text conflates these two descriptions (v. 3). Deuteronomy

4:41-43 and Joshua 20:8-9 agree in specifying the names of these cities. (Bezer may well be the Bozrah [modern Umm el-`Amad] located six miles east of Hesbon; Ramoth in Gilead is well known [modern Tell Ramith]; Golan is the modern Sahem el-Jolan.) Only Deuteronomy 4 manifests no interest in the procedures to be employed with respect to the manslayer seeking refuge.

Because Deuteronomy 4:41-43 seems to presume knowledge of the procedural details and shares no characteristic language with the Numbers passage, it must be literarily dependent on Deuteronomy 19 and independent of Numbers. On the other hand, the conflation of definitions in Joshua 20 suggests that it depends on at least one of the Deuteronomy texts as well as the Numbers passage. It is difficult to say whether Deuteronomy 4 knows Joshua 20, or vice versa, although the absence of the conflate definition suggests strongly that Joshua 20 depends on Deuteronomy 4. In contrast, Knapp,[6] who considers Deuteronomy 19 the oldest text in the family, argues that both Deuteronomy 4 and Numbers 35, although independent of one another, depend on Joshua 20.

For a more thorough discussion of the role of Cities of Refuge in Israelite culture, and especially the significance of the distinction between murder and manslaughter in Deuteronomy's explication of the commandment against killing, see the commentary on Deuteronomy 19.

Introduction to the Explication of the Law, 4:44-49

Another abrupt transition calls attention to peculiarities arising from the placement of vv. 44-49. After the lengthy historical summary (1:6–3:22), culminating in what appears to be the dismissal of Moses and the commissioning of Joshua as his successor (3:23-29), and the series of interpolations in the form of the lengthy idol polemic paranesis (4:1-40), this introduction resumes the program announced in 1:1-5. Now, finally, begins Moses' explication of the Law.

Since M. Noth first proposed the idea,[7] Deuteronomy scholarship has explained circumstances such as the silence on the Law in Deuteronomy 1–3 and the abrupt introduction in 4:44-49 as evidence that Deuteronomy 1–3—which are historiographical narrative—were originally written not as the introduction to the book of Deuteronomy, but as the introduction to the "Deuteronomistic History," Joshua, Judges, 1–2 Samuel, and 1–2 Kings. Ending with the dismissal of Moses and the commissioning of Joshua, the account resumes in Joshua, the first book of the

Deuteronomistic History. This notion implies, then, that 4:44-49, or some form of it, once stood as the introduction to the book of Deuteronomy.

As yet Deuteronomy scholarship has been unable to determine whether Deuteronomy itself was incorporated into the Deuteronomistic History from the outset. The peculiar repetition of the basic elements of the historical account in Deuteronomy 1–3 in 4:46-49 suggests either that Deuteronomy 1–3 expanded the information supplied in the pre-existing introduction to the book of Deuteronomy when it was incorporated into the Deuteronomistic History or that vv. 46-47 were summarized on the basis of Deuteronomy 1–3 at a later date by an editor.

For the purposes of this commentary, the most interesting observations concerning this passage, however, involve the existence of parallel introductions (v. 44 // v. 45) within vv. 44-49. The first defines what follows as the "Torah" (singular) that Moses placed before Israel, while the second refers to "these . . . testimonies (ʿēdôt), statutes, and ordinances (plural)." Although the terms for "statutes and ordinances" are common in Deuteronomy, v. 45 offers the first of only three occurrences (4:45; 6:17, 20) of the term for "testimonies," a term regularly encountered in the context of covenant-making to describe the text, emblem, or monument left behind to attest that a covenant has been made. The dual introduction (vv. 44, 45) can be explained in two ways. Either an editor has expanded an original simple introduction, or the duplication points forward to some feature of the following statement of the Law. In fact, Deuteronomy 5, which contains a version of the Decalogue, has its own introduction describing its contents as the covenant. Another introduction in 6:1-2 identifies subsequent material as "commandments, statutes, and ordinances." Apparently, v. 44 refers to the Torah found in Deuteronomy 5 (the Decalogue), a singular and unique entity, while v. 45 introduces the *explication* of the Torah to follow in Deuteronomy 6.[8]

Notably, vv. 45-66 telescope events between the exodus and the entry into the land, omitting any reference to the wilderness wandering or the conquest of the Transjordan. According to the verses, Moses taught the words contained in the subsequent chapters of the book of Deuteronomy "when [Israel] came out of Egypt." Was the early book of Deuteronomy unaware of the wilderness wandering tradition?

CONNECTIONS

The Authority of Biblical Traditions

Two aspects of this paranesis offer exciting possibilities for the reengagement of the modern community of faith with the rich source of its tradition. First, the apparent late date and likely phased growth of Deuteronomy 4 raises questions *about*, and it can be argued, provides a model *for* a mature understanding of the nature of the Scriptures. Second, the text itself seems to be aware of—and to endorse the distinction between—the source of faith tradition and the faithful and competent extension of the tradition in new settings and through the progression of the generations.

Biblical scholars have long recognized that many books in the Hebrew Bible have undergone sometimes rather extensive growth processes. As argued above in the commentary, Deuteronomy grew to its present form over an extended period of time and under several hands. In some modern religious circles, such observations have caused great concern for the authority of the Scriptures because of assumptions that authority depends upon known

Scenes from the Life of Moses

In the foreground, Moses destroying the Tablets of the Law. On the right, the Golden Calf.

Cosimo Rosselli. 1439–1507. *Scenes from the Life of Moses.* Fresco. Sistine Chapel. Vatican Palace. Vatican State.

authorship. If Moses did not write the entire book of Deuteronomy with his own hand, in one more-or-less continuous act, the book cannot be trusted—or so the argument goes.

Alternatively, phenomena such as those observed in Deuteronomy 4 raise the question as to whether God could have inspired a scriptural tradition or a series of authors just as reliably and authoritatively. Does the authority of scripture depend upon the reader knowing the name of the author or upon the content, the reliability, and the functionality of the text itself? But the book of Deuteronomy, it may be objected, purports to stem from Moses! Is the book lying about itself if Moses did not write it? Surely a book that makes false claims as to its authorship cannot be considered reliable, trustworthy, or authoritative! Fortunately, Deuteronomy 4 supplies its own response to this and any similar objections through four assertions:

(1) The Extrapolation of Tradition. First, according to Deuteronomy 4, YHWH instructed Moses at Horeb/Sinai that, at some later date, Moses was further to elucidate the basic provisions of the covenant as contained in the Decalogue. In other words, while, at Horeb/Sinai, YHWH revealed the essence of the divine will for the covenant people, this revelation was not and could not be a comprehensive statement of all the implications and applications of the covenant necessary for Israel throughout all its generations. YHWH charged Moses, as the mediator between YHWH and Israel, to adapt the essential provisions of the covenant to the specific circumstances Israel would later encounter. [The Oral Law in Judaism and the Extrapolation of Tradition]

(2) Interpretation and Reason. Second, in that regard, it is interesting to note the role deductive reasoning plays in the development of the arguments here. YHWH revealed himself in manifestations of cosmic proportions, but in no localizable or corporeal form. The paranesis bases a lengthy and sophisticated argument solely on the implications of this phenomenon. In a real sense much of the Bible can be described as the product of the faith community working out the implications of its encounter with God. Jesus' disciples did not begin to understand the significance of his crucifixion and resurrection until they encountered the risen Lord after Easter. Faith is not an abstract, philosophical exercise. Faith is not based upon speculative reasoning from philosophical first principles. It grows out of the experience of encounter with God. [Heschel on Faith and Reason] Theology is a second order

---

The Oral Law in Judaism and the Extrapolation of Tradition

Rabbinic Judaism distinguishes between the Written Law, or the books of Moses, and an Oral Law tradition that God taught Moses and that was subsequently handed down from generation to generation. Tractate *Gittin* (60b) of the Babylonian Talmud contains the following discussion of the relationship between the Written and Oral Law. The disagreement among the rabbis reflected here involves the proper translation of a single word in Exod 34:27. Their reverence for the interpretive tradition subsumed in the Oral Law is obvious.

Said R. Eleazar, "As to the Torah, the larger part is in writing, and the smaller part is oral: 'Though I wrote for him the major portion of my law, they were counted a strange thing' (Hos 8:12)." And R. Yohanan said, "The larger part was oral, the smaller part in writing: 'For orally, these words . . .' (Exod 34:27)." *And as to the other party, isn't it written,* "Though I wrote for him the major portion of the law?" *That is an expression of astonishment, namely,* should I have written down for him the major portion of my law?! Even now, isn't it regarded by him as a strange thing?! *And as to the other party, isn't it written,* "For orally, these words . . ."? *That is because it is a formidable task to learn them.* R. Judah var Nahmani, the interpreter of R. Simeon b. Laqish, expounded, "One version of Scripture says, 'Write these words' (Exod 34:27). [Since the word 'in accord' can be translated, 'by the oral version . . .,'] it means to tell you matters that are to be memorized you have not got the right to state in writing, and those that are to be in writing you have not got the right to state from memory." (Neusner)

The great medieval Jewish commentator, Rashi, regarded Deut 4:14 as a reference to the Oral Law. Commenting on Exod 24:12 ("And I will give you the tablets of stone, and the law, and the commandment which I have written to teach them")—which seems to differentiate between the "law" (= the Decalogue?) and the "commandment"—Rashi observed that "All the six hundred and thirteen commandments are implicitly contained in the Ten Commandments and they may therefore be regarded as having been written on the tablets" (Rosenbaum et al.).

While the historicity of the tradition that the Oral Law had been handed down in oral form unchanged since Moses may be questioned, the rabbinic notion reflects the awareness that the tradition of interpretation can lay claim to Mosaic heritage. Rashi's comment is particularly suggestive and consonant with the interpretation of the Deut 4 paraenesis forwarded in the commentary.

J. Neusner, trans., *The Talmud of Babylonia: An American Translation*, vol. 18, B: Gittin, chs. 4–5 (Brown Judaic Studies 266; Atlanta: Scholars Press, 1992), 116-17.

M. Rosenbaum et al., trans., *Pentateuch with Targum Onkelos, Haphtaroth and Prayers for Sabbath and Rashi's Commentary, vol. 2: Exodus* (London: Shapiro, Vallentine & Co., 1930), 130.

---

undertaking. It is the effort to work out the significance of God's activity in the lives of individuals and communities. Encounters such as those Israel had with YHWH in the exodus and on Mt. Horeb/Sinai become the impetus for and the content of inspired reflection on the basic issues of faith. So long as the community, under God's continued care, returns ever and faithfully to its root experiences as source and criteria, the implications it unfolds can be trusted as genuine extensions of the original revelation.

(3) A Fixed Basis. Third, the text's careful distinction between "covenant (*bĕrît*)," identified specifically with the Ten Commandments, and the exposition of this fundamental covenant in the "statutes and ordinances" confirms the biblical authors' awareness of the relationship between root event and authentic extrapolation. J. Sanders has often observed that the genius of a canon of scriptures lies in its constancy as a *fixed* tradition that is, at the same time, *adaptable* to ever-changing circumstances.[9] This need to interpret "fixed tradition" in the changing circumstances is

Heschel on Faith and Reason

The sense of the ineffable introduces the soul to the divine aspect of the universe, to a reality higher than the universe. However, in stating that to be means to be thought of by God, that the universe is an object of divine thought, we have affirmed the existence of a being who is beyond the ineffable. How do we know that God is more than the holy dimension, more than an aspect or an attribute of being? How do we go from the allusiveness of the world—to a being to whom the world alludes?

In thinking on the level of the ineffable, we do not set out with a preconceived idea of a supreme being in our possession, trying to ascertain whether He [sic] is in reality the way He is in our minds. The awareness which opens our minds to the existence of a supreme being is an awareness of reality, an awareness of a divine presence. Long before we attain any knowledge about His *essence*, we possess an intuition of a divine *presence*.

This is wherein the approach through the ineffable differs from the approach through speculation. In the latter we proceed from an idea of His essence to a belief in His existence, while in the former we proceed from an intuition of His presence to an understanding of His essence.

Abraham Heschel, *Man is Not Alone: A Philosophy of Religion* (New York: Harper & Row, 1951), 67-68.

by no means a new phenomenon in the modern world. In fact, it can be seen taking place within Scripture itself. The book of Deuteronomy explicates the Horeb/Sinai covenant in relation to entry into the promised land, Israel's embarkation on a new, landed existence. The prophets can be understood as interpreters of the fundamental, defining tradition in new settings.

The Bible itself, then, is aware that it may not always be sufficient simply to appeal to founding traditions. What does it mean to honor father and mother? Few would disagree that this principle is basic to covenant existence, to life as God's people. But the demand is ambiguous in itself, so that biblical authors return ever again to this requirement to offer restatements of it in terms of prevailing social and economic conditions.

(4) Continuity across Generations. Fourth, this awareness of the need constantly to restate the tradition in and for new settings also accounts for the emphasis in Deuteronomy 4, indeed in the whole book of Deuteronomy (see Deut 6, for example), upon *teaching* the tradition to the next generation. Thus the Bible itself models the "actualization" of defining tradition, and in turn incorporates these actualizations into the expanding defining tradition recorded in Scripture. In addition, it invites subsequent generations of the community of faith to join in the line of those responsible for the tradition. Indeed, the Bible enjoins this active involvement in handing the tradition on to the future.

Abiding Principles

The distinction between the Torah, on the one hand, and the "commandments, statutes, and ordinances" that derive from it, on the other, is fundamental to the book of Deuteronomy (see commentary and connections on 4:1-40). Deuteronomy consistently maintains that the Deuteronomic Code (12–25) and its hortatory preamble (6–11) explicate (1:5) the Decalogue (5). This observation not only provides a clue as to the structure of the Code (see commentary on Deut 12), but also invites reflection on the relationship between the fundamental principles stated in the Decalogue and the new situation Israel faces when it enters Canaan. Or, to put the problem more directly, it invites reflection on the relationship between the fundamental precedents of faith and the unprecedented situations the community of faith faces in any era. Deuteronomy 4:44-49 would remind those who assume that the Bible in general, and Deuteronomy in particular, can have nothing to contribute to the solutions for issues facing the modern believer that every generation has found it both necessary and productive to return to the abiding principles as the starting point for reflection and guidance.

NOTES

[1] A. D. H. Mayes, "Deuteronomy 4 and the Literary Criticism of Deuteronomy," in *A Song of Power and the Power of Song: Essays on the Book of Deuteronomy*, ed. D. L. Christensen (Sources for Biblical and Theological Study 3; Winona Lake: Eisenbrauns, 1993), 204.

[2] The position championed by Mayes, "Deuteronomy 4," for example.

[3] As argued, for example, by D. Knapp, *Deuteronomium 4: Literarische Analyse und theologische Interpretation* (GTA 35; Gottingen: Vandenhoeck & Ruprecht, 1987).

[4] See E. H. Merrill, *Deuteronomy* (NAC 4; Nashville: Broadman & Holman, 1994), 160 and M. Weinfeld, *Deuteronomy and the Deuteronomic School* (Oxford: Clarendon, 1972), 1-11, 326; and, especially, S. D. McBride Jr., "Polity of the Covenant People: The Book of Deuteronomy," *Int* 41 (1987): 233-34.

[5] See M. Biddle, *A Redaction History of Jeremiah 2:1–4:2* (AThANT 77; Zurich: Theologischer Verlag Zurich, 1989), 178-85; J. Van Seters, *Abraham in History and Tradition* (New Haven: Yale University Press, 1975), 263-65; and idem, "Confessional Reformulation in the Exilic Period," *VT* 22 (1972): 455-56.

[6] *Deuteronomium 4.*

[7] *Überlieferungsgeschichtliche Studien*, Schriften der Königsberger Gelerhten Gesellschaft, Geisteswissenschaftliche Klasse 18/2 (Halle: M. Niemeyer, 1948), 91; see also Timo Veijola, "Principle Observations on the Basic Story in Deuteronomy 1–3," in *A Song of Power and the Power of Song*, 142-46. Veijola also notes the

remarkable circumstance that Deuteronomy 1–3 makes no reference to the Law after the reference in 1:5.

[8] See McBride, "Polity," 233-34 and S. Balentine, *The Torah's Vision of Worship* (OBT; Minneapolis: Fortress Press, 1999), 184-86.

[9] "Adaptable for Life: The Nature and Function of Canon," in *From Sacred Story to Sacred Text: Canon as Paradigm* (Philadelphia: Fortress Press, 1987), 9-39.

ISRAEL AT MT. HOREB: THE DECALOGUE

5:1-33

After the first, historical introduction to the book of Deuteronomy (Deut 1–3[4]), a second, didactic introduction sets the law code found in Deuteronomy 12–26 in context. This second introduction hearkens back to Mt. Horeb, as did the paranesis in Deuteronomy 4. Whereas the paranesis appealed to the theophany associated with the establishment of the covenant as the phenomenological basis of Israel's aniconic faith, Deuteronomy 5 focuses on the content and substance of the covenant established there: specifically, on the Decalogue.

COMMENTARY

Moses Summons the People to Learn the Covenant, 5:1-5

The language of 5:1-5 has become familiar by now to the reader of the book of Deuteronomy. Moses calls together "all Israel" and charges them to hear "the statutes and ordinances" he is about to rehearse to them. The people are to learn of the provisions of the covenant so that they may live according to YHWH's purposes.

The opening unit deals with three matters, however, that deserve close attention. First, narrative elements of vv. 1-5 find their continuation in vv. 22-33, which specify the details of Moses' mediation of the covenant more precisely. As in Deuteronomy 4, the question of whether Israel experienced any form of *direct* contact with YHWH at Mt. Horeb seems to have held some importance for the tradents of Deuteronomy. Deuteronomy 5:4 makes the straightforward claim that YHWH spoke "face to face" with Israel at Horeb. Verse 5 immediately precludes any possible misapprehension by explaining that Israel feared such direct contact with YHWH, preferring instead to send Moses as its representative. The continuation of the narrative supplies the missing middle step. It explains (vv. 25-31) that the

Moses Receiving the Law

As reflective of his propensity for fantasy in the dream-like recollections of his Jewish life experiences, Marc Chagall evokes the face-to-face experience of the people of Israel with YHWH. Floating, subliminal images of aspects of Jewish worship inundate the right side of the painting. Looming larger than life, Moses receives the tablets as the Israelites cower below the mountain to the left, perhaps out of sight of YHWH but within earshot. Moses, functioning as their representative, is bathed in light and transfixed in the receiving of the laws of YHWH. Rays of light issue from his head. The golden calf is slight and diminished in the far distance to the left.

Marc Chagall. 1887–1985. *Moses Receives the Talet of the Law.* 1960–1966. Oil on canvas. Musée Nationaux Message Biblique Marc Chagall. Nice, France.

people had indeed heard YHWH's voice. But they became afraid and then asked Moses to mediate for them with YHWH.

In fact, the rather unusual phrase "to speak (*dbr*) in your ears" in v. 1 (Deuteronomy usually employs verbs for "teaching" or "setting before" in relation to the "statutes and ordinances"; only 5:1 refers to "speaking" them) alludes to v. 31 where YHWH agrees to "speak" the commandments, statutes, and ordinances to Moses. Moses, in turn, can now "speak" what YHWH had "spoken" to him.[1]

Second, this introductory unit makes very explicit the transgenerational emphasis implied elsewhere in the somewhat more subtle instructions concerning teaching future generations and in the multivalency of the pronoun "you" (see commentary on Deut 4). Now (v. 3), Moses boldly claims, at face value in contradiction to the facts, that YHWH had entered into covenantal relationship, not with the generation of those actually present at Mt. Horeb, but with those now hearing Moses' voice. In fact, the unusual syntax of the final clause in v. 3 calls attention to Moses' outrageous claim (literally, "YHWH did not make this covenant with our father, but with us—those here today, all of us now living!").

Third, much like Deuteronomy 4, this passage maintains a clear distinction between the Decalogue, as the substance of the covenant, and the amplification of the Decalogue to follow. Once again, the concluding unit of Deuteronomy 5 elucidates the situation more clearly when it specifies that Moses is to teach the generation about to enter the promised land (v. 31).

The Decalogue, 5:6-21

Before turning attention to the individual commandments in the Decalogue, a few general observations concerning their nature, genre, and structure are in order. First, Christian readers in particular should note, as the preamble to the Decalogue points out (see below), that, although the requirements of obedience to the covenant as expressed in the Ten Commandments are central to Israel's identity as God's people, they hold neither chronological nor theological priority. YHWH gave Israel the Decalogue, and its extension in the Torah as a whole, only *after* YHWH had redeemed and delivered Israel from Egyptian bondage in fulfillment of an unconditional promise made to the patriarchs, Abraham, Isaac, and Jacob. This commentary will return to this fundamental observation repeatedly because it is essential as a corrective against Christian misunderstandings and caricatures of the Torah and of the Old Testament as a whole.

A second, related observation involves the importance of accurately understanding the function of these Ten Commandments as indicated by their genre. Typically, they are described as the core of the Old Testament Law. Closer examination of the Decalogue reveals, however, that this designation is woefully inadequate. Almost by definition, laws must set clear boundaries on human activities and include some enforcement mechanism. In an influential study, A. Alt[2] called attention to the presence of two distinct literary genres in the legal materials in the Pentateuch. Casuistic, or case law, more closely conforms to standard definitions and patterns of law. Such case laws normally define a circumstance or behavior and prescribe a punishment, penalty, or remedy. "If the ox gores a slave, male or female, the owner of the ox shall give to the slave's master thirty shekels of silver, and the ox shall be stoned" (Exod 21:32).

The Ten Commandments, Alt pointed out, have very little in common formally with the case law tradition. First of all, the syntax of these commandments does not utilize imperative verbs— a circumstance easily overlooked in translation—but makes statements of fact. Furthermore, as a general rule (exceptions include the commandment against idol worship and the Sabbath commandment), the Decalogue does not define its terms. Does the prohibition against killing mean to include all killing? Or does it refer specifically to murder? Neither does the Decalogue impose penalties. Alt termed this type of pure pronouncement "apodictic" law. In effect, such pronouncements are not laws at all, but statements of principle. E. Gerstenberger[3] has argued that apodictic law

Decalogue, Torah, and Interpretation

📖 Hananiah son of R. Joshua's brother said: "Just as in the sea there are ripples and wavelets between each major wave, so between each of the Ten Commandments there were Torah's unwritten minutiae, as well as all of Torah's letters." (*P. Shek* 6:1)

" 'And God spoke all these words, saying . . .' [Exod 20:1] R. Isaac said: 'At Mount Sinai the prophets of each and every generation received what they were to prophesy, for Moses told Israel, "But with him that standeth here with us this day before the Lord our God, and also with him that is not here with us this day [Deut 29:14]." He did not say, "That is not standing here with us this day," but, "That is not here with us this day," a way of referring to souls that are destined to be created. Because as yet these had no substance, Moses did not use the word "standing" for them. Still, even though they did not as yet exist, each one received his share of the Torah. Nor were the future prophets the only ones who received at Sinai the prophecy they were to utter. The sages who were to rise in each and every generation—each and every one of them also received at Sinai the wisdom he was to utter.'" (*Rab. Exod.* 28:6)

---

bears greater resemblance to the teaching of values in a family setting than to legal traditions in the strict sense. "Members of our family do not lie." B. Jackson[4] has argued further that the Israelite legal system itself did not operate by means of the application of specific codified laws, but depended on the learning and wisdom of judges as they applied the principles annunciated in the legal codes, case law, and oral traditions. [Decalogue, Torah, and Interpretation]

Third, given the fact that the Ten Commandments are not "laws" after all, it is noteworthy that the basic statements of principle are sometimes expanded by clauses offering theological (not legal) motivations and rationales. The Bible consistently attests to the tradition that, at Mt. Horeb/Sinai, YHWH gave Israel a special collection of ten "words" (hence the term "Decalogue" from the Latin for "ten words") written on two tables of stone (Exod 34:28; Deut 4:13; 10:4). The Bible does not, however, offer a uniform picture of the contents of those stone tables.

In addition to the version recorded here in Deuteronomy 5, Exodus 20:1-17 offers a slightly different version and Exodus 34:1-28 reproduces still another quite divergent list of twelve laws. The two Exodus versions purport to be the contents of the first pair of tablets that Moses broke in anger over the golden calf incident (Exod 20) and the contents of the second pair of replacement tablets written afterward (Exod 34). Deuteronomy 5, the closest parallel to Exodus 20, reflects no awareness of the broken tablets.

The most obvious phenomenon that becomes apparent through comparison of these three versions of the Decalogue concerns the significant variety in the lengths of the commandments. On the one hand, one series (Deut 5:7, 17-21 and parallels, for example) consists of a single very straightforward, apodictic, either positive or negative, statement: "You shall (not). . . ." Another series (Deut 5:8-16 and parallels, for example) begins with such a statement, but goes on to complement it with sometimes extensive definitions of terms and explanations of purposes. The so-called "ethical Decalogue" (Exod 20 /Deut 5) and the so-called "cultic Decalogue" (Exod 34) share three commandments: (1) the prohibition against worshiping gods other than YHWH, (2) the prohibition against images ("graven"—ethical Decalogue; "molten"—cultic Decalogue), and (3) the injunction to keep the Sabbath. Notably, the commandments concerning idols and the Sabbath in the cultic Decalogue manifest the simple form, whereas the same commandments in the ethical Decalogue include quite lengthy amplifications. Conversely, the commandment against worshiping gods other than YHWH—in the simple form in the ethical Decalogue—appears in the cultic Decalogue along with an explanatory phrase associated with the idol commandment in the ethical parallel.

Comparison of the Sabbath commandment in the two versions of the ethical Decalogue further underscores the distinction between the basic form of the commandment and its amplification and explication. [Sabbath Theologies] The Deuteronomy version differs from the Exodus version in three significant ways. (1) The motive clause associates the Sabbath with God's rest on the seventh day of creation (Exodus) or with the rest YHWH gave Israel from its bondage and servitude in Egypt (Deuteronomy). (2) The phrase, "as YHWH your God commanded you," found in Deuteronomy 5 reflects the literary character of this version of the Decalogue. In context, Deuteronomy 5:6-21 should be a direct quotation. (3) The Deuteronomy version amplifies the demarcation of those included in the Sabbath command, specifying "ox, ass, and any cattle," to make unmistakable the radical extent of the demand.

Clearly, then, an earlier form of the commandments did not include these motivational clauses and expansive definitions. Originally, the commandments were all cast in the brief "You shall (not) . . ." form.[5] In fact, intriguing support for the conclusion that such a concise, probably oral, tradition underlies the current literary forms of the Decalogue can be found in the several examples of the "prophetic Torah" in the Hebrew Bible (Jer 7:9; Hos 4:2, for example). These passages in the prophets cite the basic commandments, clearly reflecting the Mosaic covenant tradition, often in an order that corresponds roughly to the order in the ethical Decalogue, but entirely without the motivational and definitional amplifications found in the Pentateuch. The explications supplied

Sabbath Theologies

Judging from the frequency of references to it in the Hebrew Bible (111 times), the institution of the Sabbath was well established in ancient Israel. Its origins, however, lie in obscurity. The noun *šabbat* probably derives from the verb meaning "to rest." Scholars speculate as to whether the Israelite institution may be related to the Akkadian *šabattu/šapattu*, a Babylonian festival celebrating the full moon. While the lunar month divides into four seven-day weeks, no firm evidence has been adduced linking the Hebrew institution with the Babylonian, and the absence of lunar motifs in either the Sabbath legislation or descriptions of Sabbath observance suggests that the similarities between the terms may be either accidental or traceable to the distant past. Other scholars speculate that Moses may have borrowed the Sabbath from the Kenites among whom he sojourned. In this case, it would probably have originally been a day that held some special significance for Kenite metallurgical arts. Again, no firm evidence supports the theory.

Whatever its origins, the Bible insists that YHWH commands Sabbath observance. "Six days you shall labor" (in addition to the two versions of the Decalogue, Exod 20:7 and Deut 5:12, see Gen 2:1-3; Exod 23:12; 31:13-15; 34:21; Lev 23:3, 7; Jer 17:22). Most references to the Sabbath offer nothing by way of rationale for resting one day in seven other than the simple fact that YHWH commands it. A few texts, however, offer theological motivations. In general terms, these theological reflections fall into two categories, corresponding roughly to the "priestly" and "Deuteronomic" traditions in the Pentateuch. Gen 2:1-3, Exod 20:1, and, most clearly, Exod 31:17

ground Sabbath observance in God's seventh day of rest after the act of creation. In this understanding God hallowed and ordained a cycle of work and rest as a fundamental component of the created order. Exod 31:17 describes the Sabbath perhaps most suggestively as a "sign" (*'ot*) of creation, pointing, like the rainbow (Gen 9:13), circumcision (Gen 17:11), and the plagues against Egypt (Exod 7:3, etc.), to God's grace.

Deut 5:15 stands virtually alone (compare Deuteronomy's exposition of the Sabbath commandment in the Deuteronomic Code) in relating the Sabbath to YHWH's deliverance of Israel from Egyptian bondage. In keeping with the humanitarian impetus manifest in Deuteronomy, this motivational clause calls attention to the ethical and theological implications inherent in the Exodus. YHWH has intervened on behalf of these enslaved people to set them free and give them rest. The Sabbath represents an anniversary observance of deliverance from bondage. The Deuteronomic tradition extrapolates this insight even further. Not only did YHWH intervene on behalf of enslaved Israel, but YHWH also enjoined Israel to permit its servants and slaves periodic rest on a regular basis. Israel, freed from oppression, must not become the oppressor. Unfortunately, no biblical author (in either testament) realized the logical extension of the theological observation inherent in YHWH's intervention on behalf of oppressed Israel, namely, that God desires freedom for all people. It is little wonder that oppressed peoples throughout Christian history, from slaves in the American South to peasants in modern South America, have found solace in the Exodus story and have looked forward to Sabbath rest.

by the editors of the various Pentateuchal collections (Exod 20; 34; Deut 5) represent a first level of theological reflection on the significance of the commandments and, therefore, merit close attention.

Finally, it is important to note that the Decalogue is structured in two groupings focusing on two planes of reference. The first four commandments deal with Israel's relationship to YHWH; the remaining six with the relationship of individual Israelites to one another. The significance of this structure cannot be overemphasized. In this manner, the Decalogue establishes unmistakably the fundamental connection between *religion* and *ethics*. As Jesus put it, the Torah can be summarized in the two great commandments of love for God and for one's neighbor.

Preamble, 5:6

The Decalogue begins with a statement of the basis for YHWH's relationship with Israel, or, if the singular address forms are significant, perhaps better, with individual Israelites. Although the Decalogue does not explicate the theological import of the juxta-position of this statement of YHWH's gracious intervention with the demands of the covenant, the reader cannot overlook the sequence: YHWH delivered Israel from bondage in Egypt as an expression of free grace prior to and apart from the specifications of the covenant principles. YHWH's relationship to Israel was established through redemption, not by means of Israel's fulfillment of prior conditions. Having delivered Israel and thereby established relationship with it, however, YHWH now delineates the principles that will enable and enrich the relationship. The order, grace before works, proves fundamental to the biblical witness. The mystery of election consists in the fact that YHWH chose (Gen 12:1-3) and redeemed (Exod 1–15) Israel *before* the establishment of the covenant. The free gift of relationship is only confirmed by the relationship-structuring function of the covenant.

Principles for Relationship with YHWH, 5:7-15

The tradition of two tables may be related to an obvious structuring principle in the Decalogue. Regardless of the proper system of enumeration for the first four commandments (see below), they clearly differ from the latter six in terms of the sphere of life they concern. The first four deal primarily with the individual's relationship to YHWH, although the Sabbath commandment also relates to social conditions. The second grouping of six commandments, on the other hand, refers exclusively to interpersonal relations in which the deity has no direct involvement.

The *first commandment* (5:7) declares YHWH's fundamental and total claim to Israel's devotion. Since YHWH, and no other deity, delivered Israel from Egyptian bondage, YHWH demands Israel's total (and grateful) allegiance. Notably, in relation to the history of Israelite religion, the first commandment assumes the possible existence of other deities, and does not argue against polytheism on theoretical grounds. Instead, it concerns false priorities. In fact, the phrase usually translated "before me" employs a preposition (*'al*) that can be translated "on" or "upon," often in the sense of "above." The issue is not whether other deities exist (see commentary and sidebar on Deut 4:32-40), then, but whether Israel will respond faithfully and appreciatively to the God who delivered from foreign oppression. Israelites are to give YHWH priority. The command

Adoration of the Calf

Detail. *Adoration of the Golden Calf and Moses Destroys the Tables of Law.* Psalter of Ingeburg of Denmark. Ms. 9/1965, fol. 13. c.1210. Musée Condé. Chantilly, France.

should not be read as a metaphysical or ontological statement—as though it read "There are no other gods"—but as a description of relationship.

The *second commandment* (according to the Jewish tradition of enumeration; 5:8-10) enunciates a fundamental distinctive of biblical religion—a distaste for and distrust of iconographic representations of YHWH. This commandment divides clearly into sections. Three verbs prohibit the manufacture, worship, and service of idol images. The second and third verbs, "bow down" and "serve," may be understood as near-synonyms. A detailed definition supplements the first verb, while an explication or rationale introduced by *kî,* "because," provides the only glimpse offered in the Decalogue as to the theological significance of the commandment.

Israel is not to manufacture any *pesel,* "image (as a thing hewn or carved)," in any form. To indicate unmistakably that the prohibition is meant to be total, the definition specifies that absolutely no form is suitable. References to "the heavens above," "the earth beneath the heavens," and "the waters beneath the earth" encompass the entire three-tiered universe as understood in the ancient worldview.

No image whatsoever should be manufactured to serve as an object of worship. Why not? Nowhere does the Bible offer a cogent, coherent, concise explanation of the theological significance of this commandment. Deuteronomy 4, as has been shown, argues phenomenologically from the fact that YHWH did not appear in visible form at Mt. Horeb. In contrast, the second commandment in some way attributes the prohibition to the divine nature. YHWH, the commandment claims, is a jealous God (*ʾēl qannâ*), who punishes those who disobey, but who shows mercy to those who observe the covenant. The bulk of the formula does not, as might be expected, provide a rationale for the prohibition. Of what is YHWH jealous?

A traditional understanding of this prohibition points out, probably correctly, that human beings manufacture and worship idols as expressions of the notions: (1) that the deity can be localized, that is, that the deity can be reduced to the finite; and (2) that the deity can therefore be controlled to some degree through its image. Biblical religion denies that either of these characteristics applies to YHWH, the creator of the universe and redeemer of Israel. YHWH cannot and will not be localized (see 1 Kgs 8:27-30) or manipulated (see 1 Sam 4:19-7:1).

Not only is YHWH jealous of any attempt to portray his image, but, as the *third commandment* (5:11) indicates, YHWH is also jealous of the improper use of his name. Deuteronomy 5:11 speaks of taking it "emptily," "vainly," or "lightly" (*lašāwĕ*). In a related expression, Leviticus 19:12 speaks of not swearing by the name of YHWH "falsely" (*laššeqer*; see also Deut 6:13; 10:20; 1 Sam 20:42; Hos 4:2; Ps 24:4; Ezek 13:8). Both of these terms connote insincerity or even deceit. ["If It's Not in the Bible, It Should Be"]

What would constitute such an improper use of YHWH's name? As a first step toward answering this question, it may be helpful to

---

"If It's Not in the Bible, It Should Be": The Third Commandment and Profanity

Popular wisdom has a way of reading cultural values into sacred tradition. Astonishingly, many believers are more familiar with proverbial maxims such as, "Cleanliness is next to godliness," or "God helps those who help themselves," than they are with the beatitudes of Jesus. In fact, many assume that such statements are biblical. When challenged to find these proverbial expressions of key Western values in Scripture, it is not uncommon to hear believers respond, "If it's not in the Bible, it ought to be."

Society finds other ways to co-opt Scripture to endorse its values as well. Perhaps the most common such technique is to appropriate a text for purposes quite foreign to its original intention. Parents, for example, often appropriate the third commandment, "You shall not lightly use the name of YHWH your God," and transform it into a prohibition against profanity.

From the perspective of biblical interpretation, this use of the third commandment involves a confusion of categories. Profanity is a sociolinguistic phenomenon with culture and language specific dimensions. English language speakers have access to two sets of synonyms denoting bodily functions, for example. One set of monosyllabic, usually four-letter words ("piss," etc.) derives from Anglo-Saxon roots; another set of multisyllabic, Latinate, terms—usually ending in the suffix "-ate" (urinate, defecate, copulate, etc.), came into the language as a result of the infusion of a French stratum following the Norman

Conquest of England (AD 1066). Francophone Norman aristocrats considered the Anglo-Saxon of the peasantry to be common, vulgar. This deprecation of things Anglo-Saxon survives today in the social disapproval of "dirty" words. Although "urinate" and its Anglo-Saxon synonym *denote* the same bodily function, the monosyllable also carries with it a certain *connotation* that renders it unsuitable for use in polite company. While it is certainly a parent's duty to rear children sensitive to the requirements of polite society, the third commandment hardly relates to historical vestiges of the Norman Conquest! In fact, to the extent that the Hebrew preserved in the Hebrew Bible reflects the full range of the language spoken in the biblical period, there are no signs that ancient Hebrew culture knew a similar situation. The prophets were certainly willing to use strong language to communicate a strong message (see Amos 4:1-2; Isa 26:18), and, in the New Testament, Paul expressed his contempt for his self-righteousness prior to his Damascus road encounter in the strongest terms (*skubala*, "dung, crap," Phil 3:8).

Even more troubling than the unsuitability of employing Scripture to endorse a particular culture's rules of etiquette, such interpretations of the third commandment overlook the much more fundamental problem of insensitivity to the sacredness of God's name and reputation. Every day, Christians who would never use profanity bandy about God's name as though it were a mere interjection, attribute to God their own desires and wishes, and brand the slightest personal whim a divine directive.

ask whether the Hebrew Bible gives examples of the proper use of the divine name. Taking an oath in which YHWH was invoked by name (as guarantor) is perhaps the most obvious example of "taking the name." In fact, Jeremiah 4:2 (see also Jer 5:1; 13:25-27) enjoins Israel to swear by YHWH, but to do so "in truth, in justice, and in righteousness." In such cases, the oath taker involves the deity in the transaction, indicating thereby the oath taker's honesty and reliability. A false or insincere oath would constitute taking the name of YHWH "lightly" because it would involve the deity in deception.[6] As B. Childs points out, however, oath taking did not constitute the only practice that could be done in the name of the deity. The Hebrew Bible employs a wide range of verbs in relation to the name.[7] Most notably, prophets prophesy in the name (Jer 11:21), and, not surprisingly, the issue of false (*šeqer*) prophecy—deceptively claiming divine authority for one's preaching—plays a major role in the books of Micah (3:5-8, 11) and Jeremiah (4:9-10; 5:30-31; 6:13-15 [=8:10-12]; 14:13-16; etc.), in particular. Any insincere, inauthentic, or deceitful use of the divine name to lend validity and authority to an act or statement falls under the prohibition of the third commandment. YHWH will not permit his name and reputation to be sullied in such a manner.

The *fourth commandment* concerning the Sabbath day consists of three sections. The commandment proper (5:12), already expanded from the hypothetical original short form by the addition of the motivational clause "just as YHWH your God has commanded," has attracted a series of refinements and explanatory comments. The first motivational clause, which inconsistently refers to YHWH in the third person and which does not appear in the Exodus version of the Decalogue, represents the commentary of the editor(s) of the book of Deuteronomy. A definition of what is meant by "keeping" the day—namely, abstention from all work so that the Sabbath may be devoted entirely "to YHWH your God" (v. 14)—further expands the basic statement of the commandment. Significantly, the commandment does not describe any specific act of worship or devotion to be associated with the Sabbath. In fact, to the extent that ancient Israel observed the Torah's limitations on corporate worship, especially sacrifice, as an act to be conducted at the central sanctuary (Deut 12; see also 1 Sam 1:3), one can expect that there may have been no pattern of Sabbath worship other than the abstention from work itself.

This refined definition also demarcates those in Israel subject to the prohibition against labor on the seventh day: The commandment prohibits family members, servants, livestock, and even the

Deuteronomy's Sabbath Commandment and Slavery:
A Case Study in Cultural Inertia

Although in the exodus YHWH revealed himself as the one who hears the pleas of the oppressed, and Jesus demonstrated his concern for society's outcasts, the Christian church, from Paul (see his letter to Philemon) to the church in the southern United States in recent decades, has perceived no conflict between faith in the one God, creator and redeemer of all, and the enslavement and oppression of other human beings. God's mercy and grace inevitably become at least somewhat obscured when God's people accommodate them to their own biases and to modern culture embodied in social institutions. The history of slavery, and, especially, the history of the church's appeal to scriptural warrant for the institution, should serve as a powerful reminder of the danger of failing to search the tradition for the purest revelation of God's character and will for humanity.

The Sabbath commandment in Deut 5 assumes the institution of slavery. Ironically, however, it recalls Israel's period of slavery and interprets the Sabbath in relation to YHWH's desire for rest for his people. Sadly, Israel failed to recognize the irony of a nation of freed slaves continuing to enslave others. Later, the church failed, too, to perceive the cruel disparity between bonds of slavery and freedom in Christ (Gal 3:27-28). Because Israel failed to recognize the implications of the fact that God freed them from slavery, the Decalogue must explicitly state that the Sabbath means rest for slaves as well.

---

resident alien from work on the Sabbath. This definition of the applicability of the Sabbath commandment has been supplemented by yet another motivational clause, which once again does not appear in the Exodus version. Servants of both genders and sojourners are to observe the Sabbath, because they deserve rest as much as (or more than) the Israelites themselves. Finally, yet another explanatory clause unique to the Deuteronomy version of the commandment offers a theological, or perhaps better, a humanitarian, rationale for requiring servants to observe the Sabbath. Israel, too, was once enslaved at hard labor under cruel conditions, not permitted rest, and tormented by extraordinary demands (Exod 1). By delivering Israel from Egyptian bondage, YHWH showed himself to be on the side of the outcast, the disenfranchised, and the oppressed. [Deuteronomy's Sabbath Commandment and Slavery]

Especially when compared to the Exodus version of the Sabbath commandment, the humanitarian interest of Deuteronomy's version demands attention. The theme of YHWH's partisanship on behalf of the downtrodden, in particular widows, orphans, and sojourners, plays a significant role in Deuteronomy, as will be seen below (see commentary on Deut 10:18-19; 14:29; 16:9-15; 24:17-22; 26:12, 13; 27:19), and throughout the Hebrew Bible (Exod 22:22; 1 Kgs 17; Isa 9:17; Jer 7:16; 22:3; Ezek 22:7; Zech 7:10; Mal 3:5; Job 22:9; 24:3, 21; Pss 68:5; 94:6; Prov 15:25; etc.). In Deuteronomy, the Sabbath commandment highlights the inherent contradiction between the institution of slavery and the theological implications of YHWH's deliverance of Israel from Egyptian bondage. This contradiction offers a prime example of the way the best and truest elements of the basic tradition can subvert and criticize cultural practices and beliefs.

Principles for Social Relationships, 5:16-21

Although the Sabbath commandment, in the Deuteronomy version at least, already focuses in many ways on social relationships, the fifth commandment clearly marks a shift to the interpersonal dimensions of YHWH's covenant expectations of Israel. Again, the Decalogue does not explicitly state the theological rationale for the inclusion of these basics of proper interpersonal relationship. One can only observe that, as already suggested by the Sabbath commandment, YHWH's interest in human beings extends to individuals, even foreigners. Authentic membership in the covenant community requires not only commitment to YHWH, but also a respect for other members of the community that acknowledges that they, too, are God's children. The final six commandments indicate the basic principles of this proper respect for other human beings.

The *fifth commandment* (v. 16) enjoins respect for one's parents. The addition of the phrases "just as YHWH your God commanded you" (compare v. 12 and comments there) and "so that it may go well for you" (a common phrase in Deuteronomy—4:26, 40; 5:33; 6:2; 11:9; 17:20; 22:7; 25:15; 30:18; 32:47) suggests that this commandment, which concerns the loyalty of one generation to the next, a major theme of the book, has attracted the particular attention of the editor of the book.

The phraseology and logic of this commandment deserve special attention. Members of the covenant community are asked to "honor (*kbd*)" their parents. The idea implied by this verb involves regarding someone or something as "weighty" or "significant." There can be no question that the commandment is addressed to adult members of the community, nor that it calls for Israelites to treat their elderly parents with proper respect (that is, the commandment does not call for small children to obey their parents).

The internal logic that unites the motivational clause with the basic commandment is particularly suggestive. Honor for elderly parents will ensure that the children live long, and that this long life will be prosperous. The idea seems to be that by caring for the *previous* generation, the *current* generation provides a model or establishes a cultural value that will help to assure that the *subsequent* generation will, in turn, care for the next generation of elderly, incidentally one's own generation. Children learn that parents care for grandparents. Notably, the question of what it might mean specifically to honor one's parents is not addressed. Again, the "principle" character of the Decalogue is apparent.

The placement of the Decalogue in the book of Exodus at the head of a collection of laws known to scholars as the "Covenant Code" (Exod 20–23) indicates that the precise definition of several of the commandments in the second series (concerning persons) required explication already in Israel's earliest period. Scholars have long recognized that the collection of *mišpāṭîm* (see the discussion of Deut 4:1) found in Exodus 21–23 serves in part to explicate the specific applicability of these commandments in a given cultural circumstance. Murder (Exod 21:12), maltreatment of parents (Exod 21:15), theft (Exod 21:15), and denunciation of parents (Exod 21:17) find such explications.[8]

Problems associated with the precise definition of a term are even more conspicuous with respect to the *sixth commandment*. It seems straightforward enough, lacking any definitional or motivational clauses: at first reading, it clearly and unmistakably declares that human life is not to be taken (see also Exod 21:12; Lev 19:17-19; 24:17; Deut 27:24). But, given that other passages in the Torah, some in the book of Deuteronomy itself, prescribe capital punishment and ruthless rules of engagement in times of war, and that the Hebrew Bible as a whole seems to expect that individuals may resort to even the most violent measures in self-defense or in war, the question of the precise intention of this commandment must be addressed. Should the verb *rṣḥ* be translated "murder," for example, so that the commandment would prohibit, not all killing, but only killing intentionally and with evil purpose?

Occurrences of the verb (46 times) suggest that, at least in an early period of its usage, it did not refer to killing in the limited sense of murder (Deut 4:42; 19:3, 4, 6; Num 35:6, 11, 12, 25, 26, 27, 28; Josh 20:3, 5, 6; 21:13, 21, 22, 26, 27), but to killing that called for blood vengeance (Num 35:27, 30).[9] If the verb were understood here in this older sense, the commandment would prohibit vigilante justice. It only later came to refer to killing with malice and forethought, that is, to murder (Deut 22:26; Num 35:16, 17, 18, 19, 21, 30, 31; etc.).

Remarkably, this brief, apparently straightforward commandment presents the modern interpreter with a wonderful example of the problems associated with interpreting old texts, and especially old texts that intend to enunciate fundamental, governing, ethical principles. Is the meaning of the commandment to be restricted to the old meaning of the verb (which must have surely been the original intention)? Does the commandment prohibit vigilantism? Or, is the text to be set among a body of biblical texts dealing with the issue of violence against persons (especially Gen 6:9, for example) and understood as testimony to the absolute sanctity of human life?

Modern interpreters even face a degree of cross-cultural ambiguity when dealing with the *seventh commandment*: "You will not commit adultery." The concept of adultery depends necessarily upon a given society's definition of the institution of marriage. Ancient Israel's patriarchal society permitted polygamy, concubinage, the purchase of slave girls expressly for purposes of cohabitation (Exod 21:7-11), and, in a very early period, even a form of "patrilocal" marriage in which the husband did not live with his wife who was still considered a member of her father's household. Hebrew even reserves a special term, *pîlegeš*, for the wife in such a marriage (see Judg 8:31; 19:1, 24; 20:4; compare Ezek 23:20). Considerable gender inequity characterized Israelite sexual norms. Israelite males enjoyed considerable freedom. Israelite females, on the other hand, were bound to either their fathers, or later, to their husbands or sons, and their sexuality was considered the property of the significant male in their lives. Virginity, for example, was assigned real economic value (Exod 22:16-17; Deut 22:28-29). Fathers received from the groom a "bride price" for a virgin daughter, and they were to be fully compensated in the event that a daughter lost her virginity to a man unwilling to marry her. In turn, grooms required proof of virginity on the wedding night to authenticate their investments (Deut 22:13-19). Males were subject to no such constraints.

Israelite husbands did not owe their wives fidelity. An Israelite male could not, by definition, be unfaithful to his wife—or wives. He could commit "adultery" only by having intercourse with another man's wife, in which case his crime was not against his own marriage, but against his paramour's husband.

This command, understood in its historical sense, obviously does not apply directly to modern Western culture. Like attitudes toward slavery, the institution of marriage and associated sexual norms have undergone considerable evolution in the Judeo-Christian world since this commandment first pertained. Consequently, the definition of "adultery," too, has changed—for the better. Obviously, then, the argument for monogamy must be made on grounds not limited to the sixth commandment of the

Decalogue. Still, regardless of how one defines marriage and adultery, the commandment clearly places the sanctity of the fundamental basis of human family life, marriage, in the context of YHWH's covenant with his people. Fidelity in marriage is a matter of loyalty to the God of the covenant as well.

Yet another example of a concept that has undergone development, in this instance during the biblical period rather than afterward, presents itself in the *eighth commandment* (v. 19). Exod 21:16 explicates this commandment in the Covenant Code. Employing the same verb, *gānab* "to steal," as the commandment, this "judgment" (*mišpāṭ*) deals with the theft of human beings, or kidnapping for purposes of selling into slavery. Furthermore, as A. Phillips has noted, "although *gānab* . . . carries no object [in the Decalogue], this must refer to the person of a fellow Israelite, for as the context makes clear, the objectless commandments on murder and adultery, like that on theft, are all to be understood as committed against one's neighbour [sic] as specified in the commandment on false witness."[10]

Understood in this way, then, the prohibition against theft fundamental to YHWH's covenant with Israel does not concern property, but the worth of persons. Israelite property law is generally classified and treated under civil categories.[11] Only *relationships* with YHWH himself and with other human beings merit treatment in the Decalogue. Torts and liabilities do not.

Similarly, the *ninth commandment* (v. 20) does not offer a global condemnation of dishonesty. A somewhat wooden translation would highlight the commandment's background in legal proceedings: "You will not answer concerning your neighbor (with) unreliable (*šawẽ*, see the commentary on the third commandment) testimony." Lying in the course of everyday life may not be commendable, but lying in the docket can do serious injury to an innocent. Of course, such testimony could also be intentionally offered as an attack against one's enemy. But even to offer testimony of which one is only unsure, or to overstate or understate, may endanger the very life of an innocent fellow Israelite.

Commandments five through nine then clearly deal with serious injury done another human being. The *tenth commandment* (v. 21) seemingly departs from this principle, in two obvious ways. First, it prohibits an attitude while all the others in the second series have dealt strictly with concrete actions. Second, it seems to include for the first time a concern for (potential) violations of property rights; that is, it seeks also to protect ownership of livestock.

Coveting the House

📖 A. Phillips argues that the final commandment originally existed in a short form in which only the "house" served as the object of the verb. In his view, "coveting the house" would have been an idiomatic expression describing aspirations to usurp the status of the head of a household. In early patriarchal Israel, the paternal household functioned as the focal point of the social structure. Envy of the householder's power and prestige would have threatened the very order of Israelite society and could not have been tolerated. Phillips, who argues that the Decalogue should be understood as an early criminal code, sees the final commandment as having originally been a condemnation of rebellion against established order, not as a prohibition against an attitude. The final commandment, then—in its original form—would not have been at all inconsistent with commandments five through nine.

A. Phillips, "The Decalogue: Ancient Israel's Criminal Law," in *A Song of Power and the Power of Song: Essays on the Book of Deuteronomy,* ed. D. L. Christensen (Sources for Biblical and Theological Study 3; Winona Lake: Eisenbrauns, 1993), 243-45.

The second of these apparent divergences can be easily dismissed since the taking of any of the persons or property listed in the commandment can be readily perceived as an attack on the person from whom they were taken. The first difficulty, however, cannot be so quickly dismissed. [Coveting the House] One popular line of argument maintains that the verb *ḥmd*, "to covet," implies a degree of desire that results in action. Evidence from the use of the verb elsewhere in the Hebrew Bible (Deut 7:25; Josh 7:21; Mic 2:2) and from the cognate languages, however, suggests that in order to have this meaning *ḥmd* must be accompanied by an additional verb denoting action. The argument is moot for Deuteronomy 5:21 in any case because, unlike the parallel in Exodus, it employs a near synonym (*ʾawâ,* "to desire, want") which refers exclusively to an attitude or state. Thus, this final commandment stands alone in the Decalogue in its interest in the interior life of the Israelite. Desire, the will to act, precedes action (see Jas 1:14-15) in virtually every case, if only by fractions of a moment in some. The danger presented by illicit desire, while difficult to observe, is as threatening as the act that proceeds from it.

The People's Reaction to the Theophany, 5:22-27

This account of the people's reaction to the awesome sights and sounds accompanying YHWH's revelation on Mt. Horeb/Sinai goes into much greater detail than its parallel in Exodus 20:18-21. The distinctives in the Deuteronomy account serve to highlight four points important to the argument of the book of Deuteronomy.

First, 5:22-23 emphasize the notion that the words of the Decalogue cited immediately above (vv. 6-21) are the very words YHWH spoke to the entire congregation of those assembled at Mt. Horeb/Sinai. The congregation itself heard the thunder and the voice (or sound; *qôl* can be translated as either) from the midst of the fire (v. 22)/darkness (v. 23). These very words YHWH himself inscribed on two stone tablets and entrusted into Moses' care (v. 23). There can be no doubt, then, as to the authenticity or authority of this Decalogue.

Second, the experience frightened the people such that upon Moses' descent from the mountain they petitioned him at once for permission to withdraw from YHWH's immediate presence. Unlike the Exodus parallel, which indicates that the people withdrew instinctively even before Moses' descent, the Deuteronomy account insists that the people were present to hear YHWH's voice. Proximity to the holy God, however, proved uncomfortable for them. They feared for their very lives (vv. 24-26). Having survived one such encounter, they did not wish to risk further contact with the Holy. Instead, they requested Moses to mediate their dialogue with YHWH (v. 28).

Third, since YHWH agreed to the request, Moses' status, an important theme in Deuteronomy, received dual confirmation and validation. He was chosen by both YHWH and the people to learn the stipulations and conditions of the covenant and then to report them to the people (v. 27). The people trust Moses to be an accurate and thorough messenger, and promise to hear and do all that Moses tells them.

Fourth, the central theme of obedience links the summary of concluding events at Mt. Horeb/Sinai and Moses' concluding exhortation to the audience a generation later. In response to the people's request to be permitted to withdraw because of their fear, YHWH expressed the wish that they may always be so respectful and motivated to obey the "commandments, ordinances, and statutes" that Moses will teach them (v. 29). A generation later, Moses prepared to proclaim to those standing before him those very "commandments, ordinances, and statutes" that he received from YHWH.

CONNECTIONS

The commentary has shown that the Decalogue, while key to ancient Israel's understanding of the will of God for the people of God, functions primarily as a statement of basic principles of relationship. As the relationship between the Decalogue and the so-called "Covenant Code" (Exod 20–23) and later revisions of the "statutes and ordinances" recorded particularly in Deuteronomy indicates, ancient Israel recognized from a very early period that, if the commandments were to be more than platitudes or truisms, they required further definition bearing on the actual circumstances of contemporary life. The commandments must be applied to specific situations. Furthermore, ancient Israel thought it appropriate to incorporate these definitions and extrapolations of the concepts inherent in the Decalogue into the Scriptures alongside the Decalogue. In fact, as the seedling of the "oral law" tradition found especially in Deuteronomy 4 and 5 suggests, scriptural tradition encourages and expects future generations of Israel to continue this renewal of the significance of the Decalogue.

Several implications of this phenomenon speak to circumstances prevailing in many modern communities of faith. The failure to engage the roots of biblical faith as the wellspring of a living tradition lurks as a great danger to the health and vitality of the people of God. [Anyone Can Learn Torah]

First, modern Christians tend too often to regard the "legal" portions of the Hebrew Bible as dull, dry, and deadening remnants of the "old" covenant. Luther's facile juxtaposition of "grace" and "works" lives on in the church, much to its detriment. In their context in Scripture, the Ten Commandments do not function as legalistic means for obtaining salvation but as the tools for shaping life as God's people. The call to life in the kingdom lacks substance unless that life has distinctive, qualitative character. The Decalogue, along with its amplifications, defines the parameters of such a life as the people of God.

Second, the church must overcome its fear of interpretation, of grappling with the ancient text for purposes of hearing its message for a modern world. Typically, modern Christians assume one of three stances toward texts such as the Decalogue, all three of which involve critically erroneous assumptions and misunderstandings. Some view the ancient text through (quasi) primitivist lenses. These readers of the Bible hear the Protestant slogan *sola scriptura,* "by scripture alone," as a call to conform simplistically to the scriptural norm. Yet few believers today would wish to define "adultery" as did the ancient Israelites. Likewise, since very few even know the proper name of Israel's God (YHWH), they run little risk whatsoever of using the name in vain. This approach, while admirable for its apparent devotion to the authority of Scripture, naively assumes the continuity of culture between ancient Israel and the modern

Anyone Can Learn Torah

Elijah, ever mentioned on good occasions, said: "Once, as I was walking on the road, a man who met me mocked and reviled me. I asked him, 'My son, since you have refused to learn Torah, what will you say on the Day of Judgment?' He replied, 'I have an answer: Understanding, knowledge, and spirit were not given me from Heaven [so how could I study Torah]?' I said, 'My son, what is your work?' He replied, 'I am a trapper of fowls and fish.' I asked, 'Who gave you knowledge and spirit to take flax, spin it into cords, weave the cords into nets, use the nets to trap fish and fowls, and sell them?' He replied, 'Understanding and knowledge [to do my work] were given me from Heaven.' I said, 'To take flax, spin it into cords, weave cords into nets, and use the nets to trap fish and fowls, understanding and knowledge were given to you from Heaven. But do you suppose that, for words of Torah, about which it is written, "The word is very nigh unto thee [Deut 30:14]," understanding and knowledge were not given to you?' "
(*Yal.*, 960)

West. Texts that unmistakably call for behaviors few moderns can endorse or replicate are most often simply overlooked.

Others approach texts such as the Decalogue in a mistaken effort to harmonize the two cultures. For example, key terms in the Decalogue such as "adultery," "killing," "Sabbath," and "taking the name in vain" are understood immediately and without reflection according to the definitions of the dominant modern culture. Such an approach cannot hear the message of Scripture over the din of its own presuppositions. Seen in this way, the Bible, including the Decalogue, merely endorses existing values and practices. ["A Sabbath Scene"]

Perhaps the most common approach to texts such as the Decalogue involves the notion that they are only of *historical* significance for the community of faith. In this view, the Decalogue

---

"A Sabbath Scene"

The abolitionist John Greenleaf Whittier used the jarring contradiction between Sabbath rest and culturally accepted slavery as the central image in his moving poem "A Sabbath Scene," excerpted below. It recounts a pastor's response to an escaped slave seeking refuge in his church. How many core insights into God's character continue to be misunderstood by a church bound by cultural detritus?

Like a scared fawn before the hounds,
Right up the aisle she glided,
While close behind her, whip in hand,
A lank-haired hunter strided.

She raised a keen and bitter cry,
To Heaven and Earth appealing;
Were manhood's generous pulses dead?
Had woman's heart no feeling?
. . .
"Who dares profane this house and day?"
Cried out the angry pastor.
"Why bless your soul, the wench's a slave,
And I'm her lord and master!

"I've law and gospel on my side,
And who shall dare refuse me?"
Down came the parson, bowing low,
"My good sir, pray excuse me!"

"Of course I know your right divine
To own and work and whip her;
Quick, deacon, throw that Polyglott
Before the wench, and trip her!"

"Although," said he, "on Sabbath day
All secular occupations
Are deadly sins, we must fulfill
Our Moral obligations:

"And this commends itself as one
To every conscience tender;
As Paul sent back Onesimus,
My Christian friends, we send her!"
. . .
My brain took fire: "Is this," I cried,
"The end of prayer and preaching?
Then down with pulpit, down with priest,
And give us Nature's teaching!

"Foul shame and scorn be on ye all
Who turn the good to evil,
And steal the Bible from the Lord,
To give it to the Devil!

"Than garbled text or parchment law
I own a statute higher;
And God is true, though every book
And every man's [sic] a liar!"
. . .
Thus saith the Lord: Break every yoke,
Undo the heavy burden!

John Greenleaf Whittier, *Anti-slavery Poems: Songs of Labor and Reform* (New York: Houghton, Mifflin, and Co., 1888), 160-63.

Marcion

Marcion, the wealthy son of a bishop from Sinope, a port city on the southern coast of the Black Sea, came to Rome in AD 138 or 139 and soon attracted a large following for his controversial views. He was excommunicated in or around 144 and subsequently formed his own church. He was a dualist, that is, he considered the material world to be evil. Since Israel's God, the God of the Old Testament, created the world including humanity, this God, whom he called the *Demiurge*, and humanity must also be fundamentally evil. Marcion called attention to what he perceived to be the Demiurge's cruelty, vengefulness, capriciousness, and legalism. The Father of Jesus Christ, according to Marcion, is a second God, a God of love, unknown until revealed in Christ. Since Jesus was not the creation of the Demiurge, he was not fully human. Instead, he only seemed (Greek *dokeō*) to have a body, a view known as "docetism." Taking pity on suffering humanity, the God of Love sent Christ to deliver humanity from the dominion and rule of the Demiurge whose followers crucified the Redeemer. Their resistance only served the Redeemer's purposes. Christ's death was the price paid to purchase humanity from the Demiurge.

Marcion's views led him to reject the authority of Hebrew Scriptures outright along with much of what would later become the New Testament. Marcion recognized only edited versions of the letters of Paul—of whose pointed distinction between law and grace Marcion approved—the Gospel of Luke, and Marcion's own *Antitheses*.

---

constitutes the foundational text of the Old Covenant, the Old Testament. It represents the morality of an ancient culture, for many Christians, a culture that did not know Christ. Inadvertently, this position closely resembles the early Christian heresy, perhaps the earliest, associated with Marcion who rejected the Hebrew Bible entirely as pre-Christian and who denied that the God of the Old Testament is the Father of Jesus Christ. [Marcion] From a theological and hermeneutical perspective, this position ignores the fact that, for the early church, including Jesus and Paul, the Hebrew Bible was the only Bible available. It ignores Jesus' teaching that he did not come to invalidate the Law but to perfect it (Matt 5:17-20). It misreads Paul's evaluation of the Torah. It overlooks the New Testament's insistence that God has always dealt consistently with God's people (Heb 1:1). It too easily results in a variety of Christianity that is long on piety but short on moral substance: "Faith without works is dead" (Jas 2:17).

In the place of these erroneous approaches to the Hebrew Bible generally and to the Decalogue specifically, the church must be willing to come to terms with the problem of the relevance of the ancient text for a new and different cultural context. Awareness of its significance in its original setting, sensitivity to its core message, and perceptivity with regard to the shortcomings and need manifest in modern culture must be combined in an effort to hear the Word of God in the Decalogue. To pretend that modern is ancient, to redefine the ancient as modern, or to dismiss the ancient as irrelevant is to deny the text as the source of a living tradition.

Finally, the Decalogue as set in the context of Deuteronomy 5 offers resources for improving Jewish-Christian relations. Judaism has maintained an unbroken line of interpretive tradition reaching back to the Mosaic covenant, whereas Christianity has too often seen its own identity *in contrast to* the covenant—despite the fact that Jesus and Paul, for example, claimed the covenant as part of Christianity's heritage. Christianity can learn from Judaism the benefits of a tradition of interpretation rooted in and sanctioned by Scripture itself. Christianity can incorporate Judaism's awareness of YHWH's claim on the behavior of the people of God to great advantage. The elder sibling (Judaism) and the younger (Christianity) can and should agree that faithful worship of the one God is fundamental to identity as God's people, that the one God cannot be confused with a mere representation, that honoring one's parents expresses God's will, that human life is sacred . . . How has it come to be that these two communities of faith, both claiming to be heirs of ancient Israel's faith, have allowed the covenant with Israel established through Moses to become a point of division?

NOTES

[1] See I. Wilson, *Out of the Midst of the Fire: Divine Presence in Deuteronomy* (SBLDS 151; Atlanta: Scholars Press, 1995), 103.

[2] "The Origins of Israelite Law," in *Essays on Old Testament History and Religion* (Garden City: Doubleday, 1968), 101-71. Compare H. W. Gilmer, *The If-You Form in Israelite Law* (SBLDS 15; Missoula MT: Scholars Press, 1975), 11-20.

[3] "Covenant and Commandment," *JBL* 84 (1965): 38-51.

[4] "Legalism and Spirituality: Historical, Philosophical, and Semiotic Notes on Legislators, Adjudicators, and Subjects," in *Religion and Law: Biblical-Judaic and Islamic Perspectives*, ed. E. Firmage et al. (Winona Lake IN: Eisenbrauns, 1990), 244-61.

[5] For discussions of the pre-literary history of the Decalogue see J. J. Stamm and M. E. Andrew, *The Ten Commandments in Recent Research* (SBT 2/2; Napierville IL: Allenson, 1967) and B. Lang, "Neues über den Dekalog," *TQ* 164 (1984): 58-65.

[6] For an in-depth study of the oath in the Hebrew Bible, see F. Horst, "Der Eid im Alten Testament," *Evangelische Theologie* 17 (1957): 366-84; on the false oath, see A. Klopfenstein, *Die Lüge nach dem Alten Testament: Ihr Begriff, ihre Bedeutung, und ihre Beurteilung* (Zürich: Gotthelf-Verlag, 1964), 32-34.

[7] B. S. Childs, *The Book of Exodus: A Critical, Theological Commentary* (OTL; Philadelphia: Westminster, 1974), 410.

[8] See A. Phillips, "The Decalogue: Ancient Israel's Criminal Law," in *A Song of Power and the Power of Song: Essays on the Book of Deuteronomy*, D. L. Christensen, ed. (Sources for Biblical and Theological Study 3; Winona Lake: Eisenbrauns, 1993), 241-42 (= *JJS* 34 [1983], 17-18).

[9] See B. S. Childs, *Exodus*, 419-21.

[10] "Decalogue," 241-42.

[11] "Decalogue," 242.

THE SHEMA: THE CENTRALITY OF THE FIRST COMMANDMENT

6:1-25

Following the historical preamble (Deut 1–3) and the dual treatments of the giving of the Decalogue (Deut 4 and 5), Deuteronomy 6–11 constitute a third introduction to the law code contained in chapters 12–26. That is, this introduction is the third from the perspective of a reader encountering the final form of the book. From the perspective of the history of the redaction and composition of the book of Deuteronomy, the core of Deuteronomy 6–11, together perhaps with chapter 5, constituted the original introduction to the older law code of chapters 12–26. While the law code contains material dealing with a full range of situations and circumstances pertinent to YHWH's covenant with Israel, the editor(s) of Deuteronomy responsible for this introduction considered the Decalogue the essence of the covenant (see Deut 4 and 5) and the first commandment the quintessential statement of Israel's proper relationship to YHWH. As a result, Deuteronomy 6–11 focus on this commandment, formulating a theology that was to exert influence over much of the Hebrew Bible, namely that Israel's fortunes and its faithfulness to YHWH were inextricably linked. This theology was to become the basis for the so-called "Deuteronomistic paradigm" (Judg 2:6–3:6), the thesis statement of the books of Joshua through 2 Kings (except Ruth). Several of the prophetic books, most notably Hosea and Jeremiah, also manifest affinities with this "YHWH-only" theology of history.

COMMENTARY

Introduction to the Explication
of the First Commandment, 6:1-3

For the fourth time in the book (1:4-6; 4:1; 5:1), an introduction describes what is to follow as the laws Moses was commanded to teach Israel before it entered the promised land. Notably, here as elsewhere, YHWH has commanded Moses not merely to publish these laws, but to "teach" Israel "to do them." Again, as elsewhere, each generation is to teach the next. YHWH did not intend the covenant to be treated as esoteric doctrine, but to become the basis of living life. To that end, 6:2-3 enunciate four reasons for or intended results of learning to do the covenant. First, the covenant itself will inspire reverence for YHWH. Second, this reverence for YHWH and the covenant will result in prolonged life. Third, in general terms, "keeping" and "doing" the stipulations of the covenant will benefit (literally, "be good to you") the individual. Fourth, specifically, Israel will become much more numerous just as YHWH had promised the patriarchs (Gen 12:2; 15:5, etc.). The proverbial reference to the bounty of the land of Canaan ("flowing with milk and honey") completes the picture of the blessings of covenant-keeping.

The "Shema," 6:4-9

Somewhat abruptly, the introductory exhortation to learn and observe the stipulations of the covenant gives way to the formulaic statement that has become the central confession of faith in Judaism. Named for its first word, the "Shema" continues to figure prominently in both public worship and private devotional practice, as it did already before the time of Christ. [Scribal Improvements] [The Shema in Judaism] It may be regarded as a positive restatement[1] and radicalization of the first commandment, "You shall have no other gods before me."

Theoretically, one could render YHWH only nominal devotion and still fulfill the call to revere him above all other deities. The Shema, however, lays claim to total devotion and obedience. The ambiguous syntax of the first clause of the Shema (6:4) permits two possible

Scribal Improvements

In an effort to remedy the harsh transition between vv. 3 and 4, the translators of the LXX inserted an additional introductory clause ("and these are the statutes and ordinances that the Lord commanded the sons of Israel in the desert as they were leaving Egypt") at the beginning of v. 4 modeled after v. 1. The Hebrew text is almost surely the more original on the basis of two text-critical criteria known as *lectiodifficilior* (namely, that the more "difficult" text has a higher probability of originality since scribes often resorted to "improving" the text but rarely to rendering it less smooth) and *lectio brevior* (namely, that the shorter text is more likely the original for similar reasons).

The Shema in Judaism

The role played by the Shema in medieval and modern Judaism dates to a very early period. The Nash Papyri (2d century BC) include a manuscript of the Shema together with the Decalogue. It probably served as a liturgical text. By the 2d century AD the basic text of the Shema (Deut 6:4-9) had been supplemented with Deut 11:13-21, which supplies blessings for obedience and curses for disobedience to the covenant, and Num 15:37-41, which refers to the tassels on the corners of prayer shawls worn by observant Jews. This fuller form of the Shema continues as the confession made twice daily by observant Jews during morning and evening prayers.

---

translations and interpretations: (1) "Hear, O Israel! YHWH our God is one!" a translation that underscores the unity of the deity, or (2) "Hear, O Israel! YHWH only is our God!" a translation that emphasizes the exclusivity of YHWH's claim to Israel's devotion. If the Shema intends the former, it may represent a reaction against the tendency, known especially among Israel's Canaanite neighbors, to associate deities having the same or similar names with specific locales (for example, the "Baal of Peor," Num 25:3, 5; Deut 4:3), as though the deities were somehow interchangeable. In this understanding, the Shema rejects any hint of "poly-Yahwism." YHWH is one, indivisible. The other interpretation bears closer affinities with the first commandment in terms of its disinterest in ontological matters, whether YHWH is essentially one deity. Instead, the question of relationship carries greater weight. YHWH is Israel's *only* God. No other deserves Israel's worship. Of course, the Shema's ambiguity may have been intentional so as to imply both understandings simultaneously.

The second clause (6:5) extends and radicalizes YHWH's claim to Israel's devotion even more explicitly than does the first commandment of the Decalogue (which it interprets). Not only does YHWH demand to be *first*, but he also expects Israel's *total* commitment and dedication. The Shema offers yet another example of the difficulties inherent in dealing with ancient texts at this point. It calls for the Israelite to "love" YHWH with "heart," "soul," and "strength." Three of these four expressions suggest concepts to the modern reader that would have been alien to the original readers of this text. As D. J. McCarthy and others have shown in their work on Ancient Near Eastern treaty texts,[2] "love (*ʾhb*)" regularly designated the obedience and loyalty owed one's overlord. In such cases, it involved none of the sentimentality and emotion often understood by moderns. Instead, it referred to concrete acts in the public realm. Similarly, the ancient Israelite understood the "heart," the organ often associated in modern culture with romantic love, not as the seat of emotion, but of volition, of decision-making. "For as

The Concept of the "Soul" in Hebrew Thought

AΩ The typical modern reader of the Shema will understand the term "soul (*nepeš*)" to mean that interior, intangible, invisible essence of the person that exists to a degree independently of the body. Such a viewpoint owes much more to ancient Greek philosophy, however, than it does to the Hebrew Bible. In the Greek view, human beings consist of three independent parts: the body (*sarx*), which is inferior, corruptible, and perishable; the soul (*psychē*), something like the essence of the personality, pure and immortal; and the spirit (*pneuma*), something like the animal force.

Because of the deep and widespread influence of Greek philosophy on early Christianity, and because of the historical accident that early Christians, including the authors of the New Testament, spoke and wrote Greek, the terms used by philosophers such as Socrates and Plato found their way into use in the early church, often as translations of terms in the Hebrew Bible such as *nepeš*. A survey of the use of *nepeš* in the Hebrew Bible, however, reveals first that it has a very wide range of meaning, and second that it does not represent the Greek notion of the immortal, ineffable "soul" at all. Instead, the ancient Hebrew understood the nature of human existence in a much more concrete and holistic fashion.

The Hebrew noun *nepeš* has cognates in virtually all Semitic languages in the meanings "throat," "appetite," "breath," and "self." All these senses appear in the Hebrew Bible. The common underlying notion seems to involve the throat (Num 21:5; 1 Sam 2:33; Pss 69:2; 107:9; Prov 3:22; 6:30; Eccl 6:7; Isa 58:11; Jer 4:10; Jonah 2:6; etc.) as the part of the body that experiences hunger (real or metaphorical; Exod 15:9; 16:22; Deut 23:25) and through which one breathes (1 Kgs 17:21-22); hunger and breath represent life itself. This close association with life and vitality results in the coupling of the *nepeš* with the blood (Lev 17:14; cf. Gen 9:4). Rather than depicting an abstract feature of human existence distinct from bodily existence the Hebrew term *nepeš* describes aspects of that bodily existence.

The Hebrew understanding of human nature emphasizes a holistic viewpoint. God breathes into Adam the breath of life and Adam becomes a living being, a *nepeš ḥayyâ* (Gen 2:7), just as God commanded the sea and the earth to bring forth living beings (Gen 1:20, 24). Humans do not *have* souls, in the Hebrew understanding, any more than sea and land animals do. Instead, human beings *are* "nefeshes." The emphasis lies upon the whole of bodily life. In fact, the Hebrew apparently could not conceive of life outside a body ("nefeshes" die: see Lev 19:28; 21:1; 22:4; Num 5:2; 6:11; etc.). Incidentally, this understanding of human nature underlies the fundamental distinction between the Greek notion of the immortality of the soul and the Judeo-Christian concept of resurrection.

The Shema calls for concrete, specific, real-world obedience to God with one's whole *nepeš*, one's whole self. It does not call for an abstract devotion with one's interior, ineffable, intangible "soul."

one thinks in one's heart, so is one" (Prov 27:19; compare Gen 6:5; 8:21; Exod 4:21; 25:2; Ps 10:6, 11; etc.).[3] Still further, contrary to the common understanding of the term often translated here "soul (*nepeš*)," which may perhaps be better translated "life" in this instance,[4] the Shema does not call for interior, private, or "spiritual" devotion. Instead, one is to love YHWH with *all* one's very life. The final phrase only underscores this unsentimental, radical claim to total obedience and devotion. [The Concept of the "Soul" in Hebrew Thought] The Shema calls upon the individual Israelite to exert total effort in relation to YHWH. In this vein, the Talmudic sages and later rabbinic authorities interpreted the phrase *ûbĕkol-mĕʿōdeka* "and with all your strength" as a reference to wealth (*Ber* 51a; 61b; 9:5; *Sifre Deuteronomy*, and Nachmonides on 6:5). This interpretation may underlie Jesus' admonition to the rich young ruler that it remained only for him to submit his riches to the claims of God (Mark 10:21).

In effect, then, the Shema states YHWH's claim to exclusive, indeed perhaps even unique, status. Since YHWH is the only deity of Israel's worship, or the only deity at all, devotion to him must also be absolute and total. Obedience to YHWH is a radical decision of the will ("all one's heart") involving one's whole life ("all one's soul") to be carried out without reservation or limitation ("all one's might").

To underscore further the paramount significance of the ideas expressed in the Shema, the text continues with instructions concerning the Israelites' obligation to focus continual attention on the Shema and its demands (6:6-9). The words of the Shema, which Moses commanded "upon" Israel's "heart" (that is, made a component of their decision-making process), are also to be taught (*šnn*, literally, "inscribed") "on" (the hearts of) their children (compare Jer 31:31-34; see commentary on Deut 30:6). They are to be the topic of conver-

The Kolbuszow Rebbe

As an act of public humiliation, the Nazi occupiers of Kolbuszowa, Poland, compelled Rabbi Yechiel Teitelbaum to pose in his prayer shawl (tallit) and phylacteries. Thereafter Rabbi Teitelbaum was deported to the Rzeszow ghetto where he and two granddaughters were murdered.

Norman Salsitz. *Kolbuszowa Rebbe, Yechiel Teitelbaum.* 1942. Kolbuszowa, Poland. United States Holocaust Memorial Museum, Washington DC.

sation at home and away from home, in the evening and in the morning. English speakers might expect the order "morning and evening," but the ancient Hebrew day began at sunset (as the Jewish ritual day still does). The Mishnaic and Talmudic sages devoted a great deal of discussion to whether this expression requires the worshiper to repeat the Shema in bed in the evenings and standing in the mornings (*Ber* 1:3; *B. Ber* 11a; *Tos. Ber* 1:4; *Sifre Deuteronomy*). The consensus opinion of the sages, rabbis, and modern interpreters favors the understanding of this phrase as a general reference to times of day intended as a merism ("night and day," connotating the whole by its parts) to mean "continually." As a further reminder, the words of the Shema are to be worn on hands (*těfillin*) and forehead (*phylactery*), and written on the doorposts of private dwellings and the gates of cities (*mězuzah*).

Phylacteries and Mezuzoth

Orthodox Judaism understands literally the command to bind the words of the Shema on one's head and hands, doorposts and gates. Since before the time of Christ (the oldest extant reference to phylacteries occurs in the Letter of Aristeas, v. 159; mid-2d century BC), observant Jews have twice daily donned "phylacteries" (ironically, from the Greek for "protector," "guard," in the sense of "amulet"), small leather boxes containing manuscripts with the words of the Shema plus three related texts (Exod 13:1-10, 11-16; Deut 11:13-21), each in one of four separate sections. These boxes are constructed with precisely twelve stitches representing the tribes of Israel. The Hebrew letter "*šin*" (it resembles a "W") is inscribed twice on the outside of the box, once with a fourth prong representing the four texts inside the phylactery. Orthodox young men from the age of 13

onward (*Shebu.* 111:8, 11) begin morning and evening prayers by binding these leather boxes first on their left hands and then their foreheads by means of long leather straps tied in knots resembling, along with the *šin* on the phylactery, the letters of the Hebrew divine name "Shaddai." On the assumption that Deut 6:4-9 intends that both the recital of the Shema and the donning of phylacteries be a twice daily matter, after prayers, the phylacteries are removed in reverse order.

The Hebrew term *mĕzuzah* originally referred to the doorposts themselves. At one time, Israelites may have written the Shema directly on their doorways. For centuries, however, the practice of affixing to doorposts small containers—also inscribed with the first letter of the Shema, "*šin*," with the text of the Shema inside—has been common. These containers are also called *mĕzuzah*.

[Phylacteries and Mezuzoth] For observant Jews, recitation of the Shema and the physical reminders of it called for in this passage of Deuteronomy continue to be requirements of everyday piety.

The Blessings of Obedience and Curses of Disobedience, 6:10-19

As is characteristic of Deuteronomy's logic, the argument moves on now to consider the benefits of obedience to the requirements stated in the Shema, in effect obedience to the first commandment, as well as the dangers inherent in disobedience. Deuteronomy 6:10-19 display an interesting structure. Statements of YHWH's intention to fulfill his promise to the patriarchs ("the land which YHWH swore to your fathers," vv. 10, 18; compare v. 19, "just as YHWH said") by displacing the inhabitants of the land before the entering Israelites (vv. 10b-11, 19) form parentheses around the central admonition to observe the stipulations of the covenant (vv. 12-18a). The injunction to "keep" (*šmr*, vv. 12, 17) the covenant calls attention to the boundaries of this interior section.

This dichotomy between blessing and curse numbers among the often-noted similarities between Deuteronomy and ancient Near Eastern treaties. In fact, 6:10-11 represent an interesting inversion of a specific type of curse often found in these treaties, and not infrequently in the Hebrew Bible, the so-called "futility curse" (see below on Deut 28). Such curses threaten the accursed with unexpected, ironic reversals of fortune. Should one violate treaty loyalty, one will find others in possession of vineyards one has planted, tended, but not yet harvested. Here this curse (against the Canaanite inhabitants of the land) has been transformed into a blessing for Israel. After crossing the Jordan, Israel will take possession of cities, houses, and cisterns that it did not build. Rather than starting afresh, Israel will find vineyards and olive orchards waiting to be harvested. The Canaanites' loss will be Israel's unearned gain.

The Deuteronomic author never wanders far from the basic theme of obedience to YHWH alone. Unearned prosperity, blessing, can become a snare for Israel, enticing it to forget its history (6:12; compare 4:25). An exhortation and warning (6:12-14) culminates in a threatened curse against Israel (6:15). Israel enjoys bounty because YHWH delivered it from bondage in Egypt (compare the preamble to the Decalogue in 5:6). Consequently, YHWH alone deserves Israel's worship and service (6:13). Oaths should be sworn in YHWH's name (6:13). The Hebrew Bible does not prohibit oath-taking altogether (Jer 4:1-2). Instead, it insists that oaths be sincere and free from idolatrous association.[5] Similarly, Israel is not to "walk after other gods"[6] worshiped by Israel's neighbors. Deuteronomy 6 offers Israel a clear choice: Worship and serve only YHWH, who delivered from Egyptian bondage, or face the consequences of his jealous wrath (6:15). In another apparent allusion to the Decalogue (Deut 5:9; see also 4:24), the threat concluding this section reminds Israel that YHWH is "a jealous God" who is quick to anger. Should they provoke YHWH sufficiently, he will eradicate them from the land. In the face of such a threat, who would fail to choose the blessings of obedience? Yet, as the historical example adduced in v. 16 illustrates, Israel has always demonstrated a tendency to make the wrong choice. Only a few days after YHWH had delivered them from Egypt, parting the sea to allow their passage, the Israelites "tried (*nsh*)" YHWH at Massah (Exod 17:1-7), complaining that they lacked water to drink. Their vexing question, "Is YHWH among us or not?" (Exod 17:7), exemplifies the temporary quality of human faithfulness.

Significantly, in addition to a version of the familiar charge to keep the "commandments (*miṣwôt*) of YHWH, your God, and the testimonies (*ʿēdōt*) and the ordinances (*ḥuqqîm*)" (v. 17), Moses adds the admonition to "do right (*yāšār*) and good (*ṭôb*) in the eyes of YHWH" (v. 18). These terms transcend the technical jargon of the Law to incorporate the standards of decency and goodness along with the claims of the covenant. Implicitly, this admonition acknowledges that the written Law simply cannot anticipate every situation—every ethical issue, every moral decision, or every

Thou Shalt Write Them Upon the Posts

religious choice—that the Israelite will likely face in the course of life. The absence of specific instruction in the Torah, however, does not exempt one from YHWH's more fundamental standards of "right and good."

The Responsibility to Teach Later Generations, 6:20-25

The centrality of the Deuteronomic theme of intergenerational responsibility has already been noted (see the commentary on Deut 4). Deuteronomy 6:20-25 belong to a body of texts found primarily in Deuteronomic/ Deuteronomistic literature (see Exod 12:26-27; 13:14-16; Deut 29:24-28; Josh 4:6-7, 21-24; 1 Kgs 9:8-9; Jer 5:19; 16:10-13). Such didactic questions attest to the Deuteronomic impulse to learn from history.

The text envisions a moment in the future when a son will ask his father the significance (literally "what are the testimonies, etc.," v. 20) of the covenant and its stipulations. In the prescribed response, the father is to address, not the content of the Torah, but its *basis*, deliverance from bondage in Egypt (vv. 21-23), and its *purpose* (vv. 24-25), "so that it may go well for us . . . and be righteousness for us." Significantly, the response consistently employs first person plural pronouns describing the ancient story of Israel's redemption from Egypt and the establishment of the covenant as events in which the later generation participated directly (see comments on 5:1-5). [Doers, Not Hearers Only]

CONNECTIONS

Given the key thematic role of the Shema in Deuteronomy (compare 10:12; 11:1, 13; 13:3; 30:6), its centrality in Jewish piety and worship, and the weight given it by Jesus (Mark 12:30 and parallels; compare Luke 10:27; 11:42), one could expect that Christians would take more seriously its fundamental assertions. Western Christians are unlikely to adopt Jewish practice and make recital of the Shema at regular intervals during the day part of their daily discipline, or to don phylacteries and tefillin, or to affix mezuzoth to their doorposts and gates. Nevertheless, full, rich lives of faith require foundations, points of contact with the basis for living. As such a fundamental assertion of the basics of Israel's faith, and of Jesus' faith, the Shema calls believers to re-center their lives in relationship to the one God of Israel, the father of Jesus Christ. In particular, the Shema makes three declarations that speak directly to modern life.

> **Doers, Not Hearers Only**
>
> He who says that he is interested only in the study of Torah has no reward even for the study of Torah. And the proof? The verse, said R. Papa, "That ye may learn them . . . to do them [Deut 5:1]." He who is engaged in "doing" the commandments is regarded as engaged in learning them; but he who is not engaged in "doing" them is not regarded as engaged in learning them. (*b. Yebam.* 109b)

First, it asserts the essential unity of the Creator of all reality and suggests the essential unity of the creation. The assertion that YHWH alone is God reminds those who confess the Shema that dualistic or polytheistic notions—such as the modern fascination in some conservative Christian circles with "spiritual warfare," or New Age speculations concerning the spirit world, or the practical bifurcation of individual lives into distinct realms of religious, professional, and civic allegiance—are fundamentally foreign to biblical faith. Reality, the created order, expresses the will of one Creator. The assertion that YHWH is one, that there is no division in YHWH's essence or character, reminds those who confess the Shema that God can be trusted to remain constant to God's purposes.

Second, the Shema calls for an unsentimental obedience to the claims of the one Lord on believer's lives. In a culture—including the church—that reduces many values questions to matters of mere emotion or feeling, the Shema's clarion call to covenant loyalty with the Creator and Redeemer God—its call to acts of the will, to decision, to choice—reverberates. [Jesus and the Shema] Such a God will not be satisfied to be merely the object of warm feelings. YHWH expressed "love" for Israel in and through concrete acts of redemption and provision. YHWH liberated Israel from real bondage and led them to a specific land where they might live real lives as God's people.

Third, the Shema has much to say concerning the character of the life devoted to God. Modern Western culture compartmentalizes most areas of life such that, too often, for example, the integral relationship between one's emotional life and one's physical well-being goes unappreciated. Thankfully, the medical profession increasingly recognizes the dangers of this false separation. In matters of faith, however, a similar compartmentalization continues to influence the way believers view their faith and live their lives.

Jesus and the Shema

The Synoptic Gospels (Matt 22:34-40; Mark 12:28-34; and Luke 10:25-28) all record a significant encounter between Jesus and a "lawyer," a student of the Torah, that centered on the Shema. Already by Jesus' day, the Pharisees, who were largely responsible for giving impetus to later rabbinic tradition, had well-defined notions of the oral law and had probably identified the 613 distinct requirements of the written law. Their devotion to God took the form of study of the Torah, contemplation of its significance and issues of its interpretation, and determined efforts to fulfill all the Law's requirements. The lawyer's question to Jesus concerning which of the laws held supreme status reflects well the types of scholarly debates that were common in Jesus' day and later.

The lawyer may have expected the radical young rabbi, Jesus, reputed to be a creative interpreter of tradition (see Mark 2:23-27, etc.), to give an unconventional response. Instead, Jesus called attention to the Shema, by that time already the key confession of a Jew's faith, to which Jesus added a reference to Lev 19:18 (love for neighbor). In so doing, Jesus demonstrated his understanding of the Decalogue. Biblical faith, he maintained, may be subsumed under these two rubrics: total love for and obedience to God (the first table of the Law) and unconditional love for one's fellow human being (the second table).

Significantly, perhaps, in light of the Shema's insistence on commitment to YHWH involving the will and action, the Greek texts of the Synoptic Gospels all expand the list, "heart, soul, and might," with a reference to the mind. It should also be noted that in Luke's version of the encounter, Jesus encourages the young man who seeks the key to eternal life to answer his own question. When the young man responds with the commandments to love God and neighbor, Jesus congratulates him on having found the key. The Shema, then, is as central to the New Testament as it is to the Old.

For many, faith is a matter of the emotions and feelings, but not of daily actions. For others, belief in God is an intellectual matter primarily requiring assent to correct doctrine. For most moderns, religion belongs in a distinct and quite separate sphere of life. Believers equate piety with (normally passive) church attendance.

The Shema, however, insists in a number of ways that devotion to the one YHWH, Israel's sole Redeemer, cannot be a compartmentalized matter. Three times the Shema calls for devotion to YHWH with "all" one's self. The call for obedience lays claim to all one's decisions, to one's whole life (that is, the decisions are to be carried out), and to one's determination (that is, the effort to act in a manner consistent with one's identity as a member of God's people must be total).

NOTES

[1] D. Olson, *Deuteronomy and the Death of Moses: A Theological Reading* (OBT; Minneapolis: Fortress, 1994), 50.

[2] *Treaty and Covenant: A Study in Form in the Ancient Oriental Documents and in the Old Testament* (AnBib 21A, rev. ed.; Rome: Biblical Institute, 1978).

[3] See H. W. Wolff, *Anthropology of the Old Testament* (London: SCM Press, 1974), 40-58.

[4] See Wolff, 10-25; W. Eichrodt, *Theology of the Old Testament* II (trans. J. A. Baker, OTL; Philadelphia: Westminster Press, 1967), 134-42.

[5] See the discussion of the false oath in the commentary on Deut 5:11 and 20.

[6] This phrase is very characteristic of the book of Deuteronomy and of the body of Deuteronomistic literature influenced by it. For treatments of the diction of Deuteronomic/Deuteronomistic literature, see M. Weinfeld, *Deuteronomy and the Deuteronomic School* (Oxford: Clarendon, 1972).

ISRAEL'S NEIGHBORS-TO-BE: THE DANGER POSED BY FOREIGN CULTURES

7:1-26

While Israel is paused in Moab just before entering the promised land under Joshua's leadership, Moses has reminded the people of the basic principles of YHWH's covenant with them and commented on the extreme significance of the first commandment (Deut 5). Now he turns to dangers and temptations lying ahead. Foremost among these threats to Israel's covenant loyalty, Moses warns, will be the problem of living among the non-Yahwistic peoples already inhabiting the promised land. Despite the Hebrew Bible's sometimes idealized view of Israel's political and military might, evidence both within Scripture and without suggests that the people of Israel always found the circumstances of their existence influenced by relations with neighboring peoples living around and among them. The preservation of Israel's religious and cultural identity required conscious effort. For the first readers of the book of Deuteronomy in the late seventh and early sixth centuries BC (see Introduction), these warnings concerning the threat of foreign pollution would have brought to mind the "culture war" conducted at the highest levels of Judean society during the reigns of kings Manasseh and Josiah (2 Kgs 21–23). Babylonian influence enticed Judah to apostasy and resulted ultimately in Babylonian domination. For exilic readers, the problem of living among the nations while resisting pressures to assimilate would have only acquired new urgency: the violent eradication of foreign elements was no longer an option.

COMMENTARY

No Accommodation, 7:1-5

When the Israelites enter the promised land, they will find it already occupied by well-established populations. In fact, these Canaanites—Deuteronomy 7:1 distinguishes quite carefully between seven tribes (a traditional list; see Gen 15:20; Exod 3:8, 17; 13:5)—will easily outnumber Israel. As the book of Joshua and historical and archeological evidence indicate, Canaanite society was well advanced in terms of superstructures and institutions over the society of the wandering former slaves poised to enter the land. Canaanites lived in many cases in fortified cities ruled by kings and defended by armies. By any standard measure, they were truly "greater and stronger" than Israel (v. 1).

Nevertheless, YHWH will deliver them to Israel for the most extreme destruction (v. 2). The Hebrew noun *ḥerem* and its verbal cognates refer to the institution of the ban, or, as it is sometimes called, "holy war" (for a more complete discussion of this institution, see the commentary on 3:1-7 and, especially, 20:1-18). Israel was to eradicate completely these nations from the promised land—a harsh measure indeed. [Love and Force] Furthermore, Moses forbade Israel to enter into treaty relationships with the Canaanites (v. 2) or to intermarry with them (v. 3; but see also 21:10-14). Moses predicted that future interaction with the Canaanites would result in apostasy (v. 5; compare 2 Kgs 17:7-23), inciting YHWH's anger. To ward against the dangers of interaction with the Canaanites, their culture, and especially their religion, Israel was to destroy all of the Canaanites' religious objects, specifically their

---

Love and Force

The violence called for in Deut 7 contrasts sharply with the assertion that God is love. Walter Rauschenbusch, the leading proponent of the "social gospel" in the first half of the 20th century, offered the following observations concerning the incompatibility of Christ's call to love one's fellow human being and the use of force and coercion to impose one's will. Ironically, Rauschenbusch published this work on the eve of the First World War.

The frequency with which our communities have to fall back on physical coercion is a symptom of the failure of love, for love can usually dispense with force. The more love, the less force; the more force, the less love. Despotic government had to use plentiful force to keep its unnatural structure erect. The spread of democracy has brought a great softening of the horrors of criminal law and it will yet bring us a great lessening of militarism. Every proposed increase in police force and military organization is a challenge and accusation against those institutions of society which ought to create social solidarity. If ever our country draws toward its ruin, it will bristle with efficient arsenals and hired fighters. The constant use of military violence in labor disputes in our country proves that industry is still in the despotic stage. It needs democratizing and Christianizing. (32-33)

Walter Rauschenbusch, *Dare We Be Christians?* (Cleveland OH: Pilgrim Press, 1993 [= 1914]).

stone altars, their wooden pillars (*'ăšērîm*, associated with the goddess Asherah, probably phallic fertility symbols; see [Gods of Wood and Stone]), and their idols.

The logic of this passage betrays its ex post facto ideological passion. If Israel were to have executed the *ḥerem*—totally annihilating the Canaanites—called for in v. 2, the prohibitions against alliances and intermarriage would have been unnecessary. The Deuteronomic author writes from the perspective of hindsight, aware that, in fact, Israel did *not* so eradicate the Canaanite inhabitants of the land (compare Judg 1:27-36). In addition, while vv. 1-4 consistently employ singular pronouns, v. 5 shifts suddenly to the plural. Following the warning of YHWH's wrath for apostasy in v. 4, the apparent climax of an argument focusing on personal interaction between Israelite and Canaanite, this charge to destroy cultic objects operates on another rationale altogether. It may well reflect the concerns of an editor aware of the apostasies of Israelite and Judean kings who endorsed worship at such sites (2 Kgs 17).

Deuteronomic Influence on Exodus

The language concerning Israel's status as a holy people and a peculiar possession (7:6) finds parallels in Exod 19:5-6. This parallel does not, however, indicate that Deuteronomy reflects awareness of or dependence on Exod 19. For one thing, outside Exod 19, the term *sĕgullâ*, used to describe Israel's special status, occurs only in Deuteronomy (7:6; 14:2; 26:18) and a late Psalm (135:4). As a consequence, a considerable body of scholarship regards this language to be a Deuteronomic insertion in the Sinai text.

Israel's Holiness and Insignificance, YHWH's Love, 7:6-16

The discussion in vv. 1-5 concerning Israel's need to remain separate from their more numerous neighbors raises two issues that receive further treatment in vv. 6-16, namely the mysteries of Israel's holiness and election, especially as they relate to the danger that Israel may become arrogant due to its status as the chosen people. This section relies heavily on the exodus (v. 8) and Sinai traditions (vv. 9-11), [Deuteronomic Influence on Exodus] and probably refers to the patriarchal promise as well (vv. 8, 12; see the discussion of the various meanings of references to "the fathers" in the book of Deuteronomy in [The Promise to the Patriarchs in Deuteronomy]). As such, the passage functions as a summary of the biblical understanding of Israel's place in YHWH's economy of world history.

The first issue addressed concerns the rational for the destruction of the Canaanite inhabitants of the land. Israel is a nation "holy (*qādôš*) to YHWH," chosen (*bḥr*) from all the nations on earth to be YHWH's "peculiar possession (*sĕgullâ*)." All of these terms imply separation and distinction. In fact, although the idea of holiness often includes notions of ethical purity, its basic force involves the idea of something set aside for the deity—something reserved, off limits for ordinary use.[1] This basic idea of separation begs further definition: set aside for whom or what? how? for what purpose? The Hebrew Bible answers these questions clearly. YHWH has reserved Israel for himself. Israel's holiness is manifest in keeping the covenant. Israel has been set aside as a "priestly nation" (Exod 19:6) to "bring blessing to all the families of the earth" (Gen 12:3).

The ethical and religious demands of the covenant arise from and extend this act of setting aside, as the passage makes clear a few verses later (vv. 11-12). YHWH has chosen Israel to be apart from the other nations of the world and this holiness becomes apparent in and through specific behaviors on Israel's part: namely, their responsibility to "keep the commandment, and the ordinances, and the judgments" which, through Moses, YHWH commands them (v. 11). Again, the Hebrew Bible clearly establishes the relationship between YHWH's free choice and the covenant. Both logically and chronologically, YHWH's choice, as an act of unmotivated grace, preceded the requirements of the covenant. Israel does not earn salvation; Israel manifests it.

Indeed, the text recognizes a danger for Israel inherent in its status as the chosen nation, namely a false pride. Deuteronomy 7 began with a reminder that Israel was to dispossess seven nations "more numerous and mightier than you." Now, Moses reminds Israel once again that YHWH chose them, but "not because you are more numerous than any other nation" (v. 7). If Israel's size and strength did not influence YHWH's decision to choose them, what did?

The Hebrew Bible fails to answer this question. Viewed as one nation among others, Israel was quite unremarkable, even insignificant. Yet, YHWH "clings" (*ḥšq*, v. 7, a word usually reserved for marital devotion; see Gen 2:24) to Israel; YHWH "loves" Israel. Deuteronomy 7 appeals only to the promise YHWH made to "the fathers," perhaps the definitive statement of the mystery of election in the Hebrew Bible. YHWH chose not a mighty nation, but a single, old, weak, childless man, Abraham (Gen 12:1-3), promising him children, prosperity, and protection. Why did YHWH choose Abraham and his descendants? Why not someone young, virile, and capable? Obviously, Abraham merited the choice no more than anyone else. Of course, the fact of the matter is that no one deserves to be chosen.

Like its ancestor Abraham, Israel is weak and insignificant. It cannot merit YHWH's choice. It must depend upon YHWH's character as one who keeps promises (vv. 8-9, 12). Verses 9-10 incorporate the traditional statement of YHWH's faithfulness to the faithful and anger for the unfaithful, a statement found already in the Decalogue (Exod 20:5-6 // Deut 5:9-10) and throughout the Hebrew Bible (Exod 34:6-7; Num 14:18; Jer 32:18; compare Jonah 4:2; Joel 2:13; Pss 11:4; 86:15; 103:8; 145:8; Neh 9:17; 2 Chr 30:9).[2] Israel knows YHWH to be reliable (*ne'ĕmān,* from the root *'mn,* "to stand firm") to keep his covenant and his commitment (*ḥesed,* vv. 9, 12) to the fathers. In the context of the whole scriptural witness, it is important to note that, although the Bible does not indicate the reason (answer the question "why" in the sense of causation or basis) YHWH chose Abraham instead of another, it clearly maintains that election has an objective (answering the question "why" in the sense of purpose). Abraham and his descendants, the nation of Israel, were chosen to play a facilitating role in YHWH's relationship with "all the families of the earth."

Culture War: Modern Holy War and Political Rhetoric

Despite the dominant witness of the Hebrew Bible, even of the book of Deuteronomy, concerning God's desire to see even the "sojourner, widow, and orphan" treated with justice and mercy (see commentary on Deut 5:12-15), and of the New Testament, certain segments of modern Christianity view non-Christian segments of the population as an enemy to be converted or killed, their values a problem to be contained. These Christians do not see interaction with others as an opportunity to demonstrate the love to which Christ calls his disciples.

A leading proponent of waging cultural war on non-Christians, and one suspects non-Caucasians, political commentator and sometime Presidential candidate Patrick Buchanan expressed his views to the 1992 Republican National Convention in Houston, Texas, as follows:

My friends, this election is about much more than who gets what. It is about who we are. It is about what we believe. It is about what we stand for as Americans. There is a religious war going on in our country for the soul of America. It is a cultural war, as critical to the kind of nation we will one day be as was the Cold War itself. And in that struggle for the soul of America, Clinton and Gore are on the other side, and George Bush is on our side. And so, we have to come home, and stand beside him. . . .

Hours after the violence [of the L.A. riot] ended, I visited the Army compound in south LA, where an officer of the 18th Cavalry, that had come to rescue the city, introduced me to two of his troopers. They could not have been 20 years old. He told them to recount their story.

They had come into L.A. late on the second day, and they walked up a dark street, where the mob had looted and burned every building but one, a convalescent home for the aged. The mob was heading in, to ransack and loot the apartments of the terrified old men and women. When the troopers arrived, M-16s at the ready, the mob threatened and cursed, but the mob retreated. It had met the one thing that could stop it: force, rooted in justice, backed by courage.

Greater love than this hath no man than that he lay down his life for his friend. Here were 19-year-old boys ready to lay down their lives to stop a mob from molesting old people they did not even know. And as they took back the streets of L.A., block by block, so we must take back our cities, and take back our culture, and take back our country

To liken riot conditions to cultural variety is to demagogue. To compare the armed soldier with the nonresistant Christ sacrificing his life to redeem the lost is to blaspheme: "We have to take back our country by force, if necessary, just like Jesus would!"

To be fair, of course, Patrick Buchanan and other Western Christians enjoy no monopoly on intolerance, bigotry, and oppression. Israeli Jews deprive Palestinian citizens of Israel their basic human rights. Moslems in certain parts of the world discriminate against Jews and Christians. The recent horrors in the former Yugoslavia demonstrate that Christians can ally with non-Christians against other Christians from another branch of Christendom. The human tendency to dehumanize others survives. The Crusader mentality, "convert or kill," lives still in Western Christianity.

Deuteronomy 7, however, focuses not on the purpose of Israel's election, but on the defining characteristics of it, the covenant requirements (vv. 9, 11-12). True to the theme and purpose of the book, even this discussion of the unmerited grace YHWH demonstrated for Israel includes the charge that Israel must keep the covenant. Also in a characteristic manner, Moses outlines the consequences of Israel's stewardship of the covenant: blessing for fidelity (vv. 12-16a). In specific terms, this blessing will bring fertility. Israel will multiply; and its fields, orchards, vineyards, and flocks will be fruitful (v. 13). Its herds will be free of infertile animals (v. 14). YHWH will protect Israel from the plagues and diseases with which he afflicted Egypt at the time of the exodus (v. 15; contrast 28:27, 60, 68). Finally, through YHWH's blessing, Israel will "consume" the nations who occupy the land, showing them no pity (v. 16). The overarching theme of the passage resurfaces in the final clause of this section, "for they will be a snare to you." The destruction of the Canaanites will help to assure Israel's holiness. [Culture War: Modern Holy War and Political Rhetoric]

Interestingly, this passage seems unaware of the tension between the unmerited grace promised Israel's forefathers and the requirement that Israel observe the covenant in order to receive its blessings. Perhaps the tension can best be explained in terms of the distinction between the grace that brings Israel into relationship with YHWH and the faithful behavior expected within that relationship. YHWH threatens to punish disobedience, but he does not threaten to end the relationship. This passage also fails to account for the stark contrast between the call issued to the patriarchs and reiterated to the Sinai generation that Israel serve a mediatorial role in YHWH's dealings with other nations. It is difficult to conceive of the destruction of the Canaanites as bringing them blessing! Only the extreme priority of Israel's holiness—without which its mediatorial task, its priesthood, would be powerless—and the conviction that in YHWH's management of world affairs, the time had come to curb the Canaanites' decadence (see commentary on Deut 1 and 2) can mitigate the harshness of Deuteronomy 7 and texts like it.

Israel's Insignificance and Confidence in Its Mission, 7:17-26

Whereas Israel's awareness of its objective insignificance in relation to the other nations of the world, in particular to those that occupy Canaan, can serve as a reminder that Israel did not merit YHWH's favor, it can also inspire fear. Already in the wilderness, Israel had

Exodus

Gasping, fainting, and wilting in poverty, suffering, and despair, this scene conjures up the horrific state of the Jewish people just after the Holocaust. Jewish artist Lazar Segall captures a moment in 1947 when they have not yet secured a homeland and are truly at the mercy of YHWH.

Lazar Segall. 1891–1957. *Exodus.* 1947. Oil on canvas. 132cm x 137.1cm. The Jewish Museum. New York. Gift of James Rosenberg and George Baker in memory of Felix M. Warburg.

cowered before the mightier inhabitants of the land, thereby stubbornly and rebelliously disobeying YHWH's command to take possession of the land (1:19-33 and parallels). Moses encourages them now to remember that their strength derives from the same source as their holiness. YHWH delivered Israel from Egyptian bondage; Israel did not gain its own freedom through its military might. YHWH delivered Israel and instituted the covenant with it not because Israel was mighty, but because of his promise. In the same way, Israel will gain victory over its enemies, not because of its might, but because of YHWH's steadfast loyalty to his promise.

This section opens (v. 17) with an anticipation of Israel's reaction to the Canaanites' strength. Moses charges the Israelites to be unafraid, dispelling their fears with reminders of YHWH's intervention on their behalf in Egypt (v. 18). A brief summary of YHWH's mighty acts during the exodus (v. 19ab; this language is traditional, compare Exod 3:19; 7:3; 32:11; Deut 3:24; 4:34; 5:15; 6:21; 9:26; 11:2; 26:8; Jer 32:20, 21; Ps 135:9; Neh 9:10; Dan 4:2; 6:27; etc.) culminates in the promise that YHWH will repeat this intervention in the conquest of the promised land (v. 19c). Indeed (*wĕgam*, v. 20), YHWH will exceed his acts in Egypt. He will "send hornets"[3] among the nations, and, whereas he only decimated the Egyptian population and destroyed its army, he will utterly destroy the inhabitants of the land, eradicating even the last remnant (*'ad 'abōd hannišã'rîm wĕhannistārîm mipānêka*, "until the remnant and the remainder are destroyed before you").

In a second response (vv. 21-25), Moses repeats his instruction that they be unafraid. Israel has no reason to "dread" its enemies because YHWH, an "awesome and fearful" God, is in their midst (v. 21). YHWH will give the nations over to Israel, and the destruction will be complete. Israel will destroy the very name, the very memory, of the Canaanite kings. Indeed, no one will be able to withstand the Israelite onslaught. Israel need only remember not to introduce into their households any of the "abominable" things that they may find among the conquered nations, probably a reference primarily to Canaanite religious objects (see v. 25). Since plunder is also abominable because it is subject to the ban—the sentence of total destruction—other, non-religious, Canaanite treasures may also be considered "abominable." Israel must "detest (*šqṣ*)" and "abhor (*'bh*)" everything Canaanite.

Two statements (vv. 22, 25) interrupt the flow of this argument. Remarkably, given the repeated unequivocal call for the total annihilation of the Canaanite populace and the promise that YHWH will intervene on Israel's behalf in the Canaanite campaigns, v. 22 mitigates the drastic nature of this "holy war" by announcing that the process of the conquest and eradication of the Canaanites will be gradual, "little by little." Since Israel itself is so insignificant in numbers, should it destroy the Canaanite population at once, it would be unable to occupy fully the vacant territory. The vacuum would provide the opportunity for wild beasts to multiply and pose a danger. This rationalistic explanation attempts to account for the actual circumstances that prevailed during much of the

Christ and Culture

H. Richard Niebuhr's very influential study of the relationship between the community of faith and its cultural context, *Christ and Culture*, suggests a useful model for considering the dynamics of the problem for any faith community in any age. He identified five approaches that communities of faith have pursued in the course of history.

The first type, Christ against culture, regards the relationship in terms of opposition and antagonism: "Whatever may be the customs of the society in which the Christian lives, and whatever the human achievements it conserves, Christ is seen as opposed to them, so that he confronts men with the challenge of an 'either-or' decision." On the other extreme, some believers have emphasized the "fundamental *agreement* between Christ and culture." This approach identifies the values of a society with the ideals of Christ and risks simply endorsing cultural biases.

In between lie three approaches that recognize the distinctions between authentically Christian and manifestly cultural principles. One of these approaches, Christ above culture, sees the valuable elements of cultural expression as a manifestation of Christ, but recognizes that Christ stands beyond even the best of human accomplishment. The awareness of the necessity of living within culture, while owing ultimate allegiance to Christ, leads some to adopt a Christ and culture in paradox stance. This approach views the two worlds, culture and kingdom of faith, as largely unrelated: "In the *polarity* and *tension* of Christ and culture life must be lived precariously and sinfully in the hope of a justification which lies beyond history." The fifth and final approach looks for a conversion of culture. Culture is evil, but Christ seeks ever to transform it.

Niebuhr examines the way in which, through Christian history, segments of the church have employed these approaches. In fact, although Niebuhr does not himself undertake the task, it would be possible to locate many of these five models within Scripture. Deuteronomy views the problem in terms of an antagonism to the surrounding culture. Paul seems to have seen the believer as a citizen of two kingdoms, owing appropriate allegiance to civil authority but ultimate allegiance to Christ (Rom 13). Clearly the struggle to "live in the world" is no new circumstance, and it permits no easy solution.

H. Richard Niebuhr, *Christ and Culture* (New York: Harper & Row, 1951), 40, 41, 43.

---

monarchy—namely, the fact that, despite the repeated charge to annihilate the Canaanites and the regular assertion that Israel had indeed conquered all, Canaanites continued to occupy sizeable portions of the promised land. It is, however, entirely inconsistent with the tenor of Deuteronomy 7 as a whole. The tension calls attention to the programmatic character of the anti-Canaanite polemic of Deuteronomy 7. [Christ and Culture]

As was true for v. 5, the first four words of v. 25 (*pěsîlê ělōhêhem tiśrěpûn bāʾēš*, "the idol images of their gods you shall burn in the fire") represent a sudden, intrusive statement in the second person *plural*. It deals with the same topic dealt with in the earlier intrusion, the fiery destruction of cultic objects, and probably stems from the same hand. The remainder of the verse, composed in the second person singular once again, refers to the silver and gold Israel may well find among the belongings of the conquered Canaanites. The second singular portions of vv. 25 and 26 refer to a situation such as the one involving Achan (Josh 7)—which centered on obedience to the Holy War rules themselves—not primarily to the seductive threat posed by Canaanite idolatry.

CONNECTIONS

Multiculturalism is not a new phenomenon. Ancient Israel contended with the problem of preserving its unique identity in the face of the attractions of other cultures and religions throughout its long history. Abraham wandered among the population of Canaan and sojourned for a period in Egypt (Gen 12:10-20) and Gerar (Gen 21). His descendants lived as slaves in Egypt for generations. Freed from that bondage, they came to the land promised them to find it inhabited by a well-established population, elements of which were to persist well into the monarchial period. The Assyrian and Babylonian crises of the eighth and sixth centuries, respectively, and especially the exile and its aftermath, returned the descendants of Abraham to minority status, under foreign rule, surrounded by foreigners practicing a foreign way of life and religion. Since centuries before Christ, large numbers of Jews (indeed by Jesus' day, probably most Jews) of the Diaspora have lived as small minorities in distant lands. At home in Palestine, they lived under foreign rule for twenty-three of the past twenty-four centuries.

Christianity, too, began as a minority religion. Paul preached in a world abounding in religions and philosophies: Mithraism, Stoicism, Gnosticism, etc. Not until Constantine (AD 306–337) did Christianity enjoy official approbation. It can be, and has been argued, however, that official status robbed Christianity of something of its sense of mission, of its sense of commitment. Years later, the Protestant Reformation, and especially its radical wing (Anabaptist and Baptist groups, for example), would argue that the equation of citizenship in the state and membership in the church contradicts what they considered the fundamental Christian notion of personal decision.

Many modern Western Christians perceive the growing multiculturalism of Western societies as a crisis. Some refer to a "post-Christian" era (the counterpart within Christendom is an increasing "post-denominationalism"). Values once shared throughout society can no longer be assumed. In the US—where freedom of religion once applied primarily to varieties of Christianity—the numbers of adherents to Islam, Hinduism,

Buddhism, Zoroastrianism, and even Wicca, just to name a few, grow exponentially. All of this takes place in conjunction with the numerical decline of mainline Christian denominations. Does Christianity face a future in which it returns to minority status? How should the church approach the question of its identity in a culturally and religiously diverse world?

Deuteronomy 7 makes two important statements concerning the problem of preserving uniqueness in a multicultural context. Can modern believers find resources for dealing with the challenges of an increasingly complex culture here? Yes and No.

No first. Deuteronomy 7:1-5 calls for the total annihilation of non-Israelite populations in the promised land. Israel itself found this approach impracticable. Hopefully, modern believers will find it unconscionable. [The "Radical Reformation" and Withdrawal from Society]

The "Radical Reformation" and Withdrawal from Society

At the opposite extreme from Deut 7 and contemporaries who see multicultural society as a threat to be conquered, the churches of the so-called "radical" branch of the Protestant Reformation insisted on both the absolute separation of the church from civil society and the impropriety of employing coercive methods. In fact, since office-holders in civil government must employ forms of force, these ancestors of modern Mennonites, Baptists, and other free church traditions held that believers should not hold civil office. These radical reformers ultimately bequeathed the notion of the separation of church and state to the framers of the U.S. Bill of Rights.

The second confession of faith issued by the early Mennonites, the so-called "Waterlander Confession" of 1580 or 1581, served as the statement whereby the earliest English Baptists led by John Smyth and the Waterlanders determined the compatibility of their doctrine. Its "Article XXXVII: Of the Office of Civil Magistrate" is a typical statement of the radical reformers' views:

> Government or the civil Magistrate is a necessary ordinance of God, instituted for the government of common human society and the preservation of natural life and civil good, for the defense of the good and the punishment of the evil. We acknowledge, the word of God obliging us, that it is our duty to reverence magistracy and to show to it honor and obedience in all things which are not contrary to the word of God. It is our duty to pray to the omnipotent God for them, and to give thanks to him for good and just magistrates and without murmuring to pay just tribute and customs. This civil government the Lord Jesus did not institute in his spiritual kingdom, the church of the New Testament, nor did he join it to the offices of his church: nor did he call his disciples or followers to royal, ducal or other power; nor did he teach that they should seize it and rule in a lordly manner; much less did he give to the members of his church the law, agreeable to such office or dominion: but everywhere they are called away from it (which voice heard from heaven ought to be heeded) to the imitation of his harmless life and his footsteps bearing the cross, and in which nothing is less in evidence than an earthly kingdom, power and sword. When all these things are carefully weighed (and moreover not a few things are joined with the office of civil magistracy, as waging war, depriving enemies of goods and life, etc., which [do not agree with] the lives of Christians who ought to be dead to the world), they agree either badly or plainly not at all, hence we withdraw ourselves from such offices and administrations. And yet we do not wish that just and moderate power should in any manner be despised or condemned, but that it should be truly esteemed, as in the words of Paul, the Holy Spirit dictating, it ought to be esteemed.

Obviously the Waterlanders had not resolved, if they had even noted, the tension between the assumption that God ordained magistracy but that believers ought not to hold office. They looked, apparently, to non-believers to govern justly. Their position represents one possible response to minority status. In contrast, the modern church, grown accustomed to something like majority, even established, status in some parts of the U.S. at least, has come in many ways to enjoy imposing what they see as God's will on others.

W. L. Lumpkin, *Baptist Confessions of Faith* (Philadelphia: Judson Press, 1959), 63-64.

The mission of the church and religious crusades are incompatible. The crusader's "convert or kill" mentality opposes Christ's call to love one's neighbor. Even the modern form of cultural crusade, demanding uniformity and conformity, masks a violent, domineering, conquering impulse contrary to the biblical call to serve. Neither faith nor values can be imposed.

But yes. Deuteronomy 7 warns against two diametrically opposed attitudes that can damage a faith community, or an individual, for that matter, living in a conflict of cultures: self-importance and defeatism. A sensitive observer will note evidence of both these attitudes present in the modern religious community.

Logic would seem to dictate that God would choose the most suitable individual or group for God's purposes. If, therefore, one has been chosen, called, elected, one may reasonably conclude—it would seem—that one fulfills the qualifications for the task *better* than anyone else. One can reasonably conclude, according to this logic, that one is superior, deserving of the choice, and worthy of the call. Of course, the corollary to such a conclusion is that all others are inferior, equally deserving of exclusion from the call.

Obviously, such attitudes of superiority, fueled by the universal human need to earn and deserve, hamper relations between the elect and others. "Too bad you aren't me." Such denigration of others, individuals and groups, drive class struggles, oppression, violence, war, and even genocide. Not only do such attitudes encourage abuse of others, but both the biblical witness and common experience undeniably demolish the basis for any and all notions of the superiority of God's elect. The Bible testifies that God chose the likes of frail Abraham, rebellious Saul, adulterous David, and fugitive Jonah. Any minister can testify to the foibles of his or her flock of the elect just as any church knows the shortcomings, the humanity, of its minister. No. The elect are not superior. God is gracious.

Equally damaging to the health of the community of faith is the attitude of inferiority and of despair that can arise from the sense of being outnumbered, overpowered, or disregarded. Historically, the faithful have often withdrawn from the world in such cases, withdrawn into cloistered existences, withdrawn their influence from society. Deuteronomy reminds the faithful that they will accomplish the mission before them not through their own strength, but because, and only if, their work is the work of God. God—who delivered Israel from Egyptian bondage, who raised his Christ from the grave—this God will not abandon to the whirlwinds of a complex culture those who have heeded God's call.

NOTES

[1] See H. P. Müller, "*qdš, qdš,* holy," in *Theological Lexicon of the Old Testament* III (ed. E. Jenni and C. Westermann, trans. M. Biddle; Peabody MA: Hendrickson, 1997), 1103-18.

[2] See R. C. Dentan, "The Literary Affinities of Exodus XXXIV 6f," *VT* 13 (1963): 36-39, 48-49.

[3] Scholars debate whether hornets were actually employed as weapons of war in the ancient Near East; the greater likelihood favors that this reference is a very picturesque metaphor. See E. Neufeld, "Insects as Warfare Agents in the Ancient Near East," *Orientalia* 49 (1980): 30-57.

DESERT AND PROMISED LAND: THE DANGERS POSED BY WANT AND PROSPERITY

8:1-20

Deuteronomy 8 is the third in a series of sermons dealing with the implications of the first commandment. Following explications of the necessity for diligently remembering and transmitting the first commandment in its positive form, the Shema (Deut 6), and of the danger to observance of the first commandment posed by Israel's existence among the nations (Deut 7), Deuteronomy 8 reminds its readers of the human tendencies to apostasy in the extreme conditions of both want and prosperity. This sermon divides readily into two well-balanced units, vv. 1-10 and vv. 11-20, as indicated by the new beginning in v. 11, the shift in themes from the past to the future, and the recapitulation of phrases and ideas from the first section in the second. [Structure] Each half features a prominent hymnic section (vv. 7-10 and vv. 14-16; see commentary below).

COMMENTARY

YHWH Tests and Trains Israel in the Desert, 8:1-10

The introduction to this sermon (v. 1) repeats the familiar Deuteronomic call to heed and do the commandments (6:17; 11:22; 12:1), as well as the equally standard promise that such obedience means life and prosperity for Israel in the land promised its ancestors (4:1, 40; 5:16, 29, 33; 6:18; 11:9, 21; 12:25, 28; etc.). The statement of the unique theme of this passage comes with the call to remember the wilderness experience (v. 2). Although the usual explanation for the wilderness wandering describes it as a punishment for Israel's rebellion (Num 13–14; Deut 1:19-46), Deuteronomy 8:2 maintains that YHWH's purposes were to "humble (*'nh*)" and "test (*nsh*)" them to discover whether it was in their hearts to obey the

---

Structure

AΩ The following table illustrates the manner in which phrases and ideas from the first section of this sermon on the first commandment (vv. 1-10) recur in the second (vv. 11-20).

. . . the commandment which I command you this day . . . keep his commandments . . . (vv. 1-2)	. . . keeping his commandments . . . which I command you this day . . . (v. 11)
. . . keep the commandments . . . (v. 6)	
. . . you shall eat and be full . . . (v. 10)	. . . when you have eaten and are full . . . (v. 12)
For the LORD your God is bringing you into a good land, a land of brooks of water, of fountains and springs, flowing forth in valleys and hills, a land of wheat and barley, of vines and fig trees and pomegranates, a land of olive trees and honey, a land in which you will eat bread without scarcity, in which you will lack nothing, a land whose stones are iron, and out of whose hills you can dig copper. (vv. 7-9)	. . . and when your herds and flocks multiply, and your silver and gold is multiplied, and all that you have is multiplied, then your heart be lifted up, and you forget the LORD your God, who brought you out of the land of Egypt, out of the house of bondage, who led you through the great and terrible wilderness, with its fiery serpents and scorpions and thirsty ground where there was no water, who brought you water out of the flinty rock . . . (vv. 13-15)
. . . he humbled you . . . and fed you with manna . . . as a man disciplines his son, the LORD your God disciplines you. (vv. 3-5)	. . . who fed you in the wilderness with manna which your fathers did not know, that he might humble you and test you . . . (v. 16)

Compare I. Cairns, *Word and Presence: A Commentary on the Book of Deuteronomy* (ITC; Grand Rapids: Eerdmans, 1992), 97.

---

commandments. Lest the reader conclude that Israel's relationship to YHWH depended upon its ability to "pass" a test, however, the text goes on quickly (v. 5) to compare this period of testing to a father disciplining or training (*ysr*) his child. Anticipating modern educational theory, this test was to be a learning exercise. What lesson was Israel to learn?

Many cultures associate the desert with times of testing and humility. The Bible regularly utilizes this imagery (Jer 2:1-2; Hos 2; etc.). [The Wilderness in the Bible: Personal Struggle and Encounter with God] In conditions of want and danger, one must focus on the essentials of survival. Indeed, YHWH "humbled" Israel through hunger, supplying their need in a remarkable fashion. At a much later period in Israel's history, the prophet Hosea would describe YHWH's intention to return Israel to the conditions of its wilderness experience, to reduce it once again to a situation of need and distress (2:3, 6, 9, 11-12). Israel had lost sight of the fact that its many blessings were God's gifts. Hosea described YHWH's intention to remove the distracting riches Israel had come to enjoy so that it could clearly see that all gifts come from YHWH (2:7-8, 14-15).

Interestingly, during the wilderness period, YHWH did not provide Israel with a rich array of foods, nor did he lavish upon

The Wilderness in the Bible: Personal Struggle and Encounter with God

In the Bible, the wilderness served as both the physical setting for individuals experiencing some defining crisis of the spirit and as a powerful symbol of the state of the soul reduced to utter dependence upon God. Hagar fled from the oppression of her mistress Sarah (Gen 16) and was later banished into the wilderness (Gen 21). In both cases, God sustained her (and her child) in her need. Moses fled Egypt into the wilderness of Midian, seeking to escape the conflict in his own psyche concerning his identity (Egyptian or Israelite? Moses chooses Midianite) as well as Egyptian justice (Exod 2). God appeared to him there and charged him to return to Egypt and assume his place as the leader of his true people. Despondent, the prophet Elijah fled before Ahab and Jezebel into the wilderness, and eventually to a cave near Mt. Horeb (1 Kgs 19:4-18) where God spoke to him in a "still, small voice," responding to Elijah's self-pity with a new commission. In the desert, Jesus grappled with the essential questions concerning the character of the mission and ministry he was about to undertake (Matt 4:1-11; Luke 4:1-13). After his dramatic conversion on the road to Damascus, the apostle Paul retreated to the Arabian Desert for a lengthy period of prayer and reflection (Gal 1:17).

---

them other material blessings. Instead, their hunger was met sufficiently, although only on a day-to-day basis (Exod 16:4-8; compare the clause in the Lord's Prayer, "give us today our daily bread," with the implication that enough to meet one's need should suffice) and somewhat monotonously (Num 11:4-9), by the manna, the origins of which puzzled the Israelites (the word literally means "what's this?"). Furthermore, their clothing did not wear out. Both the manna and the preservation of Israel's clothing for forty years in the desert represent God's sustenance, but neither blessing can be characterized as extravagant. YHWH saw only to their basic needs.

The oft-quoted statement in v. 3 underscores the notion that even the most basic needs are met by God's provision. In other words, in the context of desert existence—where conditions require one to focus on the essentials—it becomes apparent that even bread, water, and clothing are gifts of God. According to the Gospel of Matthew, Jesus quoted the statement in v. 3 to Satan during Jesus' temptation in the wilderness, adding a reference to God's word: "but by every word that proceeds . . . ." Luke's parallel is more faithful to the Hebrew in that it does not include the final phrase. The Hebrew of Deuteronomy 8:3 reads simply, "One shall not live by bread alone, but by all (or by everything) that proceeds from the mouth of God." In the context of Deuteronomy 8, however, "everything that proceeds from the mouth of God" refers primarily not to God's revelation in word, but to the provision God made for Israel in the wilderness—provision God spoke into being. That is, the manna resulted from God's creative word (not God's revealing Torah-word), as did the preservation of Israel's clothing. In this understanding, the lesson of the wilderness experience was

The Last Supper/Gathering of Manna

By juxtaposing these two scenes, medieval religious art recognized the extrapolation of the Pentateuchal tradition concerning God's provision of manna evident in many of Jesus' sayings, such as those in John 6, and actions, such as the Last Supper.

The Last Supper/Gathering of the Manna: Mirror of Human Salvation. 1363. Ms.139. fol.17v. Flemish. Musée Condé. Chantilly, France.

that Israel should not take for granted the most common staples of existence. Bread may seem an entirely ordinary, everyday, natural product. In the wilderness, however, bread can obviously only be supplied by a creative God. Indeed, everything that sustains human life proceeds from the mouth of God; everything upon which human beings depend is the gift of the Creator.

Characteristically for Deuteronomy, this period of training designed to teach Israel its dependence on YHWH's provision should produce a willingness "to obey his commandments, to walk in his ways, and to fear him" (v. 6). Subsistence in dependence upon YHWH will give way to plenty. YHWH will now lead them into the promised land rich in water (with flowing streams and deep springs, both in the hills and in the valleys [v. 7]—no more water from a rock!), in produce (wheat, barley, grapes, figs, pomegranates, olives, oil, and honey), and in natural resources (iron and copper). There, Israel will know neither poverty nor hunger. In this good land, Israel will "eat and be satisfied," enjoying the bounty of YHWH's blessing (v. 10).

The Danger of Abundance, 8:11-20

The imperative, "watch yourself" (*hiššāmer lĕkā*, v. 11), announces a new beginning. Failures to contemplate and teach the commandments and the dangers posed by improper attitudes toward the nations have served as the basis for similar warnings (Deut 6 and 7, respectively). Now the danger lies in the complacency born of plenty (vv. 12-14). When Israel has entered the land of plenty they may quickly forget the lessons of the desert. Agricultural bounty, homes, fertile flocks and herds, monetary wealth—all YHWH's blessings—may dull Israel's memory of its difficult past. In short, they may become arrogant (literally, "and your heart may become high"), presumptuously relying upon their own efforts, taking for granted God's blessing. They may forget that, even in the land of plenty, they live "by everything that comes from the mouth of God," that is, that everything they enjoy is God's gift. As a consequence, they may also forget to live according to "every word that comes from the mouth of God." That is, they may forget that grateful obedience is the proper response to blessing.

Like the bounties of the promised land, the lessons of YHWH's past provision for Israel inspire the Deuteronomic author to rhapsodize. The series of participles in vv. 14-18 governs the elevated, almost poetic style of this passage. Success and comfort may seduce Israel to forget the God "who brought out" from Egyptian bondage (v. 14), "who led in the wilderness," "who brought forth water from the flinty rock" (v. 15; see Num 20:1-11), and "who gave manna to eat." YHWH met Israel's need when it suffered oppression, when it wandered in a frightful, dry desert infested with serpent and scorpion, when it was thirsty in a land without water,[1] and when it was hungry. [Imaging the Wilderness]

The memory of those acts of care should predispose Israel to recognize its good fortune in the promised land as YHWH's blessing, too. But human beings find it difficult to acknowledge that every good thing is God's gift. Moses warns that Israel will one day claim credit for its success: "My strength and the might of my hand have gotten me this wealth" (v. 17). YHWH gave the manna; he gave the bounty of the land; he even gave the strength of which Israel will boast (v. 18a). Furthermore, YHWH gave both the strength and the wealth so that Israel may keep the covenant established with their fathers (v. 18b), not so that Israel may glory in its wealth.

As always in Deuteronomy, the feared result of this arrogant forgetfulness is idolatry, and ultimately Israel's own destruction (vv. 19-20). Israel must always "heed the voice of YHWH." Otherwise, Israel becomes indistinguishable from the Canaanites whom YHWH condemned for their abominable idolatry, and it will suffer the same fate.

Imaging the Wilderness

Inhabitants of the developed northern hemisphere have little or no experience of the desolation of the desert or of the harsh realities of life there. As a consequence, the power of the image of Israel's forty-year sojourn in the wilderness as a time of trial and of the formation of Israel's faith and character, its dependence upon YHWH, is often lost on readers from the developed world. Several passages from T. S. Eliot's renowned poem "The Waste Land" evoke the wilderness as poignantly as any lines in the world's literature, in part due to its very effective allusion to Scripture.

What are the roots that clutch, what branches grow
Out of this stony rubbish? Son of man [Ezek 2:1],
You cannot say, or guess, for you know only
A heap of broken images, where the sun beats,
And the dead tree gives no shelter, the cricket [Eccl 12:5] no relief,
And the dry stone no sound of water. Only
There is shadow under this red rock,
(Come in under the shadow of this red rock) [Isa 32:2],
And I will show you something different from either
Your shadow at morning striding behind you
Or your shadow at evening rising to meet you;
I will show you fear in a handful of dust [Eccl 12:7].
. . .
Here is no water but only rock
Rock and no water and the sandy road
The road winding above among the mountains

Which are mountains of rock without water
If there were water we should stop and drink
Amongst the rock one cannot stop or think
Sweat is dry and feet are in the sand
If there were only water amongst the rock
Dead mountain mouth of carious teeth that cannot spit
Here one can neither stand nor lie nor sit
There is not even silence in the mountains
But dry sterile thunder without rain
There is not even solitude in the mountains
But red sullen faces sneer and snarl
From door of mudcracked houses

If there were water
And no rock
If there were rock
And also water
And water
A Spring
A pool among the rock
If there were the sound of water only
Not the cicada
And dry grass singing
But sound of water over a rock
Where the hermit-thrush sings in the pine trees
Drip drop drip drop drop drop drop
But there is no water.

T. S. Eliot, "The Waste Land," in *The American Tradition in Literature*, vol. 2, ed. S. Bradley et al. (New York: Grosset & Dunlap, 1967), 1287-1305. Eliot himself called attention to these allusions in his own notes. These are documented in brackets in the poem above.

CONNECTIONS

Prosperity threatened to distract ancient Israel's attention from its dependence on YHWH. Historically, Israel owed its very existence as a nation to YHWH's deliverance from Egyptian bondage. It survived the wilderness and succeeded in gaining a foothold in the land of Canaan because of YHWH's guidance and protection. In the context of its contemporary life in the land, it enjoyed continued prosperity because YHWH authored all its opportunities, its strength, and its wealth. But the all-too-human temptation to take for granted posed a significant temptation.

To the distractions of wealth and distance from the defining moments in God's relationship with God's people, modern believers can add a sometimes misplaced and arrogant confidence in progress, technology, way of life, and personal accomplishment. Human beings have come to understand a great deal about the workings of the natural world. Medical science has learned to combat disease and illness. Engineers can construct barriers and protections against natural disaster. Human minds have conceived and constructed devices to protect against hazards and to multiply productivity, economic structures to maximize wealth, and a variety of technologies and media to inform and entertain. Moderns more often feel that they owe their well-being and livelihoods to corporations or governments than to the blessings of the Creator.

Ancient Israel failed to recognize that the God who provided in the desert also maintained the bounty and fertility of the promised land. They saw their prosperity either as the result of their own efforts (Deut 8) or as the gifts of the Canaanites' Baals (Hos 2). It is almost as though they considered YHWH the God of exoduses and wanderings, but not the God of everyday life. Ironically, moderns, even the most conservative Christians, often make a similar mistake, accepting uncritically the Enlightenment distinctions between "natural causation" and the supernatural. The danger inherent in this distinction is, of course, that God is banished from everyday life! In this view, God is to be sought not in the course of everyday events (the sunrise, the next breath one takes), but only in the extraordinary.

What a dilemma God must face! Having created humankind in God's own image—with godlike powers of thought, invention, and creativity—as the crowning act of creation, God finds that these creatures easily forget that the everyday world that sustains them is God's gift. They forget that the strength and intellect that permits them to manage and utilize the resources so freely given are likewise God's gifts. Must God always keep God's people in the marginal state of existence represented by the desert so that they will be forced to recognize their dependence on God's blessing? Will people turn to God only when facing potentially terminal illnesses or troubled marriages or financial crises? Surely God would rather see God's people gratefully enjoy the riches God created for purposes of their sustenance and enjoyment!

The noted German martyr and theologian Dietrich Bonhoeffer, a leading figure in the German Free Church movement during the Nazi era and a victim of Nazi evil, offered an insightful analysis of the dilemma faced by contemporary Christians. In a series of letters written from a Nazi prison,[2] he lamented that—especially in the modern era, when many phenomena can be explained scientifically

Would That All God's People Were Poets

Ancient Israelite and modern Christian alike have found it sometimes difficult to recognize God in the ordinary, everyday experiences of life. Moses once responded to Joshua's jealous accusations made against Israelites who were prophesying "without permission" with the plaintive wish, "Would that all YHWH's people were prophets . . ." (Num 11:29). The amazingly childlike sensitivity to God's presence expressed by the 19th century British poet, Gerard Manley Hopkins, in his "God's Grandeur" makes one yearn for the day when all God's people could be poets!

> The world is charged with the grandeur of God.
>   It will flame out, like shining from shook foil;
>   It gathers to a greatness, like the ooze of oil
> Crushed. Why do men then now not reck his rod?
> Generations have trod, have trod, have trod;
>   And all is seared with trade; bleared, smeared with toil;
>   And wears man's smudge and shares man's smell: the soil
> Is bare now, nor can foot fell, being shod.
>
> And for all this, nature is never spent;
>   There lives the dearest freshness deep down things;
> And though the last lights off the black West went
>   Oh, morning, at the brown brink eastward, springs—
> Because the Holy Ghost over the bent
>   World broods with warm breast and with ah! bright wings.

Gerard Manley Hopkins, in *Poems and Prose of Gerard Manley Hopkins*, ed. W. H. Gardner (New York: Penguin Books, 1985), 27.

and many problems can be managed technologically—Christians have too often resorted to belief in a "God of the gaps." God, it is argued, can be best seen at those points where human understanding and expertise break down—in the desert, as it were. In this way, not only does God become an explanation for the otherwise unexplainable, but the gaps themselves become necessary for continued belief in God. What will become of faith as these gaps are even further diminished, as the desert recedes ever further in human memory?

Common experience demonstrates the human tendency to look to God in extreme circumstances: in the desert, in sickness, in times of family crisis, at death. At such times the religious sensibility, the feeling of "total dependence," to use an expression coined by the eighteenth-century theologian and apologist Friedriah Schleiermacher, makes itself felt poignantly. Battlefield conversions, vows made to God at the bedside of a seriously ill loved one, commitments to renewed devotion in hopes of God's intervention in some family or professional crisis—all these point to the human tendency to look to God only when no other explanation or means of assistance seems available.

Bonhoeffer called for a renewed effort to recognize God in the normal and the everyday. Like the ancient Israelite, modern Westerners rely too much on the simple normalcy of daily life. Even believers give too little attention to the fact that the world itself exists because of God's creative wish, that their own abilities, opportunities, and health are God's gift, that the rains come and the sun shines because God wills it so. [Would That All God's People Were Poets] The ancient Israelites lived in close connection with the land, and yet were prone to forget that God sustained them through the bounty of nature. Modern believers live lives disconnected from God's creation. In their technological world, they purchase prepackaged, prepared food. They live in climate-controlled settings. Increasingly, they work with information and data rather than the raw materials taken from God's good earth. This distanced prosperity threatens to seduce moderns into a spiritual arrogance surpassing even that warned against in Deuteronomy 8. God will not be relegated to the gaps.

NOTES

[1] In v. 15, the text pointedly emphasizes that, in contrast to Canaan's relatively abundant supply of water, the desert was "dry" (*ṣimmāʾôn*) and "without water" (*ʾên-māyim*).

[2] *Letters and Papers from Prison*, E. Bethge, ed. (New York: Macmillan, 1967), 154-55, 174-75, 188-89.

ELECTION AND ARROGANCE

9:1–10:11

Perhaps the greatest mystery of biblical theology concerns God's reasons for calling one individual instead of some other, or for choosing one particular people for covenant relationship. Logic would seem to dictate that the Lord of the Universe must have some clearly identifiable criteria of selection. Indeed, the temptation to assume that God has chosen the best qualified or the most deserving often seduces the chosen themselves—despite the testimony of Scripture, the witness of history, and the evidence of personal experience. Israel's experience in displacing the Amorites and Canaanites, unfortunately, taken in isolation, could have the effect of confirming suspicions that YHWH favored Israel *over against* other nations. As Deuteronomy has suggested earlier, however (see commentary on Deut 1, 2, 7), the situation is much more complicated. First, as the episode at Kadesh-barnea demonstrated, YHWH's partisanship does not extend to a blatantly rebellious Israel: Israel, too, can become YHWH's enemy, if only temporarily. Second, nations other than Israel—its kinsfolk, Ammon, Moab, and Edom, indeed, even the Philistines, for example—enjoy a degree of YHWH's favor in his management of human history. Third, YHWH's grant of the promised land to Israel also results from factors other than Israel's election. The sin of the Amorites and Canaanites has reached a critical level so that YHWH can, in one action, both fulfill his promise to the patriarchs and visit justice on the inhabitants of the promised land.

In addition to these implications of external features of Israel's historical relationship with YHWH, Moses has already reminded the Israelites that YHWH did not choose them as his people because of their intrinsic strength (Deut 7:6-11), and, similarly, that they must resist the temptation to credit to their own strength their future prosperity in the land (8:11-20). Instead, Moses cautions them that they are among the weaker nations in the world, and that they will enjoy the fruits of the land solely as YHWH's blessing. Having ruled out strength and ability as the characteristics that merited YHWH's attention, Moses turns now to the question of Israel's presumably superior righteousness. Again, Moses reminds them of the historical evidence to the contrary. From the very beginning of Israel's covenant

The Zohar on God's Faithfulness to God's Purpose

The Zohar is the main text representing the Jewish mystical tradition, the Kaballah. Taking the form of a commentary on the Torah, its authorship is shrouded in mystery. It can only be traced with certainty to 13th century Spain and a certain Moses de Léon. The following passage can be found in the section dealing with Exod 32:1-14, the episode concerning the golden calf. The "Mother" mentioned in the text is *bînâ*, or "understanding," according to Kaballah, one of the ten *sĕfîrôt*, or aspects of the divine personality.

> "Rabbi Yose said,
> 'There has never been a father so compassionate to his children as the Blessed Holy One.
> This is demonstrated in a verse:
> "Not a single word has failed of all His good words . . ." (1 Kgs 8:56).
> Come and see His compassion!
> If the verse read: "Not a single word has failed of all His words,"
> and nothing more,
> it would be better for the world to have never been created!
> But since it reads: "of all His good words,"
> the bad is left behind,
> for He does not want to carry out a bad word.
> Even though He threatens and raises the lash,
> Mother comes and grabs hold of His right arm
> and the lash is suspended,
> the sentence is not carried out,
> because both of them share one design:
> He by threatening, She by holding back His right.'"

D. C. Matt, trans., *Zohar: The Book of Enlightenment* (The Classics of Western Spirituality; New York: Paulist, 1983), 137.

---

relationship with YHWH, even before Moses had descended the mountain of God with the tablets of the covenant, Israel had proven unfaithful. This unfaithfulness, not a superior righteousness, most characterizes Israel's brief history from Mt. Horeb/Sinai to the plains of Moab.

Contrary to what might be expected of the book of Deuteronomy, this summary of the history of Israel's rebellion, which closely parallels the account in Exodus 32, does not serve as the basis for an exhortation calling for obedience to the covenant. The extended call for covenant loyalties (Deut 10:12–11:32), which functions as the conclusion of the series of sermons on the Decalogue (Deut 5–11), displays no clear link to the golden calf tradition or to the account of Moses' subsequent intercession. Deuteronomy 11:12 ("And now . . .") constitutes a new beginning to a unit calling for covenant obedience. Deuteronomy 9:1–10:11, instead, warns quite pointedly against arrogance: God's gracious election distinguishes Israel from the Amorites and Canaanites, and nothing more. Conversely, in the course of this warning against arrogance based on an extended explication of Israel's history of rebellion, a moving picture of YHWH's faithfulness emerges in silhouette against the backdrop of Israel's waywardness. YHWH will be true to his word and his character regardless of Israel's sinfulness. God will persist in God's good purposes. [The Zohar on God's Faithfulness to God's Purpose]

COMMENTARY

"Not because of your righteousness," 9:1-6

This sermon begins with the familiar summons to hear and the announcement that Israel is about to take possession of the promised land. Again, as already in Deuteronomy 7, the matter of the might of the Canaanite inhabitants of the land, especially of the Anakim, a legendary race of giants (see 2:10), and of their fortified cities provides the starting point for the discussion to follow (vv. 1-2). And, once again, Moses reminds Israel that, in the face of YHWH's intervention on their behalf, the might of the Canaanites will avail nothing. YHWH is "a consuming fire" that will eradicate Israel's enemies just as he has promised (v. 3).

To this point, the sermon replicates the argument of other sections of Deuteronomy, but from v. 4 onward, the discussion takes a surprising turn. Israel is not mighty enough to confront the Canaanites in their own strength. They will prevail only because YHWH will fight for them. Why will YHWH do this? Israel may well assume that it deserves YHWH's protection—obviously on some grounds other than its might (which would render YHWH's assistance unnecessary)—because it is righteous! Emphatically, Moses insists that Israel must avoid this arrogant assumption. Three times Moses asserts that Israel has not merited YHWH's favor because of its righteousness ("do not say . . . because of my righteousness," v. 4; "it is not because of your righteousness," vv. 5, 6). [On Giving] Counter-assertions balance each of

On Giving

You often say, "I would give, but only to the deserving."

The trees in your orchard say not so, nor the flocks in your pasture.

They give that they may live, for to withhold is to perish.

Surely he who is worthy to receive his days and his nights, is worthy of all else from you.

And he who has deserved to drink from the ocean of life deserves to fill his cup from your little stream.

And what desert greater shall there be, than that which lies in the courage and the confidence, nay the charity, of receiving?

And who are you that men should rend their bosom and unveil their pride, that you may see their worth naked and their pride unabashed?

See first that you yourself deserve to be a giver, and an instrument of giving.

For in truth it is life that gives unto life—while you, who deem yourself a giver, are but a witness.

And you receivers—and you are all receivers—assume no weight of gratitude, lest you lay a yoke upon yourself and upon him who gives.

Rather rise together with the giver on his gifts as on wings;

For to be overmindful of your debt is to doubt his generosity who has the free-hearted earth for mother, and God for father.

Kahlil Gibran, *The Prophet* (New York: Alfred A. Knopf, 1973), 21-22.

these denials of Israel's superior righteousness: (1) YHWH is about to punish the evil of the Canaanites (that is, instead of rewarding the merit of the Israelites, v. 4). (2) YHWH's primary motivation is fidelity to the promise he made to the patriarchs (v. 5; an assertion that may raise in the mind of the reader the question of why YHWH chose the patriarchs, although Deuteronomy does not address this issue). (3) Finally, the evidence of Israel's past behavior contradicts any claim to superior righteousness; Israel has repeatedly shown itself to be a "stiff-necked" or "stubborn" people.

"Remember your rebellion at Horeb," 9:7-21, (22-24), 25-29

The remainder of the sermon consists primarily of an elaboration of the third of these counter-assertions. The imperative "remember" (v. 7; compare the imperative "hear," in v. 1) marks the beginning of a new section of the sermon. It is essential that Israel always remember that throughout its history ("from the day you departed from the land of Egypt until coming to this place") it has habitually rebelled against YHWH.

The example par excellence of Israel's rebelliousness is the incident involving Aaron's golden calf. The account of this incident

---

 Deuteronomy 9 and Exodus 32

Deuteronomy 9	*Exodus 32*
Then the LORD said to me, Arise, go down . . . for your people whom you have brought from Egypt have acted corruptly; they have turned aside quickly out of the way which I commanded them; they have made themselves a molten image. (v. 12)	And the LORD said to Moses, Go down; for your people, whom you brought up out of the land of Egypt, have corrupted themselves; they have turned aside quickly out of the way which I commanded them; they have made for themselves a molten calf. . . . (vv. 7-8)
Furthermore the LORD said to me, I have seen this people, and behold, it is a stubborn people; let me alone, that I may destroy them and blot out their name from under heaven; and I will make of you a nation mightier and greater than they. (vv. 13-14)	And the LORD said to Moses, I have seen this people, and behold, it is a stiff-necked people; now therefore let me alone, that my wrath may burn hot against them and I may consume them; but of you I will make a great nation. (vv. 9-10)
So I took hold of the two tables, and cast them out of my two hands, and broke them before your eyes. (v. 17)	And as soon as he came near the camp and saw the calf and the dancing, Moses' anger burned hot, and he threw the tables out of his hands and broke them at the foot of the mountain. (v. 19)

Compare also Deut 9:10 and 31:18; Deut 9:9, 11 and Exod 24:11.

Golden Calf

Idolatry reigns supreme as Moses and Aaron witness the Israelites worshiping the golden calf. Reflective of his Renaissance clarity of composition, Raphael clearly demarcates the space of idolatry from the holy space of Moses and the tablets. The laws of God are seemingly ignored as the crowd has turned their backs on Moses and they worship and celebrate in their self-sustained space. This closure is moments from being interrupted as Moses will break the tablets in rage and fury.

Raphael. 1483–1520. *Adoration of the Golden Calf* from *The Story of Moses*. Fresco. Logge, Vatican Palace. Vatican State.

preserved in Deuteronomy 9 bears striking, often verbal, resemblance to the parallel account found in Exodus 32. [Deuteronomy 9 and Exodus 32] One the other hand, however, the sequence of events differs according to the two accounts. In comparison to the Exodus account, which is somewhat complicated, the Deuteronomy account seems confused and repetitive.

According to Exodus, sometime during Moses' forty-day stay on Mt. Sinai, Aaron despaired of his return and acquiesced to the people's request for an idol (Exod 32:1-6). When YHWH had instructed Moses to descend the mountain, he informed him of the people's idolatry, and announced his intention to destroy the people and replace them with Moses' descendants (32:7-10). Immediately, before descending the mountain, Moses effectively pleaded with YHWH to pardon Israel, to consider YHWH's own reputation with the nations of the world, and to remember his promise to the patriarchs (32:11-14). When Moses then descended the mountain, he discovered Israel's sin, broke the tablets of the Law, burned the calf to dust, poured the dust into the water, and forced Israel to drink (32:15-21). The day after interrogating Aaron (32:21-24) and inciting the Levites to slaughter the idolaters among the people (32:25-29), Moses interceded once again with YHWH on behalf of the people, asking to share their fate (32:30-24). Finally, YHWH sent a plague upon Israel for its idolatry (32:25).

In contrast, Deuteronomy 9 does not narrate Aaron's role in the incident, referring to him only incidentally in v. 20. Deuteronomy shares with Exodus the sequence of events including YHWH's delivery of the tablets of the Law to Moses (Deut 9:8-11), his instruction to descend the mountain to see for himself the people's idolatry (9:12), and his announcement of his intention to destroy the people and replace them with Moses' descendants (9:13-14). Unlike the Exodus version, Deuteronomy records that Moses descended the mountain immediately—that is, before making intercession for the people. At the foot of the mountain, Moses shattered the tablets of the Law, as in Exodus. Only then, according to Deuteronomy, and not immediately upon learning of YHWH's intention to destroy Israel (as in Exodus), Moses protracted himself before YHWH to intercede for the people, and for Aaron, for forty days and nights (9:18-20). Only then did he destroy the calf (9:21). Deuteronomy makes no mention of Moses' forcing Israel to drink the polluted water, of his interrogation of Aaron, of the Levites' vengeance against the sinners, or of the plague YHWH sent on the people. Obviously, Deuteronomy is less interested in the details than Exodus, and more interested in the account for purposes of illustrating the fundamental fact of Israel's rebellion. At the very outset of its covenant relationship with YHWH—"before the ink was dry" on the tablets of the Decalogue, so to speak—Israel rebelled so heinously that, except for Moses' swift and skillful intercession, YHWH would have abandoned Israel to make Moses the patriarch of the covenant people. A close call, indeed!

YHWH Informs Moses of Israel's Sin, 9:7-14

After the statement of the theme in v. 7 (Israel has been rebellious from the very beginning), v. 8 specifies the most egregious example of this rebellion. Israel first rebelled while they were still encamped at Mt. Horeb, waiting for Moses to return from receiving the tablets of the covenant! Only days after YHWH had appeared to them in fiery theophany and spoken to them, explaining the principles of the covenant (9:10), they violated the most basic of the commandments in a most flagrant manner! Israel had, indeed, "turned aside quickly from the way YHWH had commanded" (vv. 12, 16). Little wonder, then, that YHWH considered ending the relationship so soon after having begun it.

Two elements of the narrative account merit particular attention. First, Moses' reaction upon discovering the people's sin when he descended from the mountain seems to have greater import than as a simple demonstration of Moses' anger. Moses probably broke the two tablets of the Law publicly as an indication that, in his view, the covenant relationship with YHWH had been breached. The covenant was based, after all, on the basic notion that Israel would be God's people just as he would be their God. Israel's fickle and hasty resort to the grossest form of idolatry demonstrated the degree of the people's commitment to the essentials of relationship with YHWH: "out of sight, out of mind." Moses recognized this as a crisis moment of extreme proportions. YHWH's justified "hot anger" (v. 19) threatened Israel's very existence as God's people. Israel had broken the covenant. YHWH would have been justified to feel no longer bound by it.

Second, the narrative stresses Moses' intercessory role (as does Exod 32). Israel's hopes for survival itself rested upon the success of Moses' intervention with YHWH on Israel's behalf. Aaron's future, too, depended on Moses' success as intercessor (v. 20). The fact that Moses fasted for forty days and nights, lying "prostrate before YHWH," indicates the extreme urgency of his task and the momentous degree of his determination (vv. 18, 25). The narrative omits the content of Moses' supplication, however, reserving it for separate treatment (9:25-29) and thereby highlighting it.

A Parenthetical Remark Concerning Other Rebellions, 9:22-24
The notice concerning other instances of Israelite rebellion against YHWH interrupts the flow of the passage somewhat, separating the narrative account (vv. 7-25) from the report of the content of Moses' intercession (vv. 25-29). It may be an editorial interpolation intended to call attention to the fact that the golden calf episode was only the first of a long series of Israelite rebellions. It more likely represents a delaying tactic designed to focus the reader's attention even more pointedly on the content of Moses' intercessory prayer.

Water from the Rock

Raphael. 1483–1520. *Moses Striking the Rock* from *The Story of Moses*. Fresco. Logge, Vatican Palace. Vatican State.

At any rate, except for Kadesh-barnea, the place names cited in this parenthesis all allude to the events associated with the place. At Taberah ("Fire"), Israel complained about their sparse circumstances. Provoked, YHWH sent *fire* upon the people (Num 11:1-3). Earlier, even before the giving of the covenant at Mt. Horeb, the people complained about the lack of water, accusing Moses of poor leadership (Exod 17:1-7). YHWH commanded Moses to strike a rock from which water then gushed.

Because the people put Moses and YHWH to the test, in effect, the place was named Massah ("Proof") and Meribah ("Contention"). According to the chronology of the book of Numbers, the incident at Hibroth-hataavah ("Graves of craving") followed soon after the Taberah incident. The Israelites, weary of an uninterrupted diet of manna, expressed their longing for fish, cucumbers, melons, leeks, onions, garlic, and meat. Moses took the matter to YHWH, who agreed to supply the people with meat in abundance for a brief period. A wind blew quails to Israel, who gathered them in great quantities. But YHWH was angry with them for their ingratitude, and he sent a plague upon them. Many Israelites died and were buried in "graves of craving" (Num 11:4-34).

These incidents of Israelite dissatisfaction illustrate Israel's tendency to complain. In their shortsightedness, they expressed a preference for leeks and garlic, even if slavery in Egypt were a condition, to a period of hardship as the price of freedom. Varied menus were of greater significance to them than the gifts of freedom and relationship with YHWH. Like children complaining about healthy dinner menus, their selfishness left no room for gratitude that they were able to eat at all! These are not examples of outright disobedience to YHWH's commandments like the Gold Calf episode, but of Israel's petty ingratitude. On the other hand, Israel willfully and defiantly disobeyed YHWH's direct and explicit command to move out from Kadesh-barnea to take possession of the promised land (Num 13:1–14:45; Deut 1:19-46). Israel was small-minded, ungrateful, fearful, and disobedient. Clearly, YHWH did not choose them for their exemplary righteousness!

Moses' Intercession on Israel's Behalf, 9:25-29

To this point, the case for Israel's habitual "unrighteousness" has been made forcefully. Obviously, Israel has not merited YHWH's favor. From the outset they have been disobedient malcontents. The case has been made so effectively, in fact, that the reader may now entertain the opposite question. Since Israel is so demonstrably unworthy of YHWH's favor—having broken the covenant within days of its proclamation, even before its provisions were put into writing—how is it that YHWH continues in relationship with them?

Moses' intercessory prayer on Israel's behalf (vv. 25-29), the climactic component of Deuteronomy 9, displays a keen awareness of this problem and very instructively appeals to grounds for YHWH's forgiveness of Israel and continued relationship with it that are wholly unrelated to Israel's obedience to the covenant. If Israel must rely on its own obedience as the basis for its relationship with YHWH, it is without hope! The logic of Moses' prayer develops clearly and succinctly in four steps. First, following the narrative introduction in v. 25, Moses asks YHWH not to consider Israel's sinfulness, but to remember Israel's status as the elect (v. 26)—a choice YHWH himself made. Second, Moses appeals positively to YHWH's faithfulness to his promise (v. 27). Third, Moses draws the negative inference that YHWH's reputation with the nations of the world is at stake (v. 28). Can Israel, or anyone for that matter, rely on YHWH to keep his word? Finally, Moses concludes with a reiteration of the opening reminder of Israel's unique relationship to YHWH founded in YHWH's promise—and not in Israel's obedience (v. 29).

The core of Moses' argument that YHWH should spare Israel consists, then, in his reminder of YHWH's promise and his warning concerning YHWH's reputation. Moses asks YHWH to "remember your servants Abraham, Isaac, and Jacob (*zĕkōr laʿăbādêkā lĕʾabrāhām lĕyiṣḥāq ûlĕyaʿăqōb*)," employing a phrase that is difficult to translate into English. A "literal" translation would read "remember *to* your servants, to Abraham, etc." The idiom "to remember to" (*zkr* [in the qal stem] + *lĕ*) occurs nineteen times in the Hebrew Bible.[1] With one exception (Jer 2:2), it always occurs in settings in which a petitioner appeals to YHWH for salvation or forgiveness on the basis of some situation or relationship that preceded the breech of relationship, or in which a worshiper thanks God for having done so. In all these usages, it seems to imply more than simply "remembering," serving instead as an appeal to a basis for YHWH's grace and favor that precedes and transcends the negatives of the current situation.[2] In effect, Moses calls YHWH to account for keeping his *unconditional* promise to the patriarchs, the ultimate basis for YHWH's relationship with Israel![3]

Should the challenge to remain faithful to his promise prove insufficient grounds for YHWH's forgiveness, Moses goes on to invoke the possibility that YHWH's reputation may suffer (v. 28). The nations may conclude that YHWH is incapable of bringing his people into the promised land, or—even worse—that he had never intended to deliver Israel, that the exodus was merely a deception! Moses very effectively shifts the focus of the crisis from Israel's inconstancy and rebellion to YHWH's determination, fidelity, and honor. Will YHWH allow his intention to fulfill his promise to the patriarchs to be thwarted by Israel's sin? Does Israel's relationship with YHWH hinge ultimately on Israel's faithfulness? Can frail human nature bear such weight?

It is important to remember at this point that, although Deuteronomy 9 records Moses' intercessory prayer at Sinai as it was recounted to the second generation after Sinai, it was *recorded in Deuteronomy* for subsequent generations of Israel. These later generations had more than a historical interest in the case Moses made for YHWH's forgiveness of Israel. In fact, judging from the account of the discovery of what must have been an early form of Deuteronomy in the temple during the reign of king Josiah (c. 623/622 BC), the first readers of the *book* of Deuteronomy will have been facing the covenant crisis that resulted in the Babylonian conquest of Judah and the exile of thousands of prominent Judeans. To these generations of Israel, Moses' intercessory prayer, and more importantly YHWH's response, must have been an essential foundation for hope. Although, as the prophets, especially Jeremiah and Ezekiel, had proclaimed, Judah had broken faith with YHWH, and although YHWH had delivered first Israel, then Judah to the consequences of their infidelity, the course of YHWH's relationship with his people would ultimately be determined by YHWH's constancy, not by the people's sin. Moses had established the principle already as far back as the golden calf episode. Israel sins and bears correction, to be sure, for breech of

---

God's Faithfulness and Righteousness: Romans 3 and the Debate over Paul's Theology

"Does their unfaithfulness nullify the faithfulness of God? By no means! Let God be true though every person be false . . . But now the righteousness of God has been manifested apart from law, although the law and the prophets bear witness to it, the righteousness of God through the faithfulness of Jesus Christ for all who believe. . . ." (Rom 3:2b-4a, 21-22)

As Deut 9:1–10:11 clearly demonstrate, the commonly held view of the Hebrew Bible, especially of the Torah or books of Moses, as legalistic does not accurately reflect the text itself. This caricature, which dichotomizes faith and works, grace and the Law, lies at the source of many errors in biblical interpretation, Christian theology, church practice, and private devotion. Not the least of these errors concerns what may prove to have been a long-standing misreading of the letters of Paul in the New Testament. Typically, Paul has been seen as arguing that the Law failed as a means for justifying sinners. Those familiar with the dynamics of grace and the Law in the Hebrew Bible may well wonder how Paul, trained as a rabbi, could have so skewed his portrayal of the Torah.

In recent years, scholars have begun to see Paul somewhat differently. The authors of numerous books and articles have engaged in lively debate over the meaning of key terms and phrases such as "the righteousness of God" and "the faith of Christ" in the letters of Paul. The difficulty lies, in part, in the syntactical ambiguity of the Greek expressions. The Greek grammatical feature often represented by the English preposition "of" is notoriously ambiguous. The "righteousness *of* God," for example, may be understood to refer to the righteousness that characterizes God or to the righteousness that God gives. Similarly, the "faith *of* Christ" may refer to Christ's own faith(fulness) or to faith placed in him by the believer. The question of the precise connotations of "righteousness" and "faith(fulness)" only further complicates the situation.

Until most recently, the discussion hinged around two alternatives: namely, whether Paul's doctrine of justification by faith should be understood chiefly in forensic or in ethical terms. Does God *declare* the sinner to be justified in response to the sinner's faith in Christ in a legal fiction (forensically)? Or does God *make* the sinner just as an act of regeneration (ethically)? Both of these interpretations understand the term most often translated "righteousness" in relation to what God requires of human beings.

Understood against the background of the Hebrew Bible, especially passages such as Moses' intercessory prayer, however, the phrase "righteousness of God" may not refer to God's expectations of human beings at all, but to the righteousness that is God's. In this case, the term "righteousness" (Greek *dikaisounē*, Hebrew *ṣĕdāqâ*) would not primarily refer to legal demands placed on human beings and including the punishment of the guilty, but to the notion of fidelity to one's character, to one's promises, and above all, to relationship. In relation to human sin, it would emphasize God's steadfast intention to put right that which has gone awry in God's relationship with human beings. Seen from this perspective, the righteousness of God is not that pure holiness that requires God to punish sin—the righteousness Luther so feared—but God's determination to set right those elements of individual and social existence that have gone wrong. The sinner can rely on God to be true, to be righteous, not to abandon God's creation to its own folly and sin. In the end—Paul and the book of Deuteronomy agree—neither works, nor repentance, nor even faith in God saves. God saves. God forgives and restores because God remains true to God's self.

covenant. But, as Moses successfully argued, YHWH's relationship with Israel is not, in the first instance, a function of Israel's faithfulness to the covenant. It depends not on *Israel's* righteousness, but on *YHWH's*. YHWH will be true to his promise. [God's Faithfulness and Righteousness: Romans 3 and the Debate over Paul's Theology]

YHWH Replaces the Tablets, 10:1-11

YHWH's response to Moses' prayer is remarkable. Not only does he reconsider his plan to eradicate Israel and to begin anew with Moses and his descendants, but YHWH also replaces the original, broken (both literally and metaphorically) tablets of the covenant with a second, identical pair. Even though it was necessary for Moses, fulfilling the role of the loyal opposition, to call YHWH back to his true character, YHWH's response nonetheless demonstrates beyond question YHWH's determination not to be deterred from his original purpose. YHWH will not abandon his intention expressed in the creation of a good world, in the covenant with Noah, in the call of the patriarchs, in the exodus and the giving of the covenant.

In fact, several unusual features of the summary conclusion to this account of Israel's rebellion with the golden calf only serve to underscore the fact that YHWH responded to Moses' intercession by continuing the relationship. First, the expected divine response to Moses' intercession does not follow immediately, but only after the narration, very succinct in comparison to the Exodus parallel, of the conclusion of Israel's encampment at Mt. Horeb. The phrasing of v. 10, "and YHWH heard me then, too," hints at a second intercessory prayer such as the one recorded in Exodus 33:12-16 (there, however, *prior* to Moses' second ascent). In other words, Deuteronomy's version emphasizes the fact that, because of YHWH's willingness to forgive Israel, the golden calf episode did not delay Israel's journey.

As in Exodus, Deuteronomy recounts that Moses ascended the mountain a second time to receive a replacement copy of the two tablets of the Law. Deuteronomy omits Moses' request to behold YHWH that is incorporated in the Exodus account of his second intercession (Exod 33:12-16) and provides an alternative account of the construction of the ark of the covenant.[4] Once again, Deuteronomy emphasizes the fact that YHWH persisted in his original intention for covenant relationship with Israel.

The insertion concerning the Levites (Deut 10:6-9) disrupts the continuity between Deuteronomy 10:5 and 10:10 and seems to represent an awkward adaptation of material from the book of Numbers. Again, the important feature of this information in relation to Moses' intercession has to do with Aaron's role in the golden calf episode. His guilt is unmistakable, yet YHWH permits him to continue in his priestly role until his death at Moserah. Furthermore, his son Eleazar succeeded him. The editor combined an excerpt of Israel's itinerary after departing Mt. Horeb (vv. 6-7; see Num 33:30; 31:38; 33:32-34) with an excerpt of the tradition concerning the special status of the tribe of Levi, in this case the levitical responsibility for carrying the ark (Num 3:6; 4:15) and yet another tradition explaining Levi's lack of its own territory within Israel (Num 18:20, 24). Apparently, the editor, who wished to emphasize the continuity in YHWH's relationship with Israel even after the golden calf episode, substituted for the version in Exodus 32:28-29 ("they ordained themselves" for service to YHWH by exercising vengeance on the sinners among the people) this alternate explanation for the unique role of the Levites in Israelite culture.

CONNECTIONS

The life of the great Protestant reformer, Martin Luther, stands as a powerful depiction of an individual's struggle to come to an understanding and acceptance of God's grace. His descriptions of his life prior to his discovery of the principle of justification by faith (*sola fidei*, "by faith alone") reveal a man acutely aware of the holiness of God and of his own inability to meet the requirements of this holiness. As an Augustinian monk, he strove mightily to attain purity, but his hypersensitivity to God's grandeur and his own frailty and sin tormented him continuously.

Luther recounted his experience on the occasion of celebrating his first mass as a terrible encounter with the supreme holiness of God. When the time had come for him to pronounce the words, "We offer unto thee, the living, the true, the eternal God," he was overcome. As he later described the moment:

> At these words I was utterly stupefied and terror-stricken. I thought to myself, "With what tongue shall I address such Majesty, seeing that all men [sic] ought to tremble in the presence of even an earthly prince? Who am I, that I should lift up mine eyes or raise my hands to the divine Majesty? The angels surround him. At his nod the earth trembles.

And shall I, a miserable little pygmy, say 'I want this, I ask for that'? For I am dust and ashes and full of sin and I am speaking to the living, eternal and the true God."

Following the episode, Luther's attention fastened on the question of whether one dare approach the Holy One of Israel at all unless one were oneself holy. He doubled and redoubled his efforts at penitence. He fasted unduly, for example, wore little clothing, and intentionally slept uncovered even in the depths of winter. On a pilgrimage to Rome, he climbed Pilate's stairs on his hands and knees, repeating the *Pater Noster* with each step. Moving from Erfurt to Wittenberg after this trip to Rome, he determined to obtain forgiveness and absolution for all his sins, great and small, by an exhaustive soul-searching and confession of them all. The possibility that some forgotten error could go unconfessed terrorized him. Attempts to find peace through mystical contemplation only added to his sense of dread, fear, and even hatred toward God.

Contrary to what might be expected of one who went to such lengths, Luther considered himself no great sinner. He reasoned simply that any sin whatsoever disqualified one for communion with the Holy God (compare Jas 2:10, "For whoever keeps the whole law but fails in one point has become guilty of all of it"). Luther's comments on Jesus' teachings concerning anger in the Sermon on the Mount demonstrate his sensibilities:

> This word is too high and too hard that anyone should fulfill it. This is proved, not merely by our Lord's word, but by our own experience and feeling. Take any upright man or woman. He will get along very nicely with those who do not provoke him, but let someone proffer only the slightest irritation and he will flare up in anger, . . . if not against friends, then against enemies. Flesh and blood cannot rise above it.

Eventually, Luther's struggles led him to the Scriptures, specifically to Paul's Epistle to the Romans, and to the same basis for hope upon which Moses based his appeal to YHWH on Israel's behalf— namely God's faithfulness. Again, Luther's own words relate his insights most poignantly:

> I greatly longed to understand Paul's Epistle to the Romans and nothing stood in the way but that one expression, "the justice of God," because I took it to mean that justice whereby God is just and deals justly in punishing the unjust. My situation was that, although an impeccable monk, I stood before God as a sinner troubled in conscience, and I had no confidence that my merit would assuage him. Therefore I did not love a just

and angry God, but rather hated and murmured against him. Yet I clung
to the dear Paul and had a great yearning to know what he meant.
Night and day I pondered until I saw the connection between the justice
of God and the statement that "the just shall live by his faith." Then I
grasped that the justice of God is that righteousness by which through
grace and sheer mercy God justifies us through faith. Thereupon I felt
myself to be reborn and to have gone through open doors into paradise.[5]

Conventionally, Christian interpretation of the Hebrew Bible
and its theology has emphasized the fundamentally covenantal
character of Israelite religion and of Judaism, one of its children. In
fact, several Christian Old Testament theologies written earlier in
this century took the concept of "covenant" as the organizing principle and foundation of the entire Old Testament.[6] The crisis of
Israel's experience with the golden calf at Mt. Horeb/Sinai, like
Luther's sustained and systematic attempt to attain status before
God, lays bare the inadequacy of such a view. [God's Grace and the
"Scrupulous" Conscience] Before the ink was dry on the covenant agreement between Israel and YHWH, as it were, Israel had violated the
most basic provision of that covenant: exclusive fidelity to YHWH.
Only YHWH's determination to remain true, not to the
covenant—according to its provisions, the relationship between
YHWH and Israel could be considered broken—but to his
promise and his character as deliverer spared Israel from the end of
relationship.

The experiences of Moses and Luther, though unique in many
ways, demonstrate several common aspects of the absolutely foundational nature of the believer's dependence upon God's gracious
faithfulness to God's intention to do humanity good and not ill.
First, those who know the joy of God's gracious call must accept
relationship with God in utter humility. Just as God's gift of life
itself is entirely unearned and unmerited, relationship with God
cannot be achieved. Karl Barth, the influential founder of a major
twentieth-century theological movement known variously as
"dialectical theology" or "neo-orthodoxy," often defined "religion"
as the almost universally human effort to attain relationship with
God (or the gods).[7] This "religion," he argued (no matter whether
it bears the name of Christianity or Judaism or Shinto), is tantamount to idolatry. It equates with the rich young ruler's interest in
fulfilling the requirements for inheriting eternal life (Mark 10), to
justifying oneself, to earning salvation. Instead, Barth argued, God
can only be known through God's initiative; salvation can only be
God's free gift. Humans do not and cannot come to God on their
own. God must come to humans.

God's Grace and the "Scrupulous" Conscience

Israel's outrageous sin and YHWH's angry decision to destroy his people immediately reduced Moses to a state of utter dependence upon YHWH's faithfulness to his own character—to reliance upon God's free, unmerited grace expressed in a promise. Moses simply had no other grounds for hope. Luther, on the other hand, came to the realization that this grace was his only basis for hope only after many attempts to find some basis rooted in his own human efforts for relationship with God.

The evidence of everyday human experience suggests that people more often follow Luther than Moses. Owing to a number of factors characteristic of human nature, people typically find it easier to give intellectual assent to this fundamental claim of biblical theology—that God relates benevolently to God's creation simply and solely because God chooses to do so in fidelity to God's character—than to incorporate its truth into their daily lives. How many pastors preach lofty, theologically orthodox Sunday morning sermons on the grace of God only to toil long hours the following week visiting, meeting, planning, and preparing to teach and preach, seeking to satisfy some stereotype of ministerial perfection? Sociological studies document the toll paid by ministers' families and the high incidence of ministerial "burnout." Those who preach grace often fail to accept it in their own lives.

Seward Hiltner, a pioneer in the field of pastoral theology, offers an astute analysis of the psycho-spiritual dynamics involved in the difficulties people manifest in accepting the gift of grace. Luther seems to have been an example of what the Roman Catholic tradition sometimes refers to as a "scrupulous" person. Hiltner describes such people as those who "are unable to accept assurances of forgiveness as the normal person can when he repents, confesses, and resolves to do better. Today we see such scrupulosity as a form of obsessionalism." Such scrupulosity regards sin and guilt to be more powerful than God's grace despite the ample testimony of Scripture that God values human beings, created in God's image, supremely—enough, in fact, to persist in God's efforts to redeem and bless, enough "that he gave his only begotten Son . . ." (John 3:16).

Sometimes people accept the gift of grace initially only to come later to resent it. "Even with a good and needed gift," Hiltner observes, "the power of the other to give it reminds us of our dependency. In psychiatric terms, this situation reactivates our infantile sense of helplessness and our resentment over it." Since the Garden of Eden, human beings have always longed to be self-sufficient.

It can be argued that both the scrupulous and the resentful manifest the basic human flaw of self-importance. The scrupulous person believes that his or her sin exceeds God's grace. The resentful person wishes to be free of his or her dependence upon God's grace. Either sentiment can give rise to a form of religion based on efforts to earn salvation, to legalism and perfectionism.

Seward Hiltner, *Theological Dynamics* (Nashville: Abingdon, 1972), 46-47, 84.

Second, although the resemblance on this point between Luther and ancient Israel encamped at the foot of Mt. Horeb/Sinai may escape one's attention at first glance, each fell prey to the human urge for religiosity: Luther in the form of ritual and penance and prayer; Israel in the form of the need for a visible, controllable deity. Luther's experience reminds one of the awful burden of perfectionism; ancient Israel's experience warns against the easy association of the creation with the Creator. Both testify to the inevitability of "falling short of the glory of God" (Rom 3:23).

Finally, ancient Israel and Luther were both forced to the realization that, given human frailty—sooner or later, blatantly or secretly—ultimately the only basis of hope for any and everyone is God's faithfulness. Indeed, contrary to conventional Christian understandings of the theology of the Hebrew Bible, including the interpretations of Reformers such as Luther and neo-Orthodox theologians such as Barth, the Hebrew Bible itself frequently calls attention to the priority of God's faithfulness to his character and promise over human obedience to the covenant (for example, Exod 2:24; Josh 24:2-3; Isa 40:6-8). To be sure, the dimension of covenant shapes a life of faith, but only God's steadfast "prevenient" determination enables that life.

NOTES

[1] Exod 32:13 (the parallel account of Moses' intercessory prayer); Deut 9:27; Pss 25:7; 98:3; 105:8; 106:45; 111:5; 119:47; 132:1; 136:23; 137:7; 1 Chr 16:15; 2 Chr 6:42; Neh 5:19; 6:14; 13:14, 22, 31; Jer 2:2.

[2] For detailed studies of the phrase "remember to someone['s benefit]," see B. S. Childs, *Memory and Tradition in Israel*, SBT 37 (London: SCM Press, 1962), 35-44; P. de Boer, *Gedenken und Gedächtnis in der Welt des Alten Testaments: Franz Delitzsch Vorlesungen 1960* (Stuttgart: W. Kohlhammer, 1962); W. Schottroff, *Gedenken im Alten Orient und im Alten Testament: Die Wurzel Zakar im semitischen Sprachkreis* (WMANT 15; Neukirchen-Vluyn: Neukirchener Verlag, 1964); and M. Biddle, *A Redaction History of Jeremiah 2:1–4:2* (AThANT 77; Zurich: Theologischer Verlag Zürich, 1990), 166-72.

[3] For the significance of such a claim in the history of Israel's covenant theology, see J. Van Seters, "Confessional Reformulation in the Exilic Period," *VT* 22 (1972): 448-59.

[4] Compare Deut 10:3, 5 (Moses constructs the ark to contain the tablets of the Law *before* ascending the mountain) and Exod 37:1-9 (on YHWH's instruction through Moses, Bezalel constructs the ark as a component of the furnishings for the Tent of Meeting after Moses descends the mountain).

[5] This discussion of Martin Luther's spiritual journey, including the quotations, depends heavily on Roland Bainton's magisterial *Here I Stand: A Life of Martin Luther* (Nashville: Abingdon, 1978), esp. 18-50.

[6] Most notably, W. Eichrodt's two-volume *Old Testament Theology*, trans. J. Baker (OTL; Philadelphia: Westminster, 1961).

[7] See K. Barth, "No!," in *Natural Theology: Comprising "Nature and Grace" by Emil Brunner and the reply "No!" by Karl Barth*, trans. Peter Fraenkel (London: The Centenary Press, 1946) = "Nein! Antwort an Emil Brunner," Theologische Existenz Heute 14 (München, 1934).

A SUMMARY CALL TO COVENANT OBEDIENCE

10:12–11:32

A loosely structured collection of fragments of Deuteronomic preaching on the general subject of covenant obedience concludes the extended parenetic introduction to the law code contained in Deuteronomy 12–26. Although some scholars have seen in this passage an imperfect attempt to conform to the structure of the ancient Near Eastern treaty (declaration of basic principles, 10:12–11:1; summary of the previous history of the relationship, 11:2-7; blessings and curses, 11:16-17, 22-31),[1] it can perhaps best be described as a somewhat free-form résumé of the already repetitive argument of the preceding parenetic/hortatory material. [ANE Treaty Forms] Allusions to and citations of passages in Deuteronomy 6–10, especially of the Shema, abound. [Allusions to the Shema] Despite its fragmentary structure, these linkages back to the Shema, in particular, serve to consolidate the themes of the parenetic introduction to the Deuteronomic Code under a common rubric: "Hear, O Israel, YHWH is our God, YHWH alone."

ANE Treaty Forms

Scholars have noted interesting parallels between the structure of Deuteronomy, on the whole and in its parts, and certain ancient Near Eastern treaties. Fourteenth century BC Hittite suzerainty treaties, which establish and regulate the relationship between an overlord and his vassal, for example, typically consist of six sections: (1) a prologue identifying the parties, (2) a summary of the previous history of the relationship, (3) the conditions of the covenant per se, (4) a provision for the preservation and periodic public reading of the covenant document, (5) a list of deities acting as guarantors of the covenant, and (6) the treaty curses and blessings.

See George Mendanhall, *Law and Covenant in Israel and the Ancient Near East* (Pittsburgh: Biblical Colloquium, 1955).

COMMENTARY

Israel's Duty is Clear, 10:12-19

The almost stream-of-consciousness logic of this section makes it difficult to establish clearly the boundaries of its constituents. The vocative "And now, O Israel!" unmistakably indicates a new beginning, but no similar markers occur in the following sequence of

Allusions to the Shema

AΩ The following are only a few of the parallels between Deut 6:1–10:11 and 10:12–11:32.

. . . and you shall love the LORD your God with all your heart, and with all your soul, and with all your might. (6:5)

. . . to love him, to serve the LORD your God with all your heart and with all your soul . . . (10:12)
. . . to love the LORD your God, and to serve him with all your heart and with all your soul . . . (11:13)
. . . in your heart and in your soul . . . (11:18)

And these words which I command you this day shall be upon your heart; and you shall teach them diligently to your children, and shall talk of them when you sit in your house, and when you walk by the way, and when you lie down, and when you rise. And you shall bind them as a sign upon your hand, and they shall be as frontlets between your eyes. And you shall write them on the doorposts of your house and on your gates. (6:6-9)

You shall therefore lay up these words of mine in your heart and in your soul; and you shall bind them as a sign upon your hand, and they shall be as frontlets between your eyes. And you shall teach them to your children, talking of them when you are sitting in your house, and when you are walking by the way, and when you lie down, and when you rise. And you shall write them upon the doorposts of your house and upon your gates . . . (11:18-20)

It was not because you were more in number than any other people that the LORD set his love upon you and chose you, for you were the fewest of all peoples. (7:7)

. . . to the LORD your God belong heaven and the heaven of heavens, the earth with all that is in it; yet the LORD set his heart in love upon your fathers and chose their descendants after them, you above all peoples . . . (10:14-15)

Know therefore, that the LORD your God is not giving you this good land to possess because of your righteousness; for you are a stubborn people. (9:6; cf. 9:13, 24)

Circumcise therefore the foreskin of your heart, and be no longer stubborn. (10:16)

For the LORD your God is bringing you into a good land, a land of brooks of water, of fountains and springs, flowing forth in valleys and hills, a land of wheat and barley, of vines and fig trees and pomegranates, a land of olive trees and honey, a land in which you will eat bread without scarcity, in which you will lack nothing, a land whose stones are iron, and out of whose hills you can dig copper. (8:7-9)

. . . but the land which you are going over to possess is a land of hills and valleys, which drinks water by the rain from heaven, a land which the LORD your God cares for; the eyes of the LORD your God are always upon it, from the beginning of the year to the end of the year. (11:11-12)

When the LORD your God brings you into the land which you are entering to take possession of it, and clears away many nations before you, the Hittites, the Girgashites, the Amorites, the Canaanites, the Perizzites, the Hivites, and the Jebusites, seven nations greater and mightier than yourselves . . . (7:1)

. . . then the LORD will drive out all these nations before you, and you will dispossess nations greater and mightier than yourselves. (11:23)

You shall fear the LORD your God; you shall serve him, and swear by his name. (6:13)

You shall fear the LORD your God; you shall serve him and cleave to him, and by his name you shall swear. (10:20)

. . . that you may fear the LORD your God, you and your son and your son's son, by keeping all his statutes and his commandments, which I command you, all the days of your life; and that your days may be prolonged. (6:2)

. . . and you shall love the LORD your God with all your heart, and with all your soul, and with all your might. (6:5)

You shall therefore love the LORD your God, and keep his charge, his statutes, his ordinances, and his commandments always. (11:1) admonitions and declarations. In contrast to good English style, which abhors repetitive use of the conjunction "and," Hebrew syntax relies heavily on the conjunction to link phrases and whole sentences in a coherent unit. Syntactically, the sequence of dependent clauses and conjunctively linked sentences beginning in v. 12 ends with the call to love the sojourner issued in v. 19. Even this syntactic coherence is very loose, however.

Thematically, the argument opens with a paraphrase of the Shema ("with all your heart and with all your soul," vv. 12-13), and continues with a reminder that, although the Lord of the universe with all of creation at his command and all the nations of the world at his disposal, YHWH still chose Israel. Although he is the God of gods and the Lord of lords, YHWH shows no partiality to the mighty or the powerful. Instead, YHWH demonstrates protective concern not only for insignificant Israel, but also for Israelite society's most vulnerable and powerless: widows, orphans, and resident aliens (v. 18). Indeed, YHWH demands that Israel emulate its God by "loving" the resident alien just as YHWH had loved Israel when it was a resident alien in Egypt (v. 19).

This remarkable logical sequence begins with a rhetorical question (compare Mic 6:8) that implies by its very structure that YHWH's expectations of Israel are neither complicated, nor impossible, nor obscure. By nature, rhetorical questions call attention to the obvious (compare the parent's "What did I tell you to do with the peanut butter when you're finished with it?"); they are not designed to elicit new information. The question of whether the four verbs describing YHWH's expectations of Israel should be understood as synonyms for one another or as a depiction of a hierarchy of behaviors cannot be answered with confidence. Interestingly, the verb "to love," which so dominates the Shema, occupies only third position here, alongside verbs of obedience and respect. Once again, modern readers must remember that the concept of love for YHWH found in Deuteronomy bears virtually no resemblance to present-day notions of love as a passionate emotion (see commentary on 6:5). In the book of Deuteronomy, love is either synonymous with or based upon respect for YHWH. It involves definite actions (v. 13, "walking in his ways" = "keeping his commandments"). It manifests itself in service. As in the Shema, the adverbial phrase (answering the question How?), "with all your heart and all your being," indicates the total scope of YHWH's expectation—no area of one's life falls outside the realm of YHWH's claim (see commentary on 6:4-5).

"Yet YHWH loved your ancestors"

Perhaps surprisingly for many of its readers, the Hebrew Bible very rarely asserts that YHWH "loves" Israel. Instead, the most common descriptions of YHWH's relationship with Israel involve vocabulary consistent with the image of YHWH as Israel's only God, its king, or its Redeemer. As Israel's only God, YHWH lays claim to Israel's total devotion; as king, YHWH calls Israel to some action or commands obedience to the divine will; as redeemer, YHWH brings out of bondage and leads in the wilderness. Typically, the Hebrew Bible discusses YHWH's activity on Israel's behalf and YHWH's expectations of them, but remains relatively silent with respect to YHWH's reasons for choosing to relate to Israel in this special way. Several texts trace YHWH's determination to relate to Israel in keeping with the promise made the patriarchs (see [The Promise to the Patriarchs in Deuteronomy]), but even these texts characteristically avoid any attempt to explain the reasons for YHWH's interest in Israel's ancestors.

Deut 10:15, however, represents a series of exceptional, and therefore significant, texts concentrated in Deuteronomy (7:7; 10:15; 23:6), Hosea (3:1; 11:1, for example), Jeremiah (31:3, for example), and, to a lesser degree, Ezekiel (18:8; compare also 1 Kgs 10:9 [= 2 Chr 2:10 = 9:8]; Isa 43:4; 63:9; Zeph 3:17; and Mal 1:2). These texts (especially Hosea, Jeremiah, and Ezekiel) describe YHWH's *feelings* for Israel in analogy to the love of a husband for his wife or of a father for his child (Hos 11–14). Deut 7:7 and 10:15 go so far as to describe YHWH's interest in Israel as "yearning" or "desire," employing the relatively rare verb *ḥšq* used elsewhere to denote Shechem's longing for Dinah (Gen 34:8) or the Israelite master's desire for one of the women prisoners of war (Deut 21:11). The verb also appears once to describe

the petitioner's longing for God (Ps 91:14) and twice in parallel texts concerning Solomon's wish to build the temple in Jerusalem (1 Kgs 9:19 = 2 Chr 8:6). (Isa 38:17 is textually uncertain.) The term can almost be characterized as romantic!

In the context of the doctrine of election reflected in the book of Deuteronomy, three observations are in order. First, theological language is by definition metaphorical. Humans seek to understand and describe their experience of God through the only means available to them—human experience and human language. The Bible assumes that, although God is certainly beyond total and perfect comprehension, the fact that humanity is made in God's image must mean that human beings are somehow *like* God. Therefore, human experience and language are capable of expressing something of God's nature, although, in the case at hand, few would want to argue that God longed for Israel in precisely the same way young Shechem desired the beautiful Dinah.

Second, the Bible insists relatedly that the God of Israel, the father of Jesus Christ, is not the almost mathematical First Principle of some theological and philosophical systems. The God of the Bible is not "pure love" or "pure energy" or "the life force." The God of the Bible is *personal*. Israel's God desires, can be angered or disappointed, seeks relationship, etc. Theological systems that reduce God to some "unmoved mover" reduce the image of God to the subhuman.

Third, given the insistence of 10:12-19 that Israel is an insignificant and rebellious people, the statement that YHWH "desired" the patriarchs cannot be seen as the basis for the notion that Israel merited God's favor. Election remains securely mysterious. If anything, the fact that YHWH "desired" Israel's ancestors, despite their flaws and obscurity, only heightens the mystery.

What is the basis for YHWH's claim to Israel's exclusive and total obedience? Paradoxically, the Creator and Supreme Lord of all[2] chose Israel's ancestors, the patriarchs, and their descendants. Once again, Deuteronomy lays open the mystery of divine election. This supreme God, "great, mighty, and terrible" (v. 17) "clung to" (see ["Yet YHWH loved your ancestors"]) Israel's ancestors "to love them and choose their seed after them." The paradox of election consists in the fact that this mighty deity "shows no partiality" (literally, "does not lift his face") and cannot be bribed. Since all is his by right of ownership, the wealthy and powerful have nothing to offer him. Instead, of his own gracious choosing, he devotes particular care to

Parallelismus Membrorum

Scholars employ the Latin phrase *parallelismus membrorum*, "parallelism of members," to describe a characteristic feature of Hebrew language and thought. Hebrew poetry does not utilize rhyme or any discernible system of meter. Instead, it exhibits what might be described as a "symmetry of thought units" that also appears in less concentrated form in Hebrew prose. This symmetry seems to have shaped Hebrew thought. Typically, lines of Hebrew poetry divide into two generally balanced parts that reflect an overall symmetry of grammatical structure, length, and even content. These two subdivisions of a line of poetry combine to make a single statement. The second half of the line may repeat with some variation the statement made in the first (so-called "synonymous" parallelism; Ps 67:1, for example: "May God be gracious to us and bless us, and cause his face to shine on us . . ."). The second half may expand, amplify, or further define the idea contained in the first (so-called "synthetic" or "step" parallelism; Ps 4:5: "Offer proper sacrifices; and put your trust in YHWH."). Or, the second half may state the opposite of the first so that together they encompass the whole (so-called "antithetical" parallelism; Ps 1:6: ". . . YHWH knows the way of the righteous, but the way of the wicked will perish.").

This feature of the Hebrew language often provides indispensable clues to the interpretation of a passage of Scripture. Deut 10:16 clearly exhibits this parallel structure: "Circumcise the foreskin of your heart," a very picturesque metaphorical expression, parallels "be no longer stiff-necked." The second clause can and should be understood as an alternative statement of the idea contained in the initial metaphor, that is, as a case of "synonymous parallelism." At issue is Israel's willfulness, its tendency to resist YHWH's leadership and authority. The second clause underscores the volitional, decision-making function of the heart in the ancient Hebrew understanding.

---

those at the margins—the nation Israel, on the one hand, and the powerless in Israelite society, on the other.

The fact that YHWH, the Supreme Lord of Creation, chose Israel yields two admonitions. First (v. 16), Israel should "circumcise the foreskins of their hearts." This graphic metaphor[3] calls on Israel to sanctify the organ of volition (on the heart as the seat of volition, the organ of decision-making, see the commentary on 6:4-5), to prepare for obedience to YHWH. Of course, the heart cannot be circumcised literally. Even on a metaphorical level, it is difficult to envision what might be "removed." The key to understanding the image lies in recognizing circumcision as an inaugural rite that prepares one for full membership in the covenant people. In this regard, the metaphor resembles others that contrast hearts of stone and hearts of flesh (Ezek 11:19; 36:26) and describe the covenant written on the hearts of individuals instead of on stone tablets (Jer 31:31-34). The second phrase in the *parallelismus membrorum* of v. 16 (see [Parallelismus Membrorum]) clarifies the precise intention. Israel is to cease its stubborn rebellion (literally, Israel is "stiff-necked," an idiom for "intractable") against the will of YHWH. Israel's will needs to be corrected.

Widows, Orphans, and Resident Aliens

The Hebrew Bible, especially the book of Deuteronomy, often groups the resident alien (*gēr*), the widow (*'almānâ*), and the orphan (*yātôm*) together as classes of people for whom God has particular concern (in the order alien/widow/orphan: Deut 10:18; 16:11, 14; 24:17, 19, 20, 21; 26:12, 13; 27:15; Jer 7:6; 22:3; Ezek 22:7; Ps 146:9; in the order widow/orphan/alien: Mal 3:5; Ps 94:6). For unique reasons, these groups of people did not enjoy the status of full citizenship: aliens for obvious reasons, widows because women derived legal status from their fathers, husbands, or adult sons, and orphans because they were minors. Other classes of people with diminished rights sometimes mentioned alongside orphans, widows, and resident aliens, or some subset thereof, include Levites (since the tribe of Levi was given no territory in Israel, Levites depended upon the tithes and offerings of their fellow Israelites; Deut 16:14; 26:13), the outcast (*gĕrušâ*: Lev 22:13; Num 30:10; Ezek 44:22), and the destitute (*'ānî*: Zech 7:10).

Because the legal system put these groups at disadvantage, God not only promised to care for them (Deut 10:18), but also warned against mistreating them (Jer 7:6). Deuteronomy expresses particular concern for them. In fact, the Deuteronomic Code grants them certain special privileges (14:29; 16:11, 14; 24:29-21; 26:12-13).

The book of Ruth represents a narrative example of the situation faced by widows (Naomi and Ruth) and resident aliens (Ruth). Sensing an honorable man in Boaz because he had gone above and beyond the Law's requirements for making provision for the widow, Naomi instructed Ruth, in effect, to throw herself on his mercy. Indeed, Boaz willingly took Ruth in marriage, redeeming the property belonging to her dead husband's family, and fathering a son. The precarious status of these women before Boaz's intervention illustrates the situation underlying Deuteronomy's concern for them.

Second, perhaps the most striking feature of the logical progression apparent in this unit is its concluding statement concerning ethics. The triplet "widow, orphan, and resident alien" appears frequently in Deuteronomy (10:18; 14:29; 16:11, 14; 24:17, 19, 20, 21; 26:12, 13; 27:19) and in texts influenced by it (Jer 7:6; 22:3; Zech 7:10; compare Isa 9:17; Ezek 22:7; Mal 3:5; Pss 68:5; 94:6; 146:9) as a reference to those most needful of protection. [Widows, Orphans, and Resident Aliens] From Deuteronomy's perspective, the exodus experience demonstrated once and for all YHWH's concern for the abandoned, the oppressed, and the insignificant in society's eyes. As he did for Israel in Egypt, YHWH continues to watch over those who would otherwise be left unprotected and vulnerable to the unscrupulous or the careless.

Deuteronomy charges Israel to emulate YHWH and to remember its own experience as the oppressed and powerless. These two poles constitute a firm basis for social ethics. Theologically, Israel knows its God as Redeemer, as Liberator of the needy. To love YHWH, then, is to share YHWH's concerns, to further YHWH's program of redemption and liberation. Experientially, Israel knows firsthand the hardship and injustice of powerlessness. It must never allow status and security to cloud its memory or make it insensitive to hardships suffered by elements of its own society.

It should be noted that the passage calls attention to a significant feature of the Bible's concept of "justice." Verse 18 describes YHWH as one who "does justice" for the powerless, those without legal status or rights. Modern Western society usually defines "justice" in terms of statutory rights and wrongs, crimes and torts. To bring someone to justice is to ensure that he or she is duly punished for crimes committed or penalized for civil infringements. This text, however, envisions circumstances in which the legal system fails to apply. Furthermore, the criminal is not the subject of YHWH's "doing justice." Widowhood, parentlessness, and expatriation are (usually) involuntary circumstances, not crimes. YHWH's justice in these cases does not entail punishment or penalty for the wrongdoer, but protection and provision for the needy. In fact, people in these circumstances enjoy very little or no legal protections, especially in the realm of economics and property. "To do justice" for them means to provide for them in an "extra-" or "supra-legal" fashion, to protect them when the law does not or cannot. In this context, the criteria for "justice" are not legal matters of rights and privileges, but the ethical and humanitarian values of decency, fairness, and compassion.

YHWH's Exclusive Claim to Israel's Obedience, 10:20–11:1

The next fragment in the composite sermon returns to the original theme (compare vv. 12 and 20-21), but with a new twist. The first fragment begins with a rhetorical question emphasizing the obvious nature of YHWH's requirement of exclusive obedience ("And now, O Israel, what did YHWH say he wants?"). Now, the emphasis lies on YHWH's priority. Normal Hebrew word order is verb-subject-object. Verse 20 begins a series of inverted object-verb-subject clauses that extends through v. 21 and that draws attention to YHWH's supreme and exclusive claim to Israel's devotion: "*YHWH* you shall serve, *him* you shall serve, *to him* you shall cling, *by his name* you shall swear, etc."

Apart from the emphasis on YHWH as the sole object of Israel's devotion and service, this sequence is remarkable only for the appearance of a few verbs that do not occur regularly in such admonitions in Deuteronomy ("to him you shall cling [*tidbāq*]," v. 20; "to him you shall pray [*tĕhillātĕkā*], v. 21). The intention of this series of admonitions finds expression in the final statement of v. 21: "*He* is your God."

Historical proofs of this relationship include the wonders (*haggĕdōlōt*) and horrors (*hannôrāʾōt*) that YHWH did in Israel's sight (v. 21) and the astonishing numerical growth of the Israelite population despite the hardships in Egypt (v. 22). Having arrived in Egypt a family numbering only seventy people (see Exod 1:5), they departed a people as numerous as "the stars in the heavens" (see Gen 15:5, etc.).

Yet another reiteration of the charge to love YHWH and to keep his commandments (11:1) links to Deuteronomy 10:20 and marks the end of the second fragment. It is otherwise unremarkable.

Seeing Is Believing, 11:2-7

Deuteronomy normally stresses the intergenerationally transferable quality of Israel's experiences as YHWH's people in the exodus, at Horeb/Sinai, and during the wilderness wandering (see commentary on Deut 4). The syntactically complicated fragment, 11:2-7, diverges surprisingly from the normal theme. Essentially, the unit consists of one very long, grammatically complex sentence. The main clause consists of the first phrase in v. 2 complemented by two relative clauses: (a) "that it was not your sons who knew and saw . . ." (v. 2), and (b) "but that your eyes saw . . ." (v. 7). In turn, the first of these relative clauses introduces a series of object clauses that encompass vv. 2b-6. The sons did not know or see: (a) "the discipline of YHWH," (b) his greatness," (c) "his mighty hand," (d) "his outstretched arm" (v. 2), or (e) "his signs and wonders that he did . . ." (v. 3). Next, yet another series of relative clauses further specifies the "signs and wonders" themselves: signs and wonders (a) "that he did in the midst of Egypt . . ." (v. 3), (b) "that he did to the Egyptian army . . ." (v. 4), (c) "that he did for you in the wilderness . . ." (v. 5), and (d) "that he did to Dothan and Abiram . . ." (v. 6).
[Structure of Deuteronomy 11:2-7]

The phenomena supposedly seen by the generation addressed in vv. 2-7 are largely familiar to readers of the Pentateuch and are described here in stock Deuteronomic/Deuteronomistic phraseology.[4] In a sweeping statement, the text calls attention to the plagues inflicted on Pharaoh and the land of Egypt (v. 3), the defeat of the Egyptian army at the sea crossing (v. 4), and the entire wilderness wandering

Structure of Deuteronomy 11:2-7

Schematically, Deut 11:2-7 may be diagrammed as follows:

"And you know today that
  it was not your sons who knew and saw:
    the discipline of YHWH
    his greatness
    his mighty hand
    his outstretched arm
    his signs and wonders
      that he did in the midst of Egypt
      that he did to the Egyptian army
      that he did for you in the wilderness
      that he did to Dothan and Abiram
but it was your eyes that saw."

(v. 5). The only incident that merits closer description involved Dothan and Abiram (Num 16:1-34). Even this reference, however, does not mention the nature of the sin of the sons of Eliab (offering "strange fire"). Verses 3-6 presume the reader's familiarity with the major tradition now recorded in Exodus and Numbers.

Still, the major feature of this passage remains its most puzzling. In the context of the book, and certainly in the context of later acts of *reading* the book, the assertion that the audience Moses addressed on the plains of Moab—and *no subsequent generation*— saw all YHWH's mighty acts defies explanation. In the first instance, according to the plot of the Torah as a whole, and of the book of Deuteronomy in particular, Moses' audience did *not*, in fact, witness the events described—at least not those that transpired prior to Israel's arrival at Mt. Horeb/Sinai. Furthermore, Deuteronomy makes much of the notion that later generations participate in the one revelation of YHWH's character and will that constituted the exodus/covenant-giving/wilderness wandering series of events (see the commentary on Deut 4). The assertion that only this one generation witnessed the events associated with the establishment of the covenant results, therefore, in a startling, very non-Deuteronomic discontinuity: With respect to the founding moment, the generation assembled in Moab has no point of contact with either the preceding or the following generations of Israel. One can only conclude that the editor responsible for this passage pursued a unique and somewhat obscure agenda.

Obedience and the Gift of the Land, 11:8-30

The very baroque composite sermon turns now to the function of the promised land in the matrix of the relationship constituting the covenant between YHWH and Israel. In a sense, the land represents the most tangible feature of the covenant. It is God's gift to God's people (vv. 9, 17, 21, 31). God blesses Israel by means of the land's bounty (vv. 9-12, 14-15, 17, 21). Conversely, God punishes Israel's disobedience to the covenant by withholding the land's bounty, and especially by withholding the rains (v. 17).

No well-marked divisions occur in the sermon from v. 8 onward, although the many repetitions and logical detours indicate that the section must have undergone a lengthy and complicated process of growth. The theme of Israel's possession of the land serves, however, as a unifying element (the reference to taking possession of the land in vv. 8 and 31 forms a framework). For convenience, this "land" composition may be subdivided into several subunits,

Watered with Your Feet
This scene from the Tomb of Mereruka depicts bringing cattle through the marshes; roping and throwing cattle for slaughter; planting and watering a garden; carrying fowl; boating.

Sakkarah, Tomb of Mereruka. Egypt. Bib: OIP XXI, pl. 20. The Oriental Institute Museum. Chicago, Illinois.

each dealing with some aspect of the role of the land in YHWH's covenant relationship with his people: (a) vv. 8-15 describe the advantages of the land; (b) vv. 16-17 warn against the danger of apostasy and the effects on life in the land resulting from YHWH's angry response; (c) vv. 18-21 reprise portions of the Shema, admonishing Israelites to make the covenant central in their lives in order that they may prosper in the land; (d) vv. 22-25 promise YHWH's assistance in conquering the land on the condition of Israel's obedience; and (e) vv. 26-30 conclude the sermon on the role of the land, summarizing the matrix of issues in terms of the key Deuteronomic concepts of blessing and curse.

A Description of the Land, 11:8-15

This description of the promised land emphasizes the absolute importance of obedience to the covenant, on one hand (vv. 8-9, 13), and the favorable contrast between the promised land and Egypt, a land irrigated only by human toil and labor (vv. 10-12, 14-15), on the other. Beginning with a variant of the very familiar Deuteronomic call to "keep the covenant," this unit moves quickly to promise that in response to such obedience to the covenant YHWH will grant (a) the strength Israel will require to take possession of the land (v. 8) and (b) the long life in the land that YHWH has promised (v. 9). Similarly formulaic, the opening admonition describes the land preliminarily as "flowing with milk and honey" (v. 9).

Prompted by this formulaic reference, a much less stereotypical expansion contrasts the promised land with Egypt where Israel was once enslaved. Whereas Egyptian agriculture on the plains along the Nile depended heavily on labor-intensive irrigation techniques (v. 10,), Palestinian agriculture in the ancient period depended almost exclusively on the natural rainfall sent by YHWH (vv. 11-12). Israel will possess a land under the vigilant and constant watchcare of YHWH himself (v. 12)—a watchcare manifest foremost in the essential gift of rain. There will be no need to irrigate that which YHWH himself waters!

But this watchcare will not be automatic. Yet another paraphrased condition statement of the Shema (v. 13) links YHWH's provision of life-giving rain (vv. 14-15) with life-giving obedience to the covenant. "Early rains" and "latter rains" refer to the two

---

The Former and Latter Rains

The climate of the entire "Fertile Crescent," including the Levant, is semi-arid. Israel itself receives an average of only 30 inches of rainfall per year. Egypt and Mesopotamia have major river systems that can be tapped for irrigation to compensate for the lack of rainfall. In fact, archaeological evidence suggests that inhabitants of the Nile Valley and the Tigris-Euphrates basin began systematic irrigation of their crops as early as the fifth millennium BC.

The inhabitants of the southern Levant could not employ such techniques extensively. On the one hand, the Jordan River, only 100 feet at its widest point and 10 feet at its deepest, could have supplied water in sufficient amounts to sustain large-scale agriculture. On the other, and regardless of the size of the Jordan, it runs through an often deep valley, flanked by rocky hills to the east and the west. Wells and springs, often the source of contention between neigh-

bors (see Gen 13 and 21), provided some water for human beings and livestock, but the inhabitants of the southern Levant depended almost exclusively on rainfall both to water crops and to fill the many cisterns.

In contrast to the more temperate regions of the world, the growing season in the Levant falls in the "winter" or (relatively) "rainy" season. Summer is hot and dry; winter is less hot and not so dry. Typically, a brief period of rain in the fall, the "early rains" initiated the agricultural season. These rains provided enough moisture for crops to germinate and begin to grow. A more substantial period of rainfall in the spring, the "latter rains," occurred in time to water crops as they grew to maturity. Up until most recent times, shortages in either rainy season could be catastrophic (compare Amos 4:7-8; 8:11-12). While it is true, then, that Israel would not toil in the irrigation ditches as did the Egyptians (Deut 11:10), such dependence on normally scant rainfall made life in the land of Israel precarious indeed.

principle (relatively) wet seasons in the Levant, without which there could be no agriculture. [The Former and Latter Rains] Without these rains—given the absence of a river system such as Egypt's Nile or Mesopotamia's Tigris and Euphrates—grain, grapes, olives, and grasses in pasture lands (vv. 14-15) cannot grow. In the semi-arid Levant, no blessing more essential than the bi-annual rains can so forcefully highlight the importance of obedience to the covenant.

Apostasy and Drought, 11:16-17

Given Israel's absolute dependence upon the rains YHWH sends, the warning that apostasy will motivate YHWH to withhold them (vv. 16-17) sounds a truly ominous tone. The chain of causality is clear, direct, and forceful. Should Israel worship idols (literally "other" or "strange" gods)—thereby violating the most fundamental provision of the covenant, its very basis, namely that YHWH is Israel's God and they YHWH's people—YHWH will be angered. As a result, YHWH will "shut" the heavens, closing off the sources of the rains. Crops will not grow. As a result, Israel will starve "quickly" (v. 17).

The Choice Is Clear, 11:18-21

In light of these two possibilities (fidelity to YHWH who gives the rains, or idolatry that will motivate YHWH to withhold these life-giving waters), Israel's wisest course of action is obvious. The covenant must be given central importance in the life of Israel and of individual Israelites. Verses 18-20 repeat yet again a portion of the Shema (6:6-9) almost verbatim (for a discussion of the significance of these admonitions, see the commentary on 6:6-9). In their present context, they represent Israel's hope for long life in the land. The covenant must be taken to heart, cherished, and taught to future generations. Such devotion to YHWH will assure Israel long life—"like the days of the heavens above the earth" (v. 21)! That Israel would choose otherwise is unthinkable.

Obedience and Conquest, 11:22-25

The opportunity to enjoy the blessings of life in the land depends first, of course, on Israel taking possession of it. Another beneficial result of keeping the commandments (v. 22; here equated with loving God, walking in God's ways, and clinging to God; see commentary on 7:6-16) will be that YHWH will dispossess the current inhabitants of the land, permitting Israel to displace "nations mightier and stronger" (v. 23, see also 1:28; 2:10, 21; 4:38; 9:1, 2; contrast 26:5). In fact, wherever Israel sets foot will become Israel's possession (v. 24; see commentary on 34:1), from the wilderness (to the south), to the Lebanon mountain range (to the north), to the Euphrates (in the east), and to the Mediterranean Sea (to the west). ["From the River Euphrates to the Western Sea"] So powerfully will YHWH intervene on Israel's behalf that no one will be able to withstand them: All will flee in dread and fear, leaving Israel to take possession of the land merely by traversing territory (v. 25).

Blessing and Curse in the Land, 11:26-30

Taken cumulatively, the preceding material concerning the relationship between Israel's obedience to the covenant and YHWH's gift of the land makes it clear that the land will be the most tangible realm in which YHWH and Israel will live out the covenant. The final unit in this composite sermon utilizes the complex issues revolving around Israel's existence in the land in characteristically Deuteronomic terms: blessing and curse. Simply put, Moses offers Israel a clear-cut choice between the two (v. 26): Blessing inheres in keeping the commandments (v. 27); Curse lies in failing to do so, and specifically, in idolatry—violating the first commandment (v. 28). As a ritual reminder of the unambiguous nature of the choice confronting Israel, Moses instructs the people to "put" the blessings on Mt. Gerazim and the curses on Mt. Ebal (for details see the commentary on 27:1-14). Verse 29 specifies the location of these mountains on the western side of the Jordan, in the Canaanite desert near Gilgal, in the vicinity of the oaks of Moreh (see Gen 12:6).

 **"From the River Euphrates to the Western Sea"**

The Hebrew Bible preserves two traditions concerning the extent of the geographical boundaries of ancient Israel. One tradition reflects the territory inhabited by the twelve tribes from the period of the Conquest (described in detail in Josh 13–22). Another, represented here in Deut 11:24 (see also Gen 15:17-21; etc.), describes the boundaries of David's empire (1 Sam 8). In the truest sense, the territories David conquered (Philistia, Edom, Moab, Ammon, Syria) were never incorporated into Israel proper. Many continued to be ruled directly by native kings in vassalage to David; no efforts were made to assimilate them into Israelite culture or to convert them to Yahwism; consequently, within a matter of generations, many had regained their independence from Israel. Passages such as 11:24 can, therefore, be seen as idealizations of the Davidic Empire, not as descriptions of any historical reality. Israel controlled some of this territory for brief periods (under David; the 8th century Omride dynasty in the northern kingdom also exercised control over Moab for a period), but it was never truly Israelite.

A Concluding Exhortation, 11:31-32

The composite sermon on keeping the law and enjoying the land concludes with a summary exhortation. The occasion of the sermon (indeed of the entire book of Deuteronomy) is the fact that Israel is about to "cross the Jordan and take possession of the land that YHWH your God is giving you." Since chapter 4, the constant refrain has been the exhortation to "keep" and "do" the

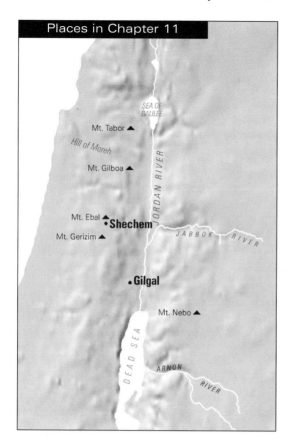

Places in Chapter 11

SEA OF GALILEE
Mt. Tabor ▲
Hill of Moreh
Mt. Gilboa ▲
JORDAN RIVER
Mt. Ebal ▲ •Shechem
Mt. Gerizim ▲
JABBOK RIVER
•Gilgal
Mt. Nebo ▲
DEAD SEA
ARNON RIVER

commandments. Finally, the exposition of these commandments announced at the beginning of the book (1:5) in the form of the statutes and ordinances contained in the so-called "Deuteronomic Code" (12–26) will now follow.

CONNECTIONS

The conclusion to the parenetic framework surrounding the Deuteronomic law code (chs. 12–26) may well leave a modern Western reader with an impression of disorder and repetitiveness. From the standpoint of the traditionists and editors responsible for its production and transmission, however, it undoubtedly represented a conviction that the quintessential experiences of God's revelation and the foundational claims of God's covenant are pregnant with implications for Israel's life before God and in the land. YHWH's deliverance of Israel from Egyptian bondage is not merely an event in the past; it reveals God's character and God's intentions for Israel, defining Israel's identity for all future generations. No one doctrinal formulation or confessional statement can exhaust the meaning of the fact that Israel worships a God who hears the cries of oppressed people, who remembers and honors ancient promises, who liberates and leads on the journey through a hostile wilderness, and who not only frees from bondage, but who provides a future, giving a home where authentic freedom can be lived out. In a sense, then, this apparently fragmentary sermon may be productively compared to an elaborate series of variations on a musical theme. The theme here, as always in the framework sections of Deuteronomy, is the first commandment, especially in its positive form, the Shema. Despite the initial sense of the text's fragmentary and confusing structure, several features of this elaboration-of-a-theme phenomenon suggest possibilities that may be significant for modern readers.

Tradition as Source

First, the technique of elaboration itself may serve as a very productive and rich model for appropriating and unfolding the inexhaustible source of meaning embodied in the key elements of the biblical tradition. Again and again, the preacher(s) of the sermon return(s) to the Shema, alluding to its key phrases, citing it almost verbatim, rephrasing it as a conditional statement, etc. From this point of departure, they then explicate some feature, draw some conclusion, or highlight some new emphasis. As was true earlier of Deuteronomy's treatment of Israel's most formative experience with YHWH at Mt. Horeb/Sinai (Deut 4–5), the preacher(s) do(es) not hesitate to extrapolate the basic tradition. For them, the truth of the basic tradition includes far more than the explicit statement. Just as the acorn implies the oak, the basic tradition can be unfolded and extended to yield truth consistent with, even contained within, its basic character.

What does it mean that Israel has been called to serve YHWH exclusively and with utter devotion, especially when seen against its experience of deliverance and failure, guidance and rebellion? What is the proper response to YHWH's determination to fulfill the ancient promise to grant this insignificant and rebellious people a land? The preacher(s) unfold(s) a picture of Israel's need gratefully, enthusiastically, and reverently to accept and value the privilege and responsibility of being God's people. Before them lies a clear choice between life and death, between blessing and curse.

Modern readers may, indeed should, approach the biblical text and tradition with a similar openness to its living significance. Viewed merely as a record of ancient Israel's historical experience, the text is lifeless. Viewed solely as a particularized statement of God's will for one ethnic group in a specific historical and geographical setting, it is powerless. Viewed as the source for the defining traditions of God's people, it engenders identity.

As one example of the way in which the Bible can engender identity and direction, one need only reflect on the central observation that the God of the Bible delivers those who need to be delivered. Does the God of the church? If so, what does this truth mean for the life of the church? Who needs to be delivered from oppression today? The God of the Bible, the God who delivers, deserves and demands exclusive devotion expressed in appropriate actions and modes of living. God does not graciously deliver to no purpose. God brings the oppressed out of bondage into prosperous and authentic life in the land. Does God still deliver to purposeful life in the world? Or has the kingdom of God become a symbol only?

If God still cares about free, authentic, productive life in this world, how does the church justify its continued otherworldliness and its relative ineffectiveness in confronting threats to authentic and purposeful human life? Why does the church seem to regard homeless children as a political problem? If God's greatest blessing continues to be rich life in a bounteous land, how does the church justify its (at least implicit) denial that God is interested in God's world? Why does the church seem to feel that God's blessings are only fully experienced in formal acts of worship and prayer? Ought not worship and prayer be properly understood as the grateful and appropriate reactions to the blessings experienced in daily life, the world of work and play, of family and community?

The preacher(s) of this sermon call(s) for Israel to place the basic truth of Israel's existence at the heart of Israel's daily life. The sermon calls for Israel to contemplate the first commandment, to repeat it, to discuss it, to teach it, to practice it—above all else—to make it a constant, never allowing it to become commonplace. How can the modern church go about reorienting itself toward the basic call to devotion, obedience, and thankfulness in relationship with the Creator and Redeemer God?

Tradition as Critique

Second, the somewhat surprising course of the argument that culminates in the charge for Israel to do justice to the disenfranchised, particularly the resident alien, provides a powerful example of the way in which the fundamental truth of the biblical witness can and does break open the limitations of human culture that so often bind the believing community, preventing the authentic expression of its identity as God's people. One could even describe this text as one in which the content of the biblical tradition criticizes its vehicle. That is, the revolutionary notion that the God of Israel sides with the powerless criticizes the structure of Israelite society that perpetuates the injustice of a hierarchically ordered, status-quo oriented society. Admittedly, this critique carries a somewhat diminished force than was true for Israel during its Egyptian sojourn. Within a very few generations after the exodus, Israel had established a society that in many ways resembled others in the ancient Near East, especially in the areas of property law and social stratification. Although Israel's laws in these areas, and especially regarding the institution of slavery, were relatively progressive, the fact remains that Israel perpetuated social structures that institutionalized the disenfranchisement of major segments of its

Remember Your Sojourn in Egypt: Pity and Love

. . . he who pities most loves most. Men aflame with a burning charity towards their neighbours are thus enkindled because they have touched the depth of their own misery, their own apparentiality, their own nothingness, and then, turning their newly opened eyes upon their fellows, they have seen that they also are miserable, apparential, condemned to nothingness, and they have pitied them and loved them.

Man yearns to be loved, or, what is the same thing, to be pitied. Man wishes others to feel and share his hardships and his sorrows. The roadside beggar's exhibition of his sores and gangrened mutilations is something more than a device to extort alms from the passer-by. True alms is pity rather than the pittance that alleviates the material hardships of life. The beggar shows little gratitude for alms thrown to him by one who hurries past with averted face; he is more grateful to him who pities him but does not help than to him who helps but does not pity, although from another point of view he may prefer the latter. Observe with what satisfaction he relates his woes to one who is moved by the story of them. He desires to be pitied, to be loved.

. . . Pity, then, is the essence of human spiritual love, of the love that is conscious of being love, of the love that is not purely animal, of the love, in a word, of a rational person. Love pities, and pities most when it loves most.

Miguel de Unamuno, *The Tragic Sense of Life*, trans. J. Flitch (New York: Dover, 1954), 136-37.

population. Somehow, these descendants of slaves saw no contradiction between celebrating Passover and buying and selling human beings as property! [Remember Your Sojourn in Egypt: Pity and Love]

In cases such as this, which aspect of the biblical tradition should be seen as normative? Israel's blind perpetuation of the societal norms of the day and region? Or the revolutionary revelation of God's liberating character? Like new wine in an old wineskin, the meaning of Passover threatens to burst open the constrictions of culture and habit. The simple reminder (10:19) that Israel must do justice to the resident alien in its midst because it remembers its own sojourn in Egypt expresses, indeed conveys, the revolutionary power of God's redemption—although Israel would be centuries coming to a fuller realization of this message. This case exemplifies the dynamics of many troublesome interpretive issues regarding the Hebrew Bible: holy war, slavery, the place of women in society, attitudes toward the ill and infirm, to name only a few. The believing community must resist unthinking acceptance and perpetuation of a status quo even in the face of evidence in the foundational tradition that the God of Israel did not (and does not) "show favoritism" (10:18).

Sadly, one can only wonder to what extent the modern community of faith unthinkingly perpetuates societal structures that directly contradict biblical assertions that there is one God, Lord of all, "who sees not as others see, but who looks upon the heart" (1 Sam 16:7), one Christ "in whom there is neither male nor female" (Gal 3:28). Will future generations regard their ancestors with the same embarrassed wonder many today feel for Christianity's conduct of the crusades, its complicity in the

Slavery: Redemption and Inertia

Remarkably, although the institution of slavery can hardly be reconciled with the fact that the God of the Bible created all, redeems the oppressed and enslaved to be God's people, and watches over the well-being of the disenfranchised, no text in the Scriptures of either the Hebrew Bible or the New Testament explicitly declares slavery an abomination and outrage. Passages such as Deut 10:17-18 abound, however, in which the central truth of the scriptural witness threatens to break through the cultural inertia of God's people.

A similar phenomenon can be observed in the masterful rhetoric of Paul's letter to Philemon concerning Philemon's slave Onesimus. Both master and slave were Christian believers; both were intimates of Paul. Onesimus had run away, presumably prior to becoming a Christian, although the text is unclear on this point. Paul, confronting the delicate conflict between Philemon's legally established "property rights" and the gospel of freedom in Christ (see Gal 3:28), chose to return Onesimus, bearing the letter preserved in the New Testament, to his "owner."

Throughout, Paul plays with the operative terms "prisoner" and "slave," reserving them largely for himself, on the one hand, and "brother" and "partner," which he uses of both Philemon and Onesimus, on the other. He contrasts goodness by compulsion with goodness by free will. Paul makes a powerful case. No one knows how Philemon responded, but it is difficult to imagine anyone turning a deaf ear to Paul's moving plea to receive Onesimus as a brother in Christ:

> . . . although I am bold enough in Christ to command you to do what is required, yet for love's sake I prefer to appeal to you . . .
>
> Perhaps this is why he was parted from you for a while, that you might have him back for ever, no longer as a slave but more than a slave, as a beloved brother, especially to me, but how much more to you, both in the flesh and in the Lord. (Phlm 8-9, 15-16)

Even Paul, however, whether through a failure of understanding or through rhetorical restraint, does not draw the logical conclusion of his insight. It would be centuries before the conscience of Western culture became sensitive to the truth of the biblical witness, namely, that God frees slaves.

Holocaust, and its endorsement of slavery in the American South as an institution ordained by God? [Slavery: Redemption and Inertia]

Tradition as Reminder

Third, the focus on Israel's life in the land reminds modern readers of ancient Israel's characteristic awareness that its God created the physical world and called it good, that God maintains this world in existence, that human beings experience God's grace first and foremost in the blessings of physical existence, that the kingdom of God does not lie solely beyond time and space, but is rightly to be experienced first in this world. It is often said that the two poles of all theology are Creation and Redemption. These two poles control the dynamics of the composite sermon, as well.

Christian theology has historically been strangely uncomfortable with the theological topic of creation. A perversion of the doctrine of sin has bred distrust of the created order as absolutely fallen and totally corrupt. Contemplation of the beauty of creation and respect for its place in God's economy is today often confused with "secular humanism" or the "New Age" movement. Theologians concerned almost exclusively with the redemption pole of the creation/redemption dyad mistrust "natural theology" as a human effort to reach out to God (see the discussion of K. Barth's skepticism of "religion" in the connections for 9:1–10:11). In the typical Christian understanding of the relationship between the two, God created a perfect world. Subsequently, however, through human arrogance and rebellion, sin and death were introduced into the world, marring its original beauty, rendering it almost totally unreliable, in the view of some, as a medium for experiencing God. It must be redeemed (re-created). Unless and until it is redeemed, it cannot be home.

Deuteronomy sees matters quite otherwise. The beginning point of YHWH's relationship with Israel is YHWH's own gracious promise, not Israel's repentance. Indeed, YHWH redeemed Israel, but not from Israel's own sin. For Deuteronomy, redemption is not exclusively, or even primarily, a "spiritual" category. YHWH redeemed Israel, as it were, from Pharaoh's sinful oppression. Israel suffered real-world, "external" hardships. Israel's redemption did not consist, first, of "forgiveness" for its own sin, or of "regeneration." Israel began its life under the demands of YHWH's will only *after* deliverance. The struggle to obey, and the inevitability of failure, results directly from deliverance!

Furthermore, YHWH enables this effort to be God's people through the good gift of the land. Deuteronomy 10:12–11:32 does not envision a land radically marred by the consequences of the sin and fall of the primal pair, but a good land that *may* suffer the results of Israel's own sin. God's good creation continues to be the arena of God's blessing. It is God's gracious gift of life! But, it is also the stage upon which Israel must play out its role as the covenant people. The choice for good or evil was not made by Adam and Eve only. It confronted Israel each and every day. Every human being makes the choice every moment of life. God's good gift of the land did not expire with the expulsion from Eden. The land YHWH gives Israel will be Israel's garden land, flowing with milk and honey.

Creation and redemption cannot be safely separated. God continues to redeem creation by taking seriously the possibilities for authentic, blessed human life, lived out in God's good creation.

NOTES

[1] See, for example, G. von Rad, *Deuteronomy: A Commentary* (OTL; Philadelphia: Westminster, 1966), 83.

[2] Verses 14, 16-17; the expressions "heaven of heavens" (v. 14), "God of gods," and "Lord of lords" (v. 17) are superlatives in the Hebrew idiom; on their face, they communicate nothing concerning a Hebrew concept of a multitiered heaven or an acceptance of the existence of other gods.

[3] See Jer 4:4; Lev 26:41; Ezek 44:7; for the metaphorical sense of circumcision in other contexts, see also Exod 6:12, 29; Lev 19:23; Jer 6:10; see also the commentary on Deut 30:6.

[4] "Discipline," Jer 2:30; 5:3; 7:28; 10:8; 17:23; 30:14; 32:33; 35:13; Hos 5:2; "mighty hand," Deut 3:24; 4:34; 5:15; 6:21; 7:8, 19; 9:26; 26:8; 1 Kgs 8:42; Jer 32:21; compare Exod 3:19; 6:1; 13:9; 32:11; Num 20:20; etc.; "outstretched arm," Deut 4:34; 5:15; 7:19; 9:29; 26:8; 1 Kgs 8:42; 17:36; Jer 21:5; 27:5; 32:17, 21; etc.

THE DEUTERONOMIC CODE: DEUTERONOMY 12–26

Fifteen chapters of Deuteronomy, less than half the book, beginning fully one-third of the way into the book (Deut 12–26) constitute the so-called "Deuteronomic Code." This very placement and proportion indicates the inadequacy of characterizing Deuteronomy simply as a law book. The extensive materials prefatory to the collection of laws proper seek to establish that the principles (or laws) governing YHWH's relationship with Israel may be subsumed under the primary commandment to "love" (see commentary on Deut 6) YHWH. Furthermore, they have called for Israel's active engagement in the process of transmitting covenant traditions to new generations (6:1-6; 11:19), for responsible interpretation of these traditions in new settings in a manner that will be both true to the tradition and responsive to changing conditions (10:12-22), and for committed actualization of the potentialities for relationship with YHWH inherent in the covenant itself (11:26-32). Several features of the Deuteronomic Code confirm that, for the book of Deuteronomy, this collection is not simply a static law code. Instead, it is, like the preface to it, the product of a process of interpretation intended to bring the covenant to life. Like the prefatory exhortations (chs. 4–11), the Code focuses on transmitting, engaging, and actualizing the fundamental principles of YHWH's covenant with Israel. As such, it functions as part of a valuable first phase in establishing an authoritative stream of interpretive tradition much more than it functions as a "law book."

A Vibrant and Growing Legal Tradition

Scholarship refers to Deuteronomy 12–26 as the "Deuteronomic Code" in order to distinguish it from two other relatively self-contained collections of legal material in the Pentateuch: the "Covenant Code" (Exod 20–23) and the "Holiness Code" (Lev 17–26). These three codes replicate a significant body of common material. All three contain legislation on at least ten matters (in the Deuteronomic order): the altar, the Sabbath year, manumission, the firstborn, Passover, Pentecost, Tabernacles, impartiality, soothsayers, usury, and oppression of the underprivileged. In addition, other passages in the Pentateuch, especially in the so-called "ritual Decalogue" (Exod 34),

AΩ **Parallels Between the Covenant and Deuteronomic Codes**

	Covenant Code (Exod 20–23)	Ritual Decalog (Exod 34)	Deuteronomic Code (Deut 12–26)
Altar Law	20:24-26		12:2-28; 14:23; 16:2, 6, 11; 26:2
Manumission	21:1-6		15:12-18
Maidservants	21:7-11		21:10-14
Homicide	21:12-14, 19-22		19:4-6, 11-13
Kidnapping	21:16		24:7
Ox in ditch	21:33-34		22:1-4
Seduction	22:16-17		22:28-29
Soothsaying	22:18		18:9-14
Oppression	22:21-24; 23:9		24:17-18
Usury/pledge	22:25-27		23:19-20; 24:9-13
First fruits	22:29a; 23:19a	34:26a	26:1-11
Firstborn	22:29b-30	34:19-20	15:19-23
Impartiality	23:3, 6		16:18-20
Sabbath Year	23:10-11		15:1-6
Three feasts	23:14-17	34:23-24	16:16-17
Unleavened	23:15	34:18	16:1-8
Harvest	23:16a	34:22a	16:9-12
Ingathering	23:16b	34:22b	16:13-15
Boil a kid	23:19b	34:26b	14:21b

also replicate some of the materials found in the Deuteronomic Code. The existence of three separate law collections that often preserve double ([Parallels Between the Covenant and Deuteronomic Codes] and [Parallels Between the Deuteronomic and Holiness Codes]), and even triple, versions of the same or very similar laws raises a number of intriguing questions for the interpreter of Deuteronomy 12–26. Also intriguing are the occasional contradictions between the codes. Leviticus 17:3-4, for example, forbids "profane" slaughter of animals. Any slaughter is sacrifice and the blood of the sacrifice must be presented to YHWH at the sanctuary. Deuteronomy 12:15-16, on the other hand, distinguishes between sacrifice, which must take place at the sanctuary, and profane slaughter of animals, which may occur anywhere. These phenomena have led scholars to discount, for example, the tradition of the Mosaic authorship of the Pentateuch. Why would Moses have written the same laws two and three times in versions that sometimes virtually contradict one another? The consensus of modern scholarship considers it likely that the law codes, which may well preserve orally-transmitted Mosaic tradition, were written in separate acts, by collectors with somewhat distinct interests, and apparently in different periods in Israel's history.

A comparison of parallels between the Covenant and Deuteronomic Codes yields two very significant observations: First, in many respects, the two codes so closely resemble one another as to suggest the possibility of some literary dependence. Did the editor/collector of the Deuteronomic Code utilize the Covenant Code as a source? Second, and for the purposes of this commentary much more importantly, the dissimilarities between the two collections are largely consistent with the assumption that the Covenant Code reflects an agrarian setting (the period of the judges) whereas the Deuteronomic Code reflects a significantly urbanized culture (the monarchial period). Regardless of whether the Deuteronomic Code depends

AΩ Parallels Between the Deuteronomic and Holiness Codes		
	Deuteronomy	Leviticus
Altar	12:1-28	17:1-16
Self-mutilation	14:1-2	19:27-28
Clean/Unclean Foods		
Beasts	14:3-8	11:2-8 (24-31, 41-44)
Fish	14:9-10	11:9-12
Fowl	14:11-20	11:13-23
Carrion	14:21a	11:31-40
Tithes	14:22	27:30-33
Sabbath year	15:1-6	25:1-7
Manumission	15:12-18	25:39-46
Firstborn	15:19-23	27:26-29
Passover	16:1-8	23:4-8
Pentecost	16:9-12	23:15-21
Tabernacles	16:13-15	23:33-44
Impartiality	16:18-20	19:15
Soothsayers	18:9-14	19:31; 20:6, 27
Rebellious son	21:18-21	(20:9)
Improper mixtures	22:9-11	19:19
Sexual impropriety		
Adultery	22:22	18:20; 20:10
Betrothed	22:23-24	(19:20-22)
Stepmother	22:30	18:7-8; 20:11
Harlotry	23:17-18	19:29
Usury	23:19-20	25:35-38
Pay vows	23:21-23	27:1-25
Gleaning	23:24-25; 24:19-22	19:9-10
Leprosy	24:8-9	13:1–14:57
Oppression	24:14-15, 17-18	19:33-34
Just measures	25:13-16	19:35-37

literarily on the Covenant Code, then, detailed comparisons of parallels should reveal what motivated the editor/collector of the Deuteronomic Code to "update" existing laws as well as the principles of interpretation utilized in this revitalization.

The Covenant Code deals primarily with what would now be described as civil or criminal law and, consequently, parallels between it and the Deuteronomic Code reveal Deuteronomy's interest in issues pertaining to life in society. A comparison with the Holiness Code, on the other hand, reveals affinities with priestly tradition. Both codes include regulations designed to make clear distinctions between clean and unclean (foods—Deut 14:3-21a; Lev 11:2-40; improper mixtures—Deut 22:9-11; Lev 19:19; and improper sexual relationships—Deut 22:22-30; Lev 18:1-30), a sphere of concern characteristic of the priesthood. In fact, Deuteronomy's affinities with priestly matters together with its program of cultic centralization (Deut 12) and its repeated provision for the welfare of the Levites, who are classed among other underprivileged groups (26:11, 12-13), form the basis for the theory that Deuteronomy represents the literary efforts of the Levites from the countryside. They may have been refugees from the northern kingdom in the aftermath of its destruction in 722 BC who found themselves stripped of their livelihoods by the reforms of Hezekiah or Josiah. The localization of the cult exclusively in the Jerusalem temple meant the end of sacrifice in the countryside and thus the end of the tithe to local priests. Not surprisingly, treatments of these issues tend to be much more extensive and detailed in the Holiness Code.

Material Peculiar to the Deuteronomic Code

When one sets aside material in the Deuteronomic Code that is paralleled in either the Covenant Code, the Holiness Code, or both, passages dealing with five topics unique to Deuteronomy remain: (1) cult centralization (12:1-32; also reflected in 14:22-29; 15:19-23; 16:1-17; 17:8-13; 18:1-8; 19:1-13), (2) deliberate apostasy (13:18), (3) the king (17:14-20), (4) war (20:1-20), and (5) unsolved homicides (21:1-9). One may assume that the Deuteronomic Code alone treats these matters because they were topics of particular interest at the time when the Deuteronomic Code was assembled and not, for example, during the period that produced the Covenant Code. The first three of these issues seem to point squarely to the monarchial period when, in the view of the Deuteronomistic movement spawned by the book of Deuteronomy, false prophecy (1 Kgs 22:13-28; Jer 14:13-16; 23:9-40; 27:1–29:32), the aberrant forms of Yahwism practiced in the countryside (2 Kgs 22–23), and the abuses of an arrogant monarch (compare Deut 17:14-20 and 1 Sam 10; 1 Kgs 11:1-13; 21:1-16), constituted the complex of interrelated problems that would eventually lead to the downfall of both Israel and Judah (2 Kgs 17).

The Literary Structure of the Deuteronomic Code

One last observation resulting from comparisons of the three major collections of legal material in the Pentateuch offers the reader of Deuteronomy a clue for interpreting the laws in Deuteronomy. While the three law codes share a significant proportion of

AΩ **The Decalogue Arrangement of the Deuteronomic Code**

12:2–13:18	First Commandment—"No other gods"
14:1-21	Second Commandment—"Misuse of God's name"
14:22–16:17	Third Commandment—"Keep the Sabbath"
16:18–18:22	Fourth Commandment—"Honor father and mother"
19:1–22:8	Fifth Commandment—"Do not kill"
22:9–23:19(23:18 Eng)	Sixth Commandment—"Do not commit adultery"
23:20(19 Eng)–24:7	Seventh Commandment—"Do not steal"
24:8–25:4	Eighth Commandment—"Do not bear false witness"
25:5-12	Ninth Commandment—"Do not covet neighbor's wife"
25:13–26:15	Tenth Commandment—"Do not covet anything of your neighbor's"

material, each arranges these laws in its own order. In other words, even if the editors/collectors of the Deuteronomic Code utilized the Covenant Code, or a common precursor, as a documentary source, they did not replicate the order of the prototype. Is there some discernible structural principle that governs the order of the statues and ordinances in Deuteronomy 12–26?

As early as the first century AD, the Jewish philosopher Philo of Alexandria maintained that the sequence of the Ten Commandments is duplicated in the laws of Deuteronomy 12–26. Calvin and Luther assumed that Deuteronomy 12–26 contain a series of explications and expansions of the Decalogue arranged in the Decalogue order. In recent years, Stephen Kaufman[1] and Georg Braulik[2] have championed this position with thorough and detailed analyses.[3] The commentary will follow the conclusions of Kaufman and Braulik and will demonstrate the ordering principle in due course. [The Decalogue Arrangement of the Deuteronomic Code]

A few peculiarities of the overall Decalogue structure of the code merit notice at the outset, however. First, ample evidence indicates that this Decalogue arrangement may not be the sole principle that influenced the shape of the collection. Within sections, in particular, individual units seemed to be placed according to a "catchword" principle.

In fact, second, transitional units pointing forward to the sexuality topic in the section devoted otherwise to killing (22:5), dealing with stealing in the section on adultery (23:16-17 [Eng 23:15-16]), and pointing back to sexuality again in the section on stealing (24:1-5), for example, suggest the highly interpretive nature of this arrangement. These transitions highlight sexual impropriety and equate it in some way with theft. Similarly, the collection of laws dealing with significant times demarcated by periods of seven units (Sabbath year, feast of weeks—or the seventh week after Passover, etc.) explicating the "Sabbath Day" commandment indicates that this commandment extends to all regular forms of rest (even with implications for "economic" rest, 15:1-18) and worship. Every section offers such commentary by way of arrangement.

Third, the decision made by the editors and arrangers of the Deuteronomic Code regarding the demarcation of the Ten Commandments themselves stands as a very early, if not the first, opinion. Apparently, the Deuteronomic editors viewed the clauses on "no other gods" and "no idol images" as constituents of the first commandment, in effect equating them. Conversely, this decision requires the clauses on coveting to be separated into the ninth and tenth commandments.

The Genre of the Deuteronomic Code

In many significant ways, as mentioned above, the title "Deuteronomic Code" implies an inaccurate categorization of the nature of this collection. In modern societies, law codes, enacted in democratic societies by legislatures, seek as far as possible completely to delimit and regulate civil interactions among citizens (i.e., contract law or family law) or to proscribe criminal behaviors and provide for penalties against infringements. A notable exception to this effort completely to define desirable interactions among citizens in Western societies involves the Enlightenment notion of the freedom of conscience, which incorporates freedom of religion. In keeping with this freedom, modern Western law codes typically avoid matters of religious belief and practice.

Thus, according to these criteria, the "Deuteronomic Code" is no law code whatsoever. As indicated by the nature of material peculiar to Deuteronomy outlined above, it is, instead, clearly a *programmatic* collection interested in advocating and promoting especially cult centralization, in curbing deliberate apostasy, etc. In contrast to modern law codes in the democratic West, Deuteronomy mixes civil, criminal, and ritual regulations. Ancient societies did not recognize distinctions between profane and sacred, societal and individual to the degree modern societies do. Finally, many of the regulations in the Deuteronomic Code fail to prescribe penalties for infringements. Instead of "criminalizing" even clearly criminal behaviors, Deuteronomy encourages certain behaviors, and even provides rationales and promises rewards in some cases. These so-called "motive clauses," such as 14:2 ("For you are a holy people to YHWH, your God, and YHWH has chosen you as a people peculiar to him above all the nations on the earth") and 15:15 ("because you remember that you were a slave in the land of Egypt, and YHWH, your God, redeemed you")[4] provide important insights into the theological interpretation given even the most mundane of civil matters in ancient Israel. Taken together, these features of the Deuteronomic Code have suggested to scholars that, rather than being a law code in the strict sense, it should be regarded as hortatory or parenetic material, "preached law" as it is often termed. The purpose of Deuteronomy and the incorporated legal material is not to legislate, but to encourage, to instruct, and to explain (see 1:5).

NOTES

[1] "The Structure of the Deuteronomic Law," *Maarav* 1/2 (1979): 105-58.

[2] "Die Abfolge der Gesetze in Deuteronomium 12–26 und der Decalog," in *Das Deuteronomium: Entstehung, Gestalt und Botschaft*, ed. N. Lohfink (Leuven: University Press, 1985), 252-72; "Zur Abfolge der Gesetze in Deuteronomium 16, 18-21, 23. Weitere Beobachtungen," *Bib* 69 (1988): 63-92.

[3] For a more extensive review of the history of research on the Decalogue order of laws in Deut 12–26, see Olson, *Deuteronomy and the Death of Moses: A Theological Reading* (OBT; Minneapolis: Fortress, 1994), 62-65, esp. n. 3.

[4] See R. Sonsino, *Motive Clauses in Hebrew Law: Biblical Forms and Near Eastern Parallels* (SBLDS 45; Missoula MT: Scholars Press, 1979).

EXPLICATION OF THE FIRST COMMANDMENT: "YOU SHALL HAVE NO OTHER GODS"

12:2–13:18

Following the brief introduction to the entire Deuteronomic Code (12:1), the peculiar character of Deuteronomy's persistent emphasis on the centrality of the first commandment manifests itself once again in the material, unique to Deuteronomy, that explicates the first commandment (understood to include both the "no other gods" and "no graven image" provisions). Specifically, the Deuteronomic Code demonstrates an interest in establishing circumstances that protect Israel from any possible contact with the attractions of idol worship by restricting cultic activity to a central location (12:2-28), where orthodox priests can supervise carefully, and by prescribing the merciless eradication of any and all individuals and communities who practice and advocate idol worship (12:29–13:18).

COMMENTARY

Cult Centralization, 12:2-28

The bulk of Deuteronomy 12 consists of three versions of the centralization law (vv. 2-7, 8-12 and 13-27[28]). Considerable scholarly debate surrounds the question of whether, and to what degree, Deuteronomy's demand for centralization of the cult represents an *innovation* in Israelite religion. The counterpart to Deuteronomy 12 in the Covenant Code, Exodus 24:24, calls for altars to be erected "in every place where I cause my name to be remembered," a provision that seems, at least, to envision a number of local sanctuaries scattered throughout Israel. [Cult Centralization: A Problem in the History of Israel]

In contrast, all three versions of the centralization law in Deuteronomy 12 agree that sacrifice to YHWH must be made only at the central sanctuary and are redundant to this extent. All three

Cult Centralization: A Problem in the History of Israel

The several passages in Deuteronomy dealing with the centralization of the cult (12:14, 26; 14:23, 25; 15:20; 16:2, 15, 16; 17:10; 18:6; 23:16; 31:11) have for over a century been the focus of considerable scholarly debate. A complex array of interrelated issues arise with respect to (a) the editorial history of the book of Deuteronomy, (b) the role of Deuteronomy, and especially its centralization regulations, in the so-called "Josianic Reform" in 7th century Judah, and (c) the status of Jerusalem in Deuteronomic theology. The debate offers a particularly interesting insight into the problems and methods confronting the historian of ancient Israel.

An early consensus of historical-critical scholarship, now sometimes questioned, held that the centralization laws belong to a layer of editorial materials that was added to an earlier form of Deuteronomy and intended to support Josiah's program of reform. In this view, they represent a late innovation calling not merely for a central or leading sanctuary, but for a sole sanctuary, namely Jerusalem.

The key issues in this as yet unresolved question suggest the intricacy of the matter. First, did the so-called "place" formula ("the place upon which I shall set my name" and variants) always and only refer to Jerusalem? Many scholars (R. E. Clements, *God and Temple* [Oxford: University Press, 1965], 92-93; J. Schreiner, *Sion— Jerusalem: Jahwes Königsitz* [Munich: Kösel-Verlag, 1963], 162) point out that the Deuteronomistic History reserves the formula for Jerusalem, that the verb "to choose" (*bḥr*) never applies to a city other than Jerusalem, and that the verb "to dwell" (*škn*) seems tied to Jerusalemite cultic tradition. Deuteronomy, however, is almost universally recognized as representing a *northern* tradition (Jerusalem is in the south) and the one-time northern sanctuary of Shiloh seems to have enjoyed significant status as the former "dwelling-place" of the divine name (Jer 7:12, 14; Ps 78:60; see also Josh 18:1; 22:9, 12; Judg 21; 1 Sam 1:21; 2:14, 22, 28).

Second, the theory that the centralization laws were innovations associated with the Josianic Reform assumes that Israelites will have once worshiped at a number of local sanctuaries. The question arises as to whether the presence of the ark of the covenant may not have lent a given site special significance and contributed to a "centralizing tendency" originating as early as the period of the judges, for example. In fact, the Bible refers, in addition to Shiloh, to Bethel (Judg 20:27; many view this verse, however, as a later addition; see J. G. McConville for the details of this discussion and for a helpful treatment of the history of scholarship on the entire question of cult centralization) in contexts suggesting that it once enjoyed preeminence.

On the other hand, if the centralization laws of Deuteronomy advocate central, but not exclusive status for a leading sanctuary, their concern for profane slaughter and provision for Levites far removed from this sanctuary becomes problematical. If the Deuteronomic Code endorses "satellite" sanctuaries—so long as the primacy of the central sanctuary, presumably the seat of the ark of the covenant, is preserved—why should Levites in the vicinity of these satellites need special care? Activity at these local sanctuaries should provide them with sufficient income (see Judg 17:1-13, for example). Profane slaughter and special concern for the economic welfare of the Levites seems to support the notion that the altar law calls for an end to sacrificial activity formerly carried out at peripheral sanctuaries. Furthermore, the Deuteronomistic history, in at least one key passage (Solomon's dedicatory address inaugurating worship in the Jerusalem temple) explicitly identifies Jerusalem as the intended central sanctuary: "Since the day that I brought my people Israel out of Egypt, I chose no city in all the tribes of Israel in which to build a house, that my name might be there" (1 Kgs 8:16).

Regardless of whether the centralization laws of Deuteronomy refer specifically and exclusively to Jerusalem, the theological impetus for the centralization laws is clear. Similar to the attitude of the Cis-Jordanian tribes reported in Judg 22, the Deuteronomic Code, either in substantially its original form or in a second edition, feared the danger of "strange worship" at outlying sanctuaries. Orthodoxy could best be assured by bringing the cult under the control of a central priestly hierarchy.

J. G. McConville, *Law and Theology in Deuteronomy* (JSOTS 33; Sheffield, 1984), 21-38.

also follow a common structure, first enunciating a negative prohibition, then its corollary positive injunction. Each, however, deals with a unique rationale for, or implication of, the centralization regulation. The first subunit (vv. 2-7) explains the need for centralization in contrast to the cultic practices of Israel's Canaanite neighbors. The second (vv. 8-12) views centralization as the appropriate model for life in the land, that is, in contrast to sacrificial practices observed during Israel's migration to the promised land [Sacrifice During the Wilderness Period]. The third (vv. 13-27) makes provisions to alleviate one impractical result of centralization, namely, the fact that since apparently all slaughter of animals had been previously considered sacrifice, Israelites far removed from the central sanctuary would now otherwise be forbidden to eat meat except on pilgrimages to the central sanctuary.

Not Like the Canaanites, 12:2-7

The first version of the centralization law begins by calling for the eradication of the cult sites and objects of the Canaanite population that inhabited Palestine when Israel arrived there (vv. 2-3). Israel is not to worship YHWH in the manner the Canaanites worshiped their gods (v. 4). To insure that Israel does not adopt Canaanite practices, YHWH will choose a place for his sanctuary, a place free of the corrupting influences of Canaanite religion. All sacrifices—both prescribed and voluntary, animal and vegetable—are to be offered there.

The description of the objects to be demolished employs very characteristic Deuteronomic/Deuteronomistic terminology and polemic. "On the high places and under every green tree" reflects

---

Sacrifice During the Wilderness Period

Lev 17, although probably formulated in its current form well after the wilderness period, reflects the ideal. Israelites could offer sacrifice "in the open field" (v. 5), but they were required to bring the blood to the mobile "tent of meeting" to be dedicated to YHWH. This provision ensured the proper respect for blood, the seat of life, and guarded against the pagan practice of offering sacrifice to "goat-demons" (v. 7). In keeping with Priestly theology, the emphasis in Lev 17 is not upon a fixed place (later Jerusalem, for example), but upon the tent. Deuteronomy thinks rather of a fixed locale.

Pillars and Asherim: "Canaanite" Elements in Israelite Religion

The pillars (Heb. *maṣṣēbôt*) mentioned in Deut 12:3 were stone columns such as are commonly found in association with ancient religions. Like many such cultic objects, they were associated with fertility. Evidence suggests that the *asherim* were wooden carvings in the form of stylized trees, probably date palms (see Saul Olyan's monograph for a thorough discussion of scholarship on the role of Asherah in ancient Israelite religion and a careful analysis of extant evidence on the matter), associated with the goddess Asherah. Deuteronomy (7:5; 12:3; 16:21) and Deuteronomistic literature (1 Kgs 14:23; 2 Kgs 13:6; 17:9-12; 18:4; 21:3, for example) describe these cult objects as though they were originally Canaanite and were borrowed into Israel's worship of YHWH after Israel's arrival in the promised land as foreign, corrupting elements.

Biblical evidence outside Deuteronomy and the Deuteronomistic History suggests, however, that these symbols were ancient and accepted components of Israel's religion until the reforms associated especially with Asa (1 Kgs 15:9-24), Hezekiah (2 Kgs 18:1-8), Josiah (2 Kgs 23), and the book of Deuteronomy itself (concerning the identification of the "book of the Torah" mentioned in 2 Kgs 22–23 with some form of the book of Deuteronomy, see the Introduction). The patriarch Abraham planted a tamarisk tree (Heb. *'eṣel*) to establish Beersheba as a cult site (Gen 26:23-25). No lesser figures than Jacob (28:11-22; 31:13, 45; 35:14, 20), Moses (Exod 24:4), and Joshua (Josh 4:8-10) erected stone pillars to commemorate significant moments and to mark sacred sites. Prophets active prior to the period of the Josianic/Deuteronomic reforms make no mention whatsoever of the asherah known to have been standing in Samaria at least since the time of Ahab (1 Kgs 16:32-33). Taken together, this evidence strongly supports the thesis that pillars and asherim were native to Yahwism.

Saul M. Olyan, *Asherah and the Cult of Yahweh in Israel* (SBL.MS 34; Atlanta: Scholars Press, 1988), 1-3.

the ancient association of height and fertility with the presence of divine beings and becomes a standard phrase in the school of thought influenced by Deuteronomy (see 1 Kgs 14:23; 2 Kgs 16:4; 17:10; 2 Chr 28:4; Isa 57:5; Jer 2:20; 3:6, 13; 17:2; Ezek 6:13; 20:47). "Pillars" and "sacred trees" were fertility symbols whose role in early and middle Israelite religion remains unclear [Pillars and Asherim], as does the precise relationship between such objects and the commandment against graven images. Although scholars often describe Israelite religion as "aniconic" (that is, a religion that does not employ graphic imagery or statuary as an element of worship), biblical and archeological evidence suggests, to the contrary, that both "official/orthodox" and "popular" Israelite religious practices involved a free use of imagery: the ark of the covenant with its cherubim-adorned covering, ornately embroidered curtains in the tabernacle, rich ornamentation in the Jerusalem temple, not to mention non-sanctioned statuettes, especially of calves, discovered in archeological digs outside Jerusalem. ["Canaanite" Elements in Israelite Religion] The key distinctions from the biblical perspective seem to involve whether the iconography attempts to represent YHWH himself or whether it may, because of its association with non-Yahwistic religion, become a syncretistic influence. ["Syncretism"] Deuteronomy and the Deuteronomistic movement detested the high places and *maṣṣēbôt* ("pillars") for the latter reason, considered them idolatrous, and advocated their eradication. The worship of YHWH was not to be confused in any way with the worship of Baal. [Baalism]

"Syncretism"

"Syncretism" is a phenomenon observable in many religions in which elements (practices, beliefs, or symbols) of another religion are adopted, borrowed, or adapted. Religion is an artifact of human cultures. The practices and beliefs associated with the worship of YHWH, for example, represent in part Israel's understanding of its God and its response to its God. Modern believers need only to worship with fellow believers, even of the same tradition, in other places in the world to discover the extent to which one's own variety of religious expression bears the marks of a specific culture, time, and place. In other words, it is not possible to practice a variety of Christianity (or Judaism or Buddhism for that matter) devoid of any and all cultural influence.

The Deuteronomic Code addressed the fear that certain practices and symbols provided a dangerous point of contact with Canaanite religion. Modern believers rarely fear such pollution from other religions, although some avoid what they feel are "pagan" influences associated with holidays such as Halloween. For the most part, the phenomenon of syncretism poses two much more subtle dangers to the modern church. First, too many assume uncritically that God has ordained their own varieties of expression—that is, they do not acknowledge the human, cultural, artificial dimensions of religious belief and practice. Pipe organs and the eleven o'clock worship hour are not in themselves sacred! Second, this sometimes willful ignorance of the cultural aspect of religion permits an easy identification of Christianity with its host culture. One need only study the history of missions to see the degree to which Christian missionaries equated evangelizing with westernizing! To be sure, churches in the West will display uniquely Western characteristics. At the same time, however, churches in the West ought to maintain constant vigilance against the consumerism, materialism, and power politics so characteristic of Western culture yet so contrary to the gospel.

"Canaanite" Elements in Israelite Religion

Archeological evidence from two Iron Age sites, Khirbet el-Qom and Kuntillet ʿAjrud, confirm that, at least among the populace, *asherah* (although it is unclear whether these inscriptions refer to the cult object or to the goddess associated with it) played a significant role in Israelite religion. Because these inscriptions were imperfectly executed, because they consist of consonants only (thus, they are said to be "unpointed"—Hebrew was written without vowels until well into the Common Era), and because they are fragmentary, however, scholars have engaged in a vigorous debate concerning their precise translation and interpretation.

Tomb inscription no. 3 from Khirbet el-Qom (c. 700 BC), lines 2-3, reads *brk* (or *brkt*) *ʿryhw lyhwh / wmṣryh lʾšrth hwšʿlh*, "Blessed be (or "I bless") Uriyahu by YHWH / and from his enemies (or "my guardian"; scholars disagree as to the proper translation of the first word of line 3. Even those who offer suggestions admit their own uncertainty.) by his asherah/Asherah deliver him." Here, the reference to asherah is unmistakable, although whether to the cult symbol (hence "asherah") or the goddess (hence "Asherah") is entirely obscure.

Several stone jars ("pithoi," singular "pithos") discovered at Kuntillet ʿAjrud mention asherah. Pithos A bears the inscription *brkt ʿtkm lyhwh šmrn wlʾšrth*, "I bless you by YHWH our guardian (or "of Samaria") and by his asherah," along with a number of crude drawings. Variations of this blessing appear on other pithoi. The proper translation of *šmrn* is disputed: Some scholars "point" (i.e., supply vowels) **šomirinu* (the asterisk indicates a conjectural form) and translate "our guardian" (Z. Meshel, "Kuntillet ʿArjud—An Israelite Religious Center in the Northern Sinai," *Expedition* 20 [1978]: 50-54; *Kuntillet ʿAjrud: A Religious Center from the Time of the Judaean Monarchy*, Museum Catalogue 175 [Jerusalem: Israel Museum, 1978]; J. Naveh, "Graffiti and Dedications," *BASOR* 235 [1979]: 27-30; and others).

Others point to the expression "YHWH of Teman" in other inscriptions from Kuntillet ʿAjrud and to the common Semitic "Divine Name of Place Name" pattern as evidence that *šmrn* should be read as the place name Samaria (Heb. *šomron*) (M. Gilula, "To Yahweh Shomron and to his Asherah," *Shnaton* 3 [1978/79]: 129-37 [Hebrew]; J. Emerton, "New Light on Israelite Religion: The Implications of the Inscriptions from Kuntillet ʿArjud," *ZAW* 94 [1982]: 2-20; and others).

The reference to asherah is unmistakable. Four figures appear on the pithos. Scholarly discussion of these figures demonstrates the difficulty involved in interpreting pictures. Is the drawing related to the text? Was it drawn by one artist or two? Who do the figures represent? What is the significance of the tree-ibex-lion figure? What are the genders of the two figures in the foreground? Who is the lyre-player seated in the background and what is the significance of music for the whole scene?

The cumulative evidence of biblical references to Asherah and archeological discoveries such as those at Khirbet el-Qom and Kuntillet ʿAjrud lead S. Olyan, for example, to conclude that: (1) the asherah was a cult symbol in the worship of YHWH from very early times (that is, it was not borrowed from the Canaanites), (2) the goddess Asherah was probably considered YHWH's consort by some Israelites at some period in history, (3) this component of Yahwism was widespread and officially sanctioned (both in the north, witness the asherah of Samaria, and the south, witness the asherah in the Jerusalem temple), and (4) motivated by an interest in a strict interpretation of the first commandment perhaps, the Deuteronomists and others mounted a successful campaign to eradicate Asherah and her cult symbol from Israelite religion (*Asherah*, 33-37).

This information may trouble some believers who assume that Israelite religion was always strictly monotheistic. It is important, however, to keep in mind two very basic realities. First, the Bible itself does not shrink from the admission that Abraham and his descendants often "worshiped other gods" (Josh 24:2). Why else would Deuteronomy insist so fervently that Israel refrain from such practices? Second, the evidence suggests that Israel worshiped YHWH first and foremost, but that it came only over time to the conviction that YHWH is the sole God. This awareness need not disturb modern believers. Christians in a prior generation endorsed and practiced slavery, regarding it a divinely ordained institution. Nothing is to be gained by denying these facts. They must be acknowledged. At the same time, however, modern Christians can be thankful that Israel gained deeper insight into God's character, insight that comprises part of Christianity's Hebrew heritage.

Asherah

Asherah was honored as a sacred tree, with upright posts or living trees to represent her.

Asherah. 1200 BC. From Minet el Beida. Ugarit, Syria. Louvre. Paris, France.

Baalism

AΩ It is not uncommon for readers of the Old Testament to assume that the Canaanite worship of Ba'al was a uniform, well-defined religion. In fact, for a number of reasons, scholars know relatively little with certainty about the nature of Ba'al worship. The term "Canaanite" itself is rather imprecise. As a linguistic designation, it equates generally with the languages and dialects comprising the "West Semitic" family that includes Hebrew, Ammonite, Moabite, Edomite, Phoenician, and other languages spoken in and around the Levant. As an ethnic term, it refers, somewhat imprecisely, to those who spoke a West Semitic language. Ethnicity is a notoriously elusive concept. By defining people groups according to their languages, anthropologists choose to categorize by cultural rather than "racial" criteria.

Just as "Canaanite" is an umbrella term for several languages and cultures, the character of "Canaanite" religion seems to have varied widely from place to place. It is much more accurate, then, to speak of Moabite or Ammonite religion, than to speak of "Canaanite" religion. Relatedly, the term "Ba'al," a common Semitic (present also in East and South Semitic languages) title meaning "lord" and sometimes "husband," can refer to any of the number of deities who were revered as the high god in a local pantheon or as the patron deity of a place or nation (compare Ba'al Peor, or the "Lord of Peor," Num 25:3, 5; Deut 4:3; Ps 106:28; Hos 9:10). Thus, the Moabites worshiped Lord Chemosh and the inhabitants of Ugarit seem to have worshiped Hadad, the storm god, as Ba'al. Ba'al did not refer to a single deity throughout the "Canaanite" world.

It is certain, however, that Deuteronomy and the Deuteronomistic history reject and despise Baalism, whatever its precise character, because of the demand for devotion to YHWH only. The Bible has no interest in describing and analyzing Baalism, its myths, or its practices. From the Bible's perspective, to worship YHWH faithfully is to reject Ba'al. Nothing more need be said.

It may seem incomprehensible that an Israelite—reared in the traditions of the patriarchs, the exodus, the wilderness wandering, and the conquest—would have been interested in "experimenting" with the worship of other gods. From a modern Judeo-Christian perspective, such behavior would be tantamount to a renunciation of one's basic beliefs. Several factors operative in the ancient context, however, explain why such experimentation was not only a real possibility, but a documented actuality in ancient Israel.

First, as discussed at several points above, Israel's faith became strictly monotheistic over the course of a period of development. Although the origins of Israel's faith are, to a degree, shrouded in the mists of time, Scripture witnesses to the fact that Israel's ancestors were polytheists (Josh 24:2, for example) and that, after they began to worship YHWH, they did not immediately or consistently deny the existence of other deities. Thus, an act that for modern Jewish or Christian believers would be an outright rejection of the fundamental tenet of monotheism was, for the ancient Israelite, a violation of allegiance to YHWH. Violation of covenant allegiance to YHWH as Israel's God was, to be sure, the most serious offense possible in the viewpoint of the book of

Deuteronomy, but it was not beyond the realm of the ancient Israelite's understanding of reality. There were, they believed, other gods than YHWH.

Second, although archeologists and historians of Israelite religion have only piecemeal evidence so that a detailed picture of the development of Israel's faith is not possible at this time, it seems very probable that, at least in some circles and at certain periods, YHWH was seen as the high god in a pantheon. In other words, clear, although incomplete, evidence suggests very strongly that Israelites continued to be polytheists differentiated from the Moabites or the Ammonites, for example, largely by the fact that they worshiped YHWH, not Molek or Chemosh, as their national god. [Ugaritic Religion] At the same time, however, a growing segment of Israelite society, with roots dating back at least to the prophet Elijah—and including Hosea, the Deuteronomic and Deuteronomistic authors, Jeremiah, and others—pushed for the exclusive worship of YHWH, and soon, for the acknowledgement that YHWH alone is God (for more on the whole question of early Israel's "henotheism" see the commentary and sidebars on 4:32-40). For the average Israelite alive when Deuteronomy was written, "secondary" allegiances to other gods were entirely conceivable.

Third, polytheism tends to think of the gods in terms of a division of labor. For example, the Greco-Roman god Hermes-Mercury, the messenger of the gods, was responsible for merchants and messengers, Aphrodite-Venus, the goddess of love and beauty, and Ares-Mars, the god of war and thieves. Similarly, in the West Semitic realm, Baal, to name only one example, was the god of fertility. To the extent that the mindset of the ancient Israelites reflected polytheistic tendencies, then, it is little wonder, given Israel's normative patriarchal and exodus traditions, that they may have associated YHWH with the needs of nomadic and seminomadic shepherds[1] and with the military affairs of the nation.[2] The prophetic polemic against the worship of Baal preserved in Hosea 2 gives explicit evidence that at least some Israelites during the eighth century had come to assume such a division of labor between YHWH, presumably viewed as guide and warrior, and Baal, giver of rain and harvest.

Not as in the Wilderness, 12:8-12

The second version of the centralization regulation reflects an awareness that it is an innovation. Presumably, during the wilderness wanderings, Israelites sacrificed as they found it necessary ("each did right in his own eyes," v. 8) along the way. Contrary to a

Ugaritic Religion

The most extensive sources concerning a particular variety of "Canaanite" religion consist of the ritual and mythical texts discovered at Ugarit, modern-day Ras Shamra. Ugarit, a commercial center on the seacoast of modern Lebanon, flourished until the middle of the 13th century BC. Obviously, its distance from the Israel addressed by Deuteronomy—geographically, chronologically, and perhaps even culturally—mitigates the usefulness of the information from Ugarit. Nevertheless, Ugarit provides the most comprehensive information available to date concerning non-Israelite, West Semitic religion in the period before Israel's rise as a nation.

Because of their subject matter and well-preserved state, the so-called "Baal and Anath" cycle of texts from Ugarit have attracted considerable scholarly attention. (For more on the Ugaritic Baal-Anath cycle, see P. Craigie, *Ugarit and the Old Testament* [Grand Rapids: Eerdmans, 1983]; N. Habel, *Yahweh versus Baal: A Conflict of Religious Cultures—A Study in the Relevance of Ugaritic Materials for the Early Faith of Israel* [New York: Bookman Associates, 1964]; J. de Moor, *The Seasonal Pattern in the Ugaritic Myth of Ba'lu According to the Version of Illimilku* [AOAT 16; Kevelaer: Butzon & Bercker, 1971]; M. Smith, *The Ugaritic Baal Cycle* [VTSup 55; New York: Brill, 1996]; G. Young, ed. *Ugarit in Retrospect: 50 Years of Ugarit and Ugaritic* [Winona Lake IN: Eisenbrauns, 1981]; etc.) They recount the story of Ba'al's ascension to the status of high god in the Ugaritic pantheon. El Elyon, the high god in many Canaanite pantheons (see also Gen 14:17-24; etc.), has apparently decided to retire from playing an active role in governing the universe. El confers authority on Ba'al, the "Rider of the Clouds." As a first order of business, Ba'al commissions Kothar-wa-Hasis, the builder god, to construct a new palace. Curiously, Ba'al specifies that the palace be windowless.

His reasoning soon becomes clear. Yamm, the sea-god, jealous of Ba'al's new authority, mounts an attack. The gods struggle mightily. Yamm can find no point of entry into Ba'al's windowless palace, and the wiser and more powerful Ba'al vanquishes his opponent.

After only a short while, however, another of Ba'al rivals, Moth, the god of death and the underworld, depicted as a great serpent with an insatiable appetite, invites Ba'al to the underworld for a banquet at which Ba'al himself is to be the main course. Against the advice of his sister-consort, Anath, the goddess of the hunt and of love, Ba'al attends the banquet only to be consumed. Since the lord of the clouds is dead, rainfall ceases, vegetation withers, animals and humans thirst and die. Anath, unaware that Ba'al has ignored her advice, searches frantically for her brother-consort while a number of lesser deities (Nahal, the god of rivers and streams, for example) attempt unsuccessfully to prove themselves competent to replace Ba'al.

After a gap resulting from a broken tablet, the account resumes with the narrative of an apparent ritual performed by Anath and involving a bull calf, another symbol associated with Ba'al (emphasizing his connection with fertility). As a result of this ritual act, Ba'al is reborn or resurrected and order returns to the cosmos.

This myth reveals a good deal about Ugaritic religion. It seems to document a shift away from primary devotion to El Elyon in favor of Ba'al (Hadad in Ugarit, Shamem, the sun god, in Syria) evidenced in other texts from the period and reflected perhaps in the Bible as well. Baal comes to be known as "Baal-Shamem," the "Lord of Heaven." A similar title is applied to YHWH in Old Testament texts primarily from the post-exilic period (Ezr 1:2; 5:11, 12; 6:9, 10; 7:12, 21, 23; Neh 1:4, 5; 2:4, 20; Dan 2:18, 19, 37, 44; Gen 24: 3, 7; Jonah 1:9; 2 Chr 36:23; cf. Ps 136:26). The Hebrew title seems to reflect exilic Israel's interest in orienting YHWH with the pantheons of the nations among whom they lived. In effect, the title is a means to claiming YHWH's superiority (see H. Niehr, *Der höchste Gott: Alttestamentlicher JHWH-Glaube im Kontext syrisch-kanaanäishcer Religion des 1. Jahrtausends v. Chr.*, BZAW 190 [New York: de Gruyter, 1990]). Regardless of the significance of the title for an understanding of the history of Semitic religion, the myth clearly points to the fertility focus of Ugaritic religion. In this myth Ba'al is described as the classical dying and rising deity like the Mesopotamian Tammuz/Dumuzi or the Greek Dionysius.

The myth does not give any clues, however, as to how Ba'al was worshiped at Ugarit. Did worshipers perform ritual reenactments of the myth? Nor can one be certain that a version of this myth was known outside Ugarit.

---

modern reader's likely expectation, this description does not hearken back to a period of romantic freedom. Instead, as the expression "to do right in the eyes of" indicates, in the Deuteronomic viewpoint, worship during the wandering period

Stone Altar
This round altar platform (with steps at left) was used as a Canaanite "high place" in Megiddo, which is located on a hill.

lacked a degree of stability and order that settlement in the land would facilitate. In the Deuteronomistic history, the expression describes the nearly anarchistic state of affairs during the period of the Judges, for example (Judg 17:6; 21:5; compare Prov 12:15; 21:1). The focal point for the cult in this period would have been the mobile Tabernacle or Tent of Meeting. Thus, geographical locale was virtually insignificant. YHWH was present all along the route.

Now, however, sedentary life would present Israel with a new circumstance involving a new mode of worship. Whereas the first statement of the centralization law offered a rationale, the second discloses a tension within Israel's theological traditions and attempts to resolve it. Theologically, the notion of a central sanctuary, whether an innovation dating to the time of Josiah or reflecting a much older practice, runs counter to the biblical affirmation of YHWH's freedom. The first commandment insists that, as creator of the universe, YHWH may not be identified with any aspect of creation. YHWH appeared to Israel's patriarchs and matriarchs at places of his choosing. During the wilderness period, YHWH led Israel from place to place through the pillars of cloud and fire. In Samuel's youth, as recounted in the so-called "Ark

Narrative" (1 Sam 4–6), Israelite and Philistine alike learned the painful lesson that, although the ark of the covenant *symbolized* YHWH's presence, control of the ark did not equate with control of YHWH's presence. On the occasion of the dedication of Solomon's temple in Jerusalem, Solomon acknowledged that YHWH, creator of heaven and earth, cannot truly be said to dwell on earth, not even in the temple Solomon had built to be his house (1 Sam 8:27).

Deuteronomic theology resolves this tension between the unassailable assertion of YHWH's freedom—a notion more consistent with Israel's "wandering" traditions than with a fixed sanctuary—and the demand for a centralized cult through the sophisticated notion of YHWH's "name" ["Name" Theology] and through the consistent claim that YHWH chose the place (12:14, 26; 14:23, 25; 15:20; 16:2, 15, 16; 17:10; 18:6; 23:16; 31:11; compare Josh 9:27; 1 Kgs 8:44, 48; 11:32, 36; 14:21; 2 Kgs 23:27; 2 Chr 6:34, 38; 12:13; Neh 1:9). The people did not choose *for* YHWH; they have no control over YHWH's presence. Deuteronomistic name theology grapples with the constant dichotomy at the core of all reflection on the nature of the deity: transcendence and immanence, God who is near yet far away.

Two other themes of Deuteronomy's doctrine of worship, which will recur as central topics in later passages, surface in v. 12. The Deuteronomic Code frequently describes sacrifice and worship as an act of rejoicing in YHWH's presence (see especially the commentary on Deut 26). Furthermore, Deuteronomy insists that no segment of Israelite society, especially not the underprivileged such as the Levites, be excluded from this joyous celebration (see especially 14:27, 29; 16:11, 14; 26:11, 12-13).

"Name" Theology

In his prayer dedicating the temple, Solomon expressed his awareness of the paradox involved in speaking of the localized presence of a deity who will not be bound to any place or symbol.

But will God indeed dwell on the earth? Even heaven and the highest heaven cannot contain you, much less this house that I have built! Regard your servant's prayer and his plea, O YHWH my God, heeding the cry and the prayer that your servant prays to you today; that your eyes may be open night and day toward this house, the place of which you said, "My name shall be there," that you may heed the prayer that your servant prays toward this place. Hear the plea of your servant and of your people Israel when they pray toward this place; O hear in heaven your dwelling place; heed and forgive. (1 Kgs 8:27-30, RSV)

Not a Hardship, 12:13-27(28)

The third version of the centralization law provides for the alleviation of an inconvenient ancillary result of cult centralization. As do many folk cultures, prior to the centralization of the cult, ancient Israel regarded all slaughter of animals to be a religious act of sacrifice. Now, however, with the prohibition of sacrifice at any site other than the central sanctuary, Israelites who live in remote regions may no longer slaughter animals for consumption—unless special provision is made. In effect, as a purely practical matter, the centralization law introduces the distinction between sacred and secular into Israelite thought.

The significance of this concession, in retrospect an innovation of some importance itself, may account for the fact that the regulation governing it appears in duplicate here. After the initial negative formulation (vv. 13-14) prohibiting sacrifice, specifically burnt offerings (an animal sacrifice), at any place other than the central sanctuary, two redundant subunits state the corollary permission of profane slaughter (vv. 15-19 and vv. 20-27). These two units parallel one another very closely in structure, and even repeat one another verbatim at points: "you may eat flesh within your towns" (vv. 15, 21); "as much as you desire" (vv. 15, 20, 21); "unclean and clean may eat" (vv. 15, 22); "as the gazelle or the hart" (vv. 15, 22); "only do not eat the blood" (vv. 16, 23); and "pour it [the blood] on the ground like water" (vv. 16, 24).

The chief distinctions between these two repetitions involve the emphasis in the first on the inclusion of one's whole household (children and servants) and the Levites in the celebration of the sacrificial meal (vv. 18-19) and the explicit recognition in the second that distance may inconvenience some Israelites (v. 20). The second also promises that obedience to this provision of the centralization law will benefit both the current and future generations (v. 25).

In order to appreciate the revolutionary significance of this concession to distance, one must consider ancient Israel's attitudes toward life and sacrifice. According to the Priestly understanding of the order ordained by God in creation, both human beings and animals were intended to be herbivores.

> And God said [to the first pair], "Behold, I have given you every plant yielding seed which is upon the face of all the earth, and every tree with seed in its fruit; you shall have them for food. And to every beast of the earth, and to every bird of the air, and to everything that creeps on the earth, everything that has the breath of life, I have given every green plant for food." (Gen 1:29-30)

Only in the aftermath of humanity's great violence (Gen 6:11) and God's angry destruction of all life, save that of Noah's family and the animals aboard the ark, did God permit human beings to eat flesh. Apparently, the fact that God destroyed animal life in the flood along with sinful humanity introduced enmity between human beings and animals (who suffered for humanity's sin). Nevertheless, God insists on a distinction between plants and animals as food. Since, like human beings who were created in

God's image, animals are *napšôt ḥayyôt* "living beings" (Gen 1:20, 21, 24; 2:19), and since life is God's alone to give and to take, humanity must never disregard the sacred nature of even the animal life it takes to sustain itself.

Furthermore, the ancient Israelite identified God's gift of life with the blood that flows in both human and animal veins. To shed blood is to take life, and to consume blood would be arrogantly and disrespectfully to transgress against life itself, God's most sacred gift.

> The fear of you and the dread of you shall be upon every beast of the earth, and upon every bird of the air, upon everything that creeps on the ground and all the fish of the sea; into your hand they are delivered. Every moving thing that lives shall be food for you; and as I gave you the green plants, I give you everything. Only you shall not eat flesh with its life, that is, its blood. For your lifeblood I will surely require a reckoning; of every beast I will require it and of human beings; of everyone's fellow I will require the life of a human being. Whoever sheds the human blood, by a human being shall this one's blood be shed; for God made human beings in God's own image. (Gen 9:2-6)

The prohibition against consuming blood (Lev 3:17; 7:26-27; 17:10, 14; 19:26; Deut 12:16, 23; 15:23; compare 1 Sam 14:33-34) and the related injunctions either to return it to God, its creator and ultimate source, in sacrifice (Lev 16:11-19) or to pour it out on the ground, its proximate source (Deut 15:23), abound in the Hebrew Bible.

Relatedly, many forms of animal sacrifice practiced in ancient Israel hinge precisely upon this understanding of blood as the essence of animal (including human) life and upon the notion, often misunderstood by modern readers of the Bible, of the sacrifice as a *communal meal with the deity* alluded to in the phrase "and you shall rejoice before YHWH your God" (v. 18). In short, the blood of the animal, representing its life, is returned to God who gave it. Then, however, in all cases of animal sacrifice except the so-called "holocaust" (whole burnt offering), the worshiper offers portions of the animal (principally, the fat and entrails; Gen 4:4; Lev 1:8, 12; 3:3, 4, 9, 10, 14, 15, 16; 7:3, 4; etc.) to God and consumes the remainder in God's presence as a communal meal.

While the Deuteronomic Code frequently assumes this understanding of sacrifice, regularly insisting that it be a joyous, inclusive experience (12:7, 12, 18; 14:26; 16:11, 14; 26:11), perhaps the clearest statement of this idea describes the communal covenant sacrificial meal that followed the giving of the Decalogue (Exod

24:3-11). This account clearly refers to the two principle aspects of animal sacrifice in Israelite practice: dedication of the lifeblood to YHWH and a meal celebrating relationship with the deity. When Moses had descended the mountain after receiving the statutes and ordinances contained in the so-called "Covenant Code," he offered them to the people for ratification. The morning after their affirmation that they intended to adhere to "all the words that YHWH has spoken," Moses

> rose early in the morning, and built an altar at the foot of the mountain, and twelve pillars, according to the twelve tribes of Israel. And he sent young men of the people of Israel, who offered burnt offerings and sacrificed peace offerings of oxen to YHWH. And Moses took half of the blood and put it in basins, and half of the blood he threw against the altar. Then he took the book of the covenant, and read it in the hearing of the people; and they said, "All that YHWH has spoken we will do, and we will be obedient." And Moses took the blood and threw it upon the people, and said, "Behold the blood of the covenant which YHWH has made with you in accordance with all these words." (Exod 24:3-8)

Then, together with Aaron and seventy-two elders, Moses ascended the mountain where "they beheld God, and ate and drank."

In contrast to modern understandings of the very idea of "sacrifice" as loss or expiation, Deuteronomy—consistent with ancient Israelite understandings—emphasizes the sacredness of all life and the idea of joyful celebration and communion with the deity. ["Imitated From the Japanese"] The worshiper does not give up something valuable. In sacrifice the worshiper acknowledges YHWH as the creator of life and enjoys the gift of meat and the privilege of table fellowship with YHWH.

In fact, Deuteronomy stresses again and again (especially chs. 14, 16, 26) that these sacrificial feasts should be characterized, above all else, by inclusiveness and joyous abandon. The worshiper celebrating God's bounteous provision must not forget those who have no inheritance (the Levites, vv. 18-19; see also 12:12, 18-19; 14:27, 29; 16:11, 14; 26:11-13), those who have fallen prey to unfortunate circumstances (orphans, widows, slaves; 14:29; 16:11, 14; 26:12-13), or even those who do not enjoy the rights of citizenship in Israel (resident aliens; 14:29; 16:11, 14; 26:12-13). Celebrations of the covenant relationship between YHWH and Israel ought to

 **"Imitated From the Japanese"**

A most astonishing thing—
Seventy years have I lived:

(Hurrah for the flowers of Spring,
For Spring is here again.)

Seventy years have I lived
No ragged beggar-man,
Seventy years have I lived,
Seventy years man and boy,
And never have I danced for joy

The Collected Poems of W. B. Yeats: Definitive Edition with the Author's Final Revisions (New York: Macmillan, 1974), 293.

["The Vagabond"]

"The Vagabond"

Dear Mother, dear Mother, the Church is cold.
But the Ale-house is healthy & pleasant & warm;
Besides I can tell where I am use'd well,
Such usage in heaven will never do well,
But if at the Church they would give us some Ale.
And a pleasant fire, our souls to regale;
We'd sing and we'd pray all the live-long day;
Nor ever once wish from the Church to stray,
Then the Parson might preach & drink & sing,
And we'd be as happy as birds in the spring:
And modest dame Lurch, who is always at Church,
Would not have bandy children nor fasting nor birch.
And God like a father rejoicing to see,
His children as pleasant and happy as he:
Would have no more quarrel with the Devil or the Barrel
But kiss him & give him both drink and apparel

The Complete Poetry and Prose of William Blake, ed. D. Erdman (New York: Doubleday, 1988), 26.

recognize the community established by this covenant. Come one, come all! These communal meals will have been anything other than solemn, somber (or even sober, if 14:26 is any indication) ceremonies. ["The Vagabond"]

Apostasy, 12:29–13:19 (Eng 12:29–13:18)

Influences exerted by the presence of "Canaanite" cultic sites and objects in Israel's social environment present one type of threat to orthodoxy. The centralization law aims at eradicating these inanimate objects altogether. Unfortunately, however, as the Deuteronomic authors recognized, sanctuaries, stone pillars, and wooden poles would be harmless but for the choices people make. Even after the eradication of these cultic sites and objects, people who are able to freely choose idolatry will remain.

The second major subsection of laws expounding the first commandment addresses the problem of apostasy resulting from human choices, especially the gross and willfully abhorrent attempt to entice others to idol worship.

The subsection divides into four units, each dealing with the danger of giving credence to a message contrary to the central, explicit demand of the Mosaic covenant: obedience to YHWH only. In each case, someone suggests or encourages the worship of other gods (12:30; 13:3, 7, 14 [Eng 13:2, 6, 13]). Three times Deuteronomy enjoins against listening to this voice (12:31; 13:3, 8). In the last case involving a community that has already succumbed to the enticements of seducers, Deuteronomy requires that the situation be well scrutinized. In the three instances in which a third party or parties suggest idolatry, Deuteronomy prescribes the death penalty for the seducer. Indeed, in the last instance it calls for the ban, *ḥerem* (13:15-18).

The identity of the seducers distinguishes these four units: one's self (12:29-31), a false prophet (13:1-6 [Eng 12:32–13:5]), a family member or close friend (13:7-13 [Eng 13:6-12]), or an entire city or community (13:14-19 [Eng 13:13-18]). The arrangement of this subsection clearly represents a movement from the private and individual to the public and communal. Along the way, the text deals with issues concerning the abhorrence of pagan religious practices (12:31), the necessity of gauging all voices against the Mosaic covenant (13:1, 19 [Eng 12:32; 13:18]), and the absolute steps to be taken to "purge the evil from your midst" (13:6 [Eng 13:5]; compare 13:9-12, 16-18 [Eng 13:8-11, 15-17]).

"Do not ask about their gods," 12:29-31

In a sense, the opening unit of this section constitutes a transition from the material dealing with worshiping YHWH at places and in ways associated with foreign gods ("You shall not worship YHWH, your God, in such ways," 12:4) to the material dealing with individuals and groups seeking to entice Israelites to worship other deities. Deuteronomy 12:29-31 combines these two topics. On the one hand, like 12:2-28, 12:29-31 prohibits Israelites from studying Canaanite worship forms in order to adapt them to the worship of YHWH (v. 31); that is, this unit does not address apostasy in the strictest sense. On the other hand, as is true of Deuteronomy 13, its primary concern is with the seductive voice, in this case, the inner voice of the individual. Curiosity concerning Canaanite practices can be fatal.

The statement that YHWH found the practices of the previous inhabitants of the land to be "abhorrent" should be read in the overall context of the Deuteronomic/Deuteronomistic theology of history. According to this viewpoint, YHWH did not indiscriminately dispossess Israel's predecessors in the land merely in order to favor his chosen. Instead, YHWH orchestrated history (Gen 15:12-16) such that the gift of the land to Israel was, at the same time, the punishment for the abominable behaviors of the Canaanites (see Deut 2:16-3:17).

It is unclear precisely what was considered "abhorrent." Because the Bible often speaks of apostasy and idolatry under the image of harlotry, describing unfaithfulness to YHWH as "whoring after other gods," for example, and because, as mentioned above (see [Baalism]), Baalism included a significant fertility element, commentators have often assumed an orgiastic component in the Canaanite cult. Other than the metaphor and a few ambiguous texts sometimes understood as references to cultic prostitution, however, little biblical or extra-biblical evidence supports the orgiastic model of Canaanite religion. The Bible's abhorrence for Canaanite religion derives, rather, from the danger it poses to exclusive Yahwism. [A Caricature of Canaanite Religion]

Baal

Stele of the God Baal with Thunderbolt. 15th century BC. Limestone. Ras Shamra (Ugarit), Syria. Louvre, Paris.

A Caricature of Canaanite Religion

The many fertility elements of Canaanite religion—some of which also appear in Israelite religion during certain phases of its history—are unmistakable. The sacred pillar and tree (see [Mt. Sinai/Jebal Musa] and [Sacrifice in the Wilderness Period]), the association of Ba'al with fecundity, and the identification of his sister-wife Anath as the goddess of love all point to the significance of reproduction in Canaanite religion.

Generations of preachers, teachers, and commentators on the Hebrew Bible have assumed rather uncritically that Canaanite religious practice also included orgiastic features such as those characteristic of the later Greek mystery cults of Dionysus or Aphrodite, for example. Closer scrutiny of the sources, however, reveals the tenuous nature of this reconstructed view. First, archeologists have discovered no direct evidence of Bacchanalia or so-called "cultic prostitution." One can reasonably expect that, were sexuality an institutionalized element of religious practice, some textual or artifactual evidence would have survived. None has. Second, biblical texts regularly understood as evidence for the perversions of Canaanite worship may be understood more reasonably as metaphorical comparisons of idolatrous Ba'al worship and adultery or harlotry—not as literal references to Canaanite religious practice. For example, Hos 1–3, often cited in support of the orgiastic portrayal of Canaanite religion, says nothing that directly links Gomer's behavior to Ba'al worship. Only the complicated metaphor of the poem in Hos 2 mentions Ba'al worship. But here, the metaphor compares Israel's relationship with Ba'al to Gomer's relationship with her unnamed lovers. The comparison does not in itself suggest that Gomer's infidelity was an act of idolatrous devotion to Ba'al. In short, the portrayal of Canaanite religion as a sex cult cannot be sustained.

The Bible, both here and in several other passages, does make specific mention of a ritual involving "passing [one's children] through fire." The details of this practice, usually associated with the so-called *mulk* sacrifice known from Phoenician and Punic sources or with a possible Moabite god, Molech, are also obscure. [Making One's Children "Pass through Fire"] Whether child sacrifice or a ritual of purification, several texts in the Deuteronomic orbit refer to it (2 Kgs 3:27; 16:3; 17:17) as the practice YHWH found most repugnant. According to the Deuteronomistic history, when the Judean king Manasseh engaged in the practice, YHWH's centuries of frustration with Israel's disobedience reached the critical point (2 Kgs 17:17). After this abomination, there could be no turning back the consequences of Israel's long history of apostasy.

"Do not listen to all prophets," 13:1-6 (Eng 12:32–13:5)

English versions of the Bible include the so-called "canonical formula" in chapter 12, whereas the Hebrew Bible considers it the first verse of chapter 13. In a sense, it can be considered the thesis of the whole subsection dealing with obedience to YHWH's word instead of to the seductive words of aberrant voices. Throughout this subsection, the Deuteronomic Code confronts a problem inherent to its nature and to the very nature of any faith tradition

Making One's Children "Pass through Fire"

AΩ The translation and significance of the phrase "to pass their children through the fire" (*'br hifil* + *bā'ēš*) is uncertain. It occurs several times in texts related to the book of Deuteronomy (2 Kgs 16:3; 17:7; 23:10; 2 Chr 28:3; Jer 32:35 omits "through the fire"; compare 2 Kgs 3:27). The KJV/RSV tradition translates, or perhaps paraphrases, the expression "burn his son or daughter" although, on its face, it could well describe a rite of purification rather than a sacrificial act.

The practice is often associated with Tophet, a cultic site outside the walls of Jerusalem in the Valley of Hinnom (2 Kgs 23:10; Jer 32:35; etc.; cf. Jer 7:30-34), and, perhaps, with the presumptive Ammonite national deity Molech/Athtar (Judg 11:28; 2 Kgs 3:27). The name Tophet, which is related to a Semitic root meaning "fire-pot," seems to reflect the nature of the fire cult celebrated at the site. Evidence for the significance of the phrase *lmlk* usually translated "to Molech" is much less clear. Just as "*ba'al* (lord)" is a title, not a name, *mlk* ("king/prince" in many Semitic languages) may be the title of the Ammonite national god. The vowels supplied to the consonants of the canonical text should likely be understood as a scribal commentary.

Masoretic scribes commonly supplied the vowels of the Hebrew word for "shame" (*bôšet*) to names for foreign gods (compare an even more radical example of this type of commentary manifest in the two forms of the name of one of Saul's sons, "Ishbaal" and "Ishbosheth" [compare 1 Chr 8:33; 9:39 and 2 Sam 3:14, 15; 4:1, 5, 8, 12]). A god "Muluk" is attested in the Mari tablets from northern Mesopotamia (c. 1700 BC), whereas a series of Punic inscriptions dating from 400–150 BC suggests that the phrase *lmlk* may mean "as a votive offering"—an interpretation some scholars find consistent with Lev 18:21; 20:35; 2 Kgs 23:10; and Jer 32:35.

For the time being, absent new archeological discoveries or philological advances, the precise nature of the abomination prohibited in Deuteronomy remains obscure. The temptation to vilify non-Israelite religions as barbaric and inhumane should be resisted pending such new insights. One need not assume that Israel practiced human sacrifice in order to account for Deuteronomy's vehement rejection of the practice of "passing children through the fire." Deuteronomy will have found such practices abhorrent on the strength of their association with foreign gods alone.

---

defined by fixed, authoritative texts. As the commentary above has repeatedly asserted, Deuteronomy encourages (see commentary and sidebars on Deut 4 in particular), even demands, that the community continue to engage, adapt, and interpret its definitive traditions and texts. In order to remain vital, even viable, the community must continually interpret, adapt, and above all, actualize the essence of its defining tradition. It risks losing its identity and its relevance otherwise. To this end, Deuteronomy portrays Moses not only as the law-giver, but also as the great prophet, the first and greatest *interpreter* of the Law (1:5). Deuteronomy 18 promises that after Moses another prophet will arise to continue the function of offering authoritative interpretations and applications of the principles of covenant with YHWH to the ever-changing circumstances of life as YHWH's people. As has been shown, Deuteronomy 12 even goes so far as to innovate precisely because the innovation is warranted by and in service of the most fundamental principle of the covenant.

Deuteronomy's emphasis on the necessity and desirability of interpretive application of the Law, however, opens the way for the possibility of the falsification of the covenant. If, in addition to the fixed documents and traditions of Israel's faith, prophetic voices can claim authority to interpret, apply, and adapt the basic tradition, the question arises as to how to distinguish between true and false prophets. That Israel faced this question during the course of its history is attested in the books of Kings and in the preaching of Hosea, Micah, Jeremiah, and others of the "classical" prophets. During the final phases of Judah's history, numbers of "prophets" arose to offer interpretations of world events dominated by Babylonian expansionism. Some appealed to election traditions and forecast Judah's survival and security. Others, like the canonical prophets Jeremiah and Ezekiel, pointed to covenant traditions and warned that Judah's infidelity would bring about its ruin. How would the people have known which message suited the situation?

The Bible offers several tests of true prophecy. A prophet can be considered authentic if his word comes true (Deut 18:22), if his word confronts the complacency of the status quo (Jer 28:8-9), or if he has been in the heavenly council (the gathering of heavenly beings who attend God, Heb. *sôd*; Jer 23:18, 22; Amos 3:7; cf. Ezek 13:9). Unfortunately, these criteria require knowledge available only beyond the time and place in which the audience must decide whether to give credence to a prophet's message. To wait for the word to come true means delaying the decision to act on the

---

Signs, Empirical Evidence, and Ambiguity

Deuteronomy warns that the prophet's fidelity to the covenant far outweighs any substantiating empirical evidence such as a wondrous act. Perhaps surprisingly, this theme of skepticism and caution with respect to the significance of "miracles" pervades Scripture. In an era when TV and radio preachers market miracles and healing over the airwaves, the Bible's warning message merits renewed attention.

At least initially, as the Bible reports, Pharaoh's priests were able to duplicate Moses' feats (Exod 7:8-25). The prophets Isaiah, Jeremiah, and Micah, in particular, complained of false prophets, diviners, and sorcerers whose messages failed to reflect the covenant tradition of responsibility to God's will (Isa 9:13-16; 28:7; 29:10; 30:10; Jer 2:8, 26; 4:9; 5:13, 31; 6:13; 8:1, 10; 14:13-16, 18; 23:9-40; 27:9, 14-15, 16-18; 28:8-9; 29:8, 15; 37:19; Mic 3:5-11). In Jesus' day, wonder-workers were apparently relatively common in Palestine. During his temptation in the wilderness, Jesus himself refused to base his ministry on miracles and sensationalism (Matt 4:3-4, 5-7; Luke 4:3-4, 9-13). He repeatedly lamented people's shallow and sensationalist interest in wonders (Matt 12:38-42; 16:1-4; Mark 8:11-13; Luke 11:29-32; 17:20-21; John 4:48) and warned against false prophets misleading through great feats (Matt 24:24; Mark 13:22). Ironically, because they were unable to discern the importance of Jesus' own acts, especially in relation to his proclamation of the kingdom of God, some of those who witnessed Jesus' public ministry attributed his power to demonic sources (Luke 11:14-23) and many were simply perplexed, unable to decide what to make of Jesus' activity (John 7:31; 9:16; 12:37). The Gospel of John emphasizes that wondrous acts alone are meaningless, indicating nothing of the character of the wonder-worker or of the validity of his message. They communicate only when, as "signs," they point beyond themselves to God (John 6:25-59; especially 20:29). This potential for transcendence also accounts for the fact that in John the accounts of Jesus' major signs are followed by discourses in which Jesus interprets the otherwise ambiguous sign in terms of the truth to which it points.

In short, the Bible is well aware that a given "wonder" may either be a sign of God's presence or mere magic—in the modern world technological manipulation must also be taken into account as a possibility. A "wonder" may accompany the message of either a true or a false prophet. The content of the wonder-worker's message offers greater surety of authenticity than the wonders worked.

word until it is too late. Who can know whether a prophet has been privy to YHWH's council?

Deuteronomy 13:2-4 (Eng 13:1-3) offers a much more practical and easily applicable criterion. Instead of the empirical evidence of mighty deeds [Signs, Empirical Evidence, and Ambiguity], Deuteronomy calls for the standard of the fixed tradition. If a prophet's message runs contrary to the basic principles of the covenant, that prophet should be judged a false spokesman. In the case at hand, Deuteronomy points out that no true spokesman of YHWH's covenant with Israel would advocate the worship of other gods! This model for the relationship between authentic interpretation of the tradition and the (fixed) tradition provides the fundamental criterion for the relationship between the community's responsibility for actualizing the covenant and the definitive character of the covenant. The community will need leaders—prophets, kings, priests, and teachers—to help it find the way to live out the covenant in particular situations. New circumstances may require creative responses. These leaders, however, must always maintain contact with the covenant. They must interpret the established tradition. They may not advocate a course of action inconsistent with the stated principles of the covenant. They certainly must not advocate a course of action, such as idolatry, in direct contradiction with the covenant foundations of Israel's existence. To do so would be blatantly to "teach rebellion against YHWH" (v. 6 [Eng v. 5]).

"Do not listen to family members," 13:7-12 (Eng 13:6-11)

The unit dealing with false prophecy admonishes Israel to resist apparent empirical validations and apply rational standards to a prophet's message. The unit dealing with family and close friends who suggest idol worship admonishes Israel to resist apparent duty to loved ones and deny emotional ties. An Israelite's primary duty to YHWH entertains no rival.

Two rhetorical features of the unit forcefully make the case for devotion to YHWH over family devotion. First, the list of potential seducers includes only nearest relations and closest friends: brother, son, daughter, wife, and friend. The list includes modifying phrases in reference to three figures designed to highlight the degree of intimacy at issue. An Israelite should not be enticed by the words of even his full[3] brother, nor of his beloved ("of your bosom") wife, nor of the friend "who is as [one's] own soul."

Second, despite the intimacy of these relationships, the crime of suggesting apostasy is of such magnitude that the text demands that the criminal be exposed and executed. Even if the enticing words are spoken "secretly" (v. 7 [Eng 6]), and could thus have been kept between the two parties involved, the Law enjoins the faithful Israelite to disclose the crime of the family member or friend. A series of verbs prescribe the actions of the faithful who is to reject the suggested apostasy ("not yield . . . or listen"), to deny any sentiment or sympathy and expose the criminal ("not pity . . . not spare . . . nor conceal"), and ultimately, even to participate in the execution of the family member or friend as the first to cast stones ("kill him . . . your hand shall be first"). Loyalty to YHWH may require that one be ruthless toward even one's family (compare Exod 32:25-35)! One could hope that news of such a horrible scenario would have a deterrent effect (v. 12 [Eng 11]).

"Do not spare even whole cities," 13:13-19 (Eng 13:12-18)

Since the crime of apostasy is grave enough that one must show even family members no mercy, it comes as no surprise that the Deuteronomic Code calls for the destruction even of entire cities guilty of it. The concluding unit of this subsection on misleading voices and apostasy deals with the only case in which the seduction succeeds. In the event that "certain base fellows" (RSV; Heb. reads "sons of Belial," *běnê bělîyaʿal*) are able to "draw away" the inhabitants of a city, Israel must subject that city to the ban, *ḥerem*, the technical term for "Holy War" (see the commentary on ch. 20). In effect, an Israelite city gone over to the worship of Canaanite gods becomes a Canaanite city like Jericho or Ai (compare Deut 13:15-17 and Josh 7:11-12). These Israelites become the enemies of YHWH and of Israel. The same rules of warfare apply to both Canaanites and "Canaanized" Israelites: everything alive must be killed, human and beast; buildings must be razed, never to be rebuilt; goods must likewise be destroyed; no Israelite may profit from the destruction of YHWH's enemies.

Such apostasy threatens Israel's very existence and must be eradicated. Israel must be merciless against the apostates so that YHWH "may turn from his anger and show mercy" on Israel (v. 18 [Eng 17]). These are harsh measures, indeed. The threat of apostasy is severe; severe are the countermeasures.

Deuteronomy 13 does reflect, in this instance, however, a typically Deuteronomic concern for the ancient equivalent of due process. Apparently, the Code envisions a circumstance in which the rumor of a city's apostasy could serve as the excuse for settling some intra-Israelite dispute. Rumor alone, then, does not justify placing an Israelite city under the ban. The case must be thoroughly investigated and the charges proven (v. 15 [Eng 14]) before the ban can be executed. Even in the face of the extreme danger to the community posed by such apostasy, the presumption of innocence and the irrevocability of the penalty require equally extreme care in determining guilt.

CONNECTIONS

The text of Deuteronomy's centralization law and the situation it describes is ancient, but the modern church still struggles with analogous issues: the perception of threats to orthodoxy, syncretism, the respect for God's gift of life, and a tendency to regard faith and worship as solemn matters only. Admittedly, the situation differs enough that it may be naïve simply to adopt the Deuteronomic solutions, especially since the Bible itself offers alternative perspectives in texts dating from a different period and reflecting different factors. Nevertheless, to regard Deuteronomy as canonical Scripture must mean, among other things, that one feels that it will be both necessary and productive to consider its insights when addressing the needs of the contemporary church of any era.

Order or Freedom?

First, Deuteronomy advocates centralization (and by implication, an administrative hierarchy) in response to a perceived threat to orthodoxy. At the transition from late antiquity to the early medieval period, the church adopted a similar stance in response especially to the threat posed by Gnosticism. [The Early Church's Reaction to Heresy] The hierarchical institutional structure ultimately embodied in Roman Catholicism would serve as the principle guarantor of orthodoxy for all of western Christianity until the Protestant Reformation. In its wake, western Christian denominations would adhere to one of two principles of church governance: (1) Roman Catholics, Episcopalians, and to a degree Methodists and several others would continue an "episcopal" model in which a(n) (arch)bishop determines doctrine and sets policy for the denomination. (2) Baptists, Mennonites, Presbyterians, Pentecostals, and others, on the other hand, appeal to another stream of scriptural tradition and, under the influence also of Enlightenment ideals of individualism and democracy, insist on some form of local church autonomy. For adherents of these denominations, the tradition of YHWH's charismatic choice of

The Early Church's Reaction to Heresy

During the first two centuries of its existence, the Christian church witnessed the rise of a number of groups who regarded themselves Christian but whose tenets and practices were perceived by the mainstream of Christianity to be perversions of the gospel. Gnostics devalued all things physical and material, denied the Incarnation, and sought salvation through esoteric knowledge. Marcionites, named for their founder, Marcion, rejected the Old Testament and accepted a New Testament canon consisting of only the letters of Paul, the Gospel of Luke, the book of Acts, and a book by Marcion himself. In Marcion's view, the vengeful God of the Old Testament could not be the Father of Jesus Christ. Montanists were hypercharismatic apocalypticists who expected the immediate inauguration of the kingdom of God.

The church quite naturally reacted to the threats posed by these movements simultaneously along three fronts, each an attempt to establish that the mainstream church was the true heir to the faith and practice of the apostles. The intended result was a clear definition of the line of demarcation between truly Christian and heretical groups. First, the church worked to determine the canon of the New Testament. Those books that could claim to have been authored by the apostles, the eyewitnesses to the life and ministry of Jesus, or to preserve apostolic memory were given special status. The writings of individuals such as Marcion could not claim such a pedigree. Second, the church insisted that the leaders of the church, the bishops, stand in a line of succession tracing back to the apostles. In this way, it was claimed, the authenticity of the church's teaching could be assured. Third, in a series of "ecumenical councils," the church addressed the thorny doctrinal issues of the Incarnation and the Trinity, producing the definitive statements of these doctrines.

Obviously, all three of these approaches were efforts to institutionalize the church and standardize the gospel. They represented a centralizing impetus in the life of the church that quickly gave birth to Catholicism. They excluded contrary and critical voices. Such are the natural reactions of religious groups whose identities are under threat.

leaders such as the judges Othniel and Ehud in the Old Testament and the idea of the priesthood of the believer in the New Testament conflict with any hierarchical structure within the church.

It is interesting to note that in the modern context of cultural diversity, materialism, and religious consumerism, even churches in the free church tradition have been prone to react to phenomena perceived as threats to orthodoxy with measures that tend toward the authoritarian, hierarchical, and centripetal. The question of proper forms of church governance may never be finally resolved in the face of ever-changing society and ever-new challenges. It may be worthwhile, however, to point out that both approaches can be said to have scriptural warrant and that both manifest strengths and weaknesses. The church must ever be alert to the need to balance order and orthodoxy with the responsibility for respecting individuals and encouraging creative freedom.

Updating or Contaminating?

Second, syncretism continues to be a problem for Christianity. Disregarding the lyrics, Rock-n-Roll developed as a musical form with roots in Blues, Gospel, and Country music. By the mid-1970s, often to the displeasure of their parents, Christian young people simply appropriated the musical form, supplying Rock-n-Roll rhythms and harmonies with Christian lyrics. "Contemporary Christian" music was born just as centuries before Bach and Handel had employed the rhythms and harmonies of their symphonies and concertos in the music they composed for church use. Increasingly, churches and church-related organizations are joining the rush to establish a presence on the World Wide Web alongside businesses, pornographers, and educational institutions.

After all, on one level, religion is a cultural phenomenon like others. God did not ordain Georgian architecture, pipe organs, or steeples. Human beings choose these modes of expression. Such symbols only convey the meaning a particular culture or subculture invests in them. The baptismal candidate's white robe speaks powerfully of innocence and new birth because the church has defined the robe in those terms.

Syncretism such as that ridiculed in the Deuteronomic Code involves the migration of symbols from one culture to another. Such migration is not, in and of itself, dangerous. If a symbol originating in a cultural context at odds with the practice and belief of the new host culture can be redefined, it can become a powerful element in the vocabulary. Danger arises only when the symbol brings along with it a contaminating influence.

The Bible and archaeology disclose ample evidence that, in fact, Israel aggressively borrowed, appropriated, and adapted symbols and practices from its neighbors. From the very outset, Christianity also did this, and still does. Deuteronomy and Deuteronomistic literature seem to have operated on the principle that certain borrowed symbols too easily reminded Israelites of the symbols' significance in another cultural context. Perhaps the church can employ a similar criterion to evaluate its interaction with the surrounding culture. Can the church employ advertising and sales models in evangelism without introducing, even encouraging, a religious consumerism at odds with the Gospel's call to discipleship? Does adapting the ideas current in pop psychology to the teachings of Jesus reduce the church to a support group and dilute the Gospel to a self-help program? Will business techniques applied in the administration of the church's affairs tend to focus attention on "bottom-line" concerns and away from the call to serve regardless of the cost?

 "The Ewes Crowd"

The ewes crowd to the mangers;
Their bellies widen, sag;
Their udders tighten. Soon
The little voices cry
In the morning cold. Soon now
The garden must be worked,
Laid off in rows, the seed
Of life to come brought down
Into the dark to rest,
Abide awhile alone,
And rise. Soon, soon again
The cropland must be plowed,
For the year's promise now
Answers the year's desire,
Its hunger and its hope.
This goes against the time
When food is bought, not grown.
O come into the market
With cash, and come to rest
In this economy
Where all we need is money
To be well-stuffed and free
By sufferance of our Lord,
The Chairman of the Board.
Because there's thus no need
To plant one's ground with seed.
Under the season's sway,
Against the best advice,
In time of death and tears,
In slow snowfall of years,
Defiant and in hope,
We keep an older way
In light and breath to stay
This household on its slope.

Wendell Berry, *A Timbered Choir: The Sabbath Poems 1979–1997* (Washington: Counterpoint, 1998), 127-28.

Commodity or Communion?

Third, modern culture isolates the typical individual from the natural world. Very few people participate in any direct way in providing food for themselves or in clothing themselves or in obtaining shelter. Foods are prepared, pre-packaged, and often pre-cooked. The food supply system in the western world is, to be sure, a marvel of efficiency, ease for consumers, and economy, and no one seriously advocates a return to pre-consumer agricultural methods. At the same time, however, one wonders whether the sterility and artificiality of modern life does not contribute to the psychological and emotional disassociation and social and religious malaise so many experience. Can one who has never even seen a field of wheat appreciate the labor required to plant, cultivate, harvest, transport, mill, and bake one's bread? ["The Ewes Crowd"] Can one truly be grateful to God for the rains sent at the proper moment and for the fact that the hailstorm did only minor damage to the crop?

Perhaps the most powerful such disassociation from the realities necessary to provide for the average westerner's daily diet may reinforce modern culture's discomfort with mortality. The ancient Israelite knew firsthand that an animal from the flock or herd lost its life to provide meat. Life and death are bound inextricably. Modern westerners insulate themselves from this most fundamental truth of nature. By doing so, they have lost a sense of wonder at the gift of life, an appreciation for the relationship between humanity and the rest of creation, and a basic gratitude to the Creator and Sustainer of life itself. [The Biblical View of Nature]

Worship: Obligation or Celebration?

Fourth, the ancient Israelite concept of sacrifice and the communal meal stands as an indictment of modern attitudes toward worship and service to God. For many, worship is an obligation, perhaps a time for meditation and reflection, usually an entirely passive experience. People go to church to fulfill a sense of duty, to be

The Biblical View of Nature

One way of categorizing religions and cultures involves their attitudes toward nature along a spectrum from mythicomagical pantheism or polytheism to empirico-secular atheism. Cultures on the one extreme view the natural world as an extension of the divine realm. Trees, rocks, animals—everything is somehow an expression of the divine. Deities and demons everywhere inhabit the natural world, giving it the numinous quality of the sacred. Typically, the religions of such cultures look to the cycles and rhythms of nature as reflections of realities in the divine realm. Human beings are regarded as but a part of the purpose of the gods. Sun, moon, stars, deer, oak, and sea are seen as siblings, like human beings, transparent to the gods. The so-called "New Age Movement" hearkens back to these cultures.

On the other extreme, mainstream modern cultures, to the extent that empiricism and scientific understandings of causation hold preeminence, make an absolute distinction between the natural world of material causation and anything "supernatural." Such a distinction typically corresponds to one of two positions concerning the influence of a deity or deities in and on everyday reality. A purely "scientific" worldview holds that any talk about God's presence or activity in the world is nonsensical. Only that which can be measured can be spoken of as real. A religious expression of this distinction between God and the world holds that, while distinct from the world, God exerts influence on it through "miracles," especially in conjunction with key events such as the exodus.

As is very often the case, the Bible holds to a middle ground between the extremes. In contrast to mythic religions and in agreement with modern perspectives, the biblical worldview does not regard nature as itself divine. The creation account in Gen 1, for example, goes to great length to make it clear that only the one God acts in creation. No other personalities or wills created. On the other hand, the objectification of the natural world characteristic of the western world since the Enlightenment is equally foreign to Scripture. Since the created order only exists as an expression of God's will, the Bible assumes that God can be and is present in and through the world God made. God can and does act even through the most mundane events and phenomena. Similarly, since the created order exists because God wills it, all parts of creation play some role in that divine will. While it is true that God gave humanity dominion over creation, the Bible clearly expects humanity to respect that creation as God's gift. Gen 2:15 expresses the proper relationship between humanity and the created order in terms of a guardianship when it speaks of God's charge that humanity "till" and "keep" the earth. Biblical injunctions concerning respect for the lifeblood of animals express the same relationship. The world is not for humans to exploit. Humans, made in God's image, are God's deputies in managing creation.

---

motivated to face a new week, to seek answers to the difficulties of life, to satisfy an esthetic urge. Worship is delivered from the platform to congregants who, for the most part, merely observe—quietly and calmly. The ministers preach and pray; the choir sings; worshipers watch and listen.

What's worse, the very term "sacrifice" conjures images of loss, denial, and suffering. Deuteronomy, on the other hand, instructs the ancient Israelite to celebrate, to feast, to party! The most significant acts of worship were opportunities to gather, enjoy, and share the bounty of God's blessing. Israel commemorates the exodus with a family meal. The first Lord's Supper was probably an "addendum" to a Passover meal. The early church, historians feel, likewise observed the Eucharist after a joyous banquet known as a "love feast" (Jude 12). Table fellowship is a fundamental and universal expression of relationship in human cultures. Why have most churches segregated the "fellowship hall" from the sanctuary? God created a wondrous world, blesses worshipers with its bounty, extends grace even to the outcast—where is the party? Unfortunately, Jesus' response to Pharisees who accused him of gluttony and drunkenness suits the modern church all too well: "John piped for you and you would not mourn, we pipe for you and you will not dance!" (Luke 7:32).

Theologians often identify four sources for doing theology: Scripture, personal experience, reason, and the teachings of the church. In terms of a doctrine of revelation, these sources correspond more or less to the belief the God can and does reveal God's self not only through inspired Scripture, but also through the voice of the Holy Spirit in individual lives and in the life of the church. Theoretically, at least (since YHWH is One), if authentic reflections of God's revelation, these sources should be in consonance: the teaching of the church, reason, and one's personal experience should confirm the witness of Scripture. In practice, however, three kinds of problems often arise.

The Necessity of Interpretation

First, all of the sources require interpretation. Scripture, and even personal experience, must be filtered and translated through the application of the canons of reason into pertinent forms. Scripture, as a fixed tradition, often seems limited to a particular sociohistorical context. It is simply not possible to apply it directly and "literally" to modern situations. What insight into the mind of God does the law of cult centralization offer the modern Christian believer? Are Christians to worship only in Jerusalem? Scripture is not alone in this need to be interpreted. Church tradition, too, requires interpretation. In the form of sacrosanct "faith of one's fathers," it often lacks a self-critical humility. Similarly, personal experience is often ambiguous as to its nature (the Holy Spirit or a hormonal imbalance?) and is susceptible to many interpretations. How does an individual evaluate that powerful and very private sense that one should embark on a new career direction? Is it the voice of God or the effects of overwork or tensions with the new boss? [Prophet or Paranoid Schizophrenic?] If it is God's voice, what precisely is God saying?

Tensions Between Sources

Second, even when one feels confident that one has understood the individual sources, taken singly, they sometimes do not confirm

Prophet or Paranoid Schizophrenic?

The authenticity of private religious experience is often particularly difficult to evaluate. Moses heard God speaking from the burning bush, commissioning him to deliver Israel from Egyptian bondage. Mental hospitals are populated with people who hear God telling them to commit murder. How does one distinguish the voice of God from the symptoms of illness?

In an insightful treatment of the pathology of unhealthy religious experience, Wayne Oates commented on the criteria for making this distinction. His comments reflect the seminal work of Anton Boisen, the founder of clinical pastoral counseling.

> One criterion . . . is the *historical continuity* of a leader like [George] Fox with previous, tested, and approved prophets like Calvin. Continuity is *one* of the "operations of common sense." Another criterion is consistency of stabilized social effectiveness in communicating the beliefs to others. This consistency is based upon a kind of humility about the contradictions and complexities that still remain. In other words, there is an openness and teachability in the true prophet that does not appear in the paranoid, grandiose, and persecutory attitudes of some mentally sick religious leaders. Such patients are not acutely disturbed . . . but are drifting and surrendering to self-concealment and deception.
>
> The genuine consistency in the true prophet prompts him to test his insights and revelations "by some stream of tradition," by social criticism and acceptance, and by the social consequences they produce.

Wayne Oates, *When Religion Gets Sick* (Philadelphia: Westminster Press, 1970), 168-69.

Anton Boisen, "The Development and Validation of Religious Faith," *Psychiatry: Journal for the Study of Interpersonal Processes 14* (1951); see also Boisen, "The Role of the Leader in Religious Movements," *Pastoral Psychology 6* (1955): 43-49.

---

one another. Christian history abounds with examples of such conflict. The Protestant Reformation pitted the Reformers' convictions concerning the centrality of Scripture against the Roman Catholics' commitment to the traditions of the church. The American Civil War pitted those who, sadly, could claim scriptural support, if not warrant, for the institution of slavery against those who heard God's voice calling for fidelity to the more basic message of the Bible (see connections and sidebars on Deut 10–11 and [Sacrifice in the Wilderness Period]). Today, virtually every Christian denomination struggles to resolve the conflict between the convictions of women who feel the call of God to ministry and the historical doctrines and practices of the church. Which Paul is to be determinative? The author of Galatians (3:28) or the author of 1 Timothy (2:11)?

Interpretation Circular

Third, the four sources must be held in some balance. The process of understanding will inevitably be circular: one's reading of Scripture is informed, if not governed, by one's tradition. Yet, one source must be the starting point or the touchstone for all others. [Members of the Dialogue]

Members of the Dialogue

In actual historical experience, not all elements or moments of experience are equally sources of the knowledge of God, and therefore of theology, at least insofar as it is Christian theology. God could in principle confront us anywhere and therefore the raw material of theology might be provided in the most unexpected places. However, it has been generally the case that Christian theology has grown out of dialogue between four primary and closely interdependent sources. Theology has usually been born out of the creative tension between the revelation of God (1) in Christ himself, (2) in the Scriptures, (3) in the church as the community of faith and the creation of God's Spirit, and (4) in the heart of the individual through forgiveness and regeneration. These are the members of the dialogue and they will prove to be the great sources out of which your theology, if it is Christian and if it is personal, will largely be drawn. The issues that confront you as you seek to understand your faith will invariably drive you to ask these four questions:

1. What did Christ teach, or what does he say on the matter?
2. What say the Scriptures?
3. What have Christians (the church) believed?
4. To what does my own experience bear witness?

Every serious expression of the Christian faith has been an attempt to bring together the testimony of each of these "moments of revelation," and every great theology has sought to draw deeply and appropriately from each and to hold them together in creative tension. And your personal theology must give evidence of this tension.

C. W. Christian, *Shaping Your Faith: A Guide to a Personal Theology* (Waco TX: Word Books, 1973), 56-57.

Deuteronomy's Model of Interpretation

Deuteronomy, especially Deuteronomy 13, reflects these problems involved in balancing the sources for theology. Inner voices, reason, prophets, the fixed covenantal tradition, and the community find themselves in conflict. Although Deuteronomy emphasizes that there is only one covenant between YHWH and Israel, Deuteronomy does not claim that God's revelation ceased with the giving of the covenant. In fact, Deuteronomy is based on the notion that the covenant must be actualized. Deuteronomy exists as a prime example of God's continued revelation through an amplification and application of the established tradition (Scripture). One can hear God's voice through personal experience, but not every inner voice is the voice of God. God will continue to speak through prophets, but some prophets will be false. The community must investigate and evaluate heterodox activities, but some communities will make the wrong choices. [Fidelity to Established Tradition: Paul and Preachers of "A Different Gospel"]

Sola scriptura, "Scripture only," was the motto of the Protestant Reformation. Heirs of this movement have often naively claimed that they simply adhere to the teachings of the Bible, unadulterated and unadorned. The motto has become a bumper-sticker slogan,

---

Fidelity to Established Tradition: Paul and Preachers of "A Different Gospel"

The apostle Paul warned the churches at Corinth and Galatia against being misled by preachers proclaiming "a different gospel." He encouraged them to measure the authenticity of those who come preaching in the name of Jesus against the established tradition.

I wish you would bear with me in a little foolishness. Do bear with me! I feel a divine jealousy for you, for I betrothed you to Christ to present you as a pure bride to her one husband. But I am afraid that as the serpent deceived Eve by his cunning, your thoughts will be led astray from a sincere and pure devotion to Christ. For if someone comes and preaches another Jesus than the one we preached, or if you receive a different spirit from the one you received, or if you accept a different gospel from the one you accepted, you submit to it readily enough . . . Such men are false apostles, deceitful workmen, disguising themselves as apostles of Christ. And no wonder, for even Satan disguised himself as an angel of light. So it is not strange if his servants also disguise themselves as servants of righteousness. Their end will correspond to their deeds. (2 Cor 11:1-4, 13-15)

I am astonished that you are so quickly deserting him who called you in the grace of Christ and turning to a different gospel—not that there is another gospel, but there are some who trouble you and want to pervert the gospel of Christ. But even if we, or an angel from heaven, should preach to you a gospel contrary to that which we preached to you, let him be accursed. As we have said before, so now I say again, if anyone is preaching to you a gospel contrary to that which you received, let him be accursed. (Gal 1:6-9)

---

almost denying that God can continue to speak to individuals and through the church: "God said it. I believe it. That settles it." Deuteronomy offers another model of the primacy of the scriptural witness. God can and does speak through prophets, to and through individuals, to and through the community. All these voices must be evaluated, however, against the fixed tradition. A new word from God may indeed be given, but if truly a word of God, it will be consistent with the fundamental principles of the covenant. Experience, reason, and church tradition must maintain contact with Scripture.

NOTES

[1] The provision of water, care of the flocks, assistance with enemies; such concerns as the protection of the flocks and guidance from one well or spring to another are, in fact, evident in the Genesis accounts of the Patriarchs.

[2] The Holy War tradition, for example.

[3] "The son of your mother"—in Israelite society, a man could have several wives so that brothers with the same father might still have different mothers; since a woman would normally have only one husband, unless she had been divorced or widowed, her sons would necessarily have the same father.

EXPLICATION OF THE SECOND COMMANDMENT: "DO NOT MISUSE THE NAME OF YHWH, YOUR GOD"

14:1-21

The hypothesis that the Deuteronomic Code is structured as an extended commentary and explication of the Decalogue seems to encounter a significant challenge in 14:1-21. At first glance, the relationship between the material in 14:1-21 and the commandment concerning the misuse of the divine name is far from apparent. According to probably the most obvious, and certainly the most common (in both Christian and Jewish traditions of exegesis), interpretation of the commandment against "lightly" or "falsely" using YHWH's name (see commentary on 5:11), the commandment addresses a category of improper speech. Deuteronomy 14:1-21, on the other hand, deal with matters of personal appearance and diet. How does one's hairstyle (14:1) relate to the improper use of the divine name?

The keys to this relationship lie in a compositional technique that figures prominently in the Deuteronomic Code, encountered for the first time here, and in the priestly understanding of "holiness," in this case as related especially to food laws. The concept of holiness serves as the point of contact between the commandment and its explication here. In effect, by juxtaposing principles concerned with the proper conduct of life in the "private" realms of personal appearance and diet with the fundamental demands of respect for the divine name, the compiler(s) and editor(s) of the Deuteronomic Code call attention to the fact that "taking the name" of YHWH can include, in fact, much more than an act of speech. To be known as YHWH's people marks Israel in all areas of its existence as a living statement. To accept the designation "people of YHWH" while behaving contrary to YHWH's will and character—even in matters of dress or diet—is to "take the name falsely." The bold statements in vv. 1 and 2 ("You are the children of YHWH, your God" and "For you are a people holy to YHWH, your God") confirm that this is the principle uniting 14:1-21 with the second commandment.

COMMENTARY

God's Name and God's People, 14:1-2, 21

For many scholars who would agree that Deuteronomy 12–13 could be understood as an explication of the first commandment, the hypothesis that the entire Deuteronomic Code is arranged in accordance with the sequence of the Ten Commandments runs afoul of the holiness laws in Deuteronomy 14. Admittedly, at first, and even second, glance, prohibitions against certain mourning practices and food laws seem to have very little to do with respecting the name of YHWH. The Deuteronomic editors have framed these laws, however, with theologically loaded statements of YHWH's relationship to Israel, statements that define what holiness means for Israel (vv. 1a, 2 and 21ab) and that give the first, very strong clue as to the relationship between the regulations assembled in 14:1-21 and the second commandment: because Israel is known as YHWH's people—that is, it bears YHWH's name—all its behaviors are "uses" of the divine name.

God's Name, Holiness, and "Being Set Apart" for YHWH

The statement, part of which occurs in both sections of the inclusio framing the unit, "For you are a people holy to YHWH, your God (vv. 2 and 21ab), and YHWH has chosen you to be a people of his own possession (v. 2)" echoes YHWH's initial offer of covenant relationship at Mt. Sinai recorded in Exodus 19:5-6. It highlights a fundamental aspect of the Hebrew concept of holiness: consecration to YHWH. In fact, the most basic meaning of the Hebrew term *qādôš*, "holy," involves the idea of separation, of being set aside for someone or for a particular use. YHWH has claimed Israel for himself. Israel has been set apart for YHWH. At this level of meaning, holiness does not yet impinge upon ethics or purity. As the parallel expressions "YHWH has chosen (*bḥr*) you" and "a people of his own possession (*sĕgullâ*)" illustrate, Israel's holiness equates first and foremost with its status as the people whom YHWH calls his own. Given the Deuteronomic Code's adaptation of regulations applied only to the priests in Leviticus (v. 1 // Lev 21:5), one cannot fail to hear echoes of the statement made at Sinai, "you shall be a nation of priests." [Deuteronomy 14 and Parallels]

Even more startling than this claim that all Israel is "holy to YHWH,"—"set aside" to be priests—the Deuteronomic editors begin the section with the very rare statement of a parent-child relationship between YHWH and Israel: "You are the children of

ΑΩ Deuteronomy 14 and Parallels

Deuteronomy	*Leviticus*
You are the children of YHWH your God. You must not lacerate yourselves or shave your forelocks for the dead. For you are a holy people to YHWH your God. . . .(14:1-2a)	You shall not eat any abhorrent thing. These are the animals you may eat: the ox. . . . Any animal that divides the hoof and has the hoof cleft in two, and chews the cud, among the animals, you may eat. Yet of those that chew the cud or have the hoof cleft you shall not eat these: the camel . . . because they chew the cud but do not divide the hoof; they are unclean for you. And the pig, because it divides the hoof but does not chew the cud, is unclean for you. You shall not eat their meat, and you shall not touch their carcasses.
No one shall defile himself for a dead person . . . They shall not make bald spots upon their heads, or shave off the edges of their beards, or make any gashes in their flesh. They shall be holy to their God, and not profane the name of their God. . . . (21:1b-6a)	
Of all that live in water you may eat these: whatever has fins and scales you may eat. And whatever does not have fins and scales you shall not eat; it is unclean for you.	These you may eat, of all that are in the waters. Everything in the waters that has fins and scales. . . . But anything in the seas or streams that does not have fins and scales . . . they are detestable to you . . . Of their flesh you shall not eat . . .
You may eat any clean birds. But these are the ones that you shall not eat: the eagle . . . And all winged insects are unclean. . . . From among all the land animals, these are the creatures that you may eat. Any animal that has divided hoofs and is cleft-footed and chews the cud. . . . But among those that chew the cud or have divided hoofs, you shall not eat the following: the camel, for even though it chews the cud, it does not have divided hoofs. . . . The rock badger. . . . The hare. . . . The pig, for even though it has divided hoofs and is cleft-footed, it does not chew the cud; it is unclean for you. Of their flesh you shall not eat, and their carcasses you shall not touch. . . .	These you shall regard as detestable among the birds. They shall not be for you; they shall not be eaten. You may eat any clean winged creature.
	You shall not eat anything that dies of itself; you may give it to aliens residing in your towns for them to eat, or you may sell it to a foreigner. (14:3-21a)
But among the winged insects that walk on all fours you may eat those that have jointed legs above their feet, with which to leap on the ground. . . .	eaten . . . the eagle . . . All winged insects that walk upon all fours are detestable to you.
If an animal of which you may eat dies, anyone who touches its carcass shall be unclean until evening. . . (11:2b-23, 39-40)	All persons . . . who eat what dies of itself or what has been torn by wild animals, shall wash . . . and be unclean until the evening . . .(17:15)

YHWH, your God!" (v. 1). As those set aside (holy) for YHWH, Israel bears YHWH's name. Here, the relationship between the regulations concerning appearance and diet in Deuteronomy 14 and the second commandment becomes most transparent. As a nation of priests standing in his service, Israel represents YHWH and

Jephthah's Daughter
The typical "use" of the Lord's name involved oath-taking and vows (see the commentary on Deut 5:11 and 23:21-23). Deuteronomy's creative interpretation of the commandment against improper use of the divine name should not be taken as a denial of the more straightforward application of the basic tenet. "Light" use of the divine name can bring disaster, as it did to the judge Jephthah and especially to his unnamed daughter (see Judg 11:29-40).

Edgar Degas. 1834–1917. *The Daughter of Jephthah.* 1859–1860. Oil on canvas. Smith College Museum of Art. Northampton, Massachusetts. Purchased, Drayton Hillyer Fund, 1933.

cooperates in maintaining the divine order of creation: Certainly, as YHWH's children, Israel bears YHWH's name!

But bearing the name of YHWH brings with it responsibilities. Any behavior contrary to YHWH's will committed by one bearing his name is tantamount to "tak[ing] the name lightly/falsely" (see commentary on 5:11). To entertain any possibility of contact with the dead—thus to disregard the boundaries between life and death ordained by YHWH—or to disregard the sanctity of the life-giving bond between ewe and kid (even the life of animals is sacred!), to name only two examples, would be to betray one's status. Jeremiah, the prophet, mounted a scathing attack against such misuse of God's name in his famous "Temple Sermon." In it, in a sense, he subsumed the entirety of the Decalogue under the commandment against misuse of the name. "Will you steal, murder, commit adultery, swear falsely, burn incense to Baal, and go after other gods that you have not known, and then come and stand before me in this house, which is called by my name, and say, 'We are saved!'—only to go on doing all these abominations?" (Jer 7:9-10).

God's Name, Holiness, and the Created Order

As noted, both the regulation concerning self-mutilation and the so-called kosher regulations in vv. 3-21 parallel regulations found in the book of Leviticus, where they constitute but a part of the priestly system of purity laws. In the priestly worldview, purity involves the maintenance of the order God established in creation.[1] As early as Genesis 1, generally recognized as the priestly account of creation, this interest in and definition of the divinely ordained order is apparent: God's act of creation was first and foremost an act of setting in order, establishing boundaries, and imposing categories of existence on creation. For the priestly tradition, then, "impurity" and "uncleanness" did not primarily involve the ethical or practical connotations often associated with them. In ancient Israel's priestly worldview, to be "unclean" was not synonymous with being "nasty," "dirty," or "perverse." Instead, crossed and confused boundaries were considered violations, or at least oddities, of the divine order of creation. Therefore, they were inherently dangerous. To be "unclean" was to be "improper" under certain

---

Clean and Unclean: "Appropriate" and "Off-limits"

AΩ Modern readers must beware of the tendency to understand the biblical concepts of "clean" (*ṭāhôr*) and "unclean" (*ṭāmēʾ*) as judgments of the value or purity of a thing, animal, or person. At issue, rather, is the system of order that God had incorporated into creation, especially with respect to the forces of life and death. In fact, the terms have to do more with assessments of whether an act or circumstance respects the established boundaries than with their inherent moral value or with sanitation. The terms "appropriate" and "off-limits" may convey the ideas more accurately to modern readers than the conventional translations "clean" and "unclean." The fact that the biblical concept of "uncleanness" does not equate with modern concepts of inferiority or impurity can be clearly seen through considerations of several features of the Bible's treatment of this sphere.

With respect to animals considered inappropriate for food, it should be remembered, first, that Gen 1, the Priestly account of creation, emphasizes that God considered *all* of creation to be "good" (Gen 1:4, 10, 12, 18, 21, 25, 31). In the Priestly view, however, intrinsically "good" creatures can nevertheless be "inappropriate" as food owing to their place in the order of creation. Second, a number of circumstances,

especially in association with the cult, are appropriate for some people, but entirely inappropriate for others. The high priest, for example, may enter the holy of holies (although only once each year), whereas for all others it is strictly off-limits. Again, the issue involves proper order and structure, not the intrinsic superiority of the high priest or the intrinsic inferiority of all other Israelites. Similarly, almost every act or condition associated with reproduction places the person concerned temporarily in a special status. The Bible views sexuality and reproduction as God's good gifts to humanity: the derogatory connotations of "uncleanness" a modern reader might well impose upon the biblical regulations concerning childbirth, etc. miss the intention. In fact, unfortunately, these mistaken connotations have historically contributed to a disdain for reproduction and sexuality in general, and for women in particular. Instead, the mystery and power of life itself, and especially the "off-limits" sphere in which women in childbirth find themselves—hovering, as it were, between life and death, risking their own lives to bring forth new life—requires that people in whom this mystery has been manifest stand apart for a time. To be "unclean" in this manner is not a negative experience, but an acknowledgment of the wonder of God's order.

circumstances, or to be "off-limits." [Clean and Unclean—"Appropriate" and "Off-limits"]

The Deuteronomic Code treats matters of personal appearance and diet from this priestly viewpoint. Deuteronomy's prohibition against self-mutilation is concerned neither with fads of fashion nor even with the psychology of self-inflicted pain: This behavior is "unclean" or taboo not because it is crude or unhealthy, but because it involves a categorical ambiguity (an area with ill-defined limits and which must, therefore, be avoided) or crossing of boundaries (which is therefore an outright violation against the divine order). Leviticus 21:5 prohibits it as an act of mourning for the dead [Self-mutilation and Mourning] in the context of a series of regulations addressing the need to preserve the holiness of priests, especially in relation to the defilement possible through contact with the dead. As YHWH's representatives, the priests may not cross the boundary between life and death, not even to the extent of adopting the visible signs of mourning. Deuteronomy takes the bold step of applying this concept of priestly holiness to all Israel (vv. 1-2).

In sum, then, by framing the laws contained in Deuteronomy 14:1-21—which admittedly, in and of themselves, have little to do with the commandment on the name—with statements concerning the nature of Israel's relationship to YHWH, the Deuteronomic editors declared that these laws explicate (1:5) what it means to be "called by YHWH's name." Respect for God's name involves respect for divine order, for the sanctity of all life, and for the boundaries between life and death, order and disorder.

Self-mutilation and Mourning

The precise purpose and origins of this practice, known also at Ugarit and attested widely in the cultures of the world, are obscure. One plausible explanation regards the practice as an act of apotropaic magic intended, in the case of shaving the head, to render the living unrecognizable to the dead and, in the case of self-mutilation, to offer some appeasing self-sacrifice. Fear of vengeful or mischievous ghosts motivates such behaviors. The Bible gives no indication that Israel remembered the original purposes of these actions. For Israel's priestly theologians and the Deuteronomists, the practice dangerously confused the boundaries between the living and the dead and was, therefore, contrary to YHWH's established order of creation.

For more on the practice of self-mutilation in the history of religion, especially in the religions of Israel's neighbors, see M. Douglas, "An Anthropology of the Afterlife," *Harvard Divinity Bulletin* 26 (1997): 20-23; J. Blenkinsopp, "Deuteronomy and the Politics of Post-Mortem Existence," *VT* 45 (1995): 1-16; P. Xella, "Death and the Afterlife in Canaanite and Hebrew Thought," *Civilizations of the Ancient Near East* 3, ed. J. Sasson et al. (New York: Charles Scribner's Sons, 1995): 2059-70; P. Johnston, "The Underworld and the Dead in the Old Testament," *Tyndale Bulletin* 45 (1994): 415-19; E. Bloch-Smith, "The Cult of the Dead in Judah: Interpreting the Material Remains," *JBL* 111 (1992): 213-24; J. McLaughlin, "The Marzeah at Ugarit: A Textual and Contextual Study," *Ugarit-Forschungen* 23 (1992): 265-81; M. Pope, "The Cult of the Dead at Ugarit," *Ugarit in Retrospect: 50 Years of Ugarit and Ugaritic*, ed. G. Young (Winona Lake IN: Eisenbrauns, 1981), 159-79; and J. Burns, "Necromancy and the Spirits of the Dead in the Old Testament," *Glasgow University Oriental Society Transcripts* 26 (1975–1976): 1-15.

Everyday Holiness and One's Diet, 14:3-21

Having discerned in the framework (vv. 1-2, 21) the key to understanding the relationship between this unit and the second commandment, attention can now be turned to the more extensive materials dealing with "appropriate" and "off-limits" animals in vv. 3-21. Here the technique of exposition by means of juxtaposition is apparent. The material in Deuteronomy 12–13 is unique to Deuteronomy and reflects the characteristic Deuteronomic style and vocabulary. Consequently, the explication of the first commandment may be viewed as a composition by the Deuteronomic author(s). Deuteronomy 14:1-21, on the other hand, parallels texts in Leviticus (14:2a // Lev 21:5; 14:3-21a // Lev 11:2-45; 14:21a // Lev 17:15, compare Exod 23:19; 34:26) almost verbatim. It represents, then, not a free composition authored, as it were, by the Deuteronomic author(s), but a redactional composition assembled from units of older tradition and edited into its present form and placement. Not surprisingly, therefore, 14:1-21 interprets the second commandment not by means of a thematic development of the concept, but by means of a classification of existing traditions. Assuming the validity of the notion that the Deuteronomic Code has been arranged as an explication of the Decalogue, a key question for modern interpreters of Deuteronomy 14 concerns what it means that the Deuteronomic editors chose to classify the laws assembled here as explications of the second commandment. The answer to this question depends upon: (a) the interpretation of the incorporated traditions apart from their current context in the book of Deuteronomy and (b) the transformation effected upon these older traditions by the Deuteronomic editors.

Like vv. 1-2, 21, the *kosher* laws of Leviticus 11 and Deuteronomy 14 reflect the Priestly concerns for two aspects of God's created order, in particular: (1) the taboo involved in the boundary between life and death (as already in the prohibition against self-mutilation), and (2) aberrance with respect to the defining characteristics of a "species." As already noted in the discussion of the cult centralization law (see commentary on Deut 12), in the biblical view, the slaughter of animals for food bears a certain sacred character owing to the sanctity of even animal life. According to Genesis 9:3, God seems to have originally intended for humans, and presumably animals as well, to be herbivorous. In the priestly view, the harmony of God's creation does not easily permit that life be sustained by death. Interestingly, the animals permitted for human consumption in the *kosher* laws, without exception, are themselves herbivores (vv. 3-6). Raptor birds are

Maintain the Boundary Between Life and Death

Scholars divide quite distinctly into two camps in relation to the interpretation of this obscure law. One group, pointing to a Ugaritic fertility ritual as a parallel, argues that the practice is outlawed in Israel because of its associations with pagan fertility rites (see Merrill, *Deuteronomy*, NAC 4 [Nashville: Broadman & Holman, 1994], 239; and P. C. Craigie, "Deuteronomy and Ugaritic Studies," *TynBul* 28 [1977]: 155-69, for example). Others, following the understanding of the priestly system of taboos outlined in the commentary, understand the regulation in relation to the ominous confusion of boundaries between life and death (see Olson, *Deuteronomy and the Death of Moses: A Theological Reading,* OBT [Minneapolis: Fortress, 1994], 77 and, most notably, J. Milgrom, "You Shall not Boil a Kid in Its Mother's Milk," *BibRev* 1 [1985]: 48-55; Milgrom also offers a concise summary of scholarship on the regulation). In this understanding, the Law reflects Israel's repulsion at the notion of consuming the flesh of an immature animal prepared in the very fluid meant to sustain its life. In some respects, this regulation recalls the Deuteronomic prohibition against capturing a mother bird and her offspring (22:6-7). As God's, life must be preserved even in the taking of life.

---

expressly forbidden (vv. 11-18), for example. Apparently, the Priestly system regarded the consumption of carnivores to be a compound taking of life. Similarly, carrion ("anything that dies of itself," v. 21a) is forbidden, perhaps because it is not possible to dispose of the lifeblood with the proper respect and care (and not as a hygienic measure; see commentary on Deut 12). Furthermore, the regulation concerning the kid boiled in its mother's milk (v. 21b), whatever its origin, seems to reflect a horror at the notion of cooking a young animal in the fluid that sustained its life! [Maintain the Boundary Between Life and Death]

All other animals prohibited as food exhibit some confusion of speciation, as the priests understood it. Based on the observation that undulates (animals that chew cuds), also usually have "cloven" hooves, all animals that conform to only one of these defining characteristics are prohibited precisely because they fit imperfectly into more than one category (vv. 7-8). Like the crossing of gender boundaries in apparel (Deut 22:5), and the mixture of crops in a field (Deut 22:9; Lev 19:19), animal species in the yoke (Deut 22:10; Lev 19:19) or textiles in a fabric (Deut 22:11; Lev 19:19), such boundary crossing renders "unclean." It is contrary to categorical order. Likewise, fins and scales constitute defining characteristics of fish. Creatures that live in water (and, therefore, should be classified among the fish) but do not have fins and scales (and, therefore, should not be classified as fish) are off-limits (vv. 9-10). Insects with legs for ground locomotion but *also* with wings for movement in the air are likewise off-limits (v. 19). [Rationalizations of the Kosher Rules]

Rationalizations of the Kosher Rules

Prompted perhaps by the Enlightenment impulse to explain everything, including the Bible, in rational terms, scholars have long sought some "reasonable" interpretation of the kosher laws. Surely, so the argument goes, the apparently capricious requirements are really consistent with some almost modern public health or public policy concerns.

Two such theories have figured most prominently. Pointing, for example, to the danger of trichinosis posed by improperly handled pork and the danger of various kinds of bacterial toxins associated with shellfish, many have argued that the kosher laws represent the ancient equivalent of public health regulations. According to this view, the kosher rules deal primarily with hygiene (compare, for example, the following definition of purity: "the condition of physical cleanliness, personal hygiene, or freedom from contamination . . ."; see A. O. Collins, "Purity," *Mercer Dictionary of the Bible*, ed. Watson E. Mills et al. [Macon GA: Mercer University Press, 1990], 725).

Others, calling attention to the fact that some of the animals categorized as unclean played prominent roles in pagan cults, have argued that the kosher laws address the need to maintain boundaries between the worship of YHWH and surrounding religions (see, for example, W. Eichrodt, *Theology of the Old Testament* I [OTL; Philadelphia: Westminster, 1961], 134). Both of these hypotheses fail to account for all the evidence, however. First, the hygiene hypothesis fails to account for the fact that in the ancient world, prior to refrigeration, all meats and fishes would have been susceptible to contamination—not just pork and shellfish. Furthermore, the vast majority of "unclean" animals listed in Deuteronomy and Leviticus are not notorious as health dangers. Similarly, whereas swine, for example, may have been cult animals in Canaanite culture, the bull, which is considered "clean," was even more prominently associated with Baal. No cultic association can be established for many animals prohibited for consumption.

The lists themselves offer the determinative information. Carnivores and scavengers are prohibited, as are animals of ambivalent phylogeny (i.e., fish without scales, cud-chewers that do not have cloven hooves). Israel's priests held a systematic, although by modern scientific criteria naïve, view of the animal kingdom. Enlightenment logic offers little to an understanding of Old Testament kosher laws.

CONNECTIONS

The problem of the authority and interpretation of the Old Testament as Scripture makes itself known perhaps nowhere as forcefully as in relation to texts that deal with matters of "ritual" or "cultic" holiness such as those discussed in 14:1-21. Since the earliest days of the church, when leaders convened in Jerusalem to decide that Gentile converts to Christianity need not at the same time convert to Judaism (Acts 15:1-21) [The Jerusalem Council], Christians have regarded Old Testament *kosher* laws, among others, to be totally inapplicable. In an effort to circumvent the obvious difficulty presented by contradictory Christian claims concerning the authority and inspiration of the Old Testament, on the one hand, and the argument that such "cultic" or "ritual" regulations are no longer incumbent upon Christians, theologians of the church have developed allegorical [A Typical Allegorical Interpretation of Kosher Rules] interpretations and doctrinal positions denigrating Jewish practice as "ritualistic."

Many modern Jews, especially in the Reformed and Reconstructed traditions, also find the requirements to keep *kosher*, to wear fetlocks and untrimmed beards, etc., to be cumbersome

The Jerusalem Council

The early church confronted the question of whether Gentile Christians are subject to the requirements of the Mosaic covenant, including the kosher regulations, almost immediately. One group of Jewish-Christians, often referred to as the "Judaizers," maintained that followers of the Jewish-Messiah must be or become Jews. At the so-called "Jerusalem Council" (Acts 15:6-23), Peter and James, Jesus' brother, whom Paul would later call the "pillars of the church in Jerusalem" (Gal 2:9), argued the contrary and prevailing position. According to Acts, Peter based his arguments on his experiences in the early Gentile mission, namely that God bestowed the Holy Spirit upon Gentile believers quite apart from conversion to Judaism. James bolstered Peter's arguments with appeals to Scripture—specifically to a series of prophetic texts that anticipate a day when Gentiles will worship Israel's God (Amos 9:11-12; Jer 12;15; Isa 45:21). James suggests, nevertheless, and the assembly agrees, that Gentile Christians be enjoined to observe three (or four) basic statutes, namely, to abstain from (1) idolatry, (2) sexual immorality, (3) food strangled, and—if not a restatement of the previous provision—(4) blood.

James's position closely resembles that held by the Talmudic rabbis with respect to the "righteous Gentile." The rabbis held, generally, that Gentiles had little to gain by converting to Judaism. The onerous requirements of Mosaic Law, incumbent upon the Jews, offer no advantage in relating to God. On the other hand, Gentiles and Jews alike descend from Noah and are heirs to God's covenant with him. Gen 6:1-7 describe the provisions of that covenant. Out of respect for life, Noah and his descendents (all of humanity) are to refrain from consuming blood (vv. 1-4) and from shedding human blood (vv. 5-6). The rabbis assumed that the covenant with Noah included provisions against idolatry and sexual immorality.

A Typical Allegorical Interpretation of Kosher Rules: Martin Luther on Deuteronomy 14

Martin Luther's exposition of Deut 14 represents a typical Christian treatment. After explaining that, on the "literal" level, these laws have to do with animals that are "literally unclean, that is harmful and unsuitable as food for the human body," Luther went on to deal with their "allegorical" meaning. In his view, "the uncleanness of animals means the doctrine of works, which the teachers of law and traditions teach, whose heart and conscience are never purified."

According to Luther, each of the unclean animals typifies some characteristic of such godless teachers:

> Well known is the stupidity of the ostrich, which thinks it is totally covered when its head is covered with some branch. Thus a godless teacher seizes upon one particular saying of Scripture and thinks his notion is fine, not noticing that he is maintaining his position as one who is bare and unarmed on every side. The owl is useful to fowlers, because the show of piety is a wonderful decoy. The night owl does not see when there is light but sees by night. Because a godless man does not hear the truth, he turns to his own tales . . . .

Martin Luther, *Lectures on Deuteronomy*, Luther's Works 9, ed. J. Pelikan and D. Poellot (St. Louis: Concordia, 1960), 134-35.

and ineffective expressions of holiness. They argue, with some justification, that, although the call to holiness voiced in these regulations deserves to be heard in the modern world, the modes of its expression no longer make sense. Moderns no longer view the world as did the ancient Israelites and their priests. [A Modern Jewish Perspective on Keeping Kosher]

The problem can neither be easily nor finally resolved. Modern Christians (and Jews) who value Scripture as authoritative, but who, for various reasons, consider keeping *kosher* inconsistent with other elements of their faith or with the demands of life in the world, can nevertheless hear God's call to holiness in and through these texts. It will not be possible here to present a thorough and well-rounded "theology of holiness" for believers suited to the day. Hopefully, however, a few observations may serve to stimulate reflection on the question and point in a fruitful direction.

A False Dichotomy

First, from a biblical perspective, the distinction, common among Christian interpreters

A Modern Jewish Perspective on Keeping Kosher

Modern Jews view *kashrut* (the rules governing the consumption of clean and unclean foods) less in terms of the ancient priestly classification of the animal kingdom and more in terms of a spiritual discipline. Rabbi Louis Finkelstein, a leading figure in American Conservative Judaism, offers the following comments.

Judaism is a way of life that endeavors to transform virtually every human action into a means of communion with God. Through this communion with God, the Jew is enabled to make his contribution to the establishment of the Kingdom of God and the brotherhood of man on earth. So far as its adherents are concerned, Judaism seeks to extend the concept of right and wrong to every aspect of their behavior. Jewish rules of conduct apply not merely to worship, ceremony, and justice between man and man, but also to such matters as philanthropy, personal friendships and kindnesses, intellectual pursuits, artistic creation, courtesy, the preservation of health and the care of diet.

So rigorous is this discipline, as ideally conceived in Jewish writing, that it may be compared to those specified for members of religious orders in other faiths. A casual conversation or a thoughtless remark may, for instance, be considered a grave violation of Jewish Law. It is forbidden as a matter not merely of good form but of religious law, to use obscene language, to rouse a person to anger or to display unusual ability in the presence of the handicapped . . . The ceremonial law expects each Jew . . . to recite a blessing before and after each meal; to thank God for any special pleasure, such as a curious sight, the perfume of a flower, or the receipt of good news . . . .

The Jews: Their History, Culture, and Religion 2 (New York: Harper and Brothers, 1949), 1739.

---

and theologians throughout the ages, between so-called "ethical" (i.e., "do not kill") and "ritual" (i.e., "do not boil a kid in its mother's milk") laws cannot be maintained. Ancient Israel saw the "ritual" requirements of the Torah as firmly grounded in the *very order of creation*. These rituals were means of honoring and even enacting the boundaries God established in creation. In fact, the requirement concerning boiling a kid in its mother's milk relates to the "ethical" commandment against killing found in the Decalogue, and, more to the point, as the editor(s) of Deuteronomy 14 clearly understood, to the very identity of Israel as YHWH's people. As God's mysterious gift, life—human and animal—must be respected and not mocked. Disdain for life, including the mysterious relationship between birth and death, is tantamount to disrespect for the order of YHWH's creation and thus for one's identity as child of God. Because moderns do not immediately discern the relationship between Old Testament ritual requirements and an ancient view of the order of creation, they may sometimes seem arbitrary. In Israel's understanding, they reflected the intrinsic moral fabric of God's world.

Dangerous Arrogance and Conceit

Second, largely because of this gap between modern Western and ancient Israelite worldviews, Christian attitudes toward modern Jewish practice continue to be ill-informed, at best, if not arrogant. A typical Christian understanding of Jewish ritual would caricature it as dead, ritualistic, and legalistic in contrast to Christian grace and heartfelt faith. Jews do not, however, keep *kosher* as a legalistic avenue toward salvation. They do so because Israel's covenant with YHWH commands it. By doing so, they incorporate even the act of taking nourishment into a life of devotion. Lunch becomes an act of worship, an affirmation of the order in God's creation, a celebration of reverence for life. Obedience to the Torah overcomes the artificial breech between sacred and secular. One serves God not just through overtly "religious" activities. Nourishment and clothing, joy and mourning, planting and harvesting, work and rest all become avenues for enacting relationship with YHWH.

A Distinct Identity

Third, sociologists of religion point out the key function played by laws such as these Old Testament *kosher* regulations in establishing and maintaining religious identity in most human cultures. It bears pointing out that the New Testament also contains regulations of this nature. Paul responds at length to questions concerning the purity of meat offered to idols in his letters to the Romans (14:1–15:6) and the Corinthians (1 Cor 8:1-13), for example. Paul recognizes that the issue confronting his readers primarily involved the believer's public identity. Given the astonishing influx of Gentiles into the church in its first century—many of whom came to the church from backgrounds in Hellenistic mystery religions or from disreputable professions and lifestyles—New Testament authors even found it necessary to offer guidance on matters of cosmetics and dress (1 Tim 2:9). In order to avoid the appearance that Christianity was another of these mystery cults—and later, to counteract charges of immorality—leaders in the early church counseled women in particular to discontinue habits of dress, appearance, and behavior often associated with priestesses in fertility religions, followers of deities such as Aphrodite, the goddess of love, or even prostitutes. No doubt, not a few early converts had been such before becoming disciples of Christ. Even today, although they are for the most part unspoken, Christian groups observe certain "cultic" or "ritual" rules concerning dress, public behavior, etc. These rules are usually defined in ways that accentuate contrasts with the surrounding culture and they are subject to modification over time. Neither Paul nor the priests of ancient Israel intended such rules as requirements to be fulfilled *in order* to earn status as God's people. For all religious groups, however, as for all cohesive social groupings, rules of identity are indispensable.

Modern Relevance

Fourth, the argument can be made that, although the cultural language of the modern Western world differs radically from that of ancient Palestine, the principles enunciated in 14:1-21 continue to lay claim to the believer: Holiness—a distinction from the surrounding culture consistent with relationship to God—for those who bear God's name; Respect for the order of God's creation; Reverence for life. To the extent that the lifestyles of modern Christians are largely indistinguishable from those characteristic of the surrounding culture, the call to visible holiness—separateness—must be reiterated. Of course, it will be difficult to identify appropriate modes for expressing this holiness—no one seriously advocates fetlocks as a mark of Christian identity at the dawn of the twenty-first century. But, with appropriate care and sensitivity to Holy Scripture, the Holy Spirit, and the dangers of modern culture, certain areas of concern can be noted. Surely the people of God can adopt "holy" behaviors with respect to the gift of the created order. Surely the people of God can find some means to bear witness to the kingdom of God amidst the modern consumption-driven economy. Surely the people of God can live in an attitude of awareness and appreciation for the wondrous gifts of daily life upon which all depend for survival. "Fast food," although in and of itself without moral implication, tends to mitigate any sense of deliberate gratitude for and true enjoyment of the bounty of God's world. Surely the people of God can reclaim the sacredness and holiness of God's gift of life itself from a society that spawns disrespect for all forms of life, a disrespect manifest in forms ranging from public rudeness to mass violence. "Be holy!"

NOTE

[1] For very insightful and informative descriptions of priestly thought, see G. Anderson, *Sacrifices and Offerings in Ancient Israel: Studies in Their Social and Political Importance* (Atlanta: Scholars Press, 1987); M. Douglas, *Purity and Danger: An Analysis of Concepts of Pollution and Taboo* (London: Routledge and Kegen Paul, 1966); F. H. Gorman Jr. *The Ideology of Ritual: Space, Time, and Status in the Priestly Theology* (Sheffield: JSOT Press, 1990); P. Jensen, *Graded Holiness: A Key to the Priestly Conception of the World* (Sheffield: JSOT Press, 1992); R. D. Nelson, *Raising Up a Faithful Priest: Community and Priesthood in Biblical Theology* (Louisville: Westminster/John Knox Press, 1993).

EXPLICATION OF THE THIRD COMMANDMENT: "REMEMBER THE SABBATH DAY"

14:22–16:17

In many of the more puritanical varieties of Judeo-Christian traditions, the Sabbath commandment carries very negative connotations. For them, the Sabbath day is above all to be solemnly observed—not only is work forbidden, but fun is, too! ["Eternal Sabbath"] Until recent decades in the southern U. S., for example, so-called "blue laws," designed to legislate observance of the Sabbath, prohibited not only commerce, but even any form of organized recreation.

In both versions of the Decalogue, however, the Sabbath commandment involves not only the prohibition of work, but also a theological basis for rest on the seventh day. The Exodus version links Sabbath observance with God's activity in creation. Even the Creator God rested after a period of work! The very fabric of the created order includes rest (Exod 20:11). Deuteronomy, on the other hand, associates the Sabbath with liberation from slavery, unending work, in Egypt. In this understanding, Sabbath commemorates and continues the exodus (Deut 5:15). The emphasis shifts from the negative—"do not work"—to the positive—"enjoy your rest."

"Eternal Sabbath"

Samuel Langhorne Clemens, Mark Twain, wrote a series of satirical essays dealing with the incongruities of society, religion, marriage, and the family published posthumously only in 1962 under the title *Letters from the Earth*. The excerpt from "Letter II," in which Satan tries to explain the absurdities he has found on earth to his heavenly colleagues Gabriel and Michael, deals with the drudgery of Sabbath. Even more horrific than the "services of praise" staged every Sunday, in Satan's view, is the fact that the worshipers expect heaven to be Sunday writ large.

Now then, in the earth these people cannot stand much church—an hour and a quarter is the limit, and they draw the line at once a week. That is to say, Sunday. One day in seven; and even then they do not look forward to it with longing. And so—consider what their heaven provides for them: "church" that lasts forever, and a Sabbath that has no end! They quickly weary of this brief hebdomadal Sabbath here, yet they long for that eternal one; they dream of it, they talk about it, they *think* they are going to enjoy it—with all their simple hearts they think they are going to be happy in it!

S. Bradley, R. Beatty, and E. Long, eds., *The American Tradition in Literature*, vol. 2 (3rd ed.; New York: Norton, 1967), 489.

The explication of the Sabbath commandment found in 14:22–16:17 expands the notion of the Sabbath rest to include all manner of rest, liberation, and celebration. Much of the material found here is also found elsewhere in the Torah in contexts unrelated to the Sabbath commandment. As in the previous section, the editors of Deuteronomy have interpreted the Sabbath commandment by means of categorizing apparently unrelated and disparate regulations and judgments together as commentary on the basic commandment. In so doing, they have both broadened and deepened the sphere of life covered by the Sabbath commandment, in effect applying the basic principle of the Sabbath universally.

In contrast to the previous section, where the relationship between *kosher* regulations and the commandment to honor YHWH's name only becomes clear upon careful examination and reflection, the editors have left a number of very perceptible verbal clues that the material in 14:22–16:17 should be read as commentary on the Sabbath commandment. First, periods of time measured in units of seven (Heb. *šebaʿ*), recalling the seventh day of rest (Heb. *šabbat*), figure prominently in 15:1–16:15 (15:1, 9, 12, 18; 16:3-4, 8, 9, 13, 15). Only three units, two at the beginning (14:22-27, 28-29) and one at the end (16:16-17), depart from this thematic use of the number seven. Deuteronomy 14:22-27 continue the motif of cult centralization, adapted here to the Sabbath theme. The unit may therefore be considered an introduction crafted by the editors for its current position. Similarly, 14:28-29 and 16:16-17 both feature the thematic number three. They deal, respectively, with the so-called "second tithe" to be offered every three years and with observance of the three feasts required of every Israelite annually. The Deuteronomic tradents preferred chiastic structures such as the one that results from this arrangement (introduction with units dealing with periods of time measured in three units framing a central section dealing with periods measured in seven units).

Second, variants of the so-called "motive clause" found in Deuteronomy's version of the Sabbath commandment, "Remember that you were a slave in the land of Egypt," constitute a refrain throughout this section (15:15; 16:12). Indeed, regulations concerning the Passover commemoration of deliverance from that servitude appear in this section (16:1-8), as if to make explicit reference to the Passover as the model for all other celebrations of liberation and rest.

Third, echoes of the commandment's concern that Sabbath rest apply to all members of the community (Exod 20:10; Deut 5:14;

see commentary above) resound throughout the unit (esp. 16:11, 14). Levites, resident aliens, widows, orphans, creditors, poor people, firstlings of the flock, sons, daughters, male and female servants—all are to rest and rejoice according to the extensions of Sabbath treated in this section. Notably, this section of the Deuteronomic Code applies the Sabbath principle to the classes of living beings listed in the Sabbath commandment ("your son and your daughter, your male or female slave, your ox or your ass, any of your livestock, or the sojourner in your towns," Exod 20:10 // Deut 5:14), although not in the same sequence (sojourner as representative of the disenfranchised: Deut 14:22-27, 28-29; 15:1-6, 7-11; slaves: 15:12-18; firstlings as representative of livestock: 15:19-23; all these classes of human beings, including family: 16:1-8, 9-12, 13-15).

Fourth, the unit makes clear that the most obvious characteristic of the Sabbath day, namely the cessation of work, also applies to the occasions treated here (15:19; 16:8). Conversely, the promise associated with observance of the regulations detailed here is that the work Israel does during the week will be blessed (14:29; 15:6, 10; 16:15). In this way, work and rest are inextricably linked. Although Deuteronomy emphasizes the Sabbath's relationship to the exodus, its recognition of the linkage between work and rest harmonizes with the Covenant Code's emphasis on rest as part of the created order. Deuteronomy also recognizes that the Sabbath participates in the rhythms of life.

COMMENTARY

Cult Centralization: Reprise I, 14:22-27

Old Testament legislation concerning tithes and offerings do not seem to represent a consistent system (contrast, for example, Deut 12; 14:22-29; 26:1-15 and Num 18:8-32). Even within the book of Deuteronomy, it is difficult to ascertain whether the so-called "second tithe" mentioned in 14:28-29 should be understood as additional to the regular tithe every third year or as an alternative procedure in those years. Furthermore, the relationship between the offering of first fruits, the sacrifice of the firstborn in the flocks and herds, and tithes is equally unclear. (Concerning this complicated issue, see the commentary on Deut 26.)

The confusion with respect to sacrificial requirements envisioned in the book of Deuteronomy arises, in part, from the fact that Deuteronomy's chief concerns are not to prescribe ritual procedure, but to set these requirements in the context of a theology of Sabbath. As may be expected, characteristic Deuteronomic issues not necessarily related to Sabbath also appear with regularity.

Deuteronomy 14:22-27, for example, make no effort precisely to define the tithe, either as to quantity, species, or schedule. Etymologically, to be sure, the Hebrew translated "tithe" (*ma'ăśer*) means "one-tenth." But, as illustrated by Jesus' criticism of Pharisaical practices (Mark 7:9-13), strict precision with respect to the amount is not the primary thrust of the biblical tithe. Similarly, v. 22 refers to "all the yield of your seed," suggesting that the tithe applies to crops planted annually. Verse 23, however, specifies "grain, wine, and oil," the latter two of which grow on vines and trees, respectively. Other passages (Lev 27:32, for example) mention

Sunday

Seen from the perspective of a Jew once grounded in Hasidic culture and now living in a Christian culture, Marc Chagall captures a glimpse of his impression of Sunday in Paris. Echoing artistic influences from Cubism, Fauvism, Surrealism, and Synchronism, Chagall uses color shapes and fragmented angles to accentuate the various subliminal images stemming from his associations of the Christian Sabbath experience. Images of the Eiffel Tower, Notre-Dame, and a kind of allegorical embodiment of the hovering presence of the Virgin Mary with Angel can be seen as if from a moving, glimpsed perspective.

Marc Chagall. 1887–1985. *Sunday.* 1953. Charcoal, ink, and gouache on vellum. Réunion des Musées Nationaux.

flocks and herds as well. Verse 23 also refers to firstborn of flock and herd, although the intention seems to be to group the tithe offering and the sacrifice of the firstborn together as subject to centralization, not to expand the definition of the tithe to include animal sacrifice.

Instead of focusing on a detailed definition of the proper constitution of the tithe, Deuteronomy explicitly (a) includes the tithe among those offerings subject to the centralization law (v. 23; compare 12:6, 11, 17; 26:12, 14), (b) makes provision for those who would find distance a hardship (vv. 24-26a), (c) enjoins Israelites joyously to offer the tithe before the LORD (v. 26b;

compare 12:7, 12, 18; 16:11, 14; 26:11; 27:7), and (d) encourages
the tither to include the Levite, who cannot own land and thus can
offer no tithe, in the celebration (compare 12:12, 18-19; 16:11, 14;
26:11-13). Deuteronomy's interest in and rationale for cult centralization has been examined above (commentary on Deut 12). As
with the provisions made for "profane" slaughter in 12:15-27,
Deuteronomy suggests a practical solution to the logistical difficulty of transporting the tithe of a bumper crop on the conceivably
long journey to Jerusalem: one may simply sell the crop at home
and convert the proceeds into "tithable" goods upon arrival in
Jerusalem. The other two features of this passage deal with key elements of Deuteronomy's theology of the Sabbath: joy before
YHWH and concern for the disadvantaged and underprivileged.

Joy Before YHWH

For readers accustomed to characterizations of Old Testament religion as somber and legalistic, the wording and tone of 14:26 is
remarkable. Twice the text encourages the worshiper to convert the
proceeds from the sale of the original tithe into "whatever you
desire" (Heb. *běkōl 'ăšer-těʾawwê napšěkā*) or "whatever your
appetite craves" (Heb. *běkōl 'ăšer tišʾālěkā napšěkā*). Possibilities even
include "wine and strong drink" (Heb. *ubayyayin ubaššēkār*). [Wine
and Strong Drink] Provisioned thus with one's favorite foods and beverages, one should "eat there (at the central sanctuary) before

---

Wine and Strong Drink

AΩ Deut 14:26 mentions two types of alcoholic beverage. "Wine" (*yayin*) is to be distinguished from
"new wine" (*tîrôš*) or grape juice. In the pre-modern world,
any grape juice not consumed within a reasonable period
after production would begin to ferment and thus,become
yayin. As an everyday beverage, wine will have often been
diluted or "mixed" (see Ps 75:9; Prov 9:2,5; 23:30, 31—
a warning against drinking undiluted wine). "Strong drink"
(*šēkār*) may be a generic term for all other alcoholic
beverages.

Partly because it was simply impossible in the pre-
modern world to preserve fruit juices except through
fermentation, the Old Testament does not consider alcohol
to be inherently evil. In general, Old Testament attitudes
toward "wine and strong drink" may be described in terms
of five positions. First, the Old Testament warns against
drunkenness (Isa 5:11; Prov 20:1), especially on the part of
the leaders of society whose drunkenness can lead to
errors of judgment or moral lapses (Isa 28:7; 56:12;

Mic 2:11; Prov 31:4,6). Second, Nazirites and priests
serving in the tabernacle/temple must not drink alcohol
(Lev 10:9; Num 6:3; Judg 13:4, 7, 14), likely because the
ancient Israelites viewed fermentation as a process of
decay. Those devoted to YHWH's service must keep themselves separate from the realm of death and decay. Third,
the staggering and reeling of the drunk can be a metaphor
of YHWH's punishment upon his enemies (Isa 29:9; Pss
60:5; 75:9; 78:65).

On the other hand, fourth, wine in particular can represent joy (Deut 29:5; Isa 24:9). As such, it is a gift of God
"to gladden the human heart" (Ps 104:15), especially of the
poor and the distressed (Prov 31:4, 6). Finally, "wine and
strong drink" play roles in worship. Since it is one of God's
gifts, a libation of "strong drink" is to be included in the
daily offering at the tabernacle/temple (Num 28:7). Since it
"gladdens the human heart," the tither, whose principle
responsibility according to Deuteronomy is to celebrate
YHWH's bounteous provision, may—no *should*—enjoy it
as part of the tithe celebration (14:26).

YHWH your God and rejoice." Obviously, Deuteronomy does not understand "tithing" as a transfer of goods to YHWH, neither in an attempt to appease him for one's sins, nor even as a gift to the temple treasury to finance the temple budget. Contrary to popular Christian understanding, the Old Testament concept of tithes, offerings, and sacrifices has virtually nothing to do with appeasing the deity for one's sins. Nor was ancient Israel's religion as bureaucratic as even the most decentralized modern Protestant denomination. What need has YHWH of the bounty he has bestowed as a blessing? Instead, after a symbolic portion has been burnt on the altar, the worshiper, together with all his household and certain invited guests, consumes the tithe in a festive and joyful celebration of YHWH's benevolence. In this interpretation, Sabbath transcends mere cessation of labor and far exceeds a mere passivity. Sabbath is the celebration of the fruits of one's labor and YHWH's blessing. Sabbath means rejoicing!

The Disadvantaged and Underprivileged

Joshua omitted the tribe of Levi from the allotment of territories in the division of the promised land (Josh 21). Instead, the tribe dispersed among the other tribes to serve as priests throughout Israel. Their livelihood came from the priest's portion of the tithe (Num 18:8-32). One argument in support of the interpretation of the Deuteronomic centralization of the cult as a radical innovation concerns the "country" priests. If they owned no property, how did they survive in the countryside unless by the priest's portion of the tithes and offerings given at local sanctuaries? In fact, Deuteronomy often, as here, expresses specific concern for the welfare of these Levites. Did cult centralization deprive them of their livelihood? (see [Cult Centralization: A Problem in the History of Israel])

At any rate, Deuteronomy insists that worshipers enjoying God's bounty must include the needy and dispossessed ["To Offer Brave Assistance"] in their celebrations. The theological rationale for this communal aspect of Sabbath expresses a key insight into the character of Israel's God and the substance of Israel's relationship with him. YHWH delivered Israel from Egyptian bondage not only because they were in bondage, but also because of his intention to bless Israel and, through them, to multiply blessing in the world. The dynamics of YHWH's deliverance from oppression and gift of blessing, commemorated in Sabbath, must also be *extended*

"To Offer Brave Assistance"

To offer brave assistance
To Lives that stand alone—
When One has failed to stop them—
Is Human—but Divine

To lend an Ample sinew
Unto a Nameless Man—
Whose Homely Benediction
No other —stopped to earn—

T. H. Johnson, ed., *The Complete Poems of Emily Dickinson* (Boston: Little, Brown and Co., c. 1960), 375.

through Sabbath. So long as needy and diminished individuals can be found among YHWH's people, the full intentions of the exodus have not yet been realized. The blessed among Israel must, in turn, be a source of blessing for the poor and distressed. Otherwise, they risk becoming oppressors themselves; otherwise, they prove to be ungrateful for YHWH's salvation.

Cult Centralization: Reprise II, 14:28-29

Deuteronomy 14:28-29 dictates a second means for transforming the impracticality of transporting the tithe the long distance to the central sanctuary into an opportunity for communal celebration. In so doing, it widens the circle of the needy to be included in the bounty of Sabbath. One year in every three,[1] the tithe should be given to the needy and dispossessed at home: the Levite without inheritance, the sojourner without citizenship in Israel, the widow without property rights, and minor orphans. This list, found often in Deuteronomy and related literature (see commentary on Deut 10:12-19 and [Widow, Orphan, and Resident Alien]), describes virtually every category of people disadvantaged by individual circumstances and the structures of Israelite society. The impulse to include any and all segments of society in the benefits of Sabbath joy appears already in the Decalogue's Sabbath commandment. Rooted in YHWH's act of deliverance from Egyptian bondage, the Sabbath cannot mean rest solely for householders while their children, servants, and animals labor on (Exod 20:10; Deut 5:14): Israel, too, was once a slave; YHWH does not want Israel to replicate Egypt's mistreatment of an underclass! To the contrary, YHWH's plan for Israel calls for blessings multiplied!

Significantly, then, 14:29 links the communal aspect of blessing shared with blessing continued for individuals with means. Israel should make this "poor tithe" (see commentary on 26:1-15) available to the needy specifically "in order that YHWH your God may bless every work of your hand you do." As subsequent units will emphasize even more explicitly, stinginess is not a principal of the Sabbath!

Sabbath "Release," 15:1-6

The Sabbath cycle of rest also applies to the burden of indebtedness. Deuteronomy defines every seventh, or Sabbatical, year as a "release" (*šĕmiṭṭâ*) from debt. Apparently, whereas the Sabbatical year tradition was firmly established in the ancient Near East generally, it was never systematized in Israel. Mesopotamian kings sometimes proclaimed "releases" (Akk. *mišarum*) to commemorate the beginnings of their reigns or other extraordinary occasions. They were not expected to do so, however, and the provisions for release varied. ["An Edict of Ammisaduqa of Babylon"] The Covenant Code that, like Deuteronomy, also relates the seventh year "release" to the Sabbath commandment (see Exod 23:12), calls for allowing crops to grow unattended and unharvested to be gleaned freely by the poor "so that the poor of your people may eat" (Exod 23:10-11). Deuteronomy replaces this provision for the sustenance of the poor with the "poor tithe" (Deut 14:28-29). The Holiness Code focuses on the Sabbath year as an occasion of rest for the land, which is YHWH's *gift* to Israel (Lev 25:2). Unlike the Covenant Code, the Holiness Code permits consumption—by landowner, servants, livestock, and wild animals alike—of whatever the land produces of itself (Lev 25:3-7). The land may not be "worked," however.

"An Edict of Ammisaduqa of Babylon"

Speak to Etel-pi-Marduk: Thus Samsu-iluna. The king my father *i[s ill]*. In order to [. . .] the land, I have taken [my seat] on the throne of [my father's] house. Moreover, in order to bol[ster up] the ten[ant(s)], [I ha]ve remitted the arrears of the [. . .], the tenant-farmers, (and) [*the shepherds*]; [the deb]t-tablets of the solder, the fisherman, and the *mushkenu* (This Akkadian term designates persons belonging to a certain socio-economic class. Its precise meaning is unclear.) I have broken, (and) I have established equity in the land. In the land of [. . .] no one *is to make demands* on the house of a soldier, a fisherman, or a *mushkenu*. As soon as you re[ad] my tablet, you and the elders of the land under your command are to come up here and have an audience with me.

Deuteronomy, on the other hand, defines the Sabbatical "release" in purely economic terms, perhaps because by the time of Deuteronomy's composition, Israel had begun the transition out of a purely agrarian economy. Assuming that the total forgiveness of all debts every seven years would destabilize any economy, some commentators suggest that Deuteronomy probably calls instead for a "debt holiday," with repayment to resume in the year following the Sabbath year. Given Deuteronomy's tendency toward radical and idealistic applications of the essential principles of the covenant, there is little to support the notion that this text reflects a fear of economic upheaval resulting from mercy! Typically, in fact, Deuteronomy shows little interest in practical details: the text specifically prescribes a radical and universal "release," not a payment holiday.

Instead of practical details, Deuteronomy concerns itself with theological rationales and ethical implications. A succession of statements commenting on the implications of the Sabbath year release (vv. 3-6) follows the basic description of the practice (v. 2). Foreign debts do not fall under the requirement (v. 3). In fact, YHWH's intentions for Israel are so benevolent that the day will come when many nations will be indebted to wealthy Israel (v. 6).

Double Standards

Drawing on a tradition of Greco-Roman philosophy that emphasized the "infertility" of money—and thus the unnatural character of the notion of money "yielding" money—and on the biblical injunction against charging interest, the medieval church outlawed "usury." As a result, Europen Jews, who were permitted under Deuteronomic law to lend at interest to non-Jews, became major sources of venture capital. In one of history's surely most ironic perversions, Jews and Christians alike appealed to the same Scripture as the basis for excluding one another. Neither was able to perceive the Torah's impulse toward economic justice for all classes and all groups in society. Sadly, this economic symbiosis contributed in some degree to the burgeoning anti-Semitism of the period. Christian merchants who needed Jewish capital nevertheless despised their Jewish bankers.

William Shakespeare's masterful play, *The Merchant of Venice*, hinges upon this uneasy relationship between banker and creditor. Shylock, the Jewish lender, himself poisoned by hatred—both as the hater and as the hated—voices an angry accusation against his nemesis, Antonio, and against Christian double standards.

> He has disgraced me, and hindered me a half a million; laughed at my losses, mocked at my gains, scorned my nation, thwarted my bargains, cooled my friends, heated mine enemies; and what's his reason? I am a Jew. Hath not a Jew eyes? Hath not a Jew hands, organs, dimensions, senses, affections, passions; fed with the same food, hurt with the same weapons, subject to the same diseases, healed by the same means, warmed and cooled by the same winter and summer, as a Christian is? If you prick us, do we not bleed? If you tickle us, do we not laugh? If you poison us, do we not die? And if you wrong us, shall we not revenge? If we are like you in the rest, we will resemble you in that. If a Jew wrong a Christian, what is his humility? Revenge. If a Christian wrong a Jew, what should his sufferance be by Christian example? Why, revenge. The villainy you teach me, I will execute, and it shall go hard but I will better the instruction. (Act III, Scene I)

A modern reader who has understood the principles of Deuteronomy's explication of the Sabbath impulse will be struck by the incongruity of this attitude toward foreigners. Instead of ever widening the scope of Sabbath rest, as has been true to this point, Deuteronomy suddenly makes a distinction between Israelite and outsider. The nationalistic, supremacist pride expressed in v. 6 seems almost absolutely contradictory to the Sabbath impulse. Israel, like the church, sometimes fell short of the liberating truth of its tradition. [Double Standards]

Verses 4-5, which deal with the question of poverty in Israel, disrupt the continuity between vv. 3 and 6 so that some commentators assign the two topics to different hands. Indeed, v. 5 seems to mitigate the absolute claims of v. 4 and may represent yet a third editor. Embarrassed by the implication of debt release, namely that some Israelites will be debtors, poor, an editor has inserted the claim that there will be no poor among YHWH's chosen people (v. 4), that is, *if* they obey the covenant (v. 5).

Debt: The Sabbath Year and Stinginess, 15:7-11

Given human nature, the Deuteronomic Code accounts for an unintended, but very predictable, consequence of the law of Sabbath-year release. If all debts are to be forgiven every Sabbath year, lenders may be hesitant to lend in the time period just prior to the beginning of a Sabbath year since time will probably be too short for them to recover their capital. The Priestly Code deals with a similar problem with respect to the return of land to its original owners in the year of Jubilees by prescribing a system of prorated payment (Lev 25:15-16). It urges against Israelites "cheating one another" by accepting full payment for land that will only be available to the "purchaser" for a brief period of time. Leviticus 25 describes a transaction resembling a secured loan, and it encourages the borrower to value the collateral fairly in view of the duration of the period of use available to the lender. The Priestly system provides for safeguards to prevent needy borrowers from taking advantage of those willing and able to assist them with a loan.

In contrast to Priestly legislation on the matter, however, Deuteronomy addresses the motivations of the lender. Calculated self-interest contradicts the joyful spirit of Sabbath release. "You shall not harden your heart (*lo' tĕammēṣ et-lĕbābĕkā*, "do not be hard-hearted") and you shall not close your hand (*wĕlo' tiqpōṣ et-yādĕka*, "or be tight-fisted")" (v. 7). Generosity is the Sabbath response to need. Otherwise, the hesitant lender may become culpable in the poverty of his fellow Israelite. With no other recourse, the poor may "cry out against" the hesitant lender to YHWH, just as the Israelites in Egypt cried out in their oppression (v. 9). YHWH, who watches over the oppressed, may well note the stinginess of the selfish lender who has himself benefited from YHWH's generosity in times of need. On the other hand, since assistance to the needy is YHWH-like and demonstrates grateful appreciation for YHWH's deliverance and blessing, YHWH will reward it with blessing on all the lender's undertakings (v. 10).

The concluding observation (v. 11) merits special comment. Jesus alluded to it in his response to those who chided Mary, sister of Lazarus and Martha, when she anointed Jesus' feet with expensive ointment, wiping them with her hair (John 12:1-8). The money, her critics scolded, could have been better spent on the poor. Jesus, however, endorsed Mary's actions as a foreshadowing of his coming burial. "You always have the poor with you (cf. Deut 15:11), but you do not always have me." Jesus' statement is often taken in an almost deterministic fashion, as if he meant "There is nothing to be done for poverty. It will always persist. Charity for the poor will never eradicate the condition." If, however, Jesus were consciously alluding to Deuteronomy 15:11, which *commands* generosity as the proper response to persistent poverty, such a conclusion perverts his intention. He means only to call attention to the more urgent responsibility, his coming death and burial, not to release his disciples from concern for the poor. One is time-sensitive; the other will always require attention.

Manumission: The Sabbath and Stinginess, Reprise, 15:12-18

Leviticus 25 deals with loans "secured" by landholdings. Ancient Israel also employed "debt slavery," loans secured by *persons*. An individual could sell himself or a family member into servitude for a period of up to six years. Two advantages made this option somewhat attractive to the poor. In addition to the cash generated for the retirement of any outstanding debts, the new master was responsible for feeding and clothing the servant.

Deuteronomy 15:12-18, which regulates the release of these indentured servants at the conclusion of the six-year period of service, parallels Exodus 21:1-6. Four revisions over against Covenant Code regulations reflect the particular concerns of the book of Deuteronomy and its understanding of the Sabbath.

Gender Equality

First, the Deuteronomic version explicitly extends protections to women (vv. 12, 18). Exodus 21:7-11 severely limits the circumstances under which a female "slave" may go free. The Covenant Code assumes that householders or their sons will take female slaves as wives or concubines. As a consequence, their status changes and they require certain special protections. Deuteronomy, on the other hand, requires women to be treated with the same respect and to be granted the same rights as men.

Protections for Families

Second, Deuteronomy makes no reference to the indentured servants' wives and children (compare Exod 21:3-4). Under the Covenant Code, a man who had married during his period of service could not take his wife and children with him into freedom. His family belonged to his master. How many "voluntarily" accepted permanent enslavement in order to remain with a beloved wife and dear children? Presumably, Deuteronomy's silence indicates that now wives and children may go with their husbands

Resistance

Here, Marc Chagall touches upon his Jewish roots as ancestral persecution seems to frame and almost engulf this painting as images of human oppression and suffering become a haunting, framing chorus around Christ, the crucified Jew. The persistence of the spirit in the face of human enslavement is perhaps embodied in the seemingly incongruous image of a leaping, joyful goat. This painting was exhibited in 1973 as part of a triptych; the other two paintings were titled *Resurrection* and *Liberation*.

Marc Chagall. 1887–1985. *Resistance*. 1937–1948. Oil on Canvas. Musée Nationaux Message biblique Marc Chagall. Nice, France.

and fathers regardless of when the marriage took place.

Desacralization of Slavery

Third, as with profane slaughter and the tithe, Deuteronomy desacralizes the procedure for making the servant relationship permanent. The Covenant Code prescribes for the conduct of the ear-piercing ceremony "before God" (Exod 21:6) whereas Deuteronomy describes the ceremony in purely secular terms (15:16).

A Fresh Start

Finally, in keeping with the radicalization of the Sabbath principle observed in the units immediately preceding, Deuteronomy adds the requirement that freedmen be sent out with liberal provision (vv. 14). The rationale or motivation for this manner of release reminds the householder that, in essence, he, too, is a freedman: "Remember! You were a slave in the land of Egypt and YHWH your God redeemed you. For this reason I command you today to do this" (v. 15). In addition to this positive injunction, Deuteronomy warns against begrudging the gifts of freedom and a "stake" to begin a new life (v. 18).

The Firstling and Sabbath Rest, 15:19-23

At first glance, regulations concerning the sacrifice of firstborn males of the herds and flocks seem unrelated to the Sabbath commandment. The key phrase in this regard, "you shall not do work with your firstling ox nor shear[2] the firstling of your flock," however, alludes to the Decalogue's requirement that the Sabbath apply also to "your ox or your ass, or any of your livestock." Like the Sabbath itself, which is to be kept "in order to consecrate it (*lĕqadĕšô*; Exod 20:8 // Deut 5:12)" because it is "a Sabbath to YHWH your God (Exod 20:10 // Deut 5:14)," the firstborn of the flocks and herds are to be consecrated to YHWH (*taqdîš layhwh ʾĕlōhêka*, v. 19). Several specific provisions of this regulation are familiar to readers of the Deuteronomic Code. The sacrifice of the firstborn is to be a celebratory meal consumed annually by the worshiper and his household in YHWH's presence, i.e., at the central sanctuary (v. 20; see Deut 12:7, 12, 18). Should there be some defect in the animal, however, it cannot be offered in sacrifice (v. 21). It may be slaughtered in accordance with Deuteronomy's provisions for profane slaughter (12:15, 21-23): It need not be slaughtered at the sanctuary (vv. 22a). Instead, it may be treated as one would treat wild game (v. 22b). Regardless of its "profane" character, however, its life-blood must be treated with the respect due all life (v. 23).

Annual "Supersabbath" Observances, 16:1-17

In its most ancient form, the Israelite festal calendar called for three annual festivals: Passover-Unleavened Bread, Harvest-Pentecost, and Booths-Ingathering. [Festal Calendars] The Deuteronomic Code discusses them in their current context in order to indicate that these annual festivals share the Sabbath principles of rest, celebration, and commemoration of blessing. A number of verbal allusions to the Sabbath commandment call attention to this linkage: the command to "observe" (*šāmôr*, Deut 16:1; cf. Exod 20:8 // Deut 5:12), the frequent references to periods of seven days or weeks (Deut 16:3, 4, 8, 9, 13), and the injunction to do no work during these festivals (Deut 16:8). More importantly, however, as it does for the Sabbath day itself, Deuteronomy consciously relates these agricultural festivals, originally based on the seasons and cycles of nature, to the exodus event (16:3, 12) and to YHWH's blessing upon Israel in the land (16:15).

Festal Calendars

Festal calendars differ slightly with respect to the names, interrelationship, and significance of these three feasts. Exod 23:14-17, for example, refer to Unleavened Bread (not Passover), Harvest, and Ingathering. Exod 34:18-24 also mention Unleavened Bread instead of Passover. These verses call the second festival the "Feast of Weeks" and relate it to the wheat harvest. The third, Ingathering, takes place "at the turn of the year," reflecting the tradition of the autumnal New Year (as opposed to the Spring New Year observed at a later stage in Israel's history, see Exod 12:2; Lev 23:5, 23-25). The Priestly tradition greatly expands the festal calendar, differentiating between Passover and the Feast of Unleavened Bread (Lev 23:5-6; Num 28:16-25) and between the offering of first fruits and firstborn (Lev 23:9) and the Feast of Weeks (Lev 23:15-16; but see Num 28:26-31 where first fruits and the Feast of Weeks are associated). The Feast of Booths, now apparently devoid of its fundamental agricultural association (Lev 23:33-36; Num 29:7-38; but see Lev 23:39-43), follows the New Year (Lev 23:23-25) and the Day of Atonement (Lev 23:26-32). The evidence from these lists suggests that the festal calendar underwent a process of development, especially with regard to the association of the primarily agricultural festival of Unleavened Bread with the celebration of the Passover and with regard to the character of the Feast of Booths or Ingathering as an autumnal New Year.

For more on the history of the Israelite festal calendar, see H. J. Kraus, *Worship in Israel: Cultic History of the Old Testament*, trans. G. Buswell (Richmond: John Knox Press, 1966); T. H. Gaster, *Festivals of the Jewish Year: A Modern Interpretation and Guide* (New York: William Morrow, 1953).

Passover, 16:1-8

The question of whether Deuteronomy intends to initiate significant reforms, such as the centralization of the cult, arises once again in view of several features of its treatment of the Passover. Especially in comparison with Exodus 12–14, the most extensive Passover regulation in the Hebrew Bible, Deuteronomy's unique provisions have elicited the attention of scholars from the time of the Mishnaic Rabbis to the present.

First, Exodus (12:5) specifically prescribes the sacrifice of a lamb or a kid at Passover. In contrast, Deuteronomy (16:2) at least seems to allow for the Passover sacrifice to be either smaller livestock ("flock," *zōʾn*) or larger cattle ("herd," *bāqār*). Does Deuteronomy intend to institute a reform designed to account for the transition of the Passover celebration from the private home setting to the public sanctuary setting? Presumably a single lamb or kid would be sufficient for a family celebration but not for a communal feast. The rabbinic tradition and a few scholars in the modern era[3] pursue a variety of avenues in the attempt to harmonize Deuteronomy 16 with the consensus position in the Hebrew Bible. Rashi[4] explains, for example, that "if they have counted themselves (formed themselves) into *too* large a company for the Passover offering (so that one lamb will not suffice for them) they bring together with it a festival offering and this is eaten first, in order that it (the Passover sacrifice) can be eaten in satiety . . . ." Nachmanides[5] resolves the difficulty by suggesting that the sacrifices from the herd are to be freewill, peace, or festal offerings in addition to the Passover sacrifice itself and adduces a number of passages with similar wording that imply such a practice (Exod 12:16; 2 Chr 35:7, 13). Others see this as another of Deuteronomy's conscious modifications of tradition in service of its overarching theological themes. J. McConville, for example, relates 16:2 to 14:26 where "there is a reflection of 7.12f. and its promise of plenty. The herd and the flock are particularly mentioned (v. 13) as an aspect of the wealth of the land. In my view, the Passover-Massot legislation picks up this promise in the way that the tithe-law does, freely adapting its material so as to reflect the deeper thrust of the book."[6]

Second, as has been true consistently since the initial enunciation of the centralization law, Deuteronomy continues its classification of institutions and practices according to whether they must be observed at the central sanctuary (16:2, 5-6). In the undoubtedly older tradition found in Exodus 12, Passover is a family celebration conducted in the home (12:3-4, 7, 21-24). The argument that

Boil or Bake?

AΩ Some commentators attempt to resolve this discrepancy by arguing that the verb *bāšal*, usually translated "to boil," is a term denoting cooking generally. This argument fails, however, to explain the usage of the term in the Hebrew Bible. It clearly denotes "boiling" in several passages that specify the liquid (Exod 12:9; 23:19; 34:26; Deut 14:21). It regularly appears together with a specific term for "baking" to describe all manner of cooking (Exod 16:23; 2 Chr 35:13), suggesting that it carried a specific connotation. Boiling seems to have been the most common method for preparing meats, especially the flesh of large cattle (1 Kgs 19:21; 2 Kgs 4:38; Ezek 24:3-5; 2 Kgs 6:29!; Lam 4:10!). In fact, whereas cereal offerings were baked, sacrificial flesh was commonly boiled (Lev 6:21 [Eng 6:28]; 8:31; 1 Sam 2:13, 15; Ezek 46:20, 24; Zech 14:21). The remaining two occurrences describe the preparation of "cakes," probably better translated "dumplings." Tamar cooks (NRSV translates "bakes," the context offers no clues as to the method she employed) cakes for Amnon (2 Sam 13:8). Num 11:8, however, explains that the people of Israel in the wilderness gathered manna, "ground it in mills or beat it in mortars, then boiled it in pots and made cakes of it."

Exodus describes only the procedures to be observed at the first Passover in Egypt[7] runs afoul of the charge in Exodus to smear the blood of the sacrifice on doorposts and lintels as a rite to be observed "as a perpetual ordinance for you and your children" (12:22-24).

Much more puzzling is the apparent disagreement between Deuteronomy and Exodus concerning the manner in which the Passover sacrifice is to be prepared for the Passover meal. Exodus (12:9) explicitly requires that the flesh of the sacrificial animal be roasted over the fire, *not boiled* (*bāšēl měbuššāl bammāyim*). Deuteronomy 16:7, on the other hand, prescribes precisely that which Exodus prohibits, namely, that the flesh be *boiled* (*ubiššaltā*). [Boil or Bake?] In short, then, usage of the term *bšl* in the Hebrew Bible offers no support whatsoever for the notion that it can be a general term meaning simply "to cook." Instead, it seems most likely that Deuteronomy innovates once again in order to accommodate the acceptability of large animals as Passover sacrifices.

The most significant feature of Deuteronomy's reinterpretation of the Passover, however, lies not in these details of observance, but in the association of Passover with Sabbath legislation. As noted above (see commentary on 5:5), the Hebrew Bible offers two major theological rationales for the Sabbath: The Priestly tradition, including the version of the Decalogue found in Exodus 20, understands the cycle of work and rest as a fundamental element of YHWH's created order (Gen 2:1-3); Deuteronomy, including its version of the Decalogue (5:15), and related texts, on the other hand, relate the Sabbath to the rest to which YHWH redeemed Israel in the exodus. Weekly, the Sabbath commemorates Israel's

Excerpts from a Passover Haggadah

We were slaves to Pharaoh in Egypt, but the Lord our God brought us out of there with a mighty hand and an outstretched arm. If the Holy One, praised be He, had not brought our forefathers out of Egypt, then we, our children and our children's children would be slaves to Pharaoh in Egypt.

Though all of us might be wise, all of us learned and all of us elders, though all of us might know the Torah well, it is our duty to tell the story of the exodus from Egypt. And the more one tells of the exodus from Egypt, the more praiseworthy he is . . .

In every generation a person is obliged to see himself as though he personally came out of Egypt, as it is written, "You shall tell your son on that day saying: This is because of what the Lord did for *me* when I left Egypt." It was not our ancestors alone that the Holy One, praised be He, redeemed, but He redeemed us as well, along with them, as it is written, "He brought *us* out of there, in order to lead us to, and give us, the Land which He promised our fathers."

Therefore are we obliged to thank, praise, laud, glorify and exalt, to honor, bless, extol and adore Him who performed all these wonders for our fathers and for us: He brought us out of slavery into freedom, out of sorrow into happiness, out of mourning into a holiday, out of darkness into daylight and out of bondage into redemption. Let us then sing Him a new song: Halleluyah!

As cited in A. Hertzberg, ed., *Judaism* (New York: George Braziller, 1962), 127-28.

---

flight from Egypt just as the Passover is the anniversary observance of that liberation. It is noteworthy that many scholars argue that the feasts of Passover and Unleavened Bread originated as agricultural festivals (that is, as observances tied to the natural order) but have been adapted as Israel's annual celebration of its liberation from Egyptian bondage (that is, as commemorations of an event in human history). In a sense Deuteronomy has only extended that process of adaptation to incorporate Sabbath as well.

Consistently, the book of Deuteronomy maintains that the health of the relationship established between YHWH and Israel in the exodus and at Horeb and the health of the natural world are interdependent (7:12-16; 11:16-17; 28:1-24, etc.). For Deuteronomy, the bounty of the land and the day of rest signify YHWH's continued blessing on freed slaves. [Excerpts from a Passover Haggadah] In Deuteronomy's understanding, the memory of slavery constitutes a defining value in Israel's ethical and political life.

Pentecost, 16:9-12

Deuteronomy's unique treatment of the Feast of Weeks continues Deuteronomy's program of theological reinterpretation, reiterating by now familiar themes. Four other passages in the Hebrew Bible discuss the Feast of Weeks. Exodus 23:16 and 34:22 simply announce that it should be observed as an offering of first fruits. Leviticus 23:15-16 and Numbers 28:26 go on to prescribe precise grain and animal sacrifices and to proscribe work. None of these passages offer theological rationales or interpretations of the festival, nor do they link it to the exodus or to the requirement of covenant generosity. Deuteronomy, on the other hand, recasts the Feast of Weeks to conform to its paradigm in a number of ways:

- Deuteronomy does not prescribe the offering appropriate to the festival. Instead, it emphasizes the relationship between blessing, bounty, and commemoration. Israelites are to offer a freewill offering "in accordance with the blessing with which YHWH your God has blessed you" (v. 10).
- Deuteronomy makes it clear that the purpose of the offerings made during the festival is not to appease or repay the deity. The bounty of YHWH's blessing should, instead, motivate joyous celebration (v. 11).
- Aware that this bounty is YHWH's blessing on former slaves, Deuteronomy maintains that prosperous Israelites should include in this celebration all those to whom YHWH offers Sabbath rest and protection: family, servants, and the dispossessed and disadvantaged Levites, aliens, orphans, and widows (v. 11).
- In accordance with Deuteronomy's program of cult centralization, the Feast of Weeks is to be a pilgrimage festival observed at the central sanctuary.
- As with Passover and the Sabbath, Deuteronomy interprets this clearly agricultural festival in relation to the exodus. "Remember that you were a slave in Egypt." Because of YHWH's redemption,

---

The Feast of Weeks, Shavuot, or Pentecost in Modern Jewish Observance

Although the Bible makes no connection between Shavuot and history, since rabbinic times it has been celebrated as the anniversary of the Giving of the Torah on Mt. Sinai. Some communities observe an all-night period of study called "Tikkun Lel Shavuot" which ends with a sunrise service, unique in Jewish observance, perhaps signifying the light of the Torah, focused around reading of the Ten Commandments. Ruth, itself set at harvest time, is also read in the synagogue on this day. It is also associated with Shavuot because Ruth, a proselyte, accepted the Torah of her own free will, just as Israel had at Mt. Sinai. According to tradition, Shavuot is also the anniversary of both the birth and death of King David, Ruth's great-grandson.

Dairy foods are consumed on Shavuot. A number of traditions explain the practice. The Bible likens the Torah to milk and honey. Some rabbinic traditions contend that Israel was like an infant after its experiences in Egypt and was able only to digest the milk of the Torah at first. Others explain that when the Israelites first received the dietary laws they were forced to consume only uncooked dairy foods since their pots were unclean.

Synagogues are decorated with flowers, especially roses, celebrating the harvest and the notion of the Torah as the Tree of Life. In a practice dating to late medieval mysticism, some communities liken the giving of the Torah to the marriage between God and Israel. By custom, children begin their Jewish education on Shavuot. Children begin the study of the Hebrew *alephbeth*. The first lesson concludes with gifts of sweets to indicate the sweetness of the Torah.

For more on the history and practice of Shavuot, see the wonderful collection of religious texts, customs, liturgy, recipes, etc., edited by Philip Goodman titled *The Shavuot Anthology* (Philadelphia: Jewish Publication Society, 1992).

Israel has gone from slavery to prosperity, from hard labor to celebration of bounty. The God who brought them *from* Egyptian slavery brought them *to* a land of bounty and rest. Bounty and rest must not be taken for granted. They must be celebrated! [The Feast of Weeks, Shavuot, or Pentecost in Modern Jewish Observance]

Feast of Booths, 16:13-15

Once again, Deuteronomy redefines an ancient agricultural festival in terms of its characteristic theological emphases. Now, however, the several elements emphasized with respect to the Feast of Weeks have been reduced to only three: celebration, community, and centralization. Quite surprisingly given its emphasis on the relationship of these feasts to the exodus, Deuteronomy omits any reference to a relationship between the Feast of Booths and the exodus. The omission here is all the more noteworthy since other traditions also associate originally agricultural festivals with the exodus tradition. Mentioned also in Exodus 23:16 and 34:22 only briefly, the Festival of Booths receives extensive treatment in Leviticus 23:33-36, 39-43. Leviticus describes not only the ritual details of sacrifice (vv. 33-36), but also explains that the purpose of living in "booths" (temporary structures, "hut" or "lean-to" may best represent the idea) is "so that your generations may know that I made the people of Israel live in booths when I brought them out of the land of Egypt" (v. 43). The reinterpretation of the once agricultural Feast of Booths in relation to salvation-history continues in the post-biblical period. Judaism associates Pentecost with the bounteous manna YHWH provided for Israel during the wilderness period and the Feast of Booths with the wilderness wandering, per se.

How is the limitation to only three elements (celebration, community, and centralization) here to be understood? May one conclude that these three elements represent the essence of Deuteronomy's festal theology? Whether these three elements represent the core elements of Sabbath rest for Deuteronomy, it cannot escape notice that 16:13-15 twice calls for Israel to "rejoice" (vv. 14, 15) during the Feast of Booths, suggesting that Sabbath joy represents, for Deuteronomy, something of the irreducible essence of Sabbath. [The Significance of Sukkoth]

Summary of the Festal Calendar, 16:16-17

Deuteronomy agrees with the Covenant Code (contrast Leviticus 23) that Israel's festal calendar consists of the three festivals

The Significance of Sukkoth

On Sukkoth, the end of the Days of Repentance, the Torah advises us to accept the exile and to consider all the world as void, as a shadow. Therefore we are told to leave permanent dwellings for a temporary one, to teach that we are strangers on the earth, without permanence, and that our days are like a shadow lasting a night, blown away by a wind. What does man profit from all his labors under the sun? All his days let his eyes be on high to the One who dwells in the heavens. Therefore one must use twigs and branches for the roof of the *Sukkah*, that the stars be clearly visible from inside it, that one might direct his heart to heaven. The Holy One, praised be He, will have compassion for the afflicted and the poor, for He knows man's low state… Thus for the seven days of the festival. But the man who fears the word of the King of the universe will have a booth not only during the festival of Sukkoth. During the whole year, everything for him will be a temporary dwelling, and he will sleep in the shadow of the *Sukkah* and leave his permanent dwelling.

Jonathan Eibschutz, *Yaarot Dvash*, cited in A. Hertzberg, ed., *Judaism* (Great Religions of Modern Man; New York: George Braziller, 1962), 133-34.

Moses with the Ten Commandments from the Steinberger Sukkah.

discussed in 16:1-15: Passover, Pentecost, and Booths. They are required observances for the adult male population, to be held at the central sanctuary, and to commemorate God's bounteous blessing.

CONNECTIONS

A modern reader's initial reaction to the material in this section of Deuteronomy will likely be that it has little to do with the Sabbath commandment. Indeed, at first glance, the component materials seem grouped only loosely in a thematic arrangement, or according to a catchword principle. As the commentary has demonstrated, however, the Deuteronomic Code offers here an extensive, subtle, and significant commentary on and extension of the Sabbath idea. Although it does not present the material in a systematic fashion, the Deuteronomic Code offers a rich source of material for a sophisticated theology of Sabbath, a theology that deserves closer attention.

A Preliminary Observation

As a prelude to a summary of Deuteronomy's Sabbath theology, Deuteronomy's positive understanding of Sabbath overall deserves particular attention. In the popular mind, the Sabbath commandment represents the negative, repressive, "thou shalt NOT," element in Old Testament faith. In this view, God has with no apparent reason simply proclaimed that every seven days work should cease. Violators will be prosecuted! The possibility that Sabbath rest may embody some deeper theological and even humanitarian value escapes popular notice. To be sure, Deuteronomy reiterates by way of reminder the charge to "do no work" on festival occasions. It focuses, however, not on the "thou shalt nots," but on the "thou shalts"; not on the Sabbath as a rule that can be violated, but as an occasion to be celebrated. Very much in the spirit of Deuteronomy, Jesus would one day remind his audience and his disciples that "humans were not made for the Sabbath, but the Sabbath for human beings" (Mark 2:27). God gave the Sabbath as a blessing and benefit, not as a restriction.

Sabbath Polarities

The major elements of the Deuteronomic Sabbath theology all derive their power from two polarities in Israel's existence: past slavery and current blessing on the one hand, and the rhythm of work and play on the other. The most foundational reality in Israel's national life is that YHWH delivered Israel from oppression and harsh slavery in Egypt to be his people. Israel—once enslaved, forced to work at hard labor under the harshest of circumstances, without respite—has been set free. What's more, YHWH blessed these newly freed slaves with a stake, a means to live, a land! Like the exodus itself, Deuteronomy's Sabbath revolves around these two poles—memory of former servitude and enjoyment of bounteous freedom. Similarly, Deuteronomy's emphasis on joy and rejoicing calls attention to the importance of the rhythm of work and play in human existence.

Past and Present: Slavery Remembered and Freedom Enjoyed
The memory of Egyptian bondage motivates Israel to be particularly sensitive toward its servants, its poor, its disenfranchised, and

Friday Evening

The matriarch of the household seated at the Sabbath table. Fellowship and celebration at meal time are key elements of Sabbath observance.

Isidor Kaufmann. 1853–1291. *Friday Evening.* c.1920. Oil on canvas. 72.4 x 90.2. Gift of Mr. and Mrs. M. R. Schweiter, JM 4-63. The Jewish Museum, New York.

foreigners. To take advantage of another's weakness (whether a member of the community or one of the resident aliens) is to behave like Pharaoh. [Slavery to an Israelite Pharaoh] Instead, fortunate Israelites can demonstrate their gratefulness for redemption by sharing their bounty with slave, Levite, orphan, widow, and foreigner. Having known the bitterness of slavery, they can *emulate YHWH* by willingly freeing their own servants in the Sabbath year of release. [Paul to Philemon] As they experience the bounty of YHWH's blessing on their crops and their herds, they can generously and liberally give to the servant leaving their service and to the needy poor alike. They are, after all, only giving a portion of that which YHWH has given them! They did not buy their own freedom, nor do they own the land they farm. Both were gifts from YHWH.

Slavery to an Israelite Pharaoh

The image of subjection to servitude and forced labor represented the negation of YHWH's blessing. In his speech warning the Israelites against the dangers of the monarchy they had asked him to institute (1 Sam 8), Samuel described the inevitable lust for power and wealth that would entice Israel's kings to become more and more like Pharaoh. In the end, after they had "taken" lands and goods, and conscripted citizens into various kinds of service to the throne, Israel's kings will have virtually enslaved their subjects, disregarding Deuteronomy's injunction that the king is to enjoy no special privilege (17:14-20). In Samuel's view, however, the greatest horror will be that, having been freed from involuntary servitude to Pharaoh, Israel will have freely chosen this new bondage to a fellow Israelite. Samuel warns that YHWH did not free his people so that they could return to slavery through their own choice. When Israel realizes the consequences of their decision to institute a monarchy and "cries out" from their oppression (1 Sam 8:17-18; cf. Exod 2:23-25), YHWH will disregard their cry. They chose freely.

Samuel's warning, issued before the establishment of the monarchy, becomes a reality by the reign of Israel's third king, Solomon. 1 Kings describes the system of forced labor Solomon relied on for his massive building projects in precisely the same terms the book of Exodus uses to depict Pharaoh's oppression of the Exodus generation (1 Kgs 5:13; compare Exod 1:11)! How easy it is to relinquish freedom!

The economic aspect of Deuteronomy's understanding of the Sabbath principle—release from slavery, release from debt, release from need—underscores the Old Testament's very this-worldly viewpoint. Deuteronomy does not speak of a "spiritual" freedom only, or of merely emotional responses to God's grace. One freed from the very real hardships of slavery in Egypt will find it difficult to enslave another! Can gratitude and greed coexist? To begrudge the needy, among whom one was formerly numbered, is to hardheartedly and tightfistedly deny YHWH's redemption and blessing. As the New Testament letter of James puts it, "If a brother or sister is naked and lacks daily food, and one of you says to them, 'Go in peace, be warm and eat your fill,' and yet you do not supply their bodily needs, what is the good of that?" Deuteronomy understands Sabbath as a principle of liberation from oppression and need. In order fully to participate in the Sabbath, then, it is not enough to have been freed. One must extend liberty! [Jesus on Extending Liberty]

Let My People Free

The God who liberates in Exodus sends others like Moses to proclaim freedom.

William H. Johnson. 1901–1970. *Let My People Free.* c.1945. Smithsonian American Art Museum. Washington DC.

Paul to Philemon

Nowhere does the Bible address the moral and ethical problem of the institution of slavery. Even Paul's oft-quoted statement concerning Greek and Jew, male and female, slave and free (Gal 3:23) announces the end of division and inequality "in Christ." It is surprising that no biblical author was able to see the connection between the *theological* claim that God liberates without reference to status and the *ethical* imperative that those so liberated must not themselves become oppressors.

Apart from passages in Deuteronomy, the Bible comes nearest the obvious ethical position in Paul's letter to Philemon concerning Philemon's slave Onesimus. Onesimus had run away from Philemon's household and come into contact with Paul. After converting to Christianity and proving invaluable to Paul as companion and friend, Onesimus returned to his "master" bearing Paul's letter imploring clemency. Choosing to convince rather than command (vv. 8-9), Paul employs a forceful logical strategy based on the contrast between the master-slave relationship and family relationships. Paul identifies himself and Epaphras as "prisoners of Christ Jesus" (vv. 1, 9, 23) and describes several individuals known to both he and Philemon, including Philemon himself, as "partners" and "fellow workers" (vv. 1, 17, 24). In contrast, Paul employs terms describing sibling relationships in reference to Timothy (v. 1), Apphia (v. 2), and Philemon (vv. 7, 20) and characterizes his relationship to the runaway slave, Onesimus, as that of father to son (v. 10)!

Paul places responsibility for resolving the tension between these spheres squarely on Philemon's shoulders when he suggests that Onesimus return to Philemon now "no longer as a slave but more than a slave, a beloved brother—especially to me but how much more to you, both in the flesh and in the Lord. So if you consider me your partner, welcome him as you would welcome me . . ." (vv. 16-17). Here Paul approaches, but does not state, the objection to slavery inherent in biblical tradition: Slaves liberated by God ought not enslave their brothers or sisters!

Work and Play

Deuteronomy's understanding of Sabbath as a celebration of freedom from past slavery and of YHWH's current blessing places special emphasis on joy. Sensitive observers of modern society, including the church, note the dwindling capacity for joy and the negligible role it plays in people's everyday lives and in the life of the church. Fundamentally, the Sabbath commandment addresses the proper rhythm of work and its opposite, rest, or even play, as Jürgen Moltmann has characterized it.[8] The commandment enjoins both work *and* rest: "six days shall you labor," but the seventh is holy to YHWH—"in it you shall do no work."

Modern Westerners have ambiguous and unhealthy relationships with both these aspects of life. The Bible sees work at its best as human cooperation with God in God's creative activity. God gave humanity, made in God's image, "dominion" over creation (Gen 1:28). God placed humankind as caretakers in the garden (Gen 2:15). Work is good, healthy, and even holy. It should be noted that work becomes toil only as the result of sin. When it cooperates with God's purpose instead of resisting it, work can become holy once again. Today, however,

Jesus on Extending Liberty

Jesus' teachings on the Sabbath are consistent with the views of the book of Deuteronomy. First, Jesus regarded Sabbath rest to be God's gift to humanity. "The Sabbath was made for humanity; humanity was not made for the Sabbath" (Mark 2:27). The notion that human beings were created for the purpose of observing certain rites or hallowing certain occasions reverses the proper relationship. Such a purpose would be tantamount to a peculiar kind of slavery. Instead, against those of his opponents who saw the Sabbath primarily as a restriction only, Jesus argued that healing on the Sabbath, for example, was not "work" but an act extending the freedom and well-being at the base of Sabbath observance. Not coincidentally, the inaugural sermon of Jesus' public ministry, according to Luke's Gospel (Luke 4:16-30), was based on a text proclaiming the eschatological Year of Jubilees (Isa 61:1-2). Jesus came to set captives free! To extend the Sabbath!

de Chardin

The biblical rhythm of work and Sabbath, which repeats the pattern of God's activity in creation, together with God's injunction to tend, till, and manage the earth, given to humanity in the beginning, elevates human work to a level above mere occupation. Human work can and should be in cooperation with God's ongoing creative activity. Sadly, for many, work is a means merely to earn a living. It is drudgery. In these circumstances, the joyful, celebratory aspects of Sabbath are difficult to realize. Sabbath rest is only an opportunity to recuperate, not to rejoice.

Among modern thinkers, Teillhard de Chardin, a noted mid-20th century scientist, theologian, and philosopher may have been one of the most insightful analysts of the role human efforts play in *cooperating* with God in ongoing creation. Not surprisingly, de Chardin's sense of joy in the world, of celebration of God's good gifts, was equally intense. The following passages from de Chardin's *Hymn of the Universe* are excerpted from sections headed "Humanity in Progress" and "The Meaning of Human Endeavour."

The world is a building. This is the basic truth which must first be understood so thoroughly that it becomes an habitual and as it were natural springboard for our thinking. At first sight, beings and their destinies might seem to us to be scattered haphazard or at least in an arbitrary fashion over the face of the earth; we could very easily suppose that each of us might equally well have been born earlier or later, at this place or that, happier or more ill-starred, as though the universe from the beginning to end of its

history formed in space-time a sort of vast flower-bed in which the flowers could be changed about at the whim of the gardener. But this idea is surely untenable. The more one reflects, with the help of all that science, philosophy and religion can teach us, each in its own field, the more one comes to realize that the world should be likened not to a bundle of elements artificially held together but rather to some organic system animated by a broad movement of development which is proper to itself. . . .

The aspect of life which most stirs my soul is the ability to share in an undertaking, in a reality, more enduring than myself: it is in this spirit and with this purpose in view that I try to perfect myself and to master things a little more. When death lays its hand upon me it will leave intact these things, these ideas, these realities which are more solid and more precious than I; moreover, my faith in Providence makes me believe that death comes at its own fixed moment, a moment of mysterious and special fruitfulness not only for the supernatural destiny of the soul but also for the further progress of the earth . . . .

In the lowliness of fear and the thrill of danger we carry on the work of completing an element which the mystical body of Christ can draw only from us. Thus to our peace is added the exaltation of creating, perilously, an eternal work which will not exist without us. Our trust in God is quickened and made firmer by the passionate eagerness of man [sic] to conquer the earth.

S. Bartholomew, trans. (New York: Harper & Row, 1965), 92-93,113-14.

people find it difficult to experience any sense of divine purpose or holiness in their lives of work. [de Chardin] Industrialization brought with it drudgery. The post-industrial economy brings insecurity in the face of rapid change, trivialization, and a sense of interchangeability.

The Sabbath rest fares no better. Many theologians and church historians have noted the ironic dual legacy of Protestant Christianity: the doctrine of justification by grace and the much-vaunted "Protestant work ethic." Ideally, work constitutes only a portion of human life. A period of work, of production, in cooperation with God's purposes and blessed by God, gives way to a period of rest, of enjoyment of the gifts, and of celebration of the Giver. It is by no means insignificant that Jesus frequently employed the imagery of the (messianic) banquet to describe the

God Blessed the Sabbath

William Blake. 1757–1872. *And God Blessed the Seventh Day and Sanctified It.* Private collection.

kingdom of God. [The Parable of the Great Dinner] As celebration and enjoyment of relationship with God, the Sabbath prefigures the goal of human history: "Purpose-free rejoicing in God."[9]

Moltmann observes that the Protestant work ethic has virtually eradicated celebration, true enjoyment, and joy from even the church. On the one hand, work has become monotonous and joyless. On the other, the ethic of efficient production has flavored the life and even the worship of the church. [Thankfulness and Joy] The joylessness of modern life, both in the everyday world of work and family life and in the church, is far from healthy and whole:

The Parable of the Great Dinner
Luke 14:12-24 (author's translation)

Now [Jesus] said to his host, "When you give a luncheon or a dinner, do not invite your friends, your brothers, your relatives, or your rich neighbors, hoping that they return the invitation and you would be repaid. Instead, when you give a banquet, call the poor, the crippled, the lame, the blind. You will be blessed because they do not have the means to repay you; for you will be repaid in the resurrection of the righteous."

Now, hearing this, one of his fellow guests said to him, "Blessed is anyone who eats bread in the kingdom of God!"

And he said to him, "There was a certain man who gave a great banquet and invited many. He sent his servant at the banquet hour to say to those invited, 'Come, for it is already prepared.' But they began to make excuses, one and all. The first said to him, 'I have purchased a field and I must go and inspect it. I beg you, allow me to be excused.' And another said, 'I have bought five yoke of oxen and I am going to try them out. I beg you, allow me to be excused.' Upon returning, the servant reported these things to his lord. Then, angered, the householder said to his servant, 'Go quickly into the streets and alleys of the city and bring the poor, the maimed, the blind, and the lame here.' And the servant said, 'Lord, your orders have been carried out and still there is room.' And the lord said to the servant, 'Go into the highways and the hedges and compel [them] to enter so that my house may be full. For I tell you that none of those men who were invited will taste my banquet.'"

. . . the joy which allows a person to breathe freely becomes a mere tool to compensate for joyless labour [sic]. This is abetted by the fact that people have lost their capacity for leisure; they no longer know how to do nothing, since constant and "full employment" has become their ideal. So they have to "do something" even with their leisure time. Having mastered their work they have to master their leisure as well. Leisure then becomes a continuation of the rhythm of work by other means.[10]

Indeed, confronted with the problems of the church's relevance on the one hand, and increasing amounts of "free" time available to its members on the other, congregations cannot resist the urge to fill nights and weekends with programs in many ways indistinguishable from those offered by the workaday world. "Christian congregations really do not know what to do with this [free time]. So they fill it with theological workshops and charitable or social activities."[11] Rather than being a foyer to the kingdom of God, the church functions as an annex to social and economic institutions.

Thankfulness and Joy

The natural man feels a genuine joy at receiving a gift, in obtaining something he has not earned. The pious man knows that nothing he has has been earned; not even his perceptions, his thoughts and words, or even his life, are his deservedly. He knows that he has no claim to anything with which he is endowed. Knowing, therefore, that he merits little, he never arrogates anything to himself. His thankfulness being stronger than his wants and desires, he can live in joy and with a quiet spirit. Being conscious of the evidences of God's blessing in all that he receives, the natural man has two attitudes toward life—joy and gloom.

The pious man has but one, for to him gloom represents an overbearing and presumptuous depreciation of underlying realities. Gloom implies that man thinks he has a right to a better, more pleasing world. Gloom is a refusal, not an offer; a snub, not an appreciation; a retreat instead of a pursuit. Gloom's roots are in pretentiousness, fastidiousness and a disregard of the good. The gloomy man . . . senses hostility everywhere, and seems never to be aware of the illegitimacy of his own complaints. He . . . stubbornly refuses to recognize the delicate grace of existence.

Abraham Heschel, *Man is Not Alone: A Philosophy of Religion* (New York: Harper & Row, 1951), 287-88.

Inevitably, on some level, the quality of one's Christian commitment comes to be measured in terms of one's level of involvement in programs and events. Inevitably, the effort to prove oneself worthy obscures the message of God's grace. Inevitably, outsiders view the church as they do the public schools or the Red Cross. How unlike Deuteronomy's call to celebrate! The modern church can neither mourn nor dance (Matt 11:17; Luke 7:32)! ["The People, Yes"]

NOTES

[1] Deuteronomy makes no attempt to coordinate this triennial observance with the seven-year cycle of Sabbatical years; once again, Deuteronomy attends to matters of purpose and intention instead of outlining details of ritual observance.

[2] Oxen were draft animals. The "work" of sheep and goats was to produce wool.

[3] For example, C. F. Keil and F. Delitzsch, *Commentary on the Old Testament, Vol. I: The Pentateuch* (Grand Rapids: Eerdmans, 1973), 374-75; J. Pedersen, "Passahfest und Passahlegende," *ZAW* 52 (1934): 162-63; A. R. Hulst, *Het Karakter van den Cultus in Deuteronomium* (Wageningen, 1938), 41.

[4] M. Rosenbaum, and others, trans., *Pentateuch with Targum Onkelos, Haphtaroth, and Prayers for Sabbath, and Rashi's Commentary*, vol. 5, Deuteronomy (London: Shapiro, Vallentine & Co., 1934), 85.

[5] *Commentary on the Torah: Deuteronomy*, trans. C. Chavel (New York: Shilo Publishing House, 1976), 185-86.

[6] McConville, *Law and Theology in Deuteronomy* (JSOTS 33; Sheffield, 1984), 116-19.

[7] See Merrill, *Deuteronomy* (NAC 4; Nashville: Broadman & Holman, 1994), 252.

[8] *Theology of Play*, trans. R. Ulrich (New York: Harper & Row, 1972); also published under the title *Theology and Joy: With an Extended Introduction by David E. Jenkins*, trans. R. Ulrich (London: SCM, 1973).

[9] *Theology of Play*, 64 (= *Joy*, 80).

[10] Ibid., 9 (= *Joy*, 33-34).

[11] (Ibid., 68 [= *Joy*, 84]).

"The People, Yes"

"The People, Yes" (excerpted)

The people will live on.
The learning and blundering people will live on.
    They will be tricked and sold and again sold
And go back to the nourishing earth for rootholds,
    The people so peculiar in renewal and comeback,
    You can't laugh off their capacity to take it.
The mammoth rests between his cyclonic dramas.

The people so often sleepy, weary, enigmatic,
Is a vast huddle with man units saying:
    "I earn my living.
    I make enough to get by
    and it takes all my time.
    If I had more time
    I could do more for myself
    and maybe for others.
    I could read and study
    and talk things over
    and find out about things.
    It takes time.
    I wish I had the time."

The people is a tragic and comic two-face: hero and hoodlum:
    phantom and gorilla twisting to moan with a gargoyle mouth:
    "They buy me and sell me . . . it's a game . . .
    sometime I'll break loose. . . ."

Carl Sandburg in S. Bradley, R. Beatty, and E. Long, eds., *The American Tradition in Literature*, vol. 2 (3rd ed.; New York: Norton, 1967), 1106-1108.

EXPLICATION OF THE FOURTH COMMANDMENT: "HONOR FATHER AND MOTHER"

16:18–18:22

The hypothesis that the Deuteronomic Code functions as an explication of each of the Ten Commandments in succession meets perhaps its greatest test, at least on its face, with regard to the theme and language of the section of laws concerning authority (16:18–18:22). In his influential article "The Sequence of the Laws in Deuteronomy 12–26 and in the Decalogue,"[1] G. Braulik, the leading proponent of the thesis that the Deuteronomic Code has been arranged as an explication of the Decalogue, limits his comments on this section to the following:

> Relating this part of the law to the fourth commandment of the Decalogue appears problematic, not least because of modern exegesis of the command to honors one's parents. Nevertheless, Philo of Alexandria (*De Decalogo* 31:165) already thought that the commandment "regarding respect for parents at the same time points toward many important laws, such as those . . . concerning rulers and the ruled." So it is possible that a redactional reinterpretation of the laws regarding office in 16:18–18:22 could have been made on the basis of the Decalogue-structure of the whole legal codex.

N. Lohfink describes the principle of organization operative in this section as "an association of ideas."[2] In fact, it is very likely that this section began as a loose collection of independent regulations gathered together largely, if not solely, because of their subject matter. Nevertheless, in the final form and placement of the material, several features strongly suggest that it, too, has been incorporated into the Decalogue scheme of the Deuteronomic Code—with surprising and significant results for interpretation.

Of course, the material surrounding the "authority" section so clearly represents the Decalogue order that it is difficult to imagine that the editors responsible for the final form of the Deuteronomic Code will have neglected to employ the principle here, as well. In fact, several allusions to the commandment to honor parents that

Allusions to the Fourth Commandment in Deuteronomy 16:18–18:22

AΩ The commandment to honor parents consists of three clauses: the commandment per se ("honor your father and your mother"), the appeal to divine authority ("just as YHWH your God commanded you"), and a bi-partite "motivational clause" ("in order that your days may be long" and "in order that it may go well for you in the land which YHWH your God gives you"). The root *kbd*, "to honor," is not characteristic of Deuteronomic diction, occurring only once more in the entire book (28:58). As can be expected if it is an explication and extension of the fourth commandment to other authority figures, 16:18–18:22 surprisingly does not mention "father and mother." The law prohibiting "passing" sons and daughters "through fire," however, clearly addresses a family situation, although it reverses the concerns of the commandment. In addition, the law of the king employs a family metaphor to emphasize the unity of Israelite society: Israel must choose a king "among your brothers" and he must not allow himself to "exalt his heart over his brothers" (17:15, 20).

The most common allusions in 16:18–18:22 to the Decalogue occur in the form of citations or paraphrases of the motivational clauses. The phrase "in order that you may live (*lĕma'an tiḥyê*)" (16:20) paraphrases, and the phrase "in order that he may prolong his days (*lĕma'an ya'ărîk yāmîm*)" (17:20) cites, the Decalogue's "in order that your days may be long (*lĕma'an ya'ărîkun yāmêkā*)" (5:16). Even more common are citations and paraphrases of the clause, "in order that it may go well for you on the land which YHWH your God gives you (*lĕma'an yîṭab lāk 'al hā'ădāmâ 'ašer-yhwh 'ĕlōhêkā nōtēn lak*)," found in 16:18 ("in all your gates which YHWH your God gives you"), 16:20 ("and you possess the land which YHWH your God gives you"), 17:2 ("in one of your gates which YHWH your God gives you"), 17:14 ("when you come to the land which YHWH your God gives you"), and 18:6 ("when you come to the land which YHWH your God gives you").

---

recur throughout the section, although not forceful enough alone to make the case for the relationship, are very suggestive in light of the overall pattern of arrangement. [Allusions to the Fourth Commandment in Deuteronomy 16:18–18:22]

As noted above in the commentary on 5:16, the commandment to honor one's parents, like much of the Decalogue, states a basic principle without precisely defining its terms or clarifying limitations of its application. How does one honor one's parents in specific situations? It is not surprising, then, that the Deuteronomic Code undertakes the task of amplification and explication. On the other hand, key features of the Deuteronomic treatment of this commandment introduce a number of themes that modern readers may not anticipate. In fact, these themes prove to be the central issues in Deuteronomy's interpretation of the commandment to honor one's parents.

Respect Authority

First, and most fundamentally, the Deuteronomic Code extends the matter of the honor due parents to incorporate virtually all authority figures in Israelite society. The principle of respect

---

Justice "in the Gate"

The appointment of "judicial authorities" described in the Deuteronomic Code seems to reflect the situation that pertained at quite a late date in Israel's history. Throughout the period of the judges and well into the monarchial period, disputes were settled and criminals were judged and sentenced by elders of the local community gathered "in the gate." Young men would have been occupied in the fields and shops, but elderly men, especially those of status in the community (Prov 31:23), gathered in the city gate (see [A Typical Casemate Wall with Gate]) to publish and hear news (Jer 17:19-27), to do business, especially transactions requiring witnesses (Gen 34:20, 24; Ruth 4:1, 10, 11), and to decide disputes and criminal cases (2 Sam 15:2; Isa 29:21; Amos 5:10, 12, 15; Zech 8:16; Prov 22:22). (For a fuller discussion of this system of folk justice, see R. Wilson, "Israel's Judicial System in the Pre-Exilic Period," *JQR* 74 [1983]: 229-48 and M. Weinfeld, "Judge and Officer in Ancient Israel and the Ancient Near East," *IOS* 7 [1977]: 67-76.) These elders represented the collective wisdom of the community and spoke for it.

Texts dating as late as the exilic period attest to this system of local, non-governmental justice. Deut 16, however, seems to describe an appointed judiciary. Scholars have long seen this as evidence that, in its present formulation, Deut 16 dates from the time period of the sweeping reforms instituted by the Judean kings Hezekiah (2 Kgs 18:1-6; 2 Chr 29:3–31:21) and Josiah (2 Kgs 22:3–23:25; 2 Chr 34:1–35:19).

Regarding Hezekiah's reform—the significance, scope, and even historicity of which is much debated, see O. Borowski, "Hezekiah's Reforms and the Revolt against Assyria," *Biblical Archaeologist* 58 (1995): 148-55; L. Handy, "Hezekiah's Unlikely Reform," *ZAW* 100 (1988): 111-15; N. Na'aman, "The Debated Historicity of Hezekiah's Reform in the Light of Historical and Archaeological Research," *ZAW* 107 (1995): 179-95; I. Provan, *Hezekiah and the Book of Kings: A Contribution to the Debate about the Composition of the Deuteronomic History* (BZAW 172; Berlin: Walter de Gruyter, 1988); J. Rosenbaum, "Hezekiah's Reform and the Deuteronomistic Tradition," *HTR* 72 (1979): 23-43; E. Todd, "Reforms of Hezekiah and Josiah," *Scottish Journal of Theology* 9 (1956): 288-93; etc. On Josiah's reform, see M. Cogan, "Israel in Exile: The View of Josianic Historian," *JBL* 97 (1978): 40-44; E. Eynikel, *The Reform of King Josiah and the Composition of the Deuteronomistic History* (Oudtestamentische Studien 33; Leiden: E. J. Brill, 1996); J. Lundbom, "Lawbook of the Josianic Reform," *CBQ* 38 (1976): 293-302; M. Sweeney, "Jeremiah 30–31 and King Josiah's Program of National Restoration and Religious Reform," *ZAW* 108 (1996): 569-83; M. Weinfeld, "Deuteronomy's Theological Revolution," *Bible Review* 12 (1996): 38-41; etc.

---

underlying the Decalogue commandment applies to any and all who would lead.

At Home and at Large

Second, and in a similar fashion, the Deuteronomic Code expands the realm in which this principle of honor pertains to include society at large. In this respect, allusions to the Decalogue's motivational clause concerning prosperity "on the land YHWH your God gives you" (5:16) found in 16:18 and 17:2 provide a significant clue. The substitution "your gates" for "land" employs the term *šaʿar*, which functions almost as a refrain throughout the section (16:18; 17:2, 5, 8; 18:6). As the site of the community's public life, the gate typifies authority in Israelite society and signals the shift from the home, where parents are honored, to the community. [Justice "in the Gate"]

Properly Constituted Authority

Third, by means of Lohfink's "principle of association," Deuteronomy in effect offers a functional definition of the "honor" due authorities. Although they deserve respect, for example, parents may not exercise *absolute power* over their children by virtue of their office, as it were (see 18:9-13). By the same token, judges must resist temptations to abuse their power (16:18-20), judges may find a case too difficult (17:8-13), the king's power is limited (17:14-20), prophets must not be believed simply by virtue of their title (18:15-22), and so forth. Deuteronomy knows of no authority other than that properly executed. Honor must, in some sense, be merited.

Limited Authority

Fourth, Deuteronomy heightens the distinction between proper respect for one in authority and absolute obedience by means of the collection in one place of regulations concerning judges, priests, kings, and prophets. With the exception of the wisdom teacher, these regulations deal with all Israel's public leaders. By treating them together, Deuteronomy reminds its readers that these roles have discrete areas of responsibility. No one may attain absolute power and control. Lohfink[3] goes so far as to compare this treatment of the proper delimitation of functions to the doctrine of the separation of powers in modern constitutions.

COMMENTARY

Judicial Authority: Limitations and Responsibilities, 16:18–17:13

In its present form, the material in 16:18–17:13 comprises a treatise on the limitations and responsibilities of judicial authority. Vocabulary and theme link the several apparently discrete units. The verbal root *špṭ* "to judge" and the related noun *mišpāṭ* "judgment" appear a total of nine times (16:18 [3x], 19; 17:8, 9 [2x], 11, 12). The related terms *ṣedeq* "righteousness, uprightness" and *ṣadîqîm* "righteous ones" (16:18, 19, 20 [2x]), *ʾemet* "reliable, true" (17:3), *yrh* "to instruct, issue a legal opinion" (17:10, 11), and *tôrâ*, here not in the sense of the written Mosaic Law, but in the sense of a legal opinion (17:11) define the concerns of the text. Vocabulary for unjust behaviors include *raʿ* "evil, bad, wrong" (17:1, 5, 7, 12), *tôʿēbâ* "abomination" (17:1, 4), and *zādôn/zdn* "insolence, contempt/to be insolent, contemptuous" (17:12, 13).

The vocabulary points to a very significant aspect of the theme of this unit, especially as it relates to the commandment to honor authority, namely, its focus on behaviors. The Deuteronomic Code concentrates here neither on the various offices nor on the qualifications and prerogatives of the office-holders, but on the *exercise* of authority. There is no discussion of the means of selection to office, the qualifications for holding office, or the terms of service. Indeed, every circumstance addressed in this unit involves the potential for misuse of authority. In effect, it is an extended treatise against corruption (16:18-20), haste (16:21–17:7), and contempt (17:8-13).

A Typical Casement Wall with Gate
Photo of the eastern gate at Shechem.

A Warning against Corruption, 16:18-20

The initial unit in this section dealing with the proper exercise of authority concerns the miscarriage of justice due to judicial misconduct. After a very cursory prescription calling for the appointment of "judges and officers" or, "judicial officers" (*šōptîm wešōtrîm*) on the local level ("in all your gates," see [A Typical Casement Wall with Gate]) to "judge the people with righteous justice" (*mišpaṭ-ṣedeq*), the unit goes on to define this justice in negative terms. These judges are not to "bend," "turn aside," or "pervert" (all possible translations of the verb *nth* employed here) justice. Specifically, they are to disregard the status and social standing (literally, the "face" *pānîm* [Face, Prestige, and Impartiality] of the parties brought before them, and they are not to accept a "bribe" (*šōḥad*). Judges must be blind to reputation because status—that is wealth—can blind even the wise to what is right and "twist" or "pervert" (*slp*) the words of the innocent/just. Apparently in ancient Israel (as in modern America), the legal system was susceptible to economic influence. The eighth-century prophets Amos and Micah, who prophesied in the north and the south, respectively,

Face, Prestige, and Impartiality

The Deuteronomic warning against judicial favoritism literally admonishes the judge to have no regard for the "face" of any party appearing before him. Western readers of the Bible often forget that ancient Israel was a Near Eastern culture. Like many Asian cultures, Hebrew society operated with a developed system of prestige and shame, i.e., it was concerned with the preservation and loss of "face." In addition to this system of social worth and the universal human tendency to judge relative to a person's reputation, at least one tendency in Israel's theology—a notion often described, ironically, as "Deuteronomic"—would seem to confirm that a judge *should* take "face" into account. According to this ancient version of the "gospel of prosperity," God blesses the righteous and curses the unrighteous. Logically, then, one might well assume, as did Job's friends, that reputation ("face") signals innocence and righteousness.

Deuteronomy does not, however, advocate an automatic relationship between prosperity and God's blessing. For example, the Deuteronomic Code admonishes Israel to emulate YHWH's care for widows, orphans, resident aliens, and Levites—society's most accursed and underprivileged. It makes special provision for the welfare of the poor. Here it warns against the influence of status.

Deuteronomy's warning still applies. Despite constitutional safeguards, it can be argued that reputation, status, and wealth continue to exercise undue influence over the modern American judicial system. How many cases, either civil or criminal, are won by the party without the financial resources to pay for top-notch legal teams, expert witnesses, and jury consultants?

castigated judges, priests, and rulers for allowing financial gain to influence the legal process (Amos 5:7, 15, 24; 6:12; Mic 3:1, 8, 9). Money's corrupting influence on justice is an abiding threat.

The unit concludes with an exhortation and a rationale. The goal is the pursuit of justice ("justice, you shall pursue justice!" *ṣedeq ṣedeq tirdōf*, v. 20) and nothing else. The health and well-being of Israelite society depends on this uncontaminated pursuit of justice. Once again, Deuteronomy links prosperity in the land to ethical and religious purity.

A Case in Point: Diligence, Caution, and Responsibility, 16:21–17:7

Deuteronomy 16:21–17:1, which reiterate prohibitions against the asherah and the massebah (see 7:5; 12:3 and the commentary), and the offering of "defective (*mûm*)" animal sacrifices (15:21), seem at first glance not only redundant, but also unrelated to the authority theme of the larger section. It is tempting to attribute the placement of these prohibitions to imprecise editing or scribal error, although it is difficult to imagine what might have prompted a scribe or editor to disrupt the "authority" topic. Given the careful and consistent editing characteristic of Deuteronomy, a more fruitful approach may be to hypothesize that these verses form an integral element in the authority discussion. The question then becomes "How?"

Scholars propose two answers (that are not mutually exclusive). Some view the inclusion of these brief and repetitive prohibitions against activity Deuteronomy considers idolatrous as a reminder of

The Awesome Authority Conferred by the State

On February 23, 1994, the State of Texas executed Bruce Edwin Callins. The Supreme Court denied a last-minute petition for a writ of certiorari. Justice Blackmun's dissenting opinion included the following observations:

Within days, or perhaps hours, the memory of Callins will begin to fade. The wheels of justice will churn again, and somewhere, another jury or another judge will have the unenviable task of determining whether some human being is to live or die. We hope, of course, that the defendant whose life is at risk will be represented by competent counsel—someone who is inspired by the awareness that a less-than-vigorous defense truly could have fatal consequences for the defendant. We hope that the attorney will investigate all aspects of the case, follow all evidentiary and procedural rules, and appear before a judge who is still committed to the protection of defendants' rights—even now, as the prospect of meaningful judicial oversight has diminished. In the same vein, we hope that the prosecution, in urging the penalty of death, will have exercised its discretion wisely, free from bias, prejudice, or political motive, and will be humbled, rather than emboldened, by the awesome authority conferred by the State.

But even if we can feel confident that these actors will fulfill their roles to the best of their human ability, our collective conscious will remain uneasy. Twenty years have passed since this Court declared that the death penalty must be imposed fairly, and with reasonable consistency, or not at all, see *Furman v. Georgia* . . . (1972), and, despite the effort of the States and courts to devise legal formulas and procedural rules to meet this daunting challenge, the death penalty remains fraught with arbitrariness, discrimination, caprice, and mistake . . . .

The United States Law Week (22 February 1994) 62 U.S.L.W. 3546.

---

the overarching significance of the first commandment. All genuine authority derives from one supreme source. Ultimately, only YHWH deserves complete allegiance. Others see 16:21–17:1 as the citation of the statutes involved in the example detailed in 17:2-7. The occurrence of *tôʿēbâ*, "abomination" in 17:1 and again in 17:3 supports this position. In this view, 16:21–17:1 cites the applicable statute, 17:2-3 postulates the violation of these commandments (with additional reference to idolatrous worship of astral entities), and 17:4-7 prescribes the proper judicial approach to be employed in such cases.

In terms of the proper exercise of judicial authority, then, 17:4-7 constitute the climactic core of this passage. Significantly, as in 16:18-20, the danger of the perversion of justice—the abuse of authority—dominates the discussion. Under the Mosaic covenant, idol worship is a capital offense to which both genders are subject (v. 5). The finality of this punishment, however, warrants extreme diligence and caution in reaching a verdict and executing the sentence. [The Awesome Authority Conferred by the State]

Three specific measures serve to guard against the execution of innocent parties falsely or erroneously accused. First, hearsay ("it is told you, and you hear," v. 4) is insufficient grounds for decision; the matter must be thoroughly investigated (*wĕdāraštā hêṭēb*, "you will investigate well," v. 4). The charge must prove to be

The Importance of Innocence: Competing Views of Justice

Ernest van den Haag, a leading proponent of capital punishment in the United States, responds to the objection that capital punishment is unjust "because it may lead to the execution of innocents" by developing a utilitarian calculus of relative justice. He argues that

> if the death of innocents because of judicial error is unjust, so is the death of innocents by murder. If some murders could be avoided by a penalty conceivably more deterrent than others—such as the death penalty—then the question becomes: Which penalty will minimize the number of innocents killed (by crime and by punishment)? It follows that the irrevocable injustice sometimes inflicted by the death penalty would not significantly militate against it, if capital punishment deters enough murder to reduce the total number of innocents killed so that fewer are lost than would be lost without it.

The Hebrew Bible offers a different view of the importance of innocence when Abraham intervenes with YHWH on the behalf of the innocent in Sodom and Gomorrah (Gen 18). Asking whether "the Judge of all the earth" can commit the injustice of punishing the innocent along with the guilty, Abraham persuades God to relent his plan simply to eradicate the populations of those two cities. Faced with a choice similar to that described in van den Haag's equation—whether it is preferable to risk unjustly punishing the innocent or to risk failing to punish the guilty—the supreme judge chooses to favor the innocent. Innocence is important.

"On Deterrence and the Death Penalty," in *Punishment and the Death Penalty: The Current Debate*, ed. Robert Baird and Stuart Rosenbaum (Amherst NY: Prometheus Books, 1995), 126-27.

"established truth" (*wĕhinnê ʾĕmet nākôn*) that, in fact, "this abomination has been done in Israel." This provision can be likened to the "innocent until proven guilty" principle of American criminal justice.

Second, the testimony of a single witness does not meet the test of "established truth" (v. 6). The Deuteronomic Code does not specify the rationale for this rule of evidence. Apparently, however, the Code anticipates the possibility of observational error or malice. Later Judaic legal doctrine emphasizes the need for independent confirmation, since even an honest eyewitness may misperceive for any of a number of reasons: obscured vision, distance, a poor angle of sight, etc. A second, independent witness also protects against convictions based on false testimony given by an enemy of the accused. Ancient Israel was very aware that the justice system could be perverted by those seeking to use it to settle scores or gain advantages over opponents. The third provision and another regulation calling for the punishment of lying witnesses with the punishment appropriate for the charge (19:16-21) suggest the level of concern. [The Importance of Innocence: Competing Views of Justice]

Third, the people, beginning with the witnesses whose testimony secured the conviction, must all participate in the execution of the condemned. Again, the Deuteronomic Code does not specify the rationale for this procedure. However, the context and general familiarity with Hebraic thought suggest two purposes. Given the overall theme of the unit—concern for abuse of authority—this requirement functions as a means for holding the witnesses and the community directly accountable for justice. Modern society employs capital punishment ostensibly as a deterrent against heinous crimes. Ancient Israel required the accusers and the entire community to participate actively in the execution as a deterrent against false and hasty convictions! If one must participate in the execution—*cause* and *witness* the death of another human being—one will likely take the whole matter much more seriously than if capital executions are carried out under artificially "sterile" conditions. Israel did not "sanitize" and "tame" this act. It was final, awful. The community, especially the witnesses, must confront the reality. [The Courage to Witness]

In addition, such crimes were "abominations" that had been done "in Israel." They are not matters merely between the criminal and the criminal's victims, or the criminal and God. The entire community has become somehow polluted. The entire community is somehow implicated. The community must take responsibility for ridding itself of the pollutant.

Judicial Humility and Respect for Authority, 17:8-13

The language of justice (*mišpāṭ*, vv. 8, 9, 11, 12) in the gate (*šaʿar*, v. 8) continues in this unit. The people are instructed, once again (see v. 3), to "investigate/seek out" (*drš*, v. 9) and to "be told" (*ngd*, v. 9). Like the preceding, this unit deals with limitations on judicial

---

The Courage to Witness

Though I've now had a hand in a dozen or more executions, I have never witnessed one. The closest I came was a conversation with Bill Allen, a lawyer from my former law firm. I ran into him at a reception and his face was gray; his eyes—usually sharp and clear—seemed out of focus.

"Not well," Bill answered when I asked how he was doing. "I lost a client. His name was Linwood Briley. I saw him die in the electric chair a couple of days ago."

"Was it rough?"

"What do you think? It was awful."

"What was it like when they turned on the juice?"

"Oh, by the time they got done strapping him down, putting the goop on his head and the mask on his face, the thing sitting in that chair hardly looked human. But the really strange part was before: looking at him, talking to him, even joking with him, fully aware that he'd be dead in half an hour."

"Why did you go?"

"I though he should have a friend with him in his final minutes."

The look on Bill's face stayed with me a long time. It was enough to persuade me that I'd never want to witness an execution. Yet I sometimes wonder whether those of us who make life-and-death decisions on a regular basis should not be required to watch as the machinery of death grinds up a human being. I ponder what it says about me that I can, with cool precision, cast votes and write opinions that seal another human being's fate but lack the courage to witness the consequences of my actions.

Alex Kozinski, "Tinkering with Death," *The New Yorker* 72 (19 February 1997), 48-53.

authority related to the limits of human ability. Several new linguistic elements and a major new theme surface, however, giving a first indication of a unique focus. For the first and only time in this section, justice stands in parallel to torah (*hattôrâ*, v. 11; compare the related verb, *yrh* "to instruct," in vv. 10-11) and attention turns to the case of one contemptuous (*zādôn*) of rightful authority (vv. 12-13).

The situation treated in this unit involves recourse to a higher court in the event the local judge finds a case beyond his ability to resolve (v. 8). The procedure described is not an appeals process instituted by one of the parties "before the bar," but a remedy made available to the baffled judge. The three circumstances detailed in the phrase "between blood and blood, between judgment and judgment, between mark and mark (*nega*ʾ)" may be meant to demarcate the major areas of jurisdiction: blood likely refers to violent crimes, although rulings concerning proper sacrifice are also blood matters; "judgment" probably refers to what would today be described as civil matters; "mark" is the term employed in priestly materials in reference to skin diseases and molds or fungi "infecting" buildings (Lev 13:1–14:54). In this latter case, Deuteronomy assigns to the local judges the responsibility reserved to the priests in Leviticus, namely for determining whether a "mark," either in a person's flesh or in some inanimate object, is "clean." The judge is to distinguish between harmless "marks" and those that pose a threat of infection and contamination.

Some cases may be beyond the expertise of the local authority. His responsibility then is to acknowledge the limits of his competency and seek the assistance of the "levitical priests" (*hakkōhănîm halĕwîyyim*, literally, "the priests, the Levites," a hendiadys—synonymous or near-synonymous terms employed to denote only one thing) at the central sanctuary (v. 9). They will be able to discern justice in the matter at hand (v. 10) and render a definitive "instruction (*hattôrâ*)" or "legal opinion (*mišpāṭ*)." The equation of these two terms, together with the joint responsibility of the levitical priests and the judge, is significant for an understanding of Israel's concept of justice, as well as for the notion of the covenant as "law" (*tôrâ*). Torah, often inadequately translated "law," derives from a verb that means "to guide" or "to teach." Only secondarily does the term describe *written* "guidelines" or "principles" (see Introduction). As it appears in 17:11, the term reverts to its original meaning. Obviously, the local judge brings a case before the authorities at the central sanctuary not because he is ignorant of the "law," but because of some difficulty in *interpreting* either the

Power and Authority

Legitimate power depends on a person's organizational role. It can be thought of as one's formal or official authority. . . . It is important to note that legitimate authority and leadership are not the same thing. Holding a position and being a leader are not synonymous, despite the relatively common practice of calling position holders in bureaucracies the leaders. The head of an organization may be a true leader, but he also may not be. Effective leaders often intuitively realize they need more than legitimate power to be successful. Before he became president, Dwight Eisenhower commanded all Allied troops in Europe during World War II. In a meeting with his staff before the Normandy invasion, Eisenhower pulled a string across a table to make a point about leadership. He was demonstrating that just as you can pull a string, not push it, officers must lead soldiers and not "push" them from the rear.

R. Hughes, R. Ginnett, and G. Curphy, *Leadership: Enhancing the Lessons of Experience* (Richard D. Irwin, 1993) as cited in J. T. Wren, ed., *The Leader's Companion: Insights on Leadership through the Ages* (New York: The Free Press, 1995), 342.

---

evidence or the pertinent regulation. The expectation, then, is that the authorities at the central sanctuary will bring to bear greater discernment, insight, and wisdom. They will render authoritative opinions meant to guide. In the end, the justice system does not succeed solely because of the superiority of the "law," but because of the wisdom, even the inspiration (compare v. 12), of human authorities. [Power and Authority]

At any rate, the opinions of the highest legal authorities must be followed without deviation "either to the right or the left" (v. 11, a characteristic Deuteronomic/Deuteronomistic phrase; see esp. 17:20 and 2:27; 5:32; 28:14; Josh 1:7; 23:6; 2 Sam 14:19; 2 Kgs 22:2). At the conclusion of this subsection on judicial authority, the code reiterates the necessity of "honoring" proper authority. In the light of the repeated emphasis on the number of ways in which judicial authority may be abused, the temptation may arise to dismiss the justice system as hopelessly flawed by human character, to "contemptuously" (*bĕzādôn*, v. 12) disregard the binding opinion of the priests and judge. Such contempt for the considered opinions of those who "stand to serve . . . YHWH your God (*ha ʿōmēd lĕšāret . . . ʾet-yhwh ʾĕlōhêkā*, v. 12) is tantamount to dishonoring parents.

Royal Authority: Power and Arrogance, 17:14-20

Given the significance of the institution of the monarchy in the history of ancient Israel and Judah, it is remarkable that only three passages (Deut 17:14-20; 1 Sam 8:11-22; 10:25) deal in any systematic way with the nature and functions of the office. It is equally remarkable that these three passages share a skepticism concerning the monarchy that seems to reflect Israel's experience: the

Peace and Justice

Many of Tiepolo's commissions paid homage to the power, yet beneficence of absolute monarchy. Here, the allegorical figures of Peace and Justice communicate such beneficence as they are buoyantly sustained upon clouds, as if at the precipice between heaven and earth. Justice, towering above the rest of the composition, has withheld the use of scales to decide the correct way to govern and is pensively and adoringly responding to the admonitions of Peace, shown turning toward her. The allegorical figure of Peace is identified with the laurel branches extending through her left hand.

Giambattista Tiepolo. 1696–1770. *Peace and Justice*. S. Lazzoro dei Mendicanti. Venice, Italy.

motive in all three texts is the limitation of royal power, which poses a grave threat if unlimited.

The unit divides roughly into four sections: the conditions for the appointment of a king (vv. 14-15), three circumstances the king must avoid (vv. 16-17), the requirement that (even or, perhaps, especially) the king must adhere to the Torah (vv. 18-19), and a summary warning and promise (v. 20). Obviously, the Deuteronomic Code fears royal authority as too easily abused. The king's "rights and duties" (mentioned, but not listed, in 1 Sam 10:25) are to be found nowhere in the Hebrew Bible.

The text begins by positing the moment, after the conquest and possession of the land, when Israel will consider establishing a monarchy. The expression "like all the surrounding nations" offers no further explanation of Israel's motives, although it recalls 1 Sam 8:5 where the implication is that Israel came to regard the system of leadership by charismatically chosen judges too unstable. At any rate, 17:15 permits ("you may surely put a king over you"), but does not prescribe, the establishment of a monarchy. Moreover, two conditions must be met: First, YHWH himself will make the choice on the people's behalf (v. 15). The Israelite monarchy is not based on political power, but upon God's decision. Second, Moses instructs the people that the prospective king must be an Israelite chosen "from among your brothers" (v. 15)—a reminder (compare v. 20) of the fact that, although he may sit on the throne, the king of Israel cannot claim inherent superiority (such as the divinity claimed by Egyptian kings).

In addition to the prerequisites for assuming the throne of Israel, the king must adhere to certain limitations of power when he sits on it (vv. 16-17). He must not acquire large stables of horses or "return the people to Egypt" in order to do so, since YHWH has expressly forbidden the practice (v. 16; there is no other record of this prohibition). Nor should he marry many wives who would be likely to "turn aside his heart" (v. 17a). Finally, he must not accumulate wealth ("silver and gold," v. 17b). In other words, the king of Israel must not depend upon military strength and the power that derives from wealth as the key principles of his government. Furthermore, he must not allow himself to forget that he is no more than an Israelite chosen for special responsibility, not extraordinary privilege.

The provision prohibiting the acquisition of many horses and, to a lesser extent, the prohibition against a large harem are somewhat puzzling. What is the significance of the phrase "and he must not return the people to Egypt in order to multiply horses" (v. 16ab)? Two possibilities suggest themselves. It may prohibit the king from hiring out his subjects to Egypt, a practice unattested in the biblical witness. More likely, it prohibits the Israelite king from putting Israelites to forced labor as did the Egyptians, and thus returning them to Egypt metaphorically.

This interpretation gains strength from comparisons of these three prohibitions to the accounts of Samuel's warnings concerning royal abuse of power and of Solomon's reign. Samuel warns that the king will accumulate wealth and power to such an extent that "you shall be his slaves. And in that day you will cry out (*z'q*, compare Exod 2:23) because of your king whom you have chosen for yourselves; but YHWH will not answer you in that day." In effect, by choosing a king who will inevitably succumb to the temptations of power, Israel—freed from bondage to an Egyptian king—will have chosen to return to slavery to an Israelite king. Already by the third king of the new monarchy, Solomon, royal construction projects, including stables (1 Kgs 9:19), demanded material and human resources to such an extent that Solomon found it necessary to institute a system of forced labor (*mas*, 1 Kgs 5:13; 9:15-22; 12:18; compare Exod 1:11; see also 1 Kgs 12:4): Israelites enslaved by their own king so that he could acquire horses from Egypt (1 Kgs 10:28)!

Like the prohibition against accumulating large numbers of horses, the prohibition against marrying many wives finds illumination by comparison with the account of Solomon's reign (1 Kgs 11:1-13). Evidence suggests that Solomon conducted foreign policy by marriage, marrying foreign princesses to seal relationships between Israel and its neighbors through ties of kinship between the royal houses. These marriages had unforeseen consequences, however:

> He had seven hundred wives, princesses, and three hundred concubines;
> and his wives turned aside his heart (compare Deut 17:17, "and he shall
> not turn aside his heart"). For when Solomon was old his wives turned
> aside his heart after other gods; and his heart was not wholly true to
> YHWH his God . . . For Solomon went after Ashtoreth the goddess of
> the Sidonians and after Milcom the abomination of the Ammonites.
> (1 Kgs 11:3-5)

The common danger underlying these prohibitions is that the king
will come to view himself as being superior to his fellow Israelites.
Even worse, he may come to rely on his own power and forget that
he is but a servant of YHWH. As a consequence, the law of the
king prescribes that, on the day of his ascension to the throne
(*kĕšibtô ʿal kissēʾ mamlaktô*, v. 18), he is to commission the preparation, in the presence of the levitical priests, of a copy of "this
Torah." Furthermore, he is to study the Torah daily so that he may
"learn to fear YHWH his God" and so that he may observe all its
provisions and act in accordance with them (v. 19). Just as even the
president of the United States is not above the law, the king of
Israel is to be subject to YHWH's covenant with his people.

The summary conclusion expressly states the two dangers facing
the king: that he may become arrogant in relation to his fellow
Israelites and that he may depart from the commandments of the
covenant. However, the king may also resist the temptation to
hoard power and wealth. He may remain true to the covenant. Just
as obedience to the covenant offers the promise of long life
(*lĕmaʿan yaʾărîk yāmîm*, Deut 5:16; 6:2; 25:15) to every Israelite,
obedience to the covenant offers the promise of a long reign
(*lĕmaʿan yaʾărîk yāmîm ʿal-mamlaktô*) to the king and his
descendants.

Levites: Honor and Dependence, 18:1-8

The unit dealing with the livelihood of the Levites manifests
perhaps the most obscure link to the commandment to honor one's
parents. Previous units in this extended section deal in some way
with the limitation of authority: judges must take care that justice
is not miscarried and judicial authority not abused; kings must not
grab for power and wealth. As will be shown below, subsequent
units continue this theme of limitation. The regulation concerning
the Levites here, however, says nothing of the exercise of the
priestly office, or the authority associated with it. Instead, the discussion focuses on the means whereby the landless Levites are to
live.

A number of possibilities may account for the inclusion of this unit at this point: (1) References to the levitical priests in the preceding material (17:9, 18) and an impulse to be exhaustive (judges, kings, priests, prophets) may have been a primary motivation for the placement of this unit. In this case, the determination to include material dealing with all four of the major institutions of leadership in Israel may have overridden the thematic relationship to the Decalogue. (2) On the other hand, the editors of Deuteronomy may have regarded the dependency of the priests on the levitical portion of the sacrifices offered to YHWH as evidence either of an inherent limitation of the Levites' power or, simultaneously, of a reminder of the source of the Levites' authority. (3) Yet another explanation for the inclusion of this unit here would rely on the implication that the country Levites discussed in vv. 6-8 have been involved in illicit worship. In this view, the unit would imply a warning that Levitical authority derives not from any inherent priestly power or holiness, but only from the proper exercise of the office. (4) Perhaps the most reasonable interpretation of the levitical material, however, would focus on the analogy between the honor due the Levites and that due one's parents. Both Levites and parents find themselves in vulnerable circumstances: the former owing to its lack of territory and its dependence on the tithe for sustenance; the latter owing to advancing age, etc. Both rely on the faithfulness of others.

The unit divides quite neatly into three sections. Verses 1-2 state the basic principle accounting for the Levites' landlessness; vv. 3-5 offer a basic definition of the sacrificial portions due the Levites; vv. 6-8 outline the concessions to be made in order to provide for provincial Levites who choose to associate with the central sanctuary.

YHWH is their inheritance, 18:1-2

As a means of establishing the unique role of the tribe of Levi, they were not assigned territory in Joshua's division of the land (Josh 13–22). Instead, unlike all other Israelites, they were privileged to partake of a portion of the sacrifices offered to YHWH. This privilege emphasizes the fact that the Levites have been set aside for YHWH; they are holy. In effect, just as YHWH has chosen Israel to be set aside for him in a unique way—to be a holy people—YHWH has chosen one tribe among this holy people to be set aside as the most holy among the holy. Levi can be said to be quintessentially Israel. Their role as mediators between YHWH and the people reaches even to their means of livelihood. On the other hand, this holiness renders them vulnerable and dependent! Israel must honor its priests.

This shall be the priests' due, 18:3-5

Typically, Deuteronomy demonstrates little interest in ritual specifics in contrast to the priestly material dealing with the priests' portions, which offers much greater detail (Lev 6:14-18; 7:28-36; Num 18:8-19, 25-32). The two traditions agree that the Levites, as those chosen to "stand and minister in the name of YHWH," are entitled to share in the sacrifices offered to YHWH. Deuteronomy 18:3, however, assigns to the Levites the shoulder, jowls, and stomach of sacrificial animals whereas the priestly discussion of the levitical portion assigns the breast and thigh (Lev 7:28-36; Num 18:18). Similarly, the priestly material prescribes carefully the procedure for handling the tithe. Levites, too, must tithe of their resources, setting aside the "tithe of the tithe" before consuming the remaining nine-tenths of the offering (Num 18:25-32). Only Deuteronomy mentions the "first fruits" of the fleece.

Any Levite may come to the central sanctuary, 18:6-8

The situation envisioned in vv. 6-8 seems at first glance quite straightforward. Any of the Levites who lived away from the central sanctuary, presumably serving as priests at local shrines, could at any time choose to "join the staff" of the central sanctuary (v. 6). Any who chose to do so were to be given full status as priests, i.e., they were to be permitted to serve (v. 7) and were to be granted an equal share in the priestly portion of the sacrifices (v. 8). This apparently straightforward prescription raises a number of vexing historical questions, however. According to the book of Deuteronomy, sacrifice could be made only at the central sanctuary. What function did these provincial Levites fulfill? How did they sustain themselves? In fact, Deuteronomy's requirement that sacrifice be centralized went unfulfilled until the time of Josiah (2 Kgs 23:4-20; 2 Chr 34:1-7). After the discovery of what must have been some form of Deuteronomy in the temple (2 Kgs 22), Josiah instituted a series of reforms. Among them, he closed the "high places" located throughout the countryside and brought the Levites who officiated there to Jerusalem. Either because they were too numerous, or because he regarded their service at these illicit local sanctuaries a disqualifying factor, Josiah did not, in fact, permit them to minister in Jerusalem (contrary to Deut 18:7), although they were permitted basic priestly provisions

(2 Kgs 23:8-9). In effect, then, Deuteronomy 18:6-8 seems to be aware of a historical situation in which Levites do, in fact, officiate at local shrines, contrary to the express requirement that all sacrifice be offered at the central sanctuary!

If 18:6-8 does, indeed, allude to a historical situation contrary to the law of cult centralization, it stands as an implicit criticism of Levites who do not choose to align with the official cult. These Levites, like the idol-worshiper discussed in the opening unit of this larger section on authority (17:2-7), the individual who "presumes to disobey the priest" officiating at the central sanctuary (17:12), the kind who disregards the covenant (18:19-20), or diviners, soothsayers, etc. treated in the next unit (vv. 9-14), have disdained, abused, or usurped authority. In this view, 18:1-6 conforms well to the theme of the larger unit, warning that the Levite's authority derives not from his office, per se, but from proper and lawful exercise of the duties and responsibilities of that office.

Authority and the Word of God, 18:9-22

Put in simplest terms, Deuteronomy is concerned with discerning and doing God's will. According to Deuteronomy, the Decalogue is the most basic statement of that will. But the principles of the Decalogue must be understood, interpreted, and applied. This interpretation and application is the duty of judges, kings, and priests. Their authority derives from their fidelity to the express will of God. What is Israel to do, however, in situations in which the covenant offers no obvious insight into God's will? Who in Israel, for example, should be chosen to replace Saul as king? Is it God's will that David build a temple in Jerusalem? The Decalogue cannot possibly be expected to indicate exhaustively God's will for these and other very specific problems that Israel will face throughout its history.

In ancient Israel, as in many other cultures, oracles and prophets met this need for direct, immediate, and specific guidance concerning the will of God. With respect to these means of determining the divine will, Deuteronomy's concern, as already expressed in another context (see commentary on ch. 13), involves the question of authenticity or proper authority. Deuteronomy 18:9-22 divides into two slightly unequal sections. The first (vv. 9-14) dismisses a number of oracular practices out of hand as non-authoritative. These would-be divine spokespersons do not merit the honor owed proper authorities because their methods are not authentic. The second (vv. 15-22) provides criteria for evaluating *apparently* authentic oracles. Only prophets who speak as

YHWH's messengers have any claim to authority. Even they, however, may be inauthentic, claiming authority not rightfully theirs.

YHWH abhors magic, 18:9-14

This subunit also divides roughly into three sections: An initial statement of the principle that Israel must avoid "learning to do" the "abhorrent" practices of its neighbors (v. 9) introduces a detailed list of the abominations (vv. 10-11). The unit concludes with a rationale for the basic principle (vv. 12-13).

Except possibly for the enigmatic practice of "passing one's children through the fire" (see 12:31), the prohibited practices—*qōsēm* "diviner," *mĕ'ônēn* "soothsayer," *mĕnaḥēs* probably "hydromancer," (observing signs in a liquid contained in cup; cf. Joseph's cup), *mĕkaššēp* "sorcerer, astrologer," *ḥōbēr* "spellcaster," (maybe by tying magic knots), *šō'ēl 'ôb wĕyidĕ'ōnî* "necromancer," (literally, "one who asks a ghost or familiar spirit"), and *dōrēš 'el-hammētîm* "necromancer" (literally, "one who inquires of the dead")—are all forms of magic.

Broadly defined, magic is the attempt to manipulate or understand reality by some mechanism. Ancient (and some modern) practitioners understood magic to be a craft or skill, not unlike that of the watchmaker or gunsmith. In order to manipulate even divine reality, one need only employ the proper techniques, learned from one's teacher. In effect, magic understood and practiced in this way reverses the proper relationship between creature and creator. The magician seeks to obtain some form of control over reality, even over the divine.

The underlying reason for Deuteronomy's abhorrence of these magical practices is obvious. YHWH is sovereign; YHWH cannot be manipulated. Israel must remain *tamîm* ("pure, clean, innocent") with YHWH. All authentic revelation will be at YHWH's initiative. YHWH will reveal himself when and how *he* chooses (cf. v. 15, "YHWH will raise up for you a prophet . . ."). Similarly, Deuteronomy clearly implies the threat inherent in practicing divination. YHWH displaced Israel's predecessors in the land because of divination. Israelites who dally in magic will be equally abhorrent to YHWH, and presumably, become subject to expulsion from the land (v. 12).

YHWH will validate his word, 18:15-22

In contrast to magicians of all sorts who seek to discern or influence God's will through manipulative techniques, the true prophet will function as YHWH's spokesperson, in YHWH's service, and at YHWH's behest. The unit follows a straightforward internal logic. An initial statement of the fact that YHWH will "raise up" a prophet like Moses introduces a series of explanatory sections. Verses 16-17 describe the need for and function of such a prophet. Verses 18-19 reiterate the original statement that YHWH will appoint a prophet like Moses, but go on to add that, since, like Moses, this prophet will act on divine commission, his message must be heeded. Verse 20 warns against prophets who may speak on their own volition, quite apart from any divine commission, or who may speak in the name of other gods. Verses 21-22 offer criteria for distinguishing the true prophet, who speaks authentically in YHWH's name, from such false prophets.

The explanation of the necessity for a prophet like Moses hearkens back to Israel's request for an intercessor at Mt. Horeb (see 5:22-33; compare Exod 19:16-25). Overwhelmed by the awesome majesty of YHWH's epiphany, and fearful that they might not survive a period in YHWH's very presence, the people asked that Moses might be their representative to God and, in turn, God's representative to them (v. 16). Just as YHWH agreed to their proposal at Mt. Horeb (v. 17), he will again appoint a prophet to represent his will to the people. Because the true prophet is YHWH's chosen spokesman, the prophet's word must be obeyed. YHWH himself will "seek out what is with (*ʾānōkî ʾedrōš mēʿimmô*)" anyone who disregards the prophet's message.

In the context of the larger section's concern for the limitations on and proper exercise of authority, the final topic in this unit is of greatest interest. The *need* for a prophet is clear. The people of God require guidance in matters not treated specifically in the covenant. The *role* of the prophet or the *definition* of the prophetic function is equally unambiguous. The true prophet speaks YHWH's message at YHWH's command. The *identification* of the true prophet, on the other hand, poses a difficult challenge. Should the people of God follow everyone who claims divine authority? No. Verse 20 specifies two examples of prophets without authority: those who counterfeit the divine commission and those who speak on the authority of other gods. Such fraudulent prophets usurp YHWH's supreme authority. They are to pay with their lives. The people's problem of recognition, however, still remains largely unsolved. Prophets who prophesy in the names of other gods can be easily recognized. But how does one recognize apparently sincere prophets impersonating true prophets of YHWH (v. 21)? Verse 22 offers only one very reliable criterion: if the prophecy fails to come to pass, the prophet was a liar. Although virtually foolproof, in practice, this criterion must have proven insufficient. Must one delay response to a prophet's message until his message has already proven true? The time for decision will have passed! Deuteronomy and literature inspired by it struggle with this problem in light of Israel's long experience of prophets—both true prophets unrecognized as such and false prophets mistakenly honored. Discernment of divinely commissioned messengers continues to be a problem for God's people (see also commentary on 13:1-6).

CONNECTIONS

This section of the Deuteronomic Code consists of an explication of the Decalogue's commandment to honor one's parents as a treatment of the broader question of authority. Once again, the Bible treats an issue that seems to be inherent to human nature and human societies regardless of the time or place. In a modern context, authority figures prominently in public discourse and private lives: Certain segments of the church attribute society's ills to absent or weak paternal authority, unsubmissive wives, and pampered children; the public mistrusts government at all levels; those who reached adulthood during the Vietnam War era are skeptical—even cynical—with respect to virtually all authority; local congregations and whole denominations tear apart under demands for submission to ordained authority. As always, perhaps, the twin evils of disrespect for genuine authority and the arrogant assertion of power as a substitute for true authority plague social institutions ranging from the family to the federal government.

Deuteronomy 16:18–18:22 provide the basis for three assertions concerning authority, its proper exercise, and dangers inherent in authority misapplied. The fact that the Bible devotes such attention to the problem of authority should at least give one reason to reflect.

Authority Is Necessary

First, Deuteronomy seems to assume that society depends upon authority structures. The alternative would be chaos and anarchy.

Justice, Order, and Israel's Social Institutions

Studies of Israelite wisdom literature have argued that it reflects an underlying Hebrew worldview that involved the basic notion that God had created the world to operate—or perhaps better to embody—a natural and moral *order* (see Prov 8). (See H. H. Schmid, *Gerechtigkeit als Weltordnung: Hintergrund und Geschichte als alttestamentlichen Gerechtigkeitsbegreiffes* [Tübingen: J. C. B. Mohr, 1968]; idem, *Altorientalische Welt in der alttestamentlichen Theologie* [Zurich: Theologischer Verlag, 1974]; R. Knieriem, "Cosmos and History in Israel's Theology," in *Werden und Wirken des Alten Testaments* [Göttingen: Vandenhoeck and Ruprecht, 1980], 59-123; idem, "The Task of Old Testament Theology," HBT 6 [1984]: 25-57.) The Hebrew language describes this state of proper order variously as "peace" (*šālôm*; emphasizing that things are as they should be), "justice" (*ṣĕdāqâ*; suggesting restoration to a proper order), or "wisdom" (*ḥokmâ*, the term for the principle of order itself). This order, built into the universe, God's will, can be known through the study of creation itself or by means of revelation in the covenant. Apocryphal literature explicitly identifies the principle of Wisdom with the revealed Torah (Sir 24:23).

Israel's major social institutions function in relation to this natural and moral order. The *king's* responsibility is to maintain it in the political and social realm. The *priest's* duty, as an expert in the revealed Torah, is to distinguish between states of order and disorder (clean and unclean, see [Clean and Unclean—"Appropriate" and "Off-limits"]) and to officiate in rituals designed to celebrate or restore order. The *wise man* discerns the divine will empirically (thus the common association of wise men such as Joseph and Daniel with dream interpretation, etc.) and often advises the king. The *prophet's* role is to sound the alarm in the event that the other institutions fail to fulfill their proper functions.

Judges must be appointed to adjudicate disputes, to seek justice and justice only. Charges of idolatry—rejection of YHWH as Israel's ultimate authority—must be investigated and evil must be purged from the land. Any case too difficult for a local judge must be taken to the high priest at the central sanctuary. His ruling must be honored so as to rid Israelite society of wickedness. The king must become learned in the covenant, living and ruling in accord with YHWH's will. Prophets commissioned by YHWH must communicate YHWH's will to God's people. No doubt, were Deuteronomy composed today, it would have devoted attention also to schoolteachers, police officers, and even medical professionals. People in positions of authority regulate and direct the smooth function of society. [Justice, Order, and Israel's Social Institutions] The exercise of genuine authority is simply necessary.

Authority, not Authoritarianism

Second, however, Deuteronomy also asserts that genuine authority is not authoritarian. Significantly, in comparison to the "honor your parents" commandment, the Deuteronomic Code shifts its primary focus to the responsibilities of those in authority. They are human beings, and must therefore take pains to guard against their

The Wise Leader

The wise leader does not intervene unnecessarily. The leader's presence is felt, but often the group runs itself. Lesser leaders do a lot, say a lot, have followers, and form cults. Even worse ones use fear to energize the group and force to overcome resistance. Only the most dreadful leaders have bad reputations. Remember that you are facilitating another person's process. It is not your process. Do not intrude. Do not control. Do not force your own needs and insights into the foreground. If you do not trust a person's process, that person will not trust you. Imagine that you are a midwife; you are assistant at someone else's birth. Do good without show or fuss. Facilitate what is happening rather than what you think ought to be happening. If you must take the lead, lead so that the mother is helped, yet still free and in charge. When the baby is born, the mother will rightly say: "We did it ourselves!"

From Lao-tzu, *Tao Te Ching* as cited in Wren, ed., *The Leader's Companion: Insights on Leadership through the Ages* (New York: The Free Press, 1995), 70-71.

own human fallibility. Judges must be careful not to pervert justice through laxity, corruption, or regard for the social status of the litigants. Persons may be executed for idolatry *only* after a thorough investigation and *only* on the authority of multiple, independent witnesses. The king, in particular, must guard against arrogance, greed, and lust for power. Fundamentally, he must remember that he is an Israelite like his brothers and sisters, like them subject to the covenant with YHWH. Similarly, would-be prophets must not presume to speak for YHWH. Prophets merit regard solely on the basis of the source and authenticity of their messages: Evaluate and heed the message, not the messenger! [The Wise Leader]

After all, true authority derives from the conscientious and competent fulfillment of valid responsibilities. The failure to recognize this dynamic lies at the heart of many ills—both ancient and modern. Parents expect respect and obedience even when they are either unwilling or unable to earn it. Conservative Christians declaim the virtues of submissive wives, idealizing dysfunction as the will of God. Narcissistic religious leaders and pastors claim divine sanction for their every whim, equating blind obedience to their authority with faith in God and fidelity to God's will. Deuteronomy warns very clearly against such arrogance of power. Power coerces; genuine authority nurtures.

Authority and Communal Responsibility

Finally, Deuteronomy asserts that the maintenance of proper authority is also the responsibility of the people. In fact, Deuteronomy issues a dual charge. One must honor authentic authority, to be sure; but one must also *disobey* incompetent, misdirected, fraudulent, arrogant, and self-serving authority. These two charges may be reduced to a basic duty to discern. Leaders have responsibilities, but so do followers. Following is not a passive role. Deuteronomy does not entertain the possibility of a "just following orders" defense. The community is responsible for its actions, even for its choice of leaders and its decision to follow their guidance.

NOTES

[1] L. Maloney, trans., in *A Song of Power and the Power of Song: Essays on the Book of Deuteronomy*, ed. D. Christensen (Winona Lake: Eisenbrauns, 1993), 313-35 (= "Die Abfolge der Gesetze in Deuteronomium 12–26 und der Dekalog," in *Das Deuteronomium: Entstehung, Gestalt und Botschaft*, ed. H. Lohfink (BEThL 68; Louvain: Louvain University Press, 1985], 252-72; citation, 327).

[2] "Distribution of the Functions of Power: the Laws Concerning Public Offices in Deuteronomy 16:18–18:22," trans. R. Walls, in *Song of Power* (= "Die Sicherung der Wirksamkeit des Gotteswortes durch das Prinzip der Schriftlichkeit der Tora und durch das Prinzip der Gewaltenteilung nach den Ämtergesetzen des Buches Deuteronomium [Dt 16,18-18,22]," in *Great Themes from the Old Testament* [Chicago: Franciscan Herald, 1981], 55-75), 341.

[3] "Distribution of the Functions of Power," 336-39.

THE PROTECTION OF INNOCENT LIFE

19:1-21

Explication of the Fifth Commandment: "Do not kill," 19:1–22:8

The Deuteronomic Code's longest and most complex explication of one of the basic principles of the covenant is devoted to the Decalogue's prohibition against taking life. Unlike the previous section, whose connection to the Sabbath commandment is subtle almost to the point of imperceptibility, the material gathered here, on the whole, clearly relates to the principle of the sanctity of life. Terms for killing (*rṣḥ*, 19:3, 4, 6), death (19:5, 6, 11, 12; 20:5, 6, 7; 21:21, 22), blood/bloodguilt (19:6, 10, 12, 13; 21:7, 8, 9; 22:8), etc. abound. In several previous sections, editors employed the technique of expanding the horizons in which a basic principle of the Decalogue should be viewed by assembling apparently unrelated materials in such a way as to demonstrate that the principle applies more broadly than might at first be imagined. Here, instead, the editors pursue the topic of the sanctity of life as manifest in a wide variety of cases in such a way as to illustrate the principle by means of multiple case studies. Either technique has the effect of broadening and deepening the applicability of the otherwise ambiguous and abstract fundamental principle—in this case, the principle of the sanctity of life. While a few "transitional" units (21:10-14, 15-17; 22:5) anticipate the subsequent explication of the commandment concerning adultery, even they involve issues concerning the diminishment of life and demonstrate that the boundaries separating the commandments governing human relationships are indefinite.

Following Olson,[1] the extended unit may be divided into four subsections: (1) 19:1-21, the protection of innocent life; (2) 20:1-20, limits on killing in warfare; (3) 21:1-23, situations involving conflicts between life and death; and (4) 22:1-8, the obligation to enhance life. This outline already suggests that, in the view of the Deuteronomic Code, the value placed on life inherent in the Decalogue's prohibition against killing extends in a number of directions. First, the supreme value of life requires that active measures be taken to prevent even its accidental loss (19:1-21). Second, even in time of war, bloodthirstiness must be restrained (20:1-18). Third, just as human life is sacrosanct, animal (22:1-4, 6-7) and even vegetable life (20:19-20) must be revered. Fourth, life's value makes the *quality* of life important as well. Diminishing the life of another is a degree of taking it (19:14, 15-21).

COMMENTARY

The Protection of Innocent Life, 19:1-21

The first subsection gathers regulations concerned with protecting three classes of innocent people from unjust loss or diminishment of life. Verses 1-13 provide for cities of refuge where those who have killed accidentally may find protection from the deceased's family. Verse 14 warns against depriving a fellow citizen of land, the principle source of livelihood in an agrarian culture. Verses 15-21 discourage those who would use the judicial system as a weapon against their enemies by falsely accusing them. In some cases, lying can be tantamount to murder.

Cities of Refuge, 19:1-13

The establishment of three cities of refuge in the Transjordan has already been discussed (4:41-43). Numbers 35 and Joshua 20 also discuss cities of refuge and make provisions for protection of the life of one who committed unintentional homicide. [Cities of Refuge in Numbers 35 and Joshua 20] The section divides neatly into four paragraphs: (1) the requirement for the establishment of three cities of refuge, evenly dispersed throughout the land (vv. 1-3); (2) the definition of accidental homicide (vv. 4-7); (3) the provision for three additional cities of refuge in the event of territorial expansion (vv. 8-10); and (4) the definition of intentional homicide (vv. 11-13).

Paragraphs (2) and (4) deal with the central issues. They reflect a period in which Israel was making the transition from clan-oriented justice to a true judicial system. The *gōʾēl*, the "kinsman-redeemer-avenger," is one's nearest male relative whose responsibility was to represent his kinsman, and thereby the interests of one's clan, in a wide range of circumstances ranging from

Cities of Refuge in Numbers 35 and Joshua 20

The provision for cities of refuge in Deut 19 finds parallels in Num 35 and Josh 20. While the three texts substantially agree, there are significant distinctions. Neither of the parallels mention the possibility of a third set of three cities, while only Numbers identifies the cities of refuge (three on either side of the Jordan, a commonality in all three texts) as six of the forty-eight "Levitical cities."

With respect to the definition of unintentional homicide and the regulations concerning the refugee, Numbers and Joshua specify that the non-Israelite resident alien (*gēr*) must enjoy the same protections as the citizen (Num 35:15; Josh 20:9) and that the refugee must reside in the city of refuge until the death of the presiding high priest (Num 35:25; Josh 20:6). Joshua conflates the terms for "accidental" manslaughter employed in Numbers ("in error," *bišgāgâ*, v. 11) and in Deuteronomy ("unintentionally," *biblî-da'at*, lit., "without knowing," 19:4) into the double phrase "accidentally and by mistake" (*bišgāgâ biblî-da'āt*, v. 3).

Numbers offers the most idiosyncratic depiction of the institution. For Numbers (vv. 16-21), intention can be deduced, under certain circumstances, from the use of a deadly weapon (iron implements, stones, wooden weapons) or deadly force (shoving, blows with the bare hands). Since, prior to the era of modern forensic science, many of these, especially stones, shoves, and barehanded blows, give only the most tenuous indication of intention, Deuteronomy's preference for the motive and premeditation criteria is understandable.

Numbers also cautions the refugee to remain within the walls of the city of refuge even *after* he or she has been declared innocent in court. According to its provision, the *gōʾēl* is free to avenge the death of his relative with impunity so long as the avenging attack occurs outside the city of refuge (v. 26). Similarly, the killer may not post bail ("ransom") to cover the period up until the death of the priest (v. 32). He or she must at least endure a period of limited freedom. In contrast, Deuteronomy mentions neither the duration of the refugee's enforced stay in the city nor the exclusion of a ransom. Instead, since, in its view, the accidental killer is guilty of no crime, it explicitly describes the *gōʾēl*'s vengeance, wherever it takes place, as a shedding of innocent blood that will bring bloodguilt upon both *gōʾēl* and people. Presumably, according to Deuteronomy, once the city of refuge has been attained and the innocence of the killer ascertained, the *gōʾēl* must respect this determination and the refugee may travel freely.

rescuing the kinsman from economic distress (redeeming property sold to escape economic difficulty, Lev 25:25; Ruth 4; redeeming persons who sell themselves into debt-slavery, Lev 25:39-55) to avenging the kinsman's death (as here).[2] Blood-feuds and cycles of escalating violence lie in the background.

Cities of refuge and the accompanying legal distinction between accidental homicide and murder are intended to end such cycles of violence. An individual who accidentally causes the death of another is innocent and not deserving of capital punishment. To execute such a person would be to take an innocent life and to bring "bloodguilt" upon the people (v. 10). Instead, this individual must be given refuge from the *gōʾēl*.

The matter hinges on the key factor that distinguishes between an accident and murder: intention. Of course, the difficulty lies in the fact that intention is highly subjective. Only the killer truly knows his or her intent. Since, naturally, the killer is an unreliable witness, triers of fact must deduce intent from the killer's actions.

Deuteronomy 19 offers two tests: motive (vv. 4-7) and premeditation (vv. 8-10). Paragraph (2) begins by declaring that unintentional killers deserve protection and by defining intention

No Place to Call Home

This work resonates with allusions to the 20th century Jewish refugee experience as encountered by Marc Chagall in his life. This village appears almost abandoned as if yet another emptying has occurred—ghosts of the past hover above as witnesses to human outrage and suffering. Yet, as a testament to Chagall's indomitable spirit, images of protection, nurture, and persistence loom larger than life above the rest, reflecting the will of his people. The rooster suggests the clarion call to take heart and survive.

Marc Chagall. 1887–1985. *The Refugees.* 1976. Private Collection.

in terms of prior enmity (v. 4). The assumption, made also in modern definitions of murder, [Modern Legal Definitions of Murder] is that intention involves motive. Where no prior enmity exists, it can be assumed that the killing was accidental. The example of such an accidental killing (v. 5) describes a very conceivable situation in which no fault can rightly be assigned. Comparison with the parallel in the Covenant Code (Exod 21:12-14) reveals an interesting distinction between the two. Exodus contrasts an intentional act of homicide with "an act of God." As is typical for Deuteronomy, its refuge law regards the situation from a more "secular" standpoint, speaking instead of "accidental" events. To make even clearer its definition of killing that does not deserve to be punished, Deuteronomy cites an example. The principle that the hewer of wood cannot be held accountable for the flight of an errant ax-head is meant to exemplify any and all other

Modern Legal Definitions of Murder

Modern American legal definitions of murder differ little from the ancient Israelite in the generalities, although modern law treats the question of intent with greater subtlety. Basically, murder is defined as "unlawful killing with malice aforethought." This definition excludes such "lawful killing" as necessary and appropriate acts committed during the discharge of one's duties in military service or as a law enforcement officer, or acts committed in self-defense, for example.

"Malice aforethought" is the basic criterion distinguishing murder from manslaughter in both ancient Israelite and modern law. Modern law further subdivides "malice" into *express* and *implied*. Express malice, the actual intent to kill, may be determined by inferring that a person intended the commonsense outcome of an act (for example, that tampering with a coworker's safety harness would result in the latter's fall and injury). Implied malice, manifest in a

flagrantly reckless and dangerous act, may be gauged by the extreme degree of risk created by an action.

The modern provision for degrees of murder (first and second) reflects this perception of a distinction in degrees of intention. Intent in first-degree murder involves either "deliberation and premeditation" or, in some states, takes place during the commission of another felony (for example, armed robbery). The passage of time between the moment of decision to kill and the act itself is immaterial. The murderer must, however, be in such a mental state as to permit consideration of the action and its consequences (for example, certain mentally ill persons or inebriated persons cannot make such deliberate and considered decisions). Second-degree murder involves the requisite malice but *without* deliberation or premeditation.

The material summarized here is drawn from Inge Dobelis, ed., *Reader's Digest Family Legal Guide: A Complete Encyclopedia of Law for the Layman* (Pleasantville NY: The Reader's Digest Association, 1981), s.v. "Murder."

such cases in which the proximate cause of death does not correspond to the purposes of the human agent.

Paragraph (4) offers an additional test: "lying in wait" (v. 11). Such behavior implies not only motive, but also premeditation and forethought. The murderer not only has motive, but he or she makes plans to kill. The progress of thought is similar to that described in James 1:14-15: emotion (in this case hatred) produces a will to act, which in turn produces the action. The intention and the action are bound together seamlessly.

The citation (v. 13) of the *lex talionis* (law of retaliation) in this context invites consideration. Despite its reputation for legalism and hard, almost cruel justice, the issues treated in the refuge law suggest that the Hebrew Bible engages in a nuanced, deliberative, subtle, and, above all, humane exegesis of the valuable demands of the Decalogue in the context of circumstances encountered in the real world. Obviously, talion law acknowledges the value of human life implied in the Decalogue—nothing equals a human life in value save another human life. To intentionally take human life is to forfeit one's own. On the other hand, in the context of clan justice, the talion law also limits vengeance. Only the taker of life forfeits. Feuds trespass the boundaries. Furthermore, to execute the hewer of wood would be to compound tragedy with injustice and to implicate both the *gōʾēl* and the community in a true murder! ["The Brother"] The notion of "a life for a life" implies the equal value of both the deceased and the unwitting manslayer. The manslayer "took" nothing; his or her life may not itself be taken.

> ### 📖 "The Brother"
>
> O KNOW you what I have done
> To avenge our sister? She,
> I thought, was wantoned with
> By a man of levity:
>
> And I lay in wait all day,
> All day did I wait for him,
> And dogged him to Bollard Head
> When twilight dwindled dim,
>
> And hurled him over the edge
> And heard him fall below:
> O would I were lying with him,
> For the truth I did not know!
> 'O where's my husband?' she asked,
> As evening wore away:
> 'Best you had one, forsooth,
> But never had you!' I say.
>
> 'Yes, but I have!' says she,
> 'My Love made it up with me,
> And we churched it yesterday
> And mean to live happily.'
>
> And now I go in haste
> To the Head, before she's aware,
> To join him in death for the wrong
> I've done them both out there!
>
> J. Gibson, ed., *The Complete Poems of Thomas Hardy* (New York: Macmillan, 1978), 880.

The Neighbor's Landmark: Stealing can be killing, 19:14

The circumstance addressed in this injunction is straightforward; its relationship to the commandment against killing, however, is subtle. In ancient Israel, real property was considered a perpetual inheritance. According to the book of Joshua, Joshua divided the entire land of Israel among the tribes, clans, and families of Israel. Since, under Mosaic Law, the land could not be sold—at most it could be "rented" for a period of up to, but not exceeding, six years, or until the next Sabbath year—boundary markers will have been permanent fixtures, established long before anyone remembered ("ancient markers," Prov 22:28; 23:10). Elijah pronounced judgment against King Ahab and his Phoenician queen Jezebel because, in order to wrest his patrimony from Naboth, they suborned perjury (compare Deut 19:15-21) against him, orchestrating state-condoned theft *and* murder (1 Kgs 21). The eighth-century prophets Amos and Micah frequently charged the upper strata of Israelite society with illegally depriving the poor of their inheritance (Amos 2:6-8; 4:1-3; 5:10-13; 8:4-6; Mic 2:1-3).

What has the theft of property to do with the commandment against killing, however? In a striking hyperbole, Micah describes those who "covet fields, and seize them; houses, and take them away," who "oppress householder and house, people and their inheritance" (Mic 2:2) as people who "tear the skin off my people, and the flesh off their bones, who eat the flesh of my people, flay their skin off them, break their bones in pieces, and chop them up like meat in a kettle, like flesh in a cauldron" (Mic 3:2-3). Underlying both Micah's statement and the placement of Deuteronomy 19:14 in the section dealing with the sanctity of life is the notion that, in a primarily agrarian society such as ancient Israel, to deprive one of the means of agricultural production is to deprive one of life. *Stealing can be killing.* In abstract terms, economic injustice is a form of killing; in even more general terms, any diminishment of life is a form of murder.

Rules of Evidence: Lying can be killing, 19:15-21

Although this treatment of "rules of evidence" seems at first sight to belong better with the treatment of judicial matters in 16:18-20; 17:2-13, it shares with the preceding two units an interest in the fact that, regardless of the means employed, *intent* defines wrongful killing or, for that matter, any wrongful diminishment of another's life. It outlines a number of safeguards designed to assure that an innocent person is not wrongfully convicted and thereby deprived of freedom or life itself.

First (v. 15), a single witness is to be considered unreliable as a rule; two or better three concurring witnesses are required. The text does not elaborate on the reasoning for this dictum, but circumstances regularly arise in which one witness's perspective proves to be mistaken or incomplete quite apart from any intent to deceive. Even worse, to rely on one witness only is to run the risk of convicting on patently false testimony, a circumstance the text goes on to address explicitly later. Although the precise rationale is left unstated, the force of this rule is clear. Balancing the possibility of convicting an innocent person on the basis of the testimony of one witness, whether mistaken or mischievous, against the possibility of

Susannah and the Elders

Bearing false witness can be killing.

Giovanni Battista Pittoni. 1687–1767. *Susannah and the Elders*. Canvas Louvre. Paris, France.

allowing the guilty to go free, Deuteronomy demonstrates a clear bias toward the presumption of innocence and the protection of the innocent.

Second (vv. 16-19), the authorities must remain alert to the danger posed by a "malicious" or "lying" witness. The terms describing such witnesses indicate the dynamics of the situation envisioned by the text. Verse 16 mentions an *ʿēd ḥāmās*, literally a "violent witness," in reference to the witness's intention to do harm (compare also *zāmam*, "to plan" in v. 19). Verses 18-19 speak of an *ʿēd šeqer*, "a lying witness (a witness who intentionally lies, not one who unintentionally makes erroneous statements)," in reference to

The Mishnah on the Responsibility of Judges: Avoiding the Rush to Judgment

Later Jewish jurisprudence is consistent with Deuteronomy's concern for protecting the innocent against possibilities for error or misuse of the judicial process. The Mishnah details the Sanhedrin's extreme reticence to convict, especially in capital cases.

> The more [a judge] examines [the evidence] the more praiseworthy is he. (*San* 5:1)

> If they found for his acquittal, they set him free; if not, they postpone his sentence until the next day. [The judges] went away in pairs [to discuss the verdict], and they indulged in little food and did not drink wine all that day, and they discussed the matter thoroughly the whole night, and rose early the following morning and came to the court. He that was for acquittal said, 'I was in favour [sic] of acquittal and I am still in favour of his acquittal;' and he that was for conviction said, 'I found him guilty and I still maintain that he is guilty.' He who argued for conviction may now argue for acquittal, but he who argued for acquittal may not retract and argue for conviction. (*San* 5:5)

> When the verdict has been announced they take him forth to stone him . . . One man stands at the entrance of the court with a scarf in his hand, (and another man riding) a horse far away from him but still able to see him. If one [of the judges] say, 'I have some point to argue on his behalf for acquittal,' he [namely, the first man mentioned] would wave the scarf and the horse runs and stops him. And even if [the condemned man] himself say, 'I have aught to argue on my own behalf for acquittal,' they must bring him back, even four or five time, only provided that there be any substance in his statement. If they found for him for acquittal, they set him free, but if not, he goes forth to be stoned. And a crier goes out before him [proclaiming], 'So-and-so, the son of so-and-so, is going forth to be stoned because he had committed such-and-such a transgression, and so-and-so and so-and-so are his witnesses. If anyone know aught in his favor or acquittal, let him come and argue on his behalf.' (*San* 6:1)

P. Blackman, trans., *Tractate Sanhedrin: Being the Fourth Tractate of the Fourth Order of the Mishnah* (New York: The Judaica Press, 1981), 40, 43, 44-45.

---

the means utilized by the witness to execute his or her evil intent. The horror to be avoided is the possibility that such a witness may pervert the court into an unwitting participant in wrongdoing, under certain conditions, even into a murder weapon! *Lying can be killing!*

Third (vv. 17-18), for these reasons, it is absolutely necessary for the judicial authorities to "make a thorough inquiry." [The Mishnah on the Responsibility of Judges] Since the intents and purposes of the human heart are hidden from view, judges and priests—assembled, together with the parties to the case, *before YHWH* (v. 17)—must strive to determine the reliability of a given witness. Truthfulness cannot be assumed: the freedom or very life of the accused is at stake!

Fourth (vv. 18-21), the penalty for such perjury is to equal that for the charge preferred against the innocent accused. This provision is designed to deter maliciously false testimony. One can only wonder whether modern legal systems might not benefit from a similar approach to perjury and frivolous litigation. *Lying can be killing!*

CONNECTIONS

In much of the modern world, the rule of law has replaced clan-enforced justice, rendering unnecessary institutions such as cities of refuge. Western concepts of property ownership are based on the notion of the owner's freedom to dispose of property as they will: family holdings rarely remain intact from one generation to the next. Modern adversarial legal systems encourage the introduction of contradictory evidence and, to a large degree, relieve parties to the dispute of responsibility for the pursuit of truth: that responsibility devolves solely on the jury. In other words, the situations and institutions addressed in Deuteronomy 19 have no direct analogy in modern life. One could easily conclude, therefore, that this material holds only historical interest.

Viewed from another perspective, however, it becomes apparent that the text addresses fundamental ethical and moral issues regarding the sanctity of human life that continue to confront modern societies—issues that apparently confront all human societies. While modern believers cannot turn to Deuteronomy for specific solutions to the unique modern manifestations of these timeless problems, they can appeal to the concerns expressed here as the basis for an approach that can rightly claim to be consistent with the biblical witness. At least three such concerns can be identified in Deuteronomy 19.

The Sanctity of Human Life and the Urge for Revenge

First, the supreme value of innocent life trumps the urge for vengeance. Law and order hawks often enlist the Old Testament in support of their calls for swift, sure, and unflinching punishment. Even more forcefully than in the earlier section concerning the danger of the abuse of judicial authority (see 16:18-20; 17:2-13), however, the laws concerning the cities of refuge and false witnesses resist pressures to "get a conviction" at all costs. Victims and their families, and society as a whole, do indeed have interests in seeing the guilty brought to account; these interests are not served, however, by punishing the innocent. Political motivations and responsiveness to public opinion must not be permitted to blind prosecutors, in particular, and the courts generally to their responsibility to find the truth. Given Deuteronomy's awareness of the inherent unreliability of human testimony (whether given in error or with intent)—disregarding for the moment the ambiguity of so-called "circumstantial" evidence—the American legal requirements that innocence be presumed and that jurors be convinced of guilt "beyond a reasonable doubt" cannot be overvalued. Nothing compares in gravity to rendering a verdict of guilty: despite even the best, most honorable efforts of the court, honest mistakes or deception may still have yielded a false conviction. Innocence matters.

The Sanctity of Human Life and Dangerous Emotions and Attitudes

Second, the supreme sanctity of human life requires that, in addition to the ultimate taking of life, all stages in the process leading to that act be subsumed under the prohibition against killing. Deuteronomy 19 does not yet work out the full implications of this awareness, as Jesus and the rabbis would later, but the basic ideas can be found in the definitions of accidental homicide and murder and in the statement of the penalty for false testimony. At issue in both cases is intent. Negatively, murder (as opposed to an accident) results from the completion of a sequence of emotion ("enmity in the past") become volition (the decision to "lie in wait," the intention to do harm) become action. The action alone can be merely accidental. As an expression of the will, it is murder. The law against false witness, on the other hand, draws a conclusion implicit in the definition of murder: namely, that even when the sequence fails to come to completion, the intention itself is tantamount to the act! ["But I say unto you, do not hate . . ."]

The Sanctity of Human Life and Quality of Life Issues

Third, the supreme sanctity of human life requires not only that it not be taken, but also that it not be diminished in quality. Understood in this way, the single, specific case of the misplaced boundary marker (19:14) becomes representative of an almost innumerable array of possible attacks on human life that fall short of actual murder: character "assassination," unfair hiring practices, racial, gender, or any other form of prejudice and discrimination. Any act or attitude that harms or devalues the life of another human being, likewise created in the image of God, is but the first step along the path that leads to murder itself.

"But I say to unto you, do not hate . . ."

Despite Jesus' explicit statement that he had come "to fulfill the law" (radically extrapolate all its implications and universalize its demands?), Christian interpreters regularly refer to Jesus' exegesis of the Decalogue found in Matt 5:21-48 as the "Antitheses"—as though Jesus set out to contrast or even replace the Torah with his teaching. In fact, Jesus *followed, extended,* and *expanded* the tradition of interpretation of the commandment against killing established in Deut 19. In this regard, in fact, Jesus' approach stands squarely in the tradition of rabbinic interpretation. Compare, for example, Rashi (M. Rosenbaum and A. M. Silbermann, trans., *Pentateuch with Targum Onkelos, Haphtaroth and Prayers for Sabbath and Rashi's Commentary: Deuteronomy* [London: Shapiro, Vallentine & Co., 1934], 98) on Deut 19:

> It is through his hatred that he comes to such a point as to "lie in wait for him." From here they [the Rabbis] derived their statement: If a man transgresses a light command he will in the end transgress a weighty command;—because he transgressed the command (Lev 19:17) "Thou shalt not hate thy brother in thine heart," he will in the end come to such a point as to shed blood. It is for this reason that it is stated here, apparently redundantly, "but if a man hate his fellow [and lie in wait for him]" for it ought to have written only: "But if a man rise up and lie in wait for his fellow and smite him mortally." (Siphre)

Jesus agrees with Deut 19 that intent defines murder, and, further, that anger and hatred give birth to intent (Matt 5:22). Since the sequence of attitude, decision, and action is seamless, Jesus argues—extending the argument of Deut 19 a step further—that the attitude itself already renders one "liable to judgment." The desire to kill makes one a killer. The act only manifests the killer's decision. Jesus also agrees with Deut 19:14 that any diminishment of another human being is a form of killing. Insults, deprecation, and murder arise from the same source (Matt 5:22).

The danger posed by anger is so great, in fact, that Jesus encourages his disciples not only to avoid it themselves, but also to seek actively to protect both friend (Matt 5:23-24) and enemy (Matt 5:25-26) from its effects. Because anger makes murderers, one should avoid becoming the irritant. One should quickly be reconciled with any who are in danger of becoming haters. In Jesus' view of the kingdom of God, in which all are their siblings' keepers, the potential victim loves the potential murderer enough to snuff out the chain of events leading to transgression.

Jesus *does not* contradict or invalidate the Decalogue. Neither does he contrast his interpretation of it with that of Deuteronomy. Instead, he aligns himself with the Deuteronomic scheme of interpretation and continues it to its most radical conclusion.

NOTES

[1] D. Olson, *Deuteronomy and the Death of Moses: A Theological Reading,* OBT (Minneapolis: Fortress, 1994), 88.

[2] See further, J. J. Stamm, "גאל *gʾl* to redeem," *TLOT* (ed. E. Jenni and C. Westermann; trans. M. Biddle; Peabody MA: Hendrickson, 1997), I, 288-96.

LIMITS ON KILLING IN WAR

20:1-20

Perhaps the single greatest apparent moral inconsistency in the Hebrew Bible lies in the harsh contrast between its insistence on the sanctity of human life and the institution of "holy war" (Heb. *herem*) discussed here in Deuteronomy 20. The inclusion of this treatment of rules governing warfare in the context of the exposition of the commandment against taking human life only heightens the sense of contradiction. A concern for the protection of innocent life dominates the previous subsection; Deuteronomy 20 calls for Israel to engage its enemies fearlessly and to eradicate whole populations including women and children. How does one reconcile these two sensibilities?

The problem for a modern interpreter requires a perspective encompassing more than the text of Deuteronomy itself. Deuteronomy's regulations on warfare must be set in the context of the broader history of human attitudes toward warfare, especially in relation to Israel's ancient Near Eastern setting. Essential is a theological perspective concerning the continuing nature of God's revelation, or better, the maturation of God's people over time enabling them to perceive more fully God's revelation of Godself. Interpreters must also guard against an air of superiority, maintaining humility in view of the bellicosity of modern nation states and the bloodthirstiness of modern communities of faith. ["Christmas: 1924"]

The first task, however, is to look closely at the text. Since the editors of Deuteronomy have placed the rules on warfare in the section explicating the commandment against killing, it may be useful to postulate that, although these rules presume the necessity and reality of warfare, they also seek in some way to limit the loss of life, perhaps according to some principle similar to the *lex talionis*. Should this hypothesis hold, the significance of these regulations for modern interpreters may prove to

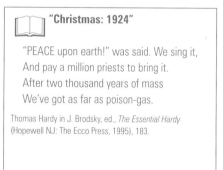

"Christmas: 1924"

"PEACE upon earth!" was said. We sing it,
And pay a million priests to bring it.
After two thousand years of mass
We've got as far as poison-gas.

Thomas Hardy in J. Brodsky, ed., *The Essential Hardy* (Hopewell NJ: The Ecco Press, 1995), 183.

consist in their insight that, even when necessary, killing in time of war must not go unrestrained.

Deuteronomy 20 divides into four unequal sections: an opening theological encouragement for Israel to engage its enemies courageously (vv. 1-4), instructions regarding those Israelites to be granted deferments from military service (vv. 5-9), rules concerning the conduct of war itself (vv. 10-18), and, finally, a prohibition against slash and burn warfare (vv. 19-20). This outline already indicates that Deuteronomy's view of warfare is complex: war is a theological issue, a humanitarian issue, an ecological issue, etc.

COMMENTARY

The Theology of Holy War, 20:1-4

The chapter on warfare begins with a statement of the fundamental, theological principle underlying Deuteronomy's understanding of the conquest. From texts such as these (see also 2:33-35; 3:3-7, 18-22; 7:1-5; 11:22-25; Josh 6:1–8:29; etc.) scholars have deduced the existence of the Israelite institution of "Holy War" (cf. Arabic *jihad*),[1] although there is increasing uncertainty as to whether it was ever an actual institution or, instead, a theological and ideological abstraction of the Deuteronomic /Deuteronomistic movement.[2] Whatever the case may be, despite its brevity and form (a priestly "pep talk"), the basic assertions of Holy War theology can all be found here. Essentially, Israel's conflicts were considered to be, in fact, YHWH's wars against *his* enemies. YHWH will fight the battles and win the victories (7:23-24; 9:1-3; Judg 7:1-23; 1 Sam 7:10; etc.), just as he fought and defeated Pharaoh's army (v. 1). So, too, the spoils of war belong to YHWH (Josh 7:1; etc.). The land conquered belongs to YHWH, the land that he grants Israel as an "inheritance" (Josh 13:6; etc.).

The common theme of Israel's relative insignificance and fear before a mightier enemy (vv. 1, 3; 7:17-21) underscores the notion that the victory is YHWH's. Israel must not rely on its might; indeed, Israel's weakness only renders unmistakable the true source of its success: YHWH has fought for them (8:11-20; etc)!

A number of Israelite beliefs and practices correlate to this notion of "YHWH wars." Property is inalienable, for example, because it does not belong to the Israelites. They hold YHWH's land in trust. They have no right to sell. In relation to the conduct of war itself, the YHWH war idea provides a theological rationale for Israel's displacement of the Canaanites (see commentary on Deut 2). Just as, centuries later, YHWH would use the Assyrians and the Babylonians as instruments for punishing errant, idolatrous Israel and Judah (2 Kgs 17), he now uses Israel to punish the Canaanites for their idolatrous and abhorrent practices (9:4-5; compare Gen 15). According to this theological view of history, YHWH did not capriciously displace the Canaanites in favor of his darling, Israel. Instead, he accomplished two just objectives at once—punishing the guilty and fulfilling his promise of land to the patriarchs.

Similarly, seen against this theological position, the ban (*herem*), the injunction for Israel to eradicate whole populations, is not as capricious or bloodthirsty as it first seems. These populations are enemies of YHWH; according to this theological scheme, they are not innocents, but egregious sinners deserving of their fate. Likewise, Israel is not to see the war as the opportunity for enrichment. The enemies' goods and livestock belong to YHWH now; they must not be plundered. In fact, the Hebrew term *herem* can also be translated "dedicated [to YHWH]" (cf. Josh 7:1).

Exemptions from Military Service, 20:5-9

Immediately after the exhortation to take courage and prior to battle, the priests are to dismiss from the ranks those falling into a number of categories—new homeowners, owners of newly planted vineyards, those soon to wed, and the fearful. In keeping with the theme of fearlessness in the face of a mighty enemy (vv. 1, 4), the text explains that the dismissal of the fearful is intended to prevent fear from spreading through the ranks like a contagion (v. 8). The other grounds for exemption hardly seem related to this interest in maintaining the fighting spirit of the troops, so interpreters offer two possible rationales. First, it may be that the priests intentionally diminished the ranks in order to accentuate the insignificance of Israel's fighting force, making it all the more clear, thereby, that YHWH—not Israel's army—will win the victory. This interpretation finds support in the account of Gideon's attack on the Midianites (Judg 7:4-8). This interpretation fails to explain, however, why the new homeowner, the vintner, and the groom should be singled out. In fact, the text explicitly states that, by going to battle, men in each of these categories risk being deprived of one of life's most significant rewards. The fruits of labor invested in homebuilding and planting a new vineyard must not be enjoyed by another! One must not woo a wife merely so that another may

wed her! Such frustrated efforts are a curse from God (Deut 28:30)!
The enemy is YHWH's; YHWH will assure the victory. No one
need risk dying as though accursed.

The Rules for Waging War, 20:10-18

This unit is usually understood to consist of two subsections: vv.
10-15, the rules of engagement with distant cities, and vv. 16-18,
the rules of engagement with nearby cities. According to this
analysis of the structure of the unit, Israel's policy toward distant
enemies differed from its policy toward neighboring enemies in
three ways. First, Israel could offer terms of peace to the former but
not the latter: It must go to war with its neighbors. Second, if
distant enemies refused terms of peace, only the males (the combatants) were to be killed. Neighboring populations must be *totally*
eradicated in any case. Third, Israel could plunder distant enemies
who had refused terms of peace. The livestock and goods of neighboring cities were to be destroyed along with the population.

Another analysis, offered first as early as Talmudic times[3] and
later strongly defended by Nachmanides, among others [Nachmanides
on Holy War], however, divides the unit as follows: vv. 10-11, the offer
of peace to be made initially to all enemies and the policy for
dealing with them should they accept peace terms; vv. 12-15, the
policy for the conduct of war against distant cities who reject
Israel's offer of peace; vv. 16-18, the policy for the conduct of war
against neighboring cities who reject Israel's offer of peace.

Both analyses are grammatically and syntactically viable. The
second option certainly appeals to one's sense of fair play, although
interpreters must guard against the possibility of reading their own
sensibilities into the text. On the other hand, the procedure envisioned in the second option, namely that even Canaanite cities
could accept terms of peace and survive—albeit as virtual slaves
(v. 11)—does correspond more closely to Israel's actual practice
during the conquest and beyond as recorded in Deuteronomy itself

---

Nachmanides on Holy War

. . . the call for peace applies even to an obligatory
war. It requires us to offer peace-terms even to the
seven nations [of Canaan], for Moses proclaimed peace to
Sihon, king of the Amorites (Deut 2:26), and he would not
have transgressed both the positive and negative commandments in this section . . . . Rather, the difference between
them [i.e., obligatory and permissible wars] is when the
enemy does not make peace and continues to make war.

Then, in the case of the *cities which are very far off,*
Scripture commanded us to *smite every male thereof* and
keep alive the woman and male children, but in *the cities of
these peoples* [i.e., the seven nations of Canaan in the event
they refuse the call to peace], it commanded us to destroy
even the women and children.

C. B. Chavel, trans., *Ramban (Nachmanides) Commentary on the Torah:
Deuteronomy* (New York: Shilo, 1976), 238-39. Nachmanides goes on to cite
two other rabbinic sources: *Devarim Rabbah* 5:13; and *Tanchuma, Shoftim* 18.

and in the Deuteronomistic history. In addition to Moses' treatment of Sihon, king of Heshbon (2:26-30), Nachmanides cites Josh 11:19-20 as evidence that the option of surrender was open even to the Canaanite inhabitants of the land: "No town made peace with the Israelite, except the Hivites, the inhabitants of Gibeon; all were taken in battle. For it was YHWH's doing to harden their hearts so that they would come against Israel in battle, in order that they might be utterly destroyed. . . ." Nachmanides' evidence can be supplemented by references to Canaanite populations at forced labor, in accordance with the provision of Deut 20:11, during the monarchical period (1 Kgs 9:20-21).

Even if one accepts the notion that this unit calls for Israel to offer peace to *all* its enemies, these rules of engagement fall far short of a modern sense of fairness and decency in the conduct of war. ["Geneva Convention"] Indeed, ironically, these regulations make of Israel an oppressor equal to Pharaoh: like him they subject threatening foreign populations to forced labor (Exod 1:14); like him they kill the male population, eliminating potential combatants (Exod 1:16, 22). Once again, however, this ironic cruelty derives

---

"Geneva Convention"

Convention for the Amelioration of the Condition of the Wounded and Sick in Armed Forces in the Field (excerpted)
Signed at Geneva, 12 August 1949.
ENTRY INTO FORCE: 21 October 1950.

Art. 3. In the case of armed conflict not of an international character occurring in the territory of one of the High Contracting Parties, each Party to the conflict shall be bound to apply, as a minimum, the following provisions:

(1) Persons taking no active part in the hostilities, including members of armed forces who have laid down their arms and those placed hors de combat by sickness, wounds, detention, or any other cause, shall in all circumstances be treated humanely, without any adverse distinction founded on race, colour [sic], religion or faith, sex, birth or wealth, or any other similar criteria. . . .

(2) The wounded and sick shall be collected and cared for. . . .

Art. 12. Members of the armed forces and other persons mentioned in the following Article, who are wounded or sick, shall be respected and protected in all circumstances.

They shall be treated humanely and cared for by the Party to the conflict in whose power they may be, without any adverse distinction founded on sex, race, nationality, religion, political opinions, or any other similar criteria. Any attempts upon their lives, or violence to their persons, shall be strictly prohibited; in particular, they shall not be murdered or exterminated, subjected to torture or to biological experiments; they shall not willfully be left without medical assistance and care, nor shall conditions exposing them to contagion or infection be created.

Only urgent medical reasons will authorize priority in the order of treatment to be administered.

Women shall be treated with all consideration due to their sex. The Party to the conflict which is compelled to abandon wounded or sick to the enemy shall, as far as military considerations permit, leave with them a part of its medical personnel and material to assist in their care. . . .

Art. 15. At all times, and particularly after an engagement, Parties to the conflict shall, without delay, take all possible measures to search for and collect the wounded and sick, to protect them against pillage and ill-treatment, to ensure their adequate care, and to search for the dead and prevent their being despoiled. . . .

from a theological rationale. In addition to doctrine that the inhabitants of the land deserve their fate as punishment for their gross sin (see commentary Deut 2), these war rules conclude with a warning against the danger the inhabitants pose as pollutants (v. 18). The absolute necessity that Israel remain faithful to YHWH alone motivates even the eradication of whole populations of idolaters.

A Prohibition against Scorched Earth Tactics, 20:19-20

A common tactic employed by invaders in the ancient Near East was to cut off and destroy the enemy's sources of supply: crops, vineyards, orchards, cisterns, wells. The Babylonians' invading and eventually conquering Judah first rampaged through the Judean countryside before marching on Jerusalem, besieging it, and, in time, plundering it (2 Kgs 24). Like Sherman's March to the Sea, these tactics, while certainly effective, had far-reaching consequences for the future viability of a regional economy. Orchards and vineyards require years to mature to the point of yielding.

The section dealing with warfare concludes with a prohibition against such scorched-earth tactics. In times of war, Israel must not unnecessarily destroy trees (vv. 19a, 20b), especially not fruit trees (v. 20a): they are non-combatants (v. 19b) after all!

This prohibition is particularly striking for at least two reasons. First, in the wider context of the explication of the commandment against killing, this prohibition takes a very long and wide view of the consequences of warfare. All-out, scorched-earth tactics can continue to harm life, even to kill by starvation, for years and decades afterward. Second, this concern for preserving ecological balance following on the heels of regulations calling for the harshest treatment of human enemies seems jarringly incongruous, almost satirical ("Are trees in the field human beings . . . ?"). One can productively ponder the incongruity: which is of greater value, the life of a human enemy or the life of a tree?

CONNECTIONS

War is a problem for Christian theology (see [Holy War, Just War, and Pacifism]). Wars fought substantially for geopolitical considerations—in order to protect a nation's oil supply, for example—hardly merit consideration. They are a particularly selfish and destructive manifestation of the evils of the modern nation-state. Even wars fought because of credible moral claims (say the struggle against Nazism), however, persist as an irritant to Christian doctrine. How does God view the inevitable death of innocents? Whose sins were punished when Allied bombs meant for Nazi factories fell on homes—Hitler's or the infant's in her crib? What level of sin deserves correction on a national scale? For Jews, heirs to Abraham's call to be blessing to the nations, and alike for Christians, called to preach the good news throughout the world, the eradication of the enemy is a poor alternative to the expansion of God's kingdom. Who *are* God's enemies?

Deuteronomy 20 and other texts like it are a particularly vexing problem for believing interpreters. One can easily and gratefully affirm the humanitarian and ecological glimmers and the theological exhortations to remember that the victory is God's and to remain unstained by the world's pollutants. Yet, the concept of YHWH's war still stands at the heart of the text: the picture of a loving God prescribing genocide! [Twain's Prayer] Such a text demands of any responsible reader the deepest and humblest theological reflection and calls for wise decision-making. What is the nature of God? The nature of Scripture? The role of God's people in a world populated by "enemies"? Surely the God concerned for even the cattle in Nineveh (Jonah 4:11), who loved the world enough to send God's Son to die (John 3:16) has been libeled here! Surely the ancient Israelite authors, in their zeal to see sin punished and idolatry eradicated, have misheard God's call to holiness! Surely the biblical calls to serve as blessing to the nations and to love even one's enemies take precedence over this xenophobia! Just as the ancient Israelites and Christians down through the ages have failed to hear clearly the exodus and Easter truth that God liberates from slavery and death (see commentary on Deut 5 and 15), so too here, Israel must surely have failed to hear clearly.

Twain's Prayer

O, Lord our Father, our young patriots, idols of our hearts, go forth to battle. Be thou near them! With them—in spirit—we also go forth from the sweet peace of our beloved firesides to smite the foe.

O Lord our God, help us to tear their soldiers to bloody shreds with our shells;

help us to cover their smiling fields with the pale forms of their patriot dead;

help us to drown the thunder of the guns with the shouts of their wounded, writhing in pain;

help us to lay waste their humble homes with a hurricane of fire;

help us to wring the hearts of their unoffending widows with unavailing grief;

help us to turn them out roofless with their little children watching and unfriended in the wastes of their desolated land in rags and hunger and thirst, sport of the sun-flames of summer and the icy winds of winter, broken in spirit, worn with travail, imploring Thee for the refuge of the grave and denied it—

For our sakes who adore Thee, Lord, blast their hopes, blight their lives, protract their bitter pilgrimage, make heavy their steps, water their way with tears, stain the white snow with the blood of their wounded feet!

We ask it, in the spirit of love, of Him Who is the Source of Love, and Who is the ever-faithful refuge and friend of all that are sore beset and seek His aid with humble and contrite hearts. Amen.

"The War Prayer," in *A Pen Warmed Up in Hell: Mark Twain in Protest,* ed. F. Anderson (New York: Harper and Row, 1972), 90-91.

Still, in a hyper-individualist era, even a difficult text such as this has something to say. It points thoughtful readers to a new consideration of God's activity on the grand stage of human history, beyond the microcosm of the individual. As jarring and discomfiting as it may be, this text, indeed much of the Bible, asserts that God works on a national and international scale. Pharaoh's Egypt, the Canaanites at the hands of Israel, Israel and Judah at the hands of the Mesopotamian powers—all have experienced the pain of God's violent correction: so says the Bible. Has Christian theology failed to grapple with the implications of God's involvement in the affairs of the world? The Bible—both Testaments—consistently maintains that God established and upholds a moral order in creation. Sin has consequences. If modern believers are rightly uncomfortable with the notion that God willed World War I, they must not flee the responsibility for examining questions of national guilt. God is not mocked. One reaps what one sows. Is it not reasonable to conclude that, after sowing generations of racial oppression, America now reaps discord on a national level?

Finally, given the human ego, a warning against too easily identifying one's own enemies as God's against too readily claiming a divine mandate for one's selfish cause may be in order. The motives of nation-states rarely align with the cause of Christ. Blessed are the peacemakers.

NOTES

[1] See, for example, G. von Rad, *Holy War in Ancient Israel*, trans. M. Dawn (Grand Rapids, 1990); J. P. U. Lilley, "The Judgment of God: The Problem of the Canaanites," *Themelios* 22 (1997): 3-12; idem, "Understanding the Herem," *Tyndale Bulletin* 44 (1993): 169-73; H. E. von Waldow, "The Concept of War in the Old Testament," *Horizons in Biblical Theology* 6 (1984): 27-48; etc.

[2] See, for example, L. Brisman, "Sacred Butchery: Exodus 32:25-29," in *Theological Exegesis: Essays in Honor of Brevard S. Childs*, ed. C. Seitz and K. Greene-McCreight (Grand Rapids: Eerdmans, 1999), 162-81; G. Mitchell, *Together in the Land: A Reading of the Book of Joshua* (JSOTSup 134; Sheffield: JSOT Press, 1993); L. Stone, "Ethical and Apologetic Tendencies in the Redaction of the Book of Joshua," *CBQ* 53 (1991): 25-36; M. Walzer, "Exodus 32 and the Theory of Holy War: The History of a Citation," *Harvard Theological Review* 61 (1968): 1-14; etc.

[3] Talmud Jer *Shevi'ith* 6:1.

LIFE AND DEATH IN TENSION

21:1-23

This collection of miscellaneous laws deals with situations in which the Decalogue's affirmation of life comes into conflict with the reality or threat of death or diminishment. The fact that the Deuteronomic editors grouped them together here demonstrates an awareness that ethical decisions must often be made in less than ideal circumstances. Wisdom consists in the ability to balance sometimes competing goods in favor of life while respecting the difficulty involved in choice. Even the Bible recognizes that obedience to the commandment against killing will sometimes force one to choose between relative evils. The regulations collected here deal with five specific situations: unsolved homicides (vv. 1-9), prisoner-of-war wives (vv. 10-14), partiality to the son of a favored wife (vv. 15-17), a recalcitrant son (vv. 18-21), and hanging an executed criminal for public display (vv. 22-23).

COMMENTARY

Unsolved Homicides, 21:1-9

Unsolved homicides presented ancient Israel with a dilemma. Blood (*dām*; see commentary on 12:13-27) was identified with life itself (*nepeš*, sometimes translated "soul"; see Gen 9:4; commentary on Deut 6:4-9 and [The Concept of the "Soul" in Hebrew Thought]). Shedding human blood was considered to be tantamount to an attack on God's own image, a crime that must be answered (Gen 9:6). Blood, life itself, once spilled, cries out from the ground (Gen 4:10) and pollutes the land (Num 35:33; cf. Deut 19:10). Justice requires that the shedder of blood, and he or she only, expiate for this taking of life; only then can the land be made clean again (Num 35:33).

But how can order be restored when the killer goes undetected? Must the land remain polluted? Clearly, such a critical situation demands some solution. This unit spells out the solemn ritual procedure for restoring the proper relationship between the people, the land, and the creator of life.

First, since the body was discovered in the open country (v. 1), the leadership of the two nearest towns gather to determine which town is closest to the body (v. 2), probably on the assumption that the actual killer will likely have been a citizen there. Thus, the obligation falls to that community (v. 3).

Second, they execute the prescribed ritual. The precise significance of many of the details of this ritual can only be deduced. The sacrificial animal, a heifer that has never been worked, probably represents purity and innocence; the site, an untilled wadi or wet-weather stream with running water, likewise represents unspoiled innocence and cleansing; the method of sacrifice, breaking the neck, may represent the community's unwillingness to compound the crime by further shedding innocent blood (vv. 3-4). At this point, in the presence of the priests—YHWH's representatives in all matters of guilt and innocence, purity and pollution (v. 5)—the leadership of the community ritually washes their hands with water from the flowing stream over the body of the dead heifer. Thus they enact their innocence while solemnly declaring themselves innocent both of the bloodshed itself and of complicity in the act (v. 7). The wording of this declaration of innocence, "our hands did not shed *this* (= the deceased's? or the heifer's?) blood," is ambiguous, and probably intentionally so. They were no guiltier of shedding the blood of the human victim than of the heifer. In view of their innocence and their ignorance of the true killer's identity— whom, naturally, they would have held responsible for the bloodshed—they ask that YHWH absolve them and remove the bloodguilt (v. 8). With that, the priests, presumably, pronounce absolution and the matter is ended. The elders have done "what is right" (v. 9): In this case, the expression may be paraphrased "the best you could under the circumstances."

Setting aside the animistic backgrounds of this ritual as accoutrements of a pre-scientific worldview, several focal points deserve to be underscored. First, in Israel's view, the supreme sanctity of human life required that, even when the guilty party could not be identified, some atonement be made for the crime. Second, in the absence of the criminal, the entire community bore the burden of the crime. Presumably, one of their citizens had taken life. From a modern legal perspective, this attitude seems unfair, perhaps. From a sociological perspective, however, it reflects the truth that individuals are the products of the communities that nurture and shelter them. To some extent, communities and families do indeed share in the guilt, or merit, of individual members. Third, ancient Israel recognized the close, sometimes mystical, connection between life and the earth that sustains it. While human beings may stand at the pinnacle of God's creation, human beings do not stand outside creation. Human life depends upon and influences the world in which it flourishes.

Enforced Transition from One Life to Another: Taking a Captive as Wife, 21:10-14

This regulation seems to be more suited to inclusion with the rules on warfare (vv. 10-13) or on the liberation of slaves (v. 14). Assuming that it is not accidental, its present location must provide some clue that the editors understood it as an explication of ambiguous situations relating to the commandment against killing.

The regulation falls clearly into three parts. First, the text merely describes, without comment, the situation—an Israelite man feels attraction for a captive woman and decides to marry her (vv. 10-11). Rabbinical interpreters found the situation, that of forcible marriage of a prisoner of war to her captor, morally reprehensible and considered it a concession made by the Mosaic Law to human nature (in this case lust for a beautiful captive): better that the man should at least marry her. [Rabbinical Interpretation of Deuteronomy 21:10-14] Second, the text prescribes a period of ritual mourning to be undergone by the woman (vv. 12-13). In the ancient world, practices such as shaving one's head and otherwise altering one's appearance often had the dual function of publicly displaying one's grief and of rendering one unrecognizable to shades of the deceased (see commentary on 14:1-2). The mourning period "for her mother and father" (presumably casualties of the war) was to last for one month, at the end of which her captor may marry her.

Rabbinical Interpretation of Deuteronomy 21:10-14

The *Sifre* argues that the prescribed ritual will eventually bring the Israelite man to his senses: ". . . the captor must divest her of her attractive raiment and clothe her in widow's weeds . . . [she is then to dwell] in a house that the captor habitually uses, so that he chance upon her when he goes in and when he goes out; if she looks like a pumpkin-shell, he will see her in all her unattractiveness" (Hammer). The regulation concerning divorcing the captive wife "is informing you that you will come to hate her . . . ." Rashi argues similarly that the purpose of these provisions was so "that she may become repulsive *to her captor*" and the marriage will not take place (Rosebaum and Silbermann).

R. Hammer, trans., *Sifre: A Tannaitic Commentary on the Book of Deuteronomy* (Yale Judaica Series 24; New Haven: Yale, 1986), 224-25.

Rosenbaum and Silbermann, *Pentateuch with Targum Onkelos, Haphtaroth and Prayers for Sabbath and Rashi's Commentary*, vol. 5, Deuteronomy (London: Shapiro, Vallentine & Co., 1934), 106.

Third, in the event that the man should later decide to divorce her, she must be treated as a wife, not as a slave. By marrying her against her will ("dishonoring her," v. 14; he was, after all, her captor and master), he had elevated her status; he may not subsequently return her to slavery. She must be sent away a free woman.

How does this regulation relate to the commandment against killing? Read out of context, the concluding prohibition against re-enslaving the woman is clearly the climactic element of this unit. Read in context, however, attention focuses on the mourning ritual. This woman has lost her family; regardless of whether they are actually dead, she is transitioning, not necessarily of her own free will, into a new life without them. She is at her master's mercy. In fact, she stands at the boundary between life and death herself. Can a situation of greater vulnerability even be imagined? Acknowledging her status, the Deuteronomic Code requires that this paradoxical passage from life through death to a new life be appropriately observed.

In fact, read in this context, even the final provision regarding a subsequent divorce becomes an exposition of the commandment against killing in the sense of diminishing life (see commentary on 19:14). Having once caused her to cross the boundary between life and death, her husband may not now diminish her life again.

Paternal Favoritism, 21:15-17

The case treated here presumes an established principle of Israelite family law and prohibits a likely exception. Like vv. 10-14, it seems out of place at first glance. Under Israel's patriarchal system, the firstborn son, the evidence of his father's virility (v. 17), inherited an extra portion of his father's estate (the Hebrew of v. 16 reads literally "two-thirds," but since only two sons are mentioned in the case, it may mean a double portion; of three sons, the elder would inherit one-half or two-fourths; of four sons, two-fifths, etc.). In addition he assumed the leadership role assigned the patriarch. The text assumes this right of primogenitor (Latin "firstborn"); it does not announce it or argue for it. Instead, it prohibits a father from indulging his favoritism contrary to the established practice. [Favored Younger Siblings]

It is important to remember that the issue addressed here is not concern for the self-esteem of either brother (one would be favored in any case), nor whether the father would act fairly (the patriarchy valued other considerations). The threat perceived in this situation involved the father's disregard for the significance of his firstborn as

Favored Younger Siblings

The situation envisioned in Deut 21:15-17, that of a man with two wives seeking to extend his preference for one wife to her son although he is not the firstborn, can be illustrated by a number of cases related in Scripture. Abraham disinherited Ishmael, Hagar's son, in favor of his younger brother, Isaac, Sarah's son (Gen 21:8-14); Jacob favored Joseph and Benjamin, the youngest two of his twelve sons, both sons of his favorite wife, Rachel (Gen 37:2-4; 42:4; 43:13-14); although sons of the same mother, the younger Jacob also supplanted his brother Esau (Gen 25:29-34; 27:1-40), and the same Jacob later granted pride of place over his elder, Manasseh, to Ephraim, the younger son of Joseph (Gen 48:8-20). Several other cases not involving inheritance per se further illustrate the Bible's fascination with the theme of preference for the younger child: Laban's gamesmanship with respect to the marriage of his daughters Rachel and Leah (Gen 29:21-30); Elkanah's preference for his wife Hannah, to whom he even granted a "double-portion" for sacrifice, over her competitor Peninah (1 Sam 1:3-8); God's choice of David, the youngest, over all his brothers (1 Sam 16:6-13); and Saul's sly offers to David of marriage to his two daughters, Meribaal and Michal (David marries the younger; 1 Sam 18:17-29).

the sign of his own ability to father children and thus to perpetuate his family and his name. A patriarchal system cannot tolerate such disdain for the continuation of the family. In essence, it would diminish one's own life by depreciating the living proof of one's virility. The biblical commandment against taking life effectively transforms here into its converse: Be fruitful and multiply; and do not undervalue the first fruits!

A Recalcitrant Son, 21:18-21

This infamously harsh prescription could easily have been included in the section explicating the command to honor one's parents. Instead, it was placed here, likely because the severity both of the circumstance and of the prescribed solution result in the most severe disruption of the boundary between life and death treated in this section.

In fact, severity is the key motif in this unit. It does not sanction the death penalty for any child, regardless of age or basic character, who disobeys his or her parents in any way whatsoever, regardless of degree or kind. It deals, instead, with adult or nearly adult sons who are stubborn (Heb. *sôrēr*, a participle, BDB defines the related noun as "stubborn,

Sloth

Deuteronomy demonstrates the fluidity of boundaries between spheres of life addressed by the Decalog. A son's sloth diminishes the life of his parents.

Hieronymous Bosch. c.1450–1516. *Sloth*. Detail from the *Seven Deadly Sins*. Museo del Prado. Madrid, Spain.

b. Sanh 71a and 72a on Deuteronomy 21:18-21

A rebellious and defiant son is condemned because of what he will become in the end.

We have been taught that R. Yose the Galilean said: Is it conceivable that merely because the young man ate a *tartemar* of meat and drank half a *log* of Italian wine, the Torah would decree that he be brought before the High Court and put to death by stoning? However, the Torah foresaw the ultimate destiny of the young man sentenced as a rebellious and defiant son. For in the end, after dissipating his father's possessions, he will continue to seek what he has become accustomed to and, unable to get it, will go out to a crossroads and rob people. There for the Torah said, "Let him die while yet innocent, and not die guilty."

R. Simeon said: Is it conceivable that just because this one ate a *tartemar* of meat and drank half a *log* of Italian wine, his father and mother should take him out to be put to death by stoning? In truth, the rebellious and defiant son never existed and never will exist. Why, then, was the account about him written? So that you will expound the possible reasons for such misconduct and receive a reward doing so. R. Jonathan, however, said: I saw one such and sat by his grave.

resentful, sullen, implacable"), rebellious (Heb. *môreh*, BDB, "contentious, refractory"), disobedient, incorrigible, gluttonous (Heb. *zôlēl*, "to make light of = be lavish with, squander"[1]), and given to drink (Heb. *sōbē'*). His disobedience far exceeds forgetting a few chores or failing to eat his vegetables. He threatens to dissipate the economic viability of the family.

The severity of his insolence is underscored by the fact that both parents bring him before the authorities. The mother who gave birth to him, nursed him, and nurtured him has reached her wit's end; the father who hoped to pass on to him name, inheritance, and future can no longer influence him. It is difficult to imagine that this regulation was often invoked. [b. Sanh 71a and 72a on Deuteronomy 21:18-21]

Now, the son's recalcitrance threatens the normal cycle of life. His parents cared for him in his youth; the time approaches for him to care for them in their advanced age. Instead, his actions threaten his parents' futures and invalidate his own. In effect, his disobedience threatens to kill them all. "Honor you father and your mother . . . that your days may be long . . ." (Deut 5:16). Dishonoring parents can be a matter of life and death for both generations.

Public Exposure of Executed Criminals, 21:22-23

It was relatively common in the ancient world to display publicly the bodies of executed criminals as a deterrent to other potential criminals and those of enemies killed in battle as a form of further humiliating the defeated (see 1 Sam 31:8-13; 2 Sam 2:4-7). [Sophocles' "Antigone"] The Deuteronomic Code acknowledges and permits the practice in Israel, but adds the requirement that such public exposure be ended and that the body be buried by sundown of the same day. The background for this restriction seems to be the belief, also common in the ancient world, that proper burial is

Sophocles' "Antigone"

Sophocles's (Athens, c. 496–406 BC) play "Antigone" relates the tragedy that befell the children of Oedipus and Jocasta, king and queen of Thebes. Two of their sons, patriotic Eteocles and traitorous Polyneices, had fallen in battle on the same day. King Creon forbade the mourning and burial of the traitor. Antigone, their sister and fiancée of Creon's son, Haemon, defied the order, which she considered contrary to the laws of nature. When his fiancée was condemned to be entombed alive by his father, Haemon committed suicide in order to join her. The warning quoted below, which was issued to Creon by the blind prophet Teiresias, addressed Creon's criminal arrogance:

. . . surely know that thou not many more
Revolving courses of the sun shalt pass,
Ere of thine own blood one, to make amends,
Dead for the dead, thou shalt have rendered up,
For that a living soul [Antigone] thou has sent below,
And with dishonour [sic] in the grave has lodged,
And that one dead [Polyneices] thou holdest here cut off
From presence of the gods who reign below,
All rites of death, all obsequies denied—
With whom thou shouldst not meddle, nor the gods
In heaven, but of their due thou robb'st the dead.
Therefore of Hades and the gods for thee
The Avengers wait, with ruin slow yet sure,
To take thee in the pit which thou hast dug.
Do I speak this for gold? Thyself shalt judge:
For, yet a little while, and wailings loud
Of men and women in thy house shall show.
Think, of each city too what gathering rage,
That sees its mangled dead entombed in maws
Of dogs and all fierce beasts, or borne by kites
With stench unhallowed to its hearth-crowned heights.

Sophocles, "Antigone," trans. Robert Whitelaw, in *An Anthology of Greek Drama: First Series*, ed. C. A. Robinson Jr. (Atlanta: Holt, Rinehart and Winston, 1949), 132-33.

---

necessary for rest in the underworld (compare, for example, Amos 2:1 and 1 Sam 28:3-25). The penalty of death and the disgrace of hanging publicly as one accursed by God is sufficient punishment. Even criminals worthy of the most extreme punishment deserve proper burial and the rest it permits.[2] Even when forced to take life as a penalty for heinous crime, the community must not dehumanize the criminal who is also created in God's image. [Criminals and the Imago Dei]

CONNECTIONS

It should perhaps be acknowledged from the outset that, for the most part, the cases treated in this unit are at best foreign to modern life, if not bizarre or even offensive—prisoners of war coerced into marriage, systematic economic favoritism for firstborn sons, capital punishment of disobedient children. These cases forcefully remind modern readers that the Bible documents not only God's revelation, but also the ancient cultures of the people who received that revelation. At the same time, however, they stand as a warning against uncritical complacency toward the institutions and systems of modern society. How will future generations view today's unexamined assumptions? What unnoticed injustices and inhumanities are built into today's family structures, economic practices, and political and legal systems?

Criminals and the Imago Dei

"His body shall not remain all night upon the tree . . . for he that is hanged is a reproach unto God." We have been taught that R. Meir said: By what parable may the meaning of the verse be made clear? By the one of twin brothers who lived in a certain city. One was appointed king, and the other took to brigandage. The king commanded that his brother be hanged, and whoever saw the corpse said, "The king is hanged." When that happened, the king commanded that the corpse be taken down. (*b. Sanh.* 46b)

Despite the justifiable unease a modern reader may feel with respect to this odd assortment of case laws, however, they attest to a compelling impulse of Deuteronomic law that should be heard as a positive challenge to modern decision-makers. The very fact that the editors of the Deuteronomic Code included legislation dealing with such extreme cases testifies to their willingness unflinchingly to recognize and confront the fact that moral and ethical decisions must often be made in messy circumstances. It is not difficult to determine the applicability of the commandment against killing in relation to the murder of a convenience store clerk by a hardened career criminal. But life regularly careens off the path of clear distinctions between right and wrong into the brambles of competing moral claims, human foibles, and temptations to acquiesce to lesser standards. This collection of laws dealing with very messy aspects of life calls for engagement in the task of consistently and intentionally conforming every area of life to the high standard of God's covenant will. The value of human life carries such weight that it must be considered even in caring for the body of an executed criminal! Human dignity demands that the captive woman, who has already been bereft of home and family, at least be given the chance to mourn properly. She must not be subjected to further indignity. In effect, one could claim that every area of life, even the most extreme and uncomfortable, relates in some way to the absolute requirement of respecting the sanctity, value, and dignity of human life. "Thou shalt not kill." Thou shalt not abuse employees. Thou shalt not denigrate your children. Thou shalt treat the most hardened criminal as a child of God . . . .

NOTES

[1] BDB, 272.

[2] J. Tigay, *Deuteronomy* (JPS Torah Commentary 5; Philadelphia: Jewish Publication Society, 1996), 198.

PROTECT LIFE

22:1-8

Three of the four laws collected here clearly expand the prohibition against taking human life into a positive injunction to respect, preserve, and protect life of all kinds. In them, the explication of the principle of the sanctity of life reaches its culmination. Life is of such supreme value that every effort must be made to guard and enhance it. Two of these cases have parallels in the Covenant Code (vv. 1-4 and Exod 23:4-5; vv. 6-7 and Exod 23:19b; compare also Deut 14:21b and Exod 34:26b), where they appear in contexts dealing with torts (Exod 23:4-5) or with cultic rules (Exod 23:4-5; cf. 34:26b). In their setting in Deuteronomy, they have been reshaped into exhortations. Some exegetes label the law concerning transvestitism (v. 5) a transitional unit anticipating the section to follow.[1] Since, however, it is unclear both how to translate and how to interpret this regulation, some as yet to be elucidated relationship to the general theme of the section may exist.

COMMENTARY

Help your neighbor however you can, 22:1-4

Oxen figure prominently in ancient Near Eastern law codes, both within and outside the Bible (compare Exod 21:28–22:4, 9-13; 23:4 and Codex Eshnunna 53-55; Codex Hammurapi 241-256, 262-263, 268, 271). Probably because of their value in agriculture and commerce, they represent the chief example of personal, or movable, property (as opposed to real estate, or immovable property). Presumably the principles of law that pertain to oxen apply to all personal property (v. 3, donkeys, garments, or "anything else" belonging to a neighbor).

This text can be considered ancient Israel's "Good Samaritan Law." Three statements render it unmistakably clear that one has an obligation actively to assist another. First, when one witnesses potential harm or loss in progress one may not "ignore" the event (v. 1). Instead, one must intervene and be willing to restore the property at the owner's request (v. 3). In fact, one must take action whenever called upon to do so (v. 4). Oxen pull plows; sheep provide milk and wool; garments keep one warm. Personal property makes living comfortable and enjoyable. In some cases, it sustains life. Its loss diminishes the life of the owner. Respect for human life is inconsistent with unconcern for the circumstances of living.

Against Transvestitism, 22:5

This regulation presents the interpreter with almost insurmountable problems. The Hebrew is unclear both as to its meaning and to its significance. The term (*kĕlî*), referring in the first clause to that which pertains to a man, is very ambiguous, roughly equivalent in semantic range to the English word "thing." The second clause prohibits a man from wearing a woman's "wrapper" (*śimlat*) suggesting that *kĕlî* refers to some "thing" a man wears. In this case, the law would prohibit cross-dressing and would invite an interpretation relating it to some pagan ritual or some sexual perversion.

In contrast, Targ Onk, R. Eliezer b. Jacob,[2] Josephus,[3] and, among modern scholars, C. Gordon,[4] C. Carmichael,[5] and others translate, "There shall not be a weapon (*kĕlî*, understood in the sense of "implement") of a man upon a woman . . . ." This translation is supported by the Hebrew term translated "man" in this context, *geber*, a term often translated "champion, warrior, hero, man of valor." Carmichael argues on the basis of this translation that the text prohibits women being smuggled into the army: "the situation contemplated is that of men deprived of women during war service."

Neither translation nor accompanying interpretation contributes to an understanding of this text in the context of an explication of the commandment against killing. Barring the future discovery of parallels, its meaning remains a mystery.

Wildlife Management, 22:6-7

The principle stated here is very practical. To prevent the depletion of the bird population (presumably, just as the oxen represents domesticated animals, the bird represents all wildlife), one must not take mother and young at the same time. To take the mother only, before the young have reached maturity, would doom the young and have the same effect as taking both together. The young may be taken, then, leaving the mother to rear other offspring in the future and assuring the continuation of the species.

Remarkably, this very practical principle of wildlife management, similar in many ways to modern practice, explicates the commandment against killing. To this point, only human life has been the subject of the Deuteronomic Code. The Hebrew Bible is not sentimentally idealistic about animal life. Ancient Israel did not value animals as equals to human beings. The young may be taken, after all. The Hebrew Bible, does, however, view animals as part of God's good creation, filled, like human beings, with the breath of life (Gen 1:30), and charged, like human beings, with multiplying and filling the earth (Gen 1:22, 28). Only respect for the balance of life in God's creation can insure humanity long life and that "it will go well . . . in the land" (v. 7).

Reckless Endangerment, 22:8

The law concerning cities of refuge distinguishes between the murderer and the accidental killer, innocent of any crime. Modern law recognizes two other categories of killing: voluntary and involuntary manslaughter. Voluntary manslaughter is the intentional killing of someone in the heat of passion, as the result of sufficient provocation, and without deliberation or premeditation. Involuntary manslaughter involves criminal negligence—"conduct that shows a reckless disregard for human life or safety and a willful indifference to the injury that is likely to follow."[6] Deuteronomy 22:8 supplements the earlier definition of murder with a warning against reckless endangerment.

In both the ancient and modern periods, homes in Palestine were typically constructed with flat roofs often utilized as courtyards or patios are elsewhere in the world. Obviously, for safety's sake, such rooftops should be walled about to prevent accidental falls. Failure to build such walls "shows a reckless disregard for human life." Not killing means not endangering as well.

CONNECTIONS

Deuteronomy's explication of the commandment against killing makes it very clear that the fundamental requirement of respect for life—especially, but not exclusively, human life—cannot be met by merely refraining from malicious behavior. Intentions and attitudes

Respect for Life Requires Active Goodness

You do well if you really fulfill the royal law according to the scripture, "You shall love your neighbor as yourself." But if you show partiality, you commit sin and are convicted by the law as transgressors. For whoever keeps the whole law but fails in one point has become accountable for all of it. For the one who said, "You shall not commit adultery," also said, "You shall not commit murder." Now if you do not commit adultery but if you murder, you have become a transgressor of the law. So speak and so act as those who are to be judged by the law of liberty. For judgment will be without mercy to anyone who has shown no mercy; mercy triumphs over judgment.

What good is it, my brothers and sisters, if you say you have faith but do not have works? Can faith save you? If a brother or sister is naked and lacks daily food, and one of you says to them, "Go in peace; keep warm and eat your fill," and yet you do not supply their bodily needs, what is the good of that? So faith by itself, if it has no works, is dead. (Jas 2:8-17)

---

that lead to violence fall under the purview of the commandment (21:1-9). Respect for another's grief (21:10-14), for one's own fertility (21:15-17), and for the dignity even of the executed criminal (21:22-23) also manifest the proper stance toward the mysterious gift of life. The final several cases treated in this explication expand the implications of the fundamental principle in two significant ways.

No Harm

First, in stark contrast to a universal human inclination, this subunit asserts that the supreme value of life demands not only that one refrain from doing intentional harm, but that, whenever possible, one must undertake not to cause harm even unintentionally; indeed, one must strive to do good. Laziness, thoughtlessness, and unconcern can kill as surely as malicious intent. Bystanders who refuse to offer assistance to someone in need are at least complicit in any harm that results. Whether individuals unwilling "to get involved" or nations hesitant to intervene in conflict or crisis in some geo-politically insignificant region of the world, those who most value their own comfort and security often become accomplices to murder. [Respect for Life Requires Active Goodness] From the perspective of the Decalogue, claims that "I didn't mean to" or "It's not my concern," are nonsensical and sinful.

Respect without Distinction

Second, respect for life as God's wondrous gift extends, in some way, to all life. Human life, created in God's image, holds particular value, to be sure. But God created all life calling it "good." Callous disrespect for any creature betrays disrespect for all creatures. It is not surprising that psychologists who have studied murderers identify cruelty to animals exhibited in childhood and adolescence as a warning sign.

NOTES

[1] Compare S. Kaufman, "The Structure of the Deuteronomic Law," *Maarav* 1/2 (1978-1979): 136 and Merrill, *Deuteronomy* (NAC 4; Nashville: Broadman & Holman, 1994), 297-98.

[2] *Sifr.* 226; *Naz* 59a.

[3] *Antigone,* IV:8:43.

[4] "A Note on the 10th Commandment," *JBR* 31 (1963): 208-209.

[5] *The Laws of Deuteronomy* (Ithaca NY: Cornell University Press, 1974), 147-48.

[6] Inge Dobelis, ed., *Reader's Digest Family Legal Guide: A Complete Encyclopedia of Law for the Layman* (Pleasantville NY: The Reader's Digest Association, 1981), 641.

EXPLICATION OF THE SIXTH COMMANDMENT: "DO NOT COMMIT ADULTERY"

22:9–23:18 (Heb 22:9–23:19)

Much as the Deuteronomic Code interprets the commandment against killing broadly in terms of the intention of the "killer" and the extensive spheres of life in which the commandment applies, it understands the commandment against committing adultery in relation to a wide range of improper boundary crossings and admixtures. Marriage consists, in part, in the establishment of a structure of relationships, not only between the marriage partners, but involving their interaction with the larger society. Boundaries are fixed; a cosmos is created. Violations of these boundaries threaten to produce social chaos. Similarly, in Deuteronomy's view, God established other such systems of relationship, including boundaries that must be honored in order to preserve order. The relationship between violations of the sixth commandment, understood in the strict sense, and violations of these non-marital boundaries corresponds to the relationship between the English words "adultery" and "adulteration." The Deuteronomic Code offers a paraphrase of the commandment. Not only is adultery improper, but "thou shalt not adulterate at all."

Significantly, this viewpoint finds expression in a number of themes that link this otherwise disparate collection of laws. Cloth and various articles of clothing, instruments of modesty, figure prominently. Issues pertaining to sex and gender are central. The concern for order, which is tantamount to holiness, underlies each and every legal case. The explication deals with three spheres in which "adulteration" must be avoided: in nature (22:9-12), in human sexual relations (22:13-30 [Heb 22:13–23:1]), and within the cultic community (23:1-18 [Heb 23:2-19]).

COMMENTARY

Crossing Boundaries: Adulterations in Nature, 22:9-12

The section begins with three brief proscriptions against mixtures in the natural realm: planting mixed crops, plowing with a mixed pair of draught animals, and wearing clothing made of blended fabric. These three cases are also treated in Leviticus 19:19. The fourth case involving the positive injunction to wear tassels on the four fringes of the outer garment does not deal with such an admixture and is not paralleled in Leviticus 19.

Since none of these prohibitions include explanations, the reasons for avoiding such admixtures must be deduced. The practices may have derived from animistic or totemistic beliefs far in Israel's past and long-since forgotten [Origins and Meaning]. Scholars have offered a number of theoretical explanations for the underlying rationale for the laws as they stand in Deuteronomy. Carmichael, for example, sees all four of the prescriptions as metaphors for improper sexuality.[1] The law against plowing with mixed pairs has been explained on humane grounds since the ancient period. Josephus argued that, since priests wore sacred vestments of mixed fabric, the law against such blends was intended to prohibit laypersons from assuming priestly holiness (cf. Exod 30:22-37).

Whatever the unique origins of these individual practices, the fact that they are collected together without explanation, except as they comment on one another, must be given full weight. The commonality between them is the interest in preserving the plant and animal realms in a clearly classified and ordered state—just as

---

Origins and Meaning

Students of religion as a phenomenon must often take pains to distinguish between the ideas originally associated with a phenomenon such as Israel's taboo against improper mixtures and the meaning they come to have in later understanding and practice. A prime example of the need to maintain this distinction is the rite of circumcision. It is widely practiced in the world's cultures, from Australia to Africa and the Middle East. Among Israel's neighbors in the ancient world, the Egyptians, most Semitic peoples (except the Babylonians and Assyrians), and all of Israel's nearest neighbors (the Ammonites, Moabites, etc.) except the Philistines practiced it. Since it was such a common practice, it can be reasonably assumed that Israel's pre-Yahwistic Hebrew ancestors practiced circumcision quite apart from the covenant significance given it in Gen 17. Scholars of comparative religion, judging from the significance given the rite among cultures other than Israel, offer three possible explanations for the practice. They are not mutually exclusive: (1) as an initiation into young manhood (compare the fact that Abraham circumcised thirteen-year-old Ishmael, Gen 17), (2) as a fertility rite creating the impression of permanent erection, and (3) as a sacrificial act to a fertility deity (compare Exod 4:24-26). By biblical times, these meanings were no longer associated with circumcision. Similarly, any earlier notion of the danger of affronting the deities associated with the ox and the ass or of contamination of the life forces of the various seed crops no longer adhere to the laws against admixture in Deuteronomy.

God created and intended. In this regard the tassel requirement provides an additional clue. Although Deuteronomy 22:12 stands without explanation,[2] the parallel in Numbers 15:37-41 describes the tassels as a mnemonic device to remind Israelites of the covenant and of their holy status. As demonstrated elsewhere (see [Clean and Unclean—"Appropriate" and "Off-limits"]), ancient Israelite notions of holiness and the proper classification and categorization of natural phenomena are closely related. Apparently the proscriptions against admixtures serve a purpose similar to that of the prescriptions concerning tassels; namely, they remind Israel of the holiness of God's created order and provide Israel the means to participate in the maintenance of that order.[3]

Crossing Boundaries: Adultery Proper, 22:13-30 (Heb 22:13–23:1)

Following the cases illustrating the need to maintain holiness by maintaining boundaries in the natural realm, the code turns to the question of adultery proper. The context leads one to expect that Deuteronomy would deal with adultery as a violation of the moral order on a par with violations of the natural order. It must be acknowledged at the outset, however, that, consonant with the patriarchal structures characteristic of the wider ancient Near Eastern culture, Israelite law does not hold a lofty conception of marriage by modern standards. Israel defined adultery not as a sin against the marriage bond itself, but as a crime against the reproductive and economic rights of the key *male* figures in a woman's life: her father and her (either potential or actual) husband. At issue is the question of whether her husband can be assured that her children are his offspring. The double standard is appalling. Indeed, with only a few possible exceptions (Gen 1–2, Song of Songs, portions of Proverbs), the Bible offers few models for healthy, redemptive, nurturing marital and family relationship.

The cases adduced here do, however, demonstrate an interest, not only in defending the reproductive "rights" of men, but also in protecting women against men who would take advantage of the power inequality between the sexes. Unfortunately, even this protection is limited to exonerating the woman from responsibility in certain cases of slander and rape. Men are not subject to the same penalties for premarital sexual activity. Women's wishes and hopes for happiness in marriage are never taken into account in Israel's legal traditions.

David and Bathsheba
Perhaps the most egregious instance of adultery recorded in the Bible. David compounded his crime by adding to it murder.

Francesco Salviati. 1510–1563. *Story of David.* Palazzo Sacchetti. Rome, Italy.

The section examines seven specific cases: vv. 13-19, the bride falsely accused; vv. 20-21, the bride justly accused; v. 22, adultery with a married woman; vv. 23-24, adultery with an engaged woman; vv. 25-27, the rape of an engaged woman; vv. 28-29, the rape of a single woman; and v. 30 (Heb. 23:1), forbidden marriage to one's (presumably widowed) stepmother. In general, these cases are arranged in order of descending severity with respect both to the availability of the woman in question (wife, engaged woman, single woman, widow) and to the punishment meted out (death by stoning, fine).

A groom's false accusation, 22:13-19

The first two cases dealing with adultery in the strict sense concern the possibility of "premarital" adultery, as it were. The Hebrew Bible outlines the basics of the first case very succinctly (vv. 13-14): "If a man takes a wife, and he goes in to her, and he hates her, and he lays against her false charges (*ʿălîlōt dĕbārîm*, "frivolous words") and gives her a bad name, saying . . . I did not find her to be a virgin (*bĕtûlîm*, literally "tokens of virginity"). . . ." The reasons for and the nature of the man's dissatisfaction with his new wife are insignificant to the case. He could simply divorce her (24:1), but apparently he seeks to avoid the loss of her dowry, in effect, by claiming breech of contract between him and her father. He had been defrauded, he claims, so that he can dismiss his wife without surrendering her dowry. It should be noted that the groom's virginity is never at issue.

Not only are the woman's reputation and thus her future at stake, but also her parent's reputations and financial well-being. They risk becoming known as parents who permitted wanton behavior, losing their daughter (vv. 20-21), as well as losing a substantial sum of money. No wonder, then, that the parents of brides in ancient

Israel took measures to guard against such accusations. Interpreters debate the precise nature of the "tokens of virginity (v. 17, *śimlâ*, "outer garment, cloak"). It is usually understood to have been a cloth placed in the nuptial bed to be produced later as evidence of first intercourse. Other interpreters suggest that the token may have been proof of the bride's menses just prior to the wedding, evidence that any child born subsequently will be the groom's.

At any rate, both parents produce this incontrovertible evidence "in the gate" (v. 15, see [Justice "in the gate"]) before the elders of the community. Now the onus of responsibility shifts to the groom. He has born false witness, charging his bride with a capital offense. One might expect a capital penalty for his crime (see 19:19), but such is not the case. His penalty is, however, quite severe: First, the elders "correct" him. The rabbis understood this statement as a reference to flogging with the prescribed thirty-nine lashes (compare 25:2-3). Second, he must pay his *father-in-law*, whom he sought to defraud, 100 shekels of silver, double the normal bride-price (see v. 29). Finally, he must remain married to the bride he slandered; he may never divorce her. Only this final provision addresses the very real injury done the young woman—although indissoluble marriage to this man who charged her with a capital offense may have seemed more like a life sentence than a remedy. Clearly, this case deals with the monetary value of the woman's virginity as a commodity traded between father and son-in-law. [Adultery with (Rape of) a Betrothed Woman in ANE Law]

A groom's true accusation, 22:20-21

On the other hand, the charges may prove to be true. In this case the bride is to be stoned at her father's doorstep. He forfeits the dowry and his reputation; she forfeits her life. Her husband's

---

Adultery with (Rape of) a Betrothed Woman in ANE Law

If a man gives bride-money for a(nother) man's daughter, but another man seizes her forcibly without asking the permission of her father and her mother and deprives her of her virginity, it is a capital offence and he shall die. (*Codex Eshnunna*, 26; ANET I, 135-36. These laws from the northern Mesopotamian city state of Eshnunna [modern Tell Asmar] date to sometime around the 19th century BC.)

If the wife of a seignior has been caught while lying with another man, they shall bind them and throw them into the water. If the husband of the woman wishes to spare his wife, then the king in turn may spare his subject.

If a seignior bound the (betrothed) wife of a(nother) seignior, who had had no intercourse with a male and was still living in her father's house, and he has lain in her bosom and they have caught him, that seignior shall be put to death, while that woman shall go free.

If a seignior's wife was accused by her husband, but she was not caught while lying with another man, she shall make affirmation by god and return to her house. (*Codex Hammurapi*, 129-31; ANET I, 152. Hammurapi was a king in the Amorite dynasty of the Old Babylonian "Empire" who reigned during the 18th century BC.)

A Jewish Marriage Contract from Elephantine (Fifth Century BC)

On the 25th (?) of Tishri that is the 6th day of the month Epiphi, year . . . of Artaxerxes the king, said Ashor b. Zeho . . . to Mahseiah Aramaean of Syene . . . as follows: I came to your house that you might give me your daughter Miphtahiah in marriage. She is my wife and I her husband from this day forever. I have given you as the price of your daughter Miphtahiah the sum of 5 shekels, royal weight. It has been received by you and your heart is content therewith. I have delivered to your daughter Miphtahiah into her hand for the cost of furniture 1 karah 2 shekels royal weight. . . . I have delivered to her into her hand 1 woolen robe, new . . . I have received, and my heart is content therewith, 1 couch of reeds. . . . Tomorrow or another day (if) Ashor should die and there is no child male or female belonging to him by Miphtahiah his wife, Miphtahiah has a right to the house of Ashor, his goods and his chattels and all that he has on the face of the earth, all of it. Tomorrow or (another) day (if) Miphtahiah should die and there is no child male or female belonging to her by Ashor her husband, Ashor shall inherit her goods and her chattels. Tomorrow or another day (if) Miphtahiah should stand up in the congregation and say, I divorce Ashor my husband, the price of divorce (shall be) on her head; she shall return to the scales and weigh out to Ashor the sum of 7 shekels 2 R and all that I have put into her hand she shall give up . . . and she shall go away whither she will, without suit or process. Tomorrow or another day (if) Ashor should stand up in the congregation and say, I divorce my wife Miphtahiah, her price shall be forfeited, but all that I have put into her hand, she shall give up . . . on one day at one time, and she shall go away whither she will, without suit or process. But if should rise up against Miphtahiah to drive her out from his, Ashor's, house and his goods and chattels, he shall give her the sum of 20 kerashin, and the provisions of this deed shall be annulled, as far as she is concerned. And I shall have no right to say I have another wife besides Miphtahiah and other children that the children whom Miphtahiah shall bear to me. If I say I have children and wife other than Miphtahiah and her children, I will pay to Miphtahiah the sum of 20 kerashin, royal weight, and I shall have no right to take away my gods and chattels from Miphtahiah; and if I remove them from her [erasure] I will pay to Miphtahiah the sum of 20 kerashin, royal weight.

A. Cowley, trans., *Aramaic Papyri of the Fifth Century B.C.* (Osnabrück: Otto Zeller, 1967), 45-46.

---

virginity, or lack of it, is inconsequential. Her presumptive lover goes unpunished.

Clear-cut Adultery, 22:22

Adultery pure and simple receives little attention in the Deuteronomic Code. A consenting man and a consenting married woman not his wife who engage in sexual relations are guilty of adultery. The penalty for their crime is death by stoning.

Adultery involving an engaged woman, 22:23-24

This case differs from the previous cases in two ways. First, it makes clear that, with respect to the laws on adultery, an engaged virgin is to be considered married. Presumably, her future husband has already paid the bride-price and agreed to the marriage contract. [A Jewish Marriage Contract from Elephantine (Fifth Century BC)] Legally, then, she is his wife even though they have not yet cohabited. Second, in order to distinguish between cases of consensual adultery and rape, the case law introduces the criterion of the "cry for help (*z‘q*)." The text envisions an encounter that took place in the city where the woman's cry for help would have elicited assistance.

Thus, she would likely have thwarted the man's advances. Since she did not cry out, her assent can be presumed. She is guilty of adultery. Most interpreters, including most notably the rabbis and Martin Luther, allow for circumstances, such as threats to her life, in which the woman could not have cried out, even in the city. The key question involves distinguishing between consensual sex and rape. In the former case, both parties are guilty of adultery; in the latter, only the man.

Rape, 22:25-27

If the incident took place in the countryside, however, it can be simply assumed that the engaged woman cried out for help and was unheard. Her situation can be likened "to the case of someone who attacks and murders a neighbor." The man has "seized her and lain with her," that is, he has attacked her forcibly and against her will. She is the victim and bears no responsibility for the attack. Since she is a "married" woman, her attacker is guilty of adultery and must be executed.

Rape of a single woman, 22:28-29

The case law now takes up the issue of illicit relations with an unbetrothed virgin. [Fornication in ANE Law] Several provisions of this law are troubling. First, it apparently deals not with consensual sex, but with rape ("seizes her," *ûtĕpāśāh*, v. 28; compare v. 25). Yet the penalty for the man is merely that he pay the bride-price of fifty shekels of silver *to the woman's father* and marry the woman. The economic value of the woman's virginity to her father outweighs the injury and humiliation suffered by the victim herself. Like the case of the falsely accused woman, this victim is virtually condemned to live out her life as the wife of her attacker. Third, it assumes that the deed will be found out (v. 28) but makes no provision to protect the young woman in the event her attacker goes undiscovered. Should she subsequently marry and be found no longer a virgin, would she be subject to the penalty imposed in vv. 20-21?

Fornication in ANE Law

If a man takes a(nother) man's daughter without asking the permission of her father and her mother and concludes no formal marriage contract with her father and her mother, even though she may live in his house for a year, she is not a housewife.

On the other hand, if he concludes a formal contract with her father and her mother and cohabits with her, she is a housewife. When she is caught with a(nother) man, she shall die, she shall not get away alive. . . .

If a man deprives another man's slave-girl of her virginity, he shall pay one-third of a mina of silver; the slave-girl remains the property of her owner. (*Codex Eshnunna*, 27-28, 31)

"Post-marital" adultery, 22:30 (Heb 23:1)

The cases treated to this point have focused on adultery as a crime against the woman's father or her living husband. The final law, which has parallels elsewhere in the context of incestuous relationships forbidden as "abominations" to YHWH (Lev 18:6-30), occurs in the present context to define certain kinds of relationships as adulterous crimes against the fathers of the men in question. Unlike the other laws in this section, this prohibition is apodictic in form: it states a principle, not a case; no penalty is prescribed. A man may not marry his stepmother—probably the significance of "his father's wife," in distinction to "his (the man's) mother" who was also, by definition, his father's wife. Presumably she is widowed. She stands in no direct relationship to the man. It was frequently customary in the ancient Near East for a son, especially a prince, to inherit his father's harem. Why is this law included here? In keeping with the persistent concern of the preceding laws, this marriage is forbidden as a crime against the woman's previous husband, the man's father. It would dishonor the father.

Crossing Boundaries: Adulteration of the Cultic Community, 23:1-18 (Heb 23:2-19)

The third area of concern addressed in the explication of the commandment against adultery (and adulteration) involves the maintenance of the purity of the cultic community. The laws assembled in this section deal with criterion for membership in the community (vv. 1-8 [Heb vv. 2-9]), the purity of the Holy War camp (vv. 10-14 [Heb vv. 11-15]), the acceptance of runaway slaves into the community (vv. 15-16 [Heb vv. 16-17]), and the prohibition of prostitution in the community and the wages of the prostitute in the temple treasury (vv. 17-18 [Heb vv. 18-19]).

Maintaining Boundaries in the Composition of the Cultic Community, 23:1-8 (Heb 23:2-9)

Six categories of people are excluded, either permanently or for a number of generations, from membership in the cultic community. Readers familiar with the Bible as a whole will find these restrictions somewhat dissonant in the larger context. In fact, Isaiah 56:3-8 looks forward to a day when these restrictions will be lifted and anyone who keeps the Sabbath and honors the covenant, eunuchs and foreigners of all nationalities alike, will be welcomed into YHWH's people. The presence of these two contradictory viewpoints in the canon of Hebrew Scriptures calls attention to the fact that it is difficult to maintain proper balance between the worthy impetus toward purity and the equally noble impulse

Ammonite and Edomite Proselytes in Rabbinic Literature

Rabbis in the Talmudic period and beyond recognized that historical events had rendered inapplicable the law concerning the admission of Ammonites, Moabites, Edomites, and Egyptians to the congregation. The following passage from the *Tosephta* (*Qid* 5:4) deals with the problem:

> An Egyptian man who married an Egyptian woman, an Edomite man who married an Edomite woman—the first generation and the second are prohibited from entering the congregation, but the third is permitted.
>
> Said R. Judah, "Benjamin, an Egyptian proselyte, had a companion from among the disciples of R. `Aqiba.
>
> "He said, 'I am an Egyptian proselyte, and I married a woman who was an Egyptian proselyte. Lo, I am planning to arrange a marriage for my son with a woman who is the daughter of an Egyptian proselyte woman, so that the son of my son will be permitted to enter into the congregation,
>
> 'since it is said, *[You shall not abhor an Edomite, for he is your brother; you shall not abhor an Egyptian, because you were a sojourner in his land.] The children of the third generation that are born to them may enter the congregation of the Lord*' (Deut 23:7-8).
>
> "Said to him R. `Aqiba, 'Benjamin you have erred in this law. After Sennacherib came up and made a mixture of all the nations, the Ammonites and Moabites no longer are found in their original location, and the Egyptians and the Edomites are no longer found in their original location.
>
> "But an Ammonite man marries and Egyptian woman, and an Egyptian man marries an Ammonite woman, and any one of all these marries any one of all the families of the earth, and any one of the families of all the earth marries any one of these.'"

toward openness and inclusiveness. [Ammonite and Edomite Proselytes in Rabbinic Literature]

The first group (v. 1 [Heb v. 2]) excluded from membership are men who have been mutilated or emasculated. Typically, the text does not specify the rationale behind their exclusion. Scholars speculate that either an interest in distancing Israel's cult from certain pagan cults in which such mutilation played a significant role, or a revulsion against blurred gender boundaries, or the sense that such mutilation represented an offense against God's injunction to procreate may have been the motivating factor. Such mutilation also disqualifies priests and renders animals unfit for sacrifice.

The second group (v. 2 [Heb v. 3]) excluded is the *mamzēr*. This term occurs only twice in the Hebrew Bible, here and in Zechariah 9:6, and its precise meaning is therefore uncertain. NRSV's translation, "those born of an illicit union," is speculative. In Zechariah, where it refers to a population that will settle in Ashdod one day, it is often translated "mongrel, mixed." The Talmud understands it as a designation for the offspring of incestuous or adulterous unions. LXX and TJon take it to mean the offspring of a prostitute. Whoever the *mamzēr* are, they may not be admitted to the assembly, nor may their offspring "for ten generations (i.e., forever)."

The third and fourth groups (vv. 3-6 [Heb vv. 4-7]) excluded, also "for ten generations," are the Ammonites and Moabites, descendants of Abraham's nephew Lot. Now the text offers a rationale: they were inhospitable to Israel during its passage through the Transjordan on the way to enter the promised land (cf. Num 21–22 and Deut 2:8-30); in fact, they hired the prophet Balaam to place Israel under a curse. Traditions concerning Israel's encounters with Ammon and Moab disagree with one another. According to Numbers, only the Moabites resisted Israel's passage. It was their king, Balak, who engaged Balaam; the Ammonites played no role. According to Deuteronomy 2, both Ammon and Moab granted Israel safe passage. No doubt the conflict between Israel and its Transjordanian neighbors, strife that persisted throughout the monarchy and into the exile, contributed to the animosity expressed in the Deuteronomic Code. Regardless of this confusion, the text at hand condemns the Ammonites along with the Moabites.

In context, the relative warmth expressed for the fifth and sixth groups (vv. 7-8 [Heb vv. 8-9]), the Edomites and the Egyptians, surprises. In fact, according to Numbers 20:14-21, it was the Edomites, not the Ammonites or Moabites, who refused Israel passage through their territory. Later, Edom would become the type for the nation at enmity with Israel and YHWH (see Isa 63; Obad; etc.). Similarly, the Egyptians had been Israel's oppressors prior to the exodus. Yet, the bonds of kinship and hospitality outweigh all other considerations. Jacob and Esau, the ancestors of Israel and Edom, respectively, were brothers. Before oppressing Israel, Egypt offered its warmest hospitality to Joseph and his brothers, Jacob/Israel's sons. Consequently, after a period of three generations dwelling among God's people, Edomites and Egyptians may be admitted to the assembly.

Maintaining Purity in the Camp, 23:9-14 (Heb 23:10-15)

These regulations concerning the Holy War camp appear here instead of together with the earlier Holy War material because of their focus on purity. Because YHWH goes out to battle with Israel and, therefore, the Holy War has a decidedly religious character, the camp must be regarded as a sacred place (v. 14). Israel must take pains to guard against every impropriety in the camp (*mikkōl dābār rā*', literally, "from every bad thing," v. 9 [Heb v. 10]). Two examples illustrate the level of purity appropriate to a camp pitched in YHWH's presence: nocturnal emissions and latrine procedures. Although the rationale for the selection of these particular cases is unclear, the text does not intend to impute any moral evil or material pollution to the very natural and normal phenomena discussed. As demonstrated above (see [Clean and Unclean—"Appropriate" and "Off-limits"]), the concept of cultic purity does not involve distinctions between good and bad. Instead, the issue of propriety governs. A good thing in one context may be entirely inappropriate in another. It is good and appropriate for levitical priests to bear the ark of the covenant in procession. In contrast, any other Israelite is forbidden any and all contact with the ark.

The first example deals with a situation (literally, "if a man becomes unclean from a chance occurrence in the night," v. 10 [Heb v. 11]) that renders one cultically unclean under any circumstance (Lev 15:16-18). In Israel's view, anything associated with the mystery of reproduction bears a holy character and places the person or persons in question temporarily in the sphere of the holy. These persons must be "set apart" (the basic idea of the Hebrew root *qdš* that denotes various aspects of "holiness") for a period. This "setting apart" is not a punitive measure, nor an effort to avoid contamination. Instead, in this case, it is an acknowledgement of the mystery and sanctity of life and reproduction. Since the Holy War camp is a holy place, such a person must exit the camp for the prescribed period. Before returning he must ritually bathe.

The second example is much more mundane. Somewhere beyond the margins of the camp, the warriors should have a marked (*yād*, v. 12 [Heb v. 13]) latrine area. Each warrior should have among his weapons and tools a spade (*yātēd*, "pin, (tent) peg," v. 13 [Heb v. 14]) with which to dig and then to cover an individual latrine. This only makes common sense. But the Deuteronomic Code relates this very mundane aspect of life and this very commonsense procedure to the presence of God in the camp. YHWH will be moving about (*mithallēk*) in the camp. It is a holy place. Israel should not run the risk that YHWH will encounter such a vulgarity or indecency (*'erwat dābār*, "nakedness of a thing," v. 14 [Heb v. 15]).

Maintaining Boundaries in Society, 23:15-16 (Heb 23:16-17)

As is often the case in the Bible, the noble impetus of the fundamental truth of God's self-revelation breaks through cultural limitations in surprising ways. Within a few verses of the somewhat xenophobic and very particularistic restrictions on membership in the cultic community (23:1-8 [Heb 23:2-9]), the Deuteronomic Code prescribes universal asylum for escaped slaves, probably

Slaves in ANE Law

 If a seignior has helped either a male slave of the state or a female slave of the state or a male slave of a private citizen or a female slave of a private citizen to escape through the city-gate, he shall be put to death.

If a seignior has harbored in his house either a fugitive male or female slave belonging to the state or to a private citizen and has not brought him forth at the summons of the police, that householder shall be put to death.

If a seignior caught a fugitive male or female slave in the open and has taken him to his owner, the owner of the slave shall pay him two shekels of silver.

If that slave has not named his owner, he shall take him to the palace in order that his record may be investigated, and they shall return him to his owner.

If he has kept that slave in his house (and) later the slave has been found in his possession, that seignior shall be put to death. (*Codex Hammurapi*, 15-19)

---

non-Israelites. They are not to be returned to their owners. They are to be permitted to live in Israel in the place of their choosing. Israel shall not oppress (*ynh*, Exod 22:20; Lev 19:33) them. Clearly, the memory of slavery in Egypt and YHWH's deliverance motivates this regulation. Liberated Israel must not become the oppressor. [Escaped Slaves in ANE Law]

Maintaining Purity in the Sanctuary Treasury, 23:17-18 (Heb 23:18-19)

Finally, the editors include legislation against "adulteration" of the cultic community through internal means. God's holy people must not include members of either gender who are prostitutes (compare Lev 19:29).[4] Similarly, the temple treasury must not be polluted by earnings from prostitution or by the wages of a "dog." The precise significance of a "dog's" wages is unclear. It may refer to the proceeds from the sale of a dog, proceeds that would be improper in the temple because, as carnivores, dogs are unclean. Alternatively, Israel may have associated dogs with pagan gods of healing, as did the Philistines and others. More likely, however, given the reference to both male and female prostitutes in v. 17 [Heb v. 18], it is a derogatory reference to the stance of a male prostitute.

CONNECTIONS

Repeatedly, Deuteronomy confronts its modern readers with reminders of the antiquity and foreignness of the cultural context in which it was written. Often these reminders come in the form of institutions unparalleled in modern society (cities of refuge, for example) or of attitudes reflecting pre-modern assumptions (kosher rules, for example). In contrast, the material explicating the commandment against adultery confronts its modern reader with theological claims and cultural assumptions that are, frankly, offensive. It is tempting simply to disregard them, but that approach undermines the canon's centrality to faith grounded in Scripture.

Instead, it may prove fruitful to address the question of the very nature of Scriptures themselves, especially as related to the idea that God continues to reveal God's self even today. At issue is whether the Bible can be considered a "perfect" instrument of revelation. If so, the attitudes toward marriage, women, and foreigners canonized in this section of the Deuteronomic Code must reflect the divine will. But careful readers of Scripture will quickly call attention to other portions of the Bible such as the description of the creation of Eve as Adam's helpmate, partner, and equal, or Isaiah's promise to eunuchs and foreigners mentioned above, or Paul's assertion that in Christ "there is neither Jew nor Greek, slave nor free, male nor female" (Gal 3:28). Clearly, then, the Bible records not only God's revelation, but also evidence of the process of the moral and spiritual maturation of God's people. The Bible bears witness to God's revelation transmitted in the words of a people often blind to the fact that their institutions and attitudes were inadequate for, and often contrary to, the revelation itself.

The task of the modern reader of Deuteronomy, then, is twofold: (1) to discriminate between the word of God and its cultural vessel, and (2) to be ever alert to the possibility of one's own blindness to modern cultural inadequacies. Just as God continues to reveal God's self, God's people continue to overlook the contradictions between God's call and the very institutions and traditions responsible for perpetuating sin and injustice.

It may be fruitful to regard this section and the problems it raises as an invitation to consider at least three very important issues treated in this section of Deuteronomy. They deserve renewed attention in light of the need to be attentive to the conflict between God's will and cultural prejudice.

First among these is the question of the significance and nature of the biblical call to purity in general. Should the people of God continue to strive for personal and collective holiness? Will the hallmarks of this holiness include a reverence for and participation in the order of the cosmos? Will they include renewed attention to the central importance of marriage as the most significant institution in human society? Will the purity of the community of those called to holiness define itself in terms of whom it excludes and condemns or in terms of whom it protects and nurtures?

Second, this section of Deuteronomy invites a reconsideration of the nature of marriage and the role of women in a holy community. Ancient Israel's patriarchy valued women as bearers of children to such a degree that it virtually traded women's virginity as a commodity. The double standard resulting from this objectification of women is downright offensive. The measures taken to insure a man's investment in his wife's womb were inhumane at the very least. What woman would *want* to be virtually condemned to an indissoluble marriage to her rapist?

Quite naturally, a society's definition of the purpose of marriage influences its attitudes toward and expectations of men and women, paternity, divorce, family life, etc. [Marriage in the U.S.] Conversely, actual practices in these areas may reveal a society's definition of this purpose more accurately than any statement of the ideal. Modern culture may pride itself in having made significant advances over Iron Age Israel, but evidence suggests that both the definition and the practice of marriage continue to reflect the flaws of human sin. Demographics suggest that modern middle-class marriages value the accumulation of wealth above all other concerns.

Marriage in the U.S.

According to the United States Census Bureau:

- In 1998, 110.6 million adults (56.0 percent of the adult population) were married and living with their spouse.
- Among people age 25 to 34 years old, 13.6 million had never been married, representing 34.7 percent of all people in the age group.
- In 1998, 19.4 million adults were currently divorced, representing 9.8 percent of this population.
- About 19.8 million children under 18 lived with one parent (27.7 percent of all children under 18).
- The majority of children who lived with a single parent in 1998 lived with their mother (84.1 percent). About 40.3 percent of these children lived with mothers who had never been married. Children who lived with their father only were more likely to be living with a divorced father (44.4 percent) than with a never-married father (33.3 percent).
- No other adults were present in the household for 55.7 percent of children living with single parents.

Terry Lugaila, "Marital Status and Living Arrangements: March 1997" (Update) (Current Population Reports P20-514).

Divorce rates suggest a number of problems: that couples are ill-equipped and ill-motivated to resolve interpersonal conflict; that young people too readily accept the culture's romantic definition of marriage, marrying based on an attraction that cannot bear the weight of life's pressures; that family and society train young people in the art of courting but not in the skills necessary for successful marriage. Education data point to parents who are uninvolved in their children's education.

Operating on ancient Israel's very simple definition of marriage as a union for purposes of procreation, fidelity could be enforced. Since the health of the relationship between husband and wife was not a stated objective, it required no support mechanism. Modern society, however, views marriage ideally, not merely as an exclusive relationship, but as a nurturing, sustaining, and sustained relationship between a woman and a man, a relationship that becomes, in many cases, the nucleus for a new family. Judging from the evidence, society must invest much more heavily in equipping individuals for marriage and in supporting existing marriages.

Third, Deuteronomy's laws on adultery and adulteration invite a reconsideration of the importance of the mundane in a life of holiness. Few modern believers would view mixed crops, mixed fabrics, or latrines as moral or religious absolutes. Ancient Israel held the conviction that, for the people of God, even the most mundane areas of life require conscious attention. ["I Would Like to Rise Very High"] Has the separation of life into profane and sacred realms robbed moderns of a sense of the unity of God's creation? Have moderns lost the ability to sense daily life as lived in the presence of God? Has the scientific worldview so objectified creation that moderns can longer see it as the creation of a God who instills order? Have moderns lost awareness of their place in the cosmos?

"I Would Like to Rise Very High"

I would like to rise very high, Lord;
Above my city,
Above the world,
Above time.
I would like to purify my glance and borrow your eyes.
I would then see the universe, humanity, history, as the Father sees them.
I would see in the prodigious transformation of matter,
In the perpetual seething of life,
Your great Body that is born of the breath of the Spirit
...
Everything summed up in you, things on earth and things in heaven.
And I would see that today, like yesterday, the most minute details are part of it.
Every man in his place,
Every group
And every object.
I would see a factory, a theatre, a collective-bargaining session and the construction of a fountain.
I would see a crowd of youngsters going to a dance,
A baby being born, and an old man dying.
I would see the tiniest particle of matter and the smallest throbbing of life,
Love and hate,
Sin and grace.
Startled, I would understand that the great adventure of love, which started at the beginning of the world, is unfolding before me ...
I would understand that everything is linked together,
That all is but a single movement of the whole of humanity and of the whole universe toward the Trinity, in you, by you, Lord.
I would understand that nothing is secular, neither things, nor people, nor events,
But that, on the contrary, everything has been made sacred in its origin by God
And that everything must be consecrated by man, who has himself been made divine ...
Then, falling on my knees, I would admire, Lord, the mystery of this world
Which, in spite of the innumerable and hateful snags of sin,
Is a long throb of love towards Love eternal. ...

Michele Quoist, *Prayers*, trans. A. Forsyth and A. M. de Commaille (New York: Avon, 1975), 13-15.

NOTES

[1] C. Carmichael, "Forbidden Mixtures," *VT* 32 (1982): 394-415; and idem, *The Laws of Deuteronomy* (Ithaca NY: Cornell University Press, 1974), 159-63. Noting that in Deut 22:8-10 "plowing" takes the place of marriage to a new wife in the sequence "house, vineyard, new wife/plowing" found in Deut 20:5-7, he considers this section a playful midrash on Genesis 34.

[2] Braulik ("Sequence," 333, citing Schultz in *Das Deuteronomium: Entstehung, Gestalt und Botschaft*, ed. N. Lohfink [Leuven: University Press, 1985], 559) suggests that "the tassels may simply have weighted and drawn down the corners of the square cloak, in order 'to protect the body, and especially the private parts, from being uncovered.'"

[3] C. Hartman, "Another Look at Forbidden Mixtures," *VT* 34 (1984): 226-28.

[4] Many translations and commentaries persist in the mistaken interpretation of this and similar texts as references to so-called "cult prostitution." There is simply no warrant for the assumption that Israel knew of such an institution. See the commentary on Deut 12:29-31 and [Baalism] and [A Caricature of Canaanite Religion].

EXPLICATION OF THE SEVENTH COMMANDMENT: "DO NOT STEAL"

23:19–24:7 (Heb 23:20–24:7)

The regulations assembled in the Deuteronomic Code as explications of the commandment against stealing deal with a wide variety of life's circumstances. Parallels elsewhere in the Torah illustrate (Exod 21:16; 22:1-14; Lev 5:20–6:6 [6:1-7 Eng]; 19:11, 13) that they by no means exhaust the areas to which the prohibition against stealing can be applied. As arranged here, the regulations exhibit an interesting concentric structure in terms of the specific topics treated. The pairs of laws (interest, unpaid vows; limitations on the taking of collateral, kidnapping) at the beginning and end of the section deal with more-or-less clear cases of stealing; the three laws at the center (plucking, remarriage to a former wife, and newlyweds) relate to the commandment against stealing in surprising and abstract ways. By including them in this section, framed by laws clearly related to the commandment, the editors creatively established the relationship between these laws and the commandment against stealing.

Collectively, these laws elucidate the basic commandment in a number of significant ways. They demonstrate that the commandment applies stealing to nonmaterial realities; they establish that one can also steal from God; they focus, in fact, not on that which is stolen, but on the damage done to the victim—theft is an attack on another's well-being. Once again, they illustrate the close connection between the commandments—stealing is diminishing, even threatening, life. In fact, even divorce and remarriage can be forms of theft.

COMMENTARY

23:19-20 (Heb 23:20-21)

Deuteronomy's law against usury parallels laws in the Covenant (Exod 22:25) and Holiness (Lev 25:35-38) Codes. In relation to these parallels, Deuteronomy expands the prohibition to exclude not only charging interest to family members (Leviticus) or the poor (Exodus) but also to any Israelite. Deuteronomy's list of forbidden types of interest ("on money . . . on foodstuffs . . . on anything that is lent") agrees with and expands the sentiment of Leviticus's prohibition against making a profit from the sale of life's necessities to needy family members.

Although Deuteronomy widens the circle of those to whom interest should not be charged, the humanitarian force of all three forms of the law against usury must not be overlooked. Deuteronomy 15:1-11 has already required the forgiveness of all debts every seventh year and strongly encouraged lending to the poor even when the Sabbath year approaches and the creditor may not reasonably expect to be repaid. As the term translated "interest" or "to charge interest" (Heb. *nšk,* literally "a bite," or "to take a bite," respectively; it is used often of a serpent's bite) indicates, ancient Israel despised taking advantage of another's misfortune. [Profit and Misfortune: Economics or Ethics?] The editors of the Deuteronomic Code saw charging interest as a form of stealing. In fact, since most traders in the ancient Near East did business

---

Profit and Misfortune: Economics or Ethics?

An excerpt from the November 13, 1998, quarterly report (SEC form 10-Q) of Dialysis Corporation of America follows. As its name suggests, it is a for-profit provider of kidney dialysis. It is obviously thriving. Is profiting from the fact that people suffering from kidney disease must pay for services or die analogous to seizing millstones?

Essential to the Company is Medicare reimbursement which is a fixed rate determined by HCFA. The level of the Company's revenues and profitability may be adversely affected by potential legislation resulting in rate cuts. Additionally, operating costs tend to increase over the years without . . . comparable increases . . . in the prescribed dialysis treatment reimbursement rates . . . . There also may be reductions in commercial third-party reimbursement rates. The Company bills Medicare, Medicaid and private third-party payors and handles its records of such reimbursements electronically. . . .

Medical service revenue decreased approximately $392,000 (31%) and $839,000 (25%) for the three months and nine months ended September 30, 1998, compared to the same periods of the preceding year. This decrease reflected lost revenues of approximately $515,000 and $1,507,000 for the three months and nine months ended September 30, 1998, compared to the same periods of the preceding year resulting from the sale of the Company's Florida dialysis operations on October 31, 1997, which were offset to some degree by increased revenues of the Company's Pennsylvania dialysis centers of approximately $103,000 and $648,000 for the three months and nine months ended September 30, 1998, including revenues of approximately $107,000 and $535,000 for the three months and nine months ended September 30, 1998 from a new dialysis center located in Carlisle, Pennsylvania, which commenced operations in July 1997.

On Vows

The rabbis recognized the danger inherent in vows, especially in an overly conscientious sense of obligation. As a consequence, they identified four categories of invalid vows (*b. Nedarim* 21a): incentive vows, considered little more than admonitions or exhortations; exaggerations, considered the equivalent of exclamations; vows made in error (compare Jephthah); and vows broken under duress. Similarly, Martin Luther argued that, in order to be valid, vows must be strictly limited by two criteria: They must not be ungodly or evil (Jephthah), and they must not promise something beyond one's power or control to fulfill (Jephthah).

Vows are no longer a regular component of Protestant religion, with the single exception of the marriage ceremony. Indeed one argument that divorce is always and absolutely wrong centers around the violation of the promise made between the marriage partners and before God. Although no serious interpreter of Jesus would suggest that Jesus' admonitions concerning divorce be too easily diluted, biblical examples such as Jephthah's vow and everyday examples of family violence, for example, may suggest that some vows should never have been made at all. In these cases, one wonders whether the rash or erroneous marital vow may be the greater "sin" than divorce. Does keeping a mistaken promise matter more to God than health and well-being?

Martin Luther, *Lectures on Deuteronomy* (Luther's Works 9, ed. J. Pelikan and D. Poellot; St. Louis: Concordia, 1960), 234-35.

---

internationally, the permission to charge interest of "foreigners" may be understood less as a form of ethnocentricity and more as drawing a distinction between lending to the needy in one's community and credit as a component of commercial transactions.

Pay Vows, 23:21-23 (Heb 23:22-24)

A vow (*neder*) is a promise to perform some act usually as an acknowledgment that the deity has granted a request (Gen 28:20-22; Deut 12:6, 11, 17; 1 Sam 14:24). Vows are distinct from oaths, which are affirmations of truth invoking the deity as witness and guarantor. The failure to pay vows is a form of theft. False oaths fall under the purview of the commandment against taking YHWH's name falsely or lightly.

Although the Bible records many examples of vows made, promises to pay vows, etc. (Lev 22:18, 21; 27:2, 8; Num 6:2-21; 15:3, 8; 21:2; 30:2-14; etc.; Mark 6:23; Acts 18:18; 21:23), they obviously border on the *quid pro quo* bargaining characteristic of business dealings in human society and raise the question of whether such bargaining is an appropriate form of worship. Two of the more infamous cases are Jacob's vow at Bethel and Jephthah's rash vow. Jacob, apparently in the market for a god to worship, virtually offered YHWH the opportunity to earn his loyalty (Gen 28:20-22). Jephthah, hopeful for victory over Israel's enemies, vowed to sacrifice the first thing he encountered upon his return home should YHWH grant victory. When his daughter rushed to meet him after the battle, his rash vow costs her life (Judg 11:1-40). A few passages, including the text at hand (compare Eccl 5:4-6; Ps 76:11; Prov 20:25), manifest an awareness of the problematic nature of vows: They must be paid—failure to do so is tantamount to theft; but there is no obligation to make them in the first place. Ecclesiastes 5:4 goes so far as to recommend against vowing. [On Vows]

Hospitality, 23:25-26

The situation addressed in these two closely related laws involves travelers[1] passing through one's field. This would have been a common occurrence in ancient times when people regularly traveled on foot and taking the shortest route was an important consideration. Apparently such passage was not considered trespass.

The surprising twist in these cases involves the definition of the refusal of hospitality as theft. One might expect that the Deuteronomic editors would have been interested in protecting the property of the landowner—a standard approach to the concept of stealing. Instead, they require landowners to permit passers-by to satisfy momentary hunger (not to harvest into containers; such would be excessive). The supreme value placed upon hospitality [Hospitality] exceeds the right to protect one's property. In effect, to fail to give hospitably of one's goods in this case is tantamount to *stealing* from the traveler!

Prohibited Remarriage, 24:1-4

The regulation prohibiting the remarriage of a woman to her first husband if she has been married to another man in the interim has

---

Hospitality

The supreme value placed in the ancient world upon the requirement to extend hospitality continues in rabbinic Judaism. Martin Buber relates the following Hasidic tale:

When Rabbi Yitzhak lived in the town of Kinzk, a very well-to-do man invited him to a banquet. When the zaddik came to the house he saw that the forecourt was lit with large lanterns and the steps covered with rugs. Then he refused to proceed unless his host had the lanterns put out and the rugs removed, or promised to receive even the most unimportant guest with like magnificence from that time on.

"We are bidden to be hospitable," the zaddik said. "And just as we must not differentiate between one ram's horn and another when it comes to blowing the ram's horn, so in his capacity of guest one man is just like another." His host begged him to retract the demand, but in vain. In the end he had to yield, and since he was unable to give the required promise he had the house restored to its everyday appearance.

Martin Buber, *Tales of the Hasidim: The Later Masters*, trans. O. Marx (New York: Schocken, 1948), 295.

attracted a great deal of scholarly interest over the centuries for at least two significant reasons. First, although it concerns a very specific situation and does not purport to offer legislation governing the divorce process itself,[2] it surprisingly offers the most thorough and explicit information available concerning legal details of divorce in ancient Israel. The whole of Jewish divorce law, an entire, lengthy tractate of the Talmud, derives from these four verses. [Jewish Divorce Law]

Second, the purpose or rationale for this prohibition is far from obvious. The relationship between this prohibition and the commandment against stealing is particularly vexing. The text states the prohibition without explanation: Remarriage between a man and a former wife who has in the interim been married to another is an abomination. Why? Interpreters have offered a range of possible explanations, none of which have gained widespread acceptance.

One view holds that the prohibition has in mind a sort of legalized wife-swapping, not unlike the "pleasure marriages" practiced in some Islamic cultures, and that it simply equates such behavior with adultery. In the absence of evidence of this practice in ancient Israel and in the light of the fact that Deuteronomy 24:1-4 does not appear in the explication of the adultery commandment, however, this explanation must be rejected. Some have suggested that the prohibition is designed to deter hasty divorce on the theory that any husband contemplating divorcing his wife may give more care to the decision if he knows that it will likely prove irreversible. [Hasty Divorce] Again, however,

Jewish Divorce Law

 Most of the basic features of Jewish divorce law derive from Deut 24:1-4: Only the husband can initiate divorce (24:1), although since the time of Rab Gershom ben Yehuda (AD 965–1028) not without his wife's consent and, in some cases and at the wife's behest, a Jewish court can compel the husband to initiate divorce. The divorce procedure itself involves the drafting of a handwritten decree of divorce (24:1) or *get* that must be drawn up and delivered to the wife ("puts it into her hand," 24:1) in the presence of witnesses. In accordance with a tradition dating to Roman times, this *get* is then destroyed and record made of the divorce in the court. Both parties receive certification of the divorce without which they cannot remarry in a Jewish ceremony.

Hasty Divorce

Although they discouraged divorce, maintaining that "even the altar [God] sheds tears when anyone divorces his wife" (*Sanh* 22a; compare Mal 2:14), the rabbis disputed what constituted sufficient grounds for a husband to seek a divorce:

. . . the School of Shammai taught: A man may not divorce his wife unless he has found her guilty of sexual misconduct, as it is said, *Because he hath found some unseemly thing in her* (24:1). The School of Hillel, however, says: (He may dismiss her) even if she has merely spoiled his meal, as it is said, *thing*. The School of Hillel retorted to the School of Shammai: If Scripture says *thing*, why does it say *unseemly*? And it if says *unseemly*, why does it say *thing*? For had it said *thing*

without saying *unseemly*, I would have said that a woman divorced for a *thing*, may remarry, whereas one divorced because of unseemliness may not. And do not be amazed, for if she is forbidden to the man who is permitted to her, should she not be forbidden to the man who is forbidden to her? Therefore Scripture says, *Unseemly (thing) . . . And she departeth out of his house, and goeth and becometh another man's wife* (24:1-2). And had it said *unseemly* without saying *thing*, I would have said that she may be divorced only for something *unseemly* but not for a *thing*. Therefore Scripture says, *Thing. . . . And she departeth out of his house*. R. Akiba says: (He may divorce her) even if he finds another woman more comely than she is, as it is said, *Then it cometh to pass, if she find no favor in his eyes*.

Sifre, Piska 269 (263-64).

the text offers little in support of this explanation. On one hand, if it were interested in discouraging hasty divorces, one could reasonably expect it to focus more attention on the husband's original decision. Instead, it seems to assume that the first husband has a valid reason for divorcing his wife. On the other, it is difficult to conceive of a logical relationship between a capricious decision to divorce and the commandment against stealing.

A related and more intriguing solution to the problem offers a possible connection to the commandment against stealing and conforms to the text's focus on the woman's second and prohibited third marriages. Assuming the possibility that the first husband may harbor some lingering affections for his ex-wife and that they may be reciprocated, the law may be intended to protect the second marriage from the residue of first.[3] The first husband may not exert his influence over his ex-wife in such a way as to destroy the second marriage. To do so would, in effect, be stealing.

Stealing Life, 24:5-7

The final three brief provisions in this section may be understood as treatments of cases involving the theft of life. The bridegroom is to be exempted from military service, indeed from all public obligations, for one year following his marriage. He should "enjoy his wife whom he has married (*śimmaḥ ʾet-ʾištô ʾăšer-lāqāḥ*, v. 5). He must not risk his life in battle, thereby potentially robbing himself [Do not steal from yourself!] of the joy and meaning of marriage and family, leaving himself without heir or name, leaving his bride childless. A full life is God's gift; it must not be squandered.

Israelite creditors could claim collateral for loans, although their right to do so was strictly limited (see Exod 22:24-26[25-27 Eng]; Lev 25:35-38). The limitation imposed here (v. 6) involves an instrument necessary for sustaining life. Without a complete, functioning mill, a householder could not grind grain for bread. His life and the lives of his family would be severely limited, if not jeopardized. Even though the creditor may have a right to collateral, he has no right to employ heavy-handed means to recover his loan.

Finally, in the most egregious example, the Deuteronomic Code prohibits, under penalty of

Do not steal from yourself!

Rabbi Yehiel Meir of Gostynin had gone to his teacher in Kotzk for the Feast of Weeks. When he came home, his father-in-law asked him: "Well, did you people over there receive the Torah differently than anywhere else?"

"Certainly!" said his son-in-law.

"What do you mean?" asked the other.

"Well, to give you an instance," said Rabbi Yehiel. "How do you here interpret 'thou shalt not steal'?"

"That we shall not steal from our fellow men," answered his father-in-law. "That's perfectly clear."

"We don't need to be told that any more," said Rabbi Yehiel. "In Kotzk this is interpreted to mean: You shall not steal from yourself."

Martin Buber, *Tales of the Hasidim: The Later Masters*, trans. O. Marx (New York: Schocken, 1948), 286.

death, the kidnapping and sale into slavery of a fellow Israelite. To do so is literally to "steal life (*gōnēb nepeš*, v. 7)."

CONNECTIONS

Typically, Western culture understands theft primarily as a matter of property rights: unlawfully taking an object that belongs to another. Deuteronomy, on the other hand, focuses its explication of the commandment against stealing on thefts that diminish the life of another. Withheld hospitality is theft. Taking advantage of an ex-wife's continued affection is theft. One can rob one's self of a full life. The creditor's property rights do not exceed the right of a fellow Israelite to live and to support his family.

As has often been highlighted elsewhere in this commentary, a modern reader's encounter with the worldview and attitudes documented in the book of Deuteronomy can be an experience of culture shock. Measured by modern standards of morality, humanity, and decency, Israel's institution of Holy War can only be condemned, for example. In this case, however, ancient Israel's standards condemn the modern world.

In order to recognize the pettiness that characterizes modern culture, one need only to contrast Deuteronomy's exhortation to refrains so often heard today. "Do not deprive even strangers passing by of the hospitality that may sustain them on their journey (Deuteronomy)." "Hey, it's not my problem!" "Go get your own!" "No trespassing!"

Increasing numbers of two-income families, trends toward longer work hours for contract employees, and ballooning percentages of the day spent commuting characterize modern society. Deuteronomy would remind many in modern society not to steal from themselves. Deuteronomy would encourage many to go home, to enjoy the love and companionship of husband or wife, to rear and cherish their children.

Modern equivalents of creditors seizing millstones abound. One need only to examine the marketing strategies of credit card companies or so-called "rent-to-own" businesses. "Pre-approved" credit card applications flood college campus mailboxes with offers to extend credit to those barely of legal age to enter into contracts and with no income other than parental support. These creditors know full well that parents will pay their children's debts rather than see them start adult life with damaged credit. In effect, they hold

Luther on Debtor's Prisons

This law, . . . with the force of a general maxim, teaches that a man's trade, by which he is nourished and sustained, is not to be taken away from him on account of debt. Such is the frenzy among us barbarians that we imprison debtors until they repay the last farthing, or we prohibit their trade and work. He says here that it is enough that he give his soul as a pledge; that is, the whole man is a debtor, and through his trade he must acquire that by which he will repay the debt. It is cruel and unjust, therefore, to halt it, namely, to force him to pay one debt with double indemnity—one, because his mill is idle meantime; the other, by heaping up new debts elsewhere or selling his property to repay.

Martin Luther, *Lectures on Deuteronomy* (Luther's Works 9, ed. J. Pelikan and D. Poellot; St. Louis: Concordia, 1960), 241-42.

---

young adults' futures hostage. "Rent-to-own" companies charge exorbitant rates of interest over the lifetime of a rental contract, gouging those in our society least able to afford. [Luther on Debtor's Prisons]

As Deuteronomy understood it, theft is less about the property stolen and more about the value of life lived well and fully.

NOTES

[1] Rabbinic interpreters (*Sifre, y. Maas.* 2:4; *b. B. Mesia* 87b; contrast *b. B. Mesia* 92a and Josephus, *Ant*. IV.8.21.) sought to limit the applicability of this hospitality provision to hired laborers in one's field at harvest time. They seem to have been motivated by a desire to protect farmers from excessive losses through hospitality. The text itself does not suggest this interpretation. The account of Jesus and his disciples snacking on grain as they pass through a field on the Sabbath (Mark 2:23-28) provides insight into the interpretation of the Deuteronomy passage in Jesus' day. Jesus' critics accost him for working on the Sabbath, not for violating any restriction of this hospitality law to hired laborers.

[2] As Merill (*Deuteronomy*, [NAC 4; Nashville: Broadman & Holman, 1994], 316 n. 217) points out, the section of the law describing the circumstances of the divorce in question (vv. 1-3) comprises the protasis (the "if" statement in an "if-then" logical relation; it states the hypothetical situation, not the point). The law is concerned only with the final pronouncement (v. 4, the apodosis).

[3] Carmichael, *The Laws of Deuteronomy* (Ithaca NY: Cornell University Press, 1974), 204-207. His very original interpretation, namely that Deut 24:1-4 is a midrash on the "endangered ancestress" accounts (Gen 12:10-20; 20; 26), is generally regarded somewhat fanciful.

EXPLICATION OF THE EIGHTH COMMANDMENT: "DO NOT BEAR FALSE WITNESS"

24:8–25:4

Technically, the commandment against bearing false witness deals with a judicial matter—perjury. In typical fashion, however, Deuteronomy situates the case law concerning such judicial impropriety among the expositions of the commandments to honor authority (17:6) and against killing (19:15-21). Deuteronomy thereby demonstrates the interrelationship of the commandments—bearing false witness can be a form of murder—as well as the broad scope of the Decalogue's prescriptions. In similar fashion, then, the explanation of the commandment against bearing false witness turns attention to extra-judicial ways in which, by word or deed, one can damage the reputation of another. By so doing, Deuteronomy asserts that these injuries to another's pride and social status should not be seen as merely rude, but also as violations of the basic honor of a person created in God's image.

Many of the series of eight very brief cases gathered here have parallels elsewhere in the Torah (compare Lev 13–14; Exod 22:26; Lev 19:9, 13; 23:10, 22). They have been arranged in order of the descending social status of the persons susceptible to defamation. This arrangement clearly indicates that all classes of society deserve basic respect. Indeed, the series culminates in admonitions to respect even the foreigner (24:17-22), the criminal (25:1-3), and the laboring ox (25:4)!

COMMENTARY

Respect for the Priest, 24:8-9

The relationship between this encouragement to follow priestly instruction and the commandment against bearing false witness becomes apparent only in light of the injunction (v. 9) to remember the case of Miriam's leprosy recorded in Numbers 12. According to this account, while Israel was encamped at Hazeroth just before Moses sent the spies into the promised land, Miriam and Aaron, Moses' sister and brother, began noising complaints that Moses had married a Cushite woman (Num 12:2). Assuming the woman in question to be Zipporah,[1] whom Moses married well before his call into YHWH's service, the point of their objection is difficult to fathom. Immediately, however, they expressed their true motivation in the jealous, self-serving rhetorical question: "Has YHWH spoken only through Moses? Has he not spoken through us also?" (v. 3). YHWH's response was swift and unambiguous. He summoned the three siblings, appeared to them in the cloud, affirmed Moses special status, and confronted Miriam and Aaron with their audacity (vv. 4-9). Despite Moses' intercession, Miriam was stricken with leprosy and banned from the camp for seven days (vv. 10-15).

Miriam
Giovanni Pisano. 1248–1314. *Miriam, Sister of Moses.* Museo dell'Opera Metropolitana. Siena, Italy.

In view of this background, Deuteronomy 24:8-9 warns against slanderous disrespect for the special status of the levitical priests, Moses' successors. They are to be heeded, their authority honored. Otherwise, YHWH may visit leprosy on the offender against the Levites' reputation just as he did Miriam.

Restrictions on Seizing Collateral, 24:10-13.

Two laws in this series deal with restrictions on seizing collateral for loans (compare Exod 22:25-27). The first involves a loan made to a "neighbor," the second a loan made to a poor person. In both cases, care must be taken not to harm the pride or reputation of the debtor. Under no circumstances is collateral to be seized. To enter the debtor's home and take collateral would be to humiliate him in the eyes of the community and, more importantly, of his family. Instead, the creditor must wait patiently outside for the debtor to produce the collateral, presumably an article of the debtor's choosing (articles essential for sustenance and livelihood have already been excluded as unsuitable for collateral).

Amos on the Mistreatment of the Poor

The 8th-century prophet Amos addressed his message to the northern kingdom well after the division of the monarchy into separate states. His accusations focused primarily on socioeconomic injustices done to the poor in Israel, specifically on violations of the very laws found in Deut 24. Apparently, Amos witnessed with horror and outrage the formation of distinct social classes: wealthy and powerful businessmen and nobles on the one hand, and poor day laborers and those facing economic hardships severe enough to force them to sell themselves or some family member into debt slavery on the other. In situations of such imbalance of power and influence, the wealthy quite easily began to multiply their wealth at the expense of the poor. To make things worse, the wealthy and powerful simply ignored the principles of the covenant—concern for the needy, protection for the underprivileged, and deliverance for the oppressed. A quotation from the book of Amos illustrates the prophet's indignation:

. . . they sell the righteous for silver,
    and the needy for a pair of sandals—
they . . . trample the head of the poor into the dust of the earth
    and push the afflicted out of the way; . . .
they lay themselves down beside every altar
    on garments taken in pledge. . . . (Amos 2:6-7)

If the debtor is poor, he will likely have few belongings other than personal items such as clothing. The garment mentioned (*śalmâ*, v. 13) was the outer garment that often served double-duty as a cloak by day and a blanket by night. It must be returned daily before sunset; otherwise the debtor would be forced to sleep without the basic comfort of warmth. [Amos on the Mistreatment of the Poor]

The point of both provisions is unmistakable: While it may be true that an individual owes an outstanding debt, perhaps even long overdue, the creditor's "right" to his money is of far less significance than the basic respect he owes a fellow human being. To assault human dignity in such a way is to bear false witness. It is to say through one's actions that a person made in God's image is of lesser value than a modest monetary sum, of lesser value than a cloak.

Pay Wages on Time, 24:14-15

The series continues its progression down the ladder of social status and esteem to deal with the case of wages owed a day laborer. In ancient Israelite society, in which one normally earned a living from farming one's inheritance or from practicing one of the few trades, a person who relied on daily wages was in a truly precarious position. It can be assumed that such a person was landless and tradeless. He would have been able to find employment only

A Laborer's Complaint

 The letter quoted below was found at an ancient fortress on the Mediterranean in the region of later Jamnia. It dates to the 7th century.

Let my lord commander hear the case of his servant! As for thy servant, thy servant was harvesting at Hazar-susim. And thy servant was (still) harvesting as they finished the storage of grain, as usual before the Sabbath. While thy servant was finishing the storage of grain with his harvesters, Hoshaiah son of Shobai came and took thy servant's mantle. While I was finishing with my harvesters, this one for no reason took thy servant's mantle. And all my companions will testify on my behalf—those who were harvesting with me in the heat . . . all my companions will testify on my behalf! If I am innocent of gui[lt, let him return] my mantle, and if not, it is (still) the commander's right to take [my case under advisement (?) and to send word] to him [(asking) that he return the] mantle of thy servant. And let not [the plea of his servant] be displeasing to him!

---

seasonally, not unlike seasonal farm workers in modern society. Often a day's wages will have been his only protection against starvation for his family and himself. But employers, both ancient and modern, typically have selfish interests in productivity. They are frequently concerned primarily to assure that, from their perspective, a full day's work has been done. Or, employers may simply have no sense of urgency—whether wages are paid today or tomorrow, so long as they are paid, what is the difference? [A Laborer's Complaint]

In contrast, the Deuteronomic Code (compare Lev 19:13; Mal 3:5) insists that wages be paid at the end of each working day, to Israelite and foreigner workers alike. Otherwise, members of these powerless classes may appeal (Heb. *z'q*, "to cry out," the same verb used of Israel's cry to YHWH from their bondage in Egypt) to their truest ally, YHWH himself. Deuteronomy never wanders far from the revolutionary awareness that, just as he heard the cries of the Israelite slaves in Egypt, Israel's God watches over especially the underprivileged, the disenfranchised, the suffering, and the oppressed. Even through such a seemingly inconsequential oversight as failure to pay wages promptly, an employer risks acting out the role of Pharaoh. The supreme value of human dignity requires the utmost respect and sensitivity.

Guilt by Association a Form of False Witness, 24:16

The attitude expressed by the Hebrew Bible toward intergenerational guilt or responsibility is far from uniform. [Inherited Guilt] Despite texts such as the Decalogue's claim that YHWH's anger toward "those who hate him" persists for three and four generations (Exod 20:5; 34:7; Deut 5:9) and Joshua's account of the execution of guilty Achan along with his presumably

Inherited Guilt

There are difficulties with the common assumption that Israelite thought concerning responsibility developed over time from the pole of hyper-collectivism to a later individualism. Usually, a presumably ancient confession found frequently in the Old Testament (Exod 20:5-6; 34:6-7; Num 14:18; Deut 5:9-10; Jer 32:18; compare Jonah 4:2; Joel 2:12; Pss 11:4; 86:15; 103:8; 145:8; Neh 9:17; 2 Chr 30:9) is regarded as the classical text supporting the notion that ancient Israel expected guilt and punishment to pass from one generation to the next. Recent scholarship has questioned the supposed early date of this confession, however. Furthermore, the confession insists that God's wrath persists for generations "of those who hate [YHWH]," suggesting that the statement concerns persistent wrath in response to persistent rebellion.

It may be significant that the laments in the Psalter and in the book of Lamentations assume that God will punish only the guilty (compare Ps 79:8; Lam 5:7). Relatedly, individual psalmists frequently base their appeals for God's assistance on assertions of their innocence. The innocence of their ancestors never plays such a role. The citation of the sour grapes proverb in Jer 31:29-30 seems to respond to the people's sarcastic claim to a false innocence. The book of Jeremiah focuses on the effort to persuade the people to acknowledge their own guilt and sin—to be sure they have continued a patter of rebelliousness established by their ancestors, but, in the end, they acted on their own.

---

innocent family (Josh 7), the Deuteronomic Code explicitly prohibits executing members of one generation in a family for the crimes of another. In the context of the explication of the commandment against bearing false witness, the point seems to be that the common assumption that the behavior of children manifest something learned in the home—or, conversely that children can be assumed to be tainted with parental flaws—is unwarranted. It "assumes facts not in evidence" and is therefore unjust. To draw a conclusion concerning the character of one generation from the behavior of another is to pass judgment on the basis of the most ambiguous evidence.

Injury to the Self-esteem and Reputation of Society's Most Defenseless, 24:17-22

The progression of thought concerning injury to the reputation or pride of various segments of society reaches the lowliest, certainly the most defenseless, segments of society in a series grouped together around the familiar theme of the disadvantage of foreigners, orphans, and widows (see above; compare Lev 19:9-10; 23:22). The case law here divides neatly into prohibitions against abuse of these individuals (vv. 17-18) and injunctions to provide for their needs in a manner that will allow them to preserve their honor (vv. 19-22). Both the prohibitions and the injunctions conclude with the theologically weighted reminder that Israel itself once occupied the lowliest station in society (vv. 18, 22).

The Widow and the Orphans

Jean-Louis Forain reflects his affinity for social commentary in this lithograph print. Forain captures the dire straits of a widow and her children after a court ruling in late 19th-early 20th century French society. A sense of hopelessness is evoked through the use of silhouette and shape within the dark, oppressive surroundings. Forain is working in a style similar to Daumier and Degas.

Jean-Louis Forain. 1852–1931. *The Widow and the Orphans.* c.1910. Galerie de la Cave. Paris, France.

In the most straightforward terms, Deuteronomy warns against depriving foreigners and orphans of justice. Because the former were not citizens and the latter were minors unprotected by the rights and standing of their deceased parents—that is, because neither had a voice in society—it would have been very easy simply to have overlooked them. But to do so would have been to assume the role of Pharaoh! Similarly, it was not permissible to take as collateral for loans a widow's outer garment. While such collateral was permitted in the case of loans made to the poor (see 24:12-13), widows, who would have had little or no means of support, must be granted even greater protection against creditors. The power imbalance could too easily become a temptation to abuse. Foreigners, orphans, and widows—although disadvantaged—deserve the basic respect due all humanity.

In positive terms, more fortunate Israelites must take active measures to meet the basic physical needs of these segments of society. And they must do so in ways that will not subject the needy to humiliation. Grain, olive tree, and vineyard must not be stripped bare of produce at harvest time. Instead, reasonable portions must be left in the field, on the tree, and on the vine so that foreigners, widows, and orphans may glean the leftovers. Would it not have been easier simply to harvest thoroughly and to *give* a portion to the needy? Perhaps. But the biblical method allows the needy the satisfaction of work. In typical fashion, Deuteronomy not only extends the scope of the commandment against bearing false witness to include prohibitions against damaging the reputation of another, but also incorporates positive injunctions to take actions designed to create conditions in which even the most underprivileged may gain a sense of accomplishment and self-reliance. From Deuteronomy's perspective, the requirement to do no harm does not exhaust the call to do justice. One must actively do good.

Even Criminals Deserve Respect, 25:1-3

Respect for the underprivileged seems nobly humanitarian. But Deuteronomy goes even further. If a person is found guilty of a crime for which the penalty is corporal punishment, care must be taken: (a) that the punishment (flogging in this case) is proportionate to the crime, (b) that the judge who rendered the verdict and passed sentence be physically present for its administration (as an inducement to weigh the decision carefully? See commentary and sidebars on Deut 17:2-13), and (c) that, in any case, the punishment not exceed forty lashes. Perhaps the most striking element

Murder and Devaluing Human Life

Here's . . . how shall I tell you?—A theory of a sort, the same one by which I, for instance, consider that a single misdeed is permissible if the principal aim is right, a solitary wrongdoing and hundreds of good deeds! It's galling too, of course, for a young man of gifts and overwhelming pride to know that if he had, for instance, a paltry three thousand, his whole career, his whole future would be differently shaped and yet not to have that three thousand. Add to that, nervous irritability from hunger, from lodging in a hole, from rags, from a vivid sense of the charm of his social position and his sister's and mother's position, too. Above all, vanity, pride and vanity, though goodness knows he may have good qualities too. . . . I am not blaming him, please don't think it; besides, it's not my business. A special little theory came in too—a theory of a sort—dividing mankind, you see, into material and superior persons, that is persons to whom the law does not apply owing to their superiority, who make laws for the rest of mankind, the material, that is. It's all right as a theory, *une theorie comme une autre*. Napoleon attracted him tremendously, that is, what effected him was that a great many men of genius have not hesitated at wrongdoing, but have overstepped the law without thinking about it.

F. Dostoevsky, *Crime and Punishment*, trans. C. Garnett (New York: Bantam Books, 1971), 423.

of this case law, and certainly its point, concerns the rationale for these precautions. One might expect them to be for the criminal's benefit—a humanitarian gesture. Instead, however, Deuteronomy specifies that they are so that the criminal may not be degraded in the eyes of the community (literally, "so that your brother not be held lightly [*niqlâ*] in your eyes"). The concern is to protect the community from the very human tendency to devalue wrongdoers, to see them as somewhat less than human beings, as animals or monsters who deserve to suffer. Even criminals are fellow human beings ("*your brother*") who bear God's image! [Murder and Devaluing Human Life]

Even Animals Deserve Respect, 24:4

As if to make the point unmistakable, the Deuteronomic Code concludes this exposition on the commandment against bearing false witness with a brief law concerning respect for the ox threshing grain. The situation is clear: Draft animals were regularly used to pull threshing sledges over the newly harvested grain spread out on the threshing floor. Typically, they were tethered so that they repeatedly circled the area. Decency demands that they be permitted to graze on the grain as they worked. This is common sense. The point, however, lies in the association of this law with the Decalogue. In Deuteronomy's view, YHWH's covenant with Israel encompasses the entire created order in some way. Israel's respect for life and living things must extend to all levels of society and beyond to incorporate even the ox! [Paul on the Muzzled Ox]

Paul on the Muzzled Ox

In 1 Cor 9:8-11, the apostle Paul appeals to the Deuteronomic law against muzzling a threshing ox in support of his argument that the church should meet the physical needs of its ministers. Paul utilizes a common technique of rabbinic biblical interpretation, the argument from the lesser to the greater (Latin—*a minore ad majus*; Heb., *qal wahomer*). If God intends, as the law explicitly states, that laboring oxen be permitted a share in the product of their labors, how much more will God be concerned for the well-being of a human being laboring in the kingdom of God? While, at first glance, this application of the text may seem somewhat far-fetched, readers familiar with the principles of interpretation manifest in the book of Deuteronomy itself will likely recognize in Paul a kinship to the Deuteronomic editors on this point. Like Paul, they were interested in extrapolating the full significance of the canonical tradition and extending its authority into virtually every area of life.

CONNECTIONS

This section is a parade example of Deuteronomy's interpretation of the covenant tradition. It demonstrates Deuteronomy's characteristically creative yet tradition-faithful extrapolation of the full implications of the covenant's basic principles. In so doing, it models a very fruitful approach available to subsequent generations of those who would remain true to their roots in tradition, to the fixed canon of Scripture as source for faith, yet who face situations not directly envisioned in the fixed tradition. The commentary above pointed out the organizing principle involving descent down the ladder of social status. It is also possible to read the entire section as a subtly framed argument concerning the vital importance of respect for others as key to the health of the covenant people as a community . . . and as individuals. The argument may be paraphrased as follows:

The commandment underlying this section deals with telling lies in court. Deuteronomy has already argued that in some cases perjury can be a very insidious form of murder. In all cases, it is a cowardly attack on the well-being of an innocent human being.

Now Deuteronomy extends that principle to include respect for both the person and the work of those responsible for mediating the teachings of the covenant itself. Seen against the background of Numbers 12, such disrespect involves a degree of disdain for the covenant God! To be sure, it does not subject the priest to physical danger, but it does put at risk the trust necessary for leaders to lead and people to follow. It endangers the covenant community.

The principle also applies, however, to acts that fall short of outright attacks on leaders, those members of the community who deserve respect by virtue of status and role. It is entirely possible to act on one's rights in such a way as to incidentally diminish the reputation, social standing, and self-respect of individuals from any and all social ranks. Regardless of intent, regardless of rights, the damage done is real and must be avoided. Not only is taking human life a violation of the moral order woven into creation, but the value of human beings, created in the image of God, is so great that any diminishment of or disregard for that value is but a degree of murder.

In fact, the dignity inherent in humanity's God-given godlikeness carries such significance that it is insufficiently respectful merely to avoid damaging it. Instead, whenever possible, one must undertake extraordinary measures to enhance the dignity of a fellow human being. One must not forsake the opportunity to do good. Supporting and nurturing the godlike dignity of a fellow human being is itself a divine act.

The alternative to the active exercise and encouragement of this basic respect for the dignity of another human being becomes the focus of the case law dealing with the punishment of the criminal. Deuteronomy warns that, if Israel allows itself to lose sight of the fact that even the criminal is created in the image of God, it runs the risk of suffering harm to its own well-being. Virtually all of the horrors of torture, mass murder, and genocide known to the modern world began at the moment when a person or group of people looked upon someone else as less than fully human. The Nazis were able coldly and efficiently to execute millions of Jews, Slavs, Gypsies, homosexuals, and intellectuals not because of hatred or passion, but because they had come to see these children of God as less than fully human, as substandard, as "degraded in their eyes." Cain slew Able in anger—the murder was no less real or abhorrent. But to disdain the worth of another human being—surely this is an even greater sacrilege!

Finally, Deuteronomy offers the law on the threshing ox as a reminder that the respect owed *human* life is but the most advanced form of the respect owed all of God's good creation. God breathed the breath of life even into the oxen. God created and pronounced everything God created good. Human beings have no right to disrespect even the lowliest of God's creatures. We are but part of God's world.

NOTE

[1] The term "Cushite" may include Midianites and other Arab tribes; see Hab 3:7.

EXPLICATION OF THE NINTH COMMANDMENT: "DO NOT COVET YOUR NEIGHBOR'S WIFE"

25:5-12

As the Deuteronomic Code draws to a conclusion, the sections devoted to explications of individual commandments in the Decalogue become quite brief and the interpretive principles underlying the choice and arrangement of materials become somewhat esoteric. Since, for Deuteronomy, exclusive allegiance to YHWH is the supreme commandment and since, consequently, the materials explicating the first commandment also deal with the prohibition against idolatry, considered in some traditions the second commandment, it can be assumed that the Deuteronomic Code considered the commandments against coveting the wife of one's neighbor and against coveting anything else belonging to one's neighbor to be distinct from one another—comprising the ninth and tenth commandments.

The hermeneutical principle underlying this section, which treats only two cases, differs from the principle evident in much of the Deuteronomic Code in that the cases treated here involve an *exception* to the Decalogue's prohibition (Deut 25:5-10, levirate marriage) and, oddly, a *restriction* to the exception (Deut 25:11-12, limits on a wife's right to defend her husband). Both cases understand reproductive rights to be the key issue addressed by the commandment against coveting another man's wife.

COMMENTARY

Levirate Marriage, 25:5-10

The Hebrew Bible mentions the ancient custom of "levirate marriage" (from the Latin *levir*, "brother") only here, in Genesis 38 (the

Boaz, the levir?

AΩ For scholars hungry to study examples of the law promulgated in Deut 25, the situation described in the book of Ruth bears tantalizing similarities to the institution of levirate marriage. In the final analysis, however, the near parallel only highlights gaps in scholarly understanding of ancient Israel's levirate institution. Several issues attract scholarly attention. First, the Deuteronomic legislation makes no mention of relatives other than the deceased husband's brother who are subject to the levirate obligation; neither Boaz nor the other unnamed kinsman is Ruth's brother-in-law. Second, while responsibility for the "redemption" of lands in danger of being lost to the family, a circumstance treated in Lev 25:25, falls to the "next-of-kin" (Heb. *gō'ēl*), no Old Testament legislation connects the two institutions of levir and kinsman-redeemer. In contrast, the negotiations between Boaz and the unnamed nearer kinsman recorded in Ruth 4 treat the parcel of unclaimed land and marriage to/responsibility for Ruth as though the two were inseparably linked: in order to acquire the land, one must marry Ruth. Third, the Deuteronomic Code attaches stigma to the refusal to fulfill the levirate obligation (in Gen 38, YHWH enforces the obligation with the death penalty!); the unnamed nearer kinsman in Ruth 4 suffers no such disgrace.

Given the dissimilarities between the situation described in Ruth and the details of the Deuteronomic legislation, and in the context of the emphasis in the book of Ruth on loyalty exceeding the requirements of law and custom, the fact that Boaz is not, in fact, subject to the levirate requirement may well be the point of the account in Ruth 4. Although, technically, he is not the levir, and despite the fact that another relative stands closer in the family lineage, Boaz exceeds all expectation in order to "spread his cloak" (Ruth 3:9) of protection and blessing over Ruth *and* Naomi (Ruth 4:14-17). In the end, all three of the major characters of Ruth—Naomi, Ruth, and Boaz—prove exemplary models of loyalty and mercy far exceeding mere requirement.

---

episode involving Judah's daughter-in-law, Tamar), and, perhaps, in the book of Ruth. [Boaz, the levir?] On its face, the institution, in which the brother of a man who died without heir is expected to marry his sister-in-law so that his dead brother may, in a legal fiction, acquire an heir posthumously, seems to be in direct violation of laws against incest and, in a peculiar fashion, the commandment against coveting another's wife. As practiced also in many other cultures that place supreme value on the continuity of the clan and family and the preservation of family estates, however, the noble purposes of the Hebrew institution effectively outweigh the negatives of incest and covetousness. The text states two important reasons for the practice, to which can be added a third on the basis of an understanding of the place of women in ancient Israelite society. First, since the earliest periods of ancient Israelite religion knew of no well-developed concept of afterlife, the possibility that one could die without an heir to perpetuate one's name and memory was a fate to be avoided at all costs (compare 2 Sam 18:18; Isa 56:5 and the Ugaritic tale of Aqhat). Second, given Israel's systems of inalienable real estate and, at least in the earliest period, of the exclusively male rights of inheritance,[1] death without heir presented a particularly thorny problem with respect to the

Joseph and the Wife of Potiphar

The Joseph story relates an instance of the inverse of the commandment against coveting one's neighbor's wife: Potiphar's unnamed wife coveted Joseph—much to Joseph's danger.

Guido Reni. 1575–1642. *Joseph and the Wife of Potiphar.* Coll. Leicester, Holkham Hall. Norfolk, Great Britain.

family lands. Third, in a culture in which women had little or independent legal or economic status—a woman began life under her father's authority and protection, passed into her husband's sphere of control, and eventually to her son(s)—a widow with no son was truly in limbo, with no man to provide for her. The institution of levirate marriage resolved all these problems at once.

The Deuteronomic treatment of levirate marriage consists of more than an outline of its purpose and practice, however. It deals more specifically with the troublesome case of a brother-in-law unwilling to fulfill his obligation. The reasons for the levir's hesitancy are not stated, although, judging from the near-parallel in the

The Sandal Ritual

The symbolism of the removal of the recalcitrant levir's sandal escapes modern readers and puzzles scholars. Several explanations have been offered on the basis of parallels in the ANE and among modern Arabs. On the basis of legal documents concerning land transactions in ancient Nuzi, some have argued that the sandal represents payment in certain types of business transactions. In reference to the levirate, in this understanding, the sandal would represent the bride price returned to the widow. Also on the basis of the Nuzi texts, others have suggested that according to ancient custom one took possession of land by walking on it (compare Ps 40:8). In this view, the sandal would symbolize this act of taking possession, now applied to taking possession of the widow as wife. Jewish tradition, perhaps on the basis of Ezek 24:17, regarded the removal of the sandal as an act of mourning, in this case, mourning for the deceased husband who will now presumably go childless.

A major shortcoming of all these explanations involves the fact that none of them have to do expressly with marriage or progeny, the major concerns of the levirate institution. In contrast, a practice also involving the removal of the sandal common even in modern times among Arabs may shed light. An Arab may divorce his wife by removing his sandal and announcing, "She was my slipper, I have cast her off." L. Levy explains this practice in terms of the widespread folk imagery of the foot as an erotic male symbol and the shoe as the female counterpart ("Die Shuhsymbolik im jüdischen Ritus," *MGWJ* 62 [1918]: 182-83). This background seems best suited to the rite described in Deuteronomy 25. It explains both the stigma attached to the removal of the sandal and the act of spitting in the face associated with it. In effect, the woman withdraws her womb from the unwilling levir and rejects his seed. In a patriarchal society such as ancient Israel, such humiliation would have been indeed stigmatizing (for more on this problem, see C. Carmichael, "A Ceremonial Crux: Removing a Man's Sandal as a Female Gesture of Contempt," *JBL* 96 [1977]: 321-36).

book of Ruth, economic factors will have sometimes motivated such reluctance. The brother-in-law would have assumed financial responsibility for his brother's wife and "son" only to see his paternal estate further subdivided as a result. It would be to his advantage, and to his children's, if his brother's portion should go unclaimed and be divided equally among the remaining heirs. At any rate, the text makes it clear that, although the brother-in-law is expected to perform his duty as levir, there is no mechanism for forcing him to do so. Such a refusal, however, is tantamount in Deuteronomy's view to an attack on his deceased brother's memory and heritage: it must be severely reprimanded! To that end, the widow may impugn his honor by calling him before the assembled elders of the community, charging him with dishonoring his brother's memory, removing the sandal from his foot—apparently a ritual act of divorce [The Sandal Ritual]—and humiliating him further by spitting in his face. He and his household will henceforth be known for this ignominy.

Limits on the Sister-in-Law's Right to Defend her Husband, 25:11-12

Both the particulars of the case of the wife who defends her husband by grasping the genitals of his attacker and its placement in this context seem somewhat absurd. First, it can hardly be imagined that the situation described occurred often enough to have presented a real problem for Israelite society: If a man fights with his brother, the wife of one should not seize her husband's attacker by the genitals. The penalty for such behavior is the loss of her hand! Does the case intend to discourage brazenness? Is there some relationship between this case and the preceding? How does it relate to the commandment against coveting?

The key to resolving this question may lie in the identification of the protagonists as "a man and his brother." This phrase may refer merely to any Israelite and any fellow Israelite. In context, however, it may indicate that the actors in this case are identical to those in the levirate regulation: a man, not yet deceased, but under attack from his brother, his wife, and her brother-in-law. In the previous case, the wife/widow is empowered to defend her deceased husband's honor and heritage, even to the extent of symbolically attacking her brother-in-law's ability to procreate (regarding the significance of the sandal in this respect, see [The Sandal Ritual]). The present case, however, seems concerned that the woman may deduce that she is within her rights actually to attack her brother-in-law even while her husband still lives. Instead, the case law makes clear that the institution of levirate marriage is a special case of the most unique sort. She may not seek to damage her brother-in-law while her husband still lives. In fact, since the nature of her attack may result in her brother-in-law's infertility, it could have the effect of rendering him unsuitable as a levir should that situation arise in the future. Ironically, her attack on her brother-in-law could harm her husband's chances to perpetuate his name!

CONNECTIONS

There are no clear analogies in modern Western culture to either levirate marriage or the circumstances and ideals surrounding the institution. As a second step in interpreting this passage, after a close reading of the text itself, it may well be important actively to exercise one's historical imagination in the effort to gain some sense of the urgency of the situation for those involved, especially for the widow. Two texts elsewhere in Scripture can be helpful in this regard. Genesis 38 narrates events that transpired between Judah and his daughter-in-law Tamar. Following a chain of occurrences that left her in a state of legal limbo—still under Judah's authority and therefore unable to marry outside Judah's family, banished without husband, heir, or status to wait in her father's household—Tamar made a way out of her distress. The account celebrates Tamar's desperate cunning and courage and illustrates the high stakes involved for such a widow in the ancient world.

The book of Ruth tells the story of not one, but three widows, a mother and her two daughters-in-law, trapped by circumstance in poverty and despair. The heroine, Ruth, a Moabitess, returns to Bethlehem with her mother-in-law, Naomi, in a free act of supreme devotion. There, Ruth's faithfulness as demonstrated in the fields where she gleans grain, the only livelihood available to the two widows, finds its counterpart in Boaz's grace. Although, technically, he is not under obligation as the levir, moved by Ruth's voluntary faithfulness to Naomi, Boaz not only opens his fields for Ruth to glean, but he manipulates events such that he may fulfill the roles of levir and *gō'ēl* ("kinsman-redeemer") for Ruth, and thus for Naomi. [African Women's Readings of Ruth]

The stakes were indeed high for such women in danger of falling between the cracks in Israel's system of family law and inheritance. As a third step in interpreting these regulations, a modern reader, acknowledging that present-day social and family structures differ significantly from those of ancient Israel, can seek to identify analogous circumstances in modern society. Where are the cracks in our system through which groups or individuals may fall? Where are the stakes for survival this high? Although it is not possible here to engage in full-scale, in-depth social analysis, a number of groups in danger of being overlooked by the system or trapped between competing structures may be readily identified. Foremost among

---

African Women's Readings of Ruth

Western women have often critiqued the cultures of ancient Palestine for making women powerless when not attached to male relatives such as fathers, brothers, uncles, and husbands. Thus within this framework of modern Western cultures, the stories in the book of Ruth are matters of ancient Palestine and, at best, something can be learned from them. Otherwise, they are read in the past tense; those stories existed in the good old Bible and now those issues are no longer burning for the lives of communities today. . . .

Africans read Ruth through their cultural lenses in the context where famine, refugee status, tribal/ethnic loyalties, levirate marriages, and polygamy are not practices of ancient Palestine but of today's normal African realities. African women, in reading the Bible, confront biblical cultures . . . closer to their own. . . .

For generations, African women have gone along with cultural prescriptions that are strictly guarded by the fear of breaking taboos. For example, childless women have been despised and marginalized by society, and widows have been obliged to yield to relatives of the dead husbands to determine their status and future. Other issues also show the problems of women's powerlessness and vulnerability in the face of cultural prescriptions. . . .

Using their lives as examples, African women ask, "How can cultural practices which do not give women a possibility to experience new life as Christian church women be used as a basis for theology?" African women are asking something new. . . .

Musimbi R. A. Kanyoro, "Biblical Hermeneutics: Ancient Palestine and the Contemporary World," *Review and Expositor* 94 (1997): 367-78.

them, of course, are children who depend on adults to create safe, nurturing, secure environments in which to mature much as women in ancient Israel depended on the men in their lives. Children do not choose their parents, or the socioeconomic conditions into which they are born, or the crime levels of the neighborhoods in which they live. Children are not at fault when they have no medical insurance, little encouragement to perform well in school, and precious little hope for social and economic futures. So far at least, society has found few successful means to encourage many of the adults responsible for children to do the right thing. Many, many children today need champions like Boaz.

NOTE

[1] Texts in Numbers (36:1-12) and Joshua (17:3-6) suggest that Israel soon came to realize the impracticability of excluding daughters as heirs in at least some cases.

EXPLICATION OF THE TENTH COMMANDMENT: "DO NOT COVET ANYTHING BELONGING TO YOUR NEIGHBOR"

25:13–26:15

As in the previous explication of the ninth commandment, this section dealing with the commandment against coveting another's property exhibits a number of the peculiarities of Deuteronomic interpretation. First, all but the final two commandments of the Decalogue deal with observable actions—killing, stealing, etc. As a consequence, Deuteronomy often explicates these commandments by examining the intentions underlying such actions and including them within the purview of the commandment. In this instance, "coveting" falls in the realm of subjective—and therefore unobservable—intention. As a result, Deuteronomy explicates the meaning of the commandment against coveting in terms of *actions* that arise from and betray covetousness. ["Abel"]

Second, as is again typical of Deuteronomy, the juxtaposition of three at first apparently unrelated cases illustrates the scope of the tenth commandment in human affairs. In essence, Deuteronomy understands the commandment to be a warning against "taking advantage" of others through dishonesty (25:13-16), or in moments when they are weak (25:17-19). The final subsection dealing with offerings of first fruits (26:1-11) and the so-called "second" or "poor tithe" (26:12-15) transpose the negative prohibition against wanting the property of others and utilizing opportunities to acquire it into a positive injunction of liberality in giving to the needy.

Abel

Covetousness cannot be observed. But as early as the story of the first fratricide, the Bible demonstrates that intention almost inexorably gives rise to action.

Lionello Spada. 1576–1622. *The Killing of Abel.* Museo Nazionale di Capodimonte. Naples, Italy.

COMMENTARY

Commercial Honesty, 25:13-16

This unit on just measures divides, characteristically, into two subsections: a statement of the case proper (vv. 13-15a) and the rationale for the regulation (vv. 15b-16). In turn, these subsections have two components each, arranged chiastically (negative-positive/positive-negative): (1) a prohibition against false measures (negative) and the inverse injunction to possess only just measures (positive); and (2) the familiar promise of long life in the land to those who observe this law (positive) and the inverse warning that dishonesty is abhorrent to YHWH (negative).

The issue addressed in this unit is straightforward and requires little comment: two sets of measures, one for weight and another for volume, would permit their owner to buy more for less and sell less for more. Significantly, however, the Deuteronomic legislation deals only with the possession of a double set of measures, not with their use. In relation to the commandment against coveting, Deuteronomy suggests that the mere possession of such false measures indicates covetousness—that is, the intention to defraud, which is in itself abhorrent.

A Historical Example, 25:17-19

According to biblical tradition (Exod 17:8-15), Israel's well-attested (Num 24:20; 1 Sam 15:7-8; 27:8; 30:1-20; 1 Chr 4:41-43; Esth 3:1) animosity toward the Amalekites, a tribe of desert raiders at home in the region around Kadesh (Gen 14:7; Num 13:29; 14:25), was born during the period immediately following the exodus, before Israel had reached Mt. Horeb. According to the Exodus account, while Israel was encamped at Rephidim, the Amalekites attacked, were defeated only by means of Moses' extraordinary intercession, and were subsequently placed under the ban as enemies, not only of Israel, but also of YHWH (Exod 17:14-15; see commentary and sidebars on Deut 2:26–3:22; 13:12-18; 20:1-20). Exodus mentions neither the Amalekites' motivation for their attack nor the reason Israel reacted so strongly. Deuteronomy 25:17-19 does not retell the story, assuming familiarity with the tradition recorded in the Exodus account. Instead, it supplies precisely the information concerning motivation and rationale missing in its predecessor. The Amalekites *took advantage* of Israel's weakness! So soon after the escape from Egypt and the crossing of the Reed Sea, and during a period of severe hardship (see Exod 17:1-7), Israel was "faint and weary (*ʿāyēp wĕyāgēaʿ*)" and many who "lagged behind" (Deut 25:18) made easy prey.

By juxtaposing this reminder of the Amalekites' ruthlessness with the legislation against false measures—both are examples of taking advantage of another's weakness—the Deuteronomic editor(s) establish a link between covetousness and predatory behavior and set the stage for the strongest possible contrast between such

Tithes and Offerings

ΑΩ The tithes and offerings described in the book of Deuteronomy cannot be easily incorporated together with those called for in Leviticus and Numbers into a single, coherent system. Leviticus and Numbers mention a "heave-offering" (*tĕrûmâ*; Num 18:8-12), tithes (*ma'ăśer*; Lev 27:30-33; Num 18:21-24), and first fruits (*bikkûrîm*; Lev 2:14; 23:17-20; Num 18:13), whereas Deuteronomy refers to tithes (*ma'ăśer*; Deut 12:6-17; 14:22-29; 26:12) and first fruits (*rē'šît*; Deut 26:2, 10). Furthermore, while Leviticus and Numbers reserve the *tĕrûmâ* exclusively for the priests and the tithes for the Levites, Deuteronomy knows of no offering designated specifically for the priesthood. In fact, Deuteronomy requires the offerer to consume the tithe himself, along with his family and the needy (including, but not limited to, the Levites). Finally, Leviticus and Numbers consider the various tithes sacred in the strictest sense, while Deuteronomy attributes to them principally humanitarian character.

Several suggestions have been made in attempts to account for this dissonance. Jewish tradition assumed that Leviticus, Numbers, and Deuteronomy refer to four or five distinct offerings: (1) first fruits (see tractate *Bik.* of the Mishnah and the Talmuds); (2) *tĕrûmâ*, given to the priests (see tractate *Terumoth*); (3) the so-called "first tithe," given to the Levites (see tractate *Ma'aserot*); (4) the so-called "second tithe," consumed by the offerer in Jerusalem in all but the third and sixth years (see tractate *Ma'aser Sheni*); and (5) the so-called "poor tithe," shared with the unfortunate of the offerer's community in the third and sixth years.

Since, however, the Scriptures themselves do not indicate the relationship of these offerings to one another (Why, for example, should the tithe given the priests come first?), and since it is unlikely that Israelites made a triple or even quadruple offering, modern scholars offer other solutions. They argue that Leviticus and Numbers, on the one hand, and Deuteronomy, on the other, record the varied practices of different time periods, of different geographical regions (Deuteronomy—Northern; Leviticus and Numbers—Jerusalemite), or of different schools of thought (Deuteronomy—wise men or country Levites; Leviticus and Numbers—Jerusalem priesthood).

---

actions and the truly charitable behavior enjoined in the subsequent section.

Three Confessions to Accompany Tithes and Offerings, 26:1-15

While at first glance this passage seems to focus on rules for bringing offerings of *first fruits* and *tithes* [Tithes and Offerings], closer inspection reveals that it is principally concerned with the confessions of faith appropriate on such occasions. In the place of detailed procedural matters [Details of the Rite of First Fruits], this passage focuses on the meaning and significance of the offerings of first fruits and tithes. The confessions modeled here clearly point to several distinctive features of the theology of the book of Deuteronomy, especially in relation to the *positive* implications of the commandment against coveting. Theologically, Israelites must respond to God's bounteous provision in *celebration* and *thankful generosity*.

Details of the Rite of First Fruits

Deut 26 offers very few stipulations as to what should be offered, when, or how. The text (v. 2) instructs the Israelite to bring some of the "first" or "best" (the Hebrew term here can mean either) produce of the harvest season. It specifies neither a date nor an amount for this offering. Farmers would not likely be eager to leave their fields and orchards when they begin bearing to make a long journey to Jerusalem, however. So "best" may be preferable. The reference to a single basket suggests that the text envisions a token amount. On the other hand, the injunction that concludes the first major section in the passage (v. 11) calls on the worshiper to "rejoice" in YHWH's gracious good gifts together with his entire household, the Levites, and the sojourners. The same groups are mentioned in vv. 12-13 in the context of a celebratory meal. One basket would be insufficient for such a thanksgiving feast. The text does not specify the types of produce appropriate for the offering of the first fruits. Similarly, the second major section in this passage (vv. 12-15) does not outline the procedure associated with the third-year tithe, but presumes it (v. 12). Other texts (Deut 12:1-28; 14:22-29; 15:19-23; 18:1-8) deal with these questions in greater detail.

Three times this passage instructs the reader to make declarations "to YHWH" (v. 3) or "before him" (vv. 5, 13). Two of these statements are to be made when the worshiper brings the first fruits to the central sanctuary (vv. 3, 5-10), and the third when the worshiper offers the tithe in the third (and presumably sixth) year(s) of the seven-year Sabbath cycle, the so-called "tithe for the poor" (see Deut 14:22-29).

Some scholars have noted the redundant declarations associated with the first fruits as well as the apparent inconsistency between v. 4—where the priest takes the basket of first fruits from the worshiper and sets it before the altar of YHWH after the first declaration—and v. 10—where the worshiper himself places the basket "before YHWH" after the second confession. These observations may suggest that the passage has undergone editorial expansion, especially in the second, lengthier confession. An earlier form may have consisted essentially of vv. 5b and 10a or vv. 3b and 10a: "A wandering Aramaean was my father. . . . And, now, I bring the first fruits" or "I declare this day that I have entered the land which YHWH . . . swore to give us. . . . And now, I bring the first fruits." The historical summary [A Wandering Aramaean] in vv. 5b-9 (except for the phrase "A wandering Aramaean," which is unique) employs language commonly used in the Hebrew Bible to describe the exodus from Egypt. It may have been included here to amplify the statement in v. 3b of v. 5b and to provide a more complete expression of the Israelite worshiper's gratitude to God. In any case, the key element is the linkage between YHWH's historical provision for Israel continued in agricultural bounty in the present and

A Wandering Aramaean

Deut 26:5-9 is perhaps the most prominent example of the so-called "brief historical credo," a literary genre found throughout the Hebrew Bible (see Deut 6:20-24; Josh 24:2b-13; etc.). In 1938 Gerhard von Rad published a very influential study of Deuteronomy (available in English as "The Form-Critical Problem of the Hexateuch," in *The Problem of the Hexateuch and Other Essays* [New York: McGraw-Hill, 1966], 1-78) that focused scholarly attention on the character and significance of these confessions. Von Rad argued that these brief statements of faith are very old, dating to the period shortly after the conquest, that they originated in Israel's worship life, and that the absence of any reference to Mt. Sinai and the Sinai covenant is significant for understanding the history of Pentateuchal traditions. In essence, von Rad argued that, when committed to writing, these brief confessions, which were originally recited in various local sanctuaries, became the nucleus around which grew the complete traditions now contained in the Torah. Furthermore, he concluded that the fact that the brief creeds do not mention Sinai suggests that, at an early stage in the growth of the tradition, the traditions concerning entry into the land on the one hand, and the Sinai covenant on the other, were unrelated.

Since von Rad's provocative suggestion, scholars have submitted it to rigorous analysis and discredited his claims. First, analysis of the phraseology of Deut 26:5-9, for example, shows that it consists of a composite of stock clauses and phrases used throughout the Hebrew Bible in relation to the patriarchs, the exodus, and the entry into Canaan ("go down to Egypt," Gen 12:10; "great and mighty people," Gen 18:18; "strong hand," Exod 3:19-20; 6:1; "signs and wonders," Deut 6:22; 29:2; 34:11; cf. Exod 4:8-9, 17, 21, 28, 30; 8:19; 10:1-2; "he brought us to this place," Deut 1:31; 9:7; 11:5; 29:6; cf. Exod 3:8; 23:20; Num 10:29). Second, since the brief credos seem to be literary constructions, they probably do not reflect ancient oral liturgical traditions after all. Finally, for the same reason, the omission of any reference to Sinai cannot be understood as evidence that the Sinai tradition was originally distinct.

J. I. Durham, "Credo, Ancient Israelite," *IDB* Supplement, 197-99.

H. Huffmon, "The Exodus, Sinai and the Credo," *CBQ* 27 (1965): 101-13.

A. D. H. Mayes, *Deuteronomy* (NCBC; Grand Rapids: Eerdmans, 1987), 332-35.

J. Muilenburg, "Form Criticism and Beyond," *JBL* 87 (1969): 1-18.

J. A. Thompson, *Deuteronomy: An Introduction and Commentary* (Tyndale Old Testament Commentaries; London: Inter-Varsity Press, 1974), 254-57.

G. von Rad, *Deuteronomy: A Commentary* (OTL; Philadelphia: Westminster Press, 1966), 157-61.

the worshiper's thankfulness celebrated by extending the blessings he has enjoyed to include the less fortunate in Israel.

The First Declaration: God's Promise Fulfilled, 26:3

The harvest of the season's first produce represents an opportunity to remember that the land that sustains is God's good and gracious gift. The land was essential for Israel's existence, just as a dwelling place and farmland are essential today for human life.

Although on its face, the text may seem to call for only the first generation of those to live in the promised land to offer first fruits and to make these accompanying declarations and confessions (v. 1), the procedure is described in such a way as to suggest that it has in view an annual rite. Jewish tradition [A Version of the First Fruits Confession from the Time of Jesus] certainly understood the offering and

A Version of the First Fruits Confession from the Time of Jesus

Philo of Alexandria (20 BC–AD 50) was an important Jewish philosopher who wrote in Greek an extensive body of apologetic works intended to portray Judaism and Jewish traditions in a light favorable to the Hellenistic world. The following version of the confession in Deut 26:5-9 appears in Philo's *De Specialibus Legibus II* xxxv:217-19:

> The leaders of our nation renounced Syria, and migrated to Egypt. Being but few in number, they increased till they became a populous nation. Their descendants being oppressed in innumerable ways by the natives of the land, when no assistance did any longer appear to be expected from men, became the supplicants of God, having fled for refuge to entreat his assistance. Therefore he, who is merciful to all who are unjustly treated, having received their supplication smote those who oppressed them with signs and wonders, and prodigies, and with all the marvellous [sic] works which he wrought at that time. And he delivered those who were being insulted and enduring every kind of perfidious oppression, not only leading them forth to freedom, but even giving them in addition a most fertile land; for it is from the fruits of this land, O bounteous God! That we now bring you the first fruits, if indeed it is a proper expression to say that he who receives them from you brings them to you. For, O Master! They are all your favours [sic] and your gifts, of which you have thought us worthy, and so enabled us to live comfortably and to rejoice in unexpected blessings which thou has given to us, who did not expect them.

The Works of Philo: Complete and Unabridged, trans. C. D. Yonge (Peabody MA: Hendrickson, 1993), 588-89.

---

the declarations and confessions to be annual requirements (see Tob 1:7; Josephus, *Ant* IV:8:22; Philo, *Spec* II., xxiv:215; as long as the temple stands so that there is an altar to receive the offering, *Bik* 2:3).

The first, very short declaration remarkably conveys the immediacy of ancient Israel's faith. Centuries before Moses and Joshua, God had promised faithful Abraham that, although he would never himself see the fulfillment of the promise, the great nation descended from him would one day take possession of his heritage (Gen 15:13-16). And now, centuries later, the individual Israelite farmer, a child of Abraham, is to make the bold declaration that he has come into his inheritance thanks to YHWH's faithfulness to his promise to Abraham. At Kadesh-Barnea, the people had refused to enter the promised land for fear of the Canaanites and were punished with forty years of wandering in the wilderness (Num 13:1–14:45; Deut 1:19-46). Given this history of Israel's hesitancy to take possession of the gift God gives, the statement "I have entered the land" takes on deep significance. This worshiper has personally experienced the fulfillment of YHWH's promise.

The Second Declaration: Israel Is One People Throughout Its Generations, 26:5-10

The second declaration unfolds the historical dimension of Israel's faith. Within the space of five short verses, this confession summarizes much of Israel's story from the patriarchs to the entry into the promised land. "Wandering Aramean" (v. 5) probably refers to Jacob, who journeyed back to Haran in Aram (modern Syria) to make his fortune and begin his family. The references to "going down to Egypt" and "a great and mighty nation" (v. 5) recall portions of the story of Abraham (Gen 12:10; 18:18), however, suggesting the whole narrative of the patriarchs with great economy of terms. The account of the slavery of the Hebrews in Egypt (Exod 1) is summarized in a single verse (v. 6), as are the references to the Hebrews' pleas for deliverance (v. 7), God's saving response (v. 8), and the journey to Canaan (v. 9). None of the details recorded in Genesis–Numbers appear in this summary. It is history reduced to the essentials: God blesses his people; they experience hardship and cry out in their pain; because God, faithful to his promise to the patriarchs, continues to care for their children, he hears their cries and delivers them; he brings his promise to completion by leading the people to the promised land. This history of YHWH's faithful dealings with Israel is the key to its faith in later times.

A striking feature of this and other such historical summaries in the Hebrew Bible is the consistent use of the first person plural pronouns "we" and "us." Through these pronouns, the speakers of these confessions identify themselves with the whole prior history of the people of Israel. In the speakers' view, the Egyptians did not merely oppress their ancestors. They maintain, instead, that the Egyptians "treated *us* harshly, and afflicted *us*, and laid upon *us* hard servitude" (v. 6). Similarly, they recall (vv. 7-8) that, "*We* cried to God; he heard *us* and saw *our* need; he delivered *us*, brought *us* here, and gave *us* this land," fulfilling his promise made for *us* to *our* forefathers (see v. 15). This sense of identity with the whole history of Israel's experience of YHWH's saving acts motivates the concluding statement. Here the speakers shift from historical résumé to a personal perspective and, "in a splendid foreshortening of time,"[1] take their places in the history of salvation: "And now, behold, I bring the first fruits of the ground which you, O YHWH, have given *me*."

This emphasis upon the direct link between the current generation and its predecessors constitutes a key element in the message of Deuteronomy, indeed of the Hebrew Bible. "Israel" is a multigenerational community. When YHWH called Abraham, he called all future generations. When the current generation enjoys the fruits of the land YHWH has given, it does so because YHWH has been faithful to his promise to Abraham, Isaac, Jacob, Joseph, and Moses. It does so also because Abraham, Isaac, Jacob, and all the rest were faithful to YHWH's call. Future generations, too, will depend both upon YHWH's faithfulness to his promise and the current generation's faithfulness to YHWH.

The Third Declaration: Covenant Fidelity, 26:13-14

The third and final declaration emphasizes a second dimension of Israelite community, not across generations, but within a single generation. Now the relationship between this material and the commandment against coveting becomes clear. Because any bounty enjoyed by individual Israelites comes as YHWH's gracious gift, his faithfulness to his promise, there can be no pride in acquisition. Because YHWH called all Israel to be his people, the proper response to his blessings is to distribute them further.

The setting for this declaration is no longer the offering of first fruits, but the so-called "poor" tithe given in the third and sixth years of the Sabbath cycle (see Deut 14:22-29 and [Tithes and Offerings]), another indication of the composite nature of the passage. The phrase "before your God" in v. 13 also seems to indicate that the affirmation to follow was originally meant to be made in the central sanctuary, although the parallel text (14:22-29) calls for the third-year tithe to be offered in the tither's hometown.

Whatever the original intention, this third affirmation has been joined to the other two to form a litany of affirmation. In two series of statements, at first positive then negative, it stresses that the worshiper has maintained covenant loyalty to the other members of the community and to YHWH. First, the worshiper affirms that he has indeed brought the offering ("I have removed") and has shared it with those members of the community most in need (Levites, sojourners, widows, and orphans) as YHWH requires (v. 13). The Bible consistently insists that the God of Israel cares in special ways for the oppressed, the needy, and the disenfranchised (Deut 14:29; 16:11; 24:19-21; 26:12-13; 27:19; Jer 7:6; 22:3; compare commentary on Deut 10:12-19; 14:28-29 and [Widow, Orphan, and Resident Alien]). Because some people fell through the cracks of Israel's system of social and economic justice, YHWH took it upon himself to see to their welfare. Because Israel was once the oppressed, the enslaved, whom God had delivered, they were to have particular sensitivity (Deut 5:15; 15:15; 16:12; 24:18, 22; the phrase "remember you were slaves in Egypt" is uniquely characteristic of Deuteronomy; see commentary on 14:22–16:17). It was YHWH's will that these people be protected; Israel was to express its gratitude to YHWH for liberation from Egyptian bondage by *liberating others in turn.*

Then, in a series of "negative affirmations of innocence" similar to those known from other ancient Near Eastern cultures,[2] the worshiper declares that he has not been involved in any way in the worship of the dead nor has any portion of the tithe been used for these purposes (v. 14). A substantial body of biblical and extra-biblical literature suggests that many of Israel's neighbors revered their ancestral dead as divine or semi-divine figures and honored them through funerary offerings at a meal, probably held annually, called a *marzēaḥ* (compare 1 Sam 28:3-25; 2 Sam 18:18; 2 Kgs 21:6; 23:24; Isa 8:19-20; 19:3; 28:15, 18; 29:4; Jer 16:5-8; Amos 6:7; Ps 106:28; *KTU* 1.161; *KTU* 1.113; *CTA* 17.1.26-34; *KTU* 6.13; 6.14; see Theodore J. Lewis, *Cults of the Dead in Ancient Israel and Ugarit* [Harvard Semitic Monographs 39; Atlanta: Scholars Press, 1989]). Often mourners mutilated themselves in association with such rites of mourning. The Torah forbids these practices in Israel (Lev 19:31; Deut 14:1; 18:9-11). Perhaps the "poor" tithe, intended to be consumed as a public meal, may have outwardly resembled a *marzēaḥ*. Since the third-year tithe was offered apart from the supervision of the priests at the central sanctuary, it may have been not only susceptible to confusion with the *marzēaḥ*, but also to ready abuse as such. While Israel's faith emphasizes solidarity across generations (see vv. 5-10), it does not condone misplaced worship. The Hebrew Bible views such reverence for the dead as idolatry—a violation of the first commandment. In effect, worshipers here affirm their solidarity with the unfortunate members of the community (v. 13a), and both their obedience (v. 13b) and their loyalty to YHWH (v. 14).

The third affirmation concludes with the only petition addressed to YHWH in the section, although this prayer may also be viewed as a postscript to the entire section (vv. 1-14). It combines standard Deuteronomic phraseology,[3] language equally characteristic of portions of the Torah outside Deuteronomy,[4] and expressions concerning God's heavenly palace otherwise found exclusively in much later literature, especially the Psalms.[5] It has probably been placed here to round off the litany with an appropriate prayer seeking God's continued blessing.

CONNECTIONS

The Hebrew Bible records God's relationship with a nation that lived, for much of the period reflected in the literature, as a political entity with national boundaries, national institutions, and, for roughly five centuries, a national government. Many of the religious traditions of the Hebrew Bible are also national traditions. The Hebrew Bible knows very little of the "spiritual," individualistic, and otherworldly notions of some versions of Christianity. Modern Christian interpretations often struggle to find some point of contact with the very this-worldly character of the Hebrew Bible. Too often, the church relegates the Hebrew Bible to merely historical significance. Or it allegorizes, or perhaps worse, disregards it.

Modern believers face the basic difficulties that confront anyone who seeks to interpret ancient literature. Deuteronomy, for example, reflects the agrarian culture and the specific social, political, and religious institutions of ancient Israel. Very few of these cultural and institutional structures can be found in modern Western culture. Yet, because it is Holy Scripture, believers cannot and should not simply dismiss, disregard, or dismember the Hebrew Bible. Jews and Christians alike must struggle to make the necessary historical and cultural translations in order to be able to see the relevance of the ancient text.

Deuteronomy 25:13–26:15 is no less foreign to modern multinational, multicultural, individualistic, heavenly-minded Christianity. Modern Christians—and Jews—do not usually conduct barter transactions. The Amalekites have long since ceased to exist as an identifiable ethnic group. No one offers first fruits under the ministry of the high priest at the temple in Jerusalem: There is no temple in Jerusalem; there is no high priest. These regulations have no literal pertinence for anyone today. Short of a dismissive observation that business should be conducted fairly, an artificial effort to equate Jerusalem's temple with some modern institution, arbitrarily to designate a modern high priest, or arrogantly to claim membership in some modern counterpart to the chosen *nation*—a perspective that biblical Israel itself ultimately found inadequate for describing its existence before God—is there a word of God for modern believers in this passage?

Indeed, the text raises at least six fundamental issues. They require that the interpreter seek to understand the dynamics of the text as God's word, not merely the cultural details.

First, life in covenant relationship with God is, in part, a very everyday matter. By means of a skillful exegesis of the commandment against coveting, Deuteronomy subtly establishes the relationship between the theological affirmation that YHWH delivers the oppressed and the ethical demands of fairness, at the minimum, and generosity. Former slaves cannot fulfill the call to holiness by oppressing others, "taking advantage" of their weakness. Once migrant Arameans cannot honor the God who blessed them with harvest and flock by stinginess.

Second, thankful response to God's grace is *never* a purely private matter. Three times the text charges the worshiper to make declarations in public settings and before God. As Fredrick Holmgren notes, "God does not want anonymous gifts. . . . God expects the covenant partner to do something. . . . Religion that comes from the heart is something other than religion that remains in the heart."[6]

Third, thankful response to God's grace focuses first on basic gifts already received. Often believers equate faith exclusively with questions of eternal and supernatural proportions—eternal life and wondrous deliverance. The starting point for this litany of confessions, however, is the simple, tangible, present gifts of dwelling place, farmland, rains, and harvests. If one cannot be grateful for the life one now lives—for health, food, family—how can one be prepared to embrace fully God's provision for life to come?

Fourth, thankful response to God depends to a degree on appreciation for one's heritage. In modern society people have become increasingly unsettled and disconnected. Few people live in their ancestral homes. Westerners do not typically know the stories of past generations of their families. Clergy, educators, and civic leaders worry that ignorance of history, disrespect for tradition, and the decline of "family values" may threaten the health and prosperity of our society. Christian doctrine correctly emphasizes the personal nature of faith. Yet this assertion sometimes encourages ungrounded, aimless, rootless, formless lives of faith. The Bible asserts frequently that faith is not chronologically discrete. The same God who calls us to personal faith called Abraham. The God who led Abraham to adventure to a foreign land, who delivered Israel from Egyptian bondage, who—incarnate as Jesus of Nazareth—dined with prostitutes and scolded preachers is the God who calls us to faith and obedience. Just as the technological advances of modern society depend upon generations of experimentation and discovery, we place our faith in the God who "in many and various ways . . . spoke of old to our fathers" (Heb 1:1); we depend upon the experience of generations of God's people to teach us. Contrary to the claims of a popular hymn, we do not "come to the garden alone." ["In the Garden"] Instead, we run the race "before a cloud of witnesses" (Heb 12:1).

Fifth, thankful response to God incorporates concern for the unfortunate. As would Jesus later, the editors of Deuteronomy consistently extrapolated positive ethical requirements from prohibitions, in this case extending the commandment against coveting into a call to generosity. Ancient Israelite society was imperfectly structured. Four classes of people were particularly disenfranchised: the Levite, whose tribe received no patrimony; the resident alien, who did not have the rights of citizens; the orphan, a minor without paternal protection; and the widow, who had no means of support. Modern Christianity tends to equate material success with God's favor and to deny that poverty, for example, results in part from the fact that our socioeconomic and political system is at least as flawed as was ancient Israel's. Undeniably, migrant workers, children, mentally handicapped people, and many others in our culture do not enjoy the same opportunities as the more fortunate. They do not, in fact, have full rights and privileges. Children cannot choose their parents. They cannot vote. They cannot create for themselves the environments necessary for successful learning and proper moral development. The mentally handicapped cannot realize the American dream simply through hard work, grit, and determination. Some people start life with virtually insurmountable disadvantages. They did not choose their starting places. Often, as a practical consequence, they are not fully enfranchised citizens. Someone must help them make their voices heard; someone must insist that they not be overlooked; someone must care. Who better than God's people—who know what it is to be redeemed from slavery—who better can exercise God's love?

Finally, thankful response to God expresses the worshiper's genuine loyalty. Although worship of the ancestral dead is not a common practice in the modern western world, many modern believers' devotion to sports and their heroes, to entertainment stars, and even to political figures rivals their devotion to God, the Creator, Redeemer, and Sustainer. Love for God must surely include loyalty in the form of exclusive worship and everyday obedience.

"In the Garden"

C. Austin Miles's popular hymn "In the Garden" is a fine expression of the post-Romantic, sentimental, hyperindividualistic pietism that characterizes much of modern Christianity. Especially in the first stanza and the refrain, it stands in stark contrast to Deuteronomy's explication of the final commandment.

I come to the garden alone,
    While the dew is still on the roses;
And the voice I hear, falling on my ear,
    The Son of God discloses.

He speaks, and the sound of His voice
    Is so sweet the birds hush their singing;
And the melody that He gave to me
    Within my heart is ringing.

I'd stay in the garden with Him
    Tho' the night around me be falling;
But He bids me go; thro' the voice of woe,
    His voice to me is calling.
Refrain
And He walks with me, and He talks with me,
    And he tells me I am His own,
And the joy we share as we tarry there,
    None other has ever known.

NOTES

[1] G. von Rad, *Deuteronomy: A Commentary* (OTL; Philadelphia: Westminster Press, 1966), 159.

[2] See, for example, the excerpt from the one hundred and twenty-fifth chapter of the Egyptian "Book of the Dead," in ANET (34-36). It contains model declarations that the deceased should make before a posthumous divine court. It begins with nearly forty protestations such as the following: "I have not committed evil against men. I have not mistreated cattle. I have not committed sin in the place of truth . . . I have not blasphemed a god. I have not *done violence to* a poor man. I have not done that which the gods abominate. Etc."

[3] "You swore to our ancestors," Deut 1:8, 35; 6:10, 23; 7:8, 12, 13; 8:1, 8 and an additional 12 times in Deuteronomy; the phrase also appears regularly in Deuteronomistic literature influenced by the book of Deuteronomy, Josh 1:6, 5:6; 21:43, 44; Judg 2:1; Jer 11:5; 32:22; Mic 7:20; outside Deuteronomy and texts influenced by it, the phrase only occurs in Exod 13:5, 11; Num 11:12; 14:23.

[4] "Land flowing with milk and honey," Exod 3:8, 17; 13:5; 33:3; Lev 20:24; Num 13:27; 14:8; 16:13, 14; it occurs in Deuteronomy only 6 times, Deut 6:3; 11:9; 26:9, 15; 27:3; 31:20.

[5] Compare 1 Kgs 8:30; Pss 14:2; 53:3; 68:6; 102:20; Jer 25:30; Lam 3:50; Zech 2:17; 2 Chr 30:27.

[6] "The Pharisee and the Tax Collector: Luke 18:9-14 and Deuteronomy 26:1-15," *Interpretation* 48 (1994): 257-59.

CONCLUSION TO THE DEUTERONOMIC CODE

26:16-19

COMMENTARY

Unlike the lengthy paranetic introduction (4:44–11:32) to the exposition of the Decalogue, the editors of Deuteronomy conclude the Deuteronomic Code with a surprisingly brief and apparently straightforward statement (26:16-19). Readers should not permit this brevity, however, to misdirect their attention. Several structural, intertextual, and rhetorical features of the unit communicate a great deal more than one might expect of a mere four verses.

Structurally, the distinct allusion in v. 16 to the Shema ("with all your heart and with all your soul," cf. 6:5) and the linkage with Moses' instructions (27:1-8) concerning the erection of plastered-stone copies of the Law on Mt. Ebal (cf. 11:29-30) signals that, although brief, the conclusion implies the entirety of the lengthy homiletic treatment in Deuteronomy 6–12. The exposition of the Decalogue now concluded must therefore be understood in terms of the requirement of all-encompassing loyalty to the one YHWH discussed in the introductory framework.

Just as it begins with a recapitulation of the Shema, this brief conclusion to the Deuteronomic Code also relates unmistakably to the other great narrative of the establishment of the covenant between YHWH and his people Israel (Exod 19–20). The phrases "treasured people" ('am sĕgullâ, v. 18) and "holy people" ('am qādōš, v. 19) also appear in the offer to enter into covenant relationship with Israel that YHWH made at Mt. Sinai ('am sĕgullâ, Exod 19:5; gôy qādōš, Exod 19:6). Although scholars debate the question of which occurrence of the two phrases can claim priority,[1] there can be no doubt that their appearance in these two passages establishes a firm linkage.[2] Just as previously, at Mt. Sinai, Moses had mediated YHWH's offer of covenant relationship to an earlier generation of Israel, he now mediates the same offer to their children!

Rhetorically, the conclusion to the Deuteronomic Code underscores the later generation's responsibility for its own participation in the covenant—one of the most basic themes of Deuteronomy (see commentary and sidebars on 4:9-14; 6:20-25)—by emphasizing repeatedly that the offer of covenant relationship is not merely a historical event. Three times ("this very day," v. 16; "today," vv. 17, 18) the text exhorts the audience/readers to recognize that the covenant is a matter of the present. YHWH is Israel's God *today*. Israel is God's people *today*. God's will for God's people as expressed in the covenant requires diligent attention and obedience *today*.

NOTES

[1] See, for example, J. Van Seters, "Cultic Laws in the Covenant Code and Their Relationship to Deuteronomy and the Holiness Code," in *Studies in the Book of Exodus: Redaction, Reception, Interpretation*, ed. M. Vervenne (Bibliotheca Ephemeridum Theologicarum Lovaniensium 126; Leuven: Leuven University Press, 1996), 319-45; A. Schenker, "Drei Mosaiksteinchen: 'Königreich von Priestern,' 'Und ihre Kinder gehen weg,' 'Wir tun und wir hören' (Exodus 19,6; 21,22; 24,7)," in *Studies in the Book of Exodus*, 367-80; B. Schwartz, "The Priestly Account of the Theophany and Lawgiving at Sinai," in *Texts, Temples, and Traditions: A Tribute to Menahem Haran*, ed. M. Fox et al. (Winona Lake: Eisenbrauns, 1996), 103-34; etc.

[2] The more unusual of the two phrases, "treasured people," also occurs alone in Deut 7:6; 14:2. The two appear in conjunction only in these two passages. This circumstance suggests that the expression as found in Exod 19 may represent a Deuteronomic editorial expansion.

THE SHECHEM CEREMONY

27:1-26

Following the conclusion to the exposition of the Decalogue, the central principles of the covenant between YHWH and his people, the book of Deuteronomy ends with a series of somewhat divergent materials: instructions concerning ceremonies to be enacted later (ch. 27), a recital of blessings and curses (ch. 28), a covenant renewal ceremony (chs. 29–30), Moses' farewell address (chs. 31–32, which includes a song), Moses' parting blessing (ch. 33), and the account of Moses' death.

It is important to recall that, in the final arrangement of the book, the "legal" material contained in the Deuteronomic Code (chs. 12–26) is framed by materials that focus attention on the momentous transition documented in the book. The presumptive audience of Moses' speeches is the second generation of Israelites privileged to be party to the covenant with YHWH—a generation that did not know bondage in Egypt and does not yet know life in the promised land, the generation that will experience the transition of leadership from Moses to Joshua, the generation that will be the first to face the dangers of encounter with Canaanite culture and the challenges of maintaining fidelity to the covenant in an environment rife with temptation.

Not surprisingly, then, even the literary structure of Deuteronomy draws attention to the opportunities and dangers inherent in transition. It often looks back to the experiences of the previous generation at Sinai (1:6-18; 4:9-40; 5:22-33; etc.) and in the wilderness (1:19–3:29; 4:3; 6:16; etc.), reminding its readers (the true audience of the *text* of the book) that in transitional moments, the past may either be endorsed and perpetuated, or repudiated and forgotten. Often, as in Deuteronomy 27, the book looks to the future, calling for its audience to maintain firm links to its heritage.

Deuteronomy 27, which exhibits a number of features that raise issues regarding the history of Israelite religion [Cult Centralization and the Shechem Ceremony] and the history of the composition of the book of Deuteronomy [Several Originally Independent Traditions?], divides roughly into three unequal sections, each marked by an introductory speech formula ("Moses and the elders of Israel commanded," v. 1; "Moses

Cult Centralization and the Shechem Ceremony

The ceremony (or ceremonies) prescribed in Deut 27 is (are) to take place on or near Mt. Ebal and Mt. Gerizim, in the vicinity of the ancient city and cultic center of Shechem (but see [Several Originally Independent Traditions?]). Shechem was founded as early as the Middle Bronze II A period (c. 2000–1800 BC). Recent archeological discoveries there include a number of Canaanite sanctuaries. Ancestral traditions in the book of Genesis (33:18–34:31; 37:12) associate the patriarch Jacob, and especially his sons Simeon and Levi, with the city. Joshua held important covenant rites at Shechem (Josh 8:30-35; 24:1-28). Later, during the period of the judges, Abimelech, son of Jerubaal (Gideon), would become "king" of Shechem (Judg 9:1-57) and Rehoboam, Solomon's son and successor, would travel there to negotiate with leaders of the northern tribes concerning whether he would rule over them (1 Kgs 12:1-15). Clearly, Shechem played an important cultural and religious role in ancient Israel, especially for the northern tribes.

Its centrality in the book of Deuteronomy points once again, however, to the complicated problem of reconstructing ancient Israel's religious history. Deut 12 calls for the centralization of worship at one location (see commentary). During the monarchical period, Jerusalem and its temple would have surely served that role. Evidence scattered across the Hebrew Bible, including Deut 27, points, however, to a number of important centers of worship other than Jerusalem. For example, the Bible records that the ark of the covenant, unmistakably Israel's most important religious symbol, could be found variously at Bethel (Judg 20:27), Shiloh (1 Sam 4:3-4; cf. Josh 18:1), and Kiriath-jearim (1 Sam 7:2) before David brought it to Jerusalem. It will also have presumably been housed at Gilgal, Joshua's base of operations during the conquest (Josh 4:19-20, 5:9-10; 9:6; etc.) During Saul's reign, Samuel also offered sacrifices at Gilgal (1 Sam 11:14-15; 15:21), suggesting that it, too, was once an important cult site during the late judges period.

How is this evidence of many cult sites to be harmonized with Deuteronomy's call for centralization? Scholars suggest two possibilities: (1) The central sanctuary "migrated" from place to place so that Gilgal, Shechem, Bethel, Shiloh, Kiriath-jearim, and Jerusalem served successively as the central worship site. Deuteronomy would then combine traditions from various periods in Israel's history. (2) Before the reforms associated with Josiah of Judah, Israel worshiped at several sites simultaneously. Deuteronomy would then combine various local traditions subsuming them under the centralization law.

and the levitical priests said," v. 9; and "Moses commanded," v. 11). The first (vv. 1-8) and third (vv. 11-26) of these speeches offer instructions for the performance of a variety of rituals of covenant confirmation to be performed by the people after they have crossed the Jordan. The second (vv. 9-10) essentially comprises a reprise of the Shema. Alternatively, vv. 9-10, which echo and expand the allusion to the Shema found already in v. 1, may be intended as the concluding element of a framework surrounding vv. 2-8. In all, Deuteronomy 27 seems to refer to at least four distinct ritual acts. The sometimes fragmentary descriptions of these acts intermingle in such a way as to obscure the picture, on the one hand, and to suggest that Deuteronomy 27 preserves elements of ritual traditions with origins widespread historically and geographically, on the other. These traditions have been combined here, not for the sake of preserving data for the reconstruction of Israelite cultic history—a concern of modern scholarship, but not of the editors of the book of Deuteronomy—but in order to accentuate the importance of ritual confirmation of the covenant at this critical juncture in Israel's history.

Several Originally Independent Traditions?

The problem discussed in the previous sidebar has bearing also on the composition history of Deut 27 itself. As noted in the commentary, the text seems to preserve elements of up to four distinct ritual prescriptions. Close examination suggests that they reflect traditions associated with Shechem (Mt. Ebal and Mt. Gerizim) and Gilgal, two sites quite remote from one another, and that they date from various periods in Israel's history. Two tensions in the text call attention to its composite nature.

First, the instruction to carry out these rituals "in the day that you cross the Jordan" (27:2) suggests that they be performed at Gilgal, where Israel camped after crossing the river. In fact, Josh 4:20 records that Joshua and Israel erected twelve memorial stones, reminiscent of the stones prescribed in Deut 27 (an alternative form of the same tradition?), in the Gilgal camp. Josh 8:30-35 and, especially,

Deut 11:29-30 seem to be aware of the difficulty and attempt to harmonize the Shechem and Gilgal forms of the tradition. Deut 11:29-20 maintains (imprecisely, see **Map of Shechem Region**) that the mountains of blessing and cursing are "as you know . . . beyond the Jordan . . . opposite Gilgal, beside the oak of Moreh."

Not only does Deut 27 combine Shechem and Gilgal traditions, it combines traditions concerning the tribes of Israel from a very early period, when Levi was still a "secular" tribe, with later traditions when Levi was the priestly cast. For discussions of this evolution in Levi's status, see A. D. H. Mayes, "The Period of the Judges and the Rise of the Monarchy," in *Israelite and Judaean History*, ed. J. H. Hayes and J. M. Miller (Old Testament Library; London: SCM, 1977), 300 and J. Bright, *A History of Israel* (3rd ed.; Philadelphia: Westminster, 1981), 135-36.

COMMENTARY

A Stone Memorial and a Stone Altar, 27:1-8

Moses' third major oration (following the prefatory historical overview of Israel's relationship to YHWH [Deut 1–4] and the paranetic exposition of the Torah [Deut 5–26]) focuses on steps the Israelites should undertake to establish firmly the centrality of Torah in their new life in the land. Subtly, but very significantly, 27:1 introduces a new element into the diction of the book of Deuteronomy. Up to this point, the principle speakers in the book have been the narrator, Moses, and YHWH himself. The latter two have been interchangeable to such a degree that it becomes unmistakable that Moses functions as YHWH's spokesman. Now, however, Moses no longer speaks alone, but in the company of "Israel's elders" (v. 1) and, later, of the "levitical priests" (v. 9). This new diction testifies to the awareness that Moses' ministry draws to a close. The transition from life in the wilderness to life in the promised land and from one generation to the next will also be a transition in leadership. This theme, introduced here without fanfare, will subsequently become central.

Horned Altar
Reconstructed stone altar (c. 63 inches high), from c. 9th–8th centuries BC, that was located at Beer-sheba in Israel. Note the "horns" on the four corners of the altar.

Central to vv. 1-8 are instructions for the erection of two stone structures to commemorate and to celebrate the covenant. After charging Israel to "keep all the commandments" (v. 1), Moses and the elders reiterate (see 11:19-23) the direction to erect, as the first order of business upon entry into the promised land, large stones (vv. 2, 4) on Mt. Ebal (v. 4), to "plaster them with plaster (*wĕśadtā ʾōtām baśśîd*)" (vv. 2, 4), and to "write upon them all the words of this Torah" (vv. 3, 8). The practice of publishing important legal and historical documents inscribed in stone monuments, or "stele," is well known in the ancient Near East. [Stele] Such combinations of "monumental architecture" and, especially, the law of the realm served to create a permeating awareness of the "rule of law." Moses and the elders, then, direct Israel to publish the Torah monumentally as something like Israel's "constitution." The Torah is not to be merely a matter of private belief or devotion. It is to be the "law of the land." This publication is to precede any effort to take possession of the land, to drive out enemies, or to establish settlements. The record of the execution of this directive can be found in Joshua 8:30-35.

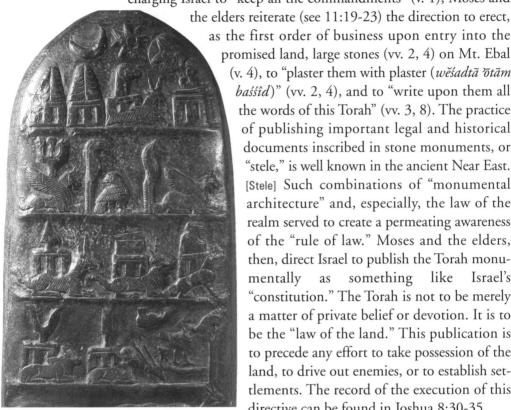

Stele

Above is a Kudurru of Babylonian king Melishishu II (1202–1188 BC) showing emblems of the chief gods Anu, Enlil, and Ea. At the top is the crescent of the moon god, the star of Ishtar, and the sun of Shamash. Seen on the bottom are the snake and scorpion of the underworld.

Kudurru. Louvre. Paris, France.

A careful reader will note the redundancy of vv. 2 and 4 and vv. 3 and 8. Apparently, editors created this duplication by imbedding a second directive within the prescription for the erection of a Torah stele. In a prescription reminiscent of Exod 20:22-26, vv. 5-8 call for the erection (on Mt. Ebal? "there," v. 5; see [Cult Centralization and the Shechem Ceremony]) of an altar of unhewn stones (literally, "stones untouched by iron, whole stones," *ʾăbānîm lōʾ-tanîp ʿălêhem barzel ʾăbōnîm šĕlēmôt*, vv. 5-6). [Why "Unhewn Stones"?] On this altar, Israel is to offer to YHWH whole burnt offerings and "peace" offerings. Before this altar, Israel is to consume the communal meal and to rejoice in YHWH's presence (see commentary on ch. 14).

Whatever the original relationship between the stele and the altar, the combination of the two structures at this point serves to emphasize the importance of two key reactions to the Torah: First, Israel must erect public reminders of the Torah. It will govern

Why "Unhewn Stones"?

Three factors probably combined to motivate ancient Israel's antipathy toward masonry altars. First, Israel's early ancestors would have erected impromptu altars constructed of readily available materials. Ancient and accepted practices become revered simply for antiquity's sake. Second, there was probably some sense that altering the stones profaned them in some way. Craftsmanship and artifice are inappropriate to sacrifice, which involves the numinous and the primal. Third, in a later period when adherents to the prophetic impulse (certainly including the Deuteronomic editors) were sensitive to the corrupting influence of non-Israelite worship practices, the primitive nature of stone altars probably appealed to "Puritan" sensibilities.

Regardless of the position taken in the Torah, opulent royal tastes favored ornate furnishings for the official sanctuary in Jerusalem (see 1 Kgs 6:1-36; 7:13-50). Archeological finds also document various forms of masonry altars at a number of sites in premonarchial and monarchial Israel. The so-called "horned" altar was especially popular. "Popular" religion and orthodoxy often conflict in these ways.

Israel's life as a community. The covenant is not to be understood as merely religious in character. It is the constitution for YHWH's people. Second, however, the Torah should inspire not only solemn obedience, but grateful celebration. It is YHWH's gift that gives life to his people as a people. It is cause for rejoicing.

A Call to Obedience, 27:9-10

Moses, joined now by the levitical priests who will succeed him as principle interpreters of the Torah, returns to the present in the next speech. Using language found throughout Deuteronomy, and, like v. 1, especially reminiscent of the Shema, Moses and the priests call on "all Israel" today to listen in silent attention to YHWH's voice and to do the commandments and statutes commanded so that they may be YHWH's people.

Rituals of Covenant Blessing and Cursing, 27:11-26

Once again, editors combine portions of descriptions of two rituals in the third and most extensive speech. In one tradition (vv. 12-13)—presumably quite old given the sociological conditions it reflects—after crossing the Jordan, six tribes, including Levi, are to take up station on Mt. Gerizim to bless the people. The remaining six are to pronounce the curses of the covenant from Mt. Ebal. In the other tradition (vv. 14-26), Levi—functioning now not as one tribe among others, but as the priestly caste—leads the entire people in a litany of covenant curses. Clearly, the first of these two traditions raises a number of questions. To begin, it is anything but certain that the blessings and curses mentioned are to be

Mount Gerizim

understood as those contained in Deuteronomy 27 and 28 as one might expect. Obviously, the tribe of Levi cannot simultaneously pronounce blessing from Mt. Gerizim and curse from Mt. Ebal. Second, it is similarly unclear how Mt. Ebal can be the site of the covenant stele, the celebratory altar, *and* the pronouncement of curse. It seems reasonable to conclude that the references to curse and to Mt. Ebal attracted the otherwise unrelated and fragmentary tradition recorded in vv. 12-13 to its present context.

The litany of "curses" to be recited by the (priestly) Levites, on the other hand, deserves special attention. First of all, it should be noted that strictly speaking in terms of literary form, as E. Merrill has pointed out,[1] this list does not contain curses at all. Properly, curses are wish statements invoking some specific ill upon some individual or group: "May your crops fail," for example. Instead, this catalog lists categories of offenders who are subject to some unspecified curse and, more importantly from a formal perspective, obtains the people's assent ("Amen," *ʾāmēn*, literally, "make it so") to the classification. The statements listed here, then, can more accurately be described as oaths by which the people subject themselves to the prohibition implied in the oath. Presumably, YHWH will see both to determining the appropriate curse and to executing it.

The people agree that the offenders listed deserve to be relegated to YHWH's curse and thereby freely subject themselves to the conditions outlined.

Second, scholars have long noted[2] that the offenses listed here correspond substantially to actions treated elsewhere in the Torah and that the number of offenses listed (twelve) closely approximates the ten of the Decalogue. The first (idol worship) even recalls the Decalogue itself. As a consequence, the list is sometimes referred to as the "Shechemite Dodecalogue," a term with implications for the history of Israelite religion (see [Cult Centralization and the Schechem Ceremony]). Others point out that the last two offenses in the list are without parallel elsewhere in the Torah and that without them, this "Dodecalogue" (from the Latin for "twelve words") would be restored to a "Decalogue" ("ten words").

Rather than attend to the reconstruction of the history of Israel's worship here, however, another principle evident in the list can be regarded as key to its interpretation. The first and the tenth items in the list address acts committed "in secret (*bassāter*)." In fact, perpetrators of all the deeds addressed in the list usually commit these acts furtively. They could easily go undetected by society. The litany intends, then, to consign to divine jurisdiction all such evildoers whose crimes go undiscovered.

Formally, items two through eleven are all constructed in Hebrew with participial clauses (for example, "cursed be the curser," *ʾārûr maqleh*, v. 16). Indeed, items six through nine employ the same verb form, "the sleeper (*šōkēb*)." The remaining participles are all piel or hiphil forms with a preformative *m-* that results in a pleasing assonance: *ʾārûr maqleh* (v. 16), *ʾārûr massîg* (v. 17), *ʾārûr mašgeh* (v. 18), *ʾārûr matteh* (v. 19), *ʾārûr makkēh* (v. 24).

In terms of content, the list may be subdivided into five unbalanced sections:

(1) The first offense (v. 15), secretive idolatry, directly violates the first, greatest, commandment of the Decalogue. (See the commentary on Deut 5 and 12.)

(2) The next four items deal with crimes characterized by deceit or abuse of power; in them, the evildoer "takes advantage" of another's weakness. It should be remembered in this regard that the parents mentioned in v. 16 are probably understood to be the elderly parents of adult children (see the commentary on Deut 5); that is, they are at the mercy of abusive children. Clearly the unscrupulous who need not fear retribution can

easily prey upon the blind and the powerless sojourners, orphans, and widows. Concerning displacing a neighbor's landmark see the commentary on 19:14.

(3) Items six through nine not only parallel one another formally (see above), but they also all deal with sexual misconduct, specifically bestiality (v. 21) and three types of incest (vv. 20, 22, 23). Leviticus 18:6-23 offers a much more extensive definition of incestuous relationships, including explanations for the prohibitions similar to that offered for only the first item in Deuteronomy's list (see the commentary on 5:18 and 22:13-30 for a discussion of sexual impropriety as an offense against the principle male in a woman's life). No rationale for the reference to the three mentioned here is apparent (the omission of incestuous relations with daughters is particularly glaring), although they are among the closest degrees of family relationship: father's wife (thus mother or stepmother, v. 20), sister (whole or half: "his sister, the daughter of his father or the daughter of his mother," v. 22), and mother-in-law (v. 23).

(4) Items ten and eleven deal with types of outright aggression committed secretively against a fellow Israelite: physical attacks (v. 24) or accepting payment to carry out such an attack (v. 25). Incidentally, the phraseology of the second of these two prohibitions sheds light on Hebrew anthropology, especially the significance of the term *nepeš*, often somewhat misleadingly translated "soul" (see [The Concept of the "Soul" in Hebrew Thought]). The ancient Hebrews knew nothing of the Platonic notion of the "tri-partite" nature of human existence as "body (Greek *sarx*)," "soul (Greek *psychē*)," and "spirit (Greek *pneuma*)." Rendered somewhat mechanically, Deuteronomy 27:25 reads, "Cursed be the one taking a bribe to smite the *nepeš* of one with innocent blood." Clearly, *nepeš* cannot be understood here to mean the ephemeral soul, which presumably cannot be "smitten." Instead, here, as elsewhere, *nepeš* refers to the living individual as a whole person.

(5) The final item in the litany remedies any omission. Through it, the people promise on penalty of the curse to "establish the words of this covenant to do them." Like the first item, this oath departs from the usual participial construction ("cursed be he who does not establish [*ʾārûr ʾăšer lōʾ-yāqîm*]") and is probably an editorial addition to the litany.

CONNECTIONS

Despite the complexity of the combination of various ritual prescriptions in Deuteronomy 27, the very public nature of the endorsement of the covenant and its stipulations unites the material into a whole. Israel is to erect monumental copies of the Torah as its constitution. Israel is to celebrate the gift of covenant. All Israel participates in antiphonal affirmations of the covenant, assuming responsibility for fulfilling its requirements, accepting the consequences of covenant violation. This Torah constitutes Israel's religious regulations, its criminal law, and its civil law in one unified whole. In ancient Israel, the religious assembly and the political entity were coterminous. This uniformity and unanimity of state and religion is without parallel in the modern Western world. Today, the Torah—or for Christians, the Bible—does *not* exercise authority over *every* area of *public* life.

So long as Roman Catholicism was the sole form of Christianity in the West, church and state were largely overlapping realms. Theoretically, at least, the Bible did occupy a position roughly analogous to that held by the Deuteronomy's Torah. But then the Reformation brought doctrinal and ecclesial variety to Christianity, and, ultimately, religious toleration and the separation of church and state. Only this measure could insure freedom to worship for adherents of minority forms of Christianity. Increasingly, as the result of immigration and other factors, practitioners of non-Christian religions have come to represent a significant proportion of the population in the West so that inner-Christian variety has given way to true pluralism. In such a context, the freedom for all to worship entails limits on all, as well. The once self-evident assumption that the moral and ethical claims of a particular version of Christianity could form the unchallenged basis for the laws of the state as well simply no longer holds.

Yet, many religious people long to return to a time when moral, ethical, and religious absolutes were the common heritage of the entire society. This nostalgia motivates many legislative and judicial efforts, such as campaigns reminiscent of Deuteronomy 27 to post the Decalogue in schoolrooms, publicly and officially to acknowledge the "fact" that this country was founded on "Judeo-Christian principles." Such "restoration" programs forget, however, that people came and still come to the New World, in part, to escape "religious tyranny," to worship as they choose. In the end, given the fact that even Christians cannot agree among themselves on even the most fundamental elements of Christian doctrine, those who wish to legislate Christian values advocate the impracticable notion

Inoffensive but Insipid Prayer

Since the Supreme Court handed down its 1962 *Engel v. Vitale* decision on prayer in public schools, both houses of Congress have held a number of hearings to debate proposed legislation, amendments to the Constitution, and resolutions designed to permit the reintroduction of public prayer into the public school classroom. Instructively, these debates have all eventually reached an impasse over two key issues:

(1) the voluntary nature of prayer and (2) the feasibility of "nondenominational" or "non-sectarian" prayer. In short, can a "voluntary" act be prescribed or regulated? If prayer is the worshiper's voluntary address to his or her deity, who can prevent it? Is it not already entirely possible, even under the *Engel v. Vitale* decision, for a public school student to silently and privately (perhaps not coincidentally, the method Jesus recommended; Matt 6:5-6) address prayer to his or her deity at any moment during a school day? Is it possible to compose a prayer that would be meaningful and inoffensive to Christian, Jew, Buddhist, Hindu, and Muslim alike? Robert S. Alley, a Baptist and a professor of religion, masterfully formulated the problems as follows in his testimony before the Senate Subcommittee on Constitutional Amendments, August 8, 1966:

The proposed amendment speaks of prayer. What is prayer? Is it religious exercise? If not, then what? What kind or kinds of prayer are involved here? These questions must be considered as unanswered by the proponents of the amendment. As a free citizen of the United States I have chosen to be a Christian. This is my religious faith. Prayer for the Christian necessarily involves the person of Jesus Christ. Every religious faith defines the essence of prayer differently. For me there is no such thing as general or non-sectarian prayer. Therefore, the promotion of prayer—and we can hardly see this amendment in other light—by the federal government inevitably raises questions not alone for the atheist, but for the religious person as well. . . . In short, if the prayer is not clearly and unapologetically sectarian it will violate my conscience and if it is of such character then it will necessarily violate the conscience of my neighbor who is not a Christian.

It may be argued that this proposal only seeks the permission of "voluntary" prayer. But the word voluntary has never been adequately defined. . . . I suggest that often the average citizen means by voluntary that the teacher may pray if he or she wishes. . . . But of course this is hardly voluntary for the students. It may be insisted that voluntary means the class deciding to pray. Does this mean majority rule while the rest close their ears or step outside? Or is this to be construed as meaning unanimous consent of students and teacher? If the latter, it requires no insight to recognize how quickly this method may become coercive where only one or two children differ from the vast majority.

The only meaningful definition of the word voluntary as related to prayer in the public schools is in terms of the individual. Voluntary prayer may be the free individual, teacher or pupil, uttering a private petition. But is not the First Amendment as it is the most adequate document ever produced by man to protect that right of voluntary prayer? The Supreme Court has never so much as hinted that true voluntary prayer would be prohibited. Obviously it could not be.

As cited in R. Alley, *School Prayer: The Court, the Congress, and the First Amendment* (Amherst NY: Prometheus, 1994), 249-51.

of imposing any set of religious values on a society as diverse as the modern West. The constant debates concerning prayer at governmental functions, such as high-school graduations, illustrate the folly. One-size-fits-all prayers designed not to offend are so denuded of content as to fail entirely *as prayers*. They are insipid. [Inoffensive but Insipid Prayer]

Rather than lament the end of a mythical era of moral purity, it should be noted that even the uniformity prescribed in Deuteronomy 27 depended upon the assent of the Israelites. Moses (like Joshua a generation later, Josh 24:14-28) gave both the Sinai (Exod 19:1-9) and the conquest generations (Deut 27:9-10; 29:2-29) the opportunity to "sign on" to the covenant, as it were—

or, by implication, to reject it. In other words, rather than lament the fact that the society at large does not give its assent to covenant with the God of Israel, the church should focus on its own participation in a covenant relationship with God.

What, then, is the church to do in relation to society at large? Surely the church wishes to influence morality and ethics. If it cannot assume that society at large shares its values and if it should not *impose* them, it still must not retreat into itself. The book of Deuteronomy is clear on the public nature of faith. The church must rely on the moral suasion of *being* the true church. If covenant life is authentic, then the church as God's people will demonstrate true humanity to a society adrift. Surely, then, others will of their choosing join the people of God.

NOTES

[1] Merrill, *Deuteronomy* (NAC 4; Nashville: Broadman & Holman, 1994), 346-47.

[2] See, for example, Gerhard von Rad, *Deuteronomy: A Commentary* (OTL; Philadelphia: Westminster, 1966), 167.

COVENANT BLESSINGS
AND CURSES

28:1-68

Before turning full attention to the transferal of leadership responsibilities from Moses to his successor, Joshua—and in harmony with the reference in 27:11-13 to the antiphonal recitation of covenant blessings and curses—the editors of the book of Deuteronomy provide a relatively full statement of the consequences of covenant obedience or disobedience, respectively. Scholars have noted that, in form, content, and placement, these covenant blessings and curses closely parallel curses included in ANE vassal treaties [Ancient Near Eastern Treaty Curses]. By including them here, the editors of Deuteronomy reinforced the "treaty" or "covenant" aspect of both the Torah and the book of Deuteronomy. [Covenantal Theology] The relationship between YHWH and his people is far from the matter of private piety typical of much of modern religion. It is a solemn contract, complete with incentives and penalties.

Ancient Near Eastern Treaty Curses

Since G. E. Mendenhall first noted similarities between ANE treaties and Old Testament covenants ("Covenant Forms in Israelite Tradition," *Biblical Archaeologist* 17 [1954]: 50-76), a number of scholars have searched ANE diplomatic and legal literature for parallels. (See, for example, D. J. McCarthy, *Treaty and Covenant: A Study in Form in the Ancient Oriental Documents and in the Old Testament* [AB 21; Rome: Pontifical Biblical Institute, 1963]; D. R. Hillers, *Treaty Curses and the Old Testament Prophets* [BibOr 16; Rome: Pontifical Biblical Institute, 1964]; J. A. Thompson, *The Ancient Near Eastern Treaties and the Old Testament* [London: Tyndale Press, 1964]; and M. Weinfeld, *Deuteronomy and the Deuteronomic School* [Oxford: Clarendon, 1972], 116-26.) The basic form of these treaties, seen already in the Hittite treaties dating to the 14th and 13th centuries BC, predominated in international diplomatic texts down to the 7th century BC and beyond. It included the following major sections: (a) preamble, (b) historical prologue, (c) stipulation of allegiance, (d) treaty agreement proper, (e) invocation of witnesses, and (f) blessings and curses.

A number of treaties established between the Mesopotamian ruler Esarhaddon and his vassals to the east dating to the early 7th century have proven particularly significant for the study of this literary form. Their very number has allowed scholars to fill in gaps in understanding the language itself. Their date demonstrates the longevity of the treaty pattern: the outline of Esarhaddon's treaties is virtually the same as the much earlier Hittite documents. Their proximity, temporally and geographically, to the Judah of king Josiah who reigned at the time of the (re?)discovery of the book of Deuteronomy may account for parallels with this covenant book.

Covenantal Theology

The covenant idea is originally and essentially secular and political. The ANE covenants that served as the model for the outline of Deuteronomy were agreements between rulers regarding vassal relationships, mutual protection pacts, international boundaries, etc. In the Old Testament, private individuals made covenants with one another similarly defining the nature of their relationships. Isaac and Abimelech covenanted together concerning water rights (Gen 21:22-32); David and Jonathan, Israel's "two musketeers," covenanted together to be lifelong friends and allies (2 Sam 20:1-17). In other words, although readers of the Bible think of "covenant" first and foremost as a religious concept, the authors and editors of Israel's Scriptures borrowed the covenant idea from the secular realm in order to express something specific about Israel's faith. The revolutionary significance of this innovation must not be missed.

As an analogy borrowed from human society and employed to describe a theological reality, however, the covenant idea has limits (see [Models]); that is, it can be pressed too far. Israel's Scripture employed it to make the claim that Israel's relationship with its God somehow resembles relationships governed by covenant in the secular realm. The key question is how. At least three points of contact seem pertinent: (1) The political backgrounds of the ANE treaty and the public dimension of the laws in Deuteronomy suggest that the covenant between YHWH and Israel is to be understood in corporate and public terms. (2) Like the water-rights "covenant," the covenant between YHWH and Israel is not to be understood as some amorphous "friendship." To love YHWH is to behave in specific ways, to respect boundaries, etc. (3) If covenants between nations or business partners are to be effective, they must include incentives and means for redressing grievances; that is, they must be enforceable. YHWH will hold violators accountable.

Structural Features

A cursory inspection of 28:1-68 reveals several features worth noting in preparation for a detailed examination of its contents. First, the ratio of curse to blessing (roughly three to one) is remarkable. Relatedly, the tone of many of the curses could hardly be harsher: total eradication as a people, reduction to cannibalism of the most reprehensible character, banishment. Third, the scope of both blessing and curse encompasses every arena of public and private life. Disobedience to the covenant will disrupt nature's balance; it will result in irrevocable damage to domestic and community life and relationships; it will create disorder on an international scale. Together, these three observations call attention once again to the solemnity of the covenant relationship.

A fourth observation relates to the difficult task of unraveling the structure and argument of the material. At first glance, Deuteronomy 28 seems best characterized as verbose and repetitive with no clear progression of thought other than the shift from blessing to curse at v. 15. Closer examination, however, reveals a careful system of framing and parallel structuring. Recognition of this system not only facilitates interpretation, but also provides clues to the composition history of, especially, the lengthy curse materials.

Blessings and Curses

The most obvious structural feature of Deuteronomy 28, of course, is the division into blessings (vv. 1-14) and curses (vv. 15-68). In addition to this shift from blessing to curse, a framework structure linking vv. 1-2 and, especially, v. 13, marks vv. 1-14 as a major unit. A second minor frame links vv. 4 and 11. Together, these dual frames produce a pleasing symmetry and, more to the point, accentuate the blessings proper. The curses are similarly framed in vv. 15 and 45-46, not, however, as one might expect, in vv. 15 and 68. [Framework Structures in Deuteronomy 28] This framework provides the first clue as to the secondary character of vv. 47-68 (see below for further discussion).

Parallels Between Blessings and Curses

In addition to the framing structures demarcating the limits of the blessings and curses (minus expansions), verbatim citations and allusions signal parallels between corresponding sections of the two subdivisions. [Parallel Structures in Deuteronomy 28] These parallels serve to portray the curses as the *inversion* of the blessings. The fact that these parallels extend only through v. 46 provides a second indication that vv. 47-68 represent an expansion of an earlier form of the curse material. Furthermore, lengthy sections of vv. 15-46 (vv. 21-24, 32-35, 38-42) have no counterpart in the blessings material. They, too, therefore, may be editorial expansions. As will be shown, the subject matter of these sections (exile) further supports this hypothesis.

Chiasm

A careful reader will note that the order of many of the parallel elements in the curses reverses that in the blessings and that a similar reversal of sequence occurs in the second half of the framing structure [Reversals of Sequence in Deuteronomy 28]. These chiasms and reversals of sequence function to underscore structurally the central

---

Framework Structures in Deuteronomy 28

AΩ Blessings Framework

28:1—"And if you truly heed the voice of YHWH your God to keep and to do all his commandments that I command you today. . . ."

28:3—"Blessed be the fruit of your womb, the fruit of your land, the fruit of your livestock, the calves of your oxen and the lambs of your flock."

28:11—"And YHWH will make abundant the fruit of your womb, the fruit of your livestock, and the fruit of your land in the land YHWH promised your fathers to give you."

28:13—"And YHWH will make you the head . . . because you heeded the commandments of YHWH your God that I command you today to keep and to do them. . . ."

Curses Framework

28:15—"And if you do not heed the voice of YHWH your God to keep and to do all his commandments and his statutes that I command you today, then all these curses will come upon you and overtake you."

28:45—"And all these curses will come upon you, pursue you, and overtake you until you are destroyed because you did not heed the voice of YHWH your God to keep his commandments and his statutes that I command you."

AΩ Parallel Structures in Deuteronomy 28

1 And if you truly heed the voice of YHWH your God to keep and to do all his commandments which I command you today. . . . 2 And all these blessings will come upon you and overtake you. . . .

3 Blessed shall you be in the city and blessed shall you be in the field. 4 Blessed shall be the fruit of your womb, the fruit of your land, the fruit of your beasts, the calves of your oxen, and the lambs of your flock. 5 Blessed shall be your basket and of your kneading trough. 6 Blessed shall you be when you come in, and blessed shall you be when you go out.

7 YHWH will cause your enemies who arise against you to be smitten before you; they will come against you on one path and they will flee before you on seven.

8 YHWH will command blessing on you in your storehouses and in everything you put your hand to and you will be blessing in the land that YHWH your God gives you.

9 YHWH will establish you as his holy people just as he promised you if you keep the commandments of YHWH your God and walk in his ways. 10 And all the peoples of the earth will see that you are called by the name of YHWH and they will fear you. 11 And YHWH will make abundant the fruit of your womb, the fruit of your cattle, and the fruit of your land in the land YHWH promised your ancestors to give you.

12 YHWH will open to you his storehouse, the heavens, to give rain for your land in its time and to bless the work of your hands. You will lend to many nations, but you will not borrow. 13 YHWH will make you the head and not the tail; you will only be at the top, never at the bottom because you heeded the commandments of YHWH your God that I command you today to keep and to do them. And you did not turn aside from the words I command you today either to the right or to the left to walk after strange gods to serve them.

15 And if you do not heed the voice of YHWH your God to keep and to do all his commandments and his statutes which I command you today. . . . And all these curses will come upon you and overtake you. . . .

16 Cursed shall you be in the city and blessed shall you be in the field. 17 Cursed shall be your basket and of your kneading trough. 18 Cursed shall be the fruit of your womb, the fruit of your land, the calves of your oxen, and the lambs of your flock. 19 Cursed shall you be when you come in and cursed shall you be when you go out.

25 YHWH will cause you to be smitten before your enemies; you will go against them on one path and you will flee before them on seven; you will be a horror to all the kingdoms of the earth.

20 YHWH will send against you curse, tumult, and rebuke in everything you put your hand to do until you are destroyed and perish swiftly because of the evil of your deeds whereby you forsake me. 21 YHWH will cause pestilence to cling to you until you are eradicated from the land you are going to possess.

36 YHWH will bring you and your kings whom you set over you to a nation neither you nor your ancestors have known and there you will serve strange gods of wood and stone. 37 And you will be a horror, a byword, and a taunt among all the nations where YHWH drives you.

43 The resident alien in your midst will ascend above you, ever higher, and you will descend ever lower. 44 He will lend to you, but you will not lend to him. He will be the head, but you will be the tail. 45 All these curses will come against you, pursue you, and overtake you because you did not heed the voice of YHWH your God to keep his commandments and his statutes that I command you. 46 And it will be a sign and a wonder for you and for your seed in perpetuity

---

Reversals of Sequence in Deuteronomy 28

AΩ *Chiasm in the Framework*

Chiasm is the reversal of a sequence in its second occurrence such that an "AB, BA" pattern results. The framework to the opening section of the treaty blessings and curses exhibits this literary technique.

A ". . . to keep and to do all (28:1)
   B the commandments that I command you today . . . ."
   B "the commandments . . . that I command you today (28:13)
A to keep and to do . . . ."

A "If you do not heed the voice of YHWH your God to keep and to do all his command-ments and statues that I command you today (28:15)
   B all these curses will come upon you and overtake you . . . ."
   B ". . . and all these curses will come upon you, pursue you, and overtake you until you are destroyed (28:45-46)
A because you did not heed the voice of YHWH your God to keep his commandments and his statutes that I command you . . . ."

Resequencing in Elements Shared by the Blessings and the Curses

(1) 28:3 city/field	city/field 28:6 (1)
(2) 28:4 fruits of womb, etc.	basket/trough 28:17 (3)
(3) 28:5 basket/trough	fruits . . . 28:18 (2)
(4) 28:6 come in/go out	come in/go out 28:19 (4)

28:12-13   lending/ head and tail/ upward and downward (A/B/C)
28:43-44   upward and downward/ lending/ head and tail (C/A/B)

---

argument of Deuteronomy 28; namely, that the wondrous order and blessing brought by obedience to YHWH and careful observance of the covenant will be totally reversed by disobedience. Order and harmony will become chaos and discord.

Multiplicity of Genres

A final preliminary observation concerning the composition of Deuteronomy 28 relates to the variety of genres found there. Although this lengthy unit is usually designated as a collection of blessings and curses, the material it contains is by no means uniform. Strictly speaking, only the two series of "futility curses" (vv. 28-33; 38-42) and the four matched sayings in vv. 3-6 and 16-19 can be classified as blessing (*bārûk*) and curse (*ʾārûr*). In addition to these simple, straightforward blessings and curses and to the framework materials described above (vv. 1-2, 13b-14; 45-46)—which are cast as typically Deuteronomic exhortations to maintain covenant loyalty—several other types of speech occur, concentrated especially in the curses section.

Futility Curses

The following curses from Esarhaddon's vassal treaties illustrate the similarity with the futility curses of Deut 28:

"May Venus, the brightest of stars, make your wives lie in your enemy's lap while your eyes look (at them)." (Essarhaddon's Succession Treaty, II. 428-29; cf. Deut 28:30a)

"May your sons not be masters of your house." (Essarhaddon's Succession Treaty, II. 429-30a; cf. Deut 28:30b)

"May a foreign enemy divide all your goods." (Essarhaddon's Succession Treaty, I. 430b; cf. Deut 28:33)

S. Parpola and K. Watanabe, *Neo-Assyrian Treaties and Loyalty Oaths, State Archives of Assyria* 2 (Helsinki: Helsinki University Press, 1988), 46.

The prophet Amos also employs the futility curse in his rebukes against those who "abhor the one who speaks the truth":

. . . you have built houses of hew stone,
    but you shall not live in them:
you have planted pleasant vineyards,
    but you shall not drink their wine. (Amos 5:11)

He warns those eager for "the day of YHWH" that it will be contrary to their expectations:

. . . as if someone fled from a lion,
    and was met by a bear;
or went into the house and rested a hand against the wall,
    and was bitten by a snake. (5:19)

Micah, too, warns of the frustration of reversed and thwarted expectations:

You shall eat, but not be satisfied,
    and there shall be a gnawing hunger within you;
you shall put away, but not save,
    and what you save, I will hand over to the sword.
You shall sow, but not reap;
    You shall tread olives, but not anoint with oil;
    You shall tread grapes, but not drink wine.
(Mic 6:14-15)

The blessings section includes a number of promises that YHWH will act in specific ways to aid Israel in certain circumstances (facing enemies, v. 7; blessing Israel's domestic endeavors, v. 8; elevating Israel's international status, vv. 9-10, 12b; bringing fertility, v. 11). The corresponding material in the curses section takes the form of threats (promises to do harm, vv. 20-21). These threats include a sequence of umbrella warnings covering virtually the entire gamut of Israel's life, each introduced with the formula "YHWH will smite (*yakkĕkâ YHWH*, vv. 22, 27, 28, 35)." Two of these threats introduce subunits (vv. 29-33; 38-42) comprised of collections of so-called "futility curses," a specialized form of treaty curse found especially in ANE treaties, eighth-century biblical prophets, and here in Deuteronomy. [Futility Curses] These curses describe a positive circumstance whose promise is left unrealized, or worse, is appropriated by another.

One threat-futility curse sequence (vv. 28-34) quite clearly develops a consistent theme—the madness that will come to those who disobey. Deuteronomy 28:28 threatens that YHWH will "smite" the disobedient "with madness (*bĕšiggā'ôn*), blindness, and bewilderment of heart" and goes on to liken this disorientation to blindness. The following futility curses enumerate the catastrophes that will cause this maddening disorientation: the rape of one's betrothed, the captivity of one's children, unharvestable vineyards, the plunder of one's livestock and produce before one's eyes. This subunit concludes (v. 34) with the explanation: "you will be maddened (*mĕšuggā'*, cf. v. 28) by what you see with your own eyes."

Except for what may be a later insertion (vv. 36-37), vv. 35-42 seem to represent a similar thematic block explicating the theme of the physical decay and corruption that will plague covenant violators. Pest and pestilence will consume everything. YHWH will "smite" the offender with "boils" everywhere (v. 35); locusts will destroy crops (v. 38); worms will consume grapes (v. 39); olives will fall prematurely to the ground (v. 40); children will go into captivity far from home (v. 41); the locusts will consume orchard fruits and field crops (v. 42).

COMMENTARY

The Blessings Conditional on Covenant Loyalty, 28:1-14

To introduce the covenant blessings, the editors of Deuteronomy recast the familiar exhortation to heed YHWH's voice and to keep and do his commandments as the condition for YHWH's benevolence. In addition to these standard formulae, the framework (vv. 1-2, 13b-14) also hints at two other themes significant in Deuteronomy. In response to obedience to the covenant, YHWH will establish Israel as the world's leading nation (v. 1); above all else, covenant obedience requires fidelity to YHWH alone (v. 14), without deviation ("neither to the right nor to the left," compare Deut 2:27; 5:32; 17:11, 20; Josh 1:7; 23:6; 1 Sam 6:12; 2 Kgs 22:2). The notion of Israel's prominence on the international stage probably accounts for the appearance of the designation of YHWH as "Most High (*ʿelyôn*, v. 1)," a term found elsewhere in Deuteronomy only in 26:19 and 32:8, two passages that also deal with Israel's place among the nations (see commentary). The possibility for Israel to attain international prominence is the subject of vv. 9-13a (see below). The anti-idolatry sentiment of v. 14b resonates primarily with the larger context of the whole book, but does recur within the blessings section (compare, however, vv. 20, 36, 64).

Before developing the prominence theme, the blessings offer Israel the possibility of prosperity and protection. The collection of blessings in vv. 3-6 gives every appearance of a self-contained collection, probably predating their inclusion here. Along with their counterparts in vv. 16-19, these couplets probably reflect a liturgical origin and likely represent a portion of the skeleton around which Deuteronomy 28 was composed.

By means of merism and parallelism, these blessings offer prosperity in every area of life—urban and rural, fertility for humans, beasts, and crops, both fruits and grains, well-being on ingress and egress. Notably, with the possible exception of the fourth,[3] these

The Usurers

Typical of this Flemish painter's emphasis upon the mercantile strength of Antwerp, Belgium, in the 16th century, this painting focuses upon the business transactions of the usurer. Here, the artist depicts a lack of balance between the "haves" and the "have-nots" as the two men in the left of the painting seem to have garnered a disproportionate amount of coins. Metsys provides an element of satire, through the attempt by the usurers at moral justification, represented by Metsys through the open Bible. Such commentary upon the hypocrisy of middle class morals and values was common among Flemish artists.

Quentin Metsys. c.1466–1530. *The Usurers.* Galleria Doria Pamphili. Rome, Italy.

blessings primarily address the life of an agrarian people concerned first and foremost with flock and field. Prosperity is also the topic of the blanket promise made in v. 8 that YHWH will open his "storehouse" of blessings to grace every Israelite undertaking ("everything you put your hand to"). Verses 3-6 and 8, then, envision life in the land YHWH gives (v. 8) in terms of natural order, vitality, and well-being. They depict the image of agrarian tranquility.

In addition to internal prosperity, YHWH promises obedient Israel protection from outside enemies. The image of an enemy approaching on one path only to flee on seven conveys a picture of the enemy's confusion and disarray. Significantly, this blessing relates to defensive conflicts ("your enemies who rise up against you") and does not, therefore, promise Israel offensive success. Like the promise of prosperity in which it is imbedded, this blessing pertains to Israel's established life in the land.

Israel's opportunity to attain international prominence involves a different perspective. Protection from enemies will be unnecessary because, as YHWH's "holy people (*ʿam qādôš*, v. 9)" who are "called by the name of YHWH" (v. 10), Israel will inspire fear in its enemies. In this context, Israel's prosperity, mentioned in terms that reprise earlier statements ("fruits of your womb, etc.," v. 11; "to bless all the work of your hand," v. 12), no longer serves a purely domestic function. Instead, it now becomes the standard of comparison whereby Israel can be assured of its supreme international status. Israel will lend to many nations, but not borrow (v. 12); YHWH will make Israel the head and not the tail; Israel's rise to prominence will be uninterrupted (v. 13).

The Curses Resulting from Covenant Disloyalty, 28:15-46

In many respects, the covenant curses detailed in vv. 15-46 mirror the previous blessings and, as demonstrated earlier, display a number of structural parallels. This relationship is self-evident for passages such as vv. 16-19 (compare vv. 3-6); other curse texts relate to their blessings counterparts in subtler ways easily overlooked owing to the variations in sequence noted above. Still other sections of the curse material have no parallels in the blessings whatsoever. In comparison to the blessings, the series of "YHWH will smite" and futility curses sayings stand out as unique elements and, together with clearly parallel materials, provide a clue as to the general outline of the curses material. [Authenticity]

The expected "antiprosperity," "antiprotection," and "antiprominence" counterthemes are treated in language mirroring the blessings and are arranged in the "antiorder" discussed above: introduction (v. 15); "anti-prosperity" (curses couplets [vv. 16-19]; comprehensive warning [vv. 20-21; compare v. 8]; pestilence and drought warnings [vv. 22, 23-24]); "anti-protection" (vv. 25-26; compare v. 7); "anti-prominence" (vv. 36-37, 43-44; compare vv. 9-13a), and conclusion (vv. 45-46). Notably, the "YHWH will smite"/futility curses units interrupt this sequence and deal with themes not addressed in the blessings: "madness" and "pestilence." Furthermore, these composite units divide the "anti-prominence" theme, effectively a treatment of the concept of exile, into two segments. Clearly, the curses have undergone a period of interpretation and expansion.

Authenticity

Some readers may be troubled by the idea that portions of the book of Deuteronomy, and of the covenant curses specifically, may have been added to the book as late as the exilic or early post-exilic periods (6th–5th centuries). They may feel that such additions are by definition inauthentic. In terms of the ancient understanding of "authenticity," an understanding evident at many points in the book of Deuteronomy, however, these concerns are unfounded. It is important to remember that the book of Deuteronomy understands itself as an "explication" of the Sinai covenant (1:5; 27:8). That is, Deuteronomy both argues for the necessity of and embodies the idea that, as a charter of basic principles, the Sinai covenant requires skillful, wise, and genuine application to new circumstances that arise in the life of the people Israel. Without such "authentic" continuation and application of the basic principles in concrete situations, the charter remains largely an abstraction. Furthermore, at several points (see commentary on Deut 4 and 6, for example), Deuteronomy *enjoins* future generations of Israelites to expand on this "authentic" tradition of interpretation. The covenant must be kept alive by continual, vigilant, careful interpretation and integration into the real life of the community. It can be helpful to bear in mind that the truth and wisdom of a statement, its "authenticity," does not depend on the identity of its author. Truth bears its own authority.

In the case at hand, the expansions to the curses have the force of making explicit (that the Assyrian and Babylonian crises are fulfillments of the covenant curses) what is surely implicit in the curses as they originally stood. They should be seen not as counterfeit, but as validations of the preceding tradition. As such, they become part of the ever-growing stream of authentic biblical witness to God's active involvement—whether to bless or to correct—in the life of God's people.

"Antiprosperity," 28:16-24

The most striking features of the "anti-prosperity" curses gathered in vv. 16-24 are (1) their focus on disasters in the natural realm with effects concentrated on Israel's agriculture and (2) the repeated insistence that these effects will extend ultimately to bring about Israel's destruction (vv. 20, 21, 22, 24). Following the traditional curse couplets in vv. 16-19, the editors have added the comprehensive statement of v. 20 (cf. 7:23) declaring that everything Israel undertakes (*bĕkol-mišlah yādĕka*, cf. v. 8) will be stricken by "curse, chaos, and rebuke" because Israel has forsaken YHWH. Employing a redundant series of somewhat rare terms[4] for illness ("consumption," "fever," and "inflammation"), meteorological disasters ("drought" and "fiery heat") and, presumably, various types of plant diseases ("smut" and "mildew"), v. 22 specifies nature as the arena in which YHWH's displeasure will become manifest. In fact, if vv. 23-24 are to be understood as a parallel to the blessing concerning the opening of YHWH's "storehouse in the heavens" in v. 12, they make clear that the treasures YHWH will grant (v. 12) or withhold (vv. 23-24) are the life-giving rains. Rather than open the doors of heaven to release the rains, YHWH will harden the skies so that they become like bronze. As a consequence, the earth beneath will be hardened like iron (v. 23). It will rain dust (v. 24)!

Ketiv/Qere

AΩ Hebrew was written with only consonants until Jewish scholars called "Massoretes" working in the 7th to 9th centuries AD invented a system of "vowel points," dots and dashes placed above and below the consonantal text. Jewish and Christian traditions, as well as modern scholarship, consider only the consonants to be constitutive of the text. The vowels supplied by the Massoretes are considered suggestions as to how the consonants should be "vocalized." The Massoretes held the consonantal text in such high regard that they refused to alter it even when they were suspicious of scribal error or when something in the consonantal text could be considered offensive. In such cases they often supplied alternative readings as marginal glosses. The consonantal text is known as the *ketiv* ("what is written") and the marginal gloss as the *qere* ("what is to be read").

Two instances of these *ketiv/qere* readings occur in 28:27-34. In v. 27, the Massoretes suggest that the *qere*, *těḥorîm* ("tumours") be read in place of the *ketiv*, *ʿŏpalîm* ("piles, hemorrhoids") because the latter was considered too vulgar to be read aloud in the synagogue. A similar situation pertains in v. 30, where the Massoretes suggest that the *qere*, *yiškābennâ* ("he will lie with her") be read in place of the *ketiv*, *yišgālennâ* ("he will rape her").

"Antiprotection," 28:25-26

In an almost verbatim reversal of the promise of protection against its enemies, the curse warns that Israel will flee in confusion. The curse supplements and amplifies the threat, however, with horrific predictions of world-wide infamy and subjection to the ultimate desecration: not only will Israelites die at the hands of their enemies, but they will be left unburied to become carrion for scavenging birds and beasts. (On the horror of being deprived burial, see commentary and sidebars on 21:22-23.)

"Madness," 28:27-34

It is difficult to determine how v. 27 fits into the structure of vv. 27-34. As one of the "YHWH will smite" sayings, it sounds a refrain heard also in vv. 22, 28, and 35. Like vv. 28 and 35, it turns attention to various ailments, diseases, and misfortunes that will impact individual Israelites personally, in this case various skin diseases and lesions ("boils of Egypt," a reminder that Israel can become YHWH's enemy in the same way Egypt was during Moses' time; "hemorrhoids" [Ketiv/Qere], "scabs," and "itch"). The smite/fertility curse unit comprised of vv. 28-34, however, deals with madness and the frustrations that contribute to it and not with physical ailments. In fact, v. 35 resumes the theme initiated in v. 27 ("boils . . . that cannot be healed," *bišḥîn . . . lōʾ-tûkal lěhērāpēʾ*), suggesting perhaps that v. 27 belongs with vv. 35-42. It may be that vv. 28-34 were inserted later, or that v. 27 was displaced through some copyist's error or through some other mishap in the process of transmission.

At any rate, vv. 28-34 develop a very unified theme by means of the juxtaposition of the "smite" and futility curse forms and through the skillful use of the literary device known as "inclusio." The madness theme is announced in v. 28, "YHWH will smite you with madness (*běšiggāʿôn*)," and concluded in v. 34 "and you will become mad (*měšuggāʿ*)." The editors elaborated the image of madness forcefully and vividly. In addition to madness, YHWH will smite Israelites with blindness and "bewilderment of heart." Even in the bright light of the noonday sun, they will be as sightless as the blind man in the black of night. In this state of confusion and disorientation, they will be at the mercy of those who would abuse and rob them (v. 29). Next, the futility curses depict a series of calamities sure to confuse and madden. All of these curses follow a set pattern: "You will do a wholesome, joyful, good thing, but your efforts will be in vain." The positive conditions described in vv. 30-33 cover the gamut of prosperous farm and domestic life: betrothal, a new home, a newly planted vineyard, oxen for slaughtering, herds of livestock, sons and daughters, and rich produce. But, one by one, these apparent blessings, holding such rich promise, are turned to bitter disappointments. Another man will rape one's bride; one's house will remain uninhabited, one's vineyard will go unharvested; one's ox slaughtered in one's presence will be consumed by another, one's donkey stolen, one's flocks given to one's enemies; one's sons and daughters will be deported before one's eyes never to return; one's crops will be consumed by foreigners. In short, one will see "only oppression and distress all one's days" (v. 33b). There is little wonder, then, that one will become "crazy from the sight that one's eyes see" (v. 34).

It is worth noting that here, as elsewhere in Deuteronomy 28, that a process of double agency characteristic of the Old Testament's view of YHWH's activity in human history can be observed. While v. 28 declares unequivocally that YHWH will smite Israel with the afflictions detailed in the futility curses, the curses themselves describe circumstances in which YHWH's hand cannot be easily discerned. In fact, the immediate agents of these calamities are usually unnamed human beings who, it may be assumed, are hardly aware of their role as executioners of YHWH's curse. Some human being will abuse the confused and blinded, rape the betrothed wife, consume the ox, steal the donkey, etc. Curiously, the intentions and purposes of these despoilers, to say nothing of their identities or of whether they are even aware that they participate in some higher plan, are apparently of no concern whatsoever to Deuteronomy. Modern readers, especially theologians and, indeed, all thoughtful believers, would be well-advised to consider carefully the mystery concerning God's activity in human history only adumbrated here (see **Connections**).

"Devastation and Decay," 28:(27)35, 38-42

As noted above, in terms of content and vocabulary, v. 27 belongs properly with the treatment of devastation and decay in vv. 35-42. Similarly, vv. 36-37, which deal with "anti-prominence" matters of exile, interrupt the argument of vv. 35-42 and will be discussed below in the context of vv. 43-44. No explanation for this disrupted arrangement is readily apparent.

Whereas the previous "madness" sequence dealt primarily with human agents of destruction, the threat of "boils . . . from the crown of [one's] head to sole of [one's] feet" (v. 35) introduces the theme of pests, disease, and decay. Again, the futility curses initially describe the most promising of situations—sowing seed in the field, planting vineyards (again), olive orchards, sons and daughters, fruit trees and crops—and, once again, hopes for the expected result are dashed. Now, however, the agents of destruction are, for the most part, natural pests: locusts, worms, and some olive-tree disease (presumably the cause for the premature loosing of the olives mentioned in v. 40). Only the captivity of sons and daughters (v. 41) implies human agency, although the context colors even this loss as a form of blight. Scholarship wisely chooses to term such curses "futility curses"! Israel will be frustrated at every turn!

"Antiprominence," 28:36-37, 43-44

Like the corresponding section in the blessings (vv. 12b-13a), vv. 43-44 focus attention primarily on Israel's status on only one small corner of the international stage, that is, in relation to its nearest neighbors or even to "the resident alien in [its] midst (v. 43)." In contrast, vv. 36-37, which disrupt the sequence of "YHWH will smite" sayings (v. 35) followed by futility curses (vv. 38-42) and which, consequently, are likely a later interpolation, transpose the "anti-prominence" theme into a premonition of the Babylonian exile. The reference to "your king whom you set over you," one of only two treatments of kings in Deuteronomy (see Deut 17), anticipates the central theme of the books of Samuel and Kings and may be an indication of the late date at which these verses were added. Similarly, the language of these two verses is very reminiscent of the

Sixth-century Parallels

Scholars have long recognized the close relationship between the language and thought of portions of Deuteronomy, the books of Joshua–2 Kings, and the book of Jeremiah. It is very difficult to ascertain in every case, however, whether Deuteronomy served as the model for the authors of the Deuteronomistic history and the book of Jeremiah or whether the portions of Deuteronomy in question are later additions to the book. It seems clear, at any rate, given the report (2 Kgs 22) of the discovery of what must have been Deuteronomy during the reign of king Josiah (c. 626 BC), that Deuteronomy underwent editorial revision during the same period that the Deuteronomistic history and

the book of Jeremiah were being written. Phraseology in 28:36-37 alone that is shared by Judges–2 Kings and Jeremiah includes the following: "A nation which you do not know" (Jer 5:15; compare 16:13; 17:4; 22:28); "serve there other gods" (Jer 16:13; 44:8, 15; ironically, this description of punishment is also a common phrase in Deuteronomy, the Deuteronomistic History, and Jeremiah describing Israel's sin: Josh 23:16; 24:2, 16; Judg 2:12, 17, 19; 10:13; 1 Sam 8:8; 26:19; 1 Kgs 9:6, 9; 11:4, 10; 14:9; 2 Kgs 5:17; 17:7, 35, 37, 38; 22:17; Jer 1:16; 7:6, 9, 18; 11:10; 13:10; 16:11; 19:4, 13; 22:9; etc.); "gods of wood and stone" (2 Kgs 19:18; Jer 2:27; 3:9); "horror, byword, taunt"—1 Kgs 9:7; 2 Kgs 22:19; Jer 2:15; 4:7; 5:30; 8:21; 18:16; 24:9; etc.).

diction of the sixth-century prophets, especially Jeremiah, who were active during the Babylonian crisis. [Sixth-century Parallels]

With astonishing economy, the interpolation (vv. 36-37) announces many of the major elements of the theology of history found in the books of Kings and in the sixth-century prophets. The kings of Israel and Judah bear significant, if not primary, responsibility for the demise of the two states. Ironically, unfaithful Israel's ultimate fate will involve forced worship of strange gods "of wood and stone" among an unknown people. Sadly, exiles will be dispersed among many nations, there to be reviled and despised. According to this brief outline of the end of Israel's history as a nation, obedience to the covenant is not merely a matter of personal success or failure, but of *survival as a nation!*

Conclusion, 28:45-46

The concluding element of the curses framework reprises the language of the opening (v. 45 // v. 15) with the addition of the ominous declaration in v. 46 that the curses of the covenant will be "a sign and a wonder" for Moses' audience and their descendants perpetually (*'ad 'ôlam*). This statement reminds a modern reader of the difference between ancient Israel's concept of "signs and wonders" and the reader's own, on the one hand, and, as though it were necessary after the preceding, of the extreme gravity with which the editors of Deuteronomy view the covenant and its incentives, on the other. For the ancient, the essence of "signs" lay in their ability to "signify" something, not necessarily in their capacity to amaze. These curses are much more than mere words of warning; they wondrously signify the supreme importance of covenant with YHWH for Israel's very survival!

An Exilic or Postexilic Insertion, 28:47-68

The framework surrounding the curses section and the scheme of parallels with the blessings section end in v. 46. Furthermore, the final section of Deuteronomy 28 (vv. 47-68) exhibits a number of other characteristics that confirm the break between vv. 46 and 47 and that suggest this material may, in fact, be an exilic or post-exilic amplification of the existent curse collection.[1] First, whereas, with the exception of only a few verses—which themselves seem to be later editorial commentary[2]—both the blessings and curses material focus primarily on natural phenomena or Israel's international reputation, vv. 47-68 generally describe siege and exile very concretely (v. 64). The ominous references to Egypt (vv. 60, 68) suggest a return to bondage.

Second, beginning in v. 48, the final section of Deuteronomy 28 adopts an even harsher tone than the preceding curse material. Repeatedly (vv. 48, 51, 61), disobedient Israel is threatened with oppression to the point of destruction (*ʿad hišmîdô ʾōtāk*, v. 48; *ʿad hiššāmdāk*, vv. 51, 61; *ʿad haʿăbîdô ʾōtāk*, v. 51; *lĕhaʿăbîd ʾetkem ûlĕhašmîd ʾetkem*, v. 63) at the hands of an enemy nation. Israel will suffer distress and affliction at the hands of this enemy (*bĕmāsôr ûbĕmāsôq ʾăšer-yāsîq lĕkā ʾōybekā*, vv. 53, 55, 57). Now covenant disloyalty brings not pestilence (v. 21), but annihilation.

Third, beginning also in v. 47, the perspective shifts from the conditional ("if," vv. 15, 46), to narrative ("because you did not serve YHWH, your God," v. 47; "because you did not heed the voice of YHWH, your God," v. 62). References to strongholds (v. 52), an enemy that speaks a language unknown to Israel (v. 62), and dispersion among the nations (v. 64) reflect awareness of conditions that Israel and Judah faced during the crises of the eighth and sixth centuries, respectively. The specificity of the description of Israel's enemy, of the distresses of siege, and especially of dispersion and exile suggest a historical perspective. Relatedly, the vocabulary of these descriptions share much in common with biblical literature dating to the period of the sixth-century Babylonian crisis (especially the "Deuteronomistic history" and Jeremiah; see the commentary below for details).

Finally, vv. 47-68 betray an awareness not only of historical conditions at the end of Israel's/Judah's existence as independent states, but also an awareness of Deuteronomy as a *book* (vv. 58, 61). In the dominant narrative scheme of Deuteronomy, the book reports the content of Moses' speeches to Israel in Moab during the final days of his life. To refer to itself as a *book* is to adopt a stance one step further removed from the purported rhetorical situation, a stance otherwise assiduously avoided.

In sum, vv. 47-68 can probably be regarded as an exilic or post-exilic amplification and extrapolation of the curse material. It exemplifies Deuteronomy's attitude toward established—in this case written—tradition and its authentic extension (see **Connections** and sidebars on Deut 4 above and [Authenticity]). For the editors of Deuteronomy, a later description of actual events consistent with, or implied in, the potential curses represents an authentic component, even a confirmation, of the tradition.

"Invaders!" 28:47-57

The blessings and curses are loosely arranged in terms of theme. Beginning in v. 47, the first addendum to the curse collection develops a linear plot in four movements: descriptions of (a) Israel's ingratitude and the resulting subjugation to a foreign power (vv. 47-48); (b) the enemy (vv. 49-50); (c) the enemy's tactics (vv. 51-52); and (d) Israel's distressed reactions (vv. 53-57). The descriptions are very specific, very graphic, and very familiar to readers of the books of Kings and the sixth-century prophets, especially Jeremiah.

Instead of the key concept of obedience expressed in the terms "hearing" and "doing," vv. 47 and 48 speak of "service" (*'bd*). Because Israel failed to serve YHWH joyfully and wholeheartedly (*běṭûb lēbāb*; literally, "with goodness of heart," v. 47), it will be forced into the service of its enemies sent by YHWH. Accompanied by famine, thirst, nakedness, and want, the enemy will subjugate Israel, placing "a yoke of iron of [its] neck" (v. 48). [Yoke of Iron]

Yoke of Iron

In the Semitic realm, the image of the yoke represents political subjugation, i.e., vassalage. Assyrian and Babylonian rulers commonly boasted of placing the yoke (*niru[m]*) of overlordship on the necks of their vassals. (See, for example, C. Gordon, *Ugaritic Textbook* [AnOr 38; Rome: Pontifical Biblical Institute, 1965], 67:II:12; 137:36-38; 118; compare J. Greenfield, "Some Aspects of Treaty Terminology in the Bible," *Fourth World Congress of Jewish Studies, Papers*, I [Jerusalem: 1967], 117-19; Z. Zevit, "The Use of *'bd* as a Diplomatic Term in Jeremiah," *JBL* 88 [1969]: 74-77.) Similarly, when used metaphorically in the Old Testament, the term always refers to political domination and oppression (Gen 27:40; Lev 26:13; 1 Kgs 12:4, 9, 10, 11, 14 [2 Chr 10:4, 9, 10, 11, 14]; Isa 9:3 [4 Eng]; 10:27;

14:25; 47:6; Jer 2:20; 27:8, 11, 12; 30:8; Ezek 34:27; Lam 1:14; 3:27).

The exchange between Jeremiah and Hananiah recorded in Jer 28 illustrates the significance of the image of an "iron yoke." Jeremiah fashioned a wooden yoke that he wore in the temple as a symbol of Babylon's domination of Judah. Hananiah removed it, broke it, and proclaimed that Babylon's imperium would be of short duration. Later, Jeremiah returned with an iron yoke around his neck and with a message for Hananiah from YHWH: "You have broken wooden bars only to forge iron bars in place of them . . . I have put an iron yoke on the neck of all these nations so that they may serve King Nebuchadnezzar of Babylon, and they shall indeed serve him" (Jer 28:14).

Defeat

The Mesopotamian powers, Assyria and later Babylon, were fierce warriors. Their tactics were designed to inspire fearful subjection to imperial authority.

Assyrian Warriors Impaling Jewish Prisoners after Conquering Laquish. Detail of a relief from the Palace of Sennacherib. 701 BC Niniveh, Mesopotamia (Iraq). British Museum. London, Great Britain.

The text seems to have in mind a specific enemy. The description of the unnamed enemy nation parallels descriptions of Israel's actual enemy, Babylon, written contemporaneously with Babylon's campaigns against Israel in the sixth century. According to vv. 49-50, four features characterize this enemy: (1) It will come "from afar, from the ends of the earth" (cf. Isa 5:26; 10:3; Jer 5:15; Hab 1:8); (2) It will swoop down upon Israel like an eagle (cf. Jer 4:13; Hab 1:8); (3) It will speak a language that Israel does not understand (cf. Jer 5:15); and (4) It will be an uncompassionate nation (*gôy 'az pānîm*, literally, "a nation strong of face," v. 50; the paraphrase "stern-faced" approximates the idea conveyed by the Hebrew) that will show neither regard for the elderly nor mercy for the young.

The narrative turns attention now to the enemy's tactics and their consequences for Israel. Skillfully, the editor(s) responsible for this addendum imitate(s) ideas from the earlier blessings and curses material, in part borrowing existing terminology, to depict the devastation of Israel's agricultural bounty. Whereas the curses attribute the destruction of Israel's crops to natural causes (see vv. 21-24), v. 51 portrays the devastation of farms and crops by military invaders who will "consume (*'kl*, vv. 51)" the "fruits of [the] cattle and of [the] land" (cf. vv. 4, 18), leaving Israel without "grain, wine, oil [terms that do not appear previously in the blessings or curses], offspring of cattle, or young of the flock" (cf. vv. 4, 18 once again). These occupation forces, besieging cities and pillaging the countryside, will prosecute the attack to its completion, eventually breaching the walls of the fortifications and strongholds that Israel has trusted as protection against such invasions (v. 52). [Trusting Walls]

Following the explanation of the cause of this situation, the vivid description of the enemy, and the equally graphic portrayal of its tactics, the addendum concentrates finally and logically on Israel's reactions. The editor(s), who devote(s) as much space to this section as to the previous three (six verses each), spare(s) nothing to depict the horror of Israel's situation. Circumstances could hardly

---

Trusting Walls

The reference in Deut 28:52 to "the walls in which you trust" recalls the prophetic critique of Israel's confidence in its military strength and its international alliances (Isa 31:1; Jer 5:17; 13:25; 46:25; 48:7; 49:4; Ezek 16:15; Hos 10:13). Even before the anointing of Israel's first king, Saul, the prophet Samuel warned (1 Sam 8 and 10) that, like any political institution, Israel's monarchy would be tempted away from trust in YHWH. Power structures deal in tangible instruments of power: armies, chariots (or tanks and missile defense systems), international treaties, fortifications, etc.

The prophets saw the monarchy's hunger for power as a threefold danger. First, in order to amass the wealth necessary to compete internationally, the state found it expedient to impose systems of heavy taxation and conscripted labor that resulted in the socioeconomic stratification of Israelite society. Second, in a quest for international prestige, Israelite kings, beginning already with Solomon, entered into alliances by marriage to foreign princesses, opening the door for the

officially sanctioned incursion of foreign religions. Both of these dangers can be seen already in the reign of King Solomon, David's son.

The expression in Deut 28:52, however, emphasizes the third and, from a prophetic perspective, perhaps most fundamental, danger. Confidence in military strength implies that trust in YHWH alone is insufficient. Such militarism is an insidious form of idolatry indeed. What king, or what president, for that matter, can easily follow the advice of the prophet Isaiah to "take heed, be quiet, and not fear" before the prospect of invasion (Isa 7:4)? The prophets were convinced, however, that to place trust in military power is to fail to understand that God, not armies, determines the course of history. A nation's might can best be judged not by its military preparedness, but by the goodness of its people, the justice of its society, and the quality of its trust in God, the ultimate source of strength. As the world's sole remaining superpower, the United States would do well to examine its internal health rather than to rely on its outward strength.

be more gruesome. The invader will "consume" Israel's agricultural products, but Israelites themselves will consume "the fruits of [their own] womb (vv. 4, 18), . . . the sons and daughters whom YHWH . . . has given," so desperate will be the shortage of food resulting from the enemy's siege ("in the deprivation and distress to which your enemy reduces you," *bĕmāṣôr ûbĕmāṣôq ʾăšer-yāṣîq lĕkā ʾōyĕbekā*, vv. 53, 55, 57). Fathers (vv. 54-55) and mothers (vv. 56-57) will be reduced not just to cannibalism, but also to cannibalizing their own children. As though the act itself were not horrendous enough, the text particularizes the horror with shocking detail. These cannibal fathers will be "the most gentle and refined" of men; the mothers so delicate that they do not even dare to place their bare feet on the ground. The terms used here often describe royalty (Isa 47:1; 1 Chr 22:5; 29:1; 2 Chr 13:7): Aristocrats will cannibalize their own children! But matters will be even more repugnant. These aristocratic cannibal-fathers will be reduced to animalistic selfishness, begrudging food, even the flesh of their own children, to brother, beloved wife, and offspring; the mothers to hoarding even their own after-births to be consumed "secretly" (v. 57)! Can a more horrifying depiction of Israel's distress be imagined?

If, however, as scholars suspect, vv. 47-57 represent a late addendum to the covenant curses, the editor(s) responsible for it may not have found it necessary to rely on imagination. Israel's historiography and poetry attest to at least two historical incidents of siege-related famine severe enough to drive people to such abhorrent cannibalism. According to 2 Kings 6:24-32, during a conflict between Israel (the northern kingdom) and Syria, circumstances in besieged Samaria became so desperate that two mothers would agree to feed upon their sons. Lamentations (2:20; 4:10) refers to maternal cannibalism during Judah's sixth-century Babylonian crisis. Similar phenomena are attested outside the Bible in other Ancient Near Eastern contexts (see ANET 298c, 300a).

"Exile!" 28:58-68

The final section is noteworthy for its commentary nature (vv. 58-63) and for introducing the possibility of exile (vv. 64-68). It functions substantially as a summary of the previous material and a theological rationale for them. Its primary contributions are to focus attention, as signaled already in its formulaic introduction, on the book of Deuteronomy *as a book*, and to describe the pathos of exile. These features alone suggest that vv. 58-68 represent a very

Captive
To the ferocity of their Assyrian predecessors, the Babylonians added the technique of hostage-taking to control conquered populations.

Jewish Captives with Camel and Baggage on Their Way into Exile. Detail of a relief from the Palace of Sennacherib. 701 BC. Niniveh, Mesopotamia (Iraq). British Museum. London, Great Britain.

late phase in the growth of the book when an editor could refer to the already extant document.

Certain stylistic characteristics offer additional confirmation of this suspicion:

(1) The phrase "to do the words of this Torah" is unique in Deuteronomy 28 (cf. "to do the commandments which I command you this day," vv. 1, 13, 15, 45). Considered alone, the distinction between these two phrases already indicates the shift in perspective. The dominant phrase refers to the commandments of YHWH delivered orally by Moses the day he addressed Israel; the phrase in v. 58 refers to words written in a book (cf. v. 61, "written in this book of the Torah").

(2) The expression "to fear the glorious and awesome name" is unique to this passage. Its nearest parallel is Malachi 1:14.

(3) The allusions to the promise to the patriarchs in v. 62 ("like the stars of the heavens") suggest that the author was familiar with the written patriarchal tradition.

(4) The reference to "the land where you are" (v. 63) contrasts with the typical Deuteronomic expressions, "the land to which you are going," "the land you are going to possess," and "the land YHWH is giving you." It suggests that, from the perspective of the author of this addendum, possession of the land is an established fact. In other words, like the references to "the book," this expression makes no effort to maintain the perspective of Moses' address in Moab.

As indicated above, the unit, which is unified by the ominous specter of Egyptian bondage (vv. 60, 68), divides neatly into two subsections governed by the shift in focus from the contents of the book in vv. 58-63 to dispersion among the nations in vv. 64-68. The first subsection begins, as noted above, with a modified version of the formula encountered frequently in Deuteronomy 28 (vv. 1, 13, 15, 45). In addition to the striking emphasis upon the book, the notion of heeding and doing the Torah by means of "fearing the name" stands out as unique in the book of Deuteronomy. Together with the modifiers "glorious and awesome," the phrase suggests a late liturgical setting. The subsection continues in logical fashion (v. 59) to warn that YHWH will bring about all the "afflictions (*makkôt*, literally "smitings") and the "illnesses" (written in the book). All the dread "diseases of Egypt," an allusion surely intended to recall the time of captivity, will "cling (*dbq*)" to Israel (v. 60). In fact, YHWH will bring upon Israel even the illnesses and afflictions (should there happen to be any such; if anything, the curses have been exhaustive!) "not recorded in this book of the Torah!" The end result? Destruction (v. 61) and decimation (v. 62). YHWH, who had hoped to make Israel number "as the stars of the heavens (v. 62)," who had rejoiced in doing Israel good and blessing it, will take delight in "annihilating (*'bd*)," "destroying (*šmd*)," and "tearing away (*nsh*)." The words of the book of the Torah hold the key to Israel's very survival!

The second and final subsection elucidates the idea that YHWH will "tear [Israel] away from the land." Again, in a very logical and linear progression, this unit outlines Israel's experience of exile. First, the text declares that Israel will be scattered among nations to the far reaches of the world, "there to serve other gods, previously unknown to you or your fathers, gods of wood and stone" (v. 64).

Then, the text describes the exiles' subjective experience of exile: they will find no rest; they will suffer despair, despondency, and hopelessness (v. 65); they will know no sense of personal security, but will be continually in fear for their lives (v. 66); they will pass their days longing for the quick passage of time (v. 67). The final statement confirms the impression that this description depicts the slave experience: YHWH will return them "in mourning"[5] to Egypt, along the same route by which they once escaped slavery. YHWH had promised that they would never see that route again, yet, as a consequence of their disobedience, they now sell themselves into (debt?) slavery. Even worse, it will be a permanent condition since there will be no one to redeem them. In the end, then, Israel's history of idolatry and defiance of YHWH's revealed will culminates in a return to the beginning: slavery in Egypt!

CONNECTIONS

Believers are accustomed to regarding the Bible as a source of answers for life and faith. Sometimes, however, the life of faith demands more than simple, pat answers. The world is complex; God is mysterious; reality is multi-faceted. In many instances, then, the Bible functions better not as the answer book, but as the source for ways of thinking. The right questions and the proper mode of thinking can often shape a faithful response to a complicated universe better than platitudes.

The covenant blessings and curses contained in Deuteronomy 28 insist on one key assertion: namely, that faithful adherence to the requirements of YHWH's covenant will result in success, security, and status for Israel, while the opposite, rebelliousness, will bring a reversal of Israel's fortunes. For Deuteronomy 28, this linkage between obedience and blessing, defiance and curse is direct, immediate, and inevitable. Explicitly and implicitly, this understanding of Israel's fate relies on absolute confidence in YHWH's sovereignty over the natural world and over human history. The grounds for this confidence are never the topic of the discussion. The text offers no arguments—theological, phenomenological, or otherwise—in support of this significant pillar of Israel's faith. The text does not provide even an outline of a doctrine of God's activity in human history. Instead, its bold claim only raises a number of problems left unresolved here. A faithful response to the complexities of the world requires careful consideration of these unresolved dimensions of biblical claims. As the broader scriptural tradition and the history of theological reflection demonstrate, these issues often become central questions for the community of faith that can shape its life and thought as deeply as many fully formed doctrines. Deuteronomy 28 gives rise to at least six such issues:

(1) The claims made in Deuteronomy 28 confront attentive readers with one of the most fundamental tensions in biblical faith: the dialectical relationship between grace and law, election and covenant. In simplest terms, the harsh description of Israel's virtual annihilation for the violation of covenant raises the question of its election status *after* violating the covenant. In more abstract terms, while the "covenant" idea obviously plays a key role in the Old Testament's conceptualization of Israel's relationship to its God, the discussion of rebellious Israel's fate offers an opportunity to contemplate the adequacy of the covenant idea.

To be sure, aspects of Israel's relationship with its God can deftly be characterized in covenant terms, but does the covenant idea have limits? From Genesis (Gen 12:1-3) to Isaiah (Isa 40), the Old Testament insists that, in fact, like most symbols and analogies, the covenant concept fails adequately to explain the full depth of God's wholly gracious commitment. Other models of relationship, especially familial models, speak more adequately to these other dimensions of YHWH's relationship with Israel [Models]. As is often the case, the challenge both for theologians in their studies and for ordinary believers in their everyday lives is to maintain the dialectic between the various useful, but inevitably limited, models. The God of the Old Testament is a loving parent, patient, kind, and forgiving. But the same God created a world with a moral dimension. This God demands to be respected. Choices have consequences, even for the most beloved child of the most merciful parent.

Models

How does one speak about God? Since the human mind cannot comprehend "godness," any God language must be based on analogies drawn from human experience. Consequently, theology is largely metaphor. This aspect of God-talk is self-evident in expressions such as "God is the Rock of my salvation" (God is most certainly not a rock). But it applies equally to all other talk about God. God is *not* a father in the everyday sense of the term; to call God "Lord" in a society that knows nothing of feudalism is virtually meaningless; in order to understand implications of the biblical notion of God as "kinsman-redeemer" (*go'ēl*), modern Westerners must first become familiar with ancient Israelite family law (see commentary, connections, and sidebars on Deut 25:5-12).

The crucial problems for theologians and believers involve (1) avoiding overextending and absolutizing these analogies and metaphors and (2) appreciating the fact that the depth and scope of the truth may require balancing a number of models. To argue that, since we call God "Father," God is male and has passed on his genes to his children through sexual reproduction is, of course, ludicrous on its face. To argue that, since we call God "Judge," God is interested only in punishing the guilty (and not also or more interested in healing and reconciling) is equally shortsighted. The idea of the covenant is another such analogy, and it must be permitted to communicate its truth without being forced to convey more than intended.

(2) In its single-minded determination to drive home its central message, Deuteronomy 28 can give the impression that the cause-and-effect relationship between obedience to the covenant and blessing, on the one hand, and violation of the covenant and curse, on the other, is automatic and invariable. Daily life and the witness of other portions of Scripture, however, contradict any notion that the Deuteronomic theology of reward and punishment applies universally—to everyone, everywhere, at all times. Common to human experience are the inexplicable suffering of the innocent and the unmerited success of the evildoer. Justice is often miscarried and even more often delayed. These phenomena provide the impetus for biblical psalms of lament, for prophetic complaints such as that of Jeremiah 12, for the lengthy and agonizing deliberations of the book of Job, and even for apocalypticism. Innocent suffering understood as redemptive, apparently first expressed in the so-called "Suffering Servant Songs" of Isaiah (see, for example, the famous song in Isa 53), becomes an important element in the Christian interpretation of the significance of the life and death of Jesus of Nazareth. Again, the whole truth is larger than any one-dimensional statement can elucidate. In faith, Scriptures maintain that Israel's God creates and sustains a moral order; at the same time, also in faith, they maintain that Israel's God governs this moral order by means more mysterious than mechanical.

(3) The system of rewards and punishments detailed in Deuteronomy's covenant theology also presents a problem in relation to the moral development of the believer. Faithful obedience motivated primarily, or exclusively, by a system of rewards and punishment can hardly be regarded a "mature" faith. The modern developmental psychologist Lawrence Kohlberg has shown that, in the typical ethical maturation of a normal human, only the very earliest stages are governed by fear of punishment and hope for reward [Kohlberg on Moral Development]. His careful research confirms what common sense and experience already suggest: namely, that to do right solely in hopes of reward and to refrain from wrong only for fear of punishment is childish. In many ways, the book of Job can be seen as an extended reflection on this basic problem. To paraphrase Satan, "Does Job serve God only because God rewards and protects him (Job 1:9-11)? Will Job continue to serve God simply

Kohlberg on Moral Development

The developmental psychologist Lawrence Kohlberg conducted extensive research on the development of moral sensibilities. Under the influence of cognitive psychologist Jean Piaget's concept of stages of development, Kohlberg theorized that individuals undergo a series of levels of moral development, each of which builds upon the previous. Kohlberg's theory of moral development in tabular form follows:

Level I: Preconventional Morality (ages 4-10)
Stage 1: Obedience and Punishment Morality. Egocentric individual motivated by a strict pleasure-pain orientation.
Stage 2: Naïve Instrumental Hedonism. Individual still motivated by need satisfaction, but has begun to see the value of deal-making.

Level II: Conventional Morality (ages 10-13)
Stage 3: "Good Boy/Nice Girl" Morality. Individual is motivated by a need for approval.
Stage 4: Authority and Social Order Morality. Individual seeks the approval of society in general by adhering rigidly to rules.

Level III: Postconventional Morality (adolescence-adulthood)
Stage 5: Contractual/Legalistic Orientation. Individual motivated by respect for others' needs; enters into contracts for the common good.
Stage 6: Universal Ethics/Individual Conscience. Individual obeys societal norms, except when in conflict with a deeper, universal justice; individual interested in doing the right thing, regardless of the rules.

L. Kohlberg, "How to Encourage Moral Development," *Learning* (March 1977): 36-44. Other researchers have suggested alternative (but not contradictory) schemes. See, for example, J. Piaget, *The Moral Judgment of the Child* (Glencoe IL: Free Press, 1948); R. H. Peck and R. J. Havighurst, *The Pyschology of Character Development* (New York: Wiley, 1960).

because it is right so to do?" For modern Christians, who celebrate "freedom in Christ" and "freedom from the law," the question has to do with whether members of the body of Christ have matured enough to do right for right's sake.

(4) Israel's prophets and historians who preached and wrote during and after the Assyrian (eighth century) and Babylonian (sixth century) crises identified the covenant curses with the military defeats dealt them by these Mesopotamian imperial powers. As might be expected, and as textual evidence from the period demonstrates (compare, for example, Lam 5), the invading armies had no interest in distinguishing between those guilty of covenant unfaithfulness and the innocent. They behaved as invading armies always do. They killed, burned, pillaged, and raped indiscriminately. Innocent people suffered the common fate. Yet, Israel's theologians insisted that the Assyrians and the Babylonians were instruments of YHWH's justice. As Walter

Brueggemann points out in his commentary on *1 & 2 Kings* in this series (Macon: Smyth & Helwys, 2000; see his discussion of 2 Kgs 22–23), YHWH's covenant with Israel is valid at a community level in a way that is difficult for modern Westerners to comprehend. Individuals may be innocent, per se, but YHWH's judgment comes against the society of which they are a part. Still, the apparent moral problem with respect to the innocent who suffer along with the guilty deserves humble and pious consideration (compare Gen 18:16-33).

(5) The flip side of this problem involves the case of the human agents who execute YHWH's judgment. Is it ever right to rape? What is the status of the executioner of YHWH's curse? As the curses and the prophets warn and the books of Kings report, YHWH brought the Babylonian invaders against Judah in punishment for the rebellion of Judah's kings and people. These invaders savagely maimed, killed, and raped. Their victims included young and old, male and female, sinner and innocent. They did not first ascertain the degree of their victims' guilt and then choose appropriate and equitable punishment. They were entirely indiscriminate and fierce. Later prophecy (Isa 14:3-27; 21:9-10; 47:1-15; Jer 50:11-18, 23-34; 51:1-14, 24-29, 34-44, 49-53), looking back on the unbridled violence worked by the Babylonians and others, recognized that, even though they had acted as instruments of YHWH's punishment for Judah, they had transgressed YHWH's expectation of justice in a number of ways. Not only had they taken malicious glee in destroying and causing injury, far exceeding what was necessary to subdue and humble the Judean population, but they had also been guilty of the fundamental sin for which Judah was being punished in the first place. The Babylonians assumed that their military success was the product of their own might! For Israel's prophets, this arrogant denial of YHWH's sovereignty over human history, parallel in many ways to Israel's chronic transgressions against the supremely important commandment to worship YHWH only as Lord, rendered Babylon worthy of a verdict similar to Judah's. YHWH did not bring the Babylonians against unfaithful Judah just so that Babylon could then behave as though it need not answer to the Lord of history for its actions. Babylon should have recognized its role as YHWH's instrument on the grand stage of human history. This recognition would surely have produced much more humble attitudes and much more humanitarian actions. [Arrogance and Malicious Glee]

Arrogance and Malicious Glee

In the context of ancient codes of honor, it is instructive to contrast the attitudes attributed to victorious Babylon with Odysseus's admonition to the nurse Eurykleia that she not gloat over the death of Odysseus's enemies. (The shameful spectacle of parties celebrating executions comes to mind: Regardless of the guilt of the condemned, and irrespective of one's position on the death penalty, the death of a human being is not a proper cause for celebration.) Jeremiah's words of judgment against Babylon stress that Babylon's joy over Judah's destruction constitutes her guilt:

Though you rejoice, though you exult,
    O plunderers of my heritage,
Though you frisk about like a heifer on the grass,
    And neigh like stallions,
Your mother shall be utterly shamed,
    And she who bore you shall be disgraced. (Jer 50:11-12a)

Babylon has acted arrogantly, without acknowledging that she has been but YHWH's instrument:

I am against you, O arrogant one,
    says YHWH God of hosts;
for your day has come,
    the time when I will punish you.
The arrogant one shall stumble and fall . . . (50:31-32a)

Odysseus, who was himself their executioner, voices the ancient code of the honor owed even to one's enemies:

. . . As she [the nurse Eurykleia] gazed
From all the corpses to the bloody man
She raised her head to cry over his triumph,
But she felt his grip upon her, checking her.
Said the great soldier then:

"Rejoice inwardly. No crowing aloud, old woman.
To glory over slain men is no piety.
Destiny and the gods' will vanquished these;
And their own hardness."

Odyssey, bk 22, ll., 406-14, trans. R. Fitzgerald, *The Odyssey* (Garden City: Doubleday, 1961), 390.

Comparisons to circumstances on the modern stage of international affairs suggest a number of caveats, especially for the only remaining superpower (as was Babylon at one time). Powerful nations must be wary of the arrogance that leads them to assume that theirs is the supreme will in human history. No doubt Babylon moved against Judah for its own reasons of national interest, but, seen from the broader perspective, their action was the fulfillment of God's will. In the modern world, the United States, the uncontested superpower, has already demonstrated the tendency to seek to impose its will on the world. Or, with an arrogance tantamount to blasphemy, the United States has on occasion, as in the Persian Gulf conflict, sought to identify its economic and security interests with the causes of justice—as though the West's ready access to Persian Gulf oil were a moral issue. Babylon's wealth and prosperity were not matters of ultimate importance for YHWH. Similarly, it is blasphemously arrogant to assume that God wills American wealth and prosperity for its own sake

The prophets charged Babylon with overreaching its mandate. In their view, Babylon had been too zealous, and too gleeful, in its prosecution of the Judean campaigns. While most would probably agree that the moral dimensions of at least one twentieth-century war (WWII) justified forceful intervention, the horror of Nazi (or Iraqi) evils was not a blanket justification for any and every response. Military leaders in the modern era often employ rhetoric that masks the horrors of modern warfare. The deaths of innocent civilians—women and children like those mourned in the biblical book of Lamentations—are described as "collateral damage." In many cases, the victims of errant bombs are the very innocents on whose behalf the war has been waged in the first place (witness events in Kosovo at the end of the twentieth century). In others, individuals comprising the enemy army are themselves opponents and victims of the oppressive regime they are forced to serve (as was true of the Iraqi forces stationed in southern Iraq). While it is true that no degree of care or preparation can ensure that combatants and only combatants will be injured, it is equally true that the God who is Judge of all the earth and Sovereign over human history notes the death of every innocent.

(6) Finally, it is important to note that Deuteronomy 28 implies an understanding of the "double agency" characteristic of God's involvement in human history. The Bible claims that YHWH acts, that he governs human affairs; but often the mechanism, i.e., human agency, obscures YHWH's presence. This mystery—that beyond the intentions and purposes of the Babylonians lies the will of YHWH—constitutes an abiding puzzle for believers and nonbelievers alike. Human beings prefer tangibles. Modern "scientific" minds require demonstrations of cause and effect. If God cannot be shown to be the "cause" of an "effect," then God language is meaningless. This is not strictly a modern bias. Even those initially attracted to Jesus during his earthly ministry awaited demonstrations of God's

power as evidence of Jesus' status (cf. Matt 16:1-4; Luke 11:14-32).

It is important to note that Jesus warned against a faith based solely on such evidentiary "signs" because they can so easily mislead. According to the Bible, God works behind—through, beyond—the invading Babylonian armies; but the Babylonians were unaware of their role, and their actions did not correspond entirely to the will of God. How does one recognize the will of God expressed so mysteriously and imperfectly in the actions of an empire? Whatever the answer to this question, two biblical assertions must be held in tension: namely, that, although the mechanism is opaque to human observers, God is at work in human history and, second, that the mysterious nature of God's activity requires humility on the part of those who would claim to have located God at work.

NOTES

[1] Contra M. Weinfeld, *Deuteronomy and the Deuteronomic School* (Oxford: Clarendon, 1972), 128-29.

[2] Verses 36-37 share many of the characteristics of vv. 47-68.

[3] In some cases, the terms "to come in" and "to go out" have military connotations. The context here does not permit a determination as to whether this connotation is intended.

[4] The terms for "consumption (*šahepet*)" and "fever (*qadahat*)" occur only here and in the related series of covenant curses found in Lev 26 (v. 16), which many scholars feel reflects knowledge of the Babylonian crisis and exile (see, for example, J. Milgrom, "Leviticus 26 and Ezekiel," in *The Quest for Context and Meaning: Studies in Biblical Intertextuality in Honor of James A. Sanders*, ed. C. Evans et al., [Biblical Interpretation Series 28; Leiden: Brill, 1997], 57-62; and B. Levine, "The Epilogue to the Holiness Code: A Priestly Statement on the Destiny of Israel," in *Judaic Perspectives on Ancient Israel*, ed. J. Neusner et al. [Philadelphia: Fortress, 1987], 9-34). "Inflammation (*dalleqet*)" and "drought (*harhur*)" occur only here in the Old Testament. "Smut (*šiddāpôn*)" and "mildew (*yērāqôn*)" appear in Solomon's prayer dedicating the temple in a recital of disasters to which a disobedient Israel may fall prey (1 Kgs 8:37 // 2 Chr 6:28), and in a few prophetic judgment oracles (Amos 4:9; Hag 2:17; "mildew" also in Jer 30:6). The linguistic milieu of these terms, then, is restricted to formulaic usage in "covenant curses" and prophetic condemnations.

[5] The Massoretic text reads "in ships," a reference that makes little sense. Israel has no natural harbors. Trade routes between Israel and Egypt were overland. The consonants of the Hebrew text can be "repointed," however, such that by means of a simple emendation of the initial vowel, the text reads "in mourning," the reading accepted in the commentary.

COVENANT RENEWAL
IN MOAB

28:69[29:1 Eng]–32:52

Scholars debate whether Deuteronomy 28:69 [29:1 Eng] represents the superscription to what follows or, as the Massoretic punctuation indicates, the conclusion to the exposition of the Horeb covenant that began at 4:1. The somewhat puzzling reference to the covenant made with Israel "in the land of Moab, distinct from the covenant made with them at Horeb" suggests the former. Furthermore, other occurrences of such formula in Deuteronomy (1:5; 33:1) function as introductions, not summations. Understood as a new superscription, 28:69 [29:1 Eng] signals the beginning of Moses' third major speech delivered to Israel as it was encamped in the Transjordan, poised to take possession of the promised land. The unit purports to contain a covenant made with Israel in Moab, a covenant that is somehow distinct from the Horeb covenant summarized and exposited in 4:1–28:68. The notion of a second, distinct covenant is difficult on its face given Deuteronomy's insistence that the Horeb covenant has binding significance for Israel throughout its generations (4:10-14; 5:2-3; etc.). Furthermore, the content of 28:69[29:1]–32:52 consists not of a clearly identifiable covenant document, but of a wide variety of hortatory, narrative, and poetic forms gathered together around the themes of a new generation's need to make a decision and of the transition in leadership. A number of scholars have attempted to reconstruct the outlines of a covenant document in chapters 29 and 30 (see ["The Covenant in Moab"]), and a few have pointed to the reconstructed document as evidence for a regular covenant-renewal institution in ancient Israel. Nevertheless, even these chapters seem better characterized, rather, as hortatory preaching on the Deuteronomic covenant idea itself and on texts from earlier in the book. In fact, allusions, especially to the opening narrative framework of the book (1–4), to the introduction to the Deuteronomic Code (5–11), especially the Shema, and to the treaty blessings and curses (27–28), suggest that this material was composed in a fashion not too different from the manner in which modern preachers expound a biblical text. The larger unit can be divided into three major subdivisions: Deuteronomy 29–30, an extended sermonic composition

"The Covenant in Moab"

A. Rofé, for example, considers 29:21-27 and 30:1-10 secondary, and further postulates that the original "stipulations" of the treaty have been moved to the Deuteronomic code. After excising the former and hypothesizing the latter, he finds a pattern that corresponds nicely to the outline of the Hittite vassal treaties. He regards the reconstruction as evidence of the antiquity of the covenant idea in Israel; that is, he disagrees with those who argue that the scribes of the 7th- to 6th-century Deuteronomic movement introduced the covenant model into Israelite theology. Rofé outlines this reconstructed ancient covenant in Moab as follows:

Inscription—28:69
Historical Prologue—29:1-9
Statement of Relationship—29:10-14
Stipulations—29:15-19a, 28
Invocation of Witnesses and Curses and Blessings—30:15-20

As I. Cairns observes, however, concerning his own similar attempt to reconstruct a covenant structure in Deut 29–30, "This suggestion would be convincing if Deut 29–30 did in fact present a clear and complete structure. Since this is not the case, however, it is safest to assume that the two chapters are intended as a literary composition rather than a report of an actual historical occurrence."

A. Rofé, "The Covenant in the Land of Moab (Deuteronomy 28:69–30:20): Historico-Literary, Comparative, and Form-critical Considerations," in *A Song of Power and the Power of Song: Essays on the Book of Deuteronomy*, ed. D. Christensen (Winona Lake: Eisenbrauns, 1993), 277-78 (= *Das Deuteronomium: Entstehung, Gestalt und Botschaft*, ed. N. Lohfink [BEThL 68; Louvain: Louvain, 1985], 310-20).

I. Cairns, *Word and Presence: A Commentary on the Book of Deuteronomy* (ITC; Grand Rapids: Eerdmans, 1992), 255-56.

dealing with the question of Israel's response to the covenant; Deuteronomy 31, Moses' farewell address and the transferal of leadership to Joshua; and Deuteronomy 32, the "Song of Moses" plus a note concerning Moses' impending death.

COMMENTARY

"Choose Life!" 28:69[29:1]–30:20

Although this extended composition refers briefly (29:8-12) to a ceremony of covenant initiation, it contains no statement of the provisions of this covenant. Instead, it apparently assumes (29:19, 20, 26; 30:10) the content of the Deuteronomic Code (chs. 12–26), including the blessings and curses (chs. 27–28), just as it frequently alludes to or cites material from the historical framework (see below). These literary dependencies suggest both that Deuteronomy 29–30 was composed at a very late stage in the growth of the book and that it was largely unconcerned with publishing covenant content. In fact, the overall tone of this "Covenant in Moab" material can better be described as exhortative or motivational. As the concluding paragraph suggests, the rhetorical objective of this composition is to motivate readers to choose wisely, to choose covenant-obedience and life. This objective governs the outline of the composition that discusses the covenant relationship in the several phases of Israel's life cycle—past (29:1-7 [2-8 Eng]), present (29:8-14 [9-15 Eng]), future punishment (29:15-28 [16-29 Eng]), and future restoration (30:1-10)—before concluding with a rousing appeal for decision (30:11-20).

The Covenant Past, 29:1-7 (2-8 Eng)

Moses' third speech begins with a retrospective summary of YHWH's acts of covenant loyalty to Israel beginning with deliverance from Egypt. The summary need not be elaborate since it reiterates earlier portions of the book, especially the initial historical retrospective (chs. 1–4) and the historical illustrations from the preamble to the Covenant code (chs. 6–11). A brief allusion or citation serves to recall the previous, fuller accounts and treatments (see the commentary on the respective texts above). With their own eyes, Israel had witnessed (v. 1 [2]; see 4:34; 7:19-20; 10:21-22; 11:2-7; cf. 3:21; 4:3) "trials, signs, and wonders" (v. 2 [3]; see 4:34; 7:19) that YHWH had performed on their behalf in Egypt. (Technically, of course, the generation Moses addressed in Moab had *not* seen these events; their parents had. This is yet another example of Deuteronomy's theological tendency to telescope generations. See commentary and sidebars on chs. 4–11, in particular.) During the forty years YHWH led his people in the wilderness, neither their clothing nor their footwear wore out, and they were sustained solely through manna, quails, and water (vv. 4-5 [5-6]; cf. 8:2-4). All this was so that they might recognize and acknowledge that YHWH provides for them. Challenged by Sihon and Og when they came to the Transjordan, Israel was victorious, conquering their territory for the Reubenites, the Gadites, and the half-tribe of Manasseh (vv. 6-7 [7-8]; cf. 2:31–3:13). In short, at every point along the way since Egypt, YHWH demonstrated his providence, his power, and his concern.

As stated, this material substantially reproduces the historical argument of Deuteronomy 1–4 and portions of Deuteronomy 6–11. The statement made in v. 3 [4], however, is both unique and enigmatic. First of all, it is unclear how to translate the final phrase, *ʿad hayyôm hazzeh*, "to this day." Two renditions are possible: (a) "YHWH did not give you an understanding heart . . . until [he did

"To this day . . ."

AΩ The expression "to this day" occurs over eighty times in the Old Testament. It appears regularly in etiologies explaining the persistence of an ancient practice (Gen 32:33, for example), an ancient landmark (Josh 4:9; 8:28, for example), a demographic circumstance (Josh 6:25; 9:27, for example), or a place name (Gen 26:33; Josh 5:9, for example) down to the time of the speaker. As a consequence of this etiological function, English translations typically render it, *as it is* to this day." In a few cases, it can be found in narrated speech (Gen 48:18; Exod 10:6; Num 22:30; Deut 11:4; Josh 22:3, 17; etc.), but by far the majority occur in narrative or editorial comments (compare Gen 26:33; 32:33; 47:26; Deut 2:22; 3:14; 10:8; 34:6; Josh 4:9; 5:9; 6:25; 7:26 [twice]; 8:28, 29; 9:27; 10:27; 13:13; 14:14; etc.).

The frequency of its occurrence in editorial comments raises the possibility that Deut 29:3[4] should also be understood in this manner, that is, as a statement made by the narrator/editor, not as the reported speech of Moses. As the commentary suggests, this interpretation remedies problems involved in understanding the statement as a reference to circumstances in Moses' day. Furthermore, it conforms to the overall impetus of chs. 29–30 to the effect that Israel has always, inexplicably, failed to fully comprehend the significance of its relationship with YHWH.

so] today" or (b) "YHWH has not given you an understanding heart . . . [a circumstance that prevails] even to this day." Second, and regardless of the proper translation of the difficult final phrase, the point of the statement is unclear. Why would YHWH withhold the understanding, discernment, and will necessary for correctly interpreting the significance of his mighty acts on Israel's behalf? The sentiment contradicts the idea, stated only a few verses later (v. 5 [6]), that YHWH's provision for Israel during the wilderness period was intended, at least in part, so that Israel would "know that I, YHWH, am your God." Furthermore, in the context of a book focused on YHWH's expectation that Israel, in all generations, can and should comprehend and obey, the statement of v. 3 [4] seems outright nonsensical.

The solution may lie in the composition history and rhetorical technique of the book of Deuteronomy. If, as scholars suspect, the book as a whole and the section at hand in particular stem from a very late period in biblical Israel's history, it may be that v. 3 [4] represents an editorial aside and not part of the reported speech of Moses. ["To this day . . ."] The "day" in question, then, would be the time of the author/editor of this passage (cf v. 27 [28]), not the day on which Moses delivered this speech to all Israel gathered in the Transjordan. In this case, the comment would convey the editor's disappointment in his people's history. Even at the late date when he wrote, he sighs, his people's continued rebelliousness and stubbornness demonstrate that they have never fully comprehended the significance of YHWH's providence, never fully obeyed his covenant. This conviction then provides the basis for the hopeful prediction later (30:6, for example) that YHWH will one day give his people the heart necessary for obedience (see below).

The Covenant Present, 29:8-14[9-16]

After the historical retrospective, intended to inspire Israel's confidence in YHWH's covenant loyalty, the text turns to the narrative present, as signaled by the shift to direct address in v. 8 [9]. Once again, as in 28:69 [29:1 Eng], the Massoretes punctuate v. 8 [9] as

"Hewers of Wood and Drawers of Water"

AΩ Josh 9:3-27 records how the Gibeonites, aware that YHWH "had commanded his servant Moses to give [Israel] all the land, and to destroy all the inhabitants of the land," tricked Joshua into making a peace treaty with them. When Joshua discovered the deception, he faced a dilemma: he had been tricked into the treaty, but was bound by his oath. According to Deut 20:11, citizens of cities that accept Israel's offer of peace may be spared death, but they are henceforth to serve Israel at forced labor. Israel's elders recommend that Joshua make the Gibeonites permanent servants of the sanctuary, "hewers of wood and drawers of water."

Why, then, are "hewers of wood and drawers of water" mentioned among the resident aliens assembled with Israel in Moab (29:10[11])? Rabbinical sources hypothesize that Moses must have already entered into covenant arrangements with segments of the Canaanite population similar to that between Joshua and the Gibeonites, although the Bible records no such agreements. Modern scholarship tends to view the reference as anachronistic. In either case, it is important to note that, despite Deuteronomy's programmatic insistence that everything Canaanite is evil, it requires the extension of covenant protections, and even of covenant status, to resident aliens, including Canaanites.

---

the conclusion to the preceding, rather than as the beginning of a new paragraph. Not only, however, does the shift to direct address contradict the Massoretic paragraph division, but the logic of the passage suggests the interpretation represented here. It is very difficult to comprehend how the statement that the lands of Sihon and Og had been distributed to the Transjordanian tribes (v. 7 [8]) should motivate the charge to keep the covenant (v. 8 [9]). Although, as noted above, the section that reports the initiation of the covenant in Moab makes no mention of specific covenant requirements, it repeats a number of familiar Deuteronomic themes: (1) obedience to the covenant as the key to Israel's prosperity (v. 8 [9]); (2) the inclusive nature of the covenant, both in terms of elements of Israel's society (tribal leaders, elders, officials, every Israelite male, children, women, even resident aliens, [see ["Hewers of Wood and Drawers of Water"]] vv. 9-10 [10-11]) and in terms of future generations (vv. 13-14 [14-15]); and (3) the "voluntary" nature of the people's entry into the covenant relationship (v. 11 [12]).

From a theological perspective, the dialectic implicit in vv. 11-12 (12-13) merits special attention. On the one hand, the covenant will be a solemn agreement, sworn by oath, whereby Israel will be YHWH's special people and he their God; on the other hand, YHWH initiates and maintains the entire relationship in fulfillment of the unmerited promise he had made to Israel's patriarchs, Abraham, Isaac, and Jacob (see the commentary on 7:6-16 and [The Promise to the Patriarchs in Deuteronomy]). Significantly, Deuteronomy nowhere seeks to resolve the tension between covenant and promise, between law and grace. Nor, for that matter, does any Old Testament text. The balance between mercy and responsibility, between faith and works, is central to biblical faith. (See **Connections** and frequently above.)

The Covenant Future I: Individual Disobedience, 29:15-28[16-29]

The reference to the fact that the covenant is valid also for coming generations of Israel suggests the future orientation that is developed in the remainder of chapter 29 (beginning in v. 15 [16]) and in all of chapter 30. The expected covenant stipulations do not follow the announcement that a covenant is to be made; nor is there any indication that, in the future, Israel will experience the blessings attendant upon fidelity to the covenant. Curiously, in fact, the entire discussion of the covenant future is governed by the assumption that Israel will be disloyal to the covenant after Moses' passing. Or—if scholarly theories concerning the date of the final phases in the history of Deuteronomy's composition are correct—the discussion reflects knowledge of the history of that infidelity.

The discussion focuses on two cases of covenant disloyalty: secretive infidelity on the part of an individual or group within Israel (vv. 15-20 [16-21]) and the apostasy of the entire nation (vv. 21-28 [22-29]). Syntactically and logically, transitions from one thought-unit to the next in this section are virtually absent. In the mind(s) of the editor/author(s) of this material, the connection between the idea that the covenant applies also to future generations and the notion that some, or all, of Israel will become apostate is self-evident. From the perspective of the editor/author(s), in fact, it is historically demonstrable.

In contrast, the flow of the argument in vv. 15-20 is quite explicit: The Egyptian and wilderness periods unfortunately brought Israel knowledge of more than YHWH's redemption and providence; Israel also become familiar with the nations' "detestable things," namely their idols of wood and stone, gold and silver (vv. 15-16 [16-17]). Fearing that some man or woman, family or tribe may have become interested in these idols and may have decided secretively to practice idol worship, the text warns that such behavior will go neither undetected nor unpunished. Even though only a minority should choose to forsake YHWH, and even though they should only do so privately, they may poison the entire nation (v. 17 [18]). For this reason, and because of their arrogance (v. 18 [19]) (see ["The Watered with the Thirsty"]), YHWH will react very harshly. YHWH is unprepared to forgive such frauds and idolaters;

"The Watered with the Thirsty"

AΩ The intention of the apparently idiomatic phrase "the watered with the thirsty" (v. 18 [19]) is obscure. The first question to be answered has to do with the nature of the imagery. The root *rwh* can refer either to being well-watered or to being sated with drink, being drunk. Does the phrase indicate that the well-watered and the drought-stricken plants will experience a common fate, or that the drunk and sober persons will do so? The horticultural image in v. 17 (18) suggests that plants are also intended in v. 18 (19).

The second question involves the identity of the speaker of this phrase. Does it express the intention (*lĕma'an*, "in order that") of the rebel, or does it represent Moses' (or the editor's) observation concerning the result (*lĕma'an*, "with the result that") of the rebel's behavior? Two factors favor the latter. First, since the verb *sph*, "to sweep away," implies judgment and destruction (compare Gen 18:23), it is unlikely that the rebel intends to bring about his own destruction. Second, the horticultural nature of the images in vv. 17-18 (18-19) suggests that they be interpreted in tandem: the root produces poison that spreads, bringing destruction to diseased and healthy plants alike. Moses (or the narrator) warns that, in fact, one bad apple can spoil the whole barrel!

---

he will "wipe out their names." Indeed "every curse recorded in this book" will come to rest upon them (v. 19 [20]); that is, they will be set apart from Israel and given over to "all the curses of this covenant written in this book of the Torah" (v. 20 [21]).

The Covenant Future II: Corporate Disobedience, 29:21-28[22-29]

Beginning in v. 21 (22), the situation envisioned in the text shifts abruptly from the elimination of the threat posed by apostate individuals or groups within Israel to the reaction of post-catastrophe generations (and foreigners) to the total destruction of the land. Once again, the declarative, as opposed to hypothetical or even persuasive, tone of this section merits attention. The text assumes (or knows firsthand) that Israel will fail (or has failed) to keep the covenant and will suffer (or, in fact, has suffered) through invasion and exile as a consequence.

Some future generation of Israelites and some group of foreigners from a distant land will investigate the state of affairs in the land of Israel only to find it smitten with disease, rendered infertile ["Sulfur and Salt"], comparable to Sodom, Gomorrah, Admah, and Zeboim [Sodom and Gomorrah]. Dismayed at the devastation, all the nations who witness it will naturally ask, "Why did this happen? Why did YHWH do this?" They answer their own question with a

Sodom and Gomorrah

Sodom and Gomorrah, whose destruction is recorded in Gen 19, frequently symbolize evil and its consequences in the Hebrew Bible (Deut 32:32; Isa 1:9-10; Jer 25:14; 49:18; 50:40; Amos 4:11; Zeph 2:9). In a few instances, Sodom alone functions in this manner (Isa 13:19; Ezek 16:46-56; Lam 4:6). Although Gen 19 does not mention Admah and Zeboim along with Sodom and Gomorrah, they appear together as four of the five confederated cities in Gen 14 (vv. 2, 8) and in a list of cities in the region in Gen 10:19. Hos 11:8 mentions the punishment of Admah and Zeboim only, omitting Sodom and Gomorrah, a circumstance that prompts some scholars to speculate that Admah and Zeboim may have taken the place of Sodom and Gomorrah in northern tradition. Deut 29 would then be a conflation of northern and southern traditions.

"Sulfur and Salt"

AΩ   The horticultural imagery of vv. 17-18 (18-19) continues here. Invading armies sometimes spread sulfur and salt on enemy fields to render them sterile. Compare Judg 9:45; Jer 17:6; Ps 107:34. For ANE examples of the practice, see S. Gervit, "Jericho and Shechem: A Religio-Literary Aspect of City Destruction," *VT* 13 (1963): 52-62. An 8th-century BC inscription in Aramaic from Sefire (in northern Syria) contains the text of a suzerainty treaty with the following intriguing reference to salting fields. It occurs in the curses section of the treaty and calls to mind both the covenant curses found in Deuteronomy and the covenant-making rite described in Gen 15:

Just as this wax is burned by fire, so may Arpad (one of the cities that was party to the treaty) be burned and [her gr]eat [daughter-cities]! May Hadad (the Syrian high-god) sow in them salt and *weeds*, and may it not be mentioned (again)! This GNB' and [ ] (are) Mati'el; it is his person. Just as this wax is burned by fire, so may Mati['el be burned by fi]re! Just as [this] bow and these arrows are broken, so may 'Inurta (a Syrian goddess) and Hadad break [the bow of Mati'el], and the bow of his nobles! And just as a man of wax is blinded, so may Mati['el] be blinded! [Just as] this calf is cut in two, so may Mati'el be cut in two, and may his nobles be cut in two! [And just as] a [ha]r[lot is stripped naked], so may the wives of Mati'el be stripped naked, and the wives of his offspring and the wives of [his] no[bles! And just as this wax woman is taken] and one strikes her on the face, so may the [wives of Mati'el be taken [and . . .] (*Sef* I, A, 35-42)

J. Fitzmyer, *The Aramaic Inscriptions of Sefire* (Biblica et Orientalia 19; Rome: Pontifical Biblical Institute, 1967), 15-17.

---

statement of quintessential Deuteronomic theology: All this has taken place "because they abandoned the covenant of YHWH, the God of their fathers, which he made with them when he brought them out of the land of Egypt; they followed after and served other gods . . . and YHWH's anger burned against this land, bringing upon it all the curses written in this book; YHWH sent them away from their land . . . to another land, as it is to this day[1]" (vv. 24-26 [25-27]).

The concluding proverb-like statement continues the theme of secret apostasy. YHWH knows the secrets of an individual's heart. Abandonment of the covenant cannot be kept secret. The Torah and its requirements, on the other hand, are public knowledge. Israel's responsibility is simply "to do all the words of this Torah."

The Covenant Future III: Repentance and Restoration, 30:1-10

Deuteronomy 30:1-10 continues to assume a future in which Israel will have suffered the full force of YHWH's wrath (v. 1, "when"—not "if"—"all these things come to you"): the land lies desolate *and* the people have been scattered among the nations of the world. But now the discussion brightens—at long last. At some point in the future, dispersed among the nations, Israel will "come to its senses" (v. 1: *hăšēbōtā 'el-lĕbābekā*, literally "you will return to your heart"), the beginning of a process (vv. 1-10 consist of a series of clauses governed by perfect verbs linked with simple conjunctions—a

Hebrew syntactic pattern characteristic of descriptions of procedures and rituals) that will culminate in Israel's return to complete covenant loyalty (v. 8) and the full restoration of the blessings of covenant fidelity (v. 9).

Three features in particular signal the theological significance of this passage. First, allusions to and citations of key texts from earlier portions of Deuteronomy make it clear that the process described here constitutes a true "restoration," a return to things as they were meant to be. In exile, Israel will once again "heed [YHWH's] voice" (vv. 2, 8, 10), doing "all his commandments that I [Moses] command you this day" (vv. 2, 8, 10). Citations of the Shema (especially Deut 6:5, "you shall love YHWH your God with all your heart, with all your soul, and with all your might") play a particularly prominent role (vv. 2, 6, 10), as do citations of the blessings and curses of chapter 28 (to vv. 3, 4 compare 28:64; to v. 9 compare 28:4, 18, 63). Ironically, this speech, set in the context of Israel's preparations for taking possession of the promised land (27:2, 4, 12, etc), predicts a day when repentant Israel will once again take possession of it (v. 5).

Second, like the material beginning at 28:58, this passage manifests an awareness of the existence of the book of Deuteronomy *as a book* (v. 10). This awareness, together with the high frequency of citations in this passage, confirm the impression that Deuteronomy 29–30 represent homiletical interpretation of the Deuteronomic code, including the covenant blessings and curses. (Regarding the "authenticity" of such extrapolations of older traditions, see **Connections** on Deuteronomy 4 and [Authenticity].)

Third, as A. Rofé has observed,[2] vv. 1-10 are a "fugue" on the theme of repentance, return, and restoration. These three English terms are all possible translations, depending on context, of the single Hebrew word, *šûb*,[3] that appears seven times in these ten verses (vv. 1, 2, 3 [twice], 8, 9, 10). The basic meaning of this powerful Hebrew term is "to turn, to turn around." By extension, it can mean "to return," "to turn [one's mind or heart]," or to turn oneself around [in attitude and behavior] = to repent," "to return [something to someone] = to restore," etc. It is a favorite term in prophetic preaching, expressing the essence of biblical repentance. As indicated by the semantics of the term *šûb* in the Hebrew Bible, "repentance" does not so much involve the emotions associated with regret. One can be "sorry" for one's sins and yet have no intention whatsoever of changing one's behavior. The picture conveyed by the Hebrew concept, in contrast, calls first and foremost for change. One finds oneself going the wrong direction in life and "turns around." Biblical repentance, then, is not merely a feeling; it involves turning away from wrong and turning toward right.

The term's multiplicity of dimensions permits 30:1-10 to elaborate the multifaceted nature of repentance. In fact, this passage is one of the more important statements concerning repentance in the Bible. An analysis of the sequence of individual occurrences of forms of *šûb* in this passage yields the following picture:

(1) Israel's repentance begins with a "return to sanity," as it were. Disobedience and rebellion are not only contrary to YHWH's intentions, but also to Israel's own best interests, its well-being, its purpose, and its nature. (v. 1)

(2) When Israel "returns to its senses" it immediately and automatically "returns to YHWH." Perhaps now Israel has finally gained the understanding (see 29:3 [4]) to recognize that YHWH has provided and will provide. All other gods are no gods at all. Turning to YHWH leaves no room for orienting oneself toward any other. One must turn to YHWH "with all [one's] heart and all [one's] soul." It is impossible to travel in two directions at once! (vv. 2, 10)

(3) "Return to YHWH" means "obedience to his voice and his commandments." Biblical repentance is not sentimental. A true change of heart results in changed behavior. (vv. 2, 8)

(4) In response to Israel's repentance, YHWH, too, will "turn," changing his direction as well. Whereas he had banished Israel to exile, he will now "gather [Israel] from all the nations to which he had driven them." That is, he will change his stance toward Israel to reflect Israel's repentance. YHWH will be able once again to rejoice over Israel. (vv. 3, 9)

As instructive as the *šûb* material is, it still begs a fundamental question: If Israel has not been in "its right mind," and it is only necessary for it to "return to its senses," why has it taken so long (from the standpoint of the editor/author, the return of Israel's sanity is still anticipated)? What is involved in Israel's return to right thinking and right behavior? Put even more fundamentally, why was Israel "insane" in the first place?

The repentance discussion highlights its response to these questions by placing it at the center (v. 6). Israel's "heart"—its will, its decision-making capacity—must be made responsive: "YHWH

Reinhold Niebuhr on Human Nature

Reinhold Niebuhr, one of the 20th century's most insightful theologians and students of human nature, offered the following assessment of the tension between humanity's capacity for good and tendency toward evil:

> The qualified optimism of an adequate religion will never satisfy the immature minds who have found some superficial harmony in the world in which the evils and threats to meaning are not taken into account. Nor will it satisfy those who think that every ill from which man [sic] suffers can be eliminated in some proximate future. It will serve men to exhaust all their resources in building a better world, in overcoming human strife, in mitigating the fury of man's injustice to man, and in establishing a society in which some minimal security for all can be achieved. But in an adequate religion there will be a recognition of the fact that nothing accomplished along the horizontal line of history can eliminate the depth of life which is revealed in every point of history. Let man stand at any point in history, even in a society which has realized his present dreams of justice, and if he surveys the human problem profoundly he will see that every perfection which he has achieved points beyond itself to a greater perfection, and that this greater perfection throws light upon his sins and imperfections. He will feel in that tension between what is and what ought to be the very glory of life, and will come to know that the perfection which eludes him is not only a human possibility and impossibility, but a divine fact.

"Optimism, Pessimism, and Religious Faith," in *The Essential Reinhold Niebuhr: Selected Essays and Addresses*, ed. R. Brown (New Haven: Yale, 1986), 16.

---

your God will circumcise your heart and the heart of your descendants so that you may love YHWH your God . . . ." Here, Deuteronomy confronts perhaps the most enigmatic aspect of being human, a problem that has occupied theology, philosophy, psychology, sociology, and politics throughout the ages. If, as Israel did, human beings *know* what is good and right, why do they *choose* to do wrong? [Reinhold Niebuhr on Human Nature] The argument made later in Deuteronomy 30 will focus on the fact that God's will for Israel is neither mysterious—it is revealed in the Torah/covenant—nor impossible—as Deuteronomy understands it, YHWH requires first and foremost only to be Israel's sole God. The puzzle is not the content of God's will, nor whether it is to Israel's advantage to obey this will. The great enigma is that, despite the fact that Israel knows what is good and right, it consistently and repeatedly chooses to do wrong. In other words, Israel is *capable* of doing right, but it does not *want* to do so. Not even Deuteronomy explains why this should be so. It does, however, promise a solution: YHWH himself will perform corrective surgery on Israel's will! [Circumcision of the Heart]

Choose Life! 30:10-20

The composition now reaches its climax in a call for decision. The previous paragraphs have repeated the underlying theme that Israel has the freedom either to accept YHWH's gracious gift of

Circumcision of the Heart

The notion that the source of Israel's problem lies in the human heart figures prominently in several key Old Testament texts. Deuteronomy suggests that the heart, the seat of the will, can be made right by "circumcision" (compare Jer 4:5); that is, it needs to be opened, laid bare, in order to be receptive to YHWH's will. Ezekiel (36:26) promises a heart transplant. YHWH will replace Israel's dead and unresponsive heart of stone with a living heart of flesh.

Perhaps the most influential text related to this theme is found in Jer 31:31-34, Jeremiah's promise of a "New Covenant." In it, the prophet predicts a day when the Law, formerly written on stone tablets (compare Jer 17:1), will be written directly in human hearts. No longer will it be necessary for experts in the Law to teach it to and interpret it for the people; everyone will have immediate and direct knowledge of YHWH's will. Since it will be written in their hearts, the seat of decision-making, their former intransigence will be remedied. Significantly, the prophet's promise of a new covenant focuses not on the novelty of its content—YHWH's will for Israel does not change—but on the new mode of its mediation. Nowhere does the Old Testament see Torah as a problem; the problem lies in the human will.

redemption and provision—that is, to obey his covenant—or to reject it by worshiping other gods. Even though YHWH demonstrated his might and his saving intention in Egypt and the wilderness, Israel failed to understand and obey (29:3[4]). Later, assembled before YHWH and his servant Moses for the purpose of reaffirming the covenant, some entertained plans privately and secretly to worship the gods of the nations they had met on the journey to Moab (29:15-18[16-29]). Judging from their knowledge of Israel's history and, presumably, their personal experience, the authors/editors soon abandon the hypothetical in his discussion of Israel's apostasy. As they know, Israel's infidelity and resulting exile are virtually inevitable (29:21-28[22-29]). But they also know that the option of covenant fidelity still remains viable. YHWH can redeem Israel, thereby giving the freedom to be his people. YHWH can offer Israel covenant relationship, thereby establishing the principles for being his people. But Israel must *choose* to live as YHWH's peculiar possession, as his nation of priests.

The appeal to make the right choice continues aspects of the preceding discussion of repentance in an effort to set aside two possible major objections (vv. 11-14). First, the requirements of the covenant are not impossibilities (literally, "they are not too wondrous for you," v. 11). They are not heavenly mysteries beyond attainment (v. 12). In the opinion of

Martin Luther on Deuteronomy 30:11

Reformer Martin Luther rejected the "plain sense" of this passage in Deuteronomy because he could not easily incorporate it into his particular understanding of grace. His comments typify a variety of Christian interpretations of the Torah:

The sophists use this passage to prove that it is possible for us to fulfill the Commandments of God, yes, even easy. That is how blind readers go astray. When Moses says: "It is not too hard for you," they understand it to mean: "It is not above your powers, not impossible." They do not consider that if this is true, the grace of God is required in vain. What need is there for the grace of God to help me in something that is possible for me and not beyond my powers? But if they had had the Hebrew text, they would have been even more puffed up. For the Hebrew says it thus: "This command which I command you this day, is not wonderful or difficult for you."

Martin Luther, *Lectures on Deuteronomy*, 277.

Good Versus Evil

In this drawing, William Blake clearly delineates the domains of these two angels. The good angel cuddles and protects the frantic child from the outreached hands of a grappling and mean-spirited evil angel. The realm of the evil angel is defined by firey blasts and shackles, whereas the realm of the good angel is defined by a spacious ocean and a brilliant, rising sun. Blake is known for the many works that express his brand of esoteric mysticism.

William Blake. 1757–1827. *The Good and Evil Angels Stuggling for Possession of a Child.* Color wash on paper. 594mm x 445mm. Tate Gallery. London.

Deuteronomy, and in contrast to a long tradition of Christian theology [Martin Luther on Deuteronomy 30:11], the covenant is immanently "doable." As the repentance discussion acknowledges, the problem lies in the human *will* for good, not the human *capacity* for good.

Second, the requirements of the covenant are not mysteries (v. 11). They are not hidden somewhere beyond the sea. YHWH has revealed the fundamental principles of his will for humankind to Israel (compare Mic 6:8, "He has told you, O mortal, what is good: What does YHWH require of you but to do justice, to love mercy, and to walk humbly with your God?"). Moses has explicated them for a new generation facing new circumstances, thereby establishing the beginning of a tradition of authoritative interpretation. Joshua stands in the wings ready to take over leadership and continue the tradition. As a consequence, Israel cannot claim ignorance of YHWH's basic intentions for its life as his people. The words of the covenant are nearby indeed. They are, in fact, "on your lips and in your heart" (v. 14; compare Deut 6:4-8).

YHWH has done all that he can: he has redeemed Israel from Egyptian bondage, given them the covenant through Moses, led them safely to Moab, and now reiterated the covenant once again. The promised land lies before them to be possessed. The words of the covenant are on their lips and in their hearts. Their future as YHWH's covenant people lies open. It is up to them to realize that future. They face a choice.

The text portrays their options starkly: Moses places before the people a choice between life and death, between good and evil. They may love YHWH—that is, they may walk in his ways, keeping his commandments, statutes, and ordinances—with the result that they will live, become numerous, and enjoy YHWH's blessings in the land he gives them. Or, their "hearts may turn away"—that is, they may fail to heed the commandments, allowing themselves to be seduced into the worship of idols—with the result that they will be destroyed (v. 18). Not coincidentally, although the terminology varies slightly (the verb "to turn away" in v. 17 is *pnh*, not *šûb*), this phrase expresses the opposite of the act of repentance discussed in 30:1.

Borrowing a technique from ANE treaties, once again the text underscores the solemnity of the choice that Israel faces by calling on cosmic witnesses to attest to Israel's choice. The choice itself is reiterated yet once more in the most forceful terms (v. 19): "I set before you life and death, blessing and curse. Choose life!" The appeal concludes by paraphrasing the decision for life in now-familiar terms: "love YHWH your God, heed his voice, cling to him, for he is your life."

CONNECTIONS

Christian readers of Deuteronomy 30 may be surprised to read the claim that observance of the stipulations of the covenant, the Law, is entirely possible. In a long tradition of Christian theology—beginning with Paul and including his interpreters ranging from St. Augustine to the Reformer Martin Luther and modern theologians as divergent as Rudolf Bultmann and Karl Barth—the demands of the Law have been regarded as beyond human fulfillment [Rudolf Bultmann on the "Failure" of the Law] and adherence to the Law has been seen as a symptom of human arrogance. This tradition emphasizes,

Rudolf Bultmann on the "Failure" of the Law

The influential 20th-century theologian, existentialist, and New Testament scholar Rudolf Bultmann typifies that variety of Christian exegesis that first mischaracterizes the demands of the Old Testament (and, not coincidentally, of Judaism. Even when not intended, this variety of Christian theology contributes to an insidious anti-Semitism.) in order to be able to reject them. His comments on Rom 10:4 ("Christ is the end of the law." It is important to note that the Greek term rendered "end" in English [and German] translations is *telos*, which can also, or better, be translated "goal, object, purpose, completion.") raise the question of whether Bultmann, and many other Christian interpreters, also mischaracterize Paul:

> The basis from which Paul combats the law is revealed in this. He does not combat it because of its contents—on the contrary, its contents are God's holy unbreakable demands. He combats it because and in so far as, it serves the Jew in satisfying his need for recognition with its help—and in *acquiring credit in God's sight*, and in earning justification by what he does. . . . In contrast to that, it is the purpose of the Christian message of "justification by faith alone" that all self-glorying based on one's achievements is rejected and a justification is preached which God gives man gratuitously.
>
> . . . Judaism, too, speaks of the *grace of God*. But here God's grace means his indulgence in regard to trespasses against the law, or the gracious guidance which makes it possible for the devout man to fulfill the law or to atone for his trespasses. The devout man, who fulfils the law, or, so far as he fulfils it, does not need grace. According to Paul the person who fulfils the law needs grace as much as the one who trespasses against it.

Rudolph Bultmann, "Christ the End of the Law," in *Essays: Philosophical and Theological*, ed. R. G. Smith (The Library of Philosophy and Theology; London: SCM, 1955), 45, 46.

---

correctly, that human beings are incapable of earning status in God's eyes, that human beings are inherently imperfect and thus prone to error, and that human beings, furthermore, demonstrate a universal leaning toward sin.

> For the promise that he would inherit the world did not come to Abraham or to his descendants through the law, but through the righteousness of faith. For if they inherit by law, faith is useless and promise is ineffectual. For the law produces wrath. But if there is no law, neither is there transgression. (Rom 4:13-15)[4]

At first glance, this perspective and the viewpoint expressed in Deuteronomy 30 seem to have very little in common. How does one account for the apparent contradiction? Is Deuteronomy 30 simply superceded by Paul?

In point of fact, the discrepancy is only apparent and can be accounted for by differences in perspective, purpose, and vocabulary. Paul and his interpreters address the Law in the context of soteriology, the doctrine of salvation. Deuteronomy (and Jesus, James, and sometimes even Paul himself; see below) focuses on ecclesiological ("who are the people of God?") or ethical ("how should the people of God behave?") concerns.

This fundamental distinction in perspectives manifests itself in a number of ways. Paul argues that, since human beings sin, obedience to the Law cannot produce the perfect righteousness necessary to be justified in God's sight. "Now, for the one who works, wages are not considered a gift, but a debt" (Rom 4:4) and "the wages of sin is death" (Rom 6:23). Deuteronomy, along with the rest of the Old Testament, on the other hand, nowhere maintains that the Law is to serve this purpose. As has been frequently pointed out above, the Old Testament consistently holds that God's relationship with Israel, and with individual Israelites, results only from *God's gracious initiative*. Apparently, Paul was in dialogue with some group of Jews or Jewish-Christians who boasted in their own righteousness as the basis for their relationship with God (Rom 2:17). But he was not in dialogue with the Old Testament itself on this point. Deuteronomy wholeheartedly agrees with Paul that Israel's only basis for relationship with God is God's grace (Deut 7:7-8).

In contrast, for Deuteronomy, the Law, which cannot be the means whereby Israel *earns* God's favor, expresses the principles for living as God's people. It is not possible to become God's people by fulfilling the requirements of the covenant; it is, however, necessary for God's people to be in accordance with God's revealed will.

On this point, too, the discrepancy between Paul—and the New Testament in general—on the one hand, and Deuteronomy on the other hand is only apparent. Deuteronomy calls on Israel, whom God redeemed from Egyptian bondage and for whom God provides in the wilderness and in the promised land, to respond in love expressed through a life of obedience to the covenant. Similarly, Paul calls on the Romans to live a holy life in Christ:

> What then shall we say? Shall we continue in sin so that grace may abound? By no means! How can we who have died to sin continue to live in it? Or do you not know that whoever is baptized in Christ Jesus is baptized into his death? Therefore, we have been buried with him through baptism into death in order that, just as Christ was raised from the dead through the Father's glory, so also we may walk in new life. (Rom 6:1-4)

Other New Testament writers are even more clearly in agreement with Deuteronomy: the salvation that comes by grace through faith *manifests itself in the conduct of the believer.* [Dietrich Bonhoeffer on "The Cost of Discipleship"] Jesus said, ". . . by their fruits you will know them" (Matt 7:20), and warned against dismissing the validity of the Law (Matt 5:17-21). John the Elder instructs his community that

Dietrich Bonhoeffer on "The Cost of Discipleship"

Cheap grace means the justification of sin without the justification of the sinner. Grace alone does everything, they say, and so everything can remain as it was before. 'All for sin could not atone.' The world goes on in the same old way, and we are still sinners 'even in the best life' as Luther said. Well, then, let the Christian live like the rest of the world, let him model himself on the world's standards in every sphere of life, and not presumptuously aspire to live a different life under grace from his old life under sin . . . That is what we mean by cheap grace, the grace which amounts to the justification of sin without the justification of the repentant sinner who departs from sin and from whom sin departs. Cheap grace is not the kind of forgiveness of sin which frees us from the toils of sin. Cheap grace is the grace we bestow on ourselves.

Cheap grace is the preaching of forgiveness without requiring repentance, baptism without church discipline, Communion without confession, absolution without personal confession. Cheap grace is grace without discipleship, grace without the cross, grace without Jesus Christ, living and incarnate.

Dietrich Bonhoeffer, *The Cost of Discipleship*, 6th English edition (London: SCM, 1959), 35-36.

---

by this we know that we know him [Jesus Christ], if we keep his commandments. The one who says, "I know him," but does not keep his commandments is a liar and the truth is not in him. Whoever keeps his word, truly in him is the love of God complete. By this we know that we are in him. The one who says, "I abide in him," ought to walk just as he walked. (1 John 2:3-6)

In a passage that almost seems to have been designed to correct a misapprehension of Paul's teaching concerning Abraham's faith (see Rom 4:1-5; Gal 3:10-14), James argues forcefully that genuine faith produces visible fruits:

But someone will say, "You have faith and I have works." Show me your faith apart from works and I will show you my faith *through* my works. You believe that there is one God; Good for you! Even the demons believe and shudder! Do you want to be shown, O foolish person, that faith apart from works is barren? Abraham, our father, was justified by works when he placed Isaac, his son, on the altar, was he not? You see that faith worked together with his works and by work faith was perfected. So the scripture was fulfilled, "Now Abraham believed in God and it was reckoned to him as righteousness" and he was called God's friend. You see that one is justified by works and not by faith only. Rahab the prostitute was similarly justified by works when she welcomed the messengers and sent them away by another route, was she not? For just as the body without the spirit is dead, so also faith without works is dead. (Jas 2:18-26)

So, Deuteronomy and the New Testament agree that God redeems as an act of grace. But God's redemptive grace is effective:

it produces holiness. Many modern Christians will read Deuteronomy's challenge to faithful obedience to God's revealed will either as a statement of the Old Testament's "failed" system of "justification through the law" or as hyperbole—a call to do the impossible. They are the modern counterparts of James's hypothetical interlocutor who argued that, in the artificial choice between grace and works, Christians must choose grace apart from works. If the church is to be the vital "nation of priests" it is called to be, it must not turn away from the Bible's call to covenant living.

NOTES

[1] Compare 29:3[4].

[2] A. Rofé, "The Covenant in the Land of Moab (Deuteronomy 28:69–30:20): Historico-Literary, Comparative, and Form-critical Considerations," in *A Song of Power and the Power of Song: Essays on the Book of Deuteronomy*, ed. D. Christensen (Winona Lake: Eisenbrauns, 1993), 277-78.

[3] For a very rich, detailed study of this supremely significant term for Old Testament theology, see W. Holladay, *The Root Šubh in the Old Testament: With Particular Reference to its Usages in Covenantal Contexts* (Leiden: E. J. Brill, 1958).

[4] New Testament citations in this section are the author's translations.

THE TRANSFERAL
OF LEADERSHIP
AND THE DEPOSIT
OF WITNESSES

31:1-29

Deuteronomy continues its treatment of matters arising from the fact that Moses' life and leadership are drawing to an end. After the sermon on Israel's opportunity to choose life by choosing obedience to the covenant, Deuteronomy 31 turns to "practical" questions. Who will lead Israel in Moses' absence? What will become of Moses' knowledge and wisdom, the "Torah" (that is, "guidance, teaching;" see Introduction and commentary on Deut 5:6-21)? Will Moses take his intimate knowledge of YHWH, YHWH's will, and YHWH's way with him to the grave?

Like the preceding section, Deuteronomy 31 is a complicated composition dating to a very late period in the history of the formation of the book of Deuteronomy. Stylistically, its historical narrative and first person divine speech depart from Deuteronomy's normal hortatory style. Similarly, the admixture of singular and plural verb forms gives the impression that many editors/authors contributed to the final form of the unit. In effect, this section abandons the fiction of Moses as speaker. Instead, here narrators report events from the distant past.[1] This narrative style, and the subject matter of the unit as well, recalls the historical introduction to the book. In fact, 31:1-8 continue the narrative left off in 3:23-29. Taken together, these features have prompted scholars to conclude that this material belongs to the framework to the book of Deuteronomy. This framework was probably supplied as the final stage in the growth of the book. It functioned to incorporate Deuteronomy into the so-called "Deuteronomistic history" as its preamble (note parallels between Deut 3:23-29; 31:1-8, 14-15, 23; and Josh 1:2-9, for example. See also the Introduction).

As one might expect of a composite section, its structure betrays something of the history of its composition. The account of the commissioning of Joshua, for example, is interrupted at several points by the insertion of material dealing with other themes (vv. 9-13 and

16-22). Perhaps as a result, the Joshua material repeats itself (vv. 6-7, 23). The discontinuity between vv. 15 and 16 on the one hand and vv. 22 and 23 on the other is particularly striking. In its present position, YHWH's statement in v. 23, the logical continuation of v. 15, is nestled between narration in vv. 22 and 24. Bracketed by these breaks, the instruction to record Moses' song seems misplaced since the song follows only after v. 30.

A first clue to the origins of the repetitive structure of this section can be seen in the secondary placement of vv. 16-22. Assuming that vv. 16-22 disrupt the original continuity between vv. 15 and 23, a hypothetical earlier form of Deuteronomy 31 (vv. 1-15, 23-29) will have exhibited the following balanced outline:

vv. 1-8—Commission of Joshua
   vv. 9-13—Deposit of the Torah Scroll
vv. 14-15, 23—Commission of Joshua
   vv. 24-29—Deposit of the Torah Scroll

With a view to Moses' immanent passing, this structure clearly highlights the central roles of Joshua as leader and the Torah book as instruction, and of both as Moses' "successors." The subsequent insertion of the material concerning the Song of Moses into the second Joshua unit resulted in the following structure [Structure of Deuteronomy 31]:

vv. 1-8—Joshua
   vv. 9-13—Torah Scroll
vv. 14-15—Joshua
   vv. 16-22—Song of Moses
v. 23—Joshua
   vv. 24-29—Torah Scroll

A comparison of the structure of the hypothetical earlier version of this unit and the structure after the insertion of vv. 16-22 makes apparent the purpose for the insertion. Now, in addition to Joshua and the Torah scroll, the song also fulfills a function as "successor" to Moses. In fact, since this structure places instructions concerning the song in the slot otherwise filled by material dealing with the Torah scroll, it elevates the song to a status comparable to the Torah scroll itself. The end result is the claim that, when Moses' departs, the people are left a leader and two documentary witnesses.

Structure of Deuteronomy 31

AΩ Of course, other analyses of the structure of Deuteronomy 31 are possible. The analysis offered in the commentary depends largely on syntactical indicators as unit dividers. N. Lohfink focuses, rather, on the speakers and subject matter and finds the following concentric structure. At the center stands the theophany recorded in vv. 14-15:

	Speaker	Topic
vv. 1-6	Moses	future—victory—divine presence
vv. 7-8	Moses	Joshua installed as successor
vv. 9-13	Moses	Torah Book
vv. 14-15	God	God appears and speaks
vv. 16-22	God	Future—defeat—divine absence
v. 23	God	Joshua installed as successor
vv. 24-29	Moses	Torah Book

N. Lohfink, "Der Bundesschluss im Land Moab," 75.

COMMENTARY

Joshua Commissioned, 31:1-8

Following the covenant sermon of chapters 29–30, Moses takes up a new topic, although it is unclear whether v. 1 introduces a new speech or marks the continuation of the speech begun at 28:69 (29:1 Eng). Instead of MT's *wylk* ("and he went"), LXX and Qumran read *wykl* ("and he continued"). MT presumes, apparently, a span of time between the speech recorded in chapters 29–30 and that introduced here. Qumran and LXX see them as parts of one great speech. Regardless of the demarcation of the units, everything Moses has to say in this section arises from the observation that he makes in v. 2 concerning his advanced age and poor health ["Aged Moses"] on the one hand and YHWH's refusal to allow him to enter the promised land on the other. In short, Moses' time with Israel is drawing both to its natural end and to the limit

---

"Aged Moses"

AΩ Moses' admission (31:2) that, at 120 years of age, he could "no longer go out or come in," sounds like a description of geriatric infirmity. If so, it contradicts the claim (34:7) that at the time of his death Moses' eyesight was still good and he was still vigorous. Contrasts such as this prompt modern scholars to hypothesize multiple traditions or editorial processes. Rabbinic scholars, on the other hand, regarded such infelicities as indicators of some subtlety.

The late medieval Jewish commentator Nachmanides, for example, assumed that the great Moses would have been in remarkable health to the end. The interpretive problem, then, is Moses' apparent misrepresentation in 31:2. Nachmanides suggested a psychological motivation for Moses' white lie; Moses' statement reveals his pastoral concern for the people who were about to be deprived of the only leader they had ever known: "he told them this in order to comfort them"; that is, so that they could find some rationale for Moses' passing.

The Talmud (Sotah 13b) harmonizes the two statements by postulating that 31:2 refers to Moses' mental condition while 34:7 refers to his physical condition. It explains that "This [31:2] teaches us that the well-springs of wisdom were stopped for him."

Ramban [Nachmanides] Commentary, 345

Moses Blesses Joshua
James Jacques Joseph Tissot. 1836–1902. *Moses Blesseth Joshua before the High Priest.* The Jewish Museum. New York.

imposed by YHWH. The only leader this generation of Israel has known—its deliverer and judge, the mediator of the covenant, their teacher and guide for over forty years—will not accompany them when they cross the Jordan. How will they go on?

Moses, aware of their quite understandable concerns, encourages them with reminders that, although he will soon leave them, their basic circumstances will not change (v. 3). First, just as has been true throughout Moses' ministry, their true leader and guide, YHWH, will continue to be with them. YHWH will go before his people, driving out their enemies ahead of them. Second, just as YHWH has promised, he will not leave his people without human leadership. Joshua will succeed Moses.

Moses explicates the thesis statement in v. 3 in vv. 4-8. YHWH's presence with his people in the future will be consistent in character with his presence with them in the past. Moses has been YHWH's spokesman, but YHWH's presence with his people does not depend on Moses' mediation. In the future, YHWH will behave "just as" he has always behaved. Specifically, YHWH will do to Israel's enemies beyond the Jordan just as he did to their enemies, Sihon and Og, on this side of the river. As a result, Israel can and must "be courageous and strong, unafraid and unwavering," because YHWH will continue to be with them whatever Moses' fate.

At the beginning of Moses' career, however, YHWH made it clear that he chooses to deliver and guide his people through a human agent: "I have seen the misery of my people in Egypt. . . . I know their sufferings, and I have come to deliver them. . . . So come, I will send you to Pharaoh to bring my people, the Israelites, out of Egypt" (Exod 3:7-8, 10). In like fashion, then, Moses calls Joshua to him, and in the presence of all Israel charges him employing the same language he has just used to encourage the people. Joshua, too, is to "be courageous and strong," because YHWH has chosen him as the human agent who will lead the people into the land. YHWH, who will precede the people into the land, will also go before Joshua, neither "leaving nor forsaking (v. 8; cf. v. 6)" him.

Provisions for the Reading of the Torah, 31:9-13

It may be significant that neither this text nor any in the series of texts dealing with Joshua's commission (Deut 1:37-38; 3:21-22, 28; 31:14-15, 23; Josh 1:2-9)[2] charges Joshua with responsibility for succeeding Moses in his prophetic role as mediator and interpreter of the covenant. Instead, Joshua's responsibility seems limited to military affairs, specifically to the conquest of the promised land. Elsewhere (18:15-22; 34:10-11), Deuteronomy describes Moses as the exemplary prophet. The Bible does not celebrate Joshua's prophetic achievement.

But Moses does not leave the people without guidance (Torah) in covenant matters either. Instead, he writes down "this Torah" ["This Torah"—Identity and Chronology]—that is, the book of Deuteronomy, his explication (1:5) of the Horeb covenant—and entrusts it to the levitical priests and the elders of Israel with instructions for its use. Notably, the nearly verbatim parallel in v. 28 does not mention the elders of the land. The reference to them in v. 9 may represent a "democratizing" editorial insertion intended to broaden the scope of Mosaic authority beyond the priests only to include the landed gentry. At any rate, in association with the seventh year of the seven-year Sabbatical cycle, here termed the "year of release (or remission)," and during Sukkoth, or the Feast of Booths [Succoth and Covenant], when all Israel is to "appear before YHWH" at the central

"This Torah"—Identity and Chronology

What did Moses write and when did he write it? The final passages in the covenant curses and portions of the account of the Moabite covenant already imply the existence of a written form of the "Torah" (28:58, 61; 30:10). According to Deut 31:9, Moses "Then . . . wrote down this Torah" and entrusted it to the levitical priests. Subsequently, however, the narrator records that Moses "wrote this song that very day" (31:22), that is, after he had written the Torah scroll. Or had he? Deut 31:24 relates once again: "Moses finished writing . . . the words of this Torah to the end." The song itself, then, follows only in Deut 32. In fact, everything else recorded in the book of Deuteronomy, including the account of his death and burial in ch. 34, occurred after Moses had "finished writing." Clearly, then, as the current form of the book of Deuteronomy understands it, the "Torah" written by Moses is not identical with the current form of Deuteronomy, and certainly not with the entire Pentateuch!

In traditional Jewish usage, of course, the term "Torah scroll" refers to the complete Pentateuch. But on the pages of the Pentateuch itself, the term has several meanings. A comparison of 10:2, which reports that Moses placed the "tablets of the Torah" inside the ark of the covenant, with 31:26, where Moses instructs the levitical priests to place "this Torah" beside the ark, proves instructive. The distinction between the Decalogue, afforded primacy through its placement inside the ark, and Moses' explication of it must be recognized. Similarly, given the fact that, beginning in Deut 28, Deuteronomy's accounts seem to refer to a document already in existence, the phrase "this Torah" must refer to the portion of the current book of Deuteronomy devoted explicitly to the explication of the Decalogue, that is, to the Deuteronomic Code. The latter portion of the book of Deuteronomy must be regarded as an "appendix," or, as modern scholarship suggests, a component of the "Deuteronomistic" framework of the book (see Introduction).

sanctuary, the levites are to publicly read the text of "this Torah" for all to hear.

Moses' instructions incorporate three typically Deuteronomic themes: (1) the inclusive nature of the assembly (v. 12a), (2) the purpose of written Torah (vv. 12b), and (3) the crucial importance of perpetuating the covenant in new generations (v. 13). The assembly gathered to hear the Torah read is to include men, women, children, and resident aliens. They are to hear Torah so that they may learn it. Hearing and learning Torah results in the fear of YHWH that, in turn, produces obedience. Obedience, then, is tantamount to "doing all the words of the Torah." Israel is to be not only hearers, but also doers of the Torah (cf. James 1:22). The children must be included in the assembly gathered to hear Torah because they, too, must learn to fear YHWH. In short, in accordance with the etymology of the term *tōrâ* ("instruction"), "this Torah" will function primarily to teach YHWH's will to coming generations of Israel, just as Moses has taught the generation assembled in Moab.

Joshua Commissioned, Part II, 31:14-15

The second sequence in this chapter also begins with a reminder of Moses' imminent death and an account of the commissioning of Joshua. In the first sequence, Moses based his address to Israel somewhat euphemistically on his advanced age and YHWH's

Leopold Pilichowski. 1869–1933. *Sukkot.* 1894–1895. Oil on canvas.
42.5" x 53". Gift of Mr. and Mrs. Oscar Gruss. The Jewish Museum. New York.

Succoth and Covenant

Jews celebrate the last, or eighth, day of the Feast of Booths, or Succoth (Deut 31:10-13; Num 29:35), as the holiday of Simchat Torah, "The Joy of Torah." In an evening service that continues into the morning hours, the congregation gathers to rejoice in God's gift of Torah. During the service the people parade one or more of the congregation's Torah scrolls around the synagogue in seven dances or processionals known as "hakkafot." Everyone present has the opportunity to carry the Torah scroll. The children follow the processional joyously waving flags. Candies and sweets abound. Simchat Torah services are above all joyous celebrations.

The highpoint of the service is the conclusion of the annual cycle of Torah readings, not coincidentally the last passage in Deuteronomy, followed immediately by the beginning of the new cycle with a reading from Genesis. The service includes many elements of wedding services. The Torah is sometimes referred to as a bride. Scripture readers are referred to as grooms of the Torah.

In this manner, Jews celebrate and commemorate very much in the spirit of Moses' intention, as described in Deut 31, that "this Torah" be Israel's guide. The presence of children ensures the transmission of Torah joy to a new generation.

prohibition. In the second, YHWH himself addresses Moses directly with the blunt reminder that the day of his death approaches and the equally blunt command to bring Joshua to the "tent of meeting" to receive the divine commission (v. 14).

Obviously, then, vv. 14-15 elevate the tenor of the narrative to a higher pitch. In fact, this narrative is quite unique in Deuteronomy: only here does the book mention the tent of meeting; this is the sole account of God's appearance in Deuteronomy. The moment when the divine presence, symbolized by the pillar of cloud that rests over the door of the tent, meets Moses and Joshua is high drama indeed. The chosen representative, Israel's leader, on the eve of his death, stands together with his divinely chosen successor, soon to be divinely commissioned, in the visible presence of Israel's God.

Moses' Testament in Song, 31:16-22

And then the account breaks off. YHWH instructed Moses to bring Joshua to the tent so that "I may commission him (*wa'ăṣawwennû*, v. 14)," but this commission goes unstated until much later. Instead, in the final form of the text, YHWH turns again to Moses, reminding him yet once more that he will soon "lie with [his] fathers" and predicting what awaits Israel after Moses' death.

As suggested above, vv. 16-21 are an insertion. Not only do they interrupt the account begun in vv. 14-15, but they also use language normally reserved for the Torah itself [Torah and Song] in reference to Moses' song. Furthermore, they are somewhat confused concerning the sequence of events narrated here (When did Moses actually write the song? When did he write the Torah?). The song introduced follows only after the intervention of another sequence dealing with Joshua and the Torah scroll.

Despite the confusion it produces in the final form of the text, however, this insertion has a clearly conceived rhetorical purpose. Cast as YHWH's words to Moses (and to Joshua, see v. 19) standing before him at the tent of meeting, it becomes the focal point of the narrative, displacing YHWH's statement of Joshua's commission. Now the Song of Moses receives the emphasis once devoted to Joshua's divine commission. Like Joshua, his successor, and the Torah scroll, the record of his Torah wisdom, YHWH commissions this song as a testament of Moses' leadership. What makes it so important?

The introduction to the song divides neatly into two parts: vv. 16-18 describe YHWH's motivation for commissioning the song and vv. 19-22 describe the function the song will serve. YHWH knows that soon after Moses' passing, the people will engage in idolatry. With acrimonious rhetoric that characterizes

---

Torah and Song

As the commentary argues, the insertion of the account of the Song of Moses at this point focuses a great deal of attention on the song. I. Cairns has noted that, in addition to the placement, the language used to describe the song serves to draw parallels between the song and the Torah book (Deuteronomy). "Like the torah, the shirah ("song") must be:

"written" (31:19, 22; cf., e.g., 27:3, 8; 28:58, 61)
"taught" (31:19, 22; cf., e.g., 4:1, 5, 10, 14; 5:31)
"placed in the mouth" (31:19, 21; cf. 30:14; Josh 1:8)
"established as a witness" (31:19, 21; cf. v.. 26)"

This comparison serves not only to accentuate the song as a parallel to Torah, however, but also to provide the Torah with a second function. Since the song does not explicate the Decalogue, the parallel must call attention to some other purpose of Torah. In addition to its role as a witness to YHWH's revealed will, therefore, Torah, like the song, now assumes the role of witness against Israel. In keeping with the tendency of the "addenda" to Deuteronomy to assume that Israel will inevitably (or already has) fail in its responsibility to keep the Torah, the editor(s) who inserted the song see it as YHWH's effort, through Moses, to leave Israel without excuse (31:19, 26, 28).

I. Cairns, *Word and Presence: A Commentary on the Book of Deuteronomy* (ITC; Grand Rapids: Eerdmans, 1992), 274.

Deuteronomistic and prophetic portrayals of Israel's infidelity, YHWH describes Israel's behavior as "harlotry" (see [Baalism] and [A Caricature of Canaanite Religion]). In so doing, YHWH says, they will "abandon me and break my covenant."

The ironic consequences will mirror Israel's faithlessness. They abandon (ʿzb, v. 16) YHWH; he will abandon (ʿzb, v. 17) them. They turn from him to other gods (v. 18); in his anger he will turn away from them, and "hide [his] face (*wěhistartî pānay*, vv. 17, 18)." ["I will hide my face"] Disaster and suffering will come to them because their God has withdrawn his protective presence, as they themselves will soon realize (v. 17).

Knowing that Israel will falter in this way, YHWH gives Moses the song and orders that it be taught to the people and recorded for posterity (v. 19). Interestingly, the imperative "write" in v. 19 is plural. If not merely a grammatical lapse on the part either of some scribe or of the author/editor, this plural may reflect awareness that, during this time of transition, both Moses and Joshua stand before YHWH in the tent of meeting. The medieval Jewish commentator, Nachmanides, explained, "In line with the plain meaning of Scripture, He commands both Moses and Joshua to write it for He wanted to make Joshua His prophet during Moses' lifetime."[3]

At any rate, YHWH intends for the song to serve as "[his] witness to the sons of Israel" (v. 19). YHWH explains the significance of this statement, in part, by reiterating the ideas expressed in vv. 16-17. When YHWH has brought them to the rich promised

---

"I will hide my face"

AΩ The expression "to hide (*str*, hiphil) one's face" belongs to a family of phrases in the Hebrew Bible indicating the absence of God. It occurs in reference to the hiding of God's face a total of twenty-six times (Deut 31:17, 18; 32:20; Pss 10:11; 13:2; 22:25; 27:9; 30:8; 44:25; 51:11; 69:18; 88:15; 102:3; 104:29; 143:7; Isa 8:17; 54:8; 59:2; 64:6; Ezek 39:23, 24, 29; Mic 3:4; Jer 33:5; Job 13:24; 34:29). In the Psalms and Job, it emphasizes the psalmist's sense of God's absence, often without indicating the cause for God's absence. In fact, psalmists frequently complain of God's absence precisely because they do not understand the reason for it.

The other occurrences differ considerably. In them, the cause for God's absence is clear: They describe a direct causal connection between the people's sin and God's absence. These "causal" passages also differ from Psalm texts in that they refer to God's absence from the community because of its sins. The psalms typically describe an individual's confusion. From a theological standpoint, it is significant that, both for individuals and the community, God's absence—not God's punitive acts—represents the extreme of human pain and despair. (For an extensive and insightful treatment of the topic of God's absence, see Samuel Balentine, *The Hidden God: The Hiding of the Face of God in the Old Testament* [Oxford Theological Monographs; Oxford: Oxford, 1983], 66-67.)

---

land and, amidst the bounty, they have forgotten the source of their blessings, they will turn to other gods (v. 20). When, as a result, "great disaster and oppression" comes upon them, this song will "answer (*wĕʿānĕta*, v. 21)" as witness.

The pessimism regarding Israel's "purity of heart" expressed as early as 29:3(4) finds expression here once again. YHWH knows their waywardness; he knows that even as they stand assembled to enter into covenant with him, some individual among them contemplates practicing idolatry (29:18-21). "I know," YHWH says, "the plan he conceives in his heart today" (v. 21). YHWH dictates Moses' song so that one day it may remind Israel that YHWH, through Moses, told them so.

The narrator concludes (v. 22) with the report that Moses wrote (a singular verb once again) the song and taught it to Israel as YHWH had instructed. The song itself follows considerably later.

Joshua Commissioned, Part III, 31:23

In context, the narrator, who speaks in v. 22, might be assumed to be the speaker of v. 23. The content of v. 23, however, clearly points to YHWH as the speaker ("the land that I promised," etc.). Verse 23, then, follows best on v. 15 as the content of YHWH's commission (*ṣwh*, vv. 14, 23). In the present arrangement of the text, YHWH spoke with both Moses (vv. 16-22) and Joshua (v. 23) as they stood before him at the tent of meeting. The divine commission itself essentially repeats the language of vv. 7-8 (and of Josh 1:2-9!). Its significance lies in the fact that now YHWH himself addresses these words directly to Joshua. Moses, heretofore YHWH's spokesman even to Joshua, is no longer needed.

Provisions for Safekeeping of the Torah and Its Role as Testament, 31:24-29

By this point in the narrative, all efforts to maintain a credible account of the sequence of events have apparently been abandoned. According to v. 9, Moses has already written down the Torah; according to v. 22, the song, now included in the Torah book (Deuteronomy) was written later; according to v. 24, Moses now completes the writing of "this Torah," although this would mean that he completed writing the book before events recorded subsequently (including most prominently his own death) had transpired. Obviously, the author/editor(s) were motivated by considerations other than journalistic accuracy. The primary focus of this final section of Deuteronomy 31 emerges clearly in v. 26. Moses instructs the levitical priests to place the completed copy of the Torah scroll beside the ark of the covenant so that it can be "a witness against you (*wĕhāyāh-šām bĕkā lĕ'ēd*)." Moses goes on to explain, as YHWH had earlier in relation to the song, that, judging from Israel's rebelliousness and stubbornness during his time with them, he can expect them only to behave worse after he has gone. They will "become truly corrupt (*hašḥēt tašḥitûn*, v. 29)" and will turn from the ways Moses has taught them. As a result of the evils they will commit in YHWH's sight, of course, disaster will befall them.

Moses knows all this full well. He assembles all the elders and leaders to warn them and to invoke heaven and earth as witnesses to the fact that he has "told them so." As a testimony for future generations, the Torah scroll will preserve Moses' teaching and commandments, his warnings and exhortations, and his prediction that the people will turn away to idolatry. Israel can never plead ignorance. They have been forewarned. The Torah scroll will always be there beside the ark of the covenant. Every seventh year the priests will read it publicly. Moses' admonitions will rebuke Israel's waywardness and explain the punishment that comes in fulfillment of the curses for disobedience. In effect, this Torah scroll will be the prophetic key to the interpretation of Israel's history.

As Thomas Mann has insightfully observed:

> . . . the introduction of the term "witness" and the prediction of the future does not turn Deuteronomy into a kind of crystal ball. Rather, it

qualifies the text as prophecy in the deeper sense. While the popular notion of a prophet is of someone who can foretell the future, the biblical notion is primarily of someone who can interpret the present in the light of the past . . . . What happens in the future is determined not by fate but by faithfulness, or the lack thereof.

In this sense, Deuteronomy is thoroughly prophetic. Its role as a witness is to bear testimony throughout Israel's subsequent history either for or against the people.[4]

CONNECTIONS

Norbert Lohfink, a prominent student of Deuteronomy and Deuteronomistic literature, has outlined four observations concerning ancient Israel's theology of leadership as evident in Deuteronomy 31.[5] To Lohfink's four, a fifth may be added. Since the transition from one leader to his or her successor will always be a period of danger and opportunity for God's people, the community of faith and its leadership—today and tomorrow—will be well-served to reflect on the dynamics of transition evident at the end of Moses' career. [Leadership: "I See the Promised Land," Martin Luther King Jr.]

(1) Moses, the departing leader, is not ready to relinquish his authority. Or, at least, he wants to see his labors bear fruit. At several points the Torah records Moses' pleas to be permitted to enter the promised land with Israel (see 3:23-29 and commentary). Here, Moses exhibits an almost universal human dissatisfaction with the rhythms of life. Youth gives way to age. Careers wax and then, inevitably, wane. Skills diminish. One's time ends. Like the professional athlete who delays retirement too long, human beings simply do not want to let go.

It is easy to feel sympathy with Moses. He championed Israel's freedom. He served as midwife at their birth as a nation. He led them in battle with their foes. He settled their disputes with one another. For over forty years, he represented God to them and them to God. But his time as leader has come to an end. He must step aside. He is not indispensable.

(2) It is also significant to note that God has determined Moses' fate as an individual, separately, in a sense, from his fate as

Leadership: "I See the Promised Land," Martin Luther King Jr.

Moses' leadership of his people has inspired and shaped the lives and work of many. Martin Luther King Jr. took inspiration from Moses' opportunity to gaze on the promised land as affirmation of the success of Moses' leadership. After all the trials, Israel was about to cross over. Even though Moses would not accompany them, his efforts had brought them to this point.

[S]everal years ago, I was in New York City autographing the first book that I had written. And while sitting there autographing books, a demented black woman came up. The only question I heard from her was, "Are you Martin Luther King?" And I was looking down writing, and I said yes. And the next minute I felt something beating on my chest. Before I knew it I had been stabbed by this demented woman. I was rushed to Harlem Hospital . . . . And . . . the X-rays revealed that the tip of the blade was on the edge of my aorta, the main artery . . . . It came out in the New York Times the next morning, that if I had sneezed, I would have died. . . . I . . . received [a letter] from the President and the Vice-President. I've forgotten what those telegrams said. I'd received a visit and a letter from the Governor of New York, but I've forgotten what the letter said. But there was another letter that came from a little girl, a young girl who was a student at the White Plains High School. And I looked at that letter, and I'll never forget it. It said simply, "Dear Dr. King: I am a ninth-grade student at the White Plains High School." She said, "While it should not matter, I would like to mention that I am a white girl. I read in the paper of your misfortune, and of your suffering. And I read that if you had sneezed, you would have died. And I'm simply writing you to say that I'm so happy that you didn't sneeze."

And I want to say tonight, I want to say that I am happy that I didn't sneeze. Because if I had sneezed, I wouldn't have been around here in 1960, when students all over the South started sitting-in at lunch counters. And I knew that as they were sitting in, they were really standing up for the best in the American dream. And taking the whole nation back to those great wells of democracy which were dug deep by the Founding Fathers in the Declaration of Independence and the Constitution. If I had sneezed, I wouldn't have been around in 1962, when Negroes in Albany, Georgia, decided to straighten their backs up. And whenever men and women straighten their backs up, they are going somewhere, because a man can't ride your back unless it is bent. If I had sneezed, I wouldn't have been here in 1963, when the black people of Birmingham, Alabama, aroused the conscience of this nation, and brought into being the Civil Rights Bill. If I had sneezed, I wouldn't have had a chance later that year, in August, to try to tell America about a dream that I had had. If I had sneezed, I wouldn't have been down in Selma, Alabama, to see the great movement there. If I had sneezed, I wouldn't have been in Memphis to see a community rally around those brothers and sisters who are suffering. I'm so happy that I didn't sneeze . . .

We've got some difficult days ahead. But it doesn't matter with me now. Because I've been to the mountaintop. And I don't mind. Like anybody, I would like to live a long life. Longevity has its place. But I'm not concerned about that now. I just want to do God's will. And He's allowed me to go up to the mountain. And I've looked over. And I've seen the Promised Land. I may not get there with you. But I want you to know tonight, that we, as a people will get to the Promised Land. And I'm happy, tonight. I'm not worried about anything. I'm not fearing any man. Mine eyes have seen the glory of the coming of the Lord.

Excerpted from Martin Luther King's last speech at the Mason Temple in Memphis, Tennessee, April 3, 1968.

Israel's leader. The problematic relationship between the two spheres of a leader's life figures prominently in the stories of Israel's subsequent leaders (King David, for example) and has become the focus of controversy in modern American politics. Both leaders and people are tempted to equate the two spheres, measuring public effectiveness in terms of private character or

Joshua Receives the Leader's Staff

Luca Signorelli. 1441–1523. *Testament and Death of Moses.* 1481–1483. Fresco. Sistine Chapel. Vatican Palace, Vatican State.

assuming that leadership successes can compensate for private failings. The story of Moses' career teaches the comforting lesson that God can and does use flawed human beings as powerful leaders. Moses learned the harsh lesson, however, that God still holds the leader personally responsible for his or her shortcomings.

(3) In a pattern that will characterize many institutions of leadership in Israel, Joshua undergoes a dual installation: once by Moses, once by God. Later, the kings of Israel will typically be chosen by God—a choice usually symbolized through prophetic anointing—and subsequently acclaimed king by the people. This two-phased process acknowledges the dual nature of leadership in Israel. As God's people, they can be truly led only by leaders whom God chooses. As God's people, they only follow those in whom they recognize God's call. From a practical standpoint, this dual process serves as a safeguard against opportunists who would falsely claim God's call in a grab for power and against fanatics who sense God's call in error. Ideally, if an individual is authentically and truly commissioned by God, the people of God will see evidence of it. History teaches,

of course, that in fact charlatans often deceive or God's people fail to recognize God's chosen.

(4) As was true in Moses' career, YHWH commissions Joshua with the reminder that Joshua will not be left to his own devices. YHWH is no absentee God. He will go before Joshua and the people; he will be with Joshua offering concrete direction. YHWH does more than confer a title. He remains the driving force in Israel's history. "YHWH leads the leader."

The book that bears his name records Joshua's career. In it, Joshua's interaction with YHWH on the one hand and the people on the other follows a typical pattern that emphasizes YHWH's leadership role: YHWH issues instructions to Joshua, Joshua relays commands to the people, the book offers a bipartite report of the execution of YHWH's plans (first a summary then a detailed expansion of the report). "Significantly, only the Ai episode departs substantially from this pattern. Here Joshua issues commands in advance of any divine commission to do so (Josh 7:2-3) with catastrophic results (Josh 7:4-5)."[6] In this case, the exception proves the rule.

(5) Finally, YHWH does not issue an abstract commission. YHWH calls Joshua specifically to lead the conquest and possession of the land. Joshua's "authority" is limited to those areas of responsibility expressly stated. Similar restrictions on "authority" can be seen in the New Testament. When the apostles admit their inadequacy as ministers to the widows in the church in Jerusalem, they lead the church in electing seven men to serve, probably, as the church's first "deacons." The apostles will limit themselves to fulfilling their calling as preachers and teachers; the newly-chosen seven will minister to the needy (Acts 6:1-6). Paul repeatedly stresses the idea that the members of the church have been given differing talents and callings and suggests the importance of fulfilling the roles for which one is equipped and to which one is called (1 Cor 12:4-31; Eph 4:7-16). The title "minister of God" can become an occasion for arrogance. The temptation to act on God's behalf without God's commission—to lead where one has not been led, to teach and preach in God's name before first hearing God's word—is the temptation to assume divine endorsement for one's own plans.

NOTES

[1] Compare G. von Rad, *Deuteronomy: A Commentary* (OTL; Philadelphia: Westminster, 1966), 188.

[2] See Lohfink, "Der Bundesschluss im Lande Moab: Redaktionsgeschichtliches zu Dt 28,69-32,47," *Biblische Zeitschrift* NS 6 (1962): 83ff.

[3] *Ramban (Nachmanides) Commentary on the Torah: Deuteronomy*, C. Chavel, trans. (New York: Shilo Publishing House, 1976), 349.

[4] T. Mann, *Deuteronomy* (Westminster Bible Companion; Louisville: Westminster/John Knox, 1995), 165.

[5] "Die deuteronomistische Darstellung des Übergangs der Führung Israels von Moses auf Josue: Ein Beitrag zur alttestamentlichen Theologie des Amtes," in *Studien zum Deuteronomium und zur deuteronomisticshen Literatur I*, Stuttgarter Biblische Aufsatzbände 8 (Stuttgart: Verlag Katholisches Bibelwerk, 1990), 96-97.

[6] M. Biddle, "Literary Structures in the Book of Joshua," *Review and Expositor* 95 (1998): 196.

MOSES' SONG

31:30–32:52

In many ways, Deuteronomy 32 is a curiosity. It includes yet another divine reminder of Moses' impending death (vv. 48-52; cf. 3:26-28), offering an alternative rationale for YHWH's refusal to permit Moses to enter the promised land. In fact, this announcement of Moses' death, with its identification of Mt. Abarim and Mt. Nebo and its reference to Meribath-kadesh (cf. Num 20:1-13), seems to be a variant of the Priestly account in Numbers 27:12-14. Furthermore, Deuteronomy 32 offers yet another concluding exhortation (vv. 44-47) identifying the words of the Song with the "words of this law" (v. 46). Strangely, it refers to Joshua as Hoshea (cf. Num 13:8, 16).

By far the most enigmatic component of Deuteronomy 32, however, is the Song of Moses itself. To start with, the very wording of the Song is a puzzle. It exists in four important, significantly divergent, manuscript traditions. [MT, Q, LXX, and Sam] Generally, the evidence of the so-called "Dead Sea Scrolls" from Qumran, in conjunction with the Samaritan Pentateuch and the Greek Septuagint (LXX), suggests that the Massoretic text tradition, which is authoritative in Judaism and is usually the basis for Christian translations of the Old Testament, probably does not preserve the oldest form of the Song of Moses. Since the passages in question deal with issues pertinent to Israel's monotheistic faith and YHWH's governance of the nations of the world, this uncertainty with respect to the wording of the Song is key to the interpretation of the Song (see the commentary on vv. 9 and 43, especially).

Second, in Hebrew, the language and style of the Song represents a bewildering mixture of archaic speech forms and late prophetic and wisdom vocabulary, of first person divine speech and third person speech about God, of legal, wisdom, and liturgical genres, and—if the evidence of the Qumran scrolls, LXX, and the Samaritan Pentateuch is credible—of theological perspectives from Israel's earliest period alongside ideas typical of the late monarchial period. Parallels with similarly complex didactic-historical psalms (78 and 82, especially; [Deuteronomy 32 and Psalm 78]) raise the possibility that the Song existed and underwent a process of transformation and growth for a long period prior to its inclusion in the book of Deuteronomy.

MT, Q, LXX, and Sam

Sorting out the significance of the multitude of ancient manuscripts in a variety of languages that attest to the text of the Hebrew Bible can be bewildering, even for scholars. For Deuteronomy, the most important families of texts are the Massoretic text (MT), the Qumran manuscripts (Q, also called "the Dead Sea Scrolls"), the Greek Septuagint (LXX), and the Samaritan Pentateuch (Sam). All except LXX are in Hebrew. The essential profiles of these families of texts are as follows:

MT is a standardized text family, produced in and authoritative for Judaism. It achieved its final form sometime in the medieval period through the activity of the Massoretes. These scribes and scholars invented the system of vowel points that were added to the existing consonantal text. Prior to this innovation (7th to 9th centuries AD), Hebrew was written entirely without vowels. The oldest complete MT manuscript of the entire Hebrew Bible, Codex Leningradensis, dates to AD 1008.

The Qumran Scrolls include one important manuscript of Deuteronomy, 4Qdeut (2d century BC). This unpointed manuscript is remarkable not only because it is nearly a millennium older than Codex Leningradensis, but also because in some cases it preserves readings quite distinct from MT and more closely akin to readings preserved in LXX and Sam.

Hellenistic Jews translated the Bible into Greek beginning during the Ptolemaic period (3rd century BC). The most important complete or nearly complete manuscripts date to the 3rd and 4th centuries AD. Although written in Greek, it is possible to "retrovert" LXX readings into the Hebrew from which they must have been translated. Remarkably, as in Deut 32:43, these reconstructed Hebrew exemplars often resemble Q more than MT.

The Samaritans preserved the text of the Pentateuch in a separate tradition (it was not subject to Massoretic standardization or vocalization, for example). Known for its ideologically motivated emendations (Mt. Gerizim is substituted for Mt. Zion regularly, for example), the oldest complete manuscript of the Samaritan Pentateuch in existence dates to the late medieval period. It, too, often agrees with LXX and Qumran against MT.

It must be remembered that no single extant text or family of texts can be identified as the original. In fact, the textual history of Deut 32 suggests that the search for an original may be misdirected. As the commentary demonstrates, it may be better to think of the development of the text of Deut 32 over time. The problem for believers, then, becomes a question of identifying the "canonical" or authoritative form of the text. Are text forms authoritative for the faith tradition that produced or transmitted them (Q for the now-defunct Qumran community, MT for Jews, Sam for Samaritans, and LXX for Christians)? Is older more authoritative? Is the final form the final word? Or, is it possible to think in terms of the authority of the entire tradition?

Whatever its origins, in its present form the Song reflects the Deuteronomistic theology of the frame to the book of Deuteronomy.

Third, scholars find the possibility that the Song contains references to historical events tantalizing, but ultimately elusive. Beginning as early as the addendum to the covenant curses (28:47-68), Deuteronomy has been concerned with the unnamed enemy who will ravage rebellious Israel, taking its population into captivity. Moses' Song continues this theme with its references to a nation that is "no people," "a foolish nation" (v. 21), "a nation void of sense," "without understanding" (v. 28) who (will be or) had been able, although vastly outnumbered, to route Israel's thousands (v. 30). On scanty evidence, no proposal for the identification of this unnamed enemy or the events described has gained widespread acceptance. Given the didactic emphasis of the Song, and of the book of Deuteronomy on the whole, it may be better to see these references as paradigmatic: Philistines, Amalekites, Assyrians,

Deuteronomy 32 and Psalm 78

AΩ While scholars have been unable to identify a specific time or setting as the background for Deut 32, parallels with other didactic poems found in the Psalter suggest a common origin and function. Ps 78 is a prime example. It can be dated to a period after the fall of Samaria (722 BC) on the basis of references to YHWH's preference for Judah and the house of David (vv. 67-72). Not coincidentally, this would place Ps 78 in the time period when the book of Deuteronomy was "discovered" in the temple (2 Kgs 22–23), the impetus for the "Deuteronomic reform" and for the prominence of "Deuteronomistic" theology and literature. The thrust of the argument of Ps 78—namely, that Israel persists in its faithlessness despite repeated evidences of YHWH's constancy, repeated episodes of Israel's rebellion, and repeated incidents in which YHWH corrects his people—approximates not only the tenor of Deut 32, but also of the entire Deuteronomistic literature (compare especially 2 Kgs 17 and, for the reference to Shiloh in v. 60, Jer 7:12, 14).

In addition to the basic Deuteronomistic theology, parallels between Deut 32 and Ps 78 include vocabulary and concepts ("give ear [*'zn*, hif.]," "words of my mouth [*'imrê pî*]"—Deut 32:1; Ps 78:1; "ancestors"—Deut 32:7; Ps 78:3, 5, 8, 12; "generations"—Deut 32:7; Ps 78:4, 6, 8; "faithful, faithfulness [*'mn*]"—Deut 32:4; Ps 78:8, 37; "God Most High"—Deut 32:8; Ps 78:17, 35; "fire"—Deut 32:22; Ps 78:21; "Rock"—Deut 32:4, 31; Ps 78:35; water from a rock—Deut 32:13; Ps 78:15-16, 20; Israel's satiation—Deut 32:15; Ps 78:29-30; Israel "provoking" YHWH and making him "jealous"—Deut 32:16, 21; Ps 78:40, 58; Israel as YHWH's "possession"—Deut 32:9; Ps 78:55) and outline. The outline of Ps 78 differs from that of Deut 32 primarily in terms of the repetition of elements: Introduction (Deut 32:1-3; Ps 78:1-4); thesis (Deut 32:4-6; Ps 78:5-11); evidence of YHWH's faithfulness (Deut 32:7-14; Ps 78:12-16, 23-29, 44-55); Israel's ingratitude (Deut 32:15-18; Ps 78:17-20, 40-43, 56-58); YHWH's reaction (Deut 32:19-25; Ps 78:21-22, 30-31, 59-64); YHWH's reconsideration/patience (Deut 32:26-33; Ps 78:32-39); and Israel/Judah vindicated (Deut 32:34-42; Ps 78:65-72).

Babylonians—all have been God's instruments of judgment against Israel; all have been nations "void of sense" unable to discern their role.

Despite, or in some instances because of, the enigmatic nature of Deuteronomy 32, its function in the context of the book is clear. At the crisis moment when Israel prepares to cross the Jordan and, at the same time, undergo a crucial change in leadership, Moses leaves Israel this Song as part of the larger Torah scroll. Thereby, the Torah scroll becomes more than a collection of laws. It becomes taught wisdom (v. 2), an occasion for praising God (v. 3) for his provision for Israel (vv. 4-14), the paradigm for understanding Israel's history—past, present, and future. In short, Moses' song summarizes the panoramic message of Deuteronomy.

COMMENTARY

Introduction, 31:30–32:3

The song begins with a complex introduction setting it in its various contexts: as Moses' oral recital before the people gathered in

Moab (31:30), as testimony in YHWH's case against Israel for covenant disloyalty (32:1), as Moses' life-giving instruction (32:2), as a call to praise (32:3). The juxtaposition of the second, third, and fourth elements of this introduction highlight the multipurpose function of the song.

Ancient Near Eastern covenants regularly include a formal "invocation of divine witnesses" to the covenant who are called upon to act as guarantors of its terms. Israelite monotheism, of course, does not permit the invocation of other deities, but the Old Testament often invokes heavens and earth, or the entire created universe, to attest to the truth of a divine accusation (Deut 4:26; 30:19; 31:28; Isa 13:13; etc.; compare 1 Chr 16:31; Pss 69:34; 96:11; Isa 49:13; etc.). Years after the passing of Moses and the people to whom he teaches this song, the universe will endure as a witness that Moses taught Israel the meaning of covenant.

In keeping with the multipurpose character of the song, the introduction shifts immediately from the legal language of the covenant lawsuit to describe the content of the song as Moses' "instruction" (v. 2). Now the picture is not that of cosmic witnesses but of nourishing moisture. Moses expresses the hope that his teaching will fall upon Israel like life-giving rain and dew. His wisdom can be the source of Israel's vitality.

Immediately, the introduction shifts once again in v. 3 to a call to praise. Moses' song will "extol (*qr*) the name of YHWH" as a motivation for Moses' hearers to "magnify [their] God." The sequence—lawsuit, instruction, praise—is remarkable. YHWH governs Israel's history according to his covenant with them: YHWH will judge Israel's commitment. But the covenant is not to be understood exclusively, or even primarily, as threat. Instead, through Moses, YHWH has revealed its principles as the key to Israel's vitality and health. The proper response is to worship the God who provides for his people in this manner and who guides them in the paths of life.

Thesis, 32:4-6

The body of the song begins with a brief statement of its basic thesis: YHWH is faithful to his people; but inexplicably, they rebel. Thematically, YHWH's *constancy* and Israel's *inconstancy* unite the song in all its sections. Stylistically, the ironic contrast between the two generates yet other ironies that propel the song's powerful poetry.

Verse 4 describes YHWH's fidelity in an unusually dense array of theologically pregnant terms cast in hymnic style (there are no verbs: "The Rock, perfect his acts, just all his ways, etc."). As if first to impress an image on the mind of the reader/hearer, the ascription of praise begins by simply naming God "The Rock." This epithet, which occurs in the Old Testament with relative frequency (1 Sam 2:2; Isa 17:10; 26:4; 30:29; 44:8; 51:1; Hab 1:12), especially in the Psalter (19:15[14 Eng]; 28:1; 28:1; 31:3; 61:3[2 Eng]; 62:3, 7, 8[2, 6, 7 Eng]; 71:3; 78:35; 89:27[26 Eng]; 92:16[15 Eng]; 94:22; 95:1; 144:1, 2), can accentuate YHWH's strength and protection especially against one's enemies (see 2 Sam 22:3, 32, 47=Ps 18:3, 32, 57[2, 31, 46 Eng]). Here, however, it represents YHWH's permanence and reliability, as the statements explicating the image illustrate.

YHWH's deeds are "perfect" (Heb. *tāmîm*). The Hebrew does not connote the Platonic notion of abstract perfection, but the idea of completion, wholeness, soundness, innocence, and integrity. The adjective occurs most often as a modifier in reference to cultic offerings that are acceptable, i.e., sound. When used to characterize people, it expresses reliable, proper, healthy relationship.[1] Thus, the term is primarily relational: YHWH acts with integrity.

The remaining phrases in v. 4 are epexegetical; they further exposit the relational idea that YHWH is the "Rock" who acts with blameless integrity. All YHWH's ways are justice (*mišpāṭ*, on the relational aspect of justice in the Old Testament, see [Righteousness and the Righteous]). YHWH is a reliable God. [Faithfulness] Just as a rock neither moves nor varies in shape and form, YHWH can be trusted to remain true to relationships. As the next phrase insists ("in him there is no perversity"), YHWH is not fickle, arbitrary, or capricious. Just as a rock neither moves nor varies in shape and form, his character and his commitment do not waver. He is ever righteous (Heb. *ṣaddîq*; for the relational component of this term, see [Righteousness and the Righteous]), ever upstanding (Heb. *yāšār*, literally, "straight").

Faithfulness

AΩ The term *'ĕmûnâ* often translated "faithful" also connotes relational integrity. It belongs to a family of words that stress constancy: the verb form *'mn*, "to be firm"; *'amen*, "confirmed, and thus valid, true"; *'emet*, "durability, dependability, and thus, truth"; and *'ĕmûnâ* itself, "firm, dependable, faithful" (see TLOT [ed. E. Jenni and C. Westermann, trans. M. Biddle; Peabody: Hendrickson, 1997] I, 134-57).

Significantly, as is characteristic of Old Testament thought, this ascription of praise does not praise God for God's abstract "attributes," but for God's faithfulness *as expressed in relationship*. Israel's "theologians" were little concerned for speculating as to YHWH's inner nature or the essence of godhood; instead, Israel knew God in relationship as expressed in God's consistent behavior toward God's people.

The contrast between YHWH's constancy and Israel's fickleness could hardly be more severe (v. 5). Whereas YHWH is the Rock of fidelity, Israel acts corruptly; whereas YHWH acts with integrity, Israel is blemished; whereas YHWH is a reliable God, Israel is a perversely (Heb. *'iqqēš*) unreliable generation; whereas YHWH is just and upright, Israel is "twisted (*pětaltol*)." To make the inequity even more apparent, the thesis statement culminates in the pointed, accusatory rhetorical question of v. 6: "Is this any way to repay YHWH?" Only a foolish people, totally devoid of wisdom, would return rebellion for constancy in this manner. In a grand climax, the final question shifts from the image of the Rock to the picture of the parent. "Is he not your father who begot[2] you, who made you, who established you?" The case against Israel is airtight. They have broken faith with the God who cared for them with the constancy of a rock and the love of a parent.

Evidence for YHWH's Faithfulness, 32:7-14

The song turns now to support the opening statement of YHWH's case against Israel with evidence of YHWH's faithfulness demonstrated toward his people in three phases of their history: YHWH's election of Israel as his own possession at the very beginning of human history (vv. 8-9), the wilderness wandering (vv. 10-12), and the settlement in the land (vv. 13-14). Throughout, the imagery emphasizes YHWH's parental concern and constancy.

A charge to review the evidence of history opens the detailed exposition of the case for YHWH's integrity (v. 7). The audience is to remember the past, to consider events through successive generations. If the audience's memory lacks scope, they are to turn to previous generations for information.

They will find that, even before Israel was a people, at the dawn of human history, when "God Most High" (*'elyôn*) was apportioning responsibility for the nations of the world among members of the heavenly council (v. 8), "God Most High" reserved Israel for himself

El Elyon and the Heavenly Council

Deut 32 is only one of several texts in the Hebrew Bible that attest to earliest Israel's tacit acceptance of the existence of deities other than YHWH. Throughout, however, the Hebrew Bible insists on YHWH's supremacy. Ps 83 (RSV) is perhaps the clearest statement of this early view.

God has taken his place in the divine council;
    In the midst of the gods he holds judgment:
"How long will you judge unjustly
    and show partiality to the wicked? [Selah]
Give justice to the weak and the fatherless;
    maintain the right of the afflicted and the destitute.
Rescue the weak and the needy;
    deliver them from the hand of the wicked."
They have neither knowledge nor understanding,
    they walk about in darkness; all the foundations of the earth are shaken.
I say, "You are gods,
    sons of the Most High, all of you;
nevertheless, you shall die like men,
    and fall like any prince."
Arise, O God, judge the earth;
    for to thee belong all the nations!

(v. 9). No underling would be charged with supervising Israel [El Elyon and the Heavenly Council]

They will remember that, at the beginning of Israel's history as a people, YHWH "found" them in the desert (compare Hos 2:16-17 [14-15 Eng]; Jer 2:2-3; Ezek 16). In the most inhospitable circumstances imaginable ("in a land of desert and void [*tōhû*, cf. Gen 1:1], a howling wasteland"), YHWH "surrounded" them protectively, attended them, guarding them "like the apple of his eye" (v. 10). The paternal care implied by these verbs is specified by the image of the eagle teaching his young to fly: "rousing" his nest, pushing the eaglets to test their wings, but hovering near to bear them upon his wings should they falter (v. 11). YHWH himself, and no other deity, parented Israel in this way.

Finally, they will recall that, presumably when brought to the promised land, they "rode the high places of the land" and fed on its riches—honey, oil, curds, milk, meat, grains, grapes, wine. From beginnings in the wilderness, Israel came to enjoy great bounty because YHWH protected and guided them.

Israel's Ingratitude, 32:15-18

YHWH's attentive care and provision for Israel produced ironic results. Rather than instilling in Israel a sense of grateful devotion, the wealth of YHWH's blessings led to decadence and disobedience. Like the spoiled child of wealthy parents, Israel rebelled. Although the phenomenon is readily observable in everyday life, especially in modern Western culture, the psychology of such self-destructive ingratitude defies common sense. [From "A Prayer for My Daughter"] Israel's historical memory, as the earlier portions of the Song emphasize, includes knowledge of the wilderness period when life was difficult. Indeed, without YHWH's provision and guidance Israel could not have attained the prosperity it enjoyed in the promised land. Central to Israel's confessions concerning its origins as a people is the recognition of YHWH's providence. How can they have allowed prosperity to delude them into forgetting their past?

The song hints at a comparison with an unmanageable animal. "Jeshurun," a rare designation for Israel (only in Deut 32:15; 33:5,

 **From "A Prayer for My Daughter"**

. . . May she be granted beauty and yet not
Beauty to make a stranger's eye distraught,
Or hers before a looking-glass, for such
Being made beautiful overmuch,
Consider beauty a sufficient end,
Lose natural kindness and maybe
The heart-revealing intimacy
That chooses right, and never find a friend . . .

. . . In courtesy I'd have her chiefly learned;
Hearts are not had as a gift but hearts are earned
By those that are not entirely beautiful;
Yet many, that have played the fool
For beauty's very self, has charm made wise,
And many a poor man that has roved,
Loved and thought himself beloved,
From a glad kindness cannot take his eyes . . .

W. B. Yeats in P. Engle and W. Carrier, eds., *Reading Modern Poetry: A Critical Anthology* (Glenview IL: Scott, Foresman and Co., 1968), 138-40.

26; Isa 44:2), "grew fat and kicked" (v. 15; compare Isa 1:3).[3] In a typically Deuteronomic hortatory aside departing from the descriptive third person discussion of Israel's rebellion, the poet confronts the hearer/reader with the fact that these decadent rebels are none other than the hearers/readers themselves: "you grew fat . . . you were sated!" After this brief outburst, the third person description immediately resumes. Self-satisfied, Israel forsook the God who made them, scoffing at the "Rock of [their] salvation."

Specifically, this abandonment of YHWH took the form of idol worship. In a wordplay involving the homonymous verbs *qnh*, "to create, beget," and *qnʾ*, "to be jealous,"[4] the song accuses Israel of making YHWH jealous. In fact, they "provoked" YHWH's anger by worshiping "new-fangled" (literally, "novelties, just arrived"— Targum Onkelos paraphrases "new things recently made") demons. Since these demons were unknown to Israel's ancestors, they cannot have been responsible for Israel's early survival and continued prosperity. In effect, Israel has ungratefully forgotten its origins, turning its back on the God who brought Israel into being in the first place.

The final statement in this indictment section of the song succinctly but powerfully portrays the horror of Israel's behavior in a complex metaphor. They have "neglected (literally, "been unmindful")" of the Rock that "begot" them; they have forgotten the God who gave them birth. The contrasts are extreme. On the one side stands YHWH, the Rock of constancy, Israel's creator and sustainer, who gave birth to Israel and loved it with a parent's love. On the other side stands disdainful, ungrateful, negligent Israel. The Father/Rock praised in vv. 4-5 has now been forgotten (v. 18). Although he alone (vv. 10-12) cared for them during their desert existence, they have now turned to "new" gods unknown to any previous generation (vv. 16-17). The riches ("fat") YHWH freely granted did not inspire gratitude; instead, the people merely became decadent and dissolute.[5]

YHWH's Reaction, 32:19-25

Again the ironic contrast between YHWH's constancy and Israel's inconstancy powers the song's description of YHWH's reaction to Israel's faithlessness. With utmost economy, the Song initiates this section in ominous simplicity: "YHWH saw!" And the sight provoked the God who had shown such loving concern for Israel, love like a parent for a child, to spurn God's sons and daughters! How terrible must the sight have been! How awful God's thoughts!

As it turns out, after this jarring announcement, the song reports God's reactions to Israel's ungrateful rebellion in God's own words. And they are awful thoughts indeed. Having seen Israel's ingratitude, YHWH decides to "hide [his] face," to turn away no longer to see to Israel's needs. YHWH will withhold protection and provision. Although the popular perception of the "wrathful" Old Testament God depicts YHWH as angry and punitive, one of the more frightening prospects discussed in the Old Testament (and in the New) involves not God's active punishment of sin, but God's withdrawal. As Paul would later describe it, "Therefore God gave them up . . ." (Rom 1:24, 26). Here, YHWH ironically decides to hide his face, to turn away, so that he cannot see what the outcome will be. Let Israel try to survive without YHWH's help! Let their foolish plans bear fruit! Let them have their way!

YHWH's decision to cease his consistent provision for Israel results from Israel's inconstancy. Previously, YHWH has been described as the "Rock" whose ways are just, a reliable God (v. 4). But Israel has not imitated God's consistent reliability. Instead, they are a fickle generation, "sons in whom there is no reliability (*'ēmun*, v. 20; see [Faithfulness])"; they are inconstant, unfaithful. Ironically, the reliable God has unreliable children. Ironically, just as they made YHWH jealous with non-gods, provoking his anger with nothings, YHWH will make them jealous with a non-nation, provoking their anger with a nation of fools (v. 21). [Babylon or the Church?] Ironically, whereas YHWH had blessed Israel with stability and wealth, now, in his anger, he will kindle a fire that will consume the depths of the underworld, the earth and all its produce, even the foundations of the mountains (v. 22). To this nearly apocalyptic vision of the destruction of the cosmos, YHWH adds a picture of disasters *within* nature. YHWH will unleash his full armory against Israel. The raggedly staccato diction of the

---

Babylon or the Church?

AΩ On the basis of Isa 23:13, the rabbis equated the "non-nation" of v. 22 with the Babylonians (see, for example, *Ramban [Nachmanides] Commentary on the Torah: Deuteronomy* [New York: Shilo, 1976], 362). Christian interpreters often see this as a reference to the supposed displacement of Israel by the church. Luther, for example, appealing to Paul's allusion to Deut 32:22 in Rom 11:11, boldly asserted: ". . . to the present day the Jews are irreconcilably angry with us for denying that they are the people of God and for asserting that according to this verse we are the people of God," *Lectures on Deuteronomy* (Luther's Works 9; J. Pelikan and D. Poellot, eds.; St. Louis: Concordia, 1960).

Closer examination of Deuteronomy and especially Paul, however, suggests that greater Christian humility is warranted. First, the song goes on to detail the punishment in store for this "non-nation," whomever it may be, because of its arrogance, and the subsequent vindication of Israel. Second, Paul's point in Rom 11 is to warn the Gentile Christians he addresses (v. 13) against precisely just such boastfulness (vv. 17-24). Indeed, Paul explicitly denies Luther's assertion that Israel is no longer God's people (v. 1). In this regard, Luther appropriates the reference apart from its context, whereas Paul takes the whole passage into account.

description of this destruction (v. 24) imparts a sense of YHWH's anger and the people's distress: "empty from famine, intestines aflame, bitter destruction, teeth of beasts I will send against them with the venom of things that crawl in the dust." Just as the whole of the cosmos will be affected according to v. 22, the whole of human society in Israel will be affected according to v. 25: those in the street and in their homes alike, male and female alike, young and old alike.

YHWH 's Constancy Motivates a Reconsideration, 32:26-33

To this point, although powerfully executed from both the literary and the theological standpoints, the song has offered a somewhat predictable portrayal of the history of YHWH's covenant relationship with his people. He chose them and reliably and consistently provided for them much as a parent cares for a child; they failed to recognize his care and became careless themselves. YHWH decided for ironic justice: Let them have what they have chosen for themselves!

In v. 26, however, the song takes a sudden, entirely unexpected turn. In the terms of the song itself, YHWH's inner dialogue takes a new direction. As Judge of all the Earth, YHWH *accounts to himself* for any unintended consequences of abandoning Israel to its own devices as he contemplates. YHWH's original intention had been to disperse Israel, eradicating all memory of it (v. 26). But the enemy through whom YHWH intends to provoke Israel's jealousy[6] might have understood its victory over Israel as evidence for YHWH's impotence, not as YHWH's deliberate act. As YHWH considers the possibilities, he becomes convinced that, like Israel, the enemy nation also lacks the insight and wisdom to comprehend correctly YHWH's direction of human affairs (v. 28). Just as Israel lacks the wisdom to foresee the outcome of its infidelity to YHWH, the enemy cannot anticipate the result of its arrogant assumption that its own might enabled it to defeat Israel. How can the enemy have routed a vastly superior Israelite force unless YHWH, Israel's "Rock," wished it so? (For the Old Testament theme of the arrogance of YHWH's instruments of punishment, see connections on Deut 28.)

Commentary interrupts YHWH's soliloquy (vv. 31-33). The reference to YHWH as Israel's Rock inspires a comparison between Israel's God and the enemy's god that intensifies the alteration in the course of the song's logic begun in v. 26. YHWH's deliberations have been based on the notions, firstly, that apostate Israel deserved to be abandoned to its fate, and only secondarily that the danger of the enemy's arrogance must somehow be avoided. Now, however, the focus shifts entirely to the enemy's folly. "Their rock" is not like "our Rock," boasts the songwriter. Furthermore, the enemies themselves are fools! They are best compared to Sodom and Gomorrah! The course alteration here is remarkable. Now Israel's unreliability and inconstancy have given way to the enemy's kinship to Sodom and Gomorrah, the very symbols of godlessness. What has become of the original theme of the song? Does the enemy's foolish arrogance divert YHWH's anger away from Israel's equally foolish apostasy?

Israel Vindicated, 32:34-42

The unexpected and ironic turn of the argument reaches an apex in the final major stanza of the song. Speaking again in vv. 34-35, YHWH declares that "vengeance" and "recompense" are stored in his treasury to be dispensed at the proper time. Indeed, the day of "their" calamity is near. The key interpretive question, of course, involves the identity of those who are subject to YHWH's vengeance. Except for vv. 26-33, one would expect that YHWH planned to repay Israel for its infidelity. After all, the framework surrounding the song describes it as YHWH's testimony against Israel, and, up to v. 26, the song consistently juxtaposes YHWH's faithfulness and Israel's waywardness. But the turn executed at v. 26 determines the direction of the rest of the song with the ironic result that the expected pronouncement of judgment against Israel takes the form of a promise of vindication—only, however, at the last possible moment. In this context, vv. 34-35 must be understood as addressing the calamity in store for Israel's arrogant enemy.

The alteration between third person speech about YHWH and divine first person speech continues in vv. 36-42. Third person speech *about* YHWH begun in v. 36 includes a *quotation* of divine speech beginning in v. 37 and continuing to the end of the stanza. Verse 36 offers a thorough statement of the ironic relationship between YHWH's disappointment in Israel and his fear that punishing them will tempt the enemy nation to arrogance. YHWH will "judge" (*dyn*) his people. In itself, this statement is ambiguous: negative should the judgment find Israel guilty; positive should it find Israel innocent. In the context of the stress on Israel's inconstancy in the first half of the song, this verb would indicate punishment; in the context of the second half, it would refer to reaching a judgment *against* Israel's enemy and, thus, on Israel's behalf. In fact, both elements figure in equal and ever ironic fashion in the continuation of v. 36. The fact that YHWH will "have compassion on his servants [= Israel]" suggests that the ambiguity may be resolved in Israel's favor. But the final explicative clause, "for he sees that strength is exhausted for both captive and free,"[7] sets a sobering precondition. YHWH will "vindicate" Israel—but only *after* exacting the price for their rebellion.

Ironic ambiguity governs YHWH's statement of the case as well. He speaks about (vv. 37-38a, 41-42) and to (vv. 38b) a group whom he describes as "my adversaries" (v. 41). Are they Israel, Israel's enemy, or both? By form and content, YHWH's taunt resembles similar sarcastic reproaches addressed elsewhere in Scripture to Israel (Pss 79:10; 115:2; especially Jer 2:28; Joel 2:17; Mic 7:10; etc.) or to a non-Israelite nation (2 Kgs 18:34 [= Isa 36:19]; 19:13 [= Isa 37:13]). Nor do YHWH's assertions of his exclusive status (v. 39a, "there is no god besides me") and of his resultant sole sovereignty over human affairs (vv. 39b-42) in and of themselves clearly indicate whether Israel or the nations are the object of his wrath. In fact, the final clause in v. 41, "I will repay those who hate me," recalls the warning associated with the Decalogue's prohibition against idolatry ("punishing children for the sin of parents to the third and fourth generation of those who hate me," Exod 20:5-6; Deut 5:9), which appears frequently in the Old Testament in affirmations of YHWH's claim to exclusive obedience (Exod 34:7; Num 14:18; Jer 32:18; compare Jonah 4:2; Joel 2:13; Pss 11:4; 86:15; 103:8; 145:8; Neh 9:17; 2 Chr 30:9). In other words, the language of this stanza exhibits affinities with other biblical texts that ridicule Israel's dalliances with idol gods and, together with the theme of the early portions of the song, suggests that the final stanza, too, maintains that YHWH will hold *Israel* accountable for exclusive fidelity to its only God. On the other hand, the figure of Israel's enemy—now, because of its arrogance, also YHWH's enemy—continues to lurk (v. 42).

Should the interpreter seek to resolve the ambiguity? It is too well and firmly incorporated into the fabric of the second half of the song, it seems. A strong case can be made that, rather than presenting the interpreter with a knot for unraveling, this ambiguity and irony represents a major point of the song in its current form. YHWH's enemies include all those who fail to recognize YHWH's sole claim to sovereignty and obedience. Israel fails to acknowledge this claim when it engages in idol worship; the unnamed enemy fails when it assumes that its victory over Israel has resulted from its own strength. In either case, "when [YHWH] whet[s his] flashing sword and [his] hand grasps [it] in judgment, [he] will take vengeance on [his] enemies" (v. 41), whomever they may be.

Call to Praise, 32:43

How did this ambiguity arise? The history of the text of Deuteronomy 32 gives a rather clear picture both of the backgrounds of the current tension in the text, and of the challenge it posed at various points in time to the various communities for whom Deuteronomy was sacred Scripture.[8] Translations of the three most significant manuscript traditions of 32:43 illustrate the problem [LXX/Q/MT].

If, as seems likely, Qumran represents the more original form of the text with LXX as a conflation and MT an abbreviation, how does one explain the motivations for the changes in MT? Qumran and LXX, picking up the motif of v. 9 once again, focus attention on YHWH's status as sovereign over the heavenly council. MT subtly recasts the hymn to focus on Israel's fate. The nations are to rejoice because Israel has been avenged and restored. [Textual Criticism and Interpretation]

More important than the reconstruction of the textual history of the passage, however, is the question of how this history informs the interpretation of the song. Here, once again, the irony and tension between judgment on Israel and vengeance against Israel's enemies evident throughout the final stanzas provides the key. Seen as testimony to the earliest tradition of interpretation, the variant textual traditions attest to the difficulties an earlier generation of interpreters faced—the same difficulties con-

LXX/Q/MT

AΩ The LXX appears first not because it is the original, nor even the oldest manuscript available, but because it is convenient for purposes of comparison to employ the line numbers of the longer LXX version (8 lines).

LXX

(1) Rejoice, O heavens, with him (Heb. *'immô*),
(2) Worship him all you sons of God,
(3) Rejoice, O nations, with his people (Heb. *'im 'ammô*)
(4) Magnify him all you angels of God,
(5) For the blood of his sons has been avenged;
(6) He has avenged and repaid the (his) enemies,
(7) He has repaid the (his) haters (cf. v. 41b),
(8) The Lord has cleansed the land of his people.

Q

(1) Rejoice, O heavens, with him (?; Heb. *'mmô*),
(2) Worship him all you gods (Heb. *kl 'lhym*; cf. Ps 97:7).
(5) For the blood of his sons has been avenged;
(6) He has taken vengeance on his enemies
(7) And has repaid those who hate him (cf. v. 41b),
(8) and atoned his land (for?/of?) his people.

MT

(3) Rejoice, O nations, (for?) his people (Heb. *'ammô*),
(5) for the blood of his servants has been avenged;
(6) He has taken vengeance on his enemies
(8) and atoned his land (for?) his people.

fronting modern interpreters of the song. The tension has its roots in the fundamental theological claim made by the song and by Deuteronomy on the whole: namely, that YHWH is both sovereign over all of human history and creator-protector-judge of Israel. YHWH cannot simply deal with Israel as though all other nations of the world were inconsequential. Israel cannot simply presume upon its status as the elect. Significantly, the final phrase of v. 43,

---

Textual Criticism and Interpretation

Several phenomena become immediately apparent: (1) The "authoritative" Massoretic text is the shortest of the three versions. (2) Both LXX and Qumran preserve the *parallelismus membrorum* (Latin, "parallelism of members") characteristic of Hebrew poetry, i.e., the lines appear in metrically and thematically balanced pairs (LXX lines 1-2, 3-4, etc.; Q lines 1-2, 5-6, etc.). In contrast, MT has no parallel for line 3, and lines 5, 6, and 7 are overbalanced. (3) The parallel lines 6 and 7 of LXX and Q reiterate the motif found earlier in v. 41b. MT makes no such allusion to its context. (4) Q begins with the introduction consisting of lines 1-2; MT begins with line 3 only. It is reasonable to assume that MT omitted a more original line 4 found in its prototype because of its reference to heavenly beings. It also seems likely that, confronted with the existence of readings similar to both Q and MT, LXX simply combined the options to produce a "conflate" text. (5) LXX and MT diverge, in part, in their resolution of the ambiguity of the consonantal Hebrew *'mmw*, which, depending upon the vowels supplied, can be translated either "his people" or "with him." Notably, however, MT's solution creates additional difficulties. MT reads, literally, "Rejoice, O nations, his people" and seems to require a preposition (that is, "Rejoice, O nations, *with* his people"). Q, which has an "unpointed" (that is, consonants only) text, should probably be translated "with him" since he (YHWH) is the object of veneration (line 2) for the actions he has taken (lines 5-8). The people (= Israel) are only incidental to Q's version of the hymn. Confronted with the options, LXX chooses both (compare lines 1 and 3), but is forced to remedy MT's lack of preposition by supplying "with" before "his people" in line 3. (6) As is true also for v. 9 (see above), LXX and Q seem to reflect a much more archaic theology than does MT. Since it is difficult to imagine why copyists and translators would introduce apparent polytheism into the song, it is likely that the scribes who produced MT expunged all references to "sons of God," indeed, even to the "heavens" in order to produce a theologically "unobjectionable" text.

---

upon which all the textual traditions substantially agree, also hints at the irony. YHWH "atones" or "cleanses" (*kpr*) the land. From what? Israel's sin? The enemy's defiling presence? Both?

Final Summary Conclusion (Song and Torah), 32:44-47

Finally, the song and the Torah are ended. The concluding summary reports succinctly that Moses (and Joshua) finished the recitation of the song (v. 44) and that Moses once again encouraged Israel to pay attention to the words (of the song, presumably) he has given "as a witness" against them so that they may observe the Torah. He reminds them once again that this Torah and obedience to it are not trivialities: they are the key to Israel's life and prosperity (v. 47). In short, the summary offers little that is new in terms of content.

As noted above, however, it is intriguing to scholars because it refers to Joshua as "Hoshea," a variant on the name that occurs chiefly in "Priestly" material (see Num 13:8, 16; 32:44). Coupled with other affinities with the priestly stratum of the Pentateuch to be found in vv. 48-52, the variant supports the hypothesis that the

Feast of Rejoicing

The Torah, the abiding witness of the Covenant, elicits a response of joy.

Solomon Alexander Hart. 1806–1881. *The Feast of the Rejoicing of the Law at the Synagogue in Leghorn, Italy.* 1850. Oil on canvas. 141.3cm x 174.6cm. Gift of Mr. and Mrs. Oscar Gruss. The Jewish Museum. New York.

"addenda" to Deuteronomy (chs. 29–34) took shape in the exilic or post-exilic period.

Moses' Death Foretold, 32:48-52

Immediately after addressing this final word of encouragement to Israel, yet once more, Moses received word from YHWH of his imminent death. YHWH's communication imparts four details: Moses is to ascend Mt. Nebo. He will die there just as Aaron died on Mt. Hor (Num 33:38-39). Moses will die not only in the same manner as his brother, but for the same reason—both had "broken faith" with YHWH by striking the rock to produce water, contrary to YHWH's command (cf. Num 20:1-13). Moses will be permitted to look over into Canaan from the mountaintop, but he will not be permitted to enter.

Mount Nebo

Again, this passage offers little in the way of new information. It is noteworthy primarily because it alludes to a number of "priestly" passages in the book of Numbers. In fact, it can be considered a variant of Numbers 27:12-14. In addition, theologically, it attributes YHWH's refusal to permit Moses to enter the promised land not to Moses' vicarious responsibility for his people's rebellion (compare Deut 1:37; 4:21), but also—for the only time in Deuteronomy (compare Num 27:12-14, for example)—to Moses' own sin (see commentary on Deut 3:23-29).

CONNECTIONS

When the believing community turns to the Bible as the major source for its doctrine and practice, it sometimes encounters puzzles. The textual history of the Song of Moses demonstrates that the tradition actively and intentionally undertook to reduce or eliminate traces of the atypical and the peculiar. On a broader scale, from very early on the teachers of the church developed techniques for homogenizing or sanitizing apparently anomalous biblical passages so that they could proceed smoothly with the task of formulating principles for living and doctrines for the preaching and teaching of the church. One well-known summary of these techniques calls for interpreting difficult or obscure passages in light of clear texts.

Unfortunately, the resulting systematic orthodoxy may unintentionally conceal subtleties, complexities, and mysteries of reality. Ecumenical creeds that reduce the mystery and complexity of the Incarnation to formulae such as "fully human, fully divine" or confessions that employ language almost mathematically and tautologically ("God . . . is infinite in being and perfection"—*Westminster Confession*, Chapter II, Article 1; "God is infinite in holiness and all other perfections"—*Baptist Faith and Message*,

Theology's Propositions and the Personal God

Theological doctrines serve an important function. But they must not be pressed beyond their purpose. The noted Christian apologist of the previous generation, C. S. Lewis, once explained the relationship between doctrine and reality as follows:

> If a man has once looked at the Atlantic from a beach, and then goes and looks at a map of the Atlantic, he will . . . be turning from something real to something less real . . . But here comes the point. The map is admittedly only coloured [sic] paper, but there are two things you have to remember about it. In the first place, it is based on what hundreds and thousands of people have found out by sailing the real Atlantic . . . while yours would be a single isolated glimpse, the map fits all those different experiences together. In the second place, if you want to go anywhere, the map is absolutely necessary . . . the map is going to be more use than walks on the beach if you want to get to America.

The obverse implication of Lewis' analogy should also be noted, however; namely, that the map can never be so thorough or up-to-date as to indicate the height of the waves on the sea where one will sail or the direction and strength of the ever-changing currents in it. Maps and doctrines are useful, almost indispensable, tools; but they will remain approximations at best. Reality has many more than the two dimensions of a map.

C. S. Lewis, *Mere Christianity* (New York: Macmillan, 1952), 135-36.

Article II, "God") illustrate the inherent insufficiency of theological axioms.

To be sure, the church needs basic statements of its fundamental understandings. In order to have and live out a clear identity, believers need at least a few more-or-less constant touchstones: God is one. Jesus is Lord. But, as ancient Israel, Judaism, and the church themselves have realized, there are dangers inherent in absolutizing and concretizing any definition. [Theology's Propositions and the Personal God]

Absolutes and Inquisitions

Church history, for example, is replete with examples of moments in which particular definitions of faith have been employed as absolute standards, usually for purposes of exclusion. People who have understood their faith differently have been excommunicated, branded heretics, and even executed because they were unwilling or unable to give assent to the majority view. Virtually every sizeable Protestant denomination has experienced the trauma of doctrinal warfare between opposing sides on some relatively minor point of Christian doctrine. Typically, one camp insists that Christian doctrine is fixed, absolute, and simple. Those who do not or cannot give assent to the majority's straightforward formulations of the truth in every detail must be excluded.

Absolutes and Heresy

Even when definitive statements of doctrine are not used to measure orthodoxy, over-dependence on them poses another more insidious threat. Theological definitions, like slogans, even if essentially true, are also inherently false because they are necessarily incomplete. As Shakespeare has Hamlet say, "There are more things in heaven and earth, Horatio, than are dreamt of in your philosophy" (*Hamlet*, Act I, Scene 5). Or, in the words of YHWH through Deutero-Isaiah, "My thoughts are not your thoughts, neither are your ways my ways . . . . For as the heavens are higher than the earth, so are my ways higher than your ways, and my thoughts than your thoughts" (Isa 55:8-9).

Biblical Curbs and Correctives

Several features of the Song of Moses may be viewed as reminders that the truth is more complicated than standard theological and philosophical systems would suggest. Admittedly, it is unwise to formulate major components of one's theology on the basis of isolated texts. Nevertheless, attention to the witness of obscure voices can enrich the church's understanding of the majestic scope and vital complexity of God's reality.

Reaffirmation of Monotheism. Most prominently, of course, the Song of Moses, along with a few other passages in the Hebrew Bible (see commentary) attests to the fact that at one stage in the history of its religion, ancient Israel had not yet understood the monotheistic implications of its faith in YHWH as Creator of all and Judge of all. In order to classify Israel's faith during this early period, scholars often distinguish between polytheism, the worship of many gods, and henotheism, the worship of one god without denying the existence of others. Surrounded by polytheistic cultures, Israel seems to have accepted, at least theoretically, the reality of these gods. It insisted, however, as in Deuteronomy 32, that these gods were subordinate to the High God, Israel's God, YHWH. Later, Israel would transform these "pagan" deities in YHWH's heavenly council into angelic beings.

Fundamentally, the distinctive insights of polytheism and monotheism have to do with competing views of the essential character of reality. Polytheism stresses the multiformity of reality. It seems to the polytheist that the complexities of the world must be the product of many divine minds. Monotheism stresses the essential unity of reality. Despite the many facets of the world, the monotheist is convinced that a unity of design and purpose underlies the cosmos. While modified in later Israelite, Jewish, and Christian theology, even ancient Israel's henotheism demonstrates the distinctively monotheistic emphasis on the oneness of fundamental reality: such secondary gods as there may be, the Song of Moses asserts, act only at the pleasure of the Supreme God whom they serve.

Post-Enlightenment scientific understandings of the universe have tended to resurrect a "polytheistic" (minus the deities) view of the universe. Every phenomenon has its cause. Apart from the principle of causation itself, no will or purpose or intention underlies the cosmos. Entropy reigns supreme. The Song of Moses challenges modern, theoretically monotheistic but practically polytheistic believers to rethink the relationship between the one God and the many facets of God's creation, to renew their confidence that one good God created one complex but good world.

God's Will and the Family of Nations

In the modern Western world another related implication of the Song of Moses deserves attention. The song seems to suggest that YHWH fashioned an economy of providence in which subordinate beings (if they are subordinate to YHWH the distinction between "gods" and "angels" seems largely semantic—a distinction without a difference) bear responsibility for the welfare of the nations of the world while reserving Israel for himself. Since the song was addressed and meant as a warning to Israel, any speculation as to the details of the divine providence for the nations on the basis of Deuteronomy 32 is unwarranted. Suffice it to say that the song warns both Israel and the nations against arrogance. The world is YHWH's.

Dependence upon God and Immaturity

The image of the eagle teaching his eaglets to fly as a metaphor for YHWH's relationship to his people (compare Hos 11:3) sounds an intriguing note of challenge. Christian piety consistently and correctly emphasizes the believer's utter dependence upon God. While it is fundamentally true that "in [God] we live and move and have our being" (Acts 17:28), it is equally true that God created human beings with capacities for reasoning, decision-making, work, responsible and ethical action, love, etc. Unfortunately, the emphasis on the believer's dependence on God—meant as an affirmation of God as Creator, Redeemer, and Sustainer—can become an excuse for irresponsibility, immaturity, and inactivity. The parent metaphor portrays God not only as provider and protector, but also as motivator and teacher. Like any good human parent, God does not want children atrophied in infancy, but growing toward mature adulthood.

God, Our Father and Our Mother

Deuteronomy 32:18 refers to "the God who gave you birth." The Old Testament was produced in a distinctly patriarchal society, so that paternal characterizations of YHWH are commonplace in the Old Testament. But the Old Testament does not entirely avoid maternal imagery as though it were inappropriate for YHWH. Modern debates, some of which qualify as disputes, concerning gender metaphors for God—some disputants argue for "traditional" (= exclusively male) language, some for a corrective swing to accentuate the "feminine" qualities of the deity—would lose much of their heat, and gain much in the way of edifying force, were the disputants to acknowledge that God encompasses and transcends both metaphors. It bears repeating that, according to Scripture and Judeo-Christian doctrine, God created human beings, *male and female*, in God's image. Everything good in humanity reflects God. It is appropriate, then, to think of God as Father *and as Mother*.

An Ethically Complex World

Human beings seem most comfortable with black and white issues, with choices between pure villainy and pure heroism. Judging from the Song of Moses, however, matters are never so clear-cut from God's vantage point, especially not in the realm of international relations. The song begins with YHWH's case against Israel for infidelity. By the midpoint, YHWH expresses the concern that the enemy nation chosen to be the instrument of judgment against Israel may arrogantly misinterpret Israel's defeat. The song concludes with language stressing YHWH's freedom to judge and promising a bittersweet vindication of Israel—after they have reached the point of exhaustion. The real world is messy.

NOTES

[1] See TLOT III, 1424-28.

[2] The Hebrew verb *qnh* can mean either "to create" or "to acquire" and, relatedly, "to beget." A homonym, *qn'*, "to be jealous," will figure in word play later in the song.

[3] Manuscripts from Qumran, the Samaritan Pentateuch, and LXX preface the phrase "Jacob ate his fill" at the beginning of v. 15. This phrase provides the kind of parallel structure typical of Hebrew poetry, and, given the apparent priority of the text of Deut 32 represented at Qumran and supported by Sam and LXX, should probably be considered the more original.

[4] See note 2 above.

[5] Merrill, *Deuteronomy* (NAC 4; Nashville: Broadman & Holman, 1994), 416. points out the crudely chiastic structure of Deut 32:4-18: A—Father/Rock; B—YHWH alone provides; C—Gift of "fatness"; C'—Corruption of "fatness"; B'—Israel worships others; A'—Father/Rock.

[6] If this enemy is to be identified with the "nonnation" of fools mentioned in v. 21—and this "nonnation" is the only possible candidate in context—v. 21 cannot be understood to suggest that YHWH intends to provoke Israel's jealousy by even feinting to replace Israel with another nation. Instead, the idea must involve the embarrassment Israel would suffer at the hands of the enemy.

[7] The syntax of this clause, as poetry, is sparse. Literally, it reads, "for he sees that strength is exhausted, neither restrained or freed."

[8] See J. W. Wevers, *Notes on the Greek Text of Deuteronomy* (SBL.SCSS 39; Atlanta: Scholars Press, 1995), 533-35; Cairns, *Word and Presence: A Commentary on the Book of Deuteronomy* (ITC; Grand Rapids: Eerdmans, 1992), 289.

MOSES' BLESSING

33:1-29

A new introduction opens Moses' final address to Israel, his blessings on the individual tribes. Just as the patriarchs Isaac and Jacob had pronounced parting blessings on their sons (Gen 27:27-29, 39-40; 49:1-28), Moses left the Israelite tribes with farewell wishes for their future. Rhetorically, the appearance of Moses' blessing at this point in Deuteronomy has the twofold effect of reinforcing the function of the entire book as Moses' parting address—his final will and testament—and of balancing the harsh judgment expressed in the song (Deut 32) with blessing (Deut 33). Thus, this placement produces the familiar judgment/blessing sequence characteristic of prophetic books in the Old Testament. In other words, the conclusion of Deuteronomy repeatedly emphasizes that the Torah as recorded in Deuteronomy functions as much more than a codification of laws; it embodies the teaching and wisdom of Moses, the first and greatest interpreter of the covenant; it provides the key for the prophetic understanding of Israel's history.

Even more than Moses' song, Moses' blessing gives evidence that it was incorporated into the book of Deuteronomy at a late stage in its development. The introduction appears abruptly, without preparation in the narrative. Apparently, Moses delivers these blessings on his own initiative. Historical and social circumstances reflected in the blessings correspond to a period much later than Moses, probably the early monarchial period. References to Moses are in the third person. Several characteristics of the theology and vocabulary of the blessings are non-Deuteronomic (see commentary below).

Moses' parting blessings, therefore, confront the interpreter with a challenging task. In short, evidence suggests that they are the result of a complicated history of composition involving at least three significant stages. First, the blessings themselves seem to be pre-Deuteronomic, dating to a period in the early monarchy, much later than Moses himself, yet earlier than the likely date of the composition of the book of Deuteronomy. [Jacob's Blessing]

Second, the blessings are framed by a generically unrelated psalm (vv. 2-5, 26-29) that also bears no clear marks of Deuteronomic origin or influence. Likely, it will have been combined with the

---

Jacob's Blessing

Comparison to Jacob's blessing (Gen 49) is illuminating. Deut 33 seems in some ways dependent: Moses' blessing on Reuben (v. 6) mitigates Jacob's harsh prediction of Reuben's instability (vv. 3-4), for example. Historical circumstances reflected in Deuteronomy, furthermore, are much later than those assumed in Genesis: Moses makes no mention of the tribe of Simeon, which is known to have been substantially absorbed into Judah as early as the late premonarchial period, for example (cf. Josh 19:1-9 and 1 Chr 4:34-43); similarly, Levi, for Jacob a warrior, is for Moses the priestly tribe. Formally, Gen 49 expands basic metaphors descriptive of the basic character of Jacob's sons (and their descendants)—mottoes of a sort ("Judah is a lion's whelp," v. 9; "Issachar is a strong ass," v. 14; "Naphtali is a hind let loose," v. 21)—into predictions concerning their futures; Moses' blessing takes the form of wishes. The tribes appear in different orders in the two collections: Jacob blesses his sons more or less in birth order, while the order in Moses' blessing manifests no clear principle, although the lengthy blessing on Joseph occupies focal position, perhaps reflecting northern origins for Moses' blessing. (For other examples of the relationship between Deut 33 and Gen 49, see the commentary.)

---

blessings in a second phase, perhaps when the blessings themselves—presumably transmitted orally prior to this moment—were committed to writing. The psalm and the blessings bear no generic relationship to one another. The distribution of key, often uncommon, and certainly not characteristically Deuteronomic terms across both the psalm and sections of the blessing [Vocabulary Links], however, confirms the editorially fashioned unity of the blessing, including the psalm. These vocabulary links also establish the importance of interpreting the blessings themselves in the context of the psalm framework. In other words, the psalm framework reflects the intention of the editor and serves as a major clue as to how the blessing should be read in its "canonical" context: namely, in praise of YHWH who provides for his people.

Finally, in the post-Deuteronomic phase of the growth of Deuteronomy responsible for the final shape of the concluding chapters of the book, the psalm/blessing composition was incorporated into the book and attributed to Moses. Through this incorporation, betrayed by infelicities such as references to Moses in the third person, the psalm/blessing composition is anchored in the covenant document and, conversely, the covenant is related to praise for YHWH who blesses his people. Law, covenant, worship, and vitality are interrelated.

Vocabulary Links

AΩ The editor(s) responsible for compiling this psalm-blessings composition masterfully unified it through a number of terms distributed throughout. These linking terms also serve to highlight the overarching theme of the composition: YHWH comes to Israel's help. In tabular form, this system of linkages is as follows (asterisked terms occur in both the psalm framework and one or more of the blessings):

*'ammîm—"peoples," vv. 3, 19
yšrwn—"Jeshurun," vv. 5, 26
*rʾš—"head," vv. 5, 16, 21
*'zr—"help," vv. 7, 21, 28
mišpāṭ—"justice," vv. 10, 21
zbḥ—"sacrifice," vv. 10, 19
rsh—"to be pleasing, pleasant," vv. 11, 16, 23, 24
škn—"to dwell," vv. 12, 16, 20, 28
*bṭh—"trust, security, safety," vv. 12, 28
*ṭal—"dew," vv. 13, 28
*grš—"to thrust," noun "produce," vv. 14, 27
*qdm—"ancient," vv. 15, 27
mlʾ—"to be full," vv. 16, 23
qdqd—"crown, pate," vv. 16, 20
ṣdq—"righteous," vv. 19, 21

The import of this composition history for interpreters of the final form of the text involves the challenge of reading the text in its various contexts. The blessings reflect conditions faced by the Israelite tribes at a specific point in their history. For the most part, those conditions no longer pertain in any way. In fact, as was already true to a degree at the moment when they were committed to writing, many of the "tribes" no longer exist. Interpreters must understand the historical situation, but they must also take into account that at some point the blessings were recontextualized through the addition of the psalm framework. Responsible interpretation of the blessings must, therefore, account for the difference in emphasis and tenor resulting from this new setting. In a final phase of literary activity, the psalm/blessing composition was incorporated into Deuteronomy as Moses' parting address. Now they must be read as part of Deuteronomy. What does it mean that Moses left this psalm/blessing as his last word of testimony to Israel? Of course, competent interpretation cannot fail to consider the final context of the composition—its place as Scripture in the life of the modern community of faith.

COMMENTARY

Introduction, 33:1

Post-Deuteronomic editor(s) have supplied the blessing with the most straightforward and abrupt of introductions. Moses' blessing, not mentioned in the narrative itself, delays the account of the fulfillment of YHWH's instructions to Moses to ascend the mountain, there to glimpse the promised land before dying. The introduction simply asserts: "this is the blessing with which Moses blessed." It details no setting, no time or place. The designation of Moses as a "man of God," unique in Deuteronomy, implies that Moses speaks here in his prophetic role, although the introduction does not specify that Moses speaks on God's behalf. [Blessing and Prophecy] Nonetheless, the parting words of the man of God, par excellence, carry great authority and power indeed.

Blessing and Prophecy

📖 In the ancient worldview, in contrast to modern practice, pronouncements such as curses and blessings were much more than mere wishes or affirmations. The spoken word was considered a force loosed in the world. Blessings offered by notable figures immediately prior to their deaths were considered especially potent. The numinous circumstance of approaching death compounded by the demonstrated wisdom of such figures—especially if aged—and their insight into the character of those they blessed enhanced the expectation that such last words would bear particular power. Both Isaac (Gen 27) and Jacob (Gen 49) "blessed" their sons by extrapolating their fates from already established characteristics. Moses' blessing more closely resembles wishes for the tribes' futures, but it too often extrapolates established circumstances or traits. Because of Moses' function as covenant-mediator, as a "man of God," his blessings take on the quality of prophecy. Significantly, neither prophecy nor blessing, then, are mere predictions of coming events. Instead, they declare the relationship between current reality and its subsequent unfolding.

In the intertestamental period, the (pseudepigraphal) blessing genre became a favored medium for comments on the circumstances facing Judaism. As with many biblical genres, these apocryphal blessings typically mutated from "prophecy" to "apocalyptic" functions (compare, for example, "The Testament of the Twelve Patriarchs").

A Psalm Celebrating Israel's Relationship with YHWH, 33:2-5

A number of interpretive difficulties and peculiarities confront the reader of the psalm opening to Moses' blessing. Only here in Deuteronomy, which otherwise consistently employs "Horeb," is the mountain of God identified as "Sinai" (v. 2). The relationship between Sinai, (the mountain in) Seir, and the mountain of Paran, which seems to elevate the two unnamed mountains to a status nearly equivalent with Sinai, is unclear and somewhat surprising (but see Exod 15:15; Judg 5:4-5; Hab 3:3; Ps 68:8). This observation alone, coupled with the fact that the psalm refers to Moses in the third person in a fashion characteristic of the addenda to the book (27:1, 9, 11; 29:1, 2; 31:1, 7, 9, 10, 14, 16, 22, 24, 25, 30; 32:44, 45, 48), constitutes strong evidence that the psalm (and probably the blessings it frames) originated quite apart from Deuteronomic traditions and was (were) added to the book well after the composition of the core of the book of Deuteronomy.

Even more puzzling, however, are a number of unclear terms and concepts. According to the psalm (v. 2), when YHWH "shines forth" from the Mountain of Paran, he comes *mēribĕbōt qōdeš mîmînô*, which can either be translated as "with/from myriads of holy ones at his right hand" or be understood as the place name "Meribah Kadesh" (cf. Num 27:14; Ezek 47:19; 48:28). In the latter case the phrase "at/in his right hand" would be construed in reference to the final clause in v. 2. Although this is possible, the parallel structure of these two phrases argues against it ("he comes with holy ones at his right hand, a fiery law with him").

"Fiery Law"

AΩ Rabbinic interpreters often made of difficulty an opportunity for a type of creative interpretation known as "haggadah." Haggadah is not doctrinal ("halakah"), but homiletic or illustrative in nature. *Sifre Deuteronomy* 48 (cf. *Rab. Song* 1:2:3 and *m. Tehar.* 1:18) accepts the very fanciful suggestion that 'ešdāt, for example, be divided into 'ēš dāt, "fiery law." It explains that

the verse asserts that words of Torah are likened to fire. As fire was given from heaven, so were words of Torah given from heaven. Even as fire is life for the world, so words of Torah are life for the world. Fire: close up to it, one is scorched; away from it, one is chilled; near but not too near, one enjoys it. So are words of Torah: as long as a man labors in them, they are life for him; but when he separates himself from them, they slay him. Even as fire is made use of in this world and in the world-to-come, so words of Torah are made use of in this world and in the world-to-come. Even as fire when used leaves a mark on a man's body, so words of Torah when used leave a mark on the body. Fire: they who work with it are readily distinguishable from other mortals. So, to—by their walk, by their speech, by their garments in the marketplace—disciples of the wise are just as readily distinguishable.

H. Bialik and Y. Ravnitzky, eds., *The Book of Legends: Legends from the Talmud and Midrash*, trans. W. Braude (New York: Schocken, 1992), 405.

Furthermore, Massoretic punctuation includes "at his right hand" with the first phrase.

The former, more likely option, however, involves its own difficulties. First, *mēribĕbōt* contains a prefixed *m*, which should usually be translated "from." Does YHWH come alone, leaving the hosts behind? What, then, would be the import of the phrase "at his right hand"? Second, the precise identification of these myriad "holy ones" is unclear. Is it a reference to Israel as in v. 3 ("Indeed, he loves the peoples, all his holy ones are in his hand")? Or, as seems more likely on the basis of biblical theophany traditions (cf. Num 10:36; Ps 3:6; Dan 11:12), are the heavenly hosts in view here?

Matters are complicated further by the difficulty of the next phrase and by the reference to YHWH's love for "the peoples ('ammîm, plural)" in the next verse. MT reads 'ešdāt lāmô, which can be roughly translated "from his mountain slopes." Rabbinic tradition divides 'ešdāt into two words resulting in the phrase "with his fiery law." ["Fiery Law"] LXX seems to have read 'išrû 'ēlîm ("with him messengers/angels," cf. Acts 7:53; Gal 3:19; Heb 2:2). Scholarly reconstructions abound.

In the context of YHWH's theophany and covenant-giving at Sinai (see commentary on Deut 4), finally, the notion that YHWH "loves the peoples"—indeed, that "all his holy ones are in his hand"—only adds to the confusion. Rabbinic commentators found this troubling and suggested that "peoples" be understood as synonymous with "tribes (of Israel)." This suggestion finds support by a comparison of LXX's "his people" and v. 5, "when the heads of the people assembled as one, the tribes of Israel." Many modern commentators agree in substance and argue that the reference in v. 3 to "holy ones" confirms the identification of "holy ones" in v. 2 with the multitudes of Israel. Unfortunately, owing in part to unclear possessive pronouns, the intent of v. 3 remains somewhat uncertain. [Unclear Pronouns]

Finally, commentators disagree as to the translation and interpretation of the initial clause of v. 5. The grammar and syntax permit two possibilities: (a) "And there was/is/will be a king in Jeshurun" or (b) "And he was/is/will be king in Jeshurun." Scholars who opt for the first of these options often see it as evidence that the psalm celebrates the establishment of Israel's monarchy. It would therefore indicate the date of the psalm in the early monarchial period. Scholars who opt for the second regard it, rather, as a celebration of YHWH's kingship over Israel. Since the psalm can be characterized as a hymn praising YHWH for his provision for Israel, and since the second half of the psalm (v. 26) boasts that "there is none like the God of Jeshurun," it is most likely that it also celebrates YHWH as "king in Jeshurun."

At every turn, it seems, 33:2-5 presents some new difficulty for translators and interpreters. Still, this much is certain beyond doubt. This psalm binds together the themes and motifs of theophany, election, law/covenant/Moses, and kingship. The cosmic Lord appeared to Israel from the mountains, surrounded by the hosts of heaven who protectively surrounded Israel. Through Moses, he delivered the Torah. He assembled the many tribes as one people. The cosmic Lord became Israel's king. In this psalm, the community ("to us," v. 4) voices its appreciative acknowledgement of YHWH's sovereignty.

Unclear Pronouns

AΩ Literally, MT reads: "Indeed, lover of peoples, all *his* holy ones are in *your* (singular) hand, and *they* are gathered (*tukkû*) at *your* (singular) feet, *he* (singular) is lifted (born up?) by *your* (singular) words." The meaning of Hebrew *tukkû*, a so-called *hapax legommenon* (that is, it occurs once and only once in the Hebrew Bible), is unknown. In context, as most commentators agree, the meaning "gathered" seems at least suitable. NRSV translates "they marched at your heels." If "holy ones" refers not to Israel but to the heavenly hosts, and if the second person singular pronouns in v. 3 refer consistently to Israel, the statement can be a description of the manner in which YHWH's heavenly hosts, having appeared with YHWH in theophany, were made subject to Israel's direction. This interpretation, however, fails to account for the initial address to the "lover of peoples" who must be understood as YHWH, the addressee and therefore the antecedent to the second person pronouns. NRSV alleviates this problem, apparently, by repointing the participle *hōbēb* as a passive "beloved of/among the peoples" and taking it as a reference to Israel. The active participle, objectionable to the rabbinic commentators, however, may echo the theme sounded earlier in Moses' song (32:8-9) that YHWH, the High God, makes provision for all peoples.

Blessings on the Individual Tribes, 33:6-25

The blessings themselves turn attention from the common welfare of the united tribes of Israel to the circumstances and fates of the individual tribes. Situations reflected in these blessings, to the extent that details permit the reconstruction of historical circumstances, vary widely. Except for the blessings on Levi and Joseph, they are all remarkably brief and, therefore, sometimes enigmatic. For the most part, in contrast to the much more broadly framed declarations in Jacob's blessing, they express some wish for a tribe's success in a particular venture rather than a portrayal of some defining trait (Dan is a notable exception).

Reuben, 33:6

Jacob's "blessing" on his firstborn, Reuben, hardly qualifies as such. Genesis 35:22 records Reuben's immorality with his father's concubine, Bilhah, the mother of several of Reuben's younger half-brothers. Jacob interpreted Reuben's shameful act as evidence of his instability and predicted that Reuben would never realize the success normally expected for the firstborn son in patriarchal societies. Historically, the tribe of Reuben settled on the fringes of Israelite territory. Both geographically and culturally, it seems to have been only loosely confederated with the united tribes. After gaining its territory in Gilead, it hesitated to join the other tribes in the conquest (see Num 32; Deut 3:18-22; and Josh 1:12-18; 22:1-9; Judg 5:15-17). During Joshua's career, it participated in the establishment of a questionably orthodox shrine east of the Jordan (Josh 22). Later, it suffered in conflicts between Israel, Syria, and Moab over its Transjordanian territory in Gilead (see 2 Kgs 10:33). Read against Jacob's "blessing"—which could better be termed a curse—and Reuben's historical experience, Moses' minimalist blessing amounts to a reprieve. The final phrase of v. 6 may be translated in either of two ways: "even though its numbers be few" or "nor its numbers few." The ambiguity, which may be intentional, adds an eerie overtone: Reuben will not enjoy success, but it may at least "live and not die."

Judah, 33:7

Jacob's blessing likens Judah to a lion, celebrating Judah's messianic preeminence in Israel ("the scepter shall not depart from Judah," Gen 49:10), its success over its enemies, and its wealth. Moses' blessing, in sharp contrast, expresses a prayer that YHWH would respond to Judah's distress, "bringing him in to his people" (a reference to reunion?) and championing Judah's cause against his enemies. Taken together with the psalm's possible allusion to a hope for reunification ("one people," v. 5) and the prominence of the key northern tribe of Joseph in the blessings (vv. 13-17), some scholars speculate that Moses' blessing represents a northern perspective on Judah's status in the period immediately following the division of Israel into northern and southern kingdoms when neighbors, including the north, sought to press their advantage against weakened Judah (see 2 Kgs 14:25-28; 15:6, 16-24).

Levi, 33:8-11

Again, a comparison of Jacob's blessing on Levi with Moses' blessing reveals the markedly different viewpoints of these two collections. Jacob notes (Gen 49:5-7) the tendency toward ferocity and violence demonstrated by Simeon and Levi, presumably in reference to the incident involving their revenge on Shechem for his violation of their sister Dinah (Gen 34), and concludes his "blessing" with the *curse* that Simeon and Levi will be scattered in Israel. In fact, Simeon virtually disappeared and Moses' blessing omits reference to the blessing—another clue as to the relatively late date of the blessing. Elsewhere, including Moses' blessing, the Old Testament regards Levi's dispersal, on the other hand, not as a curse, but as a necessary condition of Levi's priestly function. For Moses' blessing, Levi's ferocity (Deut 33:9)—now manifest apparently not in the Dinah affair, but in Levi's response to Moses' call to eradicate idolaters from Israel's midst after the incident of Aaron's golden calf (Exod 32:26-29)—rather than bringing adversity, evidences the tribe's Yahwistic devotion and suitability for the priesthood. The "test at Massah" and the struggle "at the water of Meribah" are mentioned only here; presumably oral tradition not preserved in the Bible assigned to Levi some role in the events recorded in Exodus 17:1-17 and Numbers 20:7-13. Because of this fierce piety, Levi, "the one who is faithful to you (Heb. *lĕʾîš ḥăsîdekā*)," is fit to employ the Urim and Thummim (divination stones used to obtain yes/no responses to inquiries put to God), to teach the Torah and to officiate in the cult.

It is difficult to imagine who Levi's enemies (v. 11b) might be. Because of this and the similarities in language and tone between vv. 7b and 11b, A. D. H. Mayes[1] conjectures that v. 11b may have once followed immediately on v. 7b. While this is certainly possible, the interpreter's responsibility to the final form of the text cautions against too hastily resorting to rearranging or reconstructing the text. In context, the statement in v. 11b should probably be read in relation to the tribe of Levi's willingness to strike down even its own family members should they violate YHWH's covenant (v. 9).

Benjamin, 33:12

Jacob describes Benjamin as "a ravenous wolf" always on the prowl. In contrast, Moses' blessing is irenic. Benjamin, who had been Jacob's youngest and most favored son, is also YHWH's "beloved." Benjamin "dwells in security," "[YHWH] surrounds him all day long," "he [Benjamin] dwells between his [Benjamin's/YHWH's ?] hills/shoulders [?]." The phrase "dwelling between his [Benjamin's] hills" may refer to the Benjamite sanctuary nestled among the hills at Nob (see 1 Sam 21:1). Alternatively, if translated "between his [YHWH's] shoulders," which is equally plausible, the phrase would describe Benjamin's particularly intimate relationship with YHWH. Whatever the intention of the phrase, the inseparability of translation issues and interpretation should be noted. In this case the substance of the phrase is relatively insignificant. In many other cases, familiarity with the original language of Scripture is indispensable.

Joseph, 33:13-17

In both Jacob's blessing and Moses' blessing, the blessing reserved for the tribe of Joseph that occupied Israel's rich central hill country is by far the most extensive and the most straightforward. Joseph's land will be blessed with all the abundance of heaven and earth. Watered by dew and the springs of the deep beneath the earth, nourished by the shining sun and the shimmering moon, the mountains and hills of Ephraim will produce copiously. Joseph will be known as "prince among his brothers (v. 16; a possible allusion to the northern monarchy?)." With the horns of a wild ox, Joseph will drive out all his enemies, pushing them to the ends of the earth.

Zebulun and Issacar, 33:18-19

Zebulun and Issachar regularly appear together in tribal lists and in both series of blessings. Jacob's blessing documents the commercial and geographical realities faced by these two tribes at home on Israel's far northwestern frontier. Zebulun neighbored the trading and sea-faring Phoenicians whose principle trading centers were Tyre and Sidon. The population of Issachar, apparently unable to sustain itself through agriculture or trade, had opted to make its living as hired laborers. Not coincidentally, the etymology of Issachar points to this choice (see Gen 30:14-18). Although Moses' blessing may allude to these circumstances ("in your going out" and "they suck the riches of the sea" probably refer to sea-going commerce, for example), it focuses on the sanctuary shared by these two tribes, probably on Mt. Tabor (see Hos 5:1), where they "offer right sacrifices" (v. 19). This focus on a non-centralized sanctuary conflicts with the cult regulations of Deuteronomy 12 and reflects the extra-Deuteronomic character of the blessing. Interestingly, this sanctuary and its cult will attract "peoples (*'ammîm*)." Sensitive to the image of pagan nations attracted to a non-Jerusalemite sanctuary, Targum Onkelos translates "tribes" here. Does this statement confirm the suspicion that v. 3 does, in fact, refer to YHWH's love for the non-Israelite nations?

Gad, 33:20-21

The tribe of Gad, noted for its leadership role during the conquest ("commander's portion," v. 21; see Deut 3:18-20; Num 32:17), took up residence in the fertile but vulnerable territory east of the Jordan. Situated between the city-states of Syria to the north and Ammon to the south, possession of the territory of Gad was disputed throughout much of the monarchial period in a series of border wars (see Judg 3:12-14; 10:7-9; 11:4-6; 1 Sam 11:1-11; 14:47-49; 2 Kgs 13:3-7; Amos 1:3). Both blessings collections presume this instability. Moses' blessing celebrates both YHWH's protection of Gad ("he [= YHWH] who enlarges Gad," v. 20) and Gad's own ferocity ("like a lion, he tears the arm" v. 20).

Scholars debate the function of v. 21b. LXX has a passive verb that results in a statement closely resembling the second clause of v. 5 "he [= YHWH] gathered the heads of the people together." With only slight emendation, MT can be rendered similarly. In this case, v. 21b would either be an allusion back to the ideas contained in the opening psalm or a misplaced element of that psalm: YHWH gathers the heads of the people as one people and does righteousness and justice in Israel. While possible, however, this emendation is unnecessary. This statement can be readily understood as a celebration of Gad's martial reputation (see Num 23:24; Pss 7:2; 17:12; Isa 38:13; Jer 49:19; Ezek 22:25; Hos 13:7-8).

Dan, 33:22

The tribe of Dan migrated from its original territory between Judah and Ephraim (Josh 19:40-48), which it found too confining, to capture Laish at the foot of Mt. Hermon in the far north (Josh 19:47; Judg 18:1-31). Whereas Jacob's blessing on Dan takes its impetus from the etymology of the tribal name (Heb. *dyn* means "to judge"), Moses' blessing refers to Dan's migration and may involve a play on the meaning of the place-name Laish (= "lion"). Dan, a lion's whelp, leaps forth from Bashan [to conquer?]. According to the sparse biblical record of Dan's migration, it moved from its original home through Ephraimite territory, thence to attack Laish. The reference to Bashan as the staging area for Dan's invasion is therefore puzzling. Some scholars point to a possible cognate for *bāšān* in other Semitic languages with the meaning "serpent" (cf. Gen 49:17, "Dan shall be a serpent in the path") and translate Deuteronomy 33:22b, "Dan jumps away from the serpent." Not only does this involve conjecture, however; it would also represent a different use of the image in Moses' blessing than in Jacob's. Furthermore, it makes a poor parallel to v. 22a: Dan is a lion, but he is afraid of a serpent? It seems much more likely that Deuteronomy 33:22 mirrors a tradition concerning the details of Dan's military strategy (via Bashan rather than Ephraim) not preserved elsewhere.

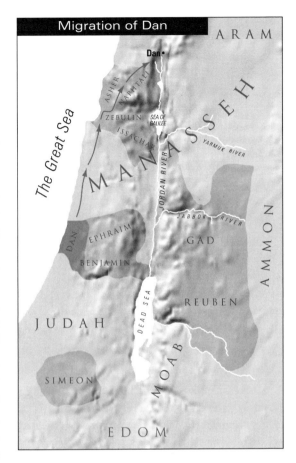

Naphtali, 33:23
Originally, Naphtali possessed a rather small region south of Hermon (Josh 20:7). Moses' blessing (and probably Jacob's, too) affirms that Naphtali's expansion toward the "sea" to the south (Chinnereth [Galilee]?) is evidence of YHWH's favor.

Asher, 33:24-25
The tribe of Asher lived in the fertile region of central Galilee noted especially for its olive production. Unfortunately, its territory also lay in the path often used by campaigning ancient Near Eastern armies for north/south travel. The name "Asher" is related etymologically either to the Hebrew term for "blessed/fortunate/happy" or for "foot." The blessing reflects all these circumstances although the significance of the plays on words is somewhat obscured by the use of etymologically unrelated

synonyms for "blessed" and "foot." It may be that, during the course of the oral transmission of this blessing, the allusions were misperceived. In any case, Asher is "blessed," a favorite among his brothers. His olive harvests will be so plentiful that he will be able to anoint his feet in olive oil. Yet, he will also find it necessary to defend his wealth against intruders.

Psalm, Part II, 33:26-29

The blessings conclude as they began, with a psalm celebrating Israel's special relationship with the Lord of the cosmos. None is like Jeshurun's God. He rides the clouds (compare Exod 34:5; Num 11:25; Pss 68:4; 104:3; Isa 19:1) when he comes to Israel's assistance. He is a sure and safe dwelling place for Israel. He vanquishes Israel's enemies. He blesses Israel with grain and wine and life-giving dews. Therefore, Israel, too, is incomparable. They are "fortunate (*ʾāšēr*; cf. the name Asher)" indeed!

CONNECTIONS

Except for the blessing on Levi, which in effect endorses Levi's priestly office, Moses' blessing of the Israelite tribes expresses wishes for, or in a few cases (Joseph, for example) celebrates, their survival and prosperity in specific historical circumstances. As a collection, these blessings testify to a period in Israel's history when individual tribes faced the challenges of existence in the difficult climate—meteorological, economic, and geo-political—of the ancient Levant. During this period, Israel focused on the very mundane, everyday matters of rain, crops, and enemies.

Moses' blessing presents a challenge for readers and interpreters who view the Bible as a vital and vibrant guide and source for the life and faith of believers and the believing community. Not only have circumstances changed (in fact, Israel's tribal organization has long since become meaningless), but, with the possible exception of the psalm (on which see below), as a rule, the blessings do not meet typical criterion for devotional literature. A modern reader who turns to the Bible expecting to find lofty theological doctrine—universally applicable and absolute ethical principles or revelation concerning the essential nature of God, to name but two examples—may justifiably be disappointed by Moses' blessing: it is supremely parochial. [Hermeneutics and History]

Hermeneutics and History

It is almost a truism that the Bible is ancient literature, mirroring the worldview and circumstances of an ancient culture. Elements such as biblical language, customs, and social structures that are foreign to modern readers must be taken into account in interpretation. Many parts of the Bible, however, present an added difficulty, namely, that they were written originally with a very specific situation in view. For example, although the Gospels were written in koine Greek and reflect the worldview and social situation of a the Hellenistic world, they were written with a wide audience in mind and, presumably, with the expectation that they would be read perhaps for generations. In other words, they were written in and from a specific setting, but they were not written to it exclusively. In contrast, Paul's Corinthian correspondence was written to the first-century church at Corinth. Indeed, Paul was prompted to write these letters by very specific issues facing that church. In fact, he wrote at least in part to answer questions the Corinthian church had posed to him.

Moses' blessing, like the Corinthian letters, is extremely specific. Asher has ceased to exist as a distinct, identifiable group. Just as the question of the suitability of eating meat offered to idols no longer confronts Western Christians, Asher's fate is hardly of consequence to modern life. Naïve interpretation attempts to make some simple one-to-one equation between ancient and modern phenomena. Unengaged interpretation is satisfied with simply noting the historical data. The difficult—but rewarding—challenge calls for sensitivity to the problem while maintaining the conviction that Scripture bears witness to the ways of God with God's people.

"Dan is a lion cub that pounces from Bashan" (v. 22). What can this blessing possibly mean for a modern believer ("I am not a Danite; in fact, there is no identifiable tribe of Dan in the modern world; I have never even been to Bashan; and I am not at all interested in pouncing on anyone!")? Remembering that these blessings were probably already long "outdated" when they were incorporated into the book of Deuteronomy, modern readers may find it necessary to broaden their expectations of Scripture if passages such as this are going to function in any way as sources for modern faith and practice. In brief, Moses' blessing serves as a reminder that real life is rarely a matter of lofty theological principles. Rain, crops, and enemies—or their equivalents in particular circumstances— will ever be first-order concerns for human beings (believers, too) trying to survive and succeed.

Perhaps it may be more accurate to state this truth as the theological principle underlying Moses' blessing. As a matter of fact, the Hebrew Bible stubbornly insists throughout, not just here, that relationship with the God of Israel involves ordinary, mundane, everyday life and its struggles. In fact, Israel came to know and continues to know its God not through mystical contemplation or intellectual speculation, but in encounter, often in circumstances of Israel's need and struggle for survival. Genesis begins with an account of God's creative activity, not with a treatise on God's

God's World or the World's God?

R. Isaac taught: A verse in Deuteronomy speaks of "the skies, the dwelling place of the eternal God" (Deut 33:27). But we would not have known whether the Holy One, blessed be He, is the dwelling place of the world or whether the world is the dwelling place of the Holy One, blessed be He, unless Moses had come and given us the answer by saying, "Lord, Thou hast been our dwelling place . . . from everlasting" (Ps 90:1).

R. Yose bar Halafta said: We would not have known whether the Holy One, blessed be He, is secondary to His world or whether His world is secondary to Him unless the Holy One Himself, blessed be He, had made the answer plain by saying, "Behold, there is a place by Me" (Exod 33:21), meaning: "The place is by Me—secondary to Me—and not I to My place."

R. Abba bar Yudan said: He is like a warrior riding upon a horse, with the caparison hanging down on one side and the other; the horse does the bidding of the rider, but the rider does not do the bidding of the horse.

R. Huna said in the name of R. Ammi: Why is the epithet "Place" used for the Name of the Holy One, blessed be He? Because He is the place of the world, and the world is not His place. (Gen. R. 68:9; *Exod. R.* 45:6; *MTeh* 90:10)

H. Bialik and Y. Ravnitzky, eds., *The Book of Legends: Legends from the Talmud and Midrash*, trans. W. Braude (New York: Schocken, 1992), 503.

omnipotence, omnipresence, and omnitemporality. Likewise, the psalm framing Moses' blessing (vv. 2-5, 26-29) begins with a celebration of YHWH's appearance to Israel at Sinai to give the Torah. Israel's God "rides the clouds to [Israel's] aid" (v. 26). Nowhere does the Hebrew Bible speculate as to the nature of God apart from God's engagement in creating, sustaining, judging and redeeming God's world. [God's World or the World's God?] The New Testament testifies, in fact, that God's engagement with God's creation extends to the Incarnation. "No one has ever seen God. It is God the only Son, who is close to the father's heart, who has made him known" (John 1:18, RSV). The God of the Bible is not an idea, but a person.

This fundamental observation concerning biblical religion prompts two reminders for modern believers concerning the authentic content and proper arena of faith. First, biblical faith is not primarily a doctrinal matter. Theology has its place as a tool for understanding, but faith is relationship (see [Theology's Propositions and the Personal God]). The questions of faith are not "Is there a God?" or "What is God's essence?" but "Who is God?" and "Who am I?" Second, biblical faith cannot be confined only to some compartmentalized domain. The God of the Bible is encountered everywhere in God's world. In fact, it may well be that one encounters God most authentically in the workplace or at the dinner table—in any moment when real life asks one to manifest who one is in relationship to the God who created human beings in God's likeness to care for the world and to live in relationship.

NOTE

[1] Mayes, *Deuteronomy* (NCBC; Grand Rapids: Eerdmans, 1979), 404.

MOSES' DEATH AND BURIAL

34:1-12

Normally, a well-conceived and well-executed conclusion resolves most, if not all, major conflicts and themes in the plot of the work in question. Significantly, however, Deuteronomy's conclusion purposely leaves many of the book's most important themes unresolved. In fact, rather than at least hinting at a final outcome, Deuteronomy only complicates the "plot" of the story of YHWH's relationship with Israel in a number of ways. It could be said that Deuteronomy simply ends with the account of Moses' death; nothing is truly finished.

From a source-critical perspective, this penultimacy is, in part, the result of the redaction history of the passage. Deuteronomy 34:1a resumes the account left off at 32:52. As noted in the commentary above, this narrative demonstrates affinities with the so-called "priestly" tradition in the Pentateuch. These similarities reappear in vv. 7-9 (to v. 9, compare Num 27:18, for example). In contrast, 34:1b-6 is related to 31:23-29, a Deuteronomic strand of tradition. Because of its defense of Moses' reputation (according to v. 5 and elsewhere in Deuteronomy, YHWH sentences Moses to die in Moab because of Moses' sin, after all), some scholars regard all or part of vv. 10-11 as a late apologetic insertion.

But the composite nature of this ending is only an element in its resistance of finality. Fundamentally, the canonical book of Deuteronomy functions as a transitional document. In that sense, the ending and the editorial effort that produced it are true to the character and purpose of the book (see **Connections**).

COMMENTARY

Moses Views the Land, Dies, and Is Buried, 34:1-6

In keeping with YHWH's command (32:48-52), Moses ascends Mt. Nebo, presumably a peak of the Pisgah mountain chain, there to survey the land promised Israel. According to the text, Moses was

The Death of Moses

Alexander Cabanel. *The Death of Moses.* 1851. Oil on canvas. Dahesh Museum of Art. New York.

able to view the regions of Gilead in the Transjordan, seeing as far north as Dan at the foot of Mt. Hermon, the Galilee (Naphtali) and the central hills of Ephraim and Manasseh to the northwest, Judah as far as the Mediterranean, and the Judean desert to the southwest. Immediately across the Jordan from Mt. Nebo lay Jericho, "the city of palms" and its environs, later to be Israel's point of entry into the promised land and its first conquest. In fact, it is possible to see the peak of Mt. Hermon from the Transjordanian mountains, although it is not possible to see to the Mediterranean. Whether Moses actually surveyed the entire land, however, is beside the point. In the legal tradition of the ancient Near East, such viewings constituted a formal act of taking possession (see Deut 3:27 and Gen 13:14-17), much like the transferal of a deed in modern practice.

Even more to the point from Deuteronomy's perspective, however, although Moses symbolically takes possession of the land, YHWH does not permit him physically to enter Canaan. Moses' career and ministry, unquestionably pivotal, have only been one element in YHWH's long-term relationship with Israel. Long before YHWH called Moses, and quite independent of Moses' obedient service, YHWH had promised this land to Israel's ancestors

Abraham, Isaac, and Jacob (v. 4). Furthermore, in relation to the fulfillment of this promise, Moses' work has only been preparatory! Joshua will lead the people across the Jordan.

Without fanfare, Deuteronomy reports that, after seeing the land "with his own eyes (v. 4)," "Moses, the servant of YHWH, died in Moab according to YHWH's command (*'al-pî YHWH*, v. 5)" and that "he [YHWH?] buried him in Moab in the valley opposite Beth Peor." The precise location of Moses' grave is unknown "to this day (v. 6)." The obscurity of the details of Moses' burial adds to the impression of penultimacy engendered by Deuteronomy's "conclusion." Moses, the great man of God, the law-giver, the only leader Israel has ever known, ascends a mountain, as he had at Sinai—this time never to return. From Israel's viewpoint, he simply disappears!

The mystery surrounding Moses' death and burial inspires the imagination. Commentators speculate that God intentionally concealed Moses' burial place in order to preclude any possibility that Israel might erect a shrine there and establish a personality cult surrounding Moses. The New Testament associates Moses with Elijah, another towering figure in the Old Testament whose life came to an extraordinary and mysterious end (2 Kgs 2:1-15; Matt 17:1-13; Mark 9:2-13; Luke 9:28-36). Jewish legend and mystical speculation have spun fantastical tales around the themes of the apparent injustice of YHWH's prohibition against Moses' entry into the land, Moses' status as God's intimate friend, and the secrecy surrounding his burial. [Moses' Grave].

Moses' Grave

"And He buried him in the valley in the land of Moab over against Beth-peor" (Deut 34:6). R. Berechyah said: "Although [Scripture provides] a clue within a clue, nevertheless 'no man knows his grave.' The wicked government once sent to Beth-peor [the message], 'Show us where Moses is buried.' When they stood above, it appeared to them to be below; when they were below, it appeared to them to be above. They divided themselves into two parties; to those who were standing above it appeared below, and to those who were below it appeared above. This is in fulfillment of what is said, 'No man knows his grave.'" R. Hama son of R. Hanina said: "Even Moses our teacher does not know where he is buried." (*Sotah* 13b).

Matteo da Lecce. 1547–1600. *Scenes from the Life of Moses: The Defense of the Body of Moses.* Sistine Chapel, Vatican Palace. Vatican State.

For a comprehensive survey and analysis of legends concerning Moses' death and burial, see Kushelevsky, *Moses and the Angel of Death* (Studies on Themes and Motifs in Literature 4; New York: Peter Lang, 1995).

In the context of Deuteronomy and the Pentateuch as a whole, however, Moses' "disappearance" on Mt. Nebo recalls his delay on Mt. Sinai and raises the crucial question of Israel's reaction. On that previous occasion, Israel had panicked over Moses' apparent disappearance and they had transgressed in the affair of the golden calf. Even while Aaron, Moses' brother and deputy and Israel' priest, had been alive, only months after witnessing YHWH's mighty acts in Egypt, the Israelites had been unfaithful. Now that Moses has truly left them, can they continue faithfully without him?

Moses' Death

It always felt to me—a wrong
To that Old Moses—done—
To let him see—the Canaan—
Without the entering—

And tho' in soberer moments—
No Moses there can be
I'm satisfied—the Romance
In point of injury—

Surpasses sharper stated—
Of Stephen—or of Paul—
For these—were only put to death—
While God's adroiter will

On Moses—seemed to fasten
With tantalizing Play
As Boy—should deal with lesser Boy—
To prove ability.

The fault—was doubtless Israel's—
Myself—had banned the Tribes—
And ushered Grand Old Moses
In Pentateuchal Robes

Upon the Broad Possession
'Twas little—But titled Him—to see—
Old Man on Nebo! Late as this—
My justice bleeds—For Thee!

T. H. Johnson, ed., *The Complete Poems of Emily Dickinson* (Boston: Little, Brown and Co., 1960), 293-94.

Israel's Initial Reaction, 34:7-9

Deuteronomy's obituary for Moses consists of two parts. First, the book reports Moses' advanced age at his death (120 years) and that, nonetheless, he was strong and healthy to the end (v. 7; see the commentary on 31:1-8). Apparently, this note calls attention to the fact that Moses' death was, in a sense, premature—he died "at YHWH's command," not because his life had run its natural course. Then follows the account of Israel's reaction: a lengthy period of mourning. Instead of the customary seven days, Israel mourned Moses' passing for an entire month in keeping with his stature as their leader, the covenant-mediator (v. 8). The loss of Moses must surely have been felt as a crisis moment. But after a month, they ceased to mourn and Joshua assumed leadership (v. 9). YHWH had commissioned him; Moses had transferred leadership through the laying on of hands; he was filled with the "spirit of wisdom"; and Israel heeded him. The end is a new beginning. "The king is dead! Long live the king!" Moses is gone, but YHWH's commandments, given through Moses, remain to be carried out. God's will is greater than an individual. The life of God's people goes on.

An Editorial Assessment of Moses' Life, 34:10-12

The final obituary notice is not a report but the editor's assessment that Moses has been without parallel. In the editor's view, no prophet equal to Moses has ever arisen in Israel (compare Deut 18:15); no one has ever been so intimately acquainted with YHWH (see Exod 33:11 and Num 12:8); YHWH has never worked such "signs and wonders" through anyone as he did through Moses in Egypt and in the sight of all Israel. [Moses' Death]

CONNECTIONS

T. W. Mann has observed that "Deuteronomy suspends Moses' audience and all subsequent readers in between end and beginning."[1] Moses symbolically takes possession of the land, but is prohibited from actually entering. Israel itself must take the land God has given in fulfillment of an ancient promise. Israel's greatest leader dies alone, his burial place forever unknown. Israel mourns him, but it soon must resume its journey. Moses has been God's intimate friend—a prophet, covenant-mediator, leader, and instrument of signs and wonders without equal. Yet under his leadership, Israel sinned. Indeed, Moses himself sinned. Moses and his entire generation were not permitted entry into the land of promise. [Moses' Death II]

Now, a new generation of Israel under new, less competent leadership stands poised to take possession of the promised land, to

---

Moses' Death II

In light of Moses' status as deliverer, mediator of the covenant, even friend of God, God's refusal to permit Moses to enter Canaan seems harsh. The text offers little explanation. Post-biblical tradition testifies to the theological imagination of readers of Deuteronomy.

The material on Deuteronomy in the *Midrash Rabbah* (H. Friedman and M. Simon, eds., *Midrash Rabbah* [London: Soncino, 1939]) devotes significant attention to the possible reasons for YHWH's decision. According to one view, YHWH buried Moses outside the promised land as a reminder to resurrect those who died in the wilderness (*Deut. Rab.* II:9). The Midrash suggests elsewhere that it was simply Joshua's turn to lead (II:5; compare the *Zohar*), that YHWH took Moses' refusal of YHWH's offer to make of Moses a great nation as a refusal to the opportunity to enter the land (VII:10-11), that Moses was punished for Adam's sins (IX:8), and that YHWH sought to prevent Moses from becoming envious of his student and successor, Joshua (IX:9).

The image of the great Moses permitted only to gaze at the promised land from a distance and buried in obscurity fascinated the rabbis. As the commentary and accompanying sidebars illustrate, it continues to serve as an ambiguous image.

establish a society based on YHWH's will revealed and interpreted by Moses, and to live out its commission as a "holy people, a kingdom of priests." Moses has placed before them the choice between authenticity and illegitimacy, between fidelity and disobedience, between life and death. But now Moses is gone. Egypt lies in the past. Ahead lies Jericho (Josh 6), and Ai (Josh 7). Joshua will lead Israel, as will Ahab (1 Kgs 16:28–22:39) one day. Jeremiah will prophesy, and so will Hannaniah (Jer 27–28). Always, however, Torah will bear witness to new generations of Israel that YHWH is faithful; always, Torah will call new generations of Israel to holiness and rightness; always, Torah will guide and instruct new generations of Israel in authentic fidelity to their destiny as people of God.

Leaders come and go. Ancestors succeed or fail. In truth, each generation stands poised to enter into God's promise, to actualize the call to be God's people, to live the authentic life described in the Torah. In truth, every day is suspended between end and beginning.

NOTE

[1] T. Mann, *Deuteronomy* (Westminster Bible Companion; Louisville: Westminster/John Knox, 1995), 167.

BIBLIOGRAPHY

Alt, A. "The Origins of Israelite Law," in *Essays on Old Testament History and Religion.* Garden City: Doubleday, 1968. Pp. 101-71.

Anderson, G. *Sacrifices and Offerings in Ancient Israel: Studies in Their Social and Political Importance.* Atlanta: Scholars Press, 1987.

Balentine, Samuel. *The Hidden God: The Hiding of the Face of God in the Old Testament,* Oxford Theological Monographs. Oxford: Oxford, 1983.

_____. *The Torah's Vision of Worship,* OBT. Minneapolis: Fortress Press, 1999.

Cairns, I. *Word and Presence: A Commentary on the Book of Deuteronomy,* ITC. Grand Rapids: Eerdmans, 1992.

Carmichael, C. *The Laws of Deuteronomy.* Ithaca, NY: Cornell University Press, 1974.

Childs, Brevard S. *The Book of Exodus: A Critical, Theological Commentary,* OTL. Philadelphia: Westminster, 1974.

_____, *Memory and Tradition in Israel.* London: SCM Press, 1962.

Christensen, Duane. *Deuteronomy 1-11,* Word Biblical Commentary 6A. Dallas: Word Books, 1991.

_____, ed. *A Song of Power and the Power of Song: Essays on the Book of Deuteronomy,* Sources for Biblical and Theological Study 3. Winona Lake: Eisenbrauns, 1993.

Douglas, Mary. *Purity and Danger: An Analysis of Concepts of Pollution and Taboo.* London: Routledge and Kegen Paul, 1966.

Emerton, J. "New Light on Israelite Religion: The Implications of the Inscriptions from Kuntillet 'Arjud," *ZAW* 94 (1982): 2-20.

Eynikel, E. *The Reform of King Josiah and the Composition of the Deuteronomistic History,* Oudtestamentische Studien 33. Leiden: E. J. Brill, 1996.

Gerstenberger, E. "Covenant and Commandment," *JBL* 84 (1965): 38-51.

Gilmer, H. W. *The If-You Form in Israelite Law,* SBLDS 15. Missoula, Mont.: Scholars Press, 1975.

Gorman, F. H., Jr. *The Ideology of Ritual: Space, Time, and Status in the Priestly Theology.* Sheffield: JSOT Press, 1990.

Groves, Joseph. *Actualization and Interpretation in the Old Testament,* SBLDS 86. Atlanta: Scholars Press, 1987.

Hammer, R. trans. *Sifre: A Tannaitic Commentary on the Book of Deuteronomy,* Yale Judaica Series 24. New Haven: Yale, 1986.

Heschel, Abraham. *Man is Not Alone: A Philosophy of Religion.* New York: Harper & Row, 1951.

Hillers, D. R. *Treaty Curses and the Old Testament Prophets,* BibOr 16. Rome: Pontifical Biblical Institute, 1964.

Jackson, B. "Legalism and Spirituality: Historical, Philosophical, and Semiotic Notes on Legislators, Adjudicators, and Subjects," in *Religion and Law: Biblical-Judaic and Islamic Perspectives*, E. Firmage, and others, eds. Winona Lake, Ind.: Eisenbrauns, 1990. Pp. 244-61.

Jensen, P. *Graded Holiness: A Key to the Priestly Conception of the World*. Sheffield: JSOT Press, 1992.

Kaufman, Stephen. "The Structure of the Deuteronomic Law," *Maarav* 1/2 (1979): 105-58.

Kushelevsky, R. *Moses and the Angel of Death*, Studies on Themes and Motifs in Literature 4. New York: Peter Lang, 1995.

Lundbom, J. "The Inclusio and Other Framing Devices in Deuteronomy I-XXVIII," *Vetus Testamentum* 56 (1996): 300-301.

Luther, Martin. *Lectures on Deuteronomy*, Luther's Works 9, J. Pelikan and D. Poellot, eds. St. Louis: Concordia, 1960.

Mann, Thomas. *Deuteronomy*, Westminster Bible Companion. Louisville: Westminster/John Knox, 1995.

Mayes, A. D. H., *Deuteronomy*, NCBC. Grand Rapids: Eerdmans, 1979.

McBride, S. D., Jr. "Polity of the Covenant People: The Book of Deuteronomy," *Int* 41 (1987): 233-34.

McCarthy, D. J. *Treaty and Covenant: A Study in Form in the Ancient Oriental Documents and in the Old Testament*, AnBib 21A, rev. ed. Rome: Biblical Institute, 1978.

McConville, J. G. *Law and Theology in Deuteronomy*, JSOTS 33. Sheffield: Sheffield, 1984.

Mendanhall, George. *Law and Covenant in Israel and the Ancient Near East*. Pittsburgh: Biblical Colloquium, 1955.

Merrill, E. H. *Deuteronomy*, NAC 4. Nashville: Broadman & Holman, 1994.

Nachmanides, *Commentary on the Torah: Deuteronomy*, C. Chavel, trans. New York: Shilo Publishing House, 1976.

Nelson, R. D. *Raising Up a Faithful Priest: Community and Priesthood in Biblical Theology*. Louisville: Westminster/John Knox Press, 1993.

Olson, D. *Deuteronomy and the Death of Moses: A Theological Reading*, OBT. Minneapolis: Fortress, 1994.

Olyan, Saul M. *Asherah and the Cult of Yahweh in Israel*, SBL.MS 34. Atlanta: Scholars Press, 1988.

Provan, I. *Hezekiah and the Book of Kings: A Contribution to the Debate about the Composition of the Deuteronomic History*, BZAW 172. Berlin: Walter de Gruyter, 1988.

Rosenbaum, M. and others, trans., *Pentateuch with Targum Onkelos, Haphtaroth, and Prayers for Sabbath, and Rashi's Commentary*, vol. 5, Deuteronomy. London: Shapiro, Vallentine & Co., 1934.

Sonsino, R. *Motive Clauses in Hebrew Law: Biblical Forms and Near Eastern Parallels*, SBL.DS 45. Missoula, Mont.: Scholars Press, 1979.

Stamm, J. J. and M. E. Andrew. *The Ten Commandments in Recent Research*, SBT 2/2. Napierville, IL: Allenson, 1967.

Thompson, J. A. *The Ancient Near Eastern Treaties and the Old Testament.* London: Tyndale Press, 1964.

_____. *Deuteronomy*, TOTC. Downers Grove: InterVarsity, 1974.

Tigay, J. *Deuteronomy*, JPS Torah Commentary 5. Philadelphia: Jewish Publication Society, 1996.

von Rad. G. *Deuteronomy: A Commentary*, OTL. Philadelphia: Westminster, 1966.

_____. *The Form-Critical Problem of the Hexateuch and Other Essays*, E. Dicken, trans. New York: McGraw Hill, 1966.

_____. *Holy War in Ancient Israel*, M. Dawn, trans. Grand Rapids, 1990.

_____. *Studies in Deuteronomy*, D. Stalker, trans. London: SCM, 1953.

Weinfeld, Moshe. *Deuteronomy and the Deuteronomic School.* Oxford: Clarendon, 1972.

_____. "Judge and Officer in Ancient Israel and the Ancient Near East," *IOS* 7 (1977): 67-76.

Wevers, J. W. *Notes on the Greek Text of Deuteronomy*, SBL.SCSS 39. Atlanta: Scholars Press, 1995.

Wilson, I. *Out of the Midst of the Fire: Divine Presence in Deuteronomy*, SBLDS 151. Atlanta: Scholars Press, 1995.

Wilson, Robert. "Israel's Judicial System in the Pre-Exilic Period," *JQR* 74 (1983): 229-48.

INDEX OF MODERN AUTHORS

INDEX OF SIDEBARS

Illustration Sidebars

INDEX OF SCRIPTURES

INDEX OF TOPICS

ILLUSTRATION CREDITS